THE WRITER'S DIGEST

CHARACTER NAMING
SOURCEBOOK

SECOND EDITION

SHERRILYN KENYON

WRITER'S DIGEST BOOKS
Cincinnati, Ohio
www.writersdigest.com

Visit our Web site at www.writersdigest.com for information on more resources for writers.

To receive a free weekly e-mail newsletter delivering tips and updates about writing and about Writer's Digest products, register directly at our Web site at http://newsletters.fwpublications.com.

09   08   07   06   05   5   4   3   2   1

Library of Congress Cataloging-in-Publication Data

Kenyon, Sherrilyn
   The Writer's digest character naming sourcebook / by Sherrilyn Kenyon.—2nd ed.
     p.   cm.
   Includes indexes.
   ISBN 1-58297-295-8 (hardcover : alk. paper)
     1. Characters and characteristics in literature. 2. Names, Personal—Dictionaries. I. Writer's Digest Books (Firm) II. Title.

PN56.4.K46   2005
809'.927—dc22   2004024957
                                                                                      CIP

Edited by Michelle Ruberg
Designed by Grace Ring
Cover designed by Matthew DeRhodes
Production coordinated by Robin Richie

Please note that many of the languages corresponding with the origins in this book use different diacritical marks that are essential to the letters in their alphabets and to the pronunciation of their names. For the most part, these diacritical marks are not included in the book. If you want to ensure complete accuracy, be sure to do independent research for the correct spelling of the names.

ONLINE RESEARCH TIPS

A Note About Accuracy

As you research names for your fictional characters, keep in mind how important accuracy is to you. All possible effort has been taken to keep errors from creeping into this book. Nonetheless, no one source of naming information can be considered infallible or perfectly objective. If accuracy is essential to the success of your story, you should verify information from any one source by cross-checking it against another source—preferably another type of source. The naming resources listed below are convenient because they can be accessed online; but, like most online information sources, they cannot be assumed to be 100 percent correct.

Genealogy Resources

Genealogists spend a lot of time researching names, and it is important for them to know historical naming practices if they want to be successful. Many genealogists post information they have uncovered in their research—from specific family history to general naming practices in certain areas of the world at specific times. Just a few of the online resources for genealogists are census and immigration records, ship passenger lists, and names taken from gravestones in cemeteries.

A huge index of genealogical information is available through Cyndi's List of Genealogy Sites at www.CyndisList.com. The information you'll find at this site not only can help you choose appropriate names for your characters, but also can provide invaluable information for settings and character background.

About.com is another good site to visit for genealogical information. The information at http://genealogy.about.com includes lists of surname meanings and information about naming practices in several countries and cultures. While you're visiting About.com, don't forget to use the search feature to check for general information about places featured in your book.

Baby Name Sites

It seems like there are dozens of Web sites designed to help you choose a first name for your child. These sites can be a source of inspiration as you choose a name for your character. Most baby name sites allow you to search for names by gender and origin, so you can specify that you're looking for a female name of Chinese origin, for instance. The meaning of each name is given, but if accuracy is important to you, you should verify the information found at baby name sites through another source.

A general search under "baby names" through Google or any other popular search engine will yield a host of sites. Some of these include:

www.BabyNames.com
www.BabyCenter.com/BabyName/
www.babynamesworld.com
www.BehindTheName.com
www.BabyNameNetwork.com

Search Engines

Using a search engine is a good way to find obscure information about naming practices. Keep cultural differences and alternate terminology in mind when you enter your search terms. For instance, a search under "first name" will probably yield different results from a search for "given name" or "Christian name." If you don't get good results with the search term "last name," try "surname," and "family name" as well. Likewise, search for both "nickname" and "byname" for information about informal names. The advanced search features of many search engines will allow you to search for sites containing at least one of several different search terms. In other words, you can save time by searching for sites that contain *either* the term "surname" *or* the term "family name," for instance. Many search-engine sites also include indexes of information by topic. Some host communities of people who share a common interest (such as genealogy or a foreign culture); as long as you are courteous and follow the rules for the community, you can join the mailing list, read correspondence among the group members, and post requests for information.

Some popular search engines include:

www.Google.com
www.Yahoo.com
www.AltaVista.com

www.Lycos.com
www.HotBot.com

Special Sources

Online encyclopedias can help out with general information about a culture and its customs and language. One particularly helpful online encyclopedia is Wikipedia at http://en.wikipedia.org. Anyone can contribute to this free encyclopedia, which means that the range of information available through this site is very broad. (In some cases, it may also mean that the information should be verified through other sources.) Wikipedia happens to have quite a bit of information on naming practices.

There are other online sources that can provide vast amounts of information, you just have to look for them. And when you find them, be careful to double check their accuracy and legitimacy.

Native Speakers and Other Experts

Travel sites can also help with your research. Look for sites put up by organizations trying to promote tourism to a specific country or city; sites created by travelers chronicling their experiences and advice for other travelers; and sites established by émigrés who wish to share their native culture with others.

If you can't find the information you need in print or online, contact the international office at a university near you. An advisor may be able to put a note with your contact information in the student newsletter or on a bulletin board. Most universities offer foreign language instruction as well as classes in culture and history. Language and history professors and graduate students may be able to supplement your research or verify information obtained from another source. Conduct as much research as you can through other channels before contacting someone at a university—that way, you are more likely to know the specific questions you need to ask in order to complete your research.

Most colleges and universities have Web sites with departmental contact information. If you can't find a specialist in the U.S., look up universities in other countries. You can often send an e-mail message to the department chair or administrator, and you may get a response, even if the university is in a non-English-speaking country.

THANKS

A special thanks to the following people who shared their time and knowledge about different cultures and their naming practices:

Dr. Alisa Smith, Centre for Maori and Indigenous Planning and Development, Lincoln University, New Zealand and Poia Rewi, Senior Lecturer Te Tumu (School of Maori, Pacific and Indigenous Studies), The University of Otago, Dunedin, New Zealand for their expertise of Maori naming practices.

Andrew HoiCung Thawnghmung and Heather Thawnghmung and Kak Tanjlain for their knowledge of Thai naming practices.

Aniket Breed, Siva Muthukrishnan, and Krishnan V Parthasarathy for sharing information on Indian names and naming practices.

Cy Bridges, Polynesian Cultural Center, for his expertise of Polynesian names.

Danielle Counotte and Gerdien de Jong for their knowledge of Dutch naming practices.

Galit Gertsenzon and Samuel Frank for their expertise of Hebrew naming practices.

Wan-Yu Jenny Lin, Chen Wei, and Ying Li for sharing information about Chinese naming practices.

Kangse Kim for sharing information about Korean naming practices.

Masoud Ghaffari and Soheil Pourshahian for sharing information about Persian names and naming practices.

Peter Szigligeti for his knowledge of Hungarian naming practices.

Kathryn Etcheverria, University Nevada, Reno, Basque Studies Program, for her knowledge of Basque naming practices.

Namy King for sharing information about Portuguese naming practices.

James Tenney, Advisor, University of Cincinnati for helping contact people with expertise in various cultures.

And finally, a special thanks to Nicole Klungle for her contributions to many of the origins.

ABOUT THE AUTHOR

Sherrilyn Kenyon is the *USA Today* and *New York Times* best-selling author of several series, including The Dark-Hunters, Brotherhood of the Sword, The MacAllisters, Sex Camp Diaries, and BAD Boys. Her novel *Fantasy Lover* was voted one of the top ten romances of 2002 by Romance Writers of America. Along with her fictional work, Sherrilyn is an accomplished nonfiction author who has contributed to such works as *The Writer's Complete Fantasy Reference.*

THE TABLE OF CONTENTS

Part 1
THE CRAFT OF NAMING, 1

Part 2
THE LISTS, 15

Sidebars

Part 3
THE INDEXES, 418

1

THE CRAFT OF NAMING

Benad, Benon, B___ Bar___ Benat, __
I, G___ GH__ Gretc___ pearl · Izaa
__ Val__o · Quemby, Quimby from the woman's estate
nping downhill · Quemby, Quimby from the woman's estate
rvest · Helenka light · Konstantin steadfast · Payton, Paden, I
Marcos, Mario, Martin, Martino, Martinez warring · Gabriella s
t fame · Tasanee beautiful view · Oksana, Oxana hospitality · Ngu
nouse · Odelia, Odella, Odelina, Odelinda, Odilia, Otha, Othilia, Odett
krikor *Armenian form of Gregory* watchful · Antton praiseworthy · Phirun rain · (
__ Alzbeta *Czechoslovakian form of Elizabeth* consecrated to God · Vilhelm *Danish for*
yth faithful · Burton, Burhtun lives in the fortified town · Saara, Sari, Saija, Si
~ Ange, Angeline, Angelina, Angelika angel · Yolanda, Yolande, Yolanthe
ilennis, Glynnes, Glynnis, Glynis from the glen · Brendan, Breandan
Lurline, Lurlina, Lurleen, Lurlene temptress · Konrad, Kurt, Kuno, K
al of the sea · Kora, Katakin, Katoka, Katica, Katus, Koto, Katinka
, Debra, Devora, Devoria bee · Mayah, Maia, Michelle, Micheline, '
oria *Hungarian form of Victoria* victorious · Tardos bald · Sakari sweet · .
Mearr, Moira, Moya, Maurya, Muire, Mairona, Mairia bitter · Bra'
· Rafaele, Raphael, Rafaello God has healed · Kaiya, Kaiyo for
Pammeli, Pamelina, Pameline, Pamella made of honey · Terenc_
s red · Kaliska coyote chasing deer · Pannoowau he lies · Kelse
n, Yasmena sweet flower · Saeed, Said, Soroush happy · Rozy
Raanui sacred · Fatima abstain, name of pilgrimage site · M
'f Christmas · Nicolai, Nikita *Russian form of Nicholas* victory ·
'ht-handed · Tira, Tyra land · Alan, Allan, Allen, Alleyn
Venceslava great glory · Boris, Borysko fighter · Brig
ss · Horacio *Spanish form of Horace* timekeeper · Salbator
nnie, Frances, Francine, Fanchon, Franziska, Franze, Fr
nd · Wolfgang wolf's way · Solada listener · Niran eternal ·
Jieu willow · Tuyet snow white · Tuan brilliant · Sang bright · C
ther · Catherine, Cathryn, Catheryn, Cate innocent · Lora, Lore
m the ledge farm · Cary, Carey from the river · Myrna, Merna, M
a untamed · Orson, Ourson little bear · Azizah, Aziza cherished · <
ya, Sofiyko wisdom · Jia lovely and good · Li strength · Wen ornam∈
`, Leena *Finnish form of Helen* (light) · Veli, Veikko, Veijo brother · Ada, Aida, A
`, Bromly from the broom-covered meadow · Harlan, Harland from the har
`, Idalie active · Anton *German form of Anthony* beyond praise · Clovis, Chlodwig far
Jus in war · Julie, Julia, Juliette, Juliet, Julietta, Julita youthful · Simone heard · L
ash-tree meadow · Farook, Farouk One who knows the truth · Gadara, Gadarine fr
n, Morgance, Morgane, Morgana dweller of the sea · Mulan magnolia blossom · Josef
Jle beautiful fairy · Ralph, Ralf, Raff, Rolf, Rolfe red wolf · Susanna, Sanna lilly · Karel, Karl,
g and masculine · Deirdre, Deidra, Deardriu raging · Bernard, Bernon, Bernot, Barnard, Bena
brave as a bear · Greta, Gretal, Grete, Gretel, Gredel, Gryta, Ghita, Gretchen pearl · Isaac, Izaa
Narayan moving water · Cassidy, Casidhe clever · Valentino, Valerio brave, strong · Hiroshi genar
, peaceful · Reka sweet · Pakuna deer jumping downhill · Quemby, Quimby from the woman's estate
a, Teresinha, Tereza, Terezinha summer harvest · Helenka light · Konstantin steadfast · Payton, Pader
nka, Nadyuiska, Nadine hope · Marco, Marcos, Mario, Martin, Martino, Martinez warring · Gabriella str
at, Roibeard, Riobart, Rupert bright fame · Tasanee beautiful view · Oksana, Oxana hospitality · Nguyen c
, Casper treasure · Xavier new house · Odelia, Odella, Odelina, Odelinda, Odilia, Otha, Othilia, Odette, Ott
sia, Ashla, Asha lively · Krikor *Armenian form of Gregory* watchful · Antton praiseworthy · Phirun rain · Gewndolen
asty name, bright moon · Alzbeta *Czechoslovakian form of Elizabeth* consecrated to God · Vilhelm *Danish form of William*
Jus · Faith, Faithe, Fayth faithful · Burton, Burhtun lives in the fortified town · Saara, Sari, Saija, Salli *Finnish for*
Angelique, Angela, Angilin, Ange, Angeline, Angelina, Angelika angel · Yolanda, Yolande, Yolanthe strong · E
indant · Glen, Glenn, Glenna, Glennis, Glynnes, Glynnis, Glynis from the glen · Brendan, Breandan, Brennan, B
mid, Diarmad free man · Lorelei, Lurline, Lurlina, Lurleen, Lurlene temptress · Konrad, Kurt, Kuno, Konni, Kur
le, Coralina, Coralin from the coral of the sea · Kora, Katakin, Katoka, Katica, Katus, Koto, Katinka, Kasienka
saving · Debora, Deborah, Debra, Devora, Devoria bee · Mayah, Maia, Michelle, Micheline, Michaele, Michalin
aim, Efrayim fruitful · Viktoria *Hungarian form of Victoria* victorious · Tardos bald · Sakari sweet · Jafar little stream · Ra
ire, Maire, Mare, Maura, Mearr, Moira, Moya, Maurya, Muire, Mairona, Mairia bitter · Brady, Bradaigh spirited ·
ary · Violet, Violetta flower · Rafaele, Raphael, Rafaello God has healed · Kaiya, Kaiyo forgiveness · Akahata su
tella, Essie star · Pamela, Pammeli, Pamelina, Pameline, Pamella made of honey · Terence, Terrence, Terry sin'
ota friend · Meoquanee wears red · Kaliska coyote chasing deer · Pannoowau he lies · Kelsey, Kelci, Kelda fror
nin, Yasmina, Yasmine, Yasmeen, Yasmena sweet flower · Saeed, Said, Soroush happy · Rozyczka, Roz, Roza
orge farmer · Nahini total woman · Raanui sacred · Fatima abstain, name of pilgrimage site · Monica advisor ·
a, Natassia, Natalia, Natyashenka born at Christmas · Nicolai, Nikita *Russian form of Nicholas* victory of the people

NAMING CHARACTERS

Without a doubt one of the hardest things a writer has to do, other than plot a book, is aptly name the characters. To quote Shakespeare's *Romeo and Juliet*, "What's in a name? That which we call a rose by any other name would smell as sweet." But would it?

A heroine named Bertha doesn't invoke the same response as a Regina or a Juliet. A memorable character name will not only define the book and shape the story, but it should invoke an instant image in the reader's mind.

Case in point, Scarlett O'Hara places a much different image in the reader's mind than Katie O'Hara or even Katherine O'Hara. The name Scarlett completely captures the spirit and fire of the Margaret Mitchell character that we all know and love as the turbulent heroine of *Gone with the Wind*. Her full name was in fact Katie Scarlett O'Hara. The name Katie is sweeter, more demure, almost childlike, while Katherine is proper and formal, neither of which would have been appropriate for our Scarlett.

NAMING GUIDELINES

For myself, when I'm asked about how I come up with names I always say that my people (I never use the term *character* because to me it makes them unreal and to me the people in my books are real, breathing entities) name themselves, and this is oddly enough true. Whenever I sit down to write, my people introduce themselves to me. I then listen to them dictate to me their stories.

But since that is seldom helpful to other writers, I have long been giving workshops and writing articles on more practical ways to get a handle on your own people. Having published works in all major genres, I have learned one thing: Most naming techniques will work no matter what you're writing.

However, you might wish to keep certain things in mind that are genre specific, which I will go into later. For now, here are the ten major guidelines that transcend genre.

1. Capture the persona.

You should always try to choose a name that captures the character's personality, an instant reader association that will allow them to know something about that character. What you wish to convey is solely up to you. But make the name mean something. Don't just arbitrarily decide on a name for any of your people, including secondary characters. You never know when that character will come back to be the hero of another book or even another series. Spend time with every character in your story, large or small. Take a little time and get to know them. Almost everyone human has some type of baggage that comes along with their names. Playing off of this will make your character seem more real.

In my suspense thrillers, the head of the Bureau of American Defense is named Joe Q. Public. His name serves a dual purpose. It shows that his father had a really sick sense of humor that Joe at times shares, and it allows me to play off the fact that the director of BAD isn't your "average Joe." His name is also a constant reminder to the agents that at the end of the day, they all serve a greater purpose. They fight not for themselves, but for the public at large.

Likewise, in my Dark-Hunter vampire novels, their leader is named Acheron, which is an ancient Greek name in keeping with his eleven-thousand-year-old heritage. The name itself is taken from the River of Woe in the Underworld that mortal souls must cross in order to reach their final resting place. The symbolism of the name and its meaning were perfect for Acheron's role in my vampire universe.

In my Brotherhood of the Sword medieval series, I have a character named Damien St. Cyr. The name Damien is a Norman French form of the Greek Daemon, which means "demon." The character in the series is a good guy turned evil, but who is ultimately redeemed. While he is evil, Demon is the perfect choice for him. His surname comes from the Catholic Saint Cyr, who was a pilgrim to the Holy Land who was persecuted because of his beliefs. Since Damien was taken prisoner in the Holy Land and tortured for his faith and political position, he took that name as his as a reminder of everything he had suffered and survived.

When deciding on names, think of your character name's connotation. In *The Three Musketeers* by Alexandre Dumas, Lady de Winter is the cold and calculating villainess. The name completely suits her.

However, if you are writing a romance novel, you might not want to name your heroine Winter or anything that makes the reader think that she is unfeeling or emotionally distant.

Choosing a name that captures your character is truly limited only by your imagination. But always remember that it is the first link your reader will have to your story.

2. Choose a name in keeping with your character's heritage and personality and/or trade.

A wonderful example of this is found in Sara Paretsky's V.I. Warshawski series. V.I. is sensitive about her name, which is a formal-sounding Victoria. She refers to herself mostly as Vic, which is in keeping with her tough PI reputation. Her last name, Warshawski, is indicative of her father's Polish heritage. A few members of her family and friends sometimes call her Vickie, but she is extremely selective about who gets to use that name with her.

Now this isn't to say that she couldn't be a PI named Victoria Warshawski or Vickie Warshawski, but that would lend itself to a whole other dimension in the series as she struggled for respectability. Most people would feel much more comfortable entrusting their lives and secrets to a Vic or V.I. than they would with a Vickie.

How you want to play the character is solely up to you, but do remember that in certain fields unorthodox names will carry a lot of personal baggage for the character.

3. Make the name harmonious.

Vary the syllables between first and last names. Jonathan Wright has a much more attractive ring to it than John Wright. However, nonvaried names can work effectively in such cases as Ian Fleming's James Bond. But I think one of the reasons why his name is so successful is because he usually introduces himself as "Bond. James Bond," which has its own unique harmony to it as well as conveying the character's trademark arrogance.

I've heard many writers say that to them the perfect harmonious blends are names that add up to a total of five syllables. I'm not sure I agree with it, but I have noticed that I stick to four- and five-syllable names myself.

The main thing is not to get in a rut. Don't make every character in the book a four- or five-syllable name, just the main characters.

4. Keep the character's name consistent with his or her time period.

Readers will be thrown off if they find a Sherri or Brandy in your tenth-century Viking novel set in Scandinavia, unless it is a time travel and they are from the modern era.

However, there's more to this than just the obvious. Having a name that is accurate to the time period is one thing, but you should always remember the reader's expectations as well. I will never forget years ago when I was on an online bulletin board where a reader was expressing her extreme anger over an author using the name Brian in a medieval set historical. When I wrote to explain to her that the name was a common ancient Irish name and was used by several Irish kings, including Irish High King Brian Boru (940–1014) the reader still accused me of being wrong because everyone knows the name Brian is a twentieth-century name.

Likewise, I have seen people say the same of the name Tiffany, which is, in fact, a common medieval French Norman name (Tifini, Tiffini, or Tiphany) as far back as the twelfth century. Tiffany with its "modern" spelling is even found in seventeenth-century records as a given name both in England and here in the New World.

But because readers associate names such as these with modern culture, be aware that should you use them even though it is accurate to your time period, some readers will never be convinced that you did your research. As a result of this, I often caution writers to stick to known historical names for their time periods or to at least be ready to defend their choices when they deviate from what readers expect.

5. Keep the character's social status in mind.

Until recently, it was virtually unheard of to find European nobility named "common" names such as Sarah, Molly, Emma, etc. They relied on the traditional names such as Elizabeth, Victoria, Anne, and such that were recycled through their families. Today they are bucking that tradition, but remember that if you have a character who does, it would be a cause for alarm to the rest of the family who might want a more traditional name chosen.

Likewise, if your character is a dirt farmer from rural Alabama circa the depression era, he most likely wouldn't have the name Rupert, Ignacio, or Pedro.

In *No Ordinary Princess,* Pamela Morsi has an interesting character named Princess whose father was an average, common man who made it rich in the oil mines. He named his daughter Princess because that is what she was to him, and Princess had a hard time living up to that name.

6. Use nicknames.

If you have a character that historically or culturally has to have a horrifically bad name such as Horatio Hornblower, you might wish to use a nickname for them. With a little imagination these can be played very well. One of the best examples of this is Stephanie Laurens, who uses nicknames to add an additional layer to her characters. In her best-selling Cynster series, all the men have traditional English noble names such as Rupert, Sylvester, Harry, etc., which are not romantic names by any means.

So, to stay historically accurate and yet give her readers names that would be evocative and sexy, she nicknamed every one of them with names such as Scandal, Devil, Demon, etc., but the neatest part about this is that none of the names are given for the reason the reader expects.

Take the name Vane for instance. Some readers might expect it to come from the fact that he is vain, but, in fact, the nickname stems from his being steadfast like a weather vane that always points true north.

7. Vary the names of the characters.

Don't get stuck on a letter or a rhythm. If you use names that sound or look alike, it can become confusing to readers. Alice, Alec, Alister, Adam, Aaron begin to look alike to the reader. I've also noticed that most writers tend to get stuck on certain letters for names. My two sins are the letters *A* and *S.* For some reason, I gravitate toward those letters and I have to force myself to use the rest of the alphabet.

8. Remember the genre.

Again, this gets back to reader expectations. If you are writing a Western and you have a hero named Giles de Givrey, it most likely won't ring true to your audience. Likewise fantasy readers aren't expecting to come across a heroine named Martha Williams.

9. If you choose a name that breaks the rules, explain it.

The above names could work, provided you let the audience know that Martha Williams fell into an enchanted tree while she was visiting a state park in Idaho and woke up in an alternate universe where she now has to battle evil to save the world. Or Giles might be the child of French immigrants who came out west to start a new life and were then murdered by the bad guy.

10. Avoid the names others have made famous.

Most character names are not trademarked; however, some are. But regardless of whether they've been trademarked, it's always a good idea to avoid the names that other people have made famous.

Yes, Anita Blake is a common name, but readers can sometimes get defensive about seeing another author use a name one of their favorite authors made famous—in this case, Laurell K. Hamilton's famous vampire hunter. Sometimes it happens inadvertently, but you should always try to stay away from other's territory.

Likewise, try to stay on top of naming trends in your chosen genre. Certain names seem to run in cycles, and I have never really figured out why. I remember a while back the name Shea was extremely popular in the fantasy genre. It seemed as if every book I picked up had a character named Shea.

When I started writing my book *Fantasy Lover*, no Julians were in sight. Yet, when my book came out, it seemed to be the year of the Julian. Every book I picked up had the name in it.

Use your character names to your advantage. Let them help you develop your story in other ways as well. One of the worksheets that I use in workshops asks the author to think about the character's birth order and how the parents felt about his or her birth. In one of my novellas, I have a character named Adrian Lesley Cole who is a man. The reason he has that name is that his mother hates men and she was determined that she would not have a son. As a result, she refused to give him a masculine name. Both the name and her feelings toward him influence their relationship and his life.

How a character feels about his or her name is a goldmine of character development just waiting to happen. Never be afraid to be creative. Remember, regardless of what you're writing, this is your world. These are your people. Make them your own.

SPECIFIC GENRE ADVICE

Writing in a specific genre often requires some extra considerations when naming your characters. Use the following advice to help create suitable genre character names.

Science Fiction/Fantasy: One of the things that I find helpful whenever I'm creating a new world is to pick a culture or language to build from. In the case of my vampire world, I use Greek as my base language for new terminology and for first and last names. It helps to build consistency, and it gives me a foundation to build from.

Case in point, my vampires are called Daimons, which is the Greek word for "demon," because they predate the origin of the word *vampire*. Everything in their world comes from ancient Greece, therefore the realm of Katoteros is taken from the Greek word meaning "nether," and Kalosis is from the Greek word *Kalasi* meaning "hell." I don't always choose a Greek term as my root word, but when I'm making up new terms, I make sure that they at least sound Greek.

One thing I would always caution against though is using names that the reader stumbles over. Most of us read aloud in our heads. If a reader has a hard time understanding the name, you run the risk of losing him or her.

However, when you create an entirely new universe or realm, your characters' names—as well as the names of the realms they inhabit—may have no direct reference to Earth or civilizations, as in the case with Margaret Weis and Tracy Hickman's Death Gate Cycle series.

For example, the elves have lyrical names such as Agah'ran and Rees'ahn. The dwarves' names, Limbeck and Jarre, summon images of solidity and strength. One of the evil magicians, Sinistrad, has a name that instantly evokes the feeling of malevolence. The main antagonist in the series is a magician named Xar, giving images of darkness and maliciousness.

The four realms they use are Arianus (air), Pryan (fire), Abarrach (stone), and Chelestra (water). Reading the names of the realms, the reader has a sense of what that world is comprised of.

As you can see, when creating worlds of this type, let your mind run free using names with sounds that suggest the image you want to portray.

Horror: Horror, much like SF/F, is a genre where you can let your mind run wild. However, I hold the belief that if Amity Beach had been named Hell Town, *Jaws* wouldn't have been half as scary. Most horror writers tend to take the mundane and make it spooky. To me, part of this is taking something as innocuous as naming your car Christine and turning that car with such a wholesome name into a lethal killer.

In Stephen King's epic Dark Tower series, readers automatically know they are going to be reading a "dark" book. In the first book of the series, King names his lead character Roland of Gilead, based on a poem "Childe Roland" by Robert Browning. The name gives the character historical complexity as well as meaning for the reader.

Another character in the Dark Tower series shows us the differing personalities that names portray. Odetta Holmes is a woman with a dual personality, one that she is unaware of. Odetta is rich, polite, and formal, just as her name suggests. Her alter ego, Detta Walker, is a tough, mean, street-smart killer. When King meshes these two personalities into one and forces them to take on each other's attributes, the result is Susannah Dean, formal and kind as well as tough and street-smart.

One thing that King has brought through several of his works from *The Stand* to *The Eyes of the Dragon* to the Dark Tower series is the consistent use of the same letters (R.F.) as the resident evil. In *The Stand* it was Randall Flagg; in *The Eyes of the Dragon*, again, it was Randall Flagg; and in the Dark Tower series it was Richard Fannin.

The constant use does not only intrigue the reader, but the implication instantly frightens, which, of course, is King's ultimate goal.

Romance: No hard, fast rules exist for naming a romance character. My personal tastes run to using a softer name for my heroines and a stronger name for my heroes. That being said, I don't always follow through with this. Romance readers seem to be open-minded about what they'll accept.

In contemporary romance, the writer can take many liberties since the names don't need to be historically accurate. In Suzanne Brockmann's *Unsung Hero*, Navy SEAL Lieutenant Tom Paoletti's name instantly brings to mind strength and dependability. When first introduced to the heroine, Dr. Kelly Ashton, the reader will picture a vibrant, spunky woman who is also intelligent and proud of it.

Regional settings often dictate the names of the people in contemporary stories. Here is where it pays to do some research. Find out what groups settled into the area. Local white pages or community phone books are an ideal resource for regional names. The surname Boudreaux might be a common name for Louisiana but would sound distinctly out of place in downtown Chicago. Armed with the knowledge of the surname origins, you can then look up the ethnic section of this book to find a larger list. Case in point, the French settled Louisiana. Therefore when naming a Cajun character, the best place to look is under French. If you have an NYPD character and have done the research to see that many of them are of Irish descent, look under Celtic, Gaelic, and Irish.

With historical romance, the readers do like to see traditional names of that time period, and as I have seen, if readers don't believe the name belongs, they could become irate.

Johanna Lindsey keeps her readers and characters rooted in the tumultuous Regency period with her Malory series. It is not just a matter of utilizing names that the reader will believe were used in the early nineteenth century, it also means having the correct use of titles as well as the names of residences, which reflected the owner.

One of the characters in the Malory series, Anthony, is a rather handsome rake. Society knows him as Lord Anthony, a name tied to power, status, and fear. Yet, his family calls him Tony, and the reader instantly knows that the persona Tony portrays to society is nothing like the real man, who is a jokester and charmer.

Another character is Regina Ashton, niece to the Malorys. Most call her Regina, invoking the image of refined beauty and elegance, of which she is. However, one of her uncles calls her Reggie, instantly making the reader picture an imp of a girl getting into all sorts of trouble without thought to consequences. Yet another uncle calls her Reagan, and we get an additional picture of the character, this one of a strong-willed and levelheaded woman. And as we read through the story we find that Regina is indeed all those things and more. Lindsey captures the heroine in each of the names.

Thrillers: In the case of the protagonists, the trend seems to be for short average names such as Tom Clancy's Jack Ryan or J.D. Robb's Eve Dallas. Again, strong names are the norm. Readers seem to expect something catchy and smart.

War/Military: In the case of W.E.B. Griffin's Corps series, the names are specific to the World War II time period, such as Edward Banning, Malcolm "Pick" Pickering, and Ernestine Sage. Military writers are careful to assign their characters names that are also geographically and culturally correct.

Griffin uses names that were common in high society at the time, as most of his characters were not only successful military men but also wealthy and prominent in society.

Teen fiction: The first teen books that usually come to mind are the Harry Potter series. With her spellbinding books, J.K. Rowling has immortalized the name Harry—a boy who starts out average but then turns out to be special. Teens want to read about people their own age. They don't want to read about a Florence, they want to read about a Carly or a Madison. Meg Cabot has also captured teens and young girls across the country with her Princess Diaries series and heroine Mia Thermopolis.

Western: One of the premiere writers of westerns, Louis L'Amour defined the genre with his unforgettable pioneer family, the Sacketts. From Barnabas to Orrin, the names fit the characters like well-worn boots. The Old West was filled with such hard names as Wyatt Earp, Billy the Kid, and Doc Holliday—and readers of Western fiction have come to expect their characters to have names along those lines.

Surnames may vary; however, one must be careful to remain true to the period and history. For example, a lot of Irish people immigrated to the West but not many Russians. One would be more likely to run into a Curly Joe O'Keefe than they would a Curly Joe Rominov.

Mystery: Agatha Christie captured the genre with her Belgian sleuth, Hercule Poirot. Hercule is a French form of Hercules, and to read that name invokes an image of a man with more strength and integrity than a normal person has. It was the perfect fit for the brilliant detective.

Another example is Elizabeth Peters and her Amelia Peabody series. The name Amelia certainly suits the brainiac Egyptologist as no other name could.

Sherlock Holmes and his famous sidekick Dr. Watson and nemesis Moriarty are three characters created by Sir Arthur Conan Doyle.

The mere mention of these characters' names invokes the image of high intellect, tenacity, perseverance, and extreme cleverness. How different would the story have been if Doyle had named the characters Robert Stanley, Dr. Brown, and Bruno?

Erotica: The erotica genre has no rules. Some readers prefer the more common names, such as Brandon and Cindy, giving rise to the idea that average, everyday people can experience erotic adventures. Others like names that have great sex appeal, like Delilah or Eve, and Slade or Tristan, which give the reader an immediate sense of sensuality and sexual prowess.

You need to be careful as names not normally associated with sex and sexuality, such as Bertha or Percy, can send the reader inaccurate images of your character. Subsequently, instead of having images of a strong, viral man they would see a scrawny, wimpy nerd.

Paranormal: Paranormal is a genre that can take a reader from modern day Houston, Texas, to Renaissance England in the space of a few pages. It allows the writer many degrees of leniency as far as names go; however, it brings its own special restrictions. Rules of both contemporary and historical fiction apply. Since paranormal can encompass any and all genres, from Western to horror to romance to erotica, the rules of the specific genres accessed must apply.

It is perfectly acceptable, and indeed desirable, to find a heroine with the name Makayla who has traveled back in time so the reader will easily identify the character and the confusion and conflict the time travel has caused.

NAMING PLACES AND THINGS

Character names are important, but so are the names you give your settings, homes, and animals. If you write SF/F, then most likely you need to create your own world or universe and aptly name it. Again, it is usually easier to pick an ethnic basis for your nomenclature. Deciding on these names for alternate or parallel universes isn't always easy.

Neither is finding the perfect name for the castle in your medieval story. If you write a historical and your character is a peer of the realm, then he needs a title, sometimes more than one.

What about your character's favorite horse, dog, cat, or any other animal? You can't name the character's dog Muhammad Ali if your book is set in the Roman period.

This is why names are so important to books. Readers have to connect on all levels—from the characters to the animals to the setting. We are known by our names, and every word in the language packs an emotional and mental wallop.

Remember the power of a single word to create an image in the mind. One of my favorite songs is written by Tal Bachman, and I use it often while teaching writing classes. "If You Sleep" is about a woman who dies, and it contains one stanza that, with only a handful of words, paints the perfect image of a funeral in your mind. You can see it vividly. People have emotional and mental associations to all words. Achilles and Samson will always be names of great strength. Percy or Cecil will always been associated with a prissy type of man.

But names also transcend the characters. If your work is set in a modern-day corporate environment, you'll have issues of liability. Even if you don't say anything negative about a company, its lawyers might be rather upset if you use its trademarked business name without permission. In my Sex Camp Diaries series, I have a publishing company. To avoid any unpleasantries, I made it a fictional company, which I named Rose Publishing.

Likewise, I seldom pick a real town to set any of my stories in, whether they are historical or contemporary. The one rare exception is New Orleans, which I use as a setting for my vampire novels for several reasons. One, I used to live there, and two, it is a perfect atmospheric setting for the paranormal.

Using an existing place is tricky unless you are extremely familiar with it. People who live there don't like to see a character go the wrong way down a one-way street. You are also limited by real-life history and culture. For that reason, I prefer to create my own realm. But that being said, Laurell K. Hamilton has done an incredible job of bringing zombies and vampires into St. Louis.

If you're like me and you want to create believable cities and towns, it's easier to base the initial layout on a town or city that you are intimately familiar with. Then choose a name that conveys the emotion you wish the reader to connect to your place. Antarctic,

Connecticut, has an entirely different feel than Sun City, Connecticut, does. Greenville casts the opposite image than Dust Bowl does.

But whether you're naming people or places, there is something to be said for searching a naming book to find the exact name that matches your image. That "aha" moment when your eyes scan the page, light on a name, and the person in your head begins to call out, "That's me!" That's when you know you've found the right name.

...rd... ...s... ...nakin, Kat...
...Dana, De...ra, De... bee · Maya...
· Efrayim fruitful · Vi...a *Hungarian form of Victoria* victorious · Tan...
...oll... ...are, Maur... ...earr, Mol... ...aurya, Muire, Mairo...
...ary · Violet... ...ta flowe... Rafaele, Raphae... ...ello God has heale...
...Essie the... Pamel... ...mmeli, ...elina, P...line, Pamella made o...
...u... ...uanee w...s red · Ka... ...hasing deer · Pannoowa...
..., Yasmina, Yasmine, Yasmeen, Yasmena sweet flower · Saeed, Said, Sorous...
...farmer · Nahini total woman · Raanui sacred · Fatima abstain, name of pilgri...
...atassia, Natalia, Natyashenka born at Christmas · Nicolai, Nikita *Russian form of Nik...*
...Niels, Nils champion · Evanna, Evina right-handed · Tira, Tyra land · Alan, Allan, A...
...Nadyuiska, Nadine hope · Wenceslaus, Wenceslava great glory · Boris, Borysko fi...
...ata, Chela consolation · Tia aunt, princess · Horacio *Spanish form of Horace* timekeepe...
...f, Olaf ancient · Rolf wolf · Fanny, Fannie, Frances, Francine, Fanchon, Franziska, ...
...a free · Hew, Hewitt heart and mind · Wolfgang wolf's way · Solada listener · Nira...
...dymyr to rule with greatness · Lieu willow · Tuyet snow white · Tuan brilliant · Sa...
...orn near the sea · Tad, Tadd father · Catherine, Cathryn, Catheryn, Cate innocen...
...y, Geoff peaceful gift · Shelby from the ledge farm · Cary, Carey from the river · My...
...amien, Damiane, Damia, Damiana untamed · Orson, Ourson little bear · Azizah, Azi...
...entious · Duhkha sorrowful · Sofiya, Sofiyko wisdom · Jia lovely and good · Li stren...
...Helja, Helli, Eila, Elina, Leena *Finnish form of Helen* (light) · Veli, Veikko, Veijo b...
...romleah, Bromleigh, Bromly from the broom-covered meadow · Harlan, ...
...s · Ida, Idaia, Idna, Idalie active · Anton *German form of Anthony* beyond pra...
...loisee famous in war · Julie, Julia, Juliette, Juliet, Julietta, Julit...
...s at the ash-tre... meadow · Farook, Farouk One who knows the ...
...organ... ... Morgane, Morgana dweller of the sea · Mulan m...
...ry · Ralph, Ralf, Raff, Rolf, Rolfe red wolf · Susanna, ...
...e · Deirdre, Deidra, Deardriu raging · Bernard, Bernon, b...
...sar · Greta, Gretal, Grete, Gretel, Gredel, Gryta, Ghita, Gretche...
...y water · Cassidy, Casidhe clever · Valentino, Valerio brave, stro...
...sweet · Pakuna deer jumping downhill · Quemby, Quimby from the...
...eza, Terezinha summer harvest · Helenka light · Konstantin steadfast ...
...Nadine hope · Marco, Marcos, Mario, Martin, Martino, Martinez warring ...
...bart, Rupert bright fame · Tasanee beautiful view · Oksana, Oxana hospitali...
...e · Xavier new house · Odelia, Odella, Odelina, Odelinda, Odilia, Otha, Othilia, ...
...ively · Krikor *Armenian form of Gregory* watchful · Antton praiseworthy · Phirun rain · G...
...moon · Alzbeta *Czechoslovakian form of Elizabeth* consecrated to God · Vilhelm *Danish form ...*
..., Fayth faithful · Burton, Burhtun lives in the fortified town · Saara, Sari, Saija, Salli *Fin...*
...a, Angilia, Ange, Angeline, Angelina, Angelika angel · Yolanda, Yolande, Yolanthe stron...
...i, Glenna, Glennis, Glynnes, Glynnis from the glen · Brendan, Breandan, Brenna...
...nan · Lorelei, Lurline, Lurlina, Lurieen, Lurlene temptress · Konrad, Kurt, Kuno, Konni, K...
...from the coral of the sea · Kora, Katakin, Katoka, Katica, Katus, Koto, Katinka, Kasienk...
...orah, Debra, Devora, Devorla bee · Mayah, Maia, Michelle, Micheline, Michaele, Michali...
...iktoria *Hungarian form of Victoria* victorious · Tardos bald · Sakari sweet · Jafar little stream · R...
...a, Mearr, Moira, Moya, Maurya, Muire, Mairona, Mairia bitter · Brady, Bradaigh spirited · ...
...er · Rafaele, Raphael, Rafaello God has healed · Kaiya, Kaiyo forgiveness · Akahata su...
...a, Pammeli, Pamelina, Pameline, Pamella made of honey · Terence, Terrence, Terry smoo...
...wears red · Kaliska coyote chasing deer · Pannoowau he lies · Kelsey, Kelci, Kelda from t...
...asmeen, Yasmena sweet flower · Saeed, Said, Soroush happy · Rozyczka, Roz, Roza, R...
...woman · Raanui sacred · Fatima abstain, name of pilgrimage site · Monica advisor · Far...

AFRICAN

Africa has no single naming system. Many different approaches are used in selecting names for children. The most common themes center around respect for ancestors and a deep desire to carry on the names of the ancestors. Coupled with this is recognition of the circumstances of birth. Thus, children born on a given day may be named for that day or for the hour or the season of their birth. Many peoples in Africa also name children in honor of relatives or friends who have recently passed on so as to preserve the name and in the belief that the person has been resurrected in the newborn child.

One naming system is that of the Gikuyu people in Kenya, who always name children after their relatives in a strict system. In this system a firstborn boy is named after his paternal grandfather and a second-born boy after his maternal grandfather; girls are named in the same way after their grandmothers. Third-borns and beyond are named after their parents' brothers and sisters, again alternating between the maternal and paternal sides in the same way. This system means that a "Mugikuyu" (Gikuyu person) will always know both the given name and surname of a child if they know the child's sex, birth order, and the names of the child's parents, grandparents, and aunts and uncles.

Hereditary surnames are not a part of native African culture, although some populations commonly use patronymics. Areas of Africa that are Muslim often use Arabic naming practices, and surnames are used in some areas heavily affected by European colonization. In some areas, a child is given a Western surname (and often a first name as well) when he or she enters school. Naming practices and forms depend on tribal culture, native language, local religion and colonization.

A few surnames:

Azzouzi	Ngoimgo
Diako	Nkansah
Emecheta	Obote
Goniwe	Olembe
Hadhari	Ramaphosa
Kabadi	Rutu
Kangwena	Shukuma
Kwei	Sudani
Mahasampo	Tengelei
Mellouk	Tsirinana

FEMALE

Aba—Thursday's child
Abebi, Abebe—asked for
Abeni—prayed for
Abiba—born after grandmother died
Aissa—gratitude
Aman—trustworthy
Amandla—strength
Aminia—faithful
Anana—gentle
Anaya—looks to God
Anisa—friendly
Arziki—wealth
Asabi—special birth
Asis—sun
Ayanna—beautiful flower
Ayoka—brings joy
Aysha—life
Baako—firstborn
Baba—Thursday's child
Badu—tenth child
Bikita—anteater
Bron—source
Caimile—proverb name
Cataya—proverb name
Cheche—small one
Chinara—God accepts
Chipo—gift
Delu—only girl
Diata—lion
Ebere—mercy
Ellema—milkmaid
Elon—God loves me
Faizah—victory
Falala—abundantly born
Fayola—walks with honor

Femi—beloved
Fisseha—joy
Fola—honor
Folake—pampered with riches
Gavivi—money is good
Gimbya—princess
Gzifa—content
Habika—sweetheart
Hada—salty place
Halima—gentle
Hanzila—path
Hawa—desire
Hazina—treasure
Hidi—root
Ifama—everything is all right
Ilori—unique treasure
Iman—faithful
Iniko—born in dark days
Isabis—beautiful
Isoke—gift
Jahzara—blessed princess
Jendayi—thankful
Jira—blood relative
Johari—gem
Juji—love in abundance
Kabibe—small lady
Kadija—wife of the prophet
Kainda—daughter of the hunter
Kambo—hard worker
Kamili—without blemish
Kanene—little thing in the eye is big
Kapera—child to die
Karasi—wisdom
Karimah—generous
Kasinda—in a family of twins

Kaula—buying
Keeya—blossom
Keisha, Keshia, Kesia—favorite
Kianga—sunshine
Kiden—first female in family of boys
Kissa—born after twins
Lateefah—gentle
Lehana—to refuse
Limber—joyful
Lisimba—lioness
Mahdi—predicted
Maizah—astute
Malaika—angel
Mandisa—sweet
Miyanda—root
Nabelung—lovely
Nafuna—breech birth
Nailah—achiever
Nala—successful
Narkeasha—beautiful
Nasha—born with the rains
Nyeki—second wife
Onaedo—golden
Ontibile—God looks out for
Palesa—flower
Qwara—tribal name
Rach—frog
Raziya—agreeable
Safara—her own space
Safiya—pure
Saidah—happy
Salihah—correct
Sanura—kitten

Sarama—pleasant
Semira—content
Shakila—lovely
Shasa—rare water
Shasmecka—princess
Sibongile—thanks
Sika—cash
Sima—prize
Sitembile—trust
Siyanda—growth
Sukutai—hug
Taifa—tribal
Takala—part of the corn
Takiyah—religious
Tale—green
Tapanga—sweet
Thandiwe—beloved
Tiombe—shy
Ujana—young
Ulan—first of twins
Vasha—language
Venda—from the Bantu
Waseme—meaning unknown
Winta—desire
Xhosa—sweet, tribal name
Xolani—begs forgiveness
Yatima—without parents
Yoruba—tribal name
Zalika—noble
Zhenga—queen
Zina—name
Ziraili—God's helper
Zula—brilliant

MALE

Abu—father
Aitan—challenge fight

Ajani—victor
Alake—honored one

Bahari—of the ocean
Barke—blessing
Braimah—father of many
Chata—finish
Chiamaka—God's greatness
Chike—power of God
Dakarai—happiness
Davu—beginning
Dembe—peace
Diallo—bold
Duka—everyone
Dume—oxen
Essien—born sixth
Fabunni—gift from God
Faraji—consolation
Gamba—warrior
Gazali—mystic
Godana—male
Haben—pride
Hajiri—to flee
Harith—farmer
Haruni—from the mountains
Hirsi—amulet
Ibeamaka—agnates are splendid
Ife—bold love
Ige—born breech
Iggi—single son
Ilom—enemy of many
Issay—hirsute
Jabilo—shaman
Jabulani—joyous
Jafuru—stream
Jayvyn—spirit
Jelani—mighty
Juma—Friday's child
Kabili—ownership
Kaikura—squirrel
Kami—desert

Kaseko—insult
Kasim—leashed anger
Katungi—wealthy
Kazi—work
Kenyi—first son after many females
Keon—meaning unknown
Kimoni—important man
Kojo—Monday's child
Leeto—travels
Lolonyo—beautiful love
Mablevi—honest one
Makalo—questioning
Mansa—ruler
Morathi—intelligent man
Nabulung—not received
Naeem—benevolent
Obiajulu—consolation
Oringo—hunter
Otieno—night born
Paulo—resting place
Polo—alligator
Raimi—sympathetic
Razi—secret
Roho—soul
Runako—good-looking
Russom—chief
Saidi—one who helps
Shakir—grateful
Silko—king of Nubia
Simba—lion
Sondo—Sunday's child
Sulaiman—peaceful (form of Solomon)
Tabansi—endurance
Tabari—historical figure
Tedros—gift of God
Tenen—Monday's child

Tumo—fame
Tupac—warrior with a message
Uba—rich
Upendo—love
Wasaki—enemy

Yobachi—honor to God
Zaid—grow
Zareb—protector
Zikomo—thanks
Zulu—heaven

HALLIE EPHRON

Hallie Ephron is part of the two-person team that creates the Dr. Peter Zak mystery series. Under the pen name G.H. Ephron, Hallie and neuropsychologist Donald A. Davidoff, Ph.D., have published four books. Hallie is one of the four writing Ephron sisters.

It took us forever to name our mystery series character. Thank goodness for the global find-and-replace feature in Word. Finally we settled on Peter for a first name because it's masculine but not macho. For the last name we wanted something short, strong, and easy to remember. We settled on Zak. We might have chosen differently if we'd realized that the name would have to be modified in the Dutch translations. In Dutch, both *Peter* and *Zak* are swear words—I believe for the same unmentionable.

ANGLO-SAXON

The hereditary surnames that we take for granted today were once unknown to the Anglo-Saxon population of England. In fact, few people had any form of identification other than their given name. Occasionally, the names of nobility would include an epithet or description, such as Alfred the Great, Aethelflaed Lady of the Mercians, Harald Bluetooth, Edward the Confessor, or Harold Godwineson (son of Godwine).

In the century before the Norman invasion in 1066, more and more of the English were referred to by their occupation, a distinguishing feature, or their home—for example, Aiken the Miller, Sherrard the Bald, or Aisley of York.

Anglo-Saxon parents searched hard to find distinctive names for their children, names that hadn't been used by an ancestor and weren't being used by anyone in the village or town. To aid in this endeavor, they turned to literature and also combined words and names to form unique names. Edwyn, for example, is a combination of the prefix *Ed-*, which means "wealthy or noble," and *Wyn*, which means "friend."

FEMALE

Acca—from Acca
Aedre—stream
Aefentid—evening
Aefre—forever
Aethelflaed—sister of King
    Edward
Aethelthryth—wife of King
    Ecgfrith
Alodie, Alodia—rich
Andswaru, Andsware—answer
Anlicnes, Anlicnisse—image
Annis—unity
Ar—mercy
Ardith—good war

Arianrod—silver wheel
Ashley, Aisley, Aisly—from the
    ash tree grove
Audrey—noble strength
Bearrocsir—from Berkshire
Bernia, Beornia—battle-maid
Bisgu—cares
Bletsung—blessing
Bliss—happy
Blythe—cheerful
Bodicea, Bodiccea, Bodicia,
    Boadicea, Boudicea,
    Boudicca—victory; also
    queen of the Iceni

Brigantia—Yorkshire goddess
Brimlad—seaway
Bysen—unique
Cartimandua—name of a queen
of Brigantes
Catherine, Cathryn, Catheryn,
Cate—pure (form of
Katherine)
Cearo—sorrow
Chelsea—seaport
Claennis—purity
Clover—clover
Coventina—name of a nymph
Cwen, Cwene—queen
Cyst—best
Daedbot—penance
Daisy—day's eye
Darlene, Darline, Darelene,
Darelle, Daryl, Darel—
tenderly loved
Dawn—dawn
Devona—from Devon
Diera—from Diera
Dohtor—daughter
Don—mother goddess
Eacnung—bears children
Eadgyth—wife of Edward the
Confessor
Eadignes—bliss
Easter, Eostre—goddess of the
dawn; myth name
Eda, Edina—wealthy
Edith, Editha, Edita, Edit, Edyt,
Edyth—wealthy gift
Edlyn, Edlynne, Edlynn, Edla,
Eadlin, Edlin—princess
Edmee, Edmunda, Edmonda—
rich protector (form of
Edmund)

Edris, Edrys—wealthy ruler
Eldrida, Elda, Eldride—wise
adviser (form of Eldred)
Elene—name of a poem
Elga—elf's spear
Ellenweorc—famous courage
Ellette—little elf
Elswyth—elf from the willow
trees
Elva, Elvia—good elf
Elvina, Elwine, Elwyna—friend
of the elves
Engel—angel
Erlina, Erline, Erlene, Aerlene—
elfin
Esma, Esme—kind defender
Estra—myth name
Etheswitha—name of a princess
Freya—queen of the gods
Garmangabis—goddess
worshipped in Lanchester
Hamia—Syrian goddess
Harimilla—Tungrian goddess
Hilda, Hild—battle-maid
Ifield—meaning unknown
Juliana—name of a poem
Kendra—prophetess
Linette, Lynet, Lynette—bird
Lora, Loretta—small sage one
Lyn, Lynn, Linn, Lynna, Lynne—
cascade
Mae, May—kinswoman
Maida, Mayda—maiden
Megan, Meghan—strong and
capable
Mercia—from Mercia
Mildred—gentle adviser
Moira, Moire—bitter

Nelda—by the alder tree
Nerthus—mother of earth
Odelia, Odella, Odelina,
    Odelinda, Odilia, Otha,
    Othilia, Odette, Ottilie,
    Odelyna, Odelyn—little
    wealthy one
Ora—money
Orva—brave friend
Osberga, Osburga—name of a
    queen
Rheda—goddess
Rowena—white-haired
Sibley—friendly

Silver—white
Shelley, Shelly—from the ledge
    meadow
Sulis—goddess who watched
    over Bath
Sunniva, Synne, Synnove,
    Sunn—gift of the sun
Taite, Tayte, Tate, Tait—happy
Udele, Udela—wealthy
Viradecthis—Tungrian goddess
Whitney—from the white island
Wilda—wild
Willa—desired
Wilona, Wilone—hoped for

MALE

Aart, Arth, Arthur, Artair—noble
    bear
Abeodan—announce
Ablendan—blind
Abrecan—storm
Ace, Acey—unity
Acennan—brings
Acwellen, Acwel—kills
Adamnan—name of an abbot
Aelle—name of several kings
Aethelbald—king of Mercia
Aethelbert—name of a king
Aethelfrith—name of a king
Aethelhere—name of a king
Aethelred—name of a king
Aethelwulf—name of a king
Agiefan, Agyfen—gives
Agilberht—name of a bishop
Aglaeca—fighter
Aheawan—cuts down
Ahebban—wages war

Ahreddan—rescues
Aidan—fiery one
Aiken—oaken
Albinus—name of an abbot
Alchfrith—meaning unknown
Alden, Aldin, Alwin, Aldwyn—
    wise protector
Aldfrith—name of a king
Aldhelm—name of a bishop
Aldred—old adviser
Alfred—name of a king
Alger, Algar—noble spearman
Almund—defender of the temple
Alwalda—all-ruler
Amaethon—god of agriculture
Anbidian—patient
Ancenned—only child
Andettan—confesses
Andsaca—enemy
Andswarian, Andswaru—
    answer

Andweard, Andwearde, Andwyrdan—present
Anfeald—simple
Anhaga—solitary
Ann, Ane—name of a king
Anna—name of a king
Anson—son of Ann
Anwealda—ruler
Archard, Archerd—sacred and powerful
Archibald—bold
Arian—spares
Arlice, Arlyss, Arlys, Arwyroe—honorable
Astyrian—remove
Atelic—horrible
Athelstan, Aethelstan—name of a king
Atol—hateful
Attor, Ator—venom
Atyhtan—entice
Audley—from the old meadow
Averil, Averill—born in April
Avery—elf ruler
Awiergan—cursed
Baecere—baker
Baldlice—bold
Bana, Banan—slayer
Banning—one who reads the bannspublic announcement especially in church of a proposed marriage
Bar—boar
Bawdewyn, Bawdewyne—bold friend
Bayen, Benwick, Benoic—from Ban
Beadurinc—warrior

Beadurof—bold in war
Bealohydig—enemy
Bearn—son
Bebeodan—commands
Bede—name of a historian
Beircheart, Bertie—intelligent army
Bellinus—name of a king
Beorn—warrior
Beornwulf—name of a king
Beowulf—intelligent wolf
Berkeley, Barclay—from the birch meadow
Bestandan—stands beside
Besyrwan—ensnares
Betlic—splendid
Birdoswald—from Birdoswald
Bliss—happy
Boniface—good
Borden, Bordan—from the boar valley
Bowden, Boden, Boyden, Bowdyn—blond
Brecc—name of a king
Brice, Bryce—son of a nobleman
Broga, Brogan—terror
Bronson—son of the dark man
Brun, Bron—dark-haired
Byrtwold—meaning unknown
Cadman—warrior
Cadwallon—name of a king
Caedmon—wise warrior
Caedwalla—name of a king
Caflice—brave
Camden, Camdene—from the winding valley
Ceawlin—name of a king
Cedd—name of a bishop

Cenwalh—name of a king
Ceolfrith—name of an abbot
Ceolwulf—name of a king
Cerdic—name of a king
Chad—name of a saint
Chapman—merchant
Cnut—name of a king
Colby—from the dark village
Corey—chosen
Courtland, Courtney, Courtnay—from the court
Cuthbert—famous; intelligent
Cynegils—name of a king
Cyneheard—meaning unknown
Cynewulf—name of a king
Cynn—family
Cynric, Cyneric—powerful
Cyst—best
Daegal, Dougal, Douglas—dweller by the dark stream
Dalston—from Dougal's place
Deman—judge
Denby—from the Danish settlement
Denisc—Danish
Deogol—secret
Derian—harm
Desmond—gracious defender
Devon, Devyn—from Devon
Drefan—trouble
Dreng—warrior
Dreogan—suffers
Drew—wise
Druce—son of Drew
Durwin, Durwyn—dear friend
Eadbert—name of a king
Eadig—blessed
Ealdian—live long

Earh—coward
Earl, Earle, Eorl—nobleman
Earm—wretched
Ebissa—meaning unknown
Ecgfrith—name of a king
Edgar, Edgard, Eadgard—wealthy spear
Edlin, Edlyn, Eadlyn—wealthy friend
Edmund, Edmond, Eamon—rich protector
Edred—name of a king
Edric—wealthy ruler
Edsel—from Edward's hall
Edson, Eddison—Ed's son
Edward, Eadward—rich guardian
Edwin, Edwyn, Eadwyn—wealthy
Edwy—name of a king
Egbert—name of a king
Egesa, Egeslic—terror
Eldred, Eldrid, Eldwin, Eldwyn—wise adviser
Ellen, Elne—courage
Elmer—noble
Erconberht—name of a king
Erian—plows
Ethelbald—name of a king
Ethelbert—name of a king
Ethelred—name of a king
Ethelwulf—name of a king
Fairfax—blond
Faran, Feran—advances
Farmon, Firman—traveler
Felix—name of a saint
Finan—name of a bishop
Fleming—from Flanders

Fraomar—name of a king
Freeman—free man
Fugol—bird
Fyren—wicked
Gaderian—gathers
Galan—sings
Gar, Garr—spear
Garberend—spear-bearer
Garrett, Gareth—strong spear
Geoffrey, Geoff—God's peace
Geraint—name of a king
Gifre—greedy
Gildas—name of a historian
Gimm—gem
Godric—rules with God
Godwine—God's friend
Gordon, Gordie, Gordy—from
    the three-cornered hill
Govannon—god of the forge
Graham, Grahem, Graeme,
    Gram—warring
Gremian—enrages
Grendel—legendary monster
Grimbold—fierce; bold
Grimm, Grimme—fierce
Grindan—sharp
Halig—holy
Halwende—lonely
Ham—home
Hengist—son of Wodan
Heolstor—darkness
Heorot—deer
Hererinc—hero
Heretoga—commander
Hilderinc—warrior
Hlaford—master
Hlisa—fame
Holt—from the forest

Hrothgar—legend name
Hrypa—shouter
Ida—name of a king
Iden—wealthy
Ine—name of a king
Irenbend—iron bend
Irwin, Irwyn—sea lover
Isen—iron
Iuwine—friend
Jeffrey—God's peace (form of
    Geoffrey)
Kenric, Kendrick, Kendryck—
    royal ruler
Kent—white
Kenway—brave in war
Kimball, Kim—royally brave
Landry—ruler
Lane, Lange, Lenge—long
Lar—teaches
Larcwide—counsel
Lathrop—from the farmstead
    with the barn
Leanian—reward
Leax—salmon
Leof—beloved
Lidmann—sailor
List—cunning
Lucan—joins
Lufian—love
Lunden—from London
Lynn, Linn, Lyn, Lin—cascade
Maccus—son of Gus
Magan—competent
Mann—vassal
Manton—from Mann's castle
Maponus—god of youth and
    music
Mars Leucetius—god
    worshipped at Bath

Maxwell—from Maccus's pool
Merton—from the farm by the sea
Modig—brave
Nechtan—name of a king
Nerian—protects
Newton—from the new farm
Nodens, Nodons—British god
Norton—from the north farm
Norville, Norvel—from the north state
Nyle—desire
Octa, Octha—son of Hengist, grandson of Wodan
Odell, Odel—wealthy
Odon, Odin, Odi, Ody—wealthy defender
Offa—name of a king
Ord—spear
Ordway—warrior armed with a spear
Orlege—battle strife
Ormod—sad
Orvin, Orvyn—brave friend
Osric—divine ruler
Oswald—divine power
Oswine—name of a king
Oswiu—name of a king
Oswy—name of a king
Oxa—ox
Page, Paige—page
Peada—name of a prince
Penda—name of a king
Pendragon—from the dragon's enclosed land
Penrith—from Penrith
Perry—from the pear tree
Piers, Pierce, Pearce—rock (form of Peter)

Pleoh—danger
Prasutagus—name of a king
Putnam—from the sire's estate
Raedan, Raedbora—advises
Raedwald—name of a king
Ramm—ram
Rand—shield
Rawlins—son of Rolfe
Recene—quick
Renweard—guardian of the house
Rheged—from Rheged
Rice, Ryce—powerful
Rinan—rain
Rinc—warrior
Ripley—from the shouter's meadow
Rolfe—meaning unknown
Rodor—sky
Rowe, Roe, Ro, Row—red-haired
Roweson, Rowson, Ruadson—Rowe's son
Russell—fox
Rypan—plunders
Sar, Sarlic—pain
Scand—disgrace
Scead, Sceadu—shade
Sceotend—archer
Scowyrhta—shoemaker
Scrydan—clothes
Scur—storm
Seamere—tailor
Seaton—from the farm by the sea
Seaver, Seber, Sever—fierce stronghold
Selwyn, Selwin—friend at court
Seward—guards the coast

Shelby—from the ledge farm

Sheldon—from the hill on the ledge

Shelley—from the ledge meadow

Shephard, Shepard—shepherd

Sheply—from the sheep meadow

Sherard—of glorious valor

Sherwin, Sherwyn—quick as the wind

Sibley—friendly

Sigebert—name of a king

Sihtric—name of a king

Slean—strikes

Slecg—hammer

Snell—bold

Stearc—severe

Stedman, Steadman—owns a farm

Stefn—stem

Stepan—exalts

Stewert, Stewart, Stuart—steward

Stillman—gentle

Stilwell—from the tranquil stream

Storm—storm

Strang—strong

Swift—swift

Swithun—name of a saint

Synn—sin

Tamar—from Tamar

Tedman, Tedmund, Theomund—national protector

Tellan—considers

Temman—tame

Teon—harms

Tilian—strives

Tobrecan, Tolucan—destroys

Tobrytan—crushes

Toland, Tolan—from the taxed land

Torht, Torhte—bright

Torr—tower

Tracy, Trace, Tracey—brave

Tredan—tramples

Treddian—leaves

Trymian—encourages

Trymman—strengthens

Upton—from the high town

Verge—owns four acres of land

Wacian—watchful

Wade—moving

Waelfwulf—wolf of slaughter

Wallace, Wallis—from Wales

Wann—dark

Ware—wise

Warian—attend

Wellington—from the wealthy estate

Werian—defends

Whitney—from the white island

Wilbur—beloved stronghold

Wilfrid—name of a saint

Willan—desired

Winchell, Wynchell—drawer of water

Wine, Wyne—friend

Winter—born in winter

Wirt, Wurt—worthy

Wissian—guide

Woden—king of the gods

Worthington—from the river's
   side
Wregan—accuses
Wright—tradesman
Wulf—wolf

Wulfgar—wolf spear
Wulfhere—name of a king
Wylie—enchanting
Wyman—fighter
Yrre—anger

ARABIC

Arabic names are patronymic in origin, meaning that they are taken from the name of the father, but religious names are also extremely popular. Additionally, names can be descriptive and occupational. Adults are seldom called by their given name except by close friends and family. It is insulting to call any parent or older person by his or her given name.

Moslem names are taken from the names of the prophet Muhammad's immediate family and from the Koran. To help in this endeavor, Muslims combine names that incorporate the necessary religious names.

An Arab's complete name follows this order: professional title, given name, title (Inb, Bin, or Binte), name of father and possibly a few ancestors (genitive indicator, or term that indicates who the child's parents were/are is dropped), Abu or Um, followed by the name of the eldest son (if they have one), then a trade, place, or tribe name. Sometimes, names are shorter and are made up of some combination of the above.

An example of a male name would be Katib Bahir Bin Kalil Kadir Hassan Abu Lufti Riyad. Translation: The Writer Bahir, son of Kalil, grandson of Kadir, great-grandson of Hassan, father of Lufti, from the garden or tribe of Riyad. To most he would simply be known as Katib Bin Kalil Abu Lufti. A female name would be Nazirah Binte Nur Um Lufti. Translation: Nazirah, daughter of Nur, mother of Lufti.

Common genitive articles are:

Ibn—son of
Bin—son of
Binte—daughter of
Abu—father of
Um—mother of
Abd—servant
Al, El—definite article

FEMALE

Aaliyah, Aliya—exalted, to ascend
Abia—great
Abir—fragrant
Abra—lesson
Adara—virgin
Aden—fiery one
Adiba—polite
Adila—similar
Adiva—gentle
Afraima—fruitful
A'ishah, Aisha, Ayisha, Ayska, Asia, Ashia, Asha—lively
Akila, Akilah—intelligent (form of Akil)
Ali—exalted
Alima—knows dance and music
Almira—princess
Altair, Altaira—flying eagle
Alula—firstborn
Alzena, Alzan, Alzina, Alzena—woman
Amal, Amala—hope
Amani—desire
Amber—jewel
Ameerah, Amira—princess
Amina, Amineh—faithful
Anan—clouds
Anisa, Annissa—gracious
Ara—opinionated
Arub, Aruba—loves her husband
Asfoureh—bird
Asima, Azima—defender (form of Asim)
Atia—ancient

Atifa—affection
Atiya—gift
Azhar, Azhara—flower
Azizah, Aziza—cherished
Azra—like a virgin
Bab—from the gateway
Bahira—sparkling (form of Bahir)
Baraka, Barakah—blessed
Bashiyra, Bashira—joyful
Basima, Basimah—always smiling (form of Basim)
Batul, Batula—virgin
Bibi, Bibsbebe—lady
Buthaynah—of a beautiful body
Cala—fortress
Cantara—bridge
Carna—horn
Dirran—unknown origin
Fadila, Fadilah—virtue
Faiza—victorious
Faridah—unique (form of Farid)
Fatima—accustom; daughter of a prophet
Fatin, Fatinah, Fatina—captivating
Ghada—graceful
Habiba—beloved (form of Habib)
Hadil—dove call
Hadiya—gift
Hadya—guide
Haifa, Hayfa—slender
Hala—moon halo
Halah—nimble
Hana—happiness

Hasna—beautiful
Helima—gentle
Iamar—moon
Imam—one who believes in God
Iman—faithful
Intisar, Intisara, Intizara—
    triumphant
Isra—night traveler
Israt—affectionate
Jala—charity
Jamilah, Jamila—beautiful
Jehan—lovely flower
Jumanah—a silver pearl
Kadira—strong
Kalila—dearly loved
Kamilah, Kamila—perfection
Karida—untouched
Karima, Karimah—generous
    (form of Karim)
Kebira—powerful
Khalidah—eternal
Latifa, Latifah—kind, gentle
    (form of Latif)
Leila, Laila, Layla—born at night
Lina—delicate
Mahala—marrow
Majida—glorious
Makarim—honorable
Malak—angel
Malika—master (form of Malik)
Manal—achieve
Manar, Manara—light
Mariam, Maryam—bitter (form
    of Mary)
Matana—gift
Maysun—has a beautiful face
Melek—angel
Meryl, Meriel, Muriel—myrrh

Muna—desire
Munira—sparkling (form of
    Munir)
Myiesha—blessing of life
Nabila—noble one (form of
    Nabil)
Nada—giving
Nadira—precious (form of
    Nadir)
Nafeeza—special
Naimah—comfortable
Nawal—gift
Nawar—flower
Nazirah—alike
Nimah—blessing
Noor, Noura, Nureh—light
Noya—ornament
Nudar, Nudara—gold
Oma—commanding
Qadira—powerful (form of
    Qadir)
Qamra—moon
Rabi—breeze
Rafa—happy
Rahimateh—grace (form of
    Rahimat)
Raja—hope
Rana—behold
Rasha—gazelle
Rashida—righteous
Rihana—sweet basil
Rima—white antelope
Saba, Sabah—morning
Sabira, Sabirah—of great
    patience (form of Sabir)
Sadira—ostrich running from
    water
Safa—innocent

Saffron—spice
Safia—pure
Safiyyah—tranquil
Sagirah—little one
Sahar—awakening
Saida, Saidah—fortunate
Sakina, Sakinah—tranquil
Salima, Salimah—safe
Salwa—comfort
Samar—conversations at night
Sameh—forgiver
Samira, Samirah—woman who
    entertains
Samma—sky
Sana—radiant one
Sara—princess (form of Sarah)
Saree—noble
Sarsoureh—bug (form of
    Sarsour)
Sawsan—lily of the valley
Shahira, Shahirah—famous
Shakira, Shahirah—grateful
    (form of Shakir)
Sharifa, Sharifah—noble
Shunnareh—pleasant (form of
    Shunnar)
Siham—arrows
Sultana—queen
Sumehra—lovely face
Tahira, Tahirah—pure (form of
    Tahir)
Talibah—scholar

Tarub—happy
Thana—gratitude
Thara—riches
Thurayya—star
Ulima—learned
Vega—falling
Wahiba, Wahibah—generous
    one (form of Wahib)
Wahida, Wahidah—unique
Walida—just born
Waqi—falling
Wasima—lovely
Widad—love
Widjan—ecstasy
Yasmin, Yasmina, Yasmeen—
    jasmine
Yusra—prosperous
Zada, Zayda, Zaida—lucky
Zafirah—victorious (form of
    Zafir)
Zahara—blossom
Zahirah—sparkling (form of
    Zahir)
Zahrah, Zahra—white
Zalika—noble
Zara—princess (form of Sarah)
Zarifa—graceful
Zayna—beauty
Zenobia—father's ornament
Zohra—full bloom
Zuleika—wise beauty
Zulema—peaceful

MALE

Aban—meaning unknown
Abba—father
Abbas—lion

Abd al'alim—servant of the all-
    knowing
Abd al Bari—servant of Allah

Abd al Hakim—servant of the wise

Abd al Jabbar—servant of the mighty

Abd al Matin—servant of the strong

Abd al Qadir—servant of the capable

Abd al Rashid—servant of the guided

Abd al Sami—servant of the all-hearing

Abdel—servant

Abd-er-Rahman, Abdalrahman—servant of the merciful one

Abdullah, Abdul—servant of God

Abir—fragrant

Absalom—father of peace

Abu Bakr—companion of Muhammad

Aden—fiery one

Adil—judicious

Adnan—meaning unknown

Ahmed—praiseworthy

Akbar—great

Akil—intelligent

Akram—generous

Aladdin—servant of God

Al'alim—omniscient

Aleser—lion

Ali—exalted

Alim—learned

Altair—flying eagle

Amal—hope

Amin—honest

Amir—prince

Ammar—builder

Ansari—helper

Anwar—shining one

Arif—knowing

Asad—lion

Asfour—bird

Ashraf—honorable

Asim—defender

Aswad—black

Avicenna—myth name

Azim—grand

Aziz—powerful

Azzam—determined

Baghel—ox

Bahir—sparkling

Barakah—blessed

Bari—of Allah

Bashshar—brings good news

Basim—always smiling

Bilal—Muhammed's first convert

Boulus—small (form of Paul)

Bruhier—name of a sultan

Burhan—proof

Butrus—rock (form of Peter)

Cemal—perfect

Coman—noble born

Dabir—teacher

Dawud—beloved (form of David)

Diya al din—faithful

Ebrahim—father of many (form of Abraham)

Eisa—God saves (form of Jesus)

Emir—prince

Fadil—generous

Fahd—lynx

Faisal, Faysal—decisive, resolute

Farid—unique
Faris—knight
Farook, Farouk—one who knows the truth
Farran, Ferran—baker
Faruq—wise
Fatin—captivating
Faxhir—proud
Feroz—successful
Firdos—paradise
Gadi—my wealth
Gadiel, Gadil—God is my wealth
Gamal—camel
Ghassan—youthful
Ginton—garden
Givon—high hill
Habib—beloved
Haddad—smith
Hafiz—guardian
Hakim, Hakeem—wise
Halim—gentle
Hamal—lamb
Hanna—gracious God (form of John)
Harb—war
Haroun, Harun—high mountain; lofty (form of Aaron)
Haroun al Rachid, Harun al Rachid—Aaron the upright
Hashim—destroys evil
Hasim—decisive
Hassan—handsome
Husain, Hussain, Hussein—small beauty
Husam al Din—sword of faith
Ibrahim—father of many (form of Abraham)
Idris—meaning unknown; prophet's name

Imam—one who believes in God
Jabbar—mighty
Jabir—comforts
Ja'far—meaning unknown
Jaleel—great
Jamal, Jamil—handsome
Jawhar—jewel
Jedidiah—hand
Jibril—archangel
Kadar, Kedar—strong
Kadin, Kaden, Khalil—companion
Kadir—green
Kalb—dog
Kalid—eternal
Kalil—good friend
Kaliq—creative
Kamal, Kamil—perfection
Kardel—meaning unknown
Karif, Kareef—born during autumn
Karim, Kareem—generous
Kasib, Kaseeb—fertile
Kasim, Kaseem—divided
Kateb—writer
Kemal—perfect
Khaldun, Khalid—eternal
Khalif—successor
Khalil—friend
Kharouf—lamb
Khayri—generous
Khayyat—tailor
Khoury—priest
Latif—kind, gentle
Lufti—kind
Mahir—skilled
Makin, Makeen—strong
Malik—master

MICHAEL CONNELLY

Michael Connelly is author of the mystery series featuring Hieronymus Bosch. His most recent novel of the series is *The Closers*. He is also the author of *The Poet* and its sequel *The Narrows*. His books have been translated into many languages and are sold worldwide.

I think the naming of characters is one of the most important elements in storytelling. If you start with the belief that your story lives or dies with character, then you begin to see how important a name could be. I believe it is important that the writer never misses an opportunity to say something about character. A name is a starting point. I choose names based on sounds sometimes, but most often I am going for a deeper or hidden meaning. I look for the use of metaphor in a name.

The choice of the name Hieronymus Bosch for a contemporary detective was not arrived at quickly. In fact, when I started writing the first book about this character I called him Pierce. No first name. Just Detective Pierce. This name came from an essay I had read regarding the creation of the fictional detective. The essay held that the detective must be able to pierce all veils and levels of society. He must go wherever the case took him. I took this direction to heart and even called my detective Pierce. It was later, when I was halfway through the first draft of the novel, that I decided to name my detective after an obscure painter from the fifteenth century that I had studied many years before in a college art class. I had a hunch that the name Hieronymus Bosch would work for me on multiple levels. If the reader knew the painter's work, then he would know the metaphor. The painter Bosch created worlds of chaos. His paintings were of a world gone wrong. My Detective Bosch would be investigating chaos. A murder is certainly a symptom of a world gone wrong. On the other hand, if the painter was too obscure for most readers, I thought that it was still a good use of the name. The name is so unusual I thought it might help plant the hook in the reader. I thought the reader would possibly press on to find out more about this detective and where his crazy name came from.

I am glad I went with Hieronymus Bosch as a name for my detective. But later I circled back and used Pierce for the name of the protagonist in another book.

Mansoor—victor
Marid—rebellious
Marwan—meaning unknown
Matin—strong
Moukib—last of the prophets
Mubarak—fortunate
Mudawar—round
Muhammad, Hamid, Hammad, Hamden, Hamdun, Humayd, Mahmoud, Mahmud, Mehemet—praised
Muhunnad—sword
Mukhtar—chosen
Munir—sparkling
Musa—taken from the water (form of Moses)
Mustafa—chosen one
Nabil—noble one
Nabi Ulmalhamah—prophet of war
Nadim—friend
Nadir—precious
Najjar—carpenter
Nasim—fresh air
Nasir—helper
Nasser—victorious
Nour, Nur—light
Omar, Omer, Ommar—first son
Osama—lion
Osman—tender youth
Qadir—powerful
Qasim, Qaseem—divides
Rabi—breeze
Rafi—exalted
Rafiq—companion
Rahimat—grace
Rahman—merciful
Ra'id—leader

Rakin—respectful
Rashad, Rashid—integrity
Riyad—garden
Sabih—handsome
Sabir—of great patience
Sadik—truthful
Sadiq—friend
Saghir—short
Sahir—wakeful
Salah—righteous
Salim, Saleem, Salem—peace
Salman—conqueror
Sami—all-hearing
Samman—grocer
Saqr—falcon
Sarsour—bug
Sayyid—master
Seif—sword of the faith
Shakir—grateful
Sharif—honest
Shunnar—pleasant
Sulaiman—peaceful (form of Solomon)
Tabari—meaning unknown
Tahir—pure
Tamir—owns palm trees
Tarafah—tree
Tarif—unique
Tarik—star; path
Taweel—tall
Taysir—makes easier
Umar, Umarah—long life
Wafiyy—loyal
Wahib—generous one
Walid—newborn male
Wasim—handsome
Xavier—intelligent

Yacoub—supplanter (form of Jacob)

Yaman—meaning unknown

Yasin—rich

Yasir—rich

Yusuf—God adds (form of Joseph)

Zafir—victorious

Zahid—altruistic

Zahir, Zuhayr—sparkling

Zaki—smart

Zero—empty

Zoltan—ruler

ARMENIAN

Armenian surnames are chosen from place names and occupational names. They also can be patronymic and descriptive.

Surnames ending in -uni or -ooni were common among Armenian aristocracy: Sasuni. Surnames ending in -ian or -yan are frequently patronymic or occupational in origin: Davidian (son of David), Najarian (son of a carpenter). Other surnames are based on place names, and were formed by adding -lian or -tsian: Marashlian (from Marash). Armenian surnames were frequently modified or shortened when the bearer moved to another country. Because Russia or the Soviet Union claimed or occupied Armenia at various times, some Armenian names have Russian endings (-ov or -ova; -sky or -skaya).

A few surnames:

Abovian	Karayan
Akopian	Kevorkian
Avdalbekian	Khodijian
Bedrosian	Kooyumjian
Bogdanian	Meliksetian
Bogosian	Missirian
Chalabov	Narekatsi
Dilbarian	Nurijanian
Draskhankertsi	Ozmanian
Egoyan	Petrosian
Fatalov	Rostomian
Gharibian	Sadoyan
Haig	Sarkissian
Hegelian	Shatverian
Hovhaness	Tumanyan
Iskandarian	Yesoyan
Izmirlian	Zarafian

FEMALE

Anahid—divine; moon goddess; myth name (form of Diana)
Ankine—valuable
Anoush—sweet tempered
Araxie—river inspired poetry
Armenouhie—woman from Armenia
Dikranouhi—queen
Elmas—diamond
Gadara, Gadarine—from the top of a mountain
Gayane—meaning unknown
Karyan—dark one
Lucine—moon
Margarid—pearl (form of Margaret)

Miriam—rebellious; biblical name
Nairi—from Armenia
Ohanna—God's gracious gift
Perouze—turquoise
Serpuhi, Sirpuhi—holy
Shakeh—meaning unknown
Shoushan—lily (form of Susan)
Siran—beautiful
Siroun—lovely
Sirvat—beautiful rose
Takouhi—queen
Vartoughi—rose
Voshki—golden
Zagir, Zagiri—flower
Ziazan—rainbow

MALE

Antranig—firstborn
Ara—legend name
Armen—Armenian
Arpiar—sunny
Arshavir—meaning unknown
Artaxiad—name of a king
Athangelos—name of a historian
Avarair—from Avarair
Avedis—brings good news
Bedrosian—rock; descended from Peter
Boghos—small (form of Paul)
Dickran, Dikran—name of a king
Eznik—name of a fifth-century philosopher
Garabed—forerunner
Ghoukas—light (form of Luke)

Hagop—supplanter (form of James)
Haig—from the hedged field
Haroutyoun—resurrection
Hovan, Hoven, Hovhaness—God's gift
Hovsep—God adds (form of Joseph)
Izmirlian—from Izmir
Jirair—hardworking
Karayan—dark
Kevork—farmer
Khachig—small cross
Kolb—from Kolb
Korian—name of a historian
Krikor—watchful (form of Gregory)

Magar—meaning unknown
Mesrop—name of a saint
Nishan—sign
Parounag—grateful
Sahak—one who laughs (form of
    Isaac)

Sarkis—royalty
Tiridates—name of a king
Vahe—victor
Vartan—giver of roses
Yervant—meaning unknown
Zeroun—wise

ARMENIAN

ARTHURIAN LEGEND NAMES

The legendary King Arthur is thought to be based on a sixth-century military leader who led the native Britons against the invading Saxons. Arthurian history is almost impossible to distinguish from Arthurian legend, and each new iteration of the legend was influenced by the language, culture, and politics at the time it was written. There are very few names associated with the historical Arthur; many of the names as we know them now have been invented or adapted from other, older names. For instance, Arthur's sword was given the name Excalibur by the twelfth-century French author Wace, who adapted the name from Geoffrey of Monmouth's Caliburn, which came from the name of a legendary Irish sword Caladbolg, which came from the Welsh Caledfwlch. Many names from Arthurian legend appear French; this is the influence of French writers, especially Chretien de Troyes, who introduced Lancelot into the legend in the twelfth century.

Surnames were not used in Arthur's time, but bynames were not unusual. A byname is a descriptive nickname, like Le Fay (the fairy) and Pendragon (head of the dragons). The names in this section should not be taken as representative of sixth-century Britain. For more information, see the sections on Anglo-Saxon, Celtic, English, French, Gaelic, Irish, Scottish, and Welsh names.

FEMALE

Acheflour, Blancheflor, Blancheflour—white flower
Ade—a mistress of Lancelot
Albiona—white
Angharat, Angharad—a love of Peredur
Anglides—mother of Alexandre (twelfth century)
Anna—Arthur's sister (twelfth century)

Argante—name of a queen (thirteenth century)
Astolat—Lady of Shalott; kills herself for the love of Lancelot (thirteenth century)
Avalon, Avilon, Avaron, Avarona—Arthur's burial place
Bedegrayne—name of a castle

Belakane—an African queen (thirteenth century)

Branwen, Branwyn—daughter of Llyr

Brengwain—unknown

Camelot—Arthur's castle (twelfth century)

Chelinde, Chelinda—Tristan's grandmother

Clarine—mother of Lancelot

Clarissant—sister of Gawain

Condwiramurs—wife of Percival

Cotovatre—name of a lake

Creiddyladl—daughter of Lludd

Cundry, Cundrie—woman who condemns Percival

Dechtire, Dechtere—unknown

Deira—unknown

Dummonia—unknown

Elaine, Elayne, Helain—mother of Lancelot

Elizabeth—sister of Mark

Elsa—rescued by Percival

Enid, Enite, Enide—faithful/ abused wife

Enygeus—grandmother of Percival

Ettard, Ettare—lover of Pelleas

Fenice—unknown

Floree—unknown

Florete—unknown

Galiene—a lady

Ganieda—Merlin's sister

Graine, Grainne—taken from Igraine

Grisandole—a princess who dresses as a man

Guenloie—a queen

Guinevere, Guanhamara, Gvenour, Wenhaver, Quinevere, Guanhumora— Arthur's queen

Gwenddydd—Merlin's sister

Gwendlolen—Arthur's wife

Gwendoloena—Merlin's wife

Gwenhwyfach—Guinevere's sister

Herzeloyde—Percival's mother

Iblis—wife of Lancelot

Igraine, Igerne, Ygerne, Igrayne—mother of Arthur

Isabella—unknown

Isolde, Isoud, Ysolde, Isoude— lover of Tristan

Kundry—unknown

Laudine—a widow

Lausanne—Lake Geneva

Lidoine—daughter of Cavalon

Llamrei—Arthur's horse

Luned, Lunet, Lunete—servant of Laudine

Lynet, Lynette—sister of Lyonors

Lyonesse, Lyones—wife of Gareth

Lyonet—sister of Lyones

Lyonors, Lysanor—mother of Boore

Maledysaunte—unknown

Matilda—mother of Merlin

Melissa—unknown

Modron—goddess; possible precursor of Morgan le Fay

Morcades—sister of Arthur

Morgan, Morgana, Morgan le Fay—half sister of Arthur; enchantress

Morguase, Morgawse, Margawse—mother of Gawain

Nineve, Nimue, Nimiane, Vivien, Viviane, Nyneve—the Lady of the Lake

Olwyn—daughter of a giant

Orguelleuse—an arrogant lady

Pridwyn, Prydwyn—name of Arthur's ship

Ragnall—Gawain's wife

Saveage—sister of Lyones

Sebille—a fairy

Shalott—land of Astolet

Sigune—Percival's cousin

Soredamors—Gawain's sister

Tyramon—a fairy princess

Yserone—unknown

MALE

Aballach, Avalloc—father of Modron

Accalon—lover of Morgan le Fay (fifteenth century)

Aglaval, Aglarale, Aglaral—brother of Percival (fourteenth century)

Agravain—brother of Gawain (thirteenth century)

Alain—from Alain le Gros, one of the Fisher kings (thirteenth century)

Albion—from Britain

Alexandre, Alixandre—nephew of King Mark (twelfth century)

Aleyn—a Fisher king

Alis—brother of Cliges (twelfth century)

Amr, Anir—son of Arthur (ninth century)

Andret—King Mark's nephew (twelfth century)

Anguysh—father of Isolde

Antfortas—keeper of the grail (thirteenth century)

Antor, Auctor—foster father of Arthur (thirteenth century)

Apollo—uncle of Tristan

Arden—unknown

Arthgallo—high honor

Arthur—king of Britain

Augwys—brother of Lot (thirteenth century)

Awarnach—a giant

Bagdemagus—father of Meleagant (twelfth century)

Baldulf—a knight (thirteenth century)

Balin, Balen—brother of Balaan (fifteenth century)

Ban—father of Lancelot (thirteenth century)

Beal—unknown

Beaumains—white hands

Bedivere, Bedver, Bedwyr—returns Excalibur to the Lady of the Lake (thirteenth century)

Bellangere—son of Alixandre
Benigied Vran—unknown
Benoyce—name of a kingdom
    (thirteenth century)
Bernlak, Bercilak, Bredbeddle—
    the Green Knight
Bersules—a knight
Bertram—a knight (twelfth
    century)
Bicoir—father of Arthur
    (seventh century)
Bladud—unknown
Blaise—a cleric (thirteenth
    century)
Blamor—unknown
Bleoberis—unknown
Bliant—healer (thirteenth
    century)
Bodwyn—brother of Mark
Bohort, Bors—uncle of Arthur
    (thirteenth century)
Borre, Boarte, Lohoot—son of
    Arthur
Brademagus—unknown
Bran—unknown (sixth century)
Brandeles, Brandelis—a knight
    (fifteenth century)
Brangore, Brangorre,
    Brangoire—unknown
    (thirteenth century)
Branor—a knight (thirteenth
    century)
Brennus, Brenius—a supposed
    king of Britain (fifteenth
    century)
Breuse, Brehus—a knight
Breri—a messenger
Briefbras—unknown

Bryan—Lord of Pendragon
Cabal, Cafall—Arthur's dog
    (ninth century)
Cacamwri—servant
Cador—nephew of Arthur
    (thirteenth century)
Cadwallon—name of a king
    (seventh century)
Caerleon—name of a battle site
Cai, Che, Ke—Arthur's brother,
    son of Ector (variant of Kay)
Caliburn, Caliborne, Caliborn,
    Caliburnus, Calibor—
    various names for Arthur's
    sword
Calles—unknown
Calogrenant—a knight (twelfth
    century)
Camlann, Camelon—site of
    Arthur's last battle
Caradoc, Caradawc—son of
    Bran
Carmelide—Guinevere's father
    (thirteenth century)
Carrado—a knight
Catterick, Catterik—name of a
    battle
Cavalon—name of a king
Caw—name of a giant
Celidone, Celidon—unknown
Chapalu, Cath—name of a
    monster
Clamedeus—name of a king
Clarion—name of a king
Claudas—name of a king
Corbenic—where the grail was
    kept
Crudel—name of a king

Culhwch—Arthur's nephew
Custennin—unknown
Cymbeline—unknown
Cynfarch—unknown
Daguenet, Dagonet—Arthur's
    fool
Dinadan—friend of Tristan
Dinas—unknown
Dodinel—unknown
Domingart—unknown
Dristan, Drystan—an adviser to
    Arthur
Druas—a murderer
Drudwyn—a knight
Drust—unknown
Dudon—unknown
Dynadin—a knight
Echoid—unknown
Ector, Ektor—father of Arthur
    (fifteenth century)
Edern—unknown
Eliaures—unknown
Elidure—unknown
Emyr—unknown
Engres—a usurper
Erbin—unknown
Erec, Erek—son of Loc
Escalibor, Excalibur—Arthur's
    sword
Escanor—knight slain by
    Gawain
Escorant—unknown
Evadeam—a dwarf
Evelake, Evalac—name of a king
Evrain—name of a king
Evrawg—unknown
Feirefiz—a mulatto heathen who
    becomes Christian

Flollo—son of Gawain
Florence—son of Gawain
Frollo, Froille—killed by Arthur
Gahariet, Gaheris—sons of Lot
Gahmuret—Percival's father
Galahad—son of Lancelot
Galahalt, Galahault—name of a
    prince
Galatyn, Galantyne—Gawain's
    sword
Galeron—a knight
Gallehant—unknown
Galvarium—a knight
Gareth—son of Lot
Gawain, Gauvain—eldest son of
    Lot
Gesnes—unknown
Giflet, Girflet, Griflet—returns
    Excalibur to the lake
Gildas—unknown
Girard—unknown
Glais, Gais—Percival's
    grandfather
Glewlwyd—unknown
Gorlois—Igraine's husband
Gorre, Gore—a kingdom
Gouvernail, Governayle,
    Gorvenal—a knight
Griffith, Griffyth—a murderer
Gringolet, Gringalet—Gawain's
    horse
Gryfflet—killed by Lancelot
Guerehes—brother of Gawain
Guiderius—unknown
Guivret—a dwarf king
Gurgalan—a pagan king
Gwyr—unknown
Hebron—unknown

Hellekin—French lover of
 Morgan le Fay (thirteenth
 century)
Hoel—father of Isolde
Houdain, Houdenc—Tristan's
 dog
Howel—killed by Arthur
Huon—meaning unknown
Isdernus—knight of Arthur
Ither—killed by Percival
Johfrit—a knight
Kadyriath—meaning unknown
Kaherdin—brother of Isolde
Kailoken—a fool
Kanelingres—father of Tristan
Kardeiz—son of Percival
Kay, Kei—Arthur's brother, son
 of Ector
Kyner—unknown
Lamorak, Lamorat—brother of
 Percival
Laodegan—unknown
Laudegrance, Leodegraunce—
 father of Guinevere
Launcelot, Lancelot—knight of
 Arthur, lover of Guinevere
Launfal—a knight
Leodegan—Guinevere's father
Lionel—cousin of Lancelot
Llacheu—Arthur's son
Llew—unknown
Lludd—name of a king
Llychlyn—unknown
Loc—father of Erec
Lohengrin—son of Percival
Lot—name of a king
Lucan—brother of Arthur
Lucius—a Roman emperor

Mabon—a knight
Mabonagrain—a knight
Mabuz—ruler of Death Castle
Madoc—unknown
Mador—accuser of Guinevere
Maheloas—lord of the Isle of
 Glass
Malduc—a wizard
Mariadok—King Mark's servant
Maris—unknown
Mark—Tristan's uncle
Marrok—a knight thought to be
 a werewolf
Medrod—unknown
Melchior—unknown
Meleagant—kidnapped
 Guinevere
Melechan—Mordred's son
Meliadus, Meliodas—Tristan's
 father
Melwas—name of a king
Melyon—son of Mordred
Merlin—Arthur's tutor
Moraunt—unknown
Mordrain—name of a king
Mordrayans—unknown
Mordred, Modred—son/nephew
 of Arthur
Morgan Tud—a physician
Morholt, Morold—prince killed
 by Tristan
Nafiens—unknown
Nantres, Nentres—name of a
 king
Nascien—unknown
Nudd—a knight
Octha—enemy of Arthur
Ocvran—father of Guinevere

Osla—unknown
Owain—son of Urien
Ozanna—unknown
Padarn—unknown
Palomydes, Palamedes—a knight
Pant—father of Lancelot
Passebreul—unknown
Pellam—father of Pelles
Pellanor, Pellinore—name of a king
Pellean—Percival's father
Pelleas, Pelles—a Fisher king
Pendragon—head of the dragons
Percival, Perceval, Percyvelle, Parzifal, Parsifal—hero of several Arthurian stories
Peredur—unknown
Peredurus—name of a king
Petrus—one of Joseph's disciples
Phelot—unknown
Pheredin—unknown
Rhongomyant—unknown
Rhydderch—unknown
Rion—a pagan giant
Rivalen—Tristan's father
Ron—unknown
Ryence, Ryons, Royns—a Welsh king
Saffire—unknown
Sagramour, Sagremor—a knight
Taliesin—sixth-century poet
Tentagil, Tintagel—land of Igraine
Tor—son of Pellinore
Tortain—unknown
Trevrizent—Percival's uncle
Tristram, Tristan—a knight
Turquine—unknown
Uriens, Urien—name of a king
Uther—Arthur's father
Uwaine, Uwayne—unknown
Vortigern—name of a king
Vortimer—Vortigern's son
Yder, Ider—unknown
Ysbaddaden—a giant

BASQUE

Basques are the most ancient identifiable ethnic group in Europe, and scholars believe they have occupied their lands in the western Pyrenees for at least several thousand years. The Basques speak Euskara, an ancient language unrelated to the Indo-European languages spoken in the rest of western Europe. Basqueland straddles the border between France and Spain, and Basques have been seeking some degree of cultural and political autonomy from those national governments since the early 1900s.

Basque naming practices have been influenced by Spanish culture, so many Basque names are similar to Spanish names (Garcia, Sanchez, Diaz). During most of the twentieth century, the use of ethnic Basque names was discouraged in Spanish culture. Since the 1970s, however, Basque first names have been used much more freely.

First names are frequently taken from Basque mythology and history, but Basque surnames are typically toponymic—based on place names. Specifically, surnames were often taken from the name of the family's *baserri*, or farmhouse. *Baserri* names were based on the location of the house (Urkialde, "beside the birch tree"), the activities of the people who lived in it (Mintegi, "nursery operator"), the name of a householder (Alonsotegi, "Alonso's house"), or a chracteristic of the house itself, like age or quality of construction (Etxeberria, "the new house"). Etxebarria is the most common Basque surname.

A few surnames:

Abaroa	Danborenea
Arrigorriaga	Durango
Aurrecoechea	Elizalde
Azkoaga	Elorrieta
Basarte	Ernaut
Basategi	Errotabarri
Beaskoetxea	Etxegarai
Belaustegi	Guerediaga
Bilbao	Ibarran
Curutchet	Ibarretxe

Iturbe
Jauregi
Larrazabal
Lizarmendi
Loidi
Lopetegi
Mendazona
Mendibe
Mintegui
Oramuno

Osabene
Osteincoechea
Pagadigorria
Sagastizabal
Ugarte
Urkialde
Urrutia
Ygartua
Zubiar

FEMALE

Agurtzane, Ainhoa, Aitziber, Alona, Arama, Arrate—reference to the Virgin Mary
Aintzane—glory
Alazne—miracle
Alesandese—defender of mankind (form of Alexander)
Amaia—end
Andere—manly (form of Andrew)
Argi—light
Arrosa—rose (form of Rosa)
Aurkene—present
Balere—strong
Barkarne, Barkarna—lonely
Bixenta—victory
Catalin—pure (form of Katherine)
Danele—God is my judge (form of Daniel)
Deiene—religious holiday
Edurne—snow
Eguskine, Eguskina—sunshine
Garaitz—victory

Gechina—graceful
Gizane—reference to Christ's incarnation
Gotzone—angel
Igone—reference to Christ's Ascension
Iratze—reference to the Virgin Mary
Jaione—reference to the Nativity
Jakinda—hyacinth (form of Hyacinth)
Kepa—stone
Kontxesi—reference to the Immaculate Conception
Mirari—miracle
Naiara, Naiaria—reference to the Virgin Mary
Nerea, Neria—mine
Osane—health
Tote—meaning unknown
Yanamari—bitter grace (form of Annamarie)
Yera—reference to the Virgin Mary
Zurine, Zurina—white

MALE

Adiran—from the Adriatic
Ager—gathers
Aingeru—messenger
Akil—from the river Akil
Ander—manly (form of Andrew)
Antton—priceless (form of Anthony)
Asentzio—ascending
Benat—bear
Bingen, Bittor—conqueror
Danel—God is my judge (form of Daniel)
Deunoro—all saints
Dunixi—god of wine (form of Dionysus)
Edorta—rich guardian (form of Edward)
Edrigu—strong ruler (form of Richard)
Edur—wine
Elazar—God helps
Erromon—from Rome
Etor—steadfast
Gabirel—God-given strength (form of Gabriel)
Gaizka—savior
Gentza—peace
Gotzon—angel
Gurutz—Holy Cross
Iker—visits

Inaki, Inogo—ardent
Ixaka—laughs
Jakome—supplanter (form of James)
Kemen—strong
Kerbasi—warrior
Mikel—godlike
Mikolas, Mikolaus—victory of the people (form of Nicholas)
Ortzi—meaning unknown
Palben—blond
Txanton—God adds, priceless (for Joseph Anthony)
Txomin—like God
Ugutz—named for John the Baptist
Unai—shepherd
Urtzi—sky
Xabier, Xavier—owner of a new home
Xanti—named for Saint James
Ximon, Ximun, Xylon—God is heard (form of Simon)
Yosu—God saves
Yuli—youthful (form of Julius)
Zadornin—god of the harvest; myth name (form of Saturn)
Zigor—punishes
Zorion—happy

CAMBODIAN

Cambodian surnames come first and given names come second. People with short names are referred to by both names.

While surnames are usually passed from father to children, a father may give a favored child his first name as a surname.

A few surnames:

Chey	Sat
Chun	Sen
Haing	Sien
Hen	Sihanouk
Heng	Sin
Him	Sok
Im	Som
Pan	Toan
Prak	Vann

FEMALE

Baen—meaning unknown
Bopha—flower
Botum—princess
Channary—full moon
Chantrea—moon
Chenda—intellect
Dara—star
Kalliyan—best
Kiri—mountain peak
Kolab—rose

Kunthea—fragrant
Mliss—flower
Pich—diamond
Samnang—lucky
Sopheap—gentle
Tevy—angel
Thirith—meaning unknown
Tola—October
Vanna—golden
Veata—wind

MALE

Arun—morning sun
Bourey—great city
Bun-Rong—meaning unknown
Chankrisna—sweet-smelling
    tree

Chay—attractive
Chhan—meaning unknown
Dara—star
Jun-Chhoun—beautiful
Kiman—meaning unknown

LORRAINE HEATH

Lorraine Heath is the author of numerous historical, contemporary, and young adult romantic titles. In 1995 and 1996, she won the *Romantic Times* Career Achievement Award for Americana Historicals.

My most memorable character names are the Leigh brothers. This Texas trilogy (*Texas Destiny*, *Texas Glory*, and *Texas Splendor*) involved three brothers, and I wanted them to be very Texas. I have a friend whose husband was named Dallas, and another friend who named her son Austin—two Texas cities. But I had three brothers and I couldn't decide which city would work as a name for the third brother. A cousin sent me a family history, and as I was looking through it, I discovered we had a relative in the late 1800s whose first name was Houston—and everything seemed to come together for this trilogy at that point. I had a clear vision for each brother. Each brother's personality also seemed to reflect the city that his name came from: Dallas was strong and bold, Austin was laid-back, and Houston struggled to find his place.

I have found that names usually have a great impact not only on the characters themselves, but because they define the characters, they also influence how the story unfolds.

Kiri—mountain peak
Makara—January
Meng—meaning unknown
Munney, Munny—wise
Nath—meaning unknown
Nghor—meaning unknown
Nhean—knowledgeable
Norodom—meaning unknown
Phirun—rain
Pich—diamond
Ranariddh—meaning unknown

Rangsey—multi colors
Rithisak—powerful
Sakngea—statesman
Samnang—lucky
Samrin—leader name
Sen—meaning unknown
Sim—meaning unknown
Solvann—of gold
Uth—meaning unknown
Varin—meaning unknown
Veasna—destiny, fate
Vibol—abundant

CELTIC

The Celtic languages are a branch of the Indo-European language group. Once spoken all across Europe, Celtic languages are now spoken only in the British Isles and France.

There aren't any Celtic surnames per se, although some modern surnames in the British Isles no doubt developed from Celtic given names or bynames. (Bynames were descriptive nicknames used before the existence of surnames to distinguish between persons with the same given name.) For more information, see the sections for English, Gaelic, Irish, Scottish, and Welsh names.

FEMALE

Adsaluta—myth name
Aife—great warrior woman; myth name
Aifric, Afric, Africa, Aphira— pleasant
Aigneis—pure (form of Agnes)
Ailidh—kind
Aina, Aine—joy
Aingeal—angel
Aithne—fire
Alanna, Alane, Alina, Aline, Alene—beautiful
Alastriona, Alastrine, Alastrina—avenger (form of Alastair)
Alice, Alys, Ailis, Elsha—sweet, noble
Alma—loving
Andraste—victory
Annwn, Annwfn—the Otherworld; myth name
Ardra—noble
Arienh—oath

Arlana, Arlene, Arela, Arleen, Arleta, Arlette, Arlina, Arline—oath (form of Arlen)
Armelle—princess
Bab, Bav—meaning unknown
Bari—spear thrower
Berit, Birgit, Berta, Birte— intelligent
Betha, Beatha—life
Birkita—strength
Blair—from the plain lands
Brangaine—character from Isolde legend
Branswen—sister of Bendigeidfran
Brenna—raven
Bretta, Bret, Brit, Brite, Brittany, Brita—from Britain
Briana—strong (form of Brian)
Bricta—meaning unknown
Brid, Bride, Brighid, Breeda, Brigid, Brigitta, Brigitte, Birgit, Britta, Brietta, Brita,

Brites, Brygid, Bridget, Birkita, Brit—strong
Brina—defender
Caoilfhionn, Keelin—slender and comely
Caoimhe—beauty, grace, gentleness
Cara—friend
Carmel—garden
Cary, Carey—from the river
Cerdwin—mother goddess
Cinnia, Cinnie—beauty
Cordelia—jewel of the sea
Corey—ravine
Coventina—name of a nymph
Culyer—chapel
Daghda—meaning unknown
Dana—from Denmark
Dechtire—nursemaid; myth name
Deirdra, Deirdre—sorrowful
Deoch—princess of Munster; myth name
Diva, Deva, Devona, Divone, Deheune—divine one
Donella—dark-haired elfin girl
Donia—dark-skinned
Doreen, Doreena—moody
Edana, Ena—passionate
Edna, Ena, Ethne—fire
Emogen, Emogene—maiden
Enid—spirit
Enys—from the islands
Epona—meaning unknown
Erina, Erin, Erie, Erea—from Ireland
Etain—sparkling
Evelyn, Engl, Evelina, Eveline—light; gives life

Fedelm—wife of Loegaire; myth name
Fenella—white shoulders (form of Finola)
Fianna—legendary tale
Findabair—daughter of Medb; myth name
Fingula—daugherof Lyr; myth name
Fiona—fair one
Genevieve—white wave
Germaine—loud of voice
Gilda, Gildas—serves God
Ginerva, Ginebra, Ginessa—white as foam
Gitta—strong
Grania—love
Guennola—white
Guinevere, Guenevere, Gwenyver—white lady
Gwendolen, Gwendolin, Gwyndolin, Gwenn, Gwynn—of the white brow
Gwenneth, Gweneth, Gwynith, Gwenith—blessed
Imogen, Imogene—maiden, girl
Iona, Ione—from the king's island
Isold, Isolde, Isolda—fair lady
Jennifer, Jennyfer, Jennyver, Jenny—white wave
Kaie—combat, battle
Keelin, Keely, Keelia—beautiful
Kendra—hill
Kennocha—lovely
Lavena—joy
Leslie, Lesley—from the gray fortress

Linette, Linnette, Lynette,
Lynet—grace
Lyonesse—little lion
Maureen, Moreen—great
Mavis, Mavelle, Mavie—
songbird
Meadghbh, Maeveen, Mabina—
nimble
Medb, Maeve—mythical queen
Melva, Melvina, Malvina—
handmaiden
Meredith—protector of the sea
Moina, Moyna—noble
Morgan, Morgance, Morgane,
Morgana—lives by the sea
Morna—dearly loved
Morrigan—war goddess
Moya, Moira, Mor—exceptional
Myrna, Merna, Mirna, Moina,
Morna, Moyna—beloved
Nantosuelta—meaning
unknown
Neala, Nealie—champion (form
of Neal)
Newlyn—from the new spring
Nola—famous
Oifa—sister of Ove; myth name

Oilell—mythical queen
Olwen, Olwyn—daughter of
Yspaddaden; myth name
Oppida—meaning unknown
Oriana—blond
Ove—daughter of Dearg; myth
name
Penarddun—daughter of Beli;
legend name
Regan, Reaghan—little king
Rhiannon—pure maiden
Ronat—seal
Rowena—white-haired
Saraid—excellent
Seanna—God's grace
Selma—comely
Shayla—fairy palace
Shela—musical
Shylah—loyal to god
Treva—prudent
Tully—peaceful
Ula—sea jewel
Una—white wave
Venetia—blessed
Wynne, Winnie, Wynnie—fair
Yseult—fair
Zenevieva, Zinerva—pale

MALE

Adair—from the ford by the oak
trees
Ahern, Ahearn—lord of the
horses
Ailbe—white
Ailill—king of Connaught; myth
name

Airell—nobleman
Alan, Allen, Allan, Allyn—
handsome
Alanson—son of Allan
Angus, Anghus, Aengus,
Aonghus—exceptionally
strong

Annan, Anant—from the stream
Ansgar—divine spear
Anwell, Anwyl—beloved
Anyon—anvil
Aod—son of Lyr; myth name
Ap Owen—son of Owen
Arawn—king of the Underworld;
    myth name
Argyle—from the land of the
    Gauls
Arlen, Arlin, Arlyn, Arlan,
    Arland—oath
Arthur, Artur, Art, Atty, Attie,
    Arturo—noble bear
Baird—bard
Barry, Bairrfhionn, Barra,
    Bearach, Bearchan—good
    marksman
Beacan, Becan—small
Bedwyr—Arthurian legend
    name
Bendigeidfran—blessed raven
Bevan, Bevin, Bevyn—young
    soldier
Blaine, Blayne, Blane, Blainey,
    Blayney—thin
Blair—from the plain lands
Boadhagh—meaning unknown
Bowden, Bowdyn, Boden,
    Bodyn, Boyden, Boyd—
    blond
Bowen, Bowyn—son of Owen
Boynton—from the white river
Bran, Brann—raven
Brasil, Breasal, Basil—battle
Breanainn, Breandan, Bredon,
    Brandan—sword
Brendan, Bran, Bram, Broin,
    Brennan—raven

Brett, Bret—a Breton
Briac—esteem
Brian, Bryan, Bryant, Briant—
    strong
Brice, Bryce—swift
Bricriu—the poison-tongued;
    myth name
Britomartus—meaning
    unknown
Burgess—town citizen
Cachamwri—servant of Arthur;
    legend name
Cadell—battle
Cadman—warrior
Caedmon—wise warrior
Calder—from the stony river
Calum—dove
Cameron, Camero, Camey—
    crooked nose
Camlin—crooked line
Caoimhghin—gentle
Caradoc—beloved
Cardew—from the black fortress
Carew, Carey, Cary—from the
    fortress
Carney, Car, Carr, Cathaoir,
    Cathair—victorious
Carrol, Carroll—manly (form of
    Charles)
Casey—brave
Cassivellaunus, Caswallan—
    Arthurian legend name
Cathal, Cahal, Conall, Connell—
    strong in battle
Cathbad—meaning unknown
Cedric—chief
Celyddon—father of Culhwch;
    myth name

Chad—warrior
Clust—son of Clustfeinad; myth name
Clustfeinad—myth name
Coalan—slender
Cocidius—hunter god; myth name
Coinneach—handsome
Conall—Ulster chieftain; myth name
Conan, Conant, Con, Conn, Cuinn—wise
Conchobar—hero; myth name
Condan, Condon—dark-haired wise man
Conlaoch—meaning unknown
Conn—son of Lir; myth name
Connla—son of Conn; myth name
Conroy—wise
Conway—hound of the plain
Corann—druid; myth name
Cormac, Cairbre, Carbry—charioteer
Cradawg—son of Bran; myth name
Cuchulainn—the Hound of Ulster; myth name
Culain, Culann—smith; myth name
Culhwch—meaning unknown
Cullen—cub
Custennin—giant; myth name
Cynyr—meaning unknown
Dallas—dwells by the waterfall
Daman—demon
Darcy—dark

Dearg—son of Daghda
Dermot—free
Desmond—from south Munster
Deverell—from the riverbank
Devin, Devyn—poet
Dillion—faithful
Dinsmore—from the hill fort
Doane—from the sand hill
Donald, Don, Doyle, Doy—ruler of the world
Donat, Donal, Domhnall, Donall, Doran, Dorran—stranger
Donnally, Donnelly—brave, dark man
Donnchadh, Donogh, Donaghy, Donovan—strong fighter
Doughlas, Douglas—dark water
Drem—son of Dremidydd; myth name
Drew—wise
Driscoll, Driscol, Driskell—interpreter
Drostan, Drystan—noisy (form of Tristan)
Druce—wise
Drudwyn—Mabon's dog; myth name
Drummond—lives on the hilltop
Duane, Dewain, Dwayne—song
Duer—hero
Duff, Dubv, Duffy—dark-faced
Dughall, Dougal, Doughal—dark stranger
Duncan, Dunham—dark warrior
Dunn—dark-skinned
Dyfed—from Dyfed
Ea, Edan—fire
Eburacon—lives near the yew-tree estate

Efnisien—son of Euroswydd; myth name

Egan, Eghan—fiery

Egomas—meaning unknown

Einion—anvil

Elidor—monk; myth name

Emrys—immortal (form of Ambrose)

Ennis—from the island

Erim—legend name

Evan—young fighter

Evnissyen—meaning unknown

Ewen, Ewan, Ewyn, Eoghann, Eoin—young

Farrel, Farrell—brave

Ferchar—son of Uisnech; myth name

Ferdiad—meaning unknown

Ferghus, Fergus, Fearghus—of manly strength

Ferris—rock

Fiacre, Fiacra—eagle

Fiallan—meaning unknown

Fiamain—meaning unknown

Finbar, Finnbar, Fynbar, Finnobarr—blond

Finian—handsome

Finn, Fingal—myth name

Fionn—fair, white

Floyd—gray

Forsa—meaning unknown

Gall—stranger

Galvin, Galvyn—sparrow

Gelban—meaning unknown

Gildas—serves God

Gilmore—servant of the Virgin Mary

Gilroy—serves the king

Girard—meaning unknown

Glen, Glyn, Glenn—from the glen

Glifieu—son of Taran; myth name

Gorsedd—from Arberth; myth name

Gruddieu—son of Muriuel; myth name

Guy—sensible

Gwalchmai—myth name

Gwawl—son of Clud; legend name

Gwefl—son of Gwastad; myth name

Gwern—son of Matholwch; myth name

Gwernach—myth name

Gwri—of the golden hair

Gwynham—father of Teithi; myth name

Hafgan—myth name

Halwn—meaning unknown

Hefeydd—father of Rhiannon; myth name

Heilyn—son of Gwyn; myth name

Henbeddestr—fastest man

Henwas—brother of Henbeddestr; myth name

Herne—hunter god; myth name

Hoel—meaning unknown

Huarwar—son of Halwn; myth name

Hueil—son of Caw; legend name

Huon—meaning unknown

Iden—wealthy

Innis, Innes—from the river island
Irvin, Irven, Irvyn, Irving—white
Kane, Kayne—intelligent
Karney, Kearney—fighter
Keane, Keene—tall and handsome
Kegan, Keegan, Keaghan—son of Egan
Keir—dark
Keith—wind
Kelvin, Kelvyn, Kelwin, Kelwyn—from the narrow river
Kembell, Kemble, Kimball—chieftain, warrior
Kendall, Kendal, Kendhal—from the clear river valley
Kendrick—hill, mountain
Kenn—clear water
Kenneth—handsome
Kent, Kentigern—head chief
Kermit, Kermode—son of Diarmaid
Kerry, Keary—dark one; county name
Kerwin, Kerwyn, Kirwin, Kirwyn, Kieran—little black one
Kevin, Kevyn, Kevan—gentle, handsome
Killian, Kilian—blind
Kunagnos—wise
Kynthelig—guide; myth name
Lairgnen—of Connaught; myth name
Lann—sword
Lee, Leigh—healer
Leith—wide river

Lesley, Leslie—from the gray fortress
Lincoln—from the settlement by the pool
Lir—a mythical king
Llewelyn—lion
Lloyd—gray
Llyr—a mythical king
Lorne—man of Lorne
Luxovious—god of Luxeuil; myth name
Mabon—god of youth; myth name
Mac, Mack—son of
Maccus—hammer
Macklin, Macklyn—son of Flann
Maddox, Maddock—beneficent
Malcolm—servant of Saint Columba
Malvin, Malvyn, Melvin, Melvyn, Melville—leader
Matholwch—myth name
Medr—myth name
Medredydd—son of Medredydd; myth name
Menw—son of Teirwaedd; legend name
Merlin, Merlyn—falcon
Morfran—ugly demon; myth name
Morgan, Morven, Morvyn, Mariner, Marvin, Marvyn, Moryn, Murray, Murry—lives by the sea
Mungo—lovable
Murdoc, Murdoch, Murdock—protector of the sea

Murtagh—protects the sea
Mynogan—father of Beli; myth name
Naois—warrior; myth name
Neal, Neil, Nealon, Nell, Neale, Niall, Neill, Niallan, Nyle—champion
Nels—chief
Nelson—son of Neil
Nemausus—god of Nimes; myth name
Newlin, Newlyn—from the new spring
Niece, Neese—choice
Nisien—son of Euroswydd; myth name
Nolan, Noland—noble
Orin, Oran—white
Oscar, Oskar, Osker, Osckar—divine spear
Ossian, Oisin—fawn
Owen, Owin, Owyn—young warrior
Pendaran—meaning unknown
Perth, Pert—from the thorn-bush thicket
Phelan—little wolf
Powell—son of Howell
Pryderi—care
Pwyll—lord of Annwn; myth name
Quin, Quinn—wise
Regan, Reghan, Reagan, Reaghan—little king
Renfrew—from the still river
Rivalin—meaning unknown
Ronan—small seal
Roy—red-haired

Sativola—name of a saint
Sawyer—cuts timber
Scilti—messenger of Arthur; legend name
Setanta—son of Sualtam; myth name
Sheridan—untamed
Sidwell—from the broad well
Sloan, Sloane—fighter
Sugn—son of Sugnedudd; myth name
Tadhg—prince of Munster; myth name
Taliesin—bard; myth name
Tanguy—fighter
Taran—meaning unknown
Teague, Teaghue—poet
Teirtu—meaning unknown
Teithi—son of Gwynham; myth name
Tegid—meaning unknown
Teyrnon, Tiernan, Tiernay—regal
Tor—rock
Torrey, Tory—lives by the tower
Trahern—strong as iron
Tremayne, Tremaine—from the town encircled by stone
Trevor—wise
Tristan, Tristen—noisy
Tristram—full of sorrows
Tuireann—meaning unknown
Turi—bear
Twrch, Trwyth—myth name
Uchdryd—son of Erim; legend name
Uisnech, Usenech—meaning unknown

MARIAN KEYES

Marian Keyes has published seven novels: *Watermelon, Lucy Sullivan Is Getting Married, Rachel's Holiday, Last Chance Saloon, Sushi for Beginners, Angels,* and *The Other Side of the Story,* all best sellers around the world, a total of nine million of her books having been sold to date. *Sushi for Beginners* and *Angels* were No. 1 best sellers on *The Sunday Times* list.

My characters' names are very, very important to me for all kinds of reasons, and I'm never entirely comfortable with a character until I feel they have a name that "fits" their personality. Because I write about "regular" women, it's important that they have a "regular" name. Names like Claire, Anna, Lisa, Lucy, Tara are all kind of friendly; they're names that most women can relate to. Unlike say, Cassandra and Saskia, which are "other woman" type names, as far as I'm concerned. I like short names, as much as possible, because I've noticed when I'm reading books where the characters have long names, that it drags the pace of the narrative slightly. Similarly, it's important that my names are pronounceable: One of my most favorite names in the whole world is Aoife, an Irish name pronounced *Eefa*, but if no one outside of Ireland knows what my character's name is, they'll never bond with her. Likewise with my male characters, their names are very important. I've tried to steer clear of calling romantic heroes names like Jake and Lance, because they're caricatures of "starring male" names.

Usk-water—meaning unknown
Varden, Vardon—from the green hill
Varney—from the alder grove
Vaughn—small

Weylin, Weylyn—son of the wolf
Wynne—fair
York—yew tree
Yspaddaden—father of Olwyn; myth name

CHINESE

Chinese names traditionally include three characters: a family name, a generational name, and a given name, in that order. In China, a person is addressed by last name first. Chinese immigrants and travelers will often reverse their names to avoid confusion, putting the family name at the end and the given name at the beginning. Chinese émigrés and their children often take a Western first name and a Chinese middle name. Naming practices vary slightly between the Cantonese and Mandarin populations, as well as in Taiwan and Hong Kong.

The Chinese character for family name is made up of the symbols for "woman" and "to give birth," so it is believed that family names were originally passed down from mother to child. Most family names consist of one character. Chinese women usually retain their maiden names after marriage, but may put the husband's family name in front of the maiden name. While many cultures have a wide variety of family names, China has relatively few in common use: about 500.

If a Chinese child is given a two-character name, the first character is often shared among all the members of the same generation in the family. It is increasingly common for the generational name to be omitted; only about half of young Chinese are given a generational name today.

In China, almost any word can be used as a given name. One word can have several pronunciations (or tones), and each tone can have a separate meaning. Hui, when pronounced with the fourth tone, means flower; when pronounced with the first tone, it means brilliance or glory. Parents may choose the name of a celebrity, a name related to the prevailing culture (red, revolution), or a name expressing a wish for the child. It can also be very important to give a child an auspicious and balanced name. Choosing such a name can be a very involved process. For instance, the Chinese believed that all things were made up of five elements: metal, wood, water, fire, and earth. From a child's birth date and time, a fortune teller can determine which elements a child is lacking, and the child can be given a name associated with that element. If the child is lacking in water, he or she can be given a name that included a word like river, tide, or rain. This is only one of the complex calculations involved in the traditional method of naming a child; in fact, there are entire books on the process. If it is important that your Chinese character be named in the traditional manner, make sure you do some additional research.

In 1977, statistics revealed that 40 percent of the Chinese population have one of the following family names. (These names are sometimes transliterated differently.)

Chen	Wu
Huang	Yang
Li	Zhao
Liu	Zhang
Wang	Zhou

Other popular family names are:

Gao	Sun
Guo	Xiao
Hu	Xu
Lin	Zheng
Ma	Zhu

FEMALE

An—peace
Bo—precious
Chao—great one
Chen—sunrise
Chow—summer
Chyou—autumn
Cong—clever
Da Xia—endless summer
Feng—maple
Genji—golden
Guan Yin—goddess of mercy
Heng—meaning unknown
Hua—blossom
Jia—lovely and good

Jie—pure
Jin—golden
Jun—truth
Le—joy
Lei—bud of the flower
Li—rose
Lian—graceful willow
Lien—lotus
Ling—dawn
Lixue—lovely snow
Mee—beautiful
Ming—bright moon;
    dynasty name
Mingmei—intelligent

Linda Needham is the author of seven historical romances with Avon Books. Several of her books have been *USA Today* best sellers.

I'm always on the lookout for clever character names. I harvest them from theater programs, maps, telephone books, TV listings. But my newest resource comes right out of the Internet age. It costs nothing if you have access to the Web. In fact, these names arrive by the bucketful every day in your e-mail in-box. That's right! It's spam! Or rather, spammers, those falsely named "senders" who are constantly flogging mortgages and Russian brides and male enhancement products. The names are usually too eccentric for your hero or heroine, but they're great for secondary characters, proving that spam is actually good for something.

The following examples arrived in my e-mail in-box on the same morning: Ellis Paige, Hollis Higgins, Isreal Cates, Jeffrey Tackett, Langdon Barr, Luther Kilgore, Magdelen Maribel, and Wilford Mock. Rusty Pitts came a day later, to a fellow writer. Boy, was I jealous of that one!

Mulan—magnolia blossom
Park—cypress tree
Ping—duckweed
Qi—finest jade
Qiao—attractive
Qing—spring water
Rong—glory
Shan—coral
Shu—kind, gentle
Shuang—bright, clear
Sun—diminishing
Tai—sun
Tao—long life
Ting—graceful
Wan—gracious
Wei—valuable

Wing—glory
Xia—summer lotus
Xiang—fragrant
Xiao—morning
Xin—happy
Xing—twin stars
Xiu—elegant
Xi Wang—hope
Xue—snow
Yan—bird, a swallow
Yi—happy
Yue—beautiful
Zhen—precious
Zhi—wise healer
Zi—graceful, beautiful

MALE

An—peace
Bo—precious
Chan—clan name
Chen—vast
Cheng—to become
Chi—youthful vitality
Chung—wise one
Cong—clever
Dewei—highly principled
Fai—bright light
Guang—light
Ho—goodness
Hsin—dynasty name
Jie—pure
Jin—golden
Jun—truth
Kong—bright
Le—joy
Li—strength
Liang—fine
Lok—joy
Long—dragon
Manchu—pure
Ming—bright moon;
   dynasty name

On—peace
Park—cypress tree
Ping—duckweed
Qiao—attractive
Qing—spring water
Rong—glory
Shan—coral
Shen—thinker
Sheng—victory
Shing—victory
Shuang—bright, clear
Sun—diminishing
Tai—sun
Tao—long life
Wang—kingly
Wen—ornamental
Wing—glory
Xiao—morning
Xing—twin stars
Xi Wang—hope
Ye—universe
Yu—pure jade
Yuan—original
Yue—beautiful
Zhi—wise healer

CZECHOSLOVAKIAN

Czech and Slovakian names follow very similar patterns, though they may have slightly different spellings. This list is Czechoslovakian because it contains names form both origins.

Czechoslovakian surnames are taken from descriptive, patronymic, occupational, and place names. Overall, they tend to be short, and female surnames always end in *-ova* or *-a*. Below are the rules to form female surnames from male surnames.

1. Add "-ova" to the male surname.
   Novak/ Novakova
   Horak /Horakova

2. If male surname ends with "y," change the "y" to an "a" to form the female surname.
   Novy/Nova
   Zeleny/Zelena

Exceptions:

1. If male surname ends with "ek," "ec," "el," then in female surname "e" is left out and -ova is added ("k," "c," or "l" stays).
   Tichacek/Tichackova
   Bobek/Bobková
   Vrabec/Vrabcová
   Havel/Havlová

2. If a male surname ends with "a" then in female surname "a" is left out and -ova is added.
   Peterka/Peterkova
   Ryba/Rybova
   Prochazka/Prochazkova
   Blaha/Blahova

3. If a male surname ends with "i" then the female version is the same as the male version
   Krejci/Krejci

A few surnames listed as male/female:

Bednar/Bednarova	Krejci/Krejci
Benes/Benesova	Kubas/Kubasova
Bily/Bila	Mlynar/Mlynarova
Bobek/Bobkova	Nemec/Nemcova
Capek/Capekova	Novak/Novakova
Cermak/Cermakova	Pekar/Pekarova
Cerny/Cerna	Polak/Polakova
Dedek/Dedkova	Ryba/Rybova
Dudek/Dudkova	Rybar/Rybarova
Hlinka/Hlinkova	Silny/Silna
Hnedy/Hneda	Slansky/Slanska
Horak/Horakova	Suchy/Sucha
Hrusosky/Hrusovska	Svec/Svecova
Kopecky/Kopecka	Tesar/Tesarova
Kozel/Kozlova	Vrba/Vrbova
Kral/Kralova	Zapotocky/Zapotocka
Krasny/Krasna	Zelenka/Zelenkova

FEMALE

Alzbeta, Beta—consecrated to God (form of Elizabeth)
Anezka—pure (form of Agnes)
Anna, Anicka—grace (form of Anne)
Barbora, Bara—stranger (form of Barbara)
Bela, Bel, Belia, Bell—white
Beta—servant of God
Bozena—meaning unknown
Dana—God is my judge (form of Daniel)
Dusana—spirit (form of Dusan)
Eliska—truthful
Frantiska—free (form of Francis)
Ivana—gracious God (form of John)

Jana—God's gift
Jirina—farmer (form of George)
Kamilla—from a noble family
Katerina—pure (form of Katherine)
Klára—clear, bright (form of Clare)
Krasava—beautiful
Kristyna—Christ's
Lenka—torch
Libuse, Libusa—myth name
Lida—cultured
Lucie, Lucia—light (form of Luke)
Ludmila, Lida—loved by the people
Marie, Marenka, Maruska—bitter (form of Mary)

Marketa—pearl (form of
	Margaret)
Michaela, Misa—who is like God
	(form of Michael)
Milada—my love
Milena—favored
Milka, Mila—industrious
Miroslava, Mirka—peaceful
	glory (form of Miroslav)
Nadezda—with hope
Nikola, Nikolka—victory of the
	people (form of Nicholas)
Otka—fortunate heroine

Pavla—small (form of Paul)
Rusalka—wood sprite
Ruzena, Ruzenka, Ruza—rose
	(form of Rosa)
Svetlana, Svetla—gift
Tereza, Terezka—reaper (form
	of Theresa)
Verushka—faith
Vlasta—myth name
Zdenka—winding sheet
Zophie—wise (form of Sophia)
Zuzana, Zuzka, Zuza—lily (form
	of Susan)

MALE

Adam—of the red earth
Antonin, Tonda—priceless
	(form of Anthony)
Bedrich—peaceful ruler
Bilko—white
Bohumil, Bohous—God's peace
Cestmir—fortress
Dusan—spirit
Eda—rich guardian (form of
	Edward)
Evzen, Eugen—well-born (form
	of Eugene)
Ferda—brave
Frantisek, Franta—free (form of
	Francis)
Holic—barber
Honza—gift from God
Jakub, Kuba—supplanter (form
	of Jacob)
Jarda—myth name
Jaroslav—famous for his power;
	myth name

Jirka, Jiri, Juraj—farmer (form of
	George)
Josef—God adds (form of
	Joseph)
Jozka—God adds (form of
	Joseph)
Kafka—birth
Kamil—from a noble family
Karel—manly (form of Charles)
Kazimir—destroys peace (form
	of Casimir)
Laco—famous ruler
Ladislav, Lada—glorious ruler
Lojza—famous warrior
Lukas—light (form of Luke)
Martinek, Marek—warlike (form
	of Marcus)
Michal—who is like God (form of
	Michael)
Miklos—victory of the people
	(form of Nicholas)
Milan, Milos—favored, beloved

Miloslav—loves glory
Mirek—peace
Miroslav—peaceful glory
Oldrich—powerful, wealthy
Ondrus, Ondras, Ondra, Ondrej—manly (form of Andrew)
Otik, Oto, Otakar—wealthy
Pavlov, Pafko, Pavel, Pavol—small (form of Paul)
Pepik—God will add
Peterka, Petr—rock (form of Peter)
Praza, Lomsky, Lomy—from Prague
Radek—happy, glad
Reznik—butcher

Risa—strong ruler (form of Richard)
Rostislav—meaning unknown
Siman—heard
Standa, Stanislav—camp glory
Tomik, Toman—twin (form of Thomas)
Tonda—meaning unknown
Vaclav—great glory (form of Wenceslas)
Vasek—victorious
Vavrin, Vavrinec—laurel (form of Lawrence)
Viktor—victorious (form of Victor)
Vilem—resolute protector (form of William)

DANISH

Danish surnames began in the late Middle Ages, but not until the nineteenth century were they used regularly as hereditary names. Even in the nineteenth century, most people continued to use just their given name without any other title. In fact, the Danish government was forced to intervene to get people to use surnames. In 1828, the government declared that children should receive both a given and family name at birth. An 1860 act made surnames permanent.

Unfortunately, most of the Danish people simply added *son* (*-sen*) or *daughter* (*-datter*) to the father's name, which produced an inordinate number of *-sen* names. To help counteract this trend, in 1904 the government begain encouraging Danish people to change their surnames. As a result, many kept their *-sen* suffixes and just added a hyphen along with their occupation.

A few surnames:

Andersdatter	Johansen
Andersen	Jørgensen
Bang	Kiersted
Bjorn	Kirkegard
Bruun	Kjaer
Christiansen	Kristoffersen
Claussen	Kruse
Dahl	Larsen
Damgaard	Lundvall
Dinesen	Madsen
Dyhr	Møller
Eriksen	Mortensen
Fabricius	Nielsen
Frederiksdatter	Nørgaard
Frederiksen	Olsen
Friis	Østergaard
Gruntvig	Petersen
Guildenstern	Rayner
Hansen	Søndergaard
Holst	Sørensen
Iversen	Vestergaard
Jensen	Yager

FEMALE

Abellona—mannish
Agneta—pure (form of Agnes)
Ailsa—consecrated to God
    (form of Elizabeth)
Aleksia—defender of mankind
    (form of Alexander)
Almeta—pearl
Andrea—manly (form of
    Andrew)
Annelise—graceful light
Annemette—bitter pearl
Arvada—eagle
Astrid—divine strength
Bergitte, Britta—strong (form of
    Bridget)
Bitten—good
Clady—lame (form of Claudia)
Dagmar—maiden of the day
Dakin—Danish, of Denmark
Dana—from Denmark
Dorothea—God's gift (form of
    Dorothy)
Ebba—strength
Else—consecrated to God (form
    of Elizabeth)
Eva—life (form of Eve)
Federikke—peaceful ruler (form
    of Frederick)
Gelsomina—jasmine
Gjerta—protection
Gudrun—divine knowledge
Gytha—warring
Hanne—gracious God (form of
    John)
Hedvig—strife (form of Hedwig)
Inga, Inger—daughter of a hero
Ingeborg—Ing's protection

Ingelise—Ing's grace
Jensine—God has blessed
Karen, Katrine—pure
Kirsten, Kristine—believes in
    Christ (form of Christian)
Kolinka—born to the
    conquering people (form of
    Kolinkar)
Laila—night
Larine, Larina—laurel (form of
    Lawrence)
Lisbet, Lise—consecrated to
    God (form of Elizabeth)
Margarethe, Meta—pearl (form
    of Margaret)
Mettalise—graceful pearl
Nielsine—champion (form of
    Neal)
Petrine, Pedrine—rock (form of
    Peter)
Rigmor—myth name
Saffi—wise
Semine—goddess of the
    heavens
Sigrid—victorious counselor
Sofie—wise (form of Sophia)
Sorine, Sorina—god of thunder;
    myth name (form of Thor)
Stinne, Stina—believes in Christ
    (form of Christian)
Thora, Thyra—god of thunder;
    myth name (form of Thor)
Trudel—strong
Vibeke—little woman
Wilhelmine—resolute protector
    (form of William)

MALE

Anders, Anker—manly (form of Andrew)

Aren, Arend—eagle (form of Arnold)

Argus—vigilant

Axel—father of peace

Balduin—bold

Bardo—hill, furrow (form of Bartholomew)

Bent—blessed

Berde, Brede—glacier

Bodil, Bo—commanding

Caesar—long-haired

Christian—believes in Christ

Christoffer—Christ-bearer (form of Christopher)

Dane—from Denmark

Diederik—ruler of the people (form of Dietrich)

Ejnar—warrior

Enok—meaning unknown

Erik—eternal ruler (form of Eric)

Eskild—meaning unknown

Frans, Franz—free (form of Francis)

Frederik—peaceful ruler (form of Frederick)

Fritz—free

Gregos—watchful (form of Gregory)

Hans—gracious God (form of John)

Harald—army ruler (form of Harold)

Henrik, Henning—rules the home (form of Henry)

Hjalmar—meaning unknown

Jakob—supplanter (form of Jacob)

Jens, Jen, Joen—gracious God (form of John)

Joren, Joris, Jory, Jorgen— farmer (form of George)

Josef—God adds (form of Joseph)

Karl—manly (form of Charles)

Klaus—victory of the people (form of Nicholas)

Knud—kind

Kolinkar—born to the conquering people

Lars, Lauritz—laurel (form of Lawrence)

Magnus—great

Mikkel—who is like God (form of Michael)

Mogens—powerful

Niel—champion (form of Neal)

Niels, Niles, Nils—son of Niel

Olaf, Ole—ancestor (form of Olaf)

Pedar—rock (form of Peter)

Poul—small (form of Paul)

Soren—god of thunder; myth name (form of Thor)

Svend—young

Tage—day

Thor—god of thunder; myth name

Ulrik—ruler of all

Valentin—valiant, strong (form of Valentine)

Vilhelm—resolute protector (form of William)

DUTCH

Dutch names consist of a first, middle, and last name. Given names are chosen by the parents, and children are sometimes named after parents or grandparents.

Hereditary surnames began in the thirteenth century in the upper classes. By the seventeenth century, the lower classes were also using surnames. Most surnames began as patronymics but also encompass occupational, place, and descriptive names. A Dutch woman usually takes her husband's name at marriage, but it is not uncommon for a woman to keep her name. If she takes her husband's surname, the husband's name is placed before the woman's maiden name. When Aleen de Vries marries Carel Jansen, she becomes Aleen Jansen de Vries. Surnames are usually passed from father to children.

Common articles are:

van—of (unlike *von* in German, *van* does not indicate nobility)
de—the (used with nicknames and, on occasion, occupational names)
van den—from the (used with place names)
van der—from the
ver—combination of *van* and *der*
ter, tor, ten, tom—at the (used with place names)
-sen, -sze, -sz, -se—son
het—the
't—the
op, on—from a farm
-man—used with place names, indicating the bearer is from there

A few surnames:

Bleecker	Dekens
Bakker	Dekker
Carstens	Deman
Christoffels	Devisser
Citroen	Devoss
de Jong	Dewitt
de Vries	Geldersman
Dehaan	Groot

Jansen	van der Klei
Kersten	van Dyck
Korstiaan	Van Ness
Lange	Vanderbilt
Rossevelt	Vanderpool
Schuylar	Vanderveer
Skipper	Verbrugge
Smedt, Smid, Smit	Vogel
Stille	Vromme
Ten Eyck	Wevers
Ter Heide	Wit
Van Aken	Woudman
van den/der Berg	Zeeman

SARI ROBINS

 Sari Robins writes Regency romances. The first novel of her Andersen Hall series, *One Wicked Night*, has been published by HarperCollins.

In *One Wicked Night*, my heroine, Lillian Kane, is a baroness in her own right, and in her circles, family name, title, and birthright are paramount. I chose her name Lillian because she blossoms like a lily and Kane because her stepfather is a blight on her family. Her family name is especially poignant for her since she does not know her biological father's identity.

I wanted her to learn that the name she creates for herself, through thought and deed, is more important than identity by birth. So the man she falls in love with, Nicholas Redford, is an orphan, named by happenstance, the location where he was abandoned as a babe.

As Nick explains to Lillian, "I was found on a snowy Christmastide near a low water junction where the town folk crossed the river. Hence, the Nicholas reference and 'reed ford' becoming Redford, thanks to the inventiveness of the local justice of the peace. The name suits me fine, but I'm starting to believe what Dunn always said. That your true name, the one you make for yourself, is the only one that counts."

FEMALE

Adrie—from the Adriatic
Alva—meaning unknown
Anke, Anika, Anki—grace (form of Anne)
Annemie—bitter grace
Arabella—beautiful eagle
Betje—devoted to God
Brandy, Brande—fine wine
Dorothea—God's gift (form of Dorothy)
Edda—poetic
Francisca—free (form of Francis)
Gisela—pledge, oath
Grishilde, Griseldis, Grushilda—gray battle-maid (form of Griselda)
Gusta, Gust—staff of God (form of Gustav)
Hendrika—rules the home (form of Henry)
Kaatje—pure (form of Katherine)
Karel—manly (form of Charles)
Lene—light
Lina, Lien—pure
Mahault—strong battle-maid (form of Matilda)
Marieke—bitter (form of Mary)
Mina—protector
Nelleke—horn
Rozamond—known defender
Saskia—Saxon
Skye, Skyla, Schyler, Skylar—sheltering
Sofie—wise (form of Sophia)
Sybylla, Sibylla—prophetess (form of Sybil)
Tryne—pure
Wigburg—young

MALE

Ambrosius—immortal (form of Ambrose)
Arend—eagle (form of Arnold)
Arje—dark; from the Adriatic (form of Adrian)
Arne—eagle (form of Arnold)
Barend—bear
Bartholomeus—hill, furrow (form of Bartholomew)
Basilius—regal (form of Basil)
Berg—mountain
Bonifacius—good (form of Boniface)
Bram—father of many (form of Abraham)
Carel—free
Cecilius—blind (form of Cecil)
Claudios—lame (form of Claude)
Claus—victory of the people (form of Nicholas)
Clementius—merciful (form of Clement)
Dirck, Dirk—God's gift (form of Theodore)
Dwight—blond
Egidius—youthful

Espen—bear of God

Eugenius—well-born (form of Eugene)

Eustatius—peaceful

Everhart—brave as a boar

Godewyn—good friend

Gottfried—God's peace (form of Godfrey)

Gotthard—divine, firm

Gregor—watchful (form of Gregory)

Hagen—heart and mind

Harold—army ruler

Henrick—rules the home (form of Henry)

Hugo—intelligent (form of Hugh)

Izaak—one who laughs (form of Isaac)

Jakob—supplanter (form of Jacob)

Jan—gracious God (form of John)

Jeremias—exalted of the Lord (form of Jeremiah)

Jilt—money

Joost—good and honest

Josef—God adds (form of Joseph)

Karel—manly (form of Charles)

Kees—horn colored

Klaas—victory of the people (form of Nicholas)

Koenraad—bold

Krisoijn—curly-haired

Kyler—archer

Larry, Lars, Larz, Lauritz—laurel (form of Lawrence)

Maarten—don't deceive

Mogens—powerful

Narve—strong

Nicolaas—victory of the people (form of Nicholas)

Noach—comfort

Piet—rock (form of Peter)

Roosevelt—from the rose field

Rutger—famous spearman (form of Roger)

Theodorus—God's gift (form of Theodore)

Thies, Thjis—God's gift (form of Matthew)

Tiebout—bold

Veit—guide (form of Guy)

Vogel—bird

Vromme—wise

Waldemar—strong ruler

Wim—strong protector

Wolter—powerful warrior (form of Walter)

EGYPTIAN

The Ptolemaic rulers, Roman Emperors and Pharaohs of Egypt could have a series of names and titles, but usually a two- or three-name system went as follows:

1. A name relating to the god Horus (names that end with -re or -ra) that also represented the bearer as a ruler of Earth and a divine spirit, and ruler of all Egypt, both North and South.

2. The individual's given name.

An example of a full name would be *Sahura Amen*.

Commoners usually had a single name, and these names frequently incorporated the names of gods: Ra, Re, Amen, Amun, Aten.

The Moslem settlers of the region use the rules listed in the section of this book on Arabic names. Other settlers use the naming system of their native tribe or land. Thus, there are no purely Egyptian surnames.

FEMALE

Ain—priceless
Akila—intelligent (form of Akil)
Amunet—goddess of mystery; myth name
Anat—wife of Seth; myth name
Annippe—daughter of the Nile
Astarte—wife of Seth; myth name
Auset—another name for Isis; myth name
Aziza—precious (form of Azizi)
Bahiti—fortune
Bast—personification of the heat of the sun; myth name
Bastet—cat; myth name
Bennu—eagle

Chione—daughter of the Nile; myth name
Cleopatra—name of a queen
Dalila—gentle
Dendera—from Dendera
Echidna—monster; myth name
Edjo—another form of Uadjit; myth name
Eshe—life
Femi—love
Fukayna—intelligent
Habibah—beloved
Hafsah—married to the prophet
Halima—gentle
Haqikah—honest
Hasina—good

Hathor, Hathor-Sakmet—
goddess of destruction;
myth name
Hatshepsut—name of a queen
Hehet—goddess of the
immeasurable; myth name
Heqet—frog-headed goddess;
myth name
Ife—love
Isis—goddess of magic; myth
name
Jamila—beauty
Jendayi—thankful
Kakra—twin
Kamilah—perfection
Kanika—black
Keket—goddess of darkness;
myth name
Kesi—born of a troubled father
Khepri—morning sun
Kissa—born after twins
Lapis—named for the lapis
stone
Layla—born at night
Lotus—lotus flower
Maat—goddess of order and
justice; myth name
Mafuane—soil
Maibe—grave
Mandisa—sweet
Mariasha—perfect one; bitter,
with sorrow
Masika—born during rain
Meht-urt—represented by a cow
Memphis—myth name
Mert, Mert-sekert—lover of
silence
Mesi—water

Meskhenet—destiny
Monifa—lucky
Mosi—born first
Moswen—light skin
Mukamutara—daughter of
Mutara
Mukantagara—born during war
Mukarramma—revered
Muminah—pious
Mut—mother; myth name
Nabirye—mother of twins
Naeemah—benevolent (form of
Naeem)
Nailah—successful
Nashwa—wonderful feeling
Nathifa—pure
Naunet—goddess of the ocean;
myth name
Nebt-het, Nephthys—nature
goddess; myth name
Neema—born to wealthy
parents
Nefertari—name of a queen
Nefertiti—name of a queen
Nekhbet—vulture-goddess;
myth name
Nephthys—daughter of Nut and
Geb; myth name
Net, Neith—divine mother
Nile—from the Nile
Nit—myth name
Niut—goddess of nothingness;
myth name
Nourbese—wonderful
Nubia—from Nubia
Nuru—born during the day
Nut—sky goddess; myth name
Ode—from the road

Olabisi—brings joy
Olufemi—beloved of the gods
Omorose—beautiful
Oni—wanted
Oseye—happy
Panya—mouse
Pili—born second
Quibilah—peaceful
Rabiah—born in the spring
Ramla—prophetess
Rashida—righteous
Raziya—agreeable
Rehema—compassionate
Renenet—goddess of fortune; myth name
Sabah—born in the morning
Safiya—pure
Sagira—little one
Sakhmet—lioness; goddess worshipped in Memphis; myth name
Salama—peaceful
Salihah—agreeable
Sanura—kitten
Sechet—myth name
Sekhet—wife of Ptah; myth name
Selma—secure

Serq, Selk—another form of Isis; myth name
Shani—wonderful
Sharifa—respected
Shukura—grateful
Siti—lady
Subira—patient
Suma—ask
Tabia—talented
Tahirah—pristine
Tale—green
Talibah—scholar
Tauret—goddess of pregnant women; myth name
Tefnut—atmospheric moisture; myth name
Thema—queen
Theoris—great
Thermuthis—another form of Renenet; myth name
Uadjit—cobra-goddess; myth name
Umayma—little mother
Umm—mother
Urbi—princess
Walidah—newly born
Yaminah—meaning unknown
Zahra—flower
Zalika, Zaliki—well-born
Zesiro—twin

MALE

Abasi—stern
Abayomi—brings joy
Abubakar—noble
Adeben—born twelfth
Adio—righteous
Adofo—fighter

Adom—receives help from the gods
Agymah—meaning unknown
Akhenaten—devoted to Aten
Akiiki—friendly
Akil—intelligent

Akins—brave

Amen, Amun, Ammon—god of a united Egypt; myth name

Amenhotep—name of a pharaoh

Amenophis—name of a pharaoh

Amen-Ra—personification of the power of the universe; myth name

Amsu, Amsi—personification of reproduction; myth name

Amun—god of mystery; myth name

An-her, Anhut—myth name

Anubis, Anpu—god of the dead; myth name

Anum—born fifth

Anzety—god of Busiris; myth name

Apis—dead bull thought to be Osiris; myth name

Apophis—meaning unknown

Asim—defender

Aswad—black

Ata—twin

Atemu—great god of Annu; myth name

Aten—sun-disk; myth name

Atsu—twin

Atum—whole

Ausar—another name for Osiris; myth name

Azibo—earth

Azizi—precious

Baal—meaning unknown

Babafemi—loved by his father

Badru—born during the full moon

Bakari—noble oath

Bankole—meaning unknown

Baruti—teacher

Beb, Bebti, Babu, Baba—Osiris's firstborn; myth name

Behdeti—myth name

Bes—brings joy; dwarf god; myth name

Bomani—warrior

Chafulumisa—fast

Chatha—ends

Chatuluka—departs

Chenzira—born on a journey

Cheops—name of a pharaoh

Chibale—kinsman

Chigaru—hound

Chike—power of God

Chisisi—secret

Chuma—wealthy

Dakarai—happiness

Darius—name of a pharaoh

Darwishi—saint

Djoser—name of a pharaoh

Donkor—humble

Ebo—born on Tuesday

Edfu—from Edfu

Fadil—generous

Faki—meaning unknown

Fenuku—born late

Fenyang—conquers

Fineas—the Nubian; dark-skinned

Funsani—a request

Gahiji—hunter

Garai—settled

Geb—earth god; myth name

Gyasi—wonderful

Haji—born during the pilgrimage

Hakizimana—God saves
Hamadi—praised
Hanbal—pristine
Hanif—believes
Hapi—god of the Nile
Hapu—name of a pharaoh
Harakhty—disguise of Horus; myth name
Hasani, Husani—handsome
Heh—god of the immeasurable; myth name
Heru—sun god; myth name
Hondo—war
Horemheb—name of a pharaoh
Horus—god of the sky; myth name
Hu—nature god; myth name
Idogbe—brother of twins
Ini-herit—he who brings back the distant one
Ishaq—laughs
Issa—God saves
Jabari—brave
Jafari—creek
Jahi—dignified
Jibade—related to royalty
Jumoke—loved by all
Kafele—would die for
Kamuzu—medical
Kaphiri—hill
Kasiya—departs
Kazemde—ambassador
Kek—god of darkness; myth name
Khafra—name of a pharaoh
Khaldun, Khalid—eternal
Khalfani—shall rule
Khentimentiu—god of the dead's destiny; myth name

Khepri—morning sun
Khnemu—to model
Khnum—reborn sun; myth name
Khons—god of the moon; myth name
Khufu—name of a pharaoh
Kneph—meaning unknown
Kontar—only son
Kosey—lion
Lateef—gentle
Lisimba—lion
Lukman—prophet
Luzige—locust
Madu—of the people
Makalani—clerk
Manu—born second
Maskini—poor
Masud—lucky
Matisimela—root
Mbizi—water
Memphis—from Memphis
Menes—name of a king
Menkaura—name of a pharaoh
Mensah—born third
Min—god of fertility; myth name
Minkah—justice
Month—god of Thebes; myth name
Mosegi—tailor
Mosi—born first
Moswen—light skin
Msamaki—fish
Msrah—born sixth
Mudada—provider
Mukhwana—twin
Musa—taken from the water (form of Moses)

Muslim—believer
Naeem—benevolent
Najja—meaning unknown
Narmer—name of a king
Nassor—victor
Neb-er-tcher—god of the universe; myth name
Nefertum—worshipped in Memphis; myth name
Nexeu—meaning unknown
Ngozi—blessed
Niu—god of nothingness; myth name
Nizam—disciplined
Nkosi—rules
Nkrumah—born ninth
Nkuku—rooster
Nun—god of the ocean; myth name
Nuru—born during the day
Oba—king
Odion—born of twins
Okpara—firstborn
Omari—high born
Onuris—brings back the distant one
Osahar—God hears me
Osaze—loved by God
Osiris, Un-nefer—god of the dead; myth name
Ottah—born third
Oubastet, Bastet—cat; myth name
Paki—witness
Petiri—meaning unknown
Pili—born second
Psamtic—name of a pharaoh
Psusennes—name of a pharaoh

Ptah—god worshipped in Memphis; myth name
Ptolemy—name of pharaoh
Qeb—father of the earth
Quaashie—born on Sunday
Ra—sun
Ramses—name of a pharaoh
Rashidi—wise
Re—midday sun
Re-Harakhty—Horus of the horizon; myth name
Reshef—myth name
Runihura—destroyer
Saa—nature god; myth name
Sabola—pepper
Sadiki—faithful
Salih—upright
Seb—god of the earth; myth name
Sebak—companion of Set; myth name
Sefu—sword
Sekani—laughs
Senusnet—name of a pharaoh
Sept—meaning unknown
Serapis—another name for Apis; myth name
Set, Sutekh—son of Seb and Nut; myth name
Seth—murdered Osiris; myth name
Sethos—name of a prince
Shabaka—name of a king
Shakir—grateful
Shu—air; myth name
Sifiye—meaning unknown
Sneferu—name of a pharaoh
Sobk—worshipped in Faiyum; myth name

Sudi—lucky
Tabari—meaning unknown
Tarik—name of a warrior
Tau—lion
Tehuti—god of earth, sky, air, and sea; myth name
Teremun—loved by his father
Thabit—strong
Thoth, Astennu—god of the moon; myth name
Thutmose—name of a pharaoh
Tor—king
Tsekani—close
Tum—great god of Annu; myth name
Tumaini—hope

Tutankhamun—name of a pharoah
Typhon—meaning unknown
Ubaid—faithful
Ufa—flour
Umi—life
Unika—meaning unknown
Ur, Ur-Atum—great; myth name
Usi—smoke
Uthman—friend of Muhammad
Wamukota—left-handed
Yafeu—bold
Yahya—given by God
Yazid—meaning unknown
Zahur—flower
Zaid, Ziyad—he shall add
Zuberi—strong
Zuka—meaning unknown

ENGLISH

The naming heritage of England has been influenced by several different cultural and linguistic groups: the Celts; Romans; Angles, Saxons, and Jutes; the Vikings and Danes; and the Normans, who invaded in 1066. In these ancient cultures, people were known by given name only, by given name and patronymic, or by given name and byname.

A byname was like a nickname used to distinguish between two people of the same given name. Bynames reflected occupation, place of origin, or personal characteristics like temperament or appearance. When the Normans centralized the relatively advanced governmental systems of England and introduced a census, they also introduced the concept of surnames. As family names were adopted from the top of the social structure down, it was not unusual for bynames like Baker, Sutton, Little, and Red to become hereditary surnames. Surnames were also constructed from personal names. By the early 1300s, surnames were common, if not universal.

Given names were primarily of Anglo-Saxon origin before the Norman invasion, but after 1066 the number of given names in common use dwindled—ultimately to only forty or fifty names for each gender—and Biblical names became more common. Since then, influence from other cultures has expanded the name pool. It has become more acceptable to use words as names or to create new names. The list of given names below represents names of Anglo-Saxon origin as well as a few other origins. A great influx of names accompanied the Norman Conquest of 1066. Traditional Hebrew (Old Testament) names such as Mary, Joseph, Miriam, Rebecca, and so on, were not used until the late Middle Ages. New Testament biblical names such as John and Peter became popular around the twelfth and thirteenth centuries. These types of names can be found in the alphabetical index.

A few surnames:

Abbott	Bottomley
Annson	Brown
Armstrong	Butler
Baker	Cartwright
Baxter	Clark

Cooper
Davidson
Faulkner
Fiske
Fletcher
Ford
Fuller
Girnwood
Goodayle
Hollister
Johnson
Jones
Lakeman
Little
Martin
Miller
Omphrey

Paddock
Peterson
Roberts
Robinson
Roper
Sawyer
Small
Smith
Statham
Taylor
Tomkin
Townsend
Tucker
Wainwright
Walker
White
Williams

FEMALE

Ada, Aida, Adda, Adia—happy

Alberta, Adalbeorht, Albertina, Albertyna, Albertine, Alberteen, Albertyne, Adalbrechta, Aldora, Aeldra—noble

Aldercy—chief

Aldis, Aldys—from the old house

Aleda, Aleta, Alita—winged

Alfreda, Aelfraed, Alfrida—elf counselor (form of Alfred)

Altheda, Altha, Althia—healer

Alura, Alhraed, Alurea, Allura—divine counselor

Alvina, Aethelwine, Aethelwyne, Aelfwine—friend of the elves

Amorica—ancient name for Britain

Anora—light

Arda, Ardelia, Ardi, Ardys, Ardine, Ardene, Ardeen, Ardella, Ardyne—warm

Arietta, Ariette—melody

Ashley, Aisley—from the ash tree grove

Attheaeldre, Atilda, Athilda—at the elder tree

Audrey, Audra, Audie, Audre—noble strength

Aurea, Auria, Aria—gentle music

Autumn—born in the fall

Avis—refuge in battle

Avril, Averil, Averyl, Avryl—born in April

Beda, Beadu—warrior maid

Berengaria, Berangari—bear-spear maid

Bertilde, Beorhthilde, Bertilda—bright battle-maid

Bertrade, Beorthtraed—bright counselor

Bethia, Betia—house of God

Beverly, Beverley—from the beaver meadow

Birdie, Birdy—birdlike

Blessing, Bletsung—blessing

Bliss, Bliths—happy

Blossom, Blostm—fresh

Blythe, Blithe—cheerful

Bonnie, Bonny, Bonie—sweet and good

Brande—firebrand

Brooke—stream

Cadena, Cadyna—rhythmic (form of Cadence)

Callie, Cally, Calli—lark

Cambria—myth name

Carmia, Carmya, Carmina, Carmine, Carmita, Charmaine—song

Carol, Caroline, Carolyn, Carolina, Carrie—manly (form of Charles)

Chelsea—seaport

Claresta—brilliant

Cleantha—glory

Cleva—dwells at the cliffs

Clover, Claefer—clover

Cody, Codie, Codi—cushion

Cordelia—myth name

Corliss—good-hearted

Cwen—queen

Cyne, Cym, Cim—ruler

Cyneburhleah, Cynburleigh, Cymberly, Cimberleigh—from the royal meadow

Daisy, Daesgesage—day's eye

Dale, Dayle, Dael—lives in the valley

Daryl—dearly loved

Dawn, Dagian—dawn

Dena, Deanna, Deana, Deane, Dina—from the valley

Devona, Defena, Devonna, Devyna—from Devon

Eadda, Ede, Eda, Eada—wealthy

Eadwine, Edwina, Edina—wealthy friend (form of Edwin)

Earlene, Erleen—noblewoman (form of Earl)

Eartha, Ertha—worldly

Earwine, Earwyn, Erwina, Erwyna, Earwyna, Aerwyna—friend of the sea

Easter, Eastre—born at Easter

Ebba—strength

Edith, Edyth, Eadgyth—wealthy gift

Edlyn, Eathelin, Eathelyn, Edlin, Edlen—noble waterfall

Edmonda, Eadmund, Edmunda, Edmanda, Eduarda—rich protector (form of Edmund)

Edrea, Earric, Edra—powerful

Eferhild, Eferhilda—bear, warrior-maiden

Egberta, Egbertina, Egbertine, Egbertyne—shining sword (form of Egbert)

Elberta, Elberte, Elbertina, Elbertine, Elbertyna—noble, glorious (form of Elbert)

Eldrida, Eldreda—wise adviser (form of Eldred)

Elethea, Elthia, Elethia—healer

Elfrida, Elfreda, Elfrieda, Elva, Elvie—good counselor

Elida, Elita, Elyta—winged

Ella, Elle—beautiful fairy

Elmira, Elmyra—noble

Elva, Elvia, Elvie, Elfie, Elivina, Elvine, Elvyne, Elvin, Elvina, Elvena—good elf

Enid, Enit, Enyd—spirit

Erna, Earna—eagle

Ernestine, Enerstyne, Enerstina, Earnestyna—serious (form of Ernest)

Ethelreda, Aethelreda, Eathelreda—noble maiden

Faith, Faithe, Fayth—faithful

Fayre—beautiful

Felabeorht, Filberta, Felberta—brilliant

Fern—fern

Fleta, Flyta—swift

Fonda—tender

Gay, Gayle, Gail, Gale—lively

Gijs—bright

Gilda, Gylda, Gyldan, Golda, Goldie, Goldy, Gildan—gilded

Glad, Gleda—happy

Gloriana, Glorianna, Gloriane—glorious grace

Godiva, Godgifu—gift from God

Goneril, Gonerilla—myth name

Gracia, Grace, Gracie—grace

Guendolen—white

Gypsy—wanderer

Gytha, Githa—gift

Hayley—from the hay meadow

Hazel, Haesel—nut

Heallfrith, Hallfrita, Halfryta, Halfrith—peaceful home

Heather—heather

Hertha—mother earth

Hilda, Hildie, Hild, Hilde—battle-maid

Hlynn—waterfall

Holly, Holea, Halig—holly

Honey, Hunig, Honbria, Honbrie—sweet

Hope—hope

Hrothbeorhta, Hrothberta, Hrothnerta, Hrothbertina—bright, famous

Huette, Huetta, Hughette, Hugiet, Hughetta—intelligent (form of Hugh)

Ilde, Ilda—heroine

Irvette, Irvetta—friend of the sea

Ivy, Ivey, Ifig—ivy

Jill—girl

Jocelyn, Joscelyne, Josceline, Jocelyne—happy

Kermeilde, Kermilda, Kermilla, Kermillie—gilded

Kerrie, Kerry—dark one; county name

Kimberly, Kim, Kimbra—from the royal fortress meadow

Kimbrought, Kimbro—from the royal field

Lark, Larke—lark

DEBBIE RALEIGH

Debbie Raleigh is the author of thirty books and novellas for Kensington Publishing, ranging from traditional regencies to paranormals. Her first novel, *Lord Carlton's Courtship*, was nominated as a *Romantic Times* Best First Regency. She has also been nominated for a Career Achievement award in Regency by *Romantic Times*.

I would like to claim that my characters flow onto the page fully formed and wearing nice, shiny name tags attached to their lapels. In reality, getting a character named is more like a twelve-round bout of mud wrestling.

Names are more than just a label that writers hand out arbitrarily. They can give us important clues to characters. They can reveal heritage, social status, or inner traits that will be exposed throughout the story. A Beowulf is not the same hero as a Corey. A heroine named Meg does not offer the reader the same expectations as Jezebel. William Hunter III would not possess the same past or family as Blade.

The first step is knowing a character. Is there a specific personality trait that I want to emphasize? A shrewish Kate or demur Sarah? Is she named for a beloved grandmother? Or a wealthy aunt in hopes of an inheritance? Is it a name she hates or takes pride in?

The time period I'm writing in as well as social and cultural influences also have to be considered. Ariel might have a devoted father who is also a classic scholar, while Shevon is a fiery Irish rebel who was orphaned as a child. Two women with two very different backgrounds.

It is also important to avoid using names that make the reader scratch their head in puzzlement. Unique names are fine, but names that are impossible to pronounce or are spelled strangely will pull the reader out of the story. The names should be an added dimension to the character, never a distraction.

In the right hands a name can help create a character that will remain in the minds of readers forever.

Lassie, Lasse, Lass—little girl
Leigh, Ley, Lee, Lea, Leah, Leia—
from the meadow
Leoma—bright
Levina, Levene, Levyna—flash
Liberty—liberty
Lindsay, Lindsey—from the
island of the linden tree
Lissa, Lyssa—honeybee
Lodema, Lodima, Lodyma—
guide
Lona, Loni—solitary
Love, Lov—affection
Luella, Louella, Luell—make
amends
Luvena, Luvina, Luvyna—little
beloved one
Lynn, Lyn, Lin, Linne—cascade
Madra, Madre—mother
Maida, Maegth, Maidie, Mady,
Maidel, Mayda, Mayde—
maiden
Maitane, Maite, Maitena—dearly
loved
Mercia—from Mercia
Mercy—mercy
Merry—happy
Mertice, Maertisa, Mertysa,
Mertise—famous
Mildred, Mildraed, Mildrid,
Mildryd—gentle adviser
Nara, Nearra—nearest
Neda—wealthy guardian
Nelda—by the alder tree
Nellwyn, Nelwin, Nelwina,
Nelwyna—bright friend
Oleda, Oleta, Olita—winged
Ora, Orabelle, Orabel—beautiful
seacoast

Oralie, Orelia—gold
Orva, Ordwin, Ordwyn,
Ordwyna, Ordwina—brave
friend
Peace, Pax—peace
Philberta—brilliant
Piper, Pipere—piper
Poppy—flower
Portia—offering
Queena, Queenie—queen
Ra, Rae—doe
Radella, Raedself—elfin
counselor
Raven, Ravyn—dark-haired;
wise
Regan—myth name
Ricarda—strong ruler (form of
Richard)
Rillette, Rilletta—stream
Roberta, Robertia—bright;
famous (form of Robert)
Sabrina—legendary princess
Saxona, Saxonia—of Saxony
Scarlett, Scarlet—red
Shelley, Scelfleah—from the
ledge meadow
Sherry, Sherri, Shirley—from the
white meadow
Starr, Starla, Star—star
Stockard, Stockhart, Stockhard,
Stokkard—hardy tree
Storm, Stormy, Stormie—storm
Summer, Suma—born during
the summer
Sunny—cheerful
Tangerine, Tangerina—from
Tangiers
Tatum, Tayte, Tait, Tate—happy

Tuesday, Tiwesdaeg—born on Tuesday
Twyla—woven
Tyne, Tyna, Tina—river
Velvet, Velouette—soft
Wallis, Waleis—from Wales
Wanetta, Wann—pale
Welcome—welcomed
Welsa, Welsie—from the west
Wenda—comely
Willa—resolute
Withypoll—twig head
Yedda—beautiful voice
Yetta—generous
Zavrina, Zabrina—legendary princess (form of Sabrina)

MALE

Adam—of the red earth
Addy—ardent
Adney, Addaneye, Addney, Adny—lives on the noble's island
Aeldra—lives at the elder tree
Aelfdane—Danish elf
Aelfdene—from the elfin valley
Aethelisdun, Athelston, Aetheston—from the noble's hill
Aiken, Adken, Adkyn, Aikin, Aickin—oaken
Ainsley, Ainslie, Ansley, Aenedleah, Ansleigh—meadow
Albern, Aethelbeorn, Alburn—noble warrior
Albert, Alburt, Aethelberht, Aethelbert—noble, intelligent
Alden, Aldwine, Aldwyn, Aldwin—wise protector
Aldo—old
Aldrich, Aldric, Aldrik—wise ruler

Alford, Alvord, Avery—from the old ford
Alfred, Alfredo, Aelfraed, Aldrid—elf counselor
Allard, Alhhard, Aethelhard—brave
All—handsome
Allred, Aldred, Aldrid—wise, red-haired man
Almo, Aethelmaer, Athemar, Athmarr—noble, famous
Alson, Alison, Adalson, Aliceson, Alycesone—son of All
Alston, Aethelstun—from the elf's home
Alton, Alden, Aldan, Aldtun—from the old manor
Ann, Ain—name of a king
Anna—name of a king
Anscom, Aenescumb, Anscomb—lives in the valley of the majestic one
Ardell, Ardel—from the hare's dell
Ardley, Ardaleah, Ardleigh—from the home-lover's meadow

Ardolf, Ardwolf, Ardolph—
home-loving wolf
Aric, Alhric, Arik, Alhrick,
Alhrik—noble ruler
Arlo—fortified hill
Arnett, Arnet, Arnatt, Arnott—
little eagle
Arthgallo—myth name
Arundel, Arndell—from the
eagle's dell
Ashley, Ashly, Aisley,
Aescleah—from the ash tree
grove
Ashlin, Aesclin—lives at the ash
tree pool
Ashton, Aiston, Aesctun—from
the ash tree farm
Ashwin, Aescwine, Ashwyn,
Aescwyn—spear friend
Aurick—noble valor
Averil, Averill, Averell—born in
April
Avery, Aelfric, Aubrey—elf ruler
Axton, Aeccestane—
swordsman's stone
Aylmer, Almer, Aethelmaere,
Aegelmaere—infamous
Aylward, Aegelweard,
Aethelweard, Athelward—
noble protector
Balder, Baldhere—bold army
Bancroft, Benecroft—from the
bean field
Barclay, Berkeley, Berkley,
Bercleah—lives at the birch
tree meadow
Barden, Bardan—lives near the
boar's den

Bardolf, Bardawulf, Bardolph,
Bardulf, Bardalph,
Barwolf—ax-wolf
Bardrick, Bardaric, Bardarik—
ax-ruler
Barnett, Beornet—leader
Baron, Barron—warrior
Barr, Barre—gateway
Barth—son of the earth
Bartram, Beorhthramm,
Barthram—glorious raven
Bayhard, Bay—reddish-brown
hair
Beacher, Beceere, Beecher—
lives by the beech tree
Beck, Bek—brook
Bede—prayer
Bert, Burt, Beorht—bright
Bertram, Beorhthram—bright
raven (form of Bertrand)
Beverly, Beverley—from the
beaver meadow
Birch, Beore, Birk—birch tree
Birkey—from the birch tree
island
Birley, Byreleah—from the
cattle shed on the meadow
Black, Claec—dark
Blade, Blaed—wealthy glory
Blaise, Blaze—stutters
Blake, Blaec—black or white
Blakeley, Blakely, Blaecleah—
from the dark meadow
Blakey, Blacey—blond
Blanford, Blandford—gray-
haired
Blayne—twin
Bliss—happy

Blyth, Blythe—cheerful
Bors—myth name
Botolf, Botewolf, Botwolf—
herald wolf
Braden, Bradyn, Brad, Bradan,
Bradene—from the broad
valley
Bradley, Bradly, Bradleah—from
the broad meadow
Brady, Bradig—from the broad
island
Brainard, Branhard, Brainerd—
bold raven
Brandon, Branddun—from the
beacon hill
Brantley, Brant, Brand—proud
Brent, Brentan—from the steep
hill
Britto—myth name
Brock, Brok, Broc—badger
Brook, Brooke—stream
Brutus—myth name
Buck, Boc—male deer
Buckley, Bocleah, Bocley—lives
at the buck meadow
Budd, Buddy, Boda—herald
Bundy, Bondig—free
Burch, Birche, Birch—birch
Burchard, Burghard—strong as
a castle
Burdon, Burhdon—lives at the
castle
Burgess, Burgeis—town citizen
Burl, Byrle—cup-bearer
Burnett, Burnet—meaning
unknown
Burney, Bureig—lives on the
brook island

Byram—from the cattle yard
Byrd, Bird, Birde—bird
Byron—from the cottage; bear
Calder, Caldre, Calldwr—cold
brook
Cale, Cal, Cayle—bold
Camber—myth name
Carswell, Caersewiella—lives at
the watercress spring
Carvell, Carvel—from the villa
by the march
Cassibellaunus—myth name
Cedric, Caddarik, Caddaric—
chief
Cenehard, Cynhard—bold
Ceneward, Cynward—bold
guardian
Cenewig, Cenewyg—bold
warrior
Chad, Cadda—warrior
Chadburn, Chadburne,
Chadbyrne—from the
wildcat brook
Charles—manly
Charleton, Charlton—from
Charles's farm
Chatwyn, Chatwin—warring
friend
Chauncey, Chance, Chancey,
Chaunce, Chancellor,
Chaunceler—chancellor
Chester, Ceaster—lives at the
camp
Cheston, Ceastun—camp
Cingeswiella, Cingeswell,
Cinwell—lives at the king's
spring
Clay, Claeg, Clayton, Claegtun—
mortal

Clifford, Cliff—lives by the ford near the cliff

Clinton, Clint, Clinttun—from the headland estate

Clive, Clyve, Cleve—lives at the cliffs

Cody, Codi, Codie—cushion

Colbert, Culbert, Culbart, Ceolbeorht, Colvert—seaman

Colby—from the dark village

Coleman, Colemann—dark-skinned

Collier, Colier, Collyer, Colyer—charcoal merchant

Collis, Colis, Colys—son of the dark man

Colter, Coltere—horse herdsman

Colton, Colt, Coletun, Cole—from the dark town

Corwin, Corwyn, Corwine, Corwan—friend of the heart

Culver, Colver, Colvyr, Colfre—dove

Cuthbert, Cuthbeorht—famous; intelligent

Cutler—makes knives

Cymbelline—myth name

Cyneleah, Cyneley—lives in the royal meadow

Cyning, Cyneric, Cynerik, Cynric, Cynrik—royal

Dalbert, Delbert, Dealbert, Dealbeorht—proud

Dale, Dael, Daley, Dayle—lives in the valley

Darrell, Daryl—dearly loved

Dean, Deanne, Dene, Dino—from the dene

Dempster—judicious

Denley—from the valley meadow

Dennis—follower of Dionysus

Derward, Deorward, Deerward—guardian of the deer

Derwin, Derwyn, Derwan—friend of wild animals

Drake, Draca—dragon

Dunn—dark-skinned

Dunstan—hill of stone

Durwin, Durwyn, Deorwine—dear friend

Earl, Eorl, Earle—nobleman

Edbert, Eadburt, Eadbeorht—wealthy

Edelmar, Edelmarr, Eadelmarr—noble

Edgar, Eadger—wealthy spear

Edmund, Edmond, Edmondo, Eadmund—rich protector

Edrick, Edrik, Edwald, Edwaldo, Eadweald, Eadric—wealthy ruler

Edsel, Eadsele—from Edward's hall

Edward, Eduard, Eda, Edvard, Ede, Eideard, Eadward, Eadweard—rich guardian

Edwin, Edwyn, Eadwyn, Eadwine—wealthy friend

Egbert, Ecgbeorht—shining sword

Eibhear, Ever, Evert, Everet, Everhard—strong as a boar

Elidure—myth name
Ellard, Eallard, Ealhhard—brave
Elmore, Elmoor, Elmer—lives at the elm tree moor
Elvy, Elvey—elf warrior
Elwald, Elwold—old Welshman
Elwell, Eadwiella—from the old spring
Elwyn, Elwin, Elwen—old friend
Emery, Emeric, Emerick—meaning unknown
Erwin, Earwyn, Earwine, Erwyn—friend of the sea
Esmond, Estmund, Esmund—protected by God
Ethelbert, Aethelbeorht—splendid
Everard, Eferhard, Ever—brave as a boar
Ewald—powerful
Ewert, Eawart, Eweheorde—shepherd
Ewing—lawyer
Fane, Fayne, Fain, Faegan, Fagan—joyful
Farold, Faerwald—powerful traveler
Farr, Faer—traveler
Ferrex—myth name
Filbert, Filburt, Felabeorht—brilliant
Filmer, Filmore, Filmarr, Felamaere—famous
Finn—blond
Firman—fair
Fiske—fish
Fitch, Fitche, Fytch—ermine
Flint, Flynt—a stream

Ford—river crossing
Foster, Forest, Forrester—keeper of the forest
Fowler—game warden
Frayne, Fraine, Freyne—foreigner
Frewin, Frewyn, Frewen, Freowine—noble friend
Frey—lord
Frick, Frika, Freca—bold
Fridolf, Fridolph, Fridwolf, Friduwulf—peaceful wolf
Frisa—curly-haired
Gail, Gayle, Gale—lively
Garman, Garrman, Garmon, Garmann—spearman
Garmond, Garmund, Garm—spear protector
Garnett, Garnet—armed with spear
Garr, Gar—spear
Garrett, Garrard, Garet—strong spear
Garrick—rules by the spear
Garroway, Garwig—spear-fighter
Garton, Garatun—lives in the triangular farmstead
Garvin, Garvyn, Garwin, Garwyn, Garwine—spear friend
Gary—carries spears
Gaukroger—Roger the clumsy
Gawain, Gawen, Gawyn—white hawk
Geary, Gerry—flexible
Gehard, Gerd, Gerrit, Gerardo, Gherardo—spear-hard
Geoffrey—God's peace

Geol—born at Christmas
Gervase—serves
Gifford, Gifuhard—gift of
　bravery
Gijs—bright
Gilbert, Gilburt, Guilbert,
　Giselbert, Gilpin—pledge
Gildas—gilded
Gilmer, Gilmar, Giselmaere—
　famous hostage
Gladwin, Gladwyn, Glaedwine—
　happy friend
Godwin, Godwyn, Godwine—
　God's friend
Gold, Golden—blond
Goldwin, Goldwyn, Goldwine—
　golden friend
Goodwin, Goodwine,
　Goodwyn—God's friend
Gorboduc—myth name
Gordon, Garadun, Garadin,
　Garadyn, Garaden—from
　the three-cornered hill
Graeham, Gram, Graeghamm—
　from the gray home
Grant, Graent—great
Grover, Grafere—lives in the
　grove
Guiderius—myth name
Hadwin, Hadwyn, Haethowine—
　friend in war
Halbert, Halburt, Halbart,
　Halebeorht—brilliant hero
Hale, Hayle, Haele—lives in the
　hall
Hardwin, Hardwyn,
　Heardwine—brave friend
Harelache, Harlak, Harlake—
　lives at the hare's lake

Hare—rabbit
Harlan, Harland—from the
　hare's land
Harley, Harleigh, Hareleah—
　from the hare's meadow
Hart, Heort—stag
Harvey, Houerv, Herve—soldier
Haslet, Haslett—from the hazel
　tree land
Hastings, Haestingas—violent
Haven, Havyn, Haefen—safety
Hayden, Haydon—from the
　hedged-in valley
Haywood, Heywood—from the
　hedged forest
Hearne, Hern, Herne—hunter;
　myth name
Heathcliff, Heathclyf, Hetheclif—
　from the heath cliff
Histion—myth name
Holden, Holdin, Holdyn—from
　the hollow in the valley
Hollis—lives by the holly trees
Howard, Heahweard—chief
　guardian
Hring—ring
Hroc—crow
Hud, Hod—hooded
Hugh, Huey, Hugi—intelligent
Humility—humble
Hunt, Hunter—hunter
Hurlbert, Hurlbart, Herlbert,
　Herlebeorht—army strong
Hurst, Hurste—lives in the
　forest
Hwistlere—piper
Innocent—innocent
Irving, Irwin, Irwyn—sea friend

Ives—little archer
Iwdael, Idal—from the yew tree valley
Jack—supplanter (derivative of James)
James—supplanter
Jasper—treasurer (form of Casper)
Keane, Keene, Keenan, Keanan—sharp
Kemp, Kempe—warrior
Kendall—from the clear river valley
Kenelm—defends the family
Kennard—bold
Kenneth, Ken—handsome
Kenrick, Kenrik, Kenryk—royal ruler
Kent—from Kent
Kenton—from a farm in Kent
Kenward—bold guardian
Kenway—brave in war
Kim—ruler
King—royal
Kinsey—victorious
Kirk, Kyrk—dwells at the church
Knight—noble, soldier
Kyne, Ken—royal
Lach, Laec, Lache—lives near water
Ladd, Lad, Ladde—attendant
Laibrook, Ladbroc—lives by the path by the brook
Langford—lives near the long ford
Leal, Lele—loyal
Lear, Lir—myth name
Lee, Lew—shelter

Leigh, Leo—from the meadow
Lind, Lynd—lives by the linden tree
Lindell, Lindael—lives by the linden tree valley
Linford, Lynford—from the linden-tree ford
Locke, Loc—lives by the stronghold
Locrine—myth name
Lorineus—myth name
Lowell, Lovell, Lyfing, Loefel—beloved
Lud—myth name
Lydell—from the open dell
Lyman, Leman, Leyman—from the valley
Lyndon, Linddun—lives by the linden tree
Malin, Malyn—little warrior
Malvin, Malvyn, Maethelwine—council friend
Manfred, Manfrid—peaceful
Mann—hero
Manning—son of a hero
Marley, Marly—from the march meadow
Marshall, Marschall, Marshall—steward
Mather, Maetthere—powerful army
Maxwell—capable
Medwin, Medwyn, Medwine—strong friend
Melvin, Melvyn, Maelwine—strong friend
Merritt, Maeret—little famous one

Mervin, Mervyn, Maerewine, Merwyn—famous friend

Mitchell, Mitchel—like God

Mordred, Modraed—brave

Napier—in charge of royal linens

Newland—lives on the new land

Norvin, Norvyn, Norwin, Norwyn—friend of the north

Nyle, Nye—island

Oakley—from the oak tree meadow

Odell, Odale, Odayle—of the valley

Odom, Odam—son-in-law

Odwulf, Odwolf, Odwolfe—wealthy wolf

Ogelsby, Oegelsby, Ogelsvy, Ogelsvie—fearsome

Orrick, Orik, Orick, Orrik, Haarac—from the ancient oak tree

Orval, Orvil, Orville, Ordwald, Orwald—spear-strength

Orvin, Orvyn, Ordwin, Ordwine—brave friend

Os, Oz—divine

Osbert, Osburt, Osbart, Osbeorht—divinely brilliant

Osborn, Osburn, Osbourne, Osbeorn—divine bear

Osmar, Osmarr—divinely glorious

Osmond, Osmund, Osmont—divine protector

Osred, Osrid, Osryd, Osraed—divine counselor

Osric, Osrik, Osrick—divine ruler

Oswald, Osweald, Oswell—divine power

Parkin, Perekin, Parle, Pierrel, Parnall, Pernel, Pernell, Pollock, Pauloc, Perkin, Perekin—little rock

Parr—from the cattle enclosure

Parsefal, Percival, Parsifal, Perceval—valley piercer

Payne, Paine—pagan

Pell, Paella—mantle

Perry, Perye—from the pear tree

Philip, Phillip—lover of horses

Pierce, Pearce, Peirce—rock (form of Peter)

Pit, Pyt—from the pit

Porrex—myth name

Prentice, Prentiss—scholar

Preston, Prestin, Preostun—from the priest's farm

Quentin, Quinton—from the queen's estate

Rad, Raed—red

Radbert, Radburt, Redman, Redamann, Readman—red-haired counselor

Radburn, Radbyrne, Radbourne, Raedburne—lives by the red stream

Radolf, Radolph, Raedwolf—red wolf

Raedeman—red-haired horseman

Ralph, Ralf, Raff, Rolf, Rolfe—wolf

Ram, Ramm—ram

Randolph, Randal, Randall, Rafe—shield wolf

Randy—coarse

Rankin, Randkin—little shield

Rans, Raven, Rand, Ren—raven

Read, Reed, Reid—red-haired

Redwald—strong counsel

Reeve, Reve, Reave—steward

Reginald, Regenweald—strong ruler

Renfred, Renfrid, Regenfrithu—peaceful raven

Richard, Rikkard—strong ruler

Richman, Ricman, Rickman—powerful

Rich—wealthy

Ricker—strong army

Rickward, Rikward, Ricweard—strong guardian

Rider, Ryder, Ridere—knight

Ridgely, Ridgeley—lives at the meadow's ridge

Ridley, Redley, Raedleah—from the red meadow

Rigby, Ricadene—lives in the ruler's valley

Rigg—lives near the ridge

Ring—ring

Roan, Rowan—from the rowan tree

Roe, Row—deer

Ronald—mighty, powerful

Roper—maker of rope

Rover, Rovere—wanderer

Royce, Royse—royal

Ruck, Rook—raven

Rudd, Ruddy, Reod—ruddy-colored

Rudyard, Ruhdugeard—from the rough enclosure

Rune—secret

Rush, Rysc—rush

Russell—fox

Rutherford—from the cattle ford

Salton, Sahhltun—lives near the willow farm

Sawyer, Sawyere—cuts timber

Scott, Scottas—from Scotland

Seabert, Seaburt, Seabright, Sebert, Saebeorht—glory at sea

Sedge, Secg—swordsman

Sedgewic, Sedgewick, Secgwic, Sedgewik—from the sword grass place

Seger, Seager, Segar, Saweger—seaman

Selby, Seleby, Shelby—from the manor house

Selwyn, Selwine, Selwin—friend at court

Severin—severe

Sewell, Sewall, Sewald, Saewald—mighty at sea

Sexton, Sextein—meaning unknown

Seymour—tailor

Shandy, Scandy—boisterous

Shattuck, Shaddock, Shaddoc, Schaddoc—shad-fish

Shawn, Shaw—from the shady grove

Sherlock, Scirloc—blond

Sherman—cuts the nap of woolen cloth

Sherwin, Sherwyn—quick as the wind

Sidney, Sydney—from Sidon

Sigehere—victorious
Skeet, Skete, Skeat, Sketes—
  swift
Spark, Sparke—gallant
Spear, Spere—spear
Speed, Sped—success
Spencer, Spenser—keeper of
  provisions
Sproule, Sproul, Sprowle—
  active
Stanley, Stan, Stanly—lives by
  the stony grove
Stanway, Stanweg—lives by the
  stony road
Starbuck—star-deer
Starling, Staerling—bird
Starr—star
Sterling, Stirling—of honest
  value
Sterne, Stern, Stearn—austere
Stewert, Stewart, Stuart,
  Steward—steward
Stillman, Stilleman, Stillmann—
  gentle
Stod, Stodd—horse
Storm, Storme—storm
Stowe—place
Strong, Strang—powerful
Styles, Stiles, Stigols—stiles
Swain, Swayn—knight's
  attendant
Talon—claw
Tate, Tayt, Tayte, Tait—happy
Tearle, Thearl—stern
Terrell, Tirell, Terrill, Tirell,
  Tyrell—thunder ruler
Thain, Thane, Thegn, Thayne,
  Thain—follower

Thaw, Thawain—thaw
Thormond, Thurmond,
  Thormund—Thor's
  protection
Thunder—stormy tempered
Thurston, Thurstun, Thurstan—
  Thor's stone
Tila, Tyla—good
Tilman, Tillman—virile
Tomkin, Thomkins—little Tom
Tomlin—little twin
Torr—tower
Tostig—name of an earl
Tripp, Trip, Trypp, Tryp,
  Tripper—traveler
True, Treowe—loyal
Trumble, Trumbald, Trumball—
  strong, bold
Trumen, Truman, Treoweman—
  loyal
Twain, Twein—cut in two
Twitchell, Twitchel—lives on a
  narrow passage
Tyler, Tylere—maker of tiles
Udolf, Udolph—wealthy wolf
Ulfred—wolf of peace
Ulger—wolf spear
Ullock, Ullok, Ulvelaik—wolf
  sport
Ulmar, Ulmarr—famous wolf
Unwin, Unwyn, Unwine—
  unfriendly
Vail, Vayle, Vale—lives in the
  valley
Valiant—brave
Vance, Vannes—grain fans
Vinn—conqueror
Wade, Wada, Waed—moving

Waite, Wait, Wayte—guard
Wake, Wacian—alert
Wallace, Waleis, Wallis, Walsh,
    Welch, Welsh—from Wales
Walwyn, Wealaworth—Welsh
    friend
War, Waer—wary
Ward, Warde, Warden, Worden,
    Weard—guard
Wareine, Warren—gamekeeper
Warrick, Warwick, Warwyk,
    Waeringawicum—fortress
Watt, Wat—hurdle
Wayne, Wain—craftsman
Wells, Welles—lives by the
    spring
Wesley, Westley, Westleah—
    from the west meadow
Whitlock, Whytlok—blond
Whitman—white-haired
Whitney—from the white island
Wilbert, Wilburt—resolute,
    brilliant
Wilbur, Willaburh—beloved
    stronghold
Wilfrid, Wilfred, Wilfryd—
    resolute peace
Will, Willa—resolute
Willard, Willhard—resolute,
    brave
William—resolute protector
Winchell, Wincel—drawer of
    water
Wine, Wyne, Win, Winn—friend
Winfred, Wynfrid, Winfrid,
    Winefrith, Wynfrith—friend
    of peace
Winter, Wynter—born in the
    winter

Witt, Witta—wise
Witter, Wittahere—wise warrior
Wolfe, Wolf, Wulf—wolf
Woodman—hunter
Woodrow—from the hedgerow
    by the forest
Woodruff—bailiff
Woolsey, Wulfsige—victorious
    wolf
Worden—defender
Wulffrith—wolf of peace
Wulfgar—wolf spear
Wyatt, Wiatt—guide
Wyman, Wigman—fighter
Wymer, Wigmaere—famous in
    battle
Yule, Yul—born during Yule

ADDITIONAL NAMES
Abbot, Abbott—abbey father
Acker, Akker—from the oak tree
Ackerley, Ackley—from the oak
    tree meadow
Ackerman—man of oak
Addis, Adamson—son of Adam
Addison—descendent of Adam
Adkins, Attkins, Atkinson,
    Atkinsone—son of Aiken
Ainsworth—from Ann's estate
Alcott—from the old cottage
Alder, Aler—from the alder tree
Aldis, Aldus, Aldous—from the
    old house
Amsden—from Ambrose's
    valley
Anglesey—from Anglesey
Archer, Archere—bowman
Arkwright—makes chests

Arledge—lives at the hare's lake

Arley, Arlie, Arleigh—from the hare's meadow

Armstrong, Armstrang—strong arm

Ascot, Ascott—lives at the east cottage

Ashburn, Aesoburne—lives near the ash tree brook

Ashby, Aescby—from the ash tree farm

Ashford, Atherton, Aethretun—lives at the spring farm

Athmore, Attmore, Atmore—from the moor

Atwater, Attewater—from the waterside

Atwell, Attwell, Attewell—lives by the spring

Atwood, Attewode—lives in the forest

Atworth, Atteworthe—lives at the farmstead

Bainbridge, Banbrigge, Bainbrydge—lives by the bridge over the stream

Banaing, Banning—son of the slayer

Barlow, Baehloew, Barhloew—lives on the bare hill

Barnum, Beornham—from the nobleman's home

Bartley, Bartleah, Bartleigh—from Bart's meadow

Barton, Bart, Beretun—from the barley farm

Baxter, Baker, Backstere, Bax—baker

Beadutun, Beaton—from the warrior's estate

Beaman, Beomann—beekeeper

Beamer, Bemeere—trumpeter

Belden, Beldan, Beldene, Beldon, Beldane—lives in the beautiful glen

Bentley, Bentleah, Bentleigh—from the bent grass meadow

Benton—lives on the moor

Beresford, Berford—from the barley ford

Berton, Burton, Beorhttun, Burhtun—from the fortified town

Berwick, Berwyk—from the barley grange

Bickford, Biecaford, Bick—from the hewer's ford

Bink—lives at the bank

Birkett, Birkhead, Birkhed—lives at the birch headland

Birney, Burneig, Burney—lives on the brook island

Birtle, Birtel, Byrtel, Birdhil, Birdhill—from the bird hill

Bishop—overseer

Bitanig—from the preserving land

Blagdon, Blagdan, Blagden—from the dark valley

Blakemore—from the dark moore

Bolton—from the manor farm

Bond—tied to the land

Booth, Boothe, Bothe—lives in a hut

Borden, Bardene, Barden—from the boar valley

Bosworth—lives at the cattle enclosure

Bradburn, Bradbourne—from the broad brook

Bradford—from the broad ford

Bradwell—from the broad spring

Bramwell, Braemwiella—from the bramble bush spring

Brawley, Brawleigh, Braleah—from the hillslope meadow

Brewster, Brewstere—brewer

Bridger, Brydger, Bryggere, Briggere—lives at the bridge

Brigham, Briggeham—lives by the bridge

Brinton—from Brinton

Brockley, Brocleah, Brocly, Brocleigh—from the badger meadow

Broderick, Brodrig, Brodrik, Broderik—from the broad ridge

Bromley, Bromleah, Bromleigh, Bromly—from the broom-covered meadow

Brooks, Brooksone, Brookson—son of Brooke

Brougher, Burghere—lives at the fortress

Broughton, Burgtun—from the fortress town

Brown, Brun—dark-haired

Burbank, Burhbank—lives on the castle's hill

Burley, Burhleag, Burleigh, Burly—lives at the castle's meadow

Burn, Byrne, Bourne, Burne, Bourn—from the brook

Burns, Bursone, Byrnes—son of Byrne

Burton, Burhtun—lives in the fortified town

Byford, Biford—lives at the river crossing

Cadby, Cadabyr—from the warrior's settlement

Caindale—from the clear river valley

Caldwell, Caldwiella—from the cold spring

Calvert, Calbert, Calfhierde—shepherd

Carland—from the land between the streams

Carleton, Carlton, Carlatun—from Carl's farm

Carlisle, Carlyle—from the walled city

Carson—son of Carr

Carter, Cartere—drives a cart

Carver—carves wood or sculpts

Caster—from the Roman camp

Chadwick, Chadwyk, Chadwik, Caddawyc—from the warrior's town

Chapman, Ceapmann—merchant

Chatham, Caddaham—from the soldier's land

Chetwey, Chetwin, Cetewind—from the cottage on the winding path

BARRY EISLER

Barry Eisler is the author of the Rain books (*Rain Fall, Hard Rain,* and *Rain Storm*), a series of three thrillers that have been translated into over a dozen languages. They have also been optioned for a film.

Sometimes what makes a great character name is the name's resonance, its associations with other words. George Lucas knows this, and uses the concept well: Darth Vader is memorable in part because the name sounds like *death*, like *dearth* (of compassion, humanity), like *invader*, all concepts that are part of the Darth Vader "brand."

Stephen King had a great one with fictional killer Alexis Machine in *The Dark Half*; the surname tells you this guy is unstoppable and unfeeling, while the first name, classy and highborn, emphasizes these concepts by contrast. And Machine's creator and progenitor, the "not a nice guy" writer George Stark, was another good one: each name a single syllable, the second one meaning in part "harsh," "grim," "desolate." All concepts that provide a chillingly accurate description of what this character is going to be up to in the story.

Another one I love is the judge from Cormac McCarthy's *Blood Meridian*. Not "Judge," with an uppercase *J*; but "the" judge, implying his uniqueness to that station, and with a lowercase *j*, perhaps implying a certain unpretentiousness or lack of conscious effort. And of course the judge does in fact sit in judgment on mankind, whether as God or the devil the reader must decide alone.

Andrew Vachss has a winner with Burke. Think a guy named Burke—no first name—could be a softy? Of course not. And iconic Burke's single syllable name, with the clipped-off *k* at the end, hints at a lot about him: his directness, his toughness, his solitary existence.

Occasionally the name a character chooses for others reveals something about the character himself: What do we learn about George Miller's Mad Max by virtue of Max's habit of calling his dog, "Dog?" A lack of imagination? A reluctance to acknowledge anything beyond the generic about the animal, perhaps born out of a reluctance to form an attachment?

Chilton, Celdtun—from the farm by the spring

Churchill, Circehyll, Churchyll—lives at the church hill

Clayborne, Claiborn, Claegborne, Claybourne, Clayburn—from the clay brook

Cleveland, Clifland, Clyfland, Clevon, Cleon—from the cliffs

Cliffton, Clifton, Cliftun, Clyftun, Clyffton—from the farm near the cliff

Cooper, Cupere, Coopersmith—makes barrels

Courtland—lives at the farmstead

Covell, Covyll, Cofahealth—lives at the cave slope

Crandall, Crandell—from the crane valley

Cranley, Cranleah, Cranly—from the crane meadow

Cranston, Cranstun—from the crane estate

Crawford—from the crow's ford

Creighton, Creketun—from the town by the creek

Crichton—from the town by the creek

Croften, Crofton—from the enclosed town

Crompton—from the winding farm

Cromwell, Crombwiella—from the crooked stream

Crosley, Crosleah, Crosly, Crosleigh—from the cross meadow

Cwentun—from the queen's estate

Dagwood—from the bright one's forest

Dalton—from the farm in the dale

Darnell, Darnall—from Darnall

Darton, Deortun—from the deer park

Davis, Davidson, Davidsone—David's son

Dearborn, Dearbourne, Derebourne—from the deer brook

Deems, Demason, Demasone—judge's son

Dempsey—from the judge's meadow

Denton—from the valley farm

Denver—lives at the valley's edge

Diamond, Deagmund, Diamont—bridge protector

Dickson, Dixon, Dikesone—son of Dick

Doane, Doune—from the sand hill

Dryden, Driden, Dridan, Drygedene—from the dry valley

Dudley—from the people's meadow

Dunley, Dunleigh, Dunly, Dunleah—from the hill meadow

Dunton—from the farm on the hill

Durward—gatekeeper

Eaton, Eatun—from the riverside village

Edison, Eadwardsone, Edwardson, Eddis—son of Edward

Egerton—from the town on the ridge

Elden, Eldan, Eldon, Ealhdun, Ealdun—from the elves' valley

Elder, Ellder, Eldur—from the elder tree

Ellison, Eallison—son of Elder

Elsdon—from the noble's hill

Elsworth—from the noble's estate

Elton—from the old town

Elwood, Ellwood, Ealdwode—from the old forest

Eoforwic—from the bear estate

Erland, Eorlland, Eorland—from the nobleman's land

Erling, Eorlson, Earlson—nobleman's son

Estcott, Estcot—from the east cottage

Everly, Eferleah, Everley, Everleigh—from Ever's meadow

Fairfax—blond

Farley, Farleigh, Farly, Faerrleah, Fairlie—from the bull's pasture

Farnell, Fearnhealh, Farnall,

Fernald—from the fern slope

Farnham, Fearnhamm—from the fern field

Farnley, Farnley, Fearnleah—from the fern meadow

Farson, Farrs, Fars—son of Farr

Felton, Feldtun, Feldun, Feldon—from the field estate

Fenton—from the farm on the fens

Fielding, Felding—lives in the field

Fitz—son

Fitz Adam, Fitsadam—son of Adam

Fitz Water, Fitzwater, Fitz Walter, Fitzwalter—son of Walter

Fitzgerald, Fitz Gerald—son of Gerald

Fitzgibbon, Fitz Gibbon, Fitzgilbert, Fitz Gilbert—son of Gilbert

Fitzhugh, Fitz Hugh—son of Hugh

Fitzjames, Fitz James—son of James

Fitzpatrick, Fitz Patrick—son of Patrick

Fitzsimon, Fitz Simon, Fitzsimmons, Fitzsimons—son of Simon

Fleming—from Flanders

Freeland—from the free land

Fuller, Fullere—cloth thickener

Fulton, Fugeltun, Fulaton—from the people's estate

Galt—from the high ground

Galton, Galeun—from the town on the high ground

Gardner, Gardiner—gardener

Garfield, Garafeld—from the triangular field

Garland, Gariland—from the spear land

Garson, Garrson, Garsone—son of Gar

Garwood, Ayrwode, Arwood—from the fir forest

Gibson, Gibbesone—Gilbert's son

Gilford—from Gill's ford

Golding—son of Gold

Granger, Grangere—farmer

Grantham, Graham—from the great meadow

Grantland, Grantley—from the large meadow

Grayson, Grayvesone—son of the reeve

Greeley, Greely, Graegleah—from the gray meadow

Gresham, Grisham—from the grazing

Haagley, Hagly, Hagalean, Haig—from the hedged enclosure

Haalstead, Heallstede—from the manor house

Hadden, Haddon, Heath, Hadon, Haden, Heathdene—from the heath

Hadley, Heathley, Heathleah—from the heath-covered meadow

Hadrian—son of Adrian

Halford—from the hall by the ford

Hall, Heall—from the manor

Hallam, Healum—from the hillside

Halley, Healleah—from the manor house meadow

Halliwell, Haligwiella, Hallwell, Holwell—lives by the holy spring

Halsey, Halsig—from Hal's island

Halton, Helton, Healhtun—from the hillslope estate

Hamilton, Hamelatun—from the grassy estate

Handord, Heanford—from the high ford

Hand—worker

Hanley, Heanleah, Hanly—from the high meadow

Harden, Hardin, Hardyn, Harding, Heardind—from the hare's valley

Harford, Haraford—from the hare ford

Hargrove—from the hare grove

Harlow, Harlowe—from the hare's hill

Harper, Hearpere—harpist

Harrison, Harris—son of Harry

Hartford, Harford—from the stag's ford

Hartley—from the stag's meadow

Hartwell, Heortwiella—lives near the stag's spring

Hawley, Hawly, Hagaleah—from the hedged meadow

Hayes—from the hedged land

Hayward, Hagaward—keeper of the hedged enclosure

Healy—from the slope land

Hillock, Hillocke—from the small hill

Hilton—from the hall on the hill

Holbrook—from the brook

Holcomb—from the deep valley

Holmes—from the river island

Holt—from the forest

Horton, Hartun—from the gray estate

Houghton—from the estate on the bluff

Howland—from the chief's land

Hraefnscaga—from the raven forest

Hristun—from the brushwood estate

Hrocby—from the crow's estate

Hrocesburh—from the crow's forest

Hrycg—from the ridge

Hrychleah—from the meadow's edge

Hrypanleah, Hrapenly—from the shouter's meadow

Hrytherford—from the cattle ford

Hudson, Hodsone—son of the hooded man

Huntingdon, Huntingden—from the hunter's hill

Huntingtun, Huntington—from the hunting farm

Huntley, Huntly—from the hunter's meadow

Hutton—from the estate on the ridge

Huxford, Huxeford—from Hugh's ford

Huxley, Huxly—from Hugh's meadow

Hwaeteleah—from the wheat meadow

Hweolere—wheel maker

Hwertun—from the estate at the hollow

Hwitby—from the white farmstead

Hwitcomb, Hwitcumb—from the white hollow

Hwitford—from the white ford

Hwithloew—from the white hill

Hwitloc—from the white fortress

Hyatt, Hiatt—from the high gate

Hyde, Hid, Hide—from the hide

Isham, Isenham—from the iron one's estate

Jackson—son of Jack

Jagger, Jager—carter

Jefferson—son of Geoffrey

Kendrick, Kendrik, Kendryk— son of Harry

Kengsley—from the king's meadow

Kenley, Kenly—from the king's meadow

Kester—from the Roman camp

Kingdon—from the king's hall

Kingston—from the king's village or estate

Kingswell—lives at the king's spring

Kipp, Kip, Kippar, Kippie—from the pointed hill

Kirkley, Kirkly—from the church's meadow

Kirkwood, Kyrkwode—from the church's forest

Kleef—from the cliff

Knox, Knocks—from the hills

Laidley, Laidly—from the creek meadow

Lander, Launder—from the grassy plain

Landon, Langdon—from the long hill

Lane, Laine—from the long meadow

Langley, Langleah—from the long meadow

Langston—from the long enclosure

Lanston—from the long estate

Lathrop—from the farmstead with the barn

Latimer—interprets Latin

Law, Lawe—from the hill

Lawford—from the ford at the hill

Lawley, Lawly—from the hill meadow

Lawson—son of Law or Lawrence

Lawton—from the hillside farm

Leicester—from Leicester

Leighton, Layton, Lay—from the meadow farm

Leland—from the meadow land

Leverton, Laefertun—from the rush farm

Lincoln—from the settlement by the pool

Lindisfarne—from Lindisfarne

Lindley, Lindleigh, Lindly—from the linden tree meadow

Link, Line, Hline, Hlink—from the bank

Linley, Linly, Linleah—from the flax field

Linton, Lintun—from the flax enclosure

Litton, Hlithtun, Lifton—from the hillside town

Livingston—from Lyfing's town

Lockwood—from the enclosed wood

Lorimer, Lorimar—saddle maker

Ludlow—from the prince's hill

Madison—son of a mighty warrior

Maitland—from the meadow

Manley, Manly, Mannleah—from the hero's meadow

Mansfield, Maunfeld—from the field by the small river

Manton—from the hero's town or farm

Marden, Mardon—from the valley with the pool

Marland, Marchman, Marland—from the march

Marlow, Marlowe, Merlow—from the hill by the lake

Marsden—from the marsh valley

Marsh, Mersc—from the marsh

Marston, Merestun—from the farm by the pool

Marwood, Merewood, Merewode—from the lake forest

Matherson, Mathers—son of Mather

Mayfield—from the warrior's field

Mead, Maed—from the meadow

Melbourne, Melburn, Melbyrne, Mylnburne, Melborn—from the mill stream

Meldon—from the hillside mill

Meldrick, Meldryk, Meldrik, Mylnric—from the powerful mill

Mercer—merchant

Merton—from the farm by the sea

Milburn, Milbyrne—from the mill stream

Milford—from the mill's ford

Miller—miller

Millman, Milman—mill worker

Milton—from the mill farm

Milward—keeper of the mill

Montgomery, Monte, Monty—from the wealthy man's mountain

More, Moreland, Morland—from the moors

Moreley, Morlee, Morly—from the meadow on the moor

Moreley, Morlee, Morly—from the moors

Morse, Morris, Morrisey, Morrison—son of More

Morton—from the farm near the moor

Moulton—from the mule farm

Newell, Niewheall—from the new hall

Newman—newcomer

Newton—from the new farm

Nixon, Nixen, Nicson, Nikson—son of Nick

Norcross—from the north crossroads

Northcliffe, Northclyf, Northclif—from the north cliff

Northrop, Northrup—from the north farm

Norton, Nortin, Northtun—from the north farm

Norwood, Northwode—from the north forest

Oakes, Okes—from the oak

Ocelfa—from the high plain

Ogden, Oakden, Ogdon—from the oak tree valley

Olney, Ollaneg—from Olney

Onslow, Onslowe—from the zealous one's hill

Oram, Orahamm, Orham—from the riverbank enclosure

Orford—from the cattle ford

Orlan, Ordland, Orland—from the pointed hill

Orman, Ordman—spearman

Ormeman—ship man

Ormemund, Ormund, Ordmund, Ormond—spear-defender

Orson, Orsen, Ordsone—Ormond's son

Orton, Ortun, Oratun—from the shore farm

Oxford, Oxnaford—from the ox ford

Oxley, Oxnaleah—from the ox enclosure

Oxton, Oxnatun—from the ox farm

Palmer, Palmere—pilgrim

Park, Parke, Pearroc—of the forest

Parker—keeper of the forest

Parkins, Parkinson—son of Parkin

Parrish, Parisch—lives near the church

Patton, Patten, Pattin, Paton—from the warrior's town

Paxton, Pax, Paxtun—from the peaceful farm

Payton, Paegastun, Peyton, Payden—from the fighter's farm

Pemton, Pelltun—from the pool farm

Penley, Penleigh, Pennleah—from the enclosed pasture meadow

Penn, Pyn—from the enclosure

Penton—from the enclosed farm

Perkins, Perkinson—son of Perkin

Phelps, Phillips, Philips—son of Philip

Pickford, Picford—from the peak ford

Pickworth, Picaworth—from the woodcutter's estate

Pierson, Piers, Pearson—son of Pierce

Pitney—from the preserving land

Prescott, Prescott, Preostcot—from the priest's dwelling

Presley, Pressley, Priestly—from the priest's meadow

Prior, Pryor—head of a monastery

Putnam—from the commander's estate

Radcliffe, Radclyf, Raedclyf, Radcliff—from the red cliff

Radley, Redley—from the red meadow

Radnor, Raedanoran—from the red shore

Radord, Raedford, Redford—from the red ford

Raleigh, Rally, Raleah, Raaley, Raawley—from the roe deer Meadow

Ralston—from Ralf's farm

Ramsay, Ramsey—from Ram's island

Ramsden—from the ram's valley

Ranfield, Renfield—from the raven's field

Ransey, Ransy—from raven's island

Ransford—from the raven ford

Ransley—from the raven's meadow

Ransom, Randson—son of Rand

Rawson, Rawlins, Rawls—son of
Rawley or Raleigh

Rayburn, Reyburn, Raybourne—
from the deer's stream

Reading, Redding—son of Reed

Redmond, Redmund, Radmund,
Raedmund—protector,
counselor

Reeves, Reaves—son of Reeve

Remington, Renton—from the
raven farm

Renshaw—from the raven forest

Rexford—from the king's ford

Rexley—from the king's
meadow

Rexton—from the king's farm

Rhodes, Rodes—lives near the
crucifix

Ridge, Rydge—from the ridge

Ridpath, Raedpath—lives near
the red path

Riggs—son of Rigg

Ripley—from the shouter's
meadow

Risley—from the brushwood
meadow

Riston—from the brushwood
farm

Rodman—lives by the road

Rodwell—lives by the spring
near the road

Romney—from Romney

Ronson—son of Ronald

Rowell, Rawiella—from the deer
spring

Rowley, Ruhleah—from the
rough meadow

Roxbury—from the raven's
fortress

Royden—from the royal hill

Ruford, Rufford—from the red
ford

Rugby—from the raven's estate

Rumford—from the wide ford

Rushford, Ryscford—lives near
the rush ford

Rutledge—from the red pool

Rutley—from the root meadow

Rycroft, Rygecroft—from the
rye field

Ryland, Rygeland—from the rye
land

Ryman, Rygemann—rye
merchant

Ryton, Rygetun—from the rye
farm

Safford, Salford, Salhford—from
the willow ford

Salisbury—from the fortified
keep

Sanborn, Sanbourne—from the
sandy brook

Sanders, Sanersone, Saunders,
Saunderson, Sanderson—
Alexander's son

Sandon—from the sandy hill

Sanford—from the sandy ford

Santon—from the sandy farm

Sawyers—son of Sawyer

Saxon, Saxan—swordsman

Seabrook, Saebroc—from the
brook by the sea

Seadon—from the hill by the sea

Seaton, Seeton, Seton—from the
farm by the sea

Sedgeley—from the swordsman's meadow

Seely, Selig, Saelig, Sceley, Sealey—from the happy meadow

Sefton—from Sefton

Seldon, Selden, Salhdene—from the manor valley

Seward, Saeweard, Seaward—guards the coast

Shadwell, Scadwiella—from the shed spring

Shandley, Scandleah—from the loud meadow

Sheffield, Scaffeld—from the crooked field

Sheldon—from the shield farm

Shelley—from the ledge meadow

Shelton, Scelftun—from the hill on the ledge

Shepherd, Shepard—shepherd

Shepley, Sheply, Sceapleigh—from the sheep meadow

Sherborne, Sherbourne, Sherbourn, Sherburne—from the clear brook

Sherwood, Scirwode—from the bright forest

Shipley—from the sheep meadow

Shipton—from the sheep farm

Siddell, Sidell, Siddael—from the wide valley

Sidwell—from the broad well

Silsby—from Sill's farm

Skelton—from the estate on the ledge

Skipper, Skippere—ship's captain

Skipton—from the sheep estate

Slade, Slaed—from the valley

Slaton, Slayton—from the valley farm

Smedley, Smetheleah—from the flat meadow

Smith, Smyth, Smythe—smith

Snowden—from the snowy hill

Somerset—from the summer settlers

Somerton, Sumertun, Sumerton—from the summer estate

Southwell—from the south spring

Spalding, Spelding—from the split meadow

Squire, Squier—shield bearer

St. Alban—from St. Alban

Stafford, Steathford—from the landing ford

Stanbury, Stanburh, Stanberry—from the stony fortress

Stancliff, Stanclyf—from the stony cliff

Standish, Stanedisc—from the stony park

Stanfield, Stanfeld—from the stony field

Stanford, Sanford, Stamford—from the stony ford

Stanhope, Stanhop—from the stony hollow

Stanton, Staunton, Stantun—from the stony farm

Stanwick, Stanwyk, Stanwik,

Stanwic—from the stony
village
Stanwood, Stanwode—from the
stony forest
Stedman, Stedeman—owns a
farm
Stock, Stok, Stoc—from the tree
stump
Stockley, Stocleah—from the
tree-stump meadow
Stockwell, Stocwiella—from the
tree-stump spring
Stoddard—keeper of horses
Stoke—from the village
Stratford—from the river ford
on the street
Stroud, Strod—from the thicket
Suffield, Suthfeld—from the
south field
Sully, Suthleah, Suthley—from
the south meadow
Sumner, Sumernor—summoner
Sutcliff, Sutclyf, Suthclif,
Suttecliff—from the south
cliff
Sutton—from the south farm
Swinton, Swintun—from the
swine farm
Symington, Symontun—from
Simon's estate
Taburer, Tab—drummer
Tanner, Tannere—leather
maker
Tanton, Tamtun—from the quiet
river farm
Tarleton, Thoraldtun—from the
thunder estate
Tedmond, Theomund,

Tedmund—national
protector
Templeton, Tempeltun—from
the temple farm
Tennyson—son of Dennis
Terris, Terrys, Teryysone—son
of Terrell
Thatcher, Thacher, Thaxter,
Thacker, Thackere—roofer
Thorley, Torley, Thurleigh,
Thurleah—from Thor's
meadow
Thorn, Torn, Thorne—from the
thorn tree
Thorndyke, Thorndike,
Thorndic—from the thorny
dike
Thornley, Thornly—from the
thorny meadow
Thornton, Thorntun—from the
thorn-tree farm
Thorpe, Thorp—from the village
Thurlow, Thurhloew—from
Thor's hill
Tilden, Tiladene—from the
fertile valley
Tilford—from the fertile ford
Tilton—from the good estate
Toft—from the small farm
Toland, Tolland—owns taxed
land
Tolman—collects taxes
Towley, Townly, Tunleah—from
the town meadow
Townsend—from the end of the
town
Tredway, Treadway,
Thrythwig—strong warrior

Trent—from the river Trent

Trowbridge, Trowbrydge, Treowbrycg—from the tree bridge

Truesdale, Truitestall, Truesdell—from the beloved one's farm

Tucker, Toukere, Tuckere—tucker of cloth

Tupper, Tuppere—ram herder

Turner, Tournour—works on the lathe

Twyford, Twiford—from the double river ford

Tye, Tyg, Teyen—from the enclosure

Tyson, Tyesone—son of Tye

Udell, Udale, Udayle, Udall—from the yew tree valley

Upchurch—from the upper church

Upton, Uptun—from the upper farm

Upwood, Upwode—from the high town

Vingon, Vinson, Vinsone—son of Vinn

Wadley—from Wade's meadow

Wadsworth—from Wade's estate

Wainwright—wagonmaker

Wakefield, Wacfeld—from Wake's field

Wakeley, Wacleah—from Wake's meadow

Wakeman, Wacuman—watchman

Walbridge, Walbrydge—from the Welshman's bridge

Walby—from the Welshman's dwellings

Walcot, Walcott, Weallcot—lives in the Welshman's cottage

Walden—from the Welshman's valley

Waldon, Waldron—from the Welshman's hill

Walford—from the Welshman's ford

Walker—thickener of cloth

Waller, Weallere—mason

Walton, Walworth, Wealaworth—from the Welshman's farm

Wardell, Weardhyll—from the guardian's hill

Warefield, Weifield—from the field by the weir

Warford, Weiford—from the farm by the weir

Warley, Warleigh, Weirley—from the weir meadow

Warton, Warun—from the farm by the weir

Washburn, Washbourne, Washburne, Waescburne—from the flooding brook

Washington—from the intelligent one's farm

Watford, Watelford—from the hurdle ford

Watkins, Wattkins, Wattikinson, Wattekinson—son of Watt

Watson, Wattesone, Watts, Wattson—son of Walter

Waverly, Waefreleah—from the quaking-aspen tree meadow

Wayland, Wegland, Weyland—from the land by the highway

Webley, Webbeleah—from the weaver's meadow

Webster, Webb, Webbe, Webbestre—weaver

Weddell, Wadanhyll—from the advancer's hill

Welborne, Welburn, Welborn, Wiellaburne—from the spring brook

Welby, Wiellaby—from the farm by the spring

Weldon, Wielladun—from the spring by the hill

Welford, Wiellaford—from the spring by the ford

Wellington, Weolingtun—from the wealthy estate

Welton, Wiellatun—from the spring farm

Wentworth, Wintanweorth—from the white one's estate

West, Wes—from the west

Westbrook, Westbroc—from the west brook

Westby—from the west farm

Westcott, Westcot—from the west cottage

Weston, Westun—from the west farm

Wetherby, Weatherby, Wethrby—from the wether-sheep farm

Wetherly, Weatherly, Wethrleah—from the wether-sheep meadow

Wharton—from the estate at the hollow

Wheatley—from the wheat meadow

Wheeler—wheel-maker

Whistler—piper

Whitby—from the white farm

Whitcomb—from the white hollow

Whitelaw, Whitlaw—from the white hill

Whitfield—from the white field

Whitford—from the white ford

Whitley—from the white meadow

Whitmore, Whitmoor—from the white moor

Whittaker—from the white field

Wickam, Wiccum, Wichamm, Wickley, Wicleah—from the village meadow

Wildon—from the wooded hill

Wilford, Wylingford—from the willow ford

Willis, Wilson, Willesone, Williams, Williamson—son of William

Willoughby, Wyligby—from the willow farm

Wilton, Wylltun—from the farm by the spring

Windsor, Winsor, Wendlesora—from Windsor

Winfield, Wynfield, Winefield—from a friend's field

Wingate, Windgate—from the winding gate

Winslow, Winslowe—from Wine's hill

Winston, Winton, Wynston—from Wine's farm

Winthrop, Wynthrop, Winthrop, Winetorp—from Wine's estate

Winward, Wynward, Winswode, Winwood, Winwodem, Wynwode—from Wine's forest

Witton, Wittatun—from the wise man's estate

Wolcott, Woolcott, Wulfcot, Wolfcot—lives in Wolfe's cottage

Woodley, Wodeleah—from the wooded meadow

Woodward, Wudoweard—forester

Worcester, Wireceaster—from the alder forest, army camp

Wordsworth, Wulfweardsweorth—world guardian

Worrell, Waerheall—from the true man's manor

Worth, Weorth—from the farm

Worton, Wyrttun—from the vegetable farm

Wright, Wryhta—tradesman

Wycliff, Wyclyf—from the white cliff

Wyndham, Windham—from the windy village

Wythe, Wyth—from the willow tree

Yale—from the slope land

Yardley, Yardly—from the enclosed meadow

Yates—lives by the gates

Yeoman, Yoman—retainer

York—from the bear estate

FINNISH

Before 1920, members of farming families in Finland were known by their given names and a patronymic. In church and tax records, these families were also identified by the name of the farm they lived on, but the farm name was not part of a person's name. Because many records were kept in Swedish prior to the 1870s, patronymics recorded then were often formed by adding "son" or "dotter" to the father's given name. In Finnish, they were formed by adding "poika" or "tytär."

Soldiers, merchants, clergy, and tradesmen (such as blacksmiths and carpenters) adopted surnames long before the farming families. These surnames were often Swedish in origin, and some were based on patronymics, descriptions, occupations, and place names. Migrant farming families, particularly in eastern Finland, also used surnames before stationary farming families. The disparity in practice might be explained by the types of records kept by tax collectors: Family name was not important to the tax collector if the family was a stationary farming family. All that was needed was the village name and farm name. People who were more likely to move around were easier to keep track of if the had a family name.

Surnames become universal in 1920, when they were required by law. Modern Finnish names consist of a first and last name and sometimes include one or two middle names.

A few surnames:

Hämäläinen	Laine
Heikkinen	Mäkelä
Hietamäki	Mäki
Järvi	Mäkinen
Järvinen	Miettlinen
Joki	Mustanen
Kilpeläinen	Nieminen
Kirkkomäki	Seppänen
Kivi	Talo
Korhonen	Valkoinen
Koskinen	Virtanen

ELIZABETH BOYLE

Elizabeth Boyle is the author of nine novels, both adventurous and romantic. Four of her novels, *No Marriage of Convenience*, *Once Tempted*, *One Night of Passion*, and *Stealing the Bride*, are *USA Today* best sellers.

Sometimes giving a character an interesting nickname and no true name at all can be more intriguing to the reader than giving them a fully stated name. One of my favorite characters that I created was the Marquis of Templeton, or Temple to his friends. I have never stated his Christian name, even on the family tree I created for my Web site, and I get mail all the time from readers who want to know what his full name is. The idea of him having another name fascinates them. In my new book, *Something About Emmaline*, I did this for the heroine. She assumes the identity of another woman, so I decided not to share with the readers her real name.

FEMALE

Aila, Aili—light bearer

Aino—legend name

Anna, Anne, Anja, Anneli, Anni, Annikki, Annukka, Anu—grace

Anttiri—manly (form of Andrew)

Aune—pure (form of Agnes)

Dorotea—God's gift (form of Dorothy)

Eeva—life (form of Eve)

Eija—meaning unknown

Emilia, Milja, Milla, Emma, Emmi—hardworking (form of Emily)

Hanna, Johanna, Hannele, Jaana, Henna—gracious God (form of John)

Helena, Heli, Helja, Helli, Eila, Elina, Leena—light (form of Helen)

Helmi—pearl

Hiija—quiet

Hikka—cap, hood

Hilma, Minna, Miina, Mimmi—resolute protector (form of William)

Ilmarinen—legend name

Inari—lake

Ingria, Inkeri, Inka—hero's daughter

Jaakkina—gracious God (form of Jukka)

Jurma—legend name

Kalle—manly (form of Charles)

Kalwa—heroine
Katariina, Kaisa, Katri, Katrikki—pure (form of Katherine)
Kerttu—strong with a spear (form of Gertrude)
Kristiina, Kirsti, Kirsi, Tiina—believes in Christ (form of Christian)
Kyllikki—woman of strength
Laila—night
Leppa—legend name
Liisa, Elisabet, Eliisa, Elsa—consecrated to God (form of Elizabeth)
Maarit, Marketta, Reeta, Reetta, Riitta—pearl (form of Margaret)
Mari, Maria, Marja, Maija, Maikki, Maaria, Maarika, Marjukka—bitter (form of Mary)
Martta—mistress (form of Martha)
Mielikki—pleasant; mistress of forest, wife of Tapio; legend name

Mirjam, Mirjami, Mirkka, Miia, Mia—rebellious; biblical name (form of Miriam)
Paula—snare, string
Paivikki, Paivi, Paiva—son of day (form of Paivio)
Pirjo, Pirkko, Riitta—strong (form of Bridget)
Preita—most loving one
Riikka, Riika—peaceful ruler (form of Frederick)
Ritva—meaning unknown
Russu, Ruusu, Roosa—rose (form of Rosa)
Saara, Sari, Saija, Salli—princess (form of Sarah)
Sisko—sister
Sofia, Sohvi—wise (form of Sophia)
Susanna, Sanna—lily (form of Susan)
Tuula—meaning unknown
Tuulikki, Tuuli—wind; legend name
Tyyne, Tyyni—calm
Vappu, Valpuri—legend name
Vellamo—protector

MALE

Aleksanteri, Aleksi—defender of mankind (form of Alexander)
Antero, Antti—manly (form of Andrew)
Armas—beloved
Eikki—powerful

Erkki—eternal ruler (form of Eric)
Heikki, Henri—rules the home (form of Henry)
Ilmarinen, Ilmari—legend name
Jaakkima, Aki—God will establish (form of Joachim)

Jani, Janne, Johan, Johannes, Juhani, Juha, Jussi, Jukka—gracious God (form of John)

Jari, Jalmari—helmet-wearing soldier

Jarmo, Jarkko, Jamo—appointed by God

Joosep, Jooseppi, Joosef, Juuso—God adds (form of Joseph)

Jorma—farmer (form of George)

Kaarle, Kaarl, Kaarlo, Kalle, Kal—manly (form of Charles)

Kaleva, Kalevi—hero; legend name

Kari—blessed (form of Markarios)

Lauri, Lasse, Lassi—laurel (form of Lawrence)

Lippo—legend name

Markus, Markku, Marko—warlike (form of Marcus)

Matti, Matias—God's gift (form of Matthew)

Mikael, Mika, Mikko, Miika, Miikka—who is like God (form of Michael)

Niles, Niilo—victory of the people (form of Nicholas)

Olavi, Olii, Uolevi—ancestor (form of Olaf)

Oskari—divine spear (form of Oscar)

Paavo, Paaveli, Pauli—small (form of Paul)

Paivio—son of day; legend name

Pekka, Petteri, Petri—rock (form of Peter)

Pentti—blessed (form of Benedict)

Perttu, Parttyli, Perttuli—hill, furrow (form of Bartholomew)

Rikkard, Riku—strong ruler (form of Richard)

Risto—Christ-bearer (form of Christopher)

Seppo—smith; legend name

Severi—severe; legend name (form of Severin)

Taavi, Taavetti—beloved

Taneli—God is my judge (form of Daniel)

Tapio—king or forest god; legend name

Tauno—docile

Teppo, Tapani—victorious

Timo—God-fearing (form of Timothy)

Toivo—hope

Tuomas, Tuomo, Tomi, Tommi—twin (form of Thomas)

Usko—faith

Vaino—legend name

Valkoinen—white

Valtteri—powerful warrior (form of Walter)

Vappu—legend name

Veli, Veikko, Veijo—brother

Viljo—resolute protector

Ville, Vilho, Vilhelmi, Viljami—resolute protector (form of William)

Yrjo—farmer (form of George)

FRENCH

French surnames are of two types: those coming from the Frankish Empire and those brought in by the Norman settlers in the tenth century. Last names began as epithets attached either after the name or to the name—for example, Pepin the Short or Charlemagne (Charles the Great). This tendency goes back to the Dark Ages but was restricted to the aristocracy.

When the Normans invaded England in 1066, they added epithets that named their estates in Normandy—Robert de Montgomerie, for example. If they didn't have an estate, they took the name of the province or town from whence they came—Piers de Paris.

By the twelfth century, some names had become hereditary, and by the thirteenth century they had become common. The handing down of a name from father to son was firmly established by the fifteenth century.

One interesting point about the Normans is that before hereditary surnames became commonplace, families stuck to a few names that alternated by generation. George would name his son after his own father, Gilbert, and when Gilbert grew to manhood and had a son, that son would be named George.

Surnames are descriptive, patronymic, or based on place or occupation.

In the twelfth and thirteenth centuries, biblical names became very popular: Peter, John, Jean, Luke, and so on. Right after the French Revolution, names were restricted to a list of French names that bore no resemblance to foreign words or names. Throughout the rest of French history, Teutonic, Norse, Slavic, Latin, and Danish names have been used.

The article *de* (of) between names was usually reserved for the nobility and denoted lands or estates the man held. *Le* means "the" and has been used with occupation or descriptive names.

A few surnames:

Bettencourt	Beaumarchais
Allain	Benoit
Baudelaire	Billaud

Bonnet
Charlebois
Cuvier
Davignon
Dubois
Dutetre
Fortier
Fournier
Frappier
Girard
Gosselin
Guignard
Hébert
Heuse

Lafontaine
Langelier
Lefèbvre
Marseau
Moreau
Olivier
Petit
Picard
Raison
Renault
Robillard
Rousseau
Severin
Therriault

FEMALE

Abella—breath (form of Abel)
Aceline—noble
Adele, Adela—pleasant
Adorlee—adored
Adrienne—dark (form of Adrian)
Afrodille—daffodil
Agathe—good (form of Agatha)
Aida—help
Aiglentine, Aiglentina—
    sweetbrier rose
Aimee, Amata, Amy, Ami—
    dearly loved
Alacoque—meaning unknown
Albertine, Albertina—noble;
    intelligent (form of Albert)
Albracca—legend name
Alcina—legend name
Alexandrine, Alexis—defender
    of mankind (form of
    Alexander)
Allegra—cheerful

Allete, Alita—winged (form of
    Aleta)
Amabelle, Amabella—beautiful,
    loving
Amarante—flower (form of
    Amarantha)
Ambre, Ambra—jewel
Amedee—loves God (form of
    Amadeus)
Amelie—hardworking (form of
    Amelia)
Amity, Amite, Amitee—friendly
Anceline, Ancelina—
    handmaiden
Andree, Andrea—manly (form of
    Andrew)
Angelette, Angeletta—little
    angel
Angelique, Angela, Angilia, Ange,
    Angeline, Angelina,
    Angelika—angel

Annette—little Ann

Antoinette—priceless (form of Anthony)

Apolline, Apollina—gift from Apollo

Aubine, Aubina—blonde (form of Aubin)

Aude, Auda—old; wealthy

Aveline, Avelaine—nut

Avice—warlike

Aya—legend name

Azura—blue

Babette—stranger

Belda—fair maiden

Belisarda—legend name

Berangaria—name of a princess

Bernadette—strong as a bear (form of Bernard)

Bertha—legend name

Blanch, Blanche—white

Blanchefleur—white flower

Bonny, Bonnie—sweet and good

Bradamate—legend name

Brucie—forest sprite

Brunella—dark-haired (form of Brun)

Cadence, Cadencia—rhythmic

Calandre—lark

Calanthe, Calantha—lovely blossom

Capucine, Capucina—cape

Caresse—endearing

Carine, Carina, Cateline—pure (form of Karen)

Carnation—flesh-colored

Carola, Carolina, Caroline, Carol, Carole—manly (form of Charles)

Chantel—song

Charlotte, Carlotta—manly (form of Charles)

Charmaine, Charleen, Charlene, Charline—manly (form of Charles)

Cherry, Cherie, Cher, Cheree, Cheri, Cherise—dear

Cheryl—beloved

Cinderella, Cendrillon—of the ashes

Claire, Clarette—clear

Clarice—clear, bright (form of Clare)

Clarimunda—legend name

Claudette, Claudine—lame (form of Claude)

Clementina—merciful (form of Clement)

Colette, Collette—necklace

Comfort, Comforte—strength

Coralie—coral

Corette, Coretta—little maiden

Cosette—victorious

Crescent, Creissant—to create

Daisi—daisy

Damien, Damiane, Damia, Damiana—untamed

Darcy, D'Arcy—from Arcy

Delight, Delit—delight

Delmare—of the sea

Demi—name taken from heraldry

Denise, Denice—follower of Dionysus (form of Dennis)

Desiree, Desire, Desirat, Desideria—desired (form of Desirata)

Diamanta—diamond

Diane, Diana—divine; moon goddess; myth name

Dixie—born tenth

Dominique—of the Lord; born on Sunday (form of Dominic)

Dorene, Dory, Doreen, Dorine, Dore—blonde

Durandana, Durindana—legend name

Edmee—rich protector (form of Edmund)

Eglantine, Eglantina—wild rose

Elinore, Elienor, Eleanor, Ellinor—light

Elisa, Elise, Eliza, Elisabeth—consecrated to God (form of Elizabeth)

Elita, Eleta—chosen

Eloise, Eloisa, Eloisee—famous in war

Emmeline—industrious

Erembourg—meaning unknown

Ermengardine—meaning unknown

Esmeraude, Emeraude—emerald

Esperanza—hope

Estelle—star (form of Esther)

Eugenia—well-born (form of Eugene)

Eulalie—well-spoken

Fabienne—bean farmer (form of Fabian)

Falerina—legend name

Fanchon, Fanchone—free

Fanette, Fanetta—crowned with laurels

Fantine, Fantina—childlike

Favor—approval

Fawnia, Faunia, Faun, Fauna—fawn

Fay, Faye, Fae—fairy

Fayette—little fairy

Fayme—famed

Fealthy—faithful

Felicienne, Filicia, Felicia, Felicity—happy (form of Felix)

Fifi, Fifine—nickname for Josephine

Fleur—flower

Fleurette—little flower

Flordelis—legend name

France—from France

Fusberta—legend name

Gaetane, Gaetana—from Gaete

Galatee—white as milk

Gallia, Gala, Galla—from Gaul

Garland—crowned with flowers

Gay—lively

Gemma—jewel

Geneva, Genevre—juniper

Genevieve—white wave

Georgette, Georgitte—farmer (form of George)

Germana, Germaine, Germain—from Germany

Gyongy—meaning unknown

Halette—little Hal

Harriet, Hanriette, Hanrietta, Harriette, Harrietta—army ruler (form of Harold); rules the home (form of Henry)

Hedvige—strife (form of Hedwig)

Heloise—famous in war (form of Louis)

Henriette, Henrietta—rules the home (form of Henry)

Hilaire—happy (form of Hilary)

Holly—holly

Honore—honor

Huette, Huguetta, Hugette—intelligent (form of Hugh)

Isla—from the island

Iva—from the yew tree

Jacqueline—supplanter (form of Jacob)

Jacquenette, Jacquenetta—little Jacques

Jeanette, Jeanetta—little Jean

Jeanne, Jehane—gracious God (form of John)

Jessamine, Jessamina—jasmine

Jewel, Jule—jewel

Joanna—gracious God (form of John)

Jolie—beautiful

Josette, Josephine, Josepha, Josephe—God adds (form of Joseph)

Joy—jewel; delight

Julienne, Julie, Julia, Juliette, Juliet, Julietta, Julita—youthful (form of Julius)

Karla—manly (form of Charles)

Karlotta, Karoline, Karolina—manly (form of Charles)

Karoly, Karcsi, Kari—joyful song

La Roux—red-haired

Laurel, Lauren, Laurene—laurel (form of Lawrence)

Laurette—little laurel

Laverna, Lavernia, La Verne, La Vergne—born in the spring

Leala, Liealia, Lealia—loyal

Leona, Leonie, Leone, Leonelle, Leonarda—brave lion (form of Leonard)

Liane, Liana—to bind; youth

Liriene, Lirienne—reads aloud

Logistilla, Logestilla—legend name

Lorraine, Loraine—from Lorraine

Lotye, Letya, Letje—tiny and womanly

Lucille, Lucile—light (form of Luke)

Lundy—born on Monday

Lynnette, Linette, Lyonette—little lion

Magnolia—flower

Manette, Mariette, Marietta, Marian, Marianne, Maria, Marie—bitter (form of Mary)

Marcelle, Marcella, Marcellia—warlike (form of Marcus)

Margo, Margauz, Margot, Marguerite, Marjori, Margery—pearl (form of Margaret)

Marjolaine, Marjolaina—flower

Marphisa—legend name

Marvel, Marveille, Marvella, Marvelle—miracle

Mathilde, Matilda, Mathilda, Mattie, Matty, Maud, Maude—strong battle-maid

Maura, Maureen, Moreen,

Maurine, Maurina—dark-skinned (form of Maurice)
Maurelle—dark and elfin
Mavis, Mavise—joy
Melisande—honeybee
Melodie—melody
Melusina—dark-skinned
Merci, Mercy—mercy
Methena, Methina—meaning unknown
Mignon, Mignonette—delicate
Millicent, Millicente—industrious
Mimi, Minna, Minnie, Minette, Minetta—resolute protector (form of William)
Mirabelle, Mirabella—of incredible beauty
Mireille—miracle
Monique—counselor (form of Monica)
Morgana—legend name
Musetta, Musette—song
Nadine—from Nada
Nanna—wife of Balder; myth name
Natalii, Natalie, Natuche—born on Christmas
Nicola, Nicolette—victory of the people (form of Nicholas)
Ninette, Ninon, Nanon—grace
Noel, Noelle, Noella—Christmas
Odelette, Odeletta—little singer
Olympe, Olympia—from Olympus
Ophelie, Ophelia—serpentine
Orane—rising
Oriel—bird

Orliena, Orlene, Orlina—gold
Ormazd—lengend name
Orva—worth gold
Paige, Page—page
Pansy—flower
Parnella—rock
Pascale, Pascala, Pascaline, Pasclina—born on Passover (form of Pascal)
Patience—patient
Patrice—noble (form of Patrick)
Pensee—thoughtful
Phillipa—lover of horses (form of Philip)
Pierrette, Pierretta—rock (form of Peter)
Prunella, Prunellie—plum
Rachelle—ewe (form of Rachel)
Raina, Reine, Reina—queen
Raissa, Raison—thinker
Renee, Rene—reborn (form of Renato)
Rive, Riva—from the shore
Robinette, Robinetta—small robin
Romaine, Romana—from Rome (form of Romano)
Rose, Rohais, Roesia, Rosamonde—rose (form of Rosa)
Rosemarie, Rosemaria—bitter rose
Roux—red
Roxane, Roxanne—bright; dawn
Royale, Roial—regal
Ruby, Rubie—red jewel
Searlait—manly (form of Charles)

SARAH MLYNOWSKI

Sarah Mlynowski is the author of the best-selling novel *Milkrun* (Red Dress Ink), which has been published in sixteen countries. She is also author of *Fishbowl*, *As Seen on TV*, and *Monkey Business* (all from Red Dress Ink), as well as teen novel *Bras & Broomsticks* (Random House).

For many of my books, I give the protagonists names I always wished my parents had given me. The star of my first book *Milkrun* is Jackie, a name I always thought had far more spunk than boring Sarah. In that first book, I named the secondary characters after people I had sat beside in elementary school, such as Jonathan and Wendy. After five novels, I still find old yearbooks an excellent source for names. High school, college, my husband's graduate school. They're the perfect springboards.

Lately I've noticed that more unusual names can be more interesting, and more memorable. So I've peppered my books with names like Sunny, Raf, Mercedes. Basically I play around on the Internet and try to find inspiration in random words and images. Or I flip through *TV Guide*s and brainstorm off celebrity names, such as Paris Hilton. I just named a secondary character London.

I find last names much harder to find, and occasionally unknowingly repeat myself. My editor once asked me if there was a reason I'd given the same surname to three different characters. Were they related? Um. No. Whoops. I still use yearbooks, but I often find myself cutting and pasting prefixes and suffixes. Such as in *Bras and Broomsticks*: Wein(berg) + (Morgan)stein = Weinstein. First name I always wished I'd had? Rachel. Enter protagonist, Rachel Weinstein.

Sidonie, Sidonia, Sydney—
    follower of Saint Denys
Simone—God is heard (form of
    Simon)
Slania, Slainie, Slanie—good
    health

Solange, Silana, Solaine,
    Solaina—dignified
Stephanie, Stefania—crowned in
    victory (form of Stephen)
Suzanne, Suzette—lily (form of
    Susan)

Sybila—prophetess (form of
    Sybil)
Tempeste—stormy
Tifini, Tiffini, Thiphany—gods
    incarnate
Tilda, Tilly—mighty in war
Trinette, Trinetta—little
    innocent
Valeria, Valere, Valara,
    Valeraine—strength (form
    of Valerius)
Vedette, Vedetta—from the
    guard tower
Veronique—honest image (form
    of Veronica)
Victorine, Victornia—victory

Vignette, Vignetta—little vine
Villette, Villetta—from the
    country estate
Viollette, Violetta—little violet
Vivienne—lively
Voleta, Voletta—veiled
Xavierre, Xavierra—owner of a
    new home (form of Xavier)
Yolanda, Yolande, Yolanthe—
    violet
Yolette—meaning unknown
Yseult—fair
Yvette, Yvonee—little archer
    (form of Yves)
Zara—light
Zuria, Zuri, Zurie—white and
    lovely

MALE

Agramant—myth name
Agrican—from the field
Ahriman—legend name
Alain—handsome (form of Alan)
Aleron—knight
Alexandre—defender of
    mankind (form of
    Alexander)
Algernon, Algrenon—bearded
Aloin, Aluin—noble friend
Amaury—name of a count
Andre—manly (form of Andrew)
Ansel, Ancil, Acel, Ansell—
    adherent of a nobleman
Arber—sells herbs
Archaimbaud, Archambault,
    Archenbaud—bold
Archard—sacred and powerful

Armand—soldier (form of
    Herman)
Arnaud—eagle (form of Arnold)
Arno—little eagle
Arnou, Arnoux—eagle wolf
Arridano—legend name
Artus—noble
Ashtaroth—legend name
Astolpho—legend name
Atlantes—legend name
Aubert—noble
Aubin—blond
Aubrey, Albaric—blond ruler
Audric, Aldrick, Aldrich—wise
    ruler
Auriville—from the gold town
Avenall, Avenelle, Aveneil—lives
    near the oatfield

Avent, Advent—born during
Advent
Aymon—legend name
Bailey, Bayley—steward
Balisarda—myth name
Barry, Barrie—lives at the
barrier
Bartlett—plowman
Bayard—legend name
Beaufort—from the beautiful
fortress
Bellamy, Bell—handsome
Beltane—legend name
Bertrand—bright raven
Bevis, Beauvais—from Beauvais
Brice—from Brieuxtown
Brigliadoro—legend name
Bruce, Brys—woods
Brunelle—dark-haired (form of
Brun)
Burkett, Burcet—from the little
stronghold
Burnell, Burel—reddish-brown
hair
Burrell—reddish-brown skin
Byron, Buiron—from the
cottage; bear
Campbell—from the beautiful
field
Carolos, Carlo, Carolus, Carlos,
Carel—manly (form of
Charles)
Chandler, Chanler—maker of
candles
Channing—member of the
bishop's council
Chapin—clergyman
Chappell, Chappel—from the
chapel

Charles, Cearbhall—manly
Charlot—name of the son of
Charlemagne
Cheney—from the oak wood
Christien, Cretiein—believes in
Christ (form of Christian)
Claude—lame
Cloridan—myth name
Clovis—name of a king
Courtland, Courtney, Court,
Curt, Courtnay, Cort—from
the court
Curtis, Curtice, Curcio—
courteous
Darcy, D'Arcy—from Arcy
Davet—beloved
Delmar, Delmer—of the sea
Denis, Dennis, Denys, Dennet—
follower of Dionysus
Desire, Didier—desired (form of
Desirata)
Dexter—right
Donatien—gift (form of Donato)
Eliot, Eliott, Elliot—believes in
God
Etienne—crowned in victory
(form of Stephen)
Ferragus—legend name
Ferrau—legend name
Fitz—son of
Fletcher—feathers arrows
Florismart—legend name
Florus—flower
Forrest—dwells in the forest
Fortun, Fortune—lucky
Frontino—legend name
Gaetan—from Gaete
Ganelon, Gan—legend name

Gano—legend name
Garland—crowned with flowers
Gaspar, Gaspard—treasurer
 (form of Casper)
Gaston, Gascon—from Gascony
Gauthier, Gautier—powerful
 warrior (form of Walter)
Geoffrey—God's peace
Georges—farmer (form of
 George)
Germain, Germano—from
 Germany
Gifford, Guifford—chubby
 cheeks
Gill, Gil—youthful (form of
 Julius)
Gradasso—legend name
Granville, Grenville—from the
 large town
Grosvenor—great hunter
Guerin—legend name
Guy—guide
Hamilton—from the mountain
 town
Harbin—glorious warrior
Harcourt—from the fortified
 farm
Hardouin—name of a count
Henri—rules the home (form of
 Henry)
Hercule—Hera's glory; myth
 name (form of Hercules)
Hugh—intelligent
Ignace—fiery (form of Ignatius)
Iven—little archer
Jacques, Jacquelin—supplanter
 (form of Jacob)
Javier—owner of a new home
 (form of Xavier)

Jay, Jaye—bluejay
Jean—gracious God (form of
 John)
Jean Baptiste—named for John
 the Baptist
Jeoffroi, Jeffrey—God's peace
 (form of Geoffrey)
Jesper, Jasper—jasper stone
Jules, Julian, Jullien—youthful
 (form of Julius)
Karel—manly (form of Charles)
Kerman—German
Lance, Lancelot, Launcelot,
 Lancelin—servant
Landers, Landis—from the
 grassy plain
Langley, L'Angley—Englishman
Latimer—interprets Latin
Leal—loyal
Legget—delegate
Leon, Leone, Leonce, Leocadie,
 Leodegrance—brave lion
 (form of Leonard)
Leroy—regal
Leverett, Leveret—young rabbit
Loring—from Lorraine
Lothair—famous warrior (form
 of Lothario)
Louis—famous in war
Lowell, Lovell, Lowe, Louvel—
 beloved
Loyal—true
Lyle, Lisle—from the island
Malagigi—legend name
Mallory, Mailhairer—ill-fated
Mandel, Mantel—makes
 garments
Manville, Manneville—from the
 great estate

Marlon—little falcon
Marmion—small one
Marshall, Marshal, Marsh—
steward
Marsilius—legend name
Maslin, Masselin—little Thomas
Mason, Masson—stone worker
Mayhew, Mahieu—God's gift
(form of Matthew)
Medoro—legend name
Melville, Malleville—from
Malleville
Mercer—merchant
Merle—blackbird
Merlin, Merlion—falcon
Michel, Michele—who is like
God (form of Michael)
Millard—strong
Montague, Montaigu—from the
peaked mountain
Moore, More, Moor—dark-
skinned
Namo—legend name
Neville, Neuveville—from the
new town
Noel—Christmas
Normand, Norman, Norm—from
the north
Norris, Norice, Noreis—
caretaker
Nouel—a kernel
Octave—born eighth
Odo—name of a bishop
Ogier—legend name
Oliver—legend name
Olivier—from the olive tree
Onfroi—peaceful Hun
Orson, Ourson—bear

Orville—from the gold town
Page, Paige, Padgett, Paget—
page
Paien—name of a nobelman
Parfait—perfect
Pascal, Pascual, Pasquale—born
on Passover
Peppin, Pippin—name of a king
Percy, Percival—pierce
Perrin, Perren, Perryn, Perry,
Pierre—rock (form of Peter)
Peverell, Piperel, Pepperell—
piper
Philip, Philippe, Phillipe—lover
of horses
Pierpone, Pierrepont—lives by
the stone bridge
Pinabel—legend name
Platt, Plat—from the flat land
Pomeroy, Pommeraie—lives
near the apple orchard
Porter, Portier, Porteur—
gatekeeper
Prewitt, Pruitt, Preruet, Pruet,
Pruie—brave
Pryor, Priour—head of a priory
Quennel, Quesnel—from the
little oak tree
Quincy, Quincey—from the
place owned by the fifth son
Rabican—legend name
Ranger, Rainger—ward of the
forest
Raoul—wolf (form of Rolf)
Ray, Roy, Rey, Rui, Royal—regal
Remy, Remi—rower
Rene—reborn (form of Renato)
Robert—bright, famous

Roch, Roche, Rocke—rock
Romain—from Rome (form of Romano)
Roslyn, Roslin, Roselin, Roselyn, Rosselin, Rosselyn, Ruff, Ruffe, Rush, Rushe, Rousse, Rushkin, Rousskin, Rust, Rousset—red-haired
Royce—son of Roy
Royden—from the royal hill
Rule, Ruelle, Reule—famous wolf
Russell, Roussel—reddish
Saber—sword
Sacripant—legend name
Sargent—military attendant
Satordi—god of the harvest; myth name (form of Saturn)
Saville, Sauville—from the willow farm
Scoville—meaning unknown
Searlas, Searle, Searlus—manly (form of Charles)
Senapus—legend name
Senior, Seignour—lord of the manor
Sennet, Sent—wise
Seymour—from Saint Maur
Sidney, Sydney—from Saint Denys
Soren, Sorel, Sorrell—reddish-brown hair
Sumner—summoner
Tabor—drum
Talbot, Talebot—bloodhound
Talon—claw

Taylor—tailor
Tearlach—manly (form of Charles)
Telford, Telfer, Taillefer, Telfor, Telfour—works in iron
Thiery, Thibaud, Tibault—people's prince
Toussaint—all saints
Travers, Travis—from the crossroads
Troy, Troyes—curly-haired
Turner—champion in a tournament
Tyson, Tyeis—son of a German
Vachel—little cow
Vaden—meaning unknown
Vail, Vayle—lives in the valley
Valiant—brave
Vallis, Vallois—Welshman
Varden, Vardan, Vardon, Verddun—from the green hill
Verney, Vernay—from the alder grove
Vernon—springlike
Verrill, Verel, Verrall, Verrell, Veryl—true
Vick, Vic, Vicq—from the village
Warrane—warden of the game
William—resolute protector
Wyatt, Wiatt—guide
Xarles—manly (form of Charles)
Yves—little archer
Yvon, Yvet—archer
Zdenek—follower of Saint Denys
Zerbino—legend name

GAELIC

In western Britain and Ireland, the Celtic language developed into Irish and Scottish Gaelic. Gaelic is very difficult to pronounce for English-speakers, and so many Gaelic names have been anglicized—given an English spelling based on the name's original pronunciation. The letters J, K, Q, V, W, X, Y, and Z do not exist in the Gaelic alphabet, so names containing these letters are almost certainly anglicized.

Surnames did not develop in Ireland and Scotland until after the tenth century. If an additional name was needed to distinguish between two people of the same given name, a byname was created. Bynames were like nicknames, and were often based on a person's occupation, birthplace, father, or personal characteristic. Some of these bynames eventually became surnames. Campbell, for instance, was originally the byname "cam beul" meaning "crooked mouth." (See the sections on Scotland and Ireland for examples of Gaelic surnames in these areas.)

FEMALE

Africa, Affrica, Apirka—pleasant
Aidan—fiery one
Aigneis, Una—pure (form of Agnes)
Ailis—sweet, noble (form of Alice)
Aimil—hardworking (form of Amelia)
Aine—bright, radiant
Aingealag—angel
Airleas—pledge
Alanna, Alain, Alayne, Allene, Allyn, Alina, Alana—beautiful
Amber—fierce
Amhuinn—lives at the alder-tree river

Annabel, Annabelle, Annabella, Anabal—lovely grace
Arienh—oath
Aselma—fair
Ashling—dream
Barabell, Barabal—stranger
Bebhinn—harmonious
Beitris—brings joy (form of Beatrice)
Bevin—sweet voice
Blaine—thin
Blair—of the fields
Breandan, Brenda—little raven
Brenna—raven
Brighde—myth name
Brodie—ditch
Cailin—small girl

Cairine—pure

Cairistiona, Ciorstag, Ciorstan—
believes in Christ (form of
Christian)

Caitlin, Caitrin—pure (form of
Katherine)

Caley—slender

Cara, Carin, Caryn—friend

Carling—little champion

Casey—brave

Cassidy, Casidhe—clever

Cathasach, Caci, Casey—brave

Catriona, Ceit, Cait, Caitlin—
pure (form of Katherine)

Cayleigh—party, celebration

Ceallach—warrior maid

Ceara—spear

Ciarda—dark

Coleen, Colleen—girl

Con—exalted

Cuini—queen

Dacey—southerner

Danu—goddess of fruitfulness

Dara—of the oak

Darby—free of envy

Darra—wealth, riches

Deirdre, Deidra, Deardriu—
raging

Dervla—from the poets

Diorbhall—God's gift (form of
Dorothy)

Donalda, Domhnulla, Donia—
ruler of the world (form of
Donald)

Donla—lady in brown

Doreen, Dorene, Doire-Ann,
Doireann—moody

Duana—dark maid

Dymphna—little poet

Ealasaid—devoted to God

Edana, Eideann—fiery one (form
of Aidan)

Eibhlin—light; gives life (form of
Eileen or Evelyn)

Eileen—sunlight

Eilidh—light

Eilionoir—light (form of
Eleanor)

Eilis—consecrated to God (form
of Elizabeth)

Eithne—fiery, ardent

Ena—ardent

Enda—like a bird

Erin, Eryn—peace

Erlina, Erline—girl from Ireland

Fiona—fair one

Fionnghuala—flower

Flanna—red-haired (form of
Flann)

Frangag—free (form of Francis)

Ghleanna—lives in the valley

Giorsal—gray battle-maid (form
of Griselda)

Glen, Glenn, Glenna, Glennis,
Glynnes, Glynnis, Glynis—
from the glen

Grainne—grace

Haley—wise, smart

Iseabal, Isobail—devoted to God

Ita—thirsty

Keeley, Keely—beautiful

Keera, Keira—dark, black

Kellan—warrior princess

Kennis—lovely

Kerry, Keriam—dark one;
county name

Keverne—saint name
Kyla—from the straits
Kyna—intelligent
Laoidheach—from the pasture meadow
Leah—light
Leitis—happy
Leslie, Lesley—from the gray fortress
Lili—lily
Liusaidh, Kelly, Kellie—warrior woman
Mab—joy
Maire, Mairin—bitter (form of Mary)
Mairearad, Mairghread—pearl (form of Margaret)
Malise—God's servant
Malvina—peaceful face
Maolmin—polished chief
Marsali—pearl
Mildread—gentle adviser (form of Mildred)

Moibeal—lovable (form of Mabel)
Mor, Mairi, Muireall—bitter
Morag—blind
Muadhnait—little, noble one
Myrna—beloved
Nairne—from the alder-tree river
Nara—happy
Neala—champion (form of Neal)
Niamh—bright and beautiful
Nola—fair champion
Nuallan—famous
Odharnait—pale
Onora—honor
Orna—pale
Peigi—peg
Raghnailt—sheep, ewe
Raonaid, Raonaild—ewe
Regan—little king
Riane—small ruler
Riley—valiant
Ronan—small seal

HAYWOOD SMITH

Haywood Smith is the author of nine novels, including *The Red Hat Club* and *The Red Hats Ride Again* (St. Martin's Press). She is a *Romantic Times* Career Achievement winner.

I named the hero from *Secrets in Satin* Garrett because it meant "strong spear" from Old English. *So* appropriate, even though I was probably the only person who got it until I started speaking about the book and told everybody. (They loved it.)

Names and their meanings are so important. (Except mine. Haywood means "conceived in the hay field beside the forest." Not!)

Rory—red ruler
Ros, Rois, Roisin, Rosheen—
  rose (form of Rosa)
Rossa—meadow
Rowan—rowan tree
Seonaid—gracious God
Sile, Silis, Sighle—blind (form of
  Cecil)
Sine—gracious God (form of
  Sean)
Siobhan, Siubhan, Shevaun,

Shivaun—gracious God
  (form of John)
Siusan—lily (form of Susan)
Sorcha—intelligent
Taithleach—quiet
Tara—from the crag of a tower
Tierney—from the lord
Toirdealbach—myth name
Treasa—reaper (form of
  Theresa)

MALE

Abboid—abbey father (form of
  Abbott)
Adair, Athdara, Athdar—from
  the ford by the oak trees
Adhamh—of the red earth (form
  of Adam)
Ahern, Aherin, Aherne—lord of
  the horses
Aidan, Aiden, Aodhan, Aodh—
  fiery one
Ailin, Ailen, Ailean—handsome
Aindreas—manly (form of
  Andrew)
Airdsgainne—from the height of
  the cliff
Airleas, Arlen—pledge
Allister, Alaster, Alai—avenger
  (form of Alastair)
Alroy—red-haired
Aod—son of Lyr; myth name
Aodh—fiery one
Aodhhan, Aidan, Aodhagan—
  ardent
Aonghus, Angus—exceptionally
  strong

Arlen—oath
Arregaithel—from the land of
  the Gaels
Artur, Art—noble bear
Bacstair—baker
Baillidh—steward
Bain, Bharain, Bheathain—lives
  near the clear stream
Bainbridge, Bainbrydge—lives
  by the bridge over the
  stream
Baird, Bard—bard
Balfour, Bailefour—from the
  pastureland
Banain, Banning—little blond
  one
Baran—noble warrior
Batair—strong warrior
Beagan, Beagen—little one
Bealantin—brave (form of
  Ballantine)
Bearach, Barry, Barra—spear
Bearnard—strong as a bear
  (form of Bernard)

Beathan—son of the right hand
Beattie, Beatie, Beatty,
    Biadhaiche—blesses
Bebhinn—harmonious
Becan—little one
Bhruic—badger
Blair—from the plain lands
Bowie, Bow, Bowen, Bowyn,
    Boyd, Buidhe—blond
Boyne, Bofind—white cow
Boynton—from the white river
Brady, Bradach—spirited
Brendan, Breandan, Brennan,
    Brendon—raven
Brom—raven
Brothaigh—from Brodie
Brus—woods (form of Bruce)
Buadhachan—victorious
Cailean, Cailen, Caillen, Colin,
    Colan, Collin, Coll—child
Caley, Caolaidhe—slender
Calhoun, Coillcumhann—from
    the narrow forest
Calum, Colm—servant of Saint
    Columba
Camden, Camdene—from the
    winding valley
Cameron, Camshron—crooked
    nose
Campbell, Caimbeul—crooked
    mouth
Canice—handsome
Caolabhuinn—from the narrow
    river
Carlin, Carlie, Cearbhallan,
    Carling—little champion
Carmichael, Caramichil—friend
    of Saint Michael

Carney, Ceanach—victorious
Carrick, Carraig, Charraigaich—
    from the rocky headland
Carroll, Carol, Carly, Carolus—
    manly (form of Charles)
Casey, Cathasach—brave
Cassidy, Casidhe—clever
Cathal—strong in battle
Cathmor, Cathmore,
    Cathaoirmore—great
    warrior
Cavan, Caomhan—handsome
Cayden—battle spirit
Ceallach—warrior
Ceannfhionn—blond
Ceileachan—little champion
Cerin—little dark one
Cian, Cein—archaic
Ciardubhan—little black one
Cinnard—from the high hill
Cinneididh—helmeted
Cinnfhail—from the head of the
    cliff
Clancy—red warrior
Cleary, Cleirach—scholar
Cluny, Clunainach—from the
    meadow
Coigleach—distaff
Coilleach, Choilleich—guards
    the forest
Coinleain—well-shaped
Coinneach—handsome
Colin, Coilin—virile
Colum, Columbanus, Calum—
    dove
Comhghan—twin
Comyn, Cuimean—meaning
    unknown

Conan—wise
Conlan, Connlan, Conlin—hero
Conn—chief
Conroy, Conaire—wise
Conway—hound of the plain
Corcoran, Corcurachan—
    reddish skin
Corey, Cori, Cory, Coire—ravine
Cormac, Cormick, Cormack—
    charioteer
Cowan, Cobhan—dwells by the
    hillside hollow
Coyle—searches for battle
Craig, Creag—dwells at the crag
Criostoir, Crisdean—Christ-
    bearer (form of
    Christopher)
Cronan—dark brown
Cuilean—cub
Cuinn—wise
Cullan, Cullin, Cully—handsome
Culley, Colle, Cully—dwells at
    the woodland
Curran, Curr, Curney,
    Curadhan—hero
Daibhidh—beloved (form of
    David)
Daley, Daly—counselor
Dall, Dallas—wise
Darby, Diarmaid, Dermot,
    Dermod, Dermott, Diarmid,
    Diarmad—free of envy
Darren, Daryn, Daron, Dearan—
    great
Darry, D'Ary, Dar, Darce—dark
Deasach, Dacey, Dacy—
    southerner
Declan—goodness

Delano—healthy black man
Dempsey, Diomasach—proud
Deorsa—farmer
Derry—red-haired
Desmond, Deasmumhan,
    Desmon—from south
    Munster
Devlin, Devlyn, Dobhailen—
    fierce
Devyn, Devin, Devan, Daimhin—
    servant
Dillon, Diolmhain—faithful
Domhnull, Donald—ruler of the
    world
Donahue, Duncan—dark warrior
Dooley, Dubhloach—dark hero
Duff, Dubhthach, Duffy, Dugan,
    Dubhgan—dark-faced
Dugal, Dugald, Dughall—dark
    stranger (form of Dougal)
Dunbar—dark branch
Duncan, Donnchadh—dark
    warrior
Dunmore—from the fortress on
    the hill
Eachann—steadfast
Eachthighearn—horse lord
Ealadhach—genius
Eamonn, Eamon—rich protector
Eanruig—rules the home
Earnan—earnest
Earvin—handsome
Edan—fiery one (form of Aidan)
Eideard—rich guardian (form of
    Edward)
Ellar—steward, servant
Eoghan, Egan, Egon, Eoghann—
    young fighter

Erin—peace
Erskine—from the top of the cliff
Euan, Ewan—of the yew
Eumann—prosperous warrior
Fagen, Faodhagan, Fagin—
ardent
Faolan—little wolf
Farrell, Fearghall—victorious
Farriss, Ferris—rock
Fearcher, Farquhar—very dear
Fergus, Fearghus, Ferghus—of
manly strength
Finbar—blond
Fingal—fair stranger
Finlay, Fionnlaoch, Fionn,
Findlay, Finn, Fionnlagh—
fair soldier
Flann, Flannan—red-haired
Flynn, Flin—son of the red-
haired man
Forbes, Fearbhirigh—wealth or
stubborn
Frang, Frannsaidh—free (form of
Francis)
Gabhan—white hawk (form of
Gavin)
Gaelbhan—sparrow
Gair, Gear—short
Galen, Gaylen, Galyn, Gaelan—
tranquil
Gall—stranger
Gallagher, Galchobhar—eager
helper
Galloway, Galaway, Galway,
Gallgaidheal—of the strange
Gauls
Galvin, Gaelbhan—sparrow
Gannon, Gannie, Gionnan—fair-
skinned

Garvey, Gairbhith, Garbhach—
rough peace
Gaynor, Gayner—son of the
blond man
Gearald—spear ruler (form of
Gerald)
Gilleasbuig—sacred and bold
Gille-Eathain—youthful (form of
Julius)
Gilmore—servant of the Virgin
Mary
Gilroy, Giollaruaidh—serves the
king
Giollamhuire—devoted
Giollanaebhin—worships the
saints
Girven, Gervin, Girvyn,
Garbhan—rough
Glen, Glenn, Gleann—from the
glen
Glendon—from the glen
Goraidh, Godfrey—God's peace
Gordan, Gordain—hero
Gorman—eyes of blue
Gow—smith
Grady, Gradey—noble
Guin—blond
Guthrie, Gaothaire—free wind
Hogan, Hagan—young
Hurley, Hurly, Hurlee—seatide
Iain—gracious God (form of
John)
Innis—from the river island
Iomar—archer
Irving—handsome
Kane, Kayne, Kaine—tribute
Keefe, Keifer—handsome
Keegan, Kegan—fiery

Keller—little champion
Kelly, Kelley—warrior
Kelvin—from the narrow river
Kendrick—son of Harry
Kennedy—helmeted
Kenyon—blond
Kermichael, Kermichil—from Michael's fortress
Kermit—free
Kern, Kerne, Kearn—little dark one
Kerr—spear
Kerry—dark one; county name
Kerwin, Kerwyn, Kerwen—little black one
Kevin, Kevyn—gentle, handsome
Key—son of Aidan
Kieran—black
Kinnard—from the high hill
Kinnell—from the head of the cliff
Kyle—from the straits
Labhruinn—laurel
Lachlann—from Scandinavia
Lawler—mumbles
Lennon, Leannan—little cloak
Lennox, Leamhnach—lives near the place abounding in elm trees
Leslie, Lesley, Liosliath—from the gray fortress
Liam—resolute protector (form of William)
Logan, Loghan—from the hollow
Lon, Lonn—fierce
Lucas—light
Luthais—famous in war

Mac a'bhaird—son of Baird
Mac a'bhiadhtaiche—son of Bhiadhtaiche
Mac Adhaimh, MacAdam, MacAdhaimh—son of Adam
Mac Ailean, MacLean, MacAilean, MacAllen—son of the handsome man
Mac Alasdair, MacAladair, MacAllister—son of Alasdair
Mac an Aba, MacNab—father's son
Mac an Bhaillidh—son of the steward
Mac an Bharain—son of the noble warrior
Mac an Bhreatannaich—son of the Briton
Mac an Tsagairt—son of the prelate
Mac an t-Saoir—son of the carpenter
Mac Artuir, MacArthur, MacArtuir—son of Arthur
Mac Asgaill—son of Asgaill
Mac Bheathain—son of the man who lives by the clear stream
Mac Bhriain—son of the strong
Mac Daraich—son of the man from the ford by the oak trees
Mac Ghille Aindries—son of the one who served the manly one
Mac Ghille-Bhuidhe—son of the one who serves the blond
Mac Ghille-Dhuibh—son of

the one who serves the dark man

Mac Ghille-Dhuinn—son of the one who serves Brown

Mac Ghille-Easpuig—son of the one who serves the sacred and bold

Mac Ghille-Laider—son of the one who serves the strong armed

Mac Ghille Mhicheil, Carmichail—son of the one who served Saint Michael

MacNair—son of an heir

Malcolm—servant of Saint Columba

Maloney, Maoldhomhnaigh—devoted to God

Malvin, Maolmin—polished chief

Manus, Mannis—great

Maoltuile—quiet

Marcus—warlike

Martainn—warlike (form of Marcus)

Mayo—lives near the yew trees

Micheil—who is like God (form of Michael)

Monroe—from the red swamp

Morvan, Morven, Morvyn, Morfinn, Morvin—pale

Muireach—Moorish

Mungan—lovable (form of Mungo)

Murchadh—protector of the sea

Murthuile—sea tide

Neacal—victory of the people (form of Nicholas)

Neall, Niall, Neil—champion (form of Neal)

Nevin, Nevyn, Nevins—worships the saints

Nolan, Noland, Nuallan—noble

Odharnait, Oran, Odran, Oren, Orin, Orran, Orren, Orrin—pale

Padraic, Padruig—noble (form of Patrick)

Parthalan—son of the furrows

Peadar—rock (form of Peter)

Phelan—little wolf

Piaras—rock

Pol—little

Proinsias—frank

Quigley—distaff; unruly hair

Quinlan—well-shaped

Quinn—wise

Rafferty, Rabhartach—wealthy

Raghnall, Raonull—mighty power

Raibeart—bright, famous (form of Robert)

Riley, Raghallach—valiant

Riordan, Rioghbhardan—royal bard

Risteard—strong ruler (form of Richard)

Roan—red-haired

Rooney, Ruanaidh—red-haired

Rory—red ruler

Roy—red

Ruairidh—famous ruler

Ryan—little king

Scully—town crier

Senach—meaning unknown

Seorus—farmer

Seosamh—God adds (form of Joseph)

Seumas—supplanter

Sholto, Siolat—teal duck

Sim—heard

Skelly, Skelley, Sguelaiche—storyteller

Slevin, Slevyn, Slavin, Slaven, Sleven, Slaibhin—mountain man

Sloan, Sloane, Sluaghan—fighter

Somhairle, Somerled—asked of God

Stiabhan—crowned in victory (form of Stephen)

Taggart—son of a prelate

Taithleach—quiet

Tavish—twin (form of Thomas)

Teague, Taidhg, Tadhg—poet

Tearlach, Tearley, Tearly—manly (form of Charles)

Tioboid—bold

Toirdealbhach—myth name

Tomas—twin (form of Thomas)

Tormod—from the north

Torrance, Terrence—from the knolls

Tully, Tulley, Tuathal—peaceful

Tynan, Teimhnean—dark

Uilleam—resolute protector (form of William)

Uisdean—intelligent

Zowie—meaning unknown

GERMAN

German surnames began in the south during the late twelfth century and moved north. By the sixteenth century, the names had become hereditary. Surnames derive from occupational, patronymic, descriptive, and place names.

Common suffixes are:

-sohn—son
-er, -mann—denote occupational names
-ke, -ish, -ush—are Slavic influences on the language

Certain common elements in German surnames relate to place names.

au—meadow or low area
bach—brook
bad—bath, spa
berg—mountain
burg—fortress or castle
fels—rock, cliff
furt—ford
hof—farm, courtyard
thal/tal—valley or dale
wald—forest, woods

Common articles:

von—can mean either "from" or "owner of a town or area"
zu—when used with names, means "at" and is usually reserved for aristocrats and used with a title

The *von* in the surname von Bremen, for example, might indicate nobility. On the other hand, it might indicate only that an ancestor moved to another area from Bremen, acquiring the surname "from Bremen." Either *von* or *zu* may be used with a title: Count von Buest (in German, *Graf von Buest*). Some members of the nobility use the phrase "von und zu," which indicated they were not only from a certain place, but still retained ownership of it: Baron von und zu Guttenberg (in German, *Freiherr von und zu Guttenberg*).

A few surnames:

Auerbach
Braun
Breit
Brugmann
Dengler
Drescher
Eichhorn
Eisenberg
Eschenbach
Finster
Fleischer
Frankenheimer
Gerhardt
Gottlieb
Gruenewald
Hammerstein
Hirsch
Huber
Kaiser
Kaufmann

Klein
Liebermann
Meier
Mendelsohn
Messerschmidt
Niemeyer
Nussbaum
Ostermann
Rahn
Reiner
Schmidt
Schuhmacher
Schuster
Stroebel
Tannenbaum
Unger
Von Schroeder
Wohlgemuth
Ziegler
Zimmermann

FEMALE

Ada—happy
Adalia, Adali, Adalie—noble
(form of Adel)
Adele, Adela—pleasant
Adeline, Adelinda, Adette,
Adelheide, Adelle, Adelina,
Adelita, Adelheid, Adal,
Adelaide, Adalheida—noble
Adelyte—has good humor
Adolpha, Adalwolfa—noble she-
wolf (form of Adolph)
Adrian, Adriane—dark
Agathe, Agatha—good (form of
Agatha)

Alarice, Alarica—noble ruler
(form of Alaric)
Alberta, Albertine, Albertyne,
Albertina—noble, intelligent
(form of Albert)
Alda, Alida, Aleda, Alyda,
Aldona—old (form of Aldo)
Alfonsine, Alphonsine—noble
and ready for battle (form of
Alphonse)
Alice, Alys, Alison, Alisz, Aliz,
Ailis, Alicia, Ailse, Aili—
sweet, noble

Alonsa—noble and ready for battle (form of Alphonse)

Aloysia, Aloisia—famous in war (form of Aloysius)

Alvar, Alva, Alvie, Alvara, Alvarie—army of elves

Amalasand, Amalasanda—industrious

Amara—eternal

Annemarie, Annamaria—bitter grace (form of Annamarie)

Antonie—priceless (form of Anthony)

Arabella—beautiful eagle

Ararinda—tenacious

Armina—warrior maid

Arnalda—eagle (form of Arnold)

Ava—like a bird

Ballard, Baldhart—bold, strong

Bathilda, Bathild, Bathilde—heroine

Berdine, Berdina—intelligent maid

Berit—intelligent

Bernadette—strong as a bear (form of Bernard)

Berta, Bertha, Bertina—bright (form of Bert)

Binga, Binge—from the kettle-shaped hollow (form of Bing)

Blas, Blasa—firebrand

Bruna, Brune—dark-haired (form of Brun)

Brunhilde, Brunhilda, Brunhild—armored battle-maid

Chriselda—strong

Clarimond, Clarimonda, Clarimonde—brilliant protectress

Clotilda, Clotilde—renowned for war

Conradina, Conradine—able counsel (form of Conrad)

Dagmar, Dagomar—maiden of the day

Della—bright

Didrika—ruler of the people (form of Dietrich)

Eadaion—joyous friendship

Ebba—strength

Edda—pleasant

Edeline, Ediline, Edelina—noble

Else, Elsie, Elsa, Elsha, Elica, Ilse, Ilyse, Elyse, Elsje—noble

Emilie—hardworking (form of Emily)

Emma—universal

Engleberta, Engelbertha, Engelbertine, Engelbertina—bright angel (form of Engelbert)

Eraman, Eramana—honorable

Erma—war goddess

Erna, Ernestine, Ernestina—serious (form of Ernest)

Ethelinda, Ethelinde—noble serpent

Etta—little one

Felda—from the field

Felisberta—intelligent

Franziska—free (form of Francis)

Frieda—peaceful

Fritzi—peaceful ruler

Gaelle—stranger
Galiena, Galiana—haughty
Genevieve, Genowefa,
Genoveva—white wave
Geraldine, Gerwalt, Gerwalta,
Gerhardine, Gerhardina,
Geraldina—spear ruler
(form of Gerald)
Gerda, Gerde, Gerdie—
protected
Gertrude, Gertrut, Gertrud,
Gertruda—strong with a
spear
Ghislaine, Guilaine—oath
Gilberta, Gisilberhta—pledge
(form of Gilbert)
Gretchen—little pearl
Griselda, Grisjahilde, Griselde—
gray battle-maid
Griswalda, Griswalde—from the
gray forest (form of
Griswald)
Gudrun, Gudruna—divine
knowledge
Guida—guide
Gunilla, Gunnel—battle-maid
Gustel—noble
Halfrida, Halifrid, Halfrid—
peaceful heroine
Hannelore, Hannelora—
meaning unknown
Harimanna, Harimanne—
protective (form of
Hariman)
Hedda, Hadu—vigorous battle-
maid
Hedwig, Haduwig—strife

Heidi, Heida, Hild, Hilda, Hilde—
nobility
Helene—light (form of Helen)
Helga, Halag—holy
Helma, Hilma—protective
Herta, Hertha—of the earth
Hida, Hide—warrior
Hildegard, Hildimar, Hildemar,
Hildemara—stronghold
Hildreth, Hildireth—battle
counselor
Holda, Holde, Holle, Hulda,
Hulde—beloved
Huberta, Hugiberahta—
intelligent (form of Hubert)
Ida, Idaia, Idna, Idalie—active
Idette, Idetta—hardworking
Ilse—noble maid
Irma, Irmine, Irmina, Irmigard,
Irmgard, Irmuska—war
goddess
Isa, Isane, Isana—strong-willed
Isolda, Isole, Isold—rule of ice
Jakoba, Jakobe, Jakobie—
supplanter (form of Jacob)
Johanna—gracious God (form of
Joan)
Jolan, Jolanka, Joli—country
Karola, Karolina, Karla,
Karoline—manly (form of
Charles)
Katharina, Katchen, Kathe—
pure (form of Katharine)
Kuonrada—wise
Leoda, Leute, Leota, Leopoldine,
Leopolda, Leopoldina—of
the people
Linda, Lind, Lindie—pretty

Lisa, Lise, Lisette—consecrated to God (form of Elizabeth)

Lorelei, Lurline, Lurlina, Lurleen, Lurlene—temptress

Lorraine, Loraine—from Lorraine

Lotte—masculine

Louise, Louisane, Luise, Lovisa, Lujza, Luijzika, Loyce—famous in war (form of Louis)

Luana, Ludkhannah, Luane—graceful battle-maid

Magd, Mady, Magda—maiden

Magnilda, Maganhildi, Magnhilda, Magnild, Magnilde—strong fighter

Malene, Maddalena, Maddalene, Maddalen, Maddalyn—from the tower (form of Madeleine)

Mallory, Madelhari—army counselor

Marelda, Marilda, Marhildi, Marhilda—famous battle-maid

Marlis, Marlisa, Maria—bitter (form of Mary)

Mathilda, Mathilde, Mathild—strong battle-maid (form of Matilda)

Millicent—industrious

Minna, Mina, Minne, Mindy—love

Nadette, Nadetta, Nadine, Nadina—courage of a bear

Nixie—little water sprite

Norberta, Norberaht,

Norberte—bright hero (form of Norbert)

Nordica, Nordika—from the north

Odile, Odelina, Odiane, Odiana, Odette, Oda, Odila, Ordella, Ordalf—elfin spear

Olinda—protector of property

Otka, Otthild, Otthilde, Otthilda, Ottila, Otilie, Ottilia, Otylia—fortunate heroine

Perahta—glorious

Petronille, Petronilla—rock (form of Peter)

Philippine, Philippina—lover of horses (form of Philip)

Rachel—ewe

Ricarda—strong ruler (form of Richard)

Rikka—mistress of all

Rilla, Rille, Rillia, Rillie—stream

Roch—glory

Roderica, Roderika—famous ruler (form of Roderick)

Rolanda, Rolande—famous (form of Roland)

Romilda, Ruomhildi, Romilde, Romhilda, Romhilde, Romhild—glorious battle-maid

Rosamund, Rozomund, Rosemunda, Rosemonde, Rozmonda, Rosa—noted protector

Rudelle, Rudella, Rupetta, Rupette—famous

Senta, Sente—assistant

Serilda, Sarohildi, Serhilda,

Serihilda, Serihilde, Serhilda, Serhild—armored battle-maid
Sigfreda, Sigfrieda, Sigfriede—victorious peace (form of Siegfried)
Solvig, Sigilwig—champion
Suzanne—lily (form of Susan)
Tibelda, Tibelde, Tibeldie—boldest
Truda, Trude, Trudchen—strong
Tugenda—virtue
Ulla—has willpower
Ulrike, Ulrica, Ulka, Uli—ruler of all
Valborga—protecting ruler
Vanda, Vande—wanderer (form of Wanda)

Verena, Verina, Verene—protector
Vibeke, Viveka—little woman
Walda, Welda—ruler
Waldburga, Walborga—protecting ruler
Wanda, Wande, Wandy—wanderer
Warda—guard
Wido—warrior maiden
Wilda, Wilde—wild
Wilhelmina, Wilhelmine—resolute protector (form of William)
Winifred, Winifrid, Winifrida, Winifride—peaceful friend
Winola—gracious friend
Yseult—ruler of ice

MALE

Abelard, Adelhard—resolute
Adal, Adel—noble
Adalard, Adalhard—brave, noble
Adalwine, Audwin, Audwine, Adalwen—noble friend
Adler, Adlar, Ahren, Aren—eagle
Adolf, Adalwolf, Adolph—noble wolf
Alaric, Alarick, Alarik, Alrik, Aurik, Aric, Arick, Arik, Aurick—noble ruler
Albrecht, Adelbert, Adalbert, Albert, Ailbe, Alvy, Ardal—noble, intelligent
Aldo, Ald—old

Alemannus—myth name
Alfonso, Alphonso—noble and ready for battle (form of Alphonse)
Alger, Adalgar—noble spearman
Alhsom—sacred fame
Alois—famous warrior
Altman, Altmann—old wise man
Alvin, Alhwin, Alwin, Adalwin—noble friend
Amory, Amery, Alhmarric—divine
Andreas—manly (form of Andrew)
Ann—name of a king
Anson—son of Ann

149

Anton—priceless (form of Anthony)

Archard—sacred and powerful

Archimbald, Archibald—bold

Armand—soldier (form of Herman)

Arndt, Arnaud, Arnot, Arnoll, Arnott, Arnet, Arnett, Arnald, Arnold, Arnd, Arend, Arno, Arnell, Arnhold, Arnall—eagle

Arne, Are, Adne, Arney, Arni, Arnt—eagle (form of Arnold)

Arnwolf—eagle wolf

Arvin—friend of the people

Audric, Audrick, Adalric, Aldrik, Adalrik—wise ruler (form of Aldrich)

Axel, Apsel, Aksel—father of peace

Baldemar—princely

Baldric, Baldrik—bold ruler

Baldwin, Baldwyn, Balduin—bold friend

Baltasar—protected by God

Bannan—commander

Bannruod—famous commander

Barret, Berowalt—mighty as a bear

Berdy—intelligent

Berg—mountain

Bern, Berne, Ber, Berrin—bear

Bernard, Bernon, Bernot, Barnard, Benat, Barrett, Bernhard, Bernd, Berend, Berinhard, Barney,

Bernardo, Bernardyn—strong as a bear

Berthold, Berchtwald—bright ruler

Bing, Binge—from the kettle-shaped hollow

Bittan, Bitten—desire

Bogart, Bogohardt—bowstring

Brandeis—dwells on a burned clearing

Brendan, Bren, Brendis—sword

Bruno, Brunon—dark-haired (form of Brun)

Burhardt, Burkhart—strong as a castle

Clovis, Chlodwig—famous warrior

Conrad, Conradin, Cord, Cort, Conrado—able counsel

Corrado—bold

Dagoberto—glorious day

Derry, Dearg—red-haired

Dick—strong leader

Diederich, Dietrich, Dedrick, Dedrik, Derrick, Dieter, Dirk, Derek, Dierck, Dietz—ruler of the people

Drugi, Drud—strong

Dutch, Deutsch—German

Eberhard, Eberhardt, Eburhardt, Eward, Evrard—strong as a boar

Edel—brave

Edingu—famous ruler

Eduard—rich guardian (form of Edward)

Edwin, Edwyn—wealthy friend

Eginhard, Eginhardt, Einhard,

Egon, Enno, Eno, Einhardt—
strong with a sword
Ehren—honorable
Ellery—lives by the alder tree
Eloy, Ely—famous fighter
Emory, Emery—joint ruler
Englbehrt, Englebert—bright
angel
Erchanbold—sacred, bold
Erchanhardt, Ekhard, Ekerd,
Eckerd, Erkerd—sacred
Erhardt, Erhard—honor
Erich—eternal ruler (form of
Eric)
Ernest, Earnest, Ernst, Erno—
serious
Errando—bold venture
Eugen—well-born (form of
Eugene)
Franz—free (form of Frank)
Fremond, Frimunt—noble
protector
Friedrich, Fritz—peaceful ruler
(form of Frederick)
Georg—farmer (form of George)
Gerhard, Gerard, Goddard—
spear ruler (form of Gerald)
Gerlach—spear thrower
Ghislain—oath
Gilleasbuig—bold
Godfrey, Godfried, Gottfried—
peaceful god
Griswold, Griswald—from the
gray forest
Hackett, Hacket—little hacker
Hamlet, Hamlett, Hamoelet—
from the little home
Hamlin—rules the home
Hans, Hann, Hanno, Han, Hanz—

gracious God (form of John)
Hardy, Harti—daring
Hariman, Harimann—protective
Hartman, Hardtman,
Hartmann—strong
Harvey—soldier
Heinrich—rules the home (form
of Henry)
Helmut, Helmutt—brave
Hernando—adventuresome
Herrick—army leader
Hewett, Hewitt, Hewlitt,
Hewlett—little Hugh
Hildebrand, Hildbrand—war
sword
Hobart, Hobbard, Hobard,
Hohberht—intelligent (form
of Hubert)
Howe, How, Hoh—high
Hugh—intelligent
Hulbert, Huldiberaht, Hubbard,
Hulbard, Hulbart—graceful
Humphrey, Hunfrid, Hunfried—
peaceful Hun
Ingel, Engel, Ingall, Ingalls—
angel
Ingelbert—bright angel
Jakob—supplanter (form of
Jacob)
Japhet—myth name
Jarman, Jarmann—German
Jarvis—sharp spear
Jay, Jaye—swift
Johan, Johann, Johannes—
gracious God (form of John)
Josef—God adds (form of
Joseph)
Jurgen—farmer (form of George)
Karl—manly (form of Charles)

DANIEL WALLACE

Daniel Wallace is the author of three novels, *Big Fish* (1998), *Ray in Reverse* (2000), and *The Watermelon King* (2003). His stories have been published far and wide in many magazines and anthologies, including *The Yale Review*, *The Massachusetts Review*, *Shenandoah*, and *Glimmer Train*. His illustrated work has appeared in the *Los Angeles Times* and Italian *Vanity Fair*. *Big Fish* has been translated into eighteen languages and was adapted for film.

I used to find my characters' names in the telephone book—opening it at random, closing my eyes, and letting my fingers do the choosing. This wasn't always successful, but it was better—and easier—than having to try and come up with something by myself. All the names I came up with seemed forced and unbelievable.

Then I named them after friends. This was fun because while almost no one else would know the origin of the name, I would; it was a little inside joke. I named dogs after old girlfriends, streets after teachers, and fathers—well, after my father. My real father's name was Eron Daniel Wallace—we called him E.D.—and most of my fictional fathers are named Ed or Edward.

But the times have changed, and so have I.

Now I get my names from spam. That's right: Those pesky unwanted e-mails are really the best place to find a name these days. All I have to do is look into the Deleted Items folder of Outlook Express, and there are dozens—no, *hundreds*—of names, right there in the From field, perfect for any character I might want to write about.

Let's take a look now!

The first name I come upon is Marina Carmichael. I think she really wants to direct me toward a porn site, but I'm not going there; instead, she'll become the attractive, mysterious, and unattainable girl-next-door.

Next? Evangelina Gunter. Hmmm, I don't know if I have a story she'll be in, but it's good to know she's there, in case I need her.

Truman Ellison—there's a name for almost anyone. Sheryl McNair. Rusty Sims. Dolores Long. These are plain yet distinctive names. Perfect for any genre.

Some, of course, will never do. Colin L. Vang. Foster Dumas. King Stud. No. No, no, and no.

But Nellie Buckner? Yes. Tracy Webb? Why not? Xavier Williams? Who *wouldn't* want Xavier Williams in a story?

Then I come upon this name, one so good I hesitate to share it with you, in case I want to use it for myself.

Faith Yankovic.

This one, this Faith—she needs a novel. Please, somebody: Write it.

Klaus—victory of the people (form of Nicholas)

Konrad, Kurt, Kuno, Konni, Kunz, Kord, Koenraad, Koen—able counsel (form of Conrad)

Kuhlbert, Kulbert, Kulbart—calm, bright

Lamar, Lamarr, Landmari—famous around the land

Lambrecht, Lambert, Lambart, Lambret, Lambrett—light of land

Leopold, Leopoldo—bold for his people

Lindberg, Lindeberg—from the linden tree hill

Lorenz, Loritz—laurel (form of Lawrence)

Loring, Lotharing, Lothar, Lothair—famous warrior (form of Lothario)

Ludwig, Lutz, Ludwik, Luki, Louis, Luis, Luduvico, Lughaidh, Lewy, Luigi, Luiginw—famous in war (form of Louis)

Mallory, Madelhari—army counselor

Mandel—almond

Manfred, Manfried, Manfrit—peaceful

Meinhard, Meinke, Meino, Maynard, Meinyard—firm

Meinrad—strong adviser

Nefen, Nefin, Nef, Neff—nephew

Orbert, Odbert, Orbart, Odbart—wealthy

Oswald—divine power

Othman, Otto, Otho, Othmann, Othomann—wealthy

Otto—born eighth

Ottokar—happy fighter

Penn—commander

Penrod—famous commander

Pepin, Peppi—petitioner

Ragnorak—myth name

Rainart, Rainhard, Reinhard, Renke—strong judgment

Rainer, Reiner—counsel

Rambert, Reginberaht, Rambart—mighty, intelligent

Raymond—mighty protector

Reginald, Reggie, Rich, Rikard,
   Richard, Riocard, Rickard,
   Ryszard, Risteard, Riccardo,
   Ricardo—strong ruler
Reynard, Reginhard, Reinhard—
   mighty brave
Richmond—strong protector
Ritter—knight
Roald, Rald—mighty, powerful
   (form of Ronald)
Roch, Rico—glory
Rosswald, Roswell, Roswalt,
   Roswald—mighty horse
Roth—red-haired
Rune—secret
Ruodrik, Rodrik, Roderick—
   famous ruler
Rupert, Ruprecht—bright fame
Rutger, Rudiger—famous
   spearman (form of Roger)
Selig, Saelac, Selik—blessed
Siegfried, Sigifrith, Sigfrid,
   Sigifrid—victorious peace
Sigwald, Sigiwald, Sigwalt—
   victorious ruler
Spangler, Spengler—tinsmith
Stein—stone
Tab, Tabbert, Tabbart—brilliant
Tibalt—people's prince
Treffen—meets
Trennen—divides
Tretan—walks
Ubel—evil
Ulrich, Uli, Ulz—ruler of all
Valdemar, Valdemarr—famous
   ruler
Vernados—courage of a bear
Volker—people's guard

Volney, Vollny—of the people
Wagner—wagonmaker
Waldemar, Waldemarr—strong
   ruler
Waldo—ruler
Waldron, Waldhramm,
   Waldrom—ruling raven
Walfred, Waldifrid, Walfrid—
   peaceful ruler
Wallache, Wallace—from Wales
Waller—army ruler
Walmond, Waldmunt—mighty
   protector
Walter, Walthari—powerful
   warrior
Walton, Walten—ruler
Warren, Waren—loyal
Weber, Webber—weaver
Wendell, Wendel—wanderer
Werner, Warner, Warenhari—
   defending warrior
Wilbur, Willaperht, Wilpert,
   Wilburt, Wilbert, Wilbart—
   resolute, brilliant
Wilfred, Willifrid, Wilfrid—
   resolute peace
Wilhelm, Williamon—resolute
   protector (form of William)
Wilmer, Willamar, Willmar,
   Wilmar, Willmarr—resolute,
   famous
Wilmot, Willimod, Wilmod—
   resolute spirit
Wolfgang—advancing wolf
Wolfric, Wolfrick, Wolfrik—wolf
   ruler
Wotan—myth name
Zelig—happy

GREEK

Greek surnames are, for the most part, patronymic in origin. In ancient Greece, *son of* suffixes *-opoulos, -akis, -adhis, -idhis, -ides* were attached to the father's name if the bearer needed more identification in addition to his given name. Present-day surnames are taken from occupational, patronymic, descriptive, and place names.

Greek's have a first name, a patronymic (the father's first name in genitive case), and a surname. The typical ending for a patronymic is -ou: Georgion becomes Georgiou. When a woman gets married, she changes her patronymic from her father's name to her husband's name, then takes the husband's surname as well.

The prefix *Papa-* means that the bearer is related to a priest, which lends prestige to the name.

A few surnames:

Anaghnostopoulos	Liatos
Adamidis	Melissanides
Androupolos	Melonakos
Antonopoulos	Mitsotakis
Arvanitidhis	Mylonas
Batsakis	Nikolaidhis
Borbokis	Nikolaou
Christofides	Panaotis
Coulouris	Panopoulos
Demarchis	Papadopoulos
Dhimitrakopoulus	Papandreou
Dimitrakos	Pappas
Giannakos	Paschalis
Houlis	Rigatos
Kalakos	Savakis
Kaloyeropoulos	Soukis
Kiriakopoulos	Spaneas
Kritopoulos	Theodorakis
Leonidis	Vamvakidis

Abdera—from Abdera

Abellona, Abellone—mannish

Acacia, Akakia—guileless

Acantha, Akantha—thorn

Achlys—dark mist

Adara—beautiful

Adelpha, Adelphie, Adelphe— dear sister

Ademia—unmarried, no husband

Admeta—from a tale of Hercules; myth name

Adonia—lover of Aphrodite (form of Adonis)

Adriano—dark (form of Adrian)

Aeaea—island of Circe; myth name

Aedon—daughter of Pandareos; myth name

Aegea—from the Aegean

Aegina—mother of Aeacus; myth name

Aello—one of the Harpies; myth name

Aethra—mother of Theseus; myth name

Aetna—from Aetna

Agafia, Agave, Agaue—good (form of Agatha)

Agalaia—splendor; myth name

Agalia—happy

Agape—love

Agatha, Agathi, Agate, Agotha, Agata—good

Agave—mother of Pentheus; myth name

Aglaia—beautiful, splendid; one of the three Graces; myth name

Aglauros—turned into stone by Hermes; myth name

Agnes, Agna, Aigneis, Agnese, Agneta, Agnek, Agnella— pure

Agueda—good (form of Agatha)

Aidoios—honored

Airlia, Airla—ethereal

Alatea—truth

Alcestis—gave her life to save her husband; myth name

Alcina—form of Alcinous

Alcippe—daughter of Ares; myth name

Alcmene—mother of Hercules; myth name

Alcyone—form of Alcyoneus

Aldara, Aldora—winged gift

Alena, Alina—light (form of Helen)

Aleris, Alerissa—meaning unknown

Alesandere, Alexandra, Alexandina, Alexine, Alexina, Aleka—defender of mankind (form of Alexander)

Alesia—helper

Alethea, Althaia, Alethia, Aletheia, Alecta—honesty

Alexia, Alexa, Alexis—aid

Alicia—sweet, noble (form of Alice)

Alpha—firstborn
Althaea, Althea, Altheda—pure
Alysia—bond
Alyssa—rational
Amalthea, Amalthia—nursed
    Zeus; myth name
Amara—eternal
Amarantha, Amarande,
    Amaranda—flower
Amaryllis—sparkling
Amazonia—warrior woman
Ambrosia—food of the gods;
    myth name
Ambrosine, Ambrotosa—
    immortal (form of Ambrose)
Amethyst—jewel
Aminta—protector
Amphitrite—sea goddess; aunt
    of Achilles; myth name
Amymone—daughter of Danaus;
    myth name
Anastasia, Anstice, Anstace—
    one who will be reborn
Anatola, Anatolia—from the east
    (form of Anatole)
Anaxarete—cruel woman
    punished by the gods; myth
    name
Andrea, Andreas—manly (form
    of Andrew)
Andromache—wife of Hector;
    myth name
Andromeda—daughter of
    Cassiopeia; myth name
Anemone—myth name
Anezka—pure (form of Agnes)
Angeliki, Angela, Angel,
    Angelique, Angelina,
    Angeline—angel

Annis, Annys—whole
Antea—form of Antaeus
Anteia—wife of sea god Proteus;
    myth name
Anthia, Anthea—flower
Anticlea—mother of Odysseus;
    myth name
Antigone—daughter of Oedipus;
    sister of Priam; myth name
Antiope—daughter of Asopus;
    myth name
Anysia—complete
Aphrodite—goddess of love;
    myth name
Apollina, Apollonia,
    Apollinaris—gift from
    Apollo
Ara—myth name
Arachne—changed into a spider
    by Athena; myth name
Arcadia—of Arcadia
Arene, Arena, Ariane, Ariana—
    holy one
Arete, Areta, Aretha—beauty
Arethusa—nymph; myth name
Aretina—virtuous
Argie, Argia—all-seeing
Ariadne—very holy
Artemia, Artemisia—gift from
    Artemis
Artemis—goddess of the hunt;
    myth name
Arva—eagle
Asia—from the east
Aspasia—welcomed
Astra, Astrea, Asta—star
Astraea—justice; surname for
    Artemis; myth name

Atalanta, Atlanta, Atalante—
huntress; myth name
Ate—goddess of irrationality;
myth name
Athanasia—immortal
Athena, Athene—goddess of
wisdom; myth name
Atropes, Antropas—one of the
Fates; myth name
Aure, Aura—gentle breeze
Autonoe—mother of Actaeon;
myth name
Autumn—myth name
Ava—an eagle
Avel—breath
Axelia—defender of mankind
(form of Alexander)
Baptista—baptizer (form of
Baptiste)
Barbara, Bairbre, Baibin,
Basham, Babita—stranger
Basilia—regal (form of Basil)
Baucis—wife of Philemon; myth
name
Berdine, Berdina—intelligent
maid
Berenice, Bernice—brings
victory
Beroe—traveled with Aeneas;
myth name
Beryl—crystal
Briseis—slave of Achilles; myth
name
Bryony—plant, vine
Caeneus—woman who asked to
become a man; myth name
Caitlin, Caitilin, Caitlyn, Caitrin,
Caitryn, Caitriona, Catia,

Catalin, Catalyn, Catherine,
Catheryn, Cathryn,
Catherin, Catharina,
Catarina, Catheryna—pure
(form of Katherine)
Calandra—lark
Calantha—lovely blossom
Calida, Calli, Callie, Calla,
Callista—the most beautiful
Callia—beautiful voice
Calligenia—born of beauty
Calliope—Muse of epic poetry;
myth name
Calliste—another name for
Artemis; myth name
Callisto—nymph; mother of
Arcas; myth name
Calypso—nymph; daughter of
Atlas; myth name
Canace—myth name
Candance, Candice, Cadis—
sparkling
Cassandra, Cassondra—
prophetess no one believed;
myth name
Cassie—purity
Cassiopeia—mother of
Andromeda; myth name
Casta—meaning unknown
Castalia—sacred fountain of the
Muses; myth name
Cathleen, Cathlin, Cathlyn—
pure (form of Katherine)
Celaeno—one of the Harpies;
one of the Pleiades; myth
name
Celandine, Celandina—swallow

Celena, Celina—goddess of the moon; myth name

Celosia—burning

Cenobia—stranger

Ceres—another name for Demeter; myth name

Cestus—Aphrodite's girdle; myth name

Ceto—goddess of the sea; myth name

Charis—grace and beauty; myth name

Charissa—loving

Charybdis—daughter of Poseidon; myth name

Cherise—grace

Chloe—blooming

Chloris, Cloris, Cloria—goddess of spring; myth name

Christa—anointed

Christine, Christen, Christiane, Christiana, Christian—believes in Christ (form of Christian)

Chruse—golden

Chryseis—daughter of Chryses; prisoner of Agamemnon; myth name

Chrysilla—hair of gold

Cinyras—founded the cult of Aphrodite; myth name

Cipriana—myth name

Circe—witch; myth name

Clematis—flower name

Cleo—famed

Cleopatra—her father's fame

Cliantha, Clianthe—glory

Clio—celebrate

Clotho—one of the Fates; myth name

Clymene, Clymena—mother of Atalanta; myth name

Clytemnestra—murdered her husband Agamemnon; myth name

Clytie, Clyte—water nymph; myth name

Colette—victory of the people (form of Nicholas)

Cora, Corella—maiden

Coral, Coralie, Coraline, Coralina, Coralin—from the coral of the sea

Corinna, Corinne, Corin, Coretta, Corette—maiden

Coronis—mother of Aesculapius; myth name

Cosimia, Cosma—of the universe

Cressida—golden one

Creusa—daughter of Erechtheus; myth name

Crocale—myth name

Crystal—sparkling

Cybele—mother of the Olympians; myth name

Cyma—flourish

Cynara—myth name

Cynere—thistle

Cynthia, Cinthia—moon

Cypriana, Cypris—from Cyprus

Cyra—myth name

Cyrene, Cyrena—mother of Aristaeus; myth name

Cyrilla—lordly (form of Cyril)

Cythera—from Cythera

Cytherea, Cytheria—another name for Aphrodite; myth name
Daffodil—flower
Damaris, Damara—gentle
Damia—myth name
Danae—mother of Perseus; myth name
Daphne—bay tree
Daria—rich
Deianira—wife of Hercules; myth name
Delbin, Delbina, Delbine—flower
Delia, Della—myth name
Delphine, Delphina, Delfine, Delfina, Delphia—from Delphi
Delta—born fourth
Demas, Demos—popular
Demetria, Demeter—goddess of the harvest; myth name
Desma, Desmoa—oath
Desmona, Desdemona—unlucky
Dia—daughter of Eineus; myth name
Dianthe, Diantha—flower
Dice, Dike—justice; myth name
Dido—queen of Carthage who killed herself; myth name
Dino—sister of the Gorgons; myth name
Dione, Diona—mother of Aphrodite; myth name
Dionysia, Dionysie—named for Dionysus, god of wine
Dirce—wife of Lycus; myth name
Dora, Dorette, Doralie, Doralia, Dorelia, Doralis, Doralice, Doretta—gift

Dorcas, Dorkas—gazelle
Dordie, Dordei—divine gift
Doreen—beautiful
Dorinda—beautiful gift
Doris, Dorice, Doria, Dorea, Dorian, Dorien, Doriana—of the sea
Dorothy, Dorothea, Dollie, Dolly, Doll, Dorita, Dorlisa, Dorte, Drew—God's gift
Dryope—nymph; myth name
Dyna—strong, powerful
Dysis—sundown
Ebony—dark wood, black
Ecaterina, Ekaterina, Ecterine—pure (form of Katherine)
Echidna—monster; myth name
Echo—attended Hera; myth name
Ede, Eda—generation
Effie—fair flame
Efterpi—beauty of face
Egeria—water nymph; one of the Camenae; myth name
Eidothea—sea nymph; myth name
Eileithyia—goddess of childbirth; myth name
Eirene—goddess of peace; myth name
Elaine, Elena, Eleanor, Eleanora, Eleanore, Ellen, Elnora, Elora, Endora, Eleni, Elenitsa—light
Eldoris—of the sea
Electra—sparkling
Elefteria, Elepheteria, Elephteria—free

Elisabet, Elisabeth, Elissa, Elisia, Ellice—consecrated to God
Elma—friendly
Elpida, Elpide—hope
Endocia—unknown virtue
Ennea—born ninth
Enora—light
Enyo—goddess of war; one of the Graeae; myth name
Eos—goddess of dawn; myth name
Erasma—friendly
Erato—Muse of erotic poetry; myth name
Erianthe, Eriantha, Erianthia—sweet
Erigone—daughter of Icarius; myth name
Erinyes—one of the Furies; myth name
Eriphyle—wife of Amphiaraus; myth name
Eris—goddess of discord; myth name
Errita—pearl (form of Margaret)
Erytheia—one of the Hesperides; myth name
Esmerelda, Esmeralda—emerald
Eudosis, Eudoxia, Eduocia, Eudosia, Eudocia, Eudokia—highly regarded
Eugenia, Evgenia—well-born (form of Eugene)
Eulallia—well-spoken
Eunice—joyous victory
Eunomia—order; myth name
Euphemia, Euphemie, Ephie—well-spoken

Euphrasia—joyful
Euphrosyne—good cheer
Eurayle—wanders far
Europa—mother of Minos; myth name
Eurycleia—nurse of Odysseus; myth name
Eurydice—wife of Orpheus; myth name
Eurynome—goddess of all things; myth name
Eustella—fair star
Euterpe—Muse of the flute; myth name
Evadne—wife of Capaneus; myth name
Evangeline, Evangelia—bringer of good news
Evania—peaceful
Evanthe, Evanth—flower
Fate—destiny; myth name
Fedora—God's gift (form of Theodore)
Fern—feather
Filia—amity
Filipina—lover of horses (form of Philip)
Filomena, Filomenia—lover of man
Fotini—light
Gaea, Gaia—mother earth; myth name
Galatea—white as milk
Galen—helper, tranquil
Gelasia—inclined to laughter (form of Gelasius)
Gemina—twin
Georgia, Georgiana, Georgine,

Georgette—farmer (form of George)

Geranium—crane

Giancinta, Giancinte—hyacinth (form of Hyacinth)

Gina—well-born

Glauce—murdered by Medea; myth name

Gregoria, Gregoriana—watchful (form of Gregory)

Greta, Gretal, Grete, Gretel, Gredel, Gryta, Ghita, Gretchen—pearl (form of Margaret)

Haidee—modest

Halcyone, Alcyone—daughter of Aeolus; myth name

Halia, Helia—of the sun

Halimeda—thinking of the sea

Harmonia—daughter of Ares; myth name

Hebe—goddess of youthful beauty; myth name

Hecate—one of the Titans; myth name

Hecuba, Hekuba—wife of Priam; mother of Paris and Hector; myth name

Hedia, Hedy, Hedyla—pleasant

Helen, Helena, Helli, Helene, Helenka, Halina—light

Helice, Helike—from Helicon

Helle—daughter of Athamas; myth name

Hemera—day; myth name

Henrika—rules the home (form of Henry)

Hera, Here—wife of Zeus; myth name

Hermione, Hermandine, Hermia, Hermandina—well-born

Hero—priestess of Aphrodite; myth name

Hesione—daughter of Laomedon; myth name

Hesper, Hester—evening star

Hesperia—daughter of Cebren; one of the Hesperides; myth name

Hestia—goddess of hearth and home; myth name

Hibiscus—flower

Hilaeira—girl carried off by Pollux and Castor; myth name

Hippodamia—wife of Pirithous; myth name

Hippolyte, Hippolyta—queen of the Amazons; myth name

Horae—goddess of the season; myth name

Hyacinthe, Hyacinth—hyacinth

Hyades—name for the nymphs; myth name

Hydra—dragon killed by Hercules; myth name

Hygeia, Hygieia—goddess of health; myth name

Hypatia, Hypate—exceptional

Hypermnestra—refused to kill her husband on their wedding night; myth name

Hypsipyle—daughter of Thoas; myth name

Ianthe, Iantha, Ianthina—flower

Iasus—mother of Atalanta; myth name

Ida—name of a mountain; myth name

Idalia—myth name

Idola—vision

Ileana, Iliona—from Troy

Ilithya, Ilithia—myth name

Ilona, Ilke, Ilka, Ica, Ilay, Ilon, Ilonka, Ilu, Ilusak—light

Inesa, Inese, Ines, Inez—pure (form of Agnes)

Ino—daughter of Cadmus; myth name

Iola, Iloe—sister of Iphitus; myth name

Iolanthe, Iolantha—violet

Iona, Ione, Ionia, Ionessa—amethyst

Iphegenia—sacrificed by her father Agamemnon; myth name

Irena, Irene, Irini, Irina, Irinia, Iryna, Irynia—peace

Iris, Irisa—rainbow

Irta—pearl

Isadora, Isidora, Isadore—gift of Isis

Isaura, Isaure—gentle breeze

Ismene, Ismini—daughter of Oedipus; myth name

Ivanna—gracious God (form of John)

Ivy—ivy

Jacinta, Jacintha, Jacinthe—hyacinth (form of Hyacinth)

Jarina, Jarine—farmer

Jeno—well-born

Jocasta—queen of Thebes; myth name

Kaethe—pure

Kaia—from the earth

Kairos—myth name

Kalliope—beautiful voice

Kalonice—victory of beauty

Kalyca, Kaly, Kali, Kalie, Kalika—rosebud

Kanake—myth name

Kandake—glittering

Katherine, Kathrine, Katheryn, Kethryn, Katrina, Katarina, Katarin, Kate, Kit, Kitty, Karen, Karin, Koren, Karena, Kara, Kasia, Kassia, Kaisa, Kasen, Kasin, Katie, Katy, Katri, Kaethe, Katja, Katya, Kolina, Koline, Kora, Katakin, Katoka, Katica, Katus, Koto, Katinka, Kasienka, Kaska, Katarzyna, Kolina, Kore—pure

Kay—glory

Keleos—flaming

Kepa, Kepe—stone

Keres—evil spirits

Kineta, Kinetikos—active

Kirsten, Krista, Kristina, Khrustina, Kirsty, Kristell, Kristel, Kirstie, Krisztina, Kriszta, Kriska, Krysta, Krysia—believes in Christ (form of Christian)

Kleopatra—her father's fame

Kolete, Kolette, Klazina—victory of the people (form of Nicholas)

Kore—another name for Persephone; myth name
Koren—maiden
Kosmo, Kosma, Kasma, Kasmo—universal
Kristin, Kristen—anointed
Kynthia—moon
Lachesis—one of the Fates; myth name
Lais—favorite name with poets
Lalage, Lalia—verbose
Lamia—evil spirit who abducts and devours children; myth name
Lampetia—myth name
Lana, Lenci, Lena, Lina, Lenore, Leonora, Leora, Leonore, Leonarda—light
Laodamia—daughter of Bellerophon; wife of Protesilaus; myth name
Larissa, Larisse—happy
Layna—truth
Leda—mother of Helen; myth name
Lelia—well-spoken
Lethe—river of oblivion; myth name
Lethia, Letha, Leitha—forgetful
Leucippe—mother of Teuthras; myth name
Leucothea, Leucothia—sea nymph; myth name
Lexine, Lexina—defender of mankind
Lia, Lea—bringer of good news
Ligia—beautiful voice
Lilis, Lilia, Lillis, Lili, Lily, Lilch, Lila, Lilla—lily

Lissa—honeybee
Loni—short form of Apollonia
Lotus—lotus flower
Luigina—well-born
Lycoris—twilight
Lydia, Lydea—from Lydia
Lykaios—like the wolf
Lyris, Lyra—lyrical
Lysandra—liberator
Macaria—daughter of Hercules; myth name
Madge—approval
Madora, Medora—ruler
Magaere, Megara—one of the Furies; myth name
Maia—mother of Hermes; myth name
Malinda, Melinda—gentle
Malva, Malvina, Malvine—soft
Marmara, Marmee—shining
Marpessa—daughter of Alcippe and Evenus; myth name
Mathilde, Matilda—strong battle-maid
Medea—wife of Jason who murders her children; myth name
Medusa—cunning; one of the Gorgons; myth name
Melania, Melanie—dark
Melantha, Melanthe—dark flower
Melantho—serving girl; myth name
Melina, Melena—yellow as a canary
Melissa, Melisse, Mellisa—honeybee; nymph; myth name

Melita, Melleta, Meleta,
Meleda—sweet as honey
Melpomene—Muse of tragedy;
myth name
Merope—foster mother of
Oedipus; myth name
Metanira—wife of Celeus; myth
name
Metea—gentle
Metis—resourcefulness; myth
name
Minerva—wise
Minta, Mintha—plant name
Mnemosyne—goddess of
memory; myth name
Moerae, Moirai—one of the
Fates; myth name
Moira, Moirai—merit
Moly—herb Hermes gave to
Odysseus to protect him;
myth name
Mona—solitary
Monica, Moniqua, Monika,
Monique—counselor
Musidora, Musadora—gift of the
Muses
Myra, Mira, Mirias—abundance
Myrtle, Mytra, Merta, Myrtis,
Myrtice, Myrtisa, Myrtia,
Myrta—myrtle
Naia—flowing
Naida—water nymph; myth
name
Narkissa, Narcissa, Narcisa—
self-love (form of Narcissus)
Nathacha, Natasha, Natassia—
born on Christmas (form of
Natalie)

Nausicaa—princess who finds
Odysseus; myth name
Nella, Nell, Nelly, Nellie, Nellis,
Nelma—light
Nemesis—goddess of
vengeance; myth name
Neola—youthful
Neoma, Neomia, Neomenia,
Neomea—new moon
Nephele—cloud Hera made by
Zeus that birthed the
Centaurs; myth name
Nerine, Nerina, Neried—named
for the Nereides, sea
nymphs; myth name
Nerissa, Nerita, Nireta, Nerice—
from the sea
Neysa, Nessa, Nessia—pure
Nicia, Nicea, Nicolette, Nicoletta,
Niki, Nikolia, Nicola,
Nicole—victory of the
people (form of Nicholas)
Nike—goddess of victory; myth
name
Niobe—fern
Nitsa—peace
Norah, Nora—honor
Nox—goddess of night; myth
name
Nympha—bride
Nysa, Nyse, Nyssa—goal
Nyx—goddess of night; myth
name
Obelia, Obelie—pointed pillar
Ocypete—one of the Harpies;
myth name
Odele, Odelle—harmonious
Odelet, Odelette—little singer

Odessa, Odysseia—wrathful

Oenone—daughter of Cebren; lover of Paris; myth name

Oighrig—well-spoken

Oleisia—protector of man

Olympia, Olympe—from Olympus

Omphale—queen of Lydia; myth name

Onella, Olena, Olina—light

Ophelia—serpentine

Ophelie—wisdom

Ophira—gold

Orea, Oria—from the mountain

Orithyia—myth name

Ortygia—Calypso's island; myth name

Page—child

Pallas—wise; another name for Athene; myth name

Pamela—made from honey

Panagiota—holy (form of Panagiotis)

Pandora—released misery and hope into the world; myth name

Panphila—all-loving

Pansy—flower

Panthea—all the gods

Parthenia, Parthenie—chaste

Pasha, Pesha—born on Passover (form of Pascal)

Pasiphae—wife of Minos; myth name

Peg, Peggy, Pegeen—pearl (form of Margaret)

Pelagia—dweller by the sea

Pelicia—weaver

Pelopia—mother of Aegisthus; myth name

Pemphredo—sister of the Gorgons; myth name

Penelope—faithful wife of Odysseus; myth name

Penthea, Penthia—born fifth

Penthesilea—queen of the Amazons; myth name

Peony, Penny—flower

Pephredo—dread; myth name

Persephone, Persephonie—wife of Hades; myth name

Persis—from Persia

Petrina, Pierette, Petronella, Perrine, Petronelle, Petra, Petrine—rock (form of Peter)

Phaedra—daughter of Minos; myth name

Phaethusa—myth name

Phemie—well-spoken

Pheodora, Phedora—supreme gift

Phila—loving

Philana—lover of man

Phillida, Phillina, Philina, Philida—loving

Phillipa, Philippa—lover of horses (form of Philip)

Philomela, Philomel—nightingale

Philomena, Philomina—greatly loved

Philothea—loves God

Phoebe, Phebe—shining (form of Phoebus)

Phoenix—bird that built its own

pyre and then was reborn from the ashes; myth name

Phyllis, Phillis, Phylis, Philis—green bough

Pleasure—myth name

Podarge—one of the Harpies; myth name

Polyhymnia—Muse of sacred song; myth name

Polyxena—daughter of Priam; myth name

Procne—wife of Pandion; myth name

Psyche—lover of Cupid; myth name

Pyrena, Pyrene, Pyrenie, Pyrenia—ardent

Pyrrha—daughter of Epimetheus; myth name

Pythia—prophetess

Rena, Rina—peaceful

Resi, Rezi—gatherer

Rhea—wife of Cronus; mother of the gods; myth name

Rheta, Rita, Rhete, Reta, Reit—speaker

Rhoda, Rhodanthe, Rhodantha, Rhodia—rose

Ritsa, Ritza—protector of man

Rizpah—hope

Saba—from Sheba

Sandra, Sandrine, Sondar—defender of mankind (form of Alexander)

Sapphira, Sapphire—blue jewel

Scylla—sea monster; myth name

Sebastene, Sebastienne, Sebastiana—revered (form of Sebastian)

Selena, Selene, Selina, Selia—moon

Semele—mother of Dionysus; myth name

Sibley, Sibyl, Sybil, Sybyl, Sibylla, Sybilla—prophetess

Sinovia, Sinobia—stranger

Sirena, Sirina—named for the Sirens

Solon, Solonie, Solona, Solone—wise

Sophia, Sophie, Sofia, Sofronia, Sofi, Saffi—wise

Sophronia—of judicious mind

Stasia, Steise, Stacie, Stacy, Stacey—shall be reborn

Stephana, Stephania, Stephanie, Stephene, Stefina, Stefinia, Stevie—crowned in victory (form of Stephen)

Stheno—mighty

Strephon, Strephonn, Strep—one who turns

Styx—river of the underworld; myth name

Suadela—goddess of persuasion; myth name

Symaethis—mother of Acis; myth name

Syna—together

Syrinx—nymph; myth name

Tabitha—gazelle

Terentia—guardian

Teresa, Terese, Teresina, Terisita, Therese, Theresa, Tess, Tessie, Tressam, Terry, Tracy, Tassos, Tosia—reaper

Terpsichore—Muse of dance and lyric poetry; myth name
Tessa—born fourth
Tethys—daughter of Gaea; wife of Oceanus; myth name
Thaddea, Thaddia—brave
Thais—beloved
Thalassa—sea goddess; myth name
Thalia, Talia, Thaleia—joyous; Muse of comedy; myth name
Thea, Thia, Theola—divine
Thecla, Thekla, Tecla, Tekla—divine fame
Thelma—nursing
Themis—righteousness; myth name
Theodora, Theda, Tedra, Tedre, Theodosia—God's gift (form of Theodore)
Theone, Thenoma, Thenomia, Theona—godly (form of Theon)
Theophania, Theophaneia—God appears
Theophilia, Tesia—divinely loved (form of Theophile)
Theora, Theore, Thora—watcher
Thera, Thira, Thyra, Tyra—untamed
Thetis—mother of Achilles; myth name
Thisbe—lover of Pyramus; myth name
Tienette, Tynet—crowned in victory
Timothea, Timothia—God-fearing (form of Timothy)
Tiphanie, Theophanie, Theophane, Tifany, Tiffany, Tiffeny—gods incarnate
Tisiphone—one of the Furies; myth name
Titania—giant
Trina, Trine, Tryn, Taryn, Taren, Terran, Terrian, Terriana, Tyrna, Tryne—innocent
Tyro—nymph; myth name
Urania—heavenly
Ursa, Ursel, Ursula—little bear
Vara, Varvara, Vavara—stranger
Venessa, Vania, Vanny, Vanna—butterfly
Veronica, Veronika, Veronicha—honest image
Xanthe, Xantha, Xanthia—blonde
Xenia—welcome
Xylia, Xylina, Xylona, Xyliana, Xylinia—from the forest (form of Xylon)
Yalena, Yalene—light (form of Helen)
Yolanda, Yolande—violet
Zandra, Zondra—defender of mankind (form of Alexander)
Zanita—long teeth
Zelia, Zelina, Zelinia—zealous
Zenaide, Zenaida—myth name
Zenia, Zena, Zene—friendly
Zenobia, Zenobe, Zena, Zenna, Zenina, Zenda, Zenaida—born of Zeus

Zephyr, Zyphire, Zefiryn,
    Zephyra, Zephira—of the
    west wind
Zeta—born last
Zeva—sword
Zoe, Zoelie, Zoelle, Zoel, Zoya,
    Zoia—alive

Zosima—lively
Zsofia, Zsofie, Zofia, Zofie—wise
    (form of Sophia)
Zyta, Zita—reaper

MALE

Abderus—friend of Hercules;
    myth name
Absyrtus—murdered by his
    sister Medea; myth name
Abydos—from Abydos
Acastus—one of the Argonauts;
    son of Pelias; myth name
Acestes, Agestes—myth name
Achates—friend of Aeneas;
    myth name
Achelous—river god; myth
    name
Acheron—river of woe; myth
    name
Achilles—lipless; hero of the
    Greeks; myth name
Acis—son of Faunus; lover of
    Galatea; myth name
Aconteus—myth name
Acrisius—father of Danae;
    grandfather of Perseus;
    myth name
Acteon, Actaeon—hunter torn
    apart by his own dogs; myth
    name
Admetus—king of Pherae; myth
    name

Adonis—lover of Aphrodite;
    myth name
Adrastus—one of the Seven
    against Thebes; myth name
Aeacus—grandfather of
    Achilles; myth name
Aeetes—Medea's father; myth
    name
Aegeus—second husband of
    Medea; myth name
Aegis—shield of Zeus; myth
    name
Aegisthus—cousin of
    Agememnon; myth name
Aegyptus—brother of Danaus;
    father of the Danaides; myth
    name
Aeneas—praiseworthy
Aeolus—god of the winds; myth
    name
Aesculapius, Asklepios—god of
    medicine; myth name
Aeson—father of Jason; myth
    name
Agamedes—murdered by his
    brother for theft; myth name
Agamemnon—leader of the

Greek forces against Troy;
myth name

Agenor—son of Poseidon; myth
name

Ajax—one of the Greeks at Troy;
myth name

Akil—from the river Akil

Alastair, Alastor, Alasdair—
avenger

Alicides—descended from
Alcaeus

Alcinous, Alcinoos—father of
Nausicaa; helped Odysseus
return home; myth name

Alcmaeon—son of Amphiaraus;
myth name

Alcyoneus—fought against
Athena; myth name

Alexander, Alexis, Alec, Alex,
Aleksandur, Alessandro,
Alexandros, Alexandras,
Alexandrukas, Alix,
Aleksandr, Aleksy, Alexio,
Alexei, Alyosha,
Alyoshenka—defender of
mankind

Aloeus—father of giants; myth
name

Alphenor—myth name

Alpheus—river god; myth name

Ambrose, Ambrus, Ambrocio,
Athan, Athanasius,
Anstice—immortal

Amphiaraus—one of the Seven
against Thebes; myth name

Amphion—son of Zeus; myth
name

Amphitryon—husband of
Alcmene; myth name

Ampyx—father of Mopsus; myth
name

Amycus—son of Poseidon; myth
name

Anastasius, Anasztaz, Anastagio,
Anastasio—one who will be
reborn (form of Anastasia)

Anatole, Anatoli, Anatolio,
Anatolijus, Anatol—from the
east

Ancaeus—one of the Argonauts;
myth name

Anchises—father of Aeneas;
myth name

Anderson, Anders, Papandrou—
son of Ander

Andraemon—myth name

Andrew, Ander, Andres, Anker,
Antti, Adras, Andor,
Aindreas, Aindriu, Androu,
Aniol, Anndra, Andrea,
Andries—manly

Androgeus—son of Minos; myth
name

Angell, Angel, Angelo—angel

Anibal—graced by God

Anstice, Anastasios, Anstiss—
resurrected

Antaeus—killed by Hercules;
myth name

Anteros—brother of Eros; myth
name

Anthony, Anton, Antony—
priceless

Anthor—myth name

Antilochus—son of Nestor; myth
 name
Antinous—one of Penelope's
 suitors; myth name
Antiphates—king of the
 Laestrygones; myth name
Aonghas, Angus—exceptionally
 strong
Apollo, Apoloniusz—manly
 beauty; myth name
Arcas—son of Callisto and Zeus;
 myth name
Archemorus—son of Lycurgus;
 myth name
Ares—god of war; myth name
Argo—name of Jason's ship;
 myth name
Argus, Argos—all-seeing
Arion—horse of Adrastus; myth
 name
Aristaeus—son of Apollo; myth
 name
Aristid—son of a great man
Aristotle—intelligent
Arsene, Arsenio—strong
Artemas, Artemus, Artemesio—
 gift from Artemis
Ascalaphus—turned into an owl
 by Persephone; myth name
Asopus—river god; myth name
Astyanax—son of Hector killed
 at Troy; myth name
Athamas—brother of Sisyphus;
 father of Phrixus and Helle;
 myth name
Athanasios—noble
Atlas—one of the Titans; myth
 name

Atreides—descended from
 Atreus
Atreus—father of Agamemnon;
 myth name
Attis—son of Manes; myth name
Auster—myth name
Autolycus—son of Hermes;
 myth name
Avernus—portal to Hades; myth
 name
Balasi—flat-footed
Baltsaros, Balthasar—one of the
 three wise men (form of
 Balthazar)
Baptiste—baptizer
Baruch—blessed
Basil, Basile, Basilio, Bazyli—
 regal
Bastien, Bastiaan, Baste—
 revered (form of Sebastian)
Baucis, Baccus, Baccaus—name
 of Dionysus; myth name
Bellerophon—son of Glaucus;
 slew Chimera; myth name
Biton—son of priestess; myth
 name
Boethius—myth name
Boreas—north wind; myth name
Briareus—one of the Titans;
 myth name
Cadmon—myth name
Cadmus—from the east; son of
 Agenor; myth name
Calais—son of Boreas; myth
 name
Calchas—seer; myth name
Capaneus—one of the Seven
 against Thebes; myth name

Castor—twin of Polydeuces and brother of Helen of Troy; myth name

Cebriones—myth name

Cecrops—founder of Athens; myth name

Celeus—father of Triptolemus; myth name

Cenon—friendly

Cephalus—husband who killed Procris; myth name

Cepheus—father of Andromeda; myth name

Cerberus—guardian to the gate of Hades; myth name

Cercyon—name of a king; myth name

Cesare, Caesare, Caseareo—long-haired (form of Caesar)

Cetus—sea monster of Poseidon; myth name

Ceyx—husband of Alcyone; myth name

Charon—ferryman across the river Styx; myth name

Chimera—monster killed by Bellerophon; myth name

Chiron—centaur; myth name

Christian, Cretien, Chris, Christiano—believes in Christ

Christopher, Cristophe, Christobel, Christoph, Christophoros, Cristoforo, Christoffel—Christ-bearer

Christos—Christ

Chryses—priest of Apollo; myth name

Chrysostom—golden-mouthed

Claus, Claas, Colum, Cole—victory of the people (form of Nicholas)

Cleobis—son of a priestess; myth name

Cletus—summoned

Cocytus—river of lamenting; myth name

Coeus—father of Leto; myth name

Corineus—myth name

Corybantes—priest of Rhea; myth name

Corydon, Coridan—ready to fight

Cosmas, Cosmo, Cosima, Cos—order

Cottus—one of the Titans; myth name

Creon—Jocasta's brother; myth name

Cronus—one of the Titans; myth name

Cycnus—swan

Cyprian—from Cyprus

Cyr, Cyril, Cyryl, Cyrek, Coireall, Cirilo, Ciro, Cirio—lordly

Cyrano—from Cyrene

Cyrus, Ciro, Cy—sun

Daedalus—killed his nephew; myth name

Daemon—guardian spirit; myth name

Damaskenos, Damaskinos—from Damascus

Damian, Damen, Damae—tame

Damocles—tyrant of Syracuse; myth name

Danaus—king of Argos; father of the Danaides; myth name

Daphnis—shepherd blinded for his infidelity; myth name

Dardanus—founder of Troy; father of Erichthonius; myth name

Deiphobus—son of Priam; myth name

Delphinus—scout of Poseidon; myth name

Demetrius, Demetri, Demetre, Demetrios—gift from Demeter

Demodocus—blind bard; myth name

Demogorgon—thought to be the name for Satan; myth name

Demophon—son of Theseus; myth name

Deucalion—son of Prometheus; myth name

Dhimitrios—myth name

Diomedes—evil king; myth name

Dionysus, Denes, Dion, Dunixi, Denys, Dionysios, Dionysius—god of wine; myth name

Dolius—shepherd; myth name

Doran—gift

Dorian—of the sea

Echion—myth name

Egidio—shield-bearer

Elek, Eli—defender of mankind (form of Alexander)

Eleutherios, Eleftherios—free

Elpenor—one of Odysseus' men; myth name

Enceladus—giant; myth name

KARYN LANGHORNE

Karyn Langhorne has written three nonfiction books, a play, screen-plays, and novels. Her first novel, *A Personal Matter*, was published with HarperCollins.

It's very popular in the African-American culture for new moms to make up their own names based on an existing name—"updating them" with a new rhythm, usually by adding sounds to the beginning or the end. For example, in *A Personal Matter*, I created several young black women who had made-up names like Diamonique, T'keysa, and Nalexi. In *Gansta Psychic*, I made up LaTae and Carmenique. The names suit younger women in particular—and makes the story very realistic—something you want in a contemporary novel.

Endre—manly (form of Andrew)

Endymion—shepherd; myth name

Enea—born ninth

Eneas—praised

Epeius—maker of the Trojan horse; myth name

Epopeus—myth name

Erasmus—worthy of love

Ercole—gift from God

Erebus—father of Charon; myth name

Erechtheus—king of Athens; myth name

Erichthonius—king of Athens; myth name

Erymanthus—son of Apollo; myth name

Erysichthon—cursed with an insatiable hunger that caused his death; myth name

Estebe, Estevao—crowned in victory (form of Stephen)

Eteocles—son of Oedipus; myth name

Etor, Ettore, Eachann—steadfast

Eubuleus—told Demeter about her daughter; myth name

Eugene, Eugen, Eugenios, Eugenio, Evasn, Eoghan—well-born

Eumaeus—swineherd who fought with Odysseus; myth name

Eupeithes—father of one of Penelope's suitors; myth name

Eurus—god of the east wind; myth name

Euryalus—taunted Odysseus; myth name

Eurylochus—turned into a pig by Circe; myth name

Eurymachus—one of Penelope's suitors; myth name

Eurypylus—soldier against Greece in the Trojan War; myth name

Eurystheus—cousin of Hercules; myth name

Euryton—giant; myth name

Eusebius—pious

Eustace, Eustis, Eustachy—fruitful

Evzen—noble

Farris—rock

Fedor, Feodor—God's gift (form of Theodore)

Feodras—stone

Filippo, Fulop, Flip, Filips—lover of horses (form of Philip)

Galen—helper, tranquil

Galinthias—servant of Alcmene; myth name

Ganymede, Genymede—cup-bearer to the gods; myth name

Gelasius—inclined to laughter

George, Georg, Georges, Georget, Gorka, Gyorgy, Gyoergy, Gyuri, Gyurka, Geordie, Goran, Gheorghe—farmer

Geryon—monster killed by Hercules; myth name

Giles, Gilles—shield-bearer

Glaucus—son of Minos; myth name

Gregory, Gregoire, Gregorie, Gregor, Grigor, Gruev, Grigorov, Gregos, Gergely, Gergor, Gregorio—watchful

Guilio—youthful (form of Julian)

Gyes—one of the Titans; myth name

Haemon—son of Creon; myth name

Hali—sea

Halirrhothius—son of Poseidon; myth name

Halithersis—seer who warns Penelope's suitors; myth name

Haralambos—meaning unknown

Hasione—myth name

Hector—steadfast

Helenus—son of Priam; myth name

Helios—god of the sun; myth name

Hephaestus—god of the crafts; myth name

Herakles, Hercules—Hera's glory; myth name

Hermes—messenger of the gods; myth name

Hesperos—evening star

Hieronim—meaning unknown

Hipolit, Hippolytus—freer of horses

Hippocampus—Poseidon's horse; myth name

Hippogriff—part horse, part griffin; myth name

Hippolytus—son of Theseus; myth name

Hippomedon—one of the Seven against Thebes; myth name

Hippomenes—winner of Atalanta; myth name

Homer, Homerus, Homeros—security

Hyancinthe, Hyacinthus—hyacinth (form of Hyacinth)

Hylas—son of Theiodamas; myth name

Hymen—god of marriage; myth name

Hypnos—god of sleep; myth name

Hyrieus—myth name

Iapetus—one of the Titans; myth name

Iasion—father of Plutus; myth name

Iasius—myth name

Iason—healer

Ibycus—bard; myth name

Icarius—gave wine to the citizens of Athens, who mistook it for poison and killed him; myth name

Icarus—son of Daedalus; myth name

Icelos—son of Hypnos; myth name

Idas—one of the Argonauts; myth name

Idomeneus—king of Crete; myth name

Ignatius—fiery

Inachus—river god; father of Io; myth name

Iobates—myth name

Ion—son of Apollo; myth name

Iorgas, Igor—farmer

Iphicles—twin of Hercules; myth name

Iphis—hanged himself over unrequited love; myth name

Iphitus—brother of Iole; myth name

Irus—challenged Odysseus on his return to Ithaca; myth name

Isidore, Isadore, Ixidor, Isidoro, Isidro—strong gift

Istvan—crowned in victory (form of Stephen)

Ivan, Ivanko—gracious God (form of John)

Ixion—father of the centaurs; myth name

Jacinto—hyacinth (form of Hyacinth)

Jason, Jasun, Jay—healer; sought the Golden Fleece with the Argonauts; myth name

Jeno, Jencir—well-born

Jerome, Jeroen—sacred

Jiri, Jirkar, Jurgisr, Jorisr, Jerzyr, Jorgenr, Jornr, Jorgr, Jorenr—farmer (form of George)

Julian, Julius—youthful

Kadmus—from the east

Kaj—earth

Karsten, Kristr—believes in Christ (form of Christian)

Kedalion—myth name

Keril, Kiril, Kyrillos, Kuirilr, Kirylr—lordly

Kester, Kestorr, Kitr, Kipr, Krisr, Kristor, Kristofr, Krystupasr—Christ-bearer (form of Christopher)

Khristos—Christ

Klaus, Klaas—victory of the people (form of Nicholas)

Kolya—victorious army

Korudon—helmeted

Kosmy, Kosmos—order

Kratos—strength

Krikor—watchful (form of Gregory)

Kristian, Krischanr, Krzysztofr, Khrystiyanr—believes in Christ (form of Christian)

Kyrillos—lordly

Kyros—master

Ladon—Hera's dragon; myth name

Laertes—father of Odysseus; myth name

Laestrygones—tribe of giants; myth name

Laius—father of Oedipus; myth name

Laocoon—son of Priam; myth name

Laomedon—father of Priam; myth name

Lasse—victory of the people (form of Nicholas)

Leander, Lander, Leandro—
brave lion (form of Leonard)
Leksi—defender of mankind
(form of Alexander)
Lethe—river of oblivion; myth
name
Lichas—friend of Hercules;
myth name
Lidio—meaning unknown
Linus—flaxen-haired
Lippi, Lipp, Lippio—lover of
horses (form of Philip)
Loxias—crooked
Lycaon—king of Arcadia; myth
name
Lycomedes—king of Scyros;
myth name
Lycurgus—king of the Edones;
myth name
Lynceus—one of the Argonauts;
myth name
Lysander—liberator
Macaire, Makarioa, Marcario—
blessed
Machaon—son of Aesculapius;
myth name
Marsyas—satyr; myth name
Maur, Maurice—dark-skinned
Medus—son of Medea by
Aegeus; myth name
Melampus—seer; myth name
Melanippus—helped defend
Thebes from the Seven
against Thebes; myth name
Melanthius—sides with
Penelope's suitors against his
master Odysseus; myth name

Meleager—one of the
Argonauts; myth name
Melecertes—son of Ino; myth
name
Meletios—meaning unknown
Menelaus—brother of
Agamemnon; myth name
Menoeceus—father of Jocasta;
myth name
Mentor—wise counselor
Mette—pearl
Mezentius—myth name
Midas—turned everything he
touched to gold; myth name
Mikolas—victory of the people
(form of Nicholas)
Mimis—myth name
Minos—king of Crete; son of
Zeus; myth name
Momus—god of ridicule; myth
name
Mopsus—seer; myth name
Morpheus—bringer of dreams;
myth name
Myles, Miles, Milo—destroyer
Myron—myrrh
Nape—myth name
Napolean, Napoleon—of the
new city
Narcissus, Narkis, Narcisse—
self-love; myth name
Nauplius—one of the Argonauts;
myth name
Nectarios—name of a saint
Neleus—son of Poseidon; myth
name
Nemo, Nemos—from the glen
Neotolemus—son of Achilles;
myth name

Nereus—god of the sea; father of the Nereids; myth name

Nestor—wisdom

Nicholas, Nicholaus, Nicolas, Niles, Nils, Nokolai, Nik, Nick, Nicodemus, Nikodem, Nicole, Nicolaus, Nicol, Nilo, Nikita, Nikolos, Nilos, Niocole, Niocol, Niklaus, Nikolajis—victory of the people

Nisus—father of Scylla; myth name

Notus—south wind; myth name

Obelix—pillar of strength

Obiareus—one of the Titans; myth name

Oceanus—father of the Oceanids; myth name

Ocnus—incompetent

Odysseus—wrathful; Greek hero whose return from the Trojan War took ten years; myth name

Oedipus—swollen foot; killed his father and married his mother; myth name

Oeneus—king of Calydon; myth name

Oenomaus—son of Ares; myth name

Oighrig—well-spoken

Oles—defender of mankind (form of Alexander)

Ophion—serpent; myth name

Orestes, Oreste, Oreias—from the mountain; killed his mother and her lover to avenge his murdered father; myth name

Orion—son of fire

Orpheus—son of Apollo; myth name

Orthros—guardian of Geryon; myth name

Otis, Otos, Otus—keen of hearing

Owen—young warrior

Palaemon—sea god; myth name

Palamedes—son of Nauplius; myth name

Pan—god of flocks; myth name

Panagiotis—holy

Pancratius—supreme ruler

Pandareos—thief; myth name

Pandarus—Trojan soldier killed for breaking a truce; myth name

Panteleimon—merciful

Parthenios—virgin

Parthenopaeus—one of the Seven against Thebes; myth name

Paris—son of Priam; abductor of Helen of Troy; myth name

Patroclus—friend of Achilles; myth name

Pegasus—winged horse; myth name

Peisistratus—son of Nestor; myth name

Peleus—father of Achilles; myth name

Pelias—son of Poseidon; myth name

Pelops—father of Atreus; myth name

Peneus—myth name
Pentheus—king of Thebes; myth name
Perdix—apprentice Daedalus murdered; myth name
Pericles—myth name
Persius, Perseus—son of Danae; myth name
Peter, Pedro, Petr, Piotr, Peder, Perrin, Pekka, Petros, Panos, Pierro, Pietro, Pero, Peterke, Piero, Pello, Peru, Piarres, Preben, Per, Petter, Pierre, Pertras, Petrukas, Petrelis, Piet, Pieter, Pietr, Pedar, Peadair, Prophyrios, Piaras—rock
Phaethon—son of Helios; myth name
Phantasos—son of Hypnos; myth name
Phaon—ferryman; myth name
Phemius—bard; myth name
Philander—lover of man
Philemon—loves thought
Philip, Pippo, Philippe, Phillip, Philipp, Pilib—lover of horses
Philo, Phylo—friend
Philoctetes—killed Paris; myth name
Philoetius—cowherd; myth name
Phineas, Phinees, Phineus—oracle
Phlegethon—river of fire; myth name
Phoebus—shining

Phoenix—bird that built its own pyre and then was reborn from the ashes; myth name
Phrixus—son of Nephele; myth name
Phorbas, Phorbus—myth name
Phorcys—sea god; myth name
Pirithous—friend of Theseus; myth name
Pirro—red-haired
Pittheus—king of Trozen; myth name
Pityocamptes—pine-bender
Plato—broad
Plexippus—one of the Argonauts; myth name
Plutus—wealthy; myth name
Polites—myth name
Pollux—brother of Helen; myth name
Polycarp—much fruit
Polydamas—Trojan soldier; myth name
Polydeuces—twin of Castor and brother of Helen of Troy; myth name
Polydorus—son of Priam; myth name
Polyeidus—seer; myth name
Polymestor—son-in-law of Priam; myth name
Polynices—son of Oedipus; one of the Seven against Thebes; myth name
Polyphemus—son of Poseidon; myth name
Pontus—sea
Porfirio—purple stone

Poseidon—god of the sea and ocean; myth name
Priam—king of Troy; myth name
Priapus—god of fertility; myth name
Procrustes—stretcher; myth name
Prokopios—declared leader
Prometheus—gave fire to man; myth name
Protesilaus—offered himself as a sacrifice for the Greeks when they arrived at Troy; myth name
Proteus—sea god; myth name
Pygmalion—king of Cyprus; myth name
Pylades—friend of Orestes; myth name
Pyramus—lover of Thisbe; myth name
Pyrrhus—king of Epirus; myth name
Rasmus—amiable
Rhadamanthus—judge in the underworld; myth name
Rhesus—king of Thrace; myth name
Rhoecus—saved Hamadryad; myth name
Risto—Christ-bearer (form of Christopher)
Rodas—rose garden
Salmoneus—king of Elis who, during Trojan War, pretended to be Zeus; myth name
Sanders, Saunders, Sander,

Sandor—defender of mankind (form of Alexander)
Sarpedon—Trojan soldier killed by Patroclus during the Trojan War; myth name
Sebastian, Sebastien, Sebestyen, Sebastiano—revered
Seoirse, Seorsa—farmer (form of George)
Sidney, Sydney—from Sidon
Simon, Simeon, Symeon—God is heard
Sinon—convinced the Trojans to pull the horse inside the city walls; myth name
Sisyphus—son of Aelous; myth name
Socrates—name of philosopher
Soterios—savior
Spyridon—round basket
Stamitos—enduring
Stephen, Steven, Stefan, Stefano, Stephano, Steverino, Stavros, Stefanos, Steafan, Staffen—crowned in victory
Stoffel—Christ-bearer (form of Christopher)
Takis—all-holy
Talus—mechanical man made by Hephaestus; myth name
Tantalus—condemned to eternal torment; myth name
Taxiarchai—archangel
Telamon—father of Ajax; myth name
Telegonus—son of Odysseus; myth name

Telemachus—son of Odysseus;
myth name
Telephus—son of Hercules;
myth name
Tereus—king of Thrace; myth
name
Teucer—archer; myth name
Teuthras—king of Mysia; myth
name
Thamyris—musician punished
for hubris; myth name
Thanatos—death; myth name
Thanos, Thanasis—noble
Thaumas—father of the Harpies;
myth name
Theoclymenus—befriended by
Telemachus; myth name
Theodore, Theodosios, Teadoir,
Teodors, Theodrekr, Todor,
Tuder, Tudor, Tivadar—
God's gift
Theon—godly
Theophile, Teofile—divinely
loved
Theron—hunter
Thersites—soldier in the Trojan
War; myth name
Theseus—son of Aegeus; myth
name
Thyestes—brother of Atreus;
myth name
Tigris—myth name
Timothy, Timon, Timun,
Timotheos, Timothea,
Tiomoid, Tymon, Tymek,
Tymoteusz—God-fearing
Tiresias—blind seer; myth name
Titos, Tito, Titus—giant

Tityus—giant; myth name
Toxeus—brother of Althaea;
myth name
Tracy, Tracey—bold
Triptolemus—taught
agriculture by Demeter;
myth name
Triton—sea god; son of
Poseidon; myth name
Trophonius—brother of
Agamedes; myth name
Tydeus—father of Diomedes;
one of the Seven against
Thebes; myth name
Tyndareus—father of Castor
and Polydeuces; myth name
Typhon, Typhoeus—child of the
Titans; myth name
Tyrone, Turannos—lord
Ulysses—wrathful
Uranus—sky; myth name
Urian—from heaven
Vanko—gracious God
Vasilis, Vasos, Vasileios, Vasyl,
Vasylko, Vasyltso—regal
(form of Basil)
Xanthus—immortal horse
belonging to Achilles; myth
name
Xenophon, Xeno—strange voice
Xenos—stranger
Xerxes—leaving
Xuthus—son of Helen; myth
name
Xylon—from the forest
Yrjo, Yurii, Yura, Yurochka,
Yure, Yuri, Yehor—farmer
(form of George)

Zale—power of the sea
Zarek—God protect the king
Zelotes—zealous
Zelus—myth name
Zenas—living
Zeno, Zeus—supreme ruler of
the gods; myth name

Zenon—friendly
Zephyrus—myth name
Zetes—son of Boreas; myth
name
Zoltan, Zoltar—life
Zotikos—meaning unknown

HEBREW

Since the Hebrews have no single national identity, surnames developed at odd intervals in communities throughout the world. Most last names were patronymic in a fashion similar to Arabic names. Now they tend to be more place oriented. Before hereditary surnames became common, Hebrews used *Ben* (son of) followed by their father's name, or they used the name of their home or a name from the Bible.

The first Hebrew surnames occurred in Spain. During the Middle Ages, Hebrews in Germany used the name of their houses for a surname. In 1785 in Austria, they were required to take surnames, and in 1787 they were restricted to using biblical names only.

In 1804, Russia prevented the Hebrews from altering their names. And in 1844, Russia compelled them to adopt surnames.

Poland passed laws in 1821 to require Hebrews to choose surnames. As late as 1942, France forbade them to change their names.

Again, there is wide variety in Hebrew surnames, when they came into being, and what form they took. Many Jewish surnames are indistinguishable from other surnames of the cultures in which they arose. I would caution writers to do more research on the nomenclature of the region and branch of the Hebrews they are interested in.

A few surnames:

Aboab	Daoud
Abrams	Einstein
Altschul	Farache
Amselem	Gabra
Baruch	Ginsberg
Benabu	Goldstein
Ben-David	Greenberg
Benjamin	Grün
Ben-Shlomo	Halevi
Berliner	Hasson
Blum	Herzhaft
Cardoso	Hitzig
Cassel	Isaac

Joseph
Kantor
Kleinlerer
Kohn
Levine
Levy
Malka
Mindel
Myer

Rabbinowitz
Reis
Rosenberg
Rosenthal
Schwab
Segal
Serrafe
Sinai
Tischler

FEMALE

Abarrane—father of many (form of Abraham)

Abelia, Abelie—breath (form of Abel)

Abigail, Abegayle, Abaigael, Abaigeal, Abby, Abbie, Avichayil, Abichail, Avigail—gives joy

Abir, Abira—strong

Abra—father of many (form of Abraham)

Achazia—held by the Lord

Adah—beautiful

Adama—of the red earth (form of Adam)

Adar, Adara—fire

Aderes—protector

Adiel—God's ornament

Adine, Adinam, Adena, Adene—tender

Admina—of the red earth (form of Adam)

Afra—doe

Ahuva, Ahava, Ahuda, Ahave—dearly loved

Ailat, Ayalah—behind

Ailsa, Ailsie—consecrated to God (form of Elizabeth)

Akiva, Akibe, Akiba—protected

Aleeza, Aliza, Alizah, Alitza, Aleezah—joyous

Alona, Allona, Allonia, Alonia—strong as an oak

Alumit, Aluma—girl

Amaris, Amariah, Amarisa, Amarise, Amarissa—given by God

Anamari, Annamarie, Anamarie—bitter grace

Anat, Anate, Anata, Anatie—singer

Ann, Anne, Ane, Annie, Anny, Ayn, Anna, Ana, Annette, Anetta, Anita, Anitra, Annora, Annorah, Anora, Anais, Antje, Ance, Aneta, Anka, Asenka, Anyuta, Asenke, Annze, Anica, Anichka, Asya, Anku—grace

Anneliese, Annaliese, Annalisa, Analise—grace, consecrated to God

Annikki, Aniki, Aniko, Annikka, Anika, Annikke—grace
Annot—light
Aoife—life (form of Eve)
Araminta, Araminte—lofty
Ardath, Aridatha—flowering field
Ariel, Arielle, Ariela, Ariellel, Athaleyah—lioness of God
Ashira—wealthy
Ateret, Atarah, Atara—crowned
Athalia, Athalie, Atalia, Atalie—God is great
Atira, Atera—pray
Avera—transgresses
Avivit, Avivi, Aviva—innocent
Axelle, Axella—father of peace (form of Axel)
Aya, Aiya—bird
Azalea, Azelia, Azelie, Aziel—flower
Aziza—meaning unknown
Bathsheba, Bethsheba—oath
Battseeyon, Battzion—daughter of Zion
Batya, Bitya—daughter of God
Beathag—to serve God
Becky—captivating
Benta—wise
Beruriah—selected by God
Bethel, Betheli—house of God
Bethseda, Bethsaida—merciful
Bettina, Bettine, Betti, Betty, Bozi, Bella, Betje, Betsy—consecrated to God (form of Elizabeth)
Beulah, Beula—to marry
Bina—intelligence; musical instrument

Bracha, Brachah—blessed
Carmel—garden
Carmella, Carmela, Carmeline, Carmelina—garden (form of Carmel)
Carmen—guard
Cassia—cinnamon
Chanah, Chana—graceful
Chasidah—pious
Chasya, Chasye—shelter
Chava, Chaya, Chabah, Chaba, Chayka, Chaka—life
Chaviva, Chavive—dearly loved (form of Chavivi)
Chedva—joyous
Chephzibah—she is our delight
Cochava—star
Csilla—defender
Daba—kind words
Daganyah, Daganya—ceremonial grain
Dalit, Dalis—drawing water
Daliyah, Daliah—tree branch
Danette, Daniela, Danita, Danele, Danelle, Danielle, Danae, Danya, Danila, Dania, Danetta, Danit—God is my judge (form of Daniel)
Daphna, Daphnah, Daphne—victory
Dara—compassion
Davina, Davinia, Davinah, Davida, Davi, Davite, Davitah—beloved (form of David)
Dayla—branch
Debora, Deborah, Debra, Devora, Devoria—bee

Delilah, Delila, Dalila—desired
Dena, Dina, Dinah—avenged
Derora, Derorit, Derorice—free
Divsha, Divshah—honey
Dodie—beloved
Eden, Edan—perfect
Edra, Edrea, Edria—powerful
Efrosina—fawn
Eliora, Eleora, Elora—God is
    light
Elka, Elke—oath to God
Ellice, Eliane, Elia, Eliana—
    Jehovah is God
Elspeth, Elli, Elizabeth,
    Elisabeth, Elisabet, Elsie,
    Eliza, Erzsebet, Elisheva, Els,
    Elzira, Elizaveta, Elisaveta,
    Elisavet—consecrated to
    God
Emmanuelle, Emunah,
    Emmanuella—God is with us
    (form of Emmanuel)
Endora—fountain
Erelah, Erela—angel
Erith, Eritha—flower
Ester, Eszter, Esther, Estrela—
    star
Etana—determined
Etel, Etilka, Ethel—noble
Eva, Eve, Eeva, Evika, Evike,
    Evacska, Ewa—life
Evelyn—light; gives life
Fifne, Fifna, Fina—God adds
    (form of Joseph)
Gabrielle, Gabriella, Gavra,
    Gavrila, Gavrilla, Gabriele—
    God-given strength (form of
    Gabriel)

Gail, Gayle, Gayleen, Gaylene—
    father's joy
Galia, Gallia, Galilah, Galila,
    Galya, Galina, Galenka,
    Galochka—God shall
    redeem
Galit, Gali, Galice—fountain
Ganit, Ganet, Gana, Ganice—
    garden
Gazit, Gisa, Giza—cut stone
Geva—hill
Gilah, Gila, Gilit, Geela, Gilia, Gili,
    Gilala, Gilal, Gilana, Gilat—
    eternal joy
Giuseppina, Giuseppie—God
    adds (form of Joseph)
Grazyna, Grazina, Grazinia—
    grace (form of Grace)
Guiditta—praise
Gurit, Gurice—cub
Hadar, Hadara—glory
Hadassah—myrtle
Hagar—flight
Hali—necklace
Hannah, Hanan, Hanna, Hanne,
    Hannele, Hannela—gracious
    God (form of John)
Haya—life
Heba—gift of God
Hedia—God's voice
Hedva—joy
Helsa—devoted to God
Hephzibah, Hepsiba,
    Hepzibeth—she is my
    delight
Hulda, Holda—weasel
Ideh—praise
Ilana, Ilanit—tree
Ilia—God is Lord

Ilse—God's word
Ionanna—grace
Iris—flower
Isabel, Izabella, Isabelle, Isabella, Isibeal—consecrated to God (form of Elizabeth)
Ivana, Ivane, Iva, Ivanna—gracious God (form of John)
Izso—God's salvation
Jacoba, Jakoba, Jakobah, Jaquenette, Jaquetta, Jocelin, Joceline, Jocelyn, Jaqueline, Jaquelina—supplanter (form of Jacob)
Jada—wise
Jael—mountain goat
Jaen—ostrich
Jaffa, Jafit, Jafita—beauty
Janet, Jane, Jayne, Janetta, Janette, Janice, Janis, Joan, Joanna, Johanna, Jone, Jan, Jenda, Jana, Jaine, Janie, Janne, Janine, Janka, Janina, Janita, Jansje, Jans, Jaantje, Juana, Juanita, Joka—gracious God (form of John)
Jardena, Jardina—meaning unknown
Jemima, Jonati—dove
Jemina—listened to
Jensine, Jensina—God has blessed
Jerusha—married
Jessica, Jessie—wealthy
Joakima, Jokine, Jokina, Joaquina, Joaquine—God will establish (form of Joachim)

Jobina, Jobyna—persecuted (form of Job)
Jochebed—God's glory (form of Jocheved)
Joelle, Joella, Joelliane, Joelliana, Jola—Jehovah is God
Jora—rain in autumn
Jordane, Jordan—descended
Josepha, Josephine, Josette, Josetta, Josepina, Joxepa, Josebe, Jose, Josie, Josee, Jozsa—God adds (form of Joseph)
Judith, Judy, Judie, Jodie, Judit, Juci, Jutka, Jucika—praised (form of Jude)
Kadisha—holy
Kalanit—flower
Karmia, Karmit, Karmelit, Karmelita, Karmelite—Lord's vineyard
Kazia, Ketzia, Kezia—cinnamon
Kefira—lion cub
Kelilah, Kelula, Kyla—victorious
Keren, Keryn, Keran—horn
Ketura—incense
Kinneret, Kinnette—harp
Kiva, Kivi, Kiba—protected
Ksena—praise be to God
Laila, Lailie, Laili, Laylie—night
Lea, Leah—tired
Ledah—birth
Lemuela, Lise, Liza, Lisabette, Lisabet, Lisavet, Liesbeth, Liesbet, Lizbeth, Lizbet—consecrated to God (form of Elizabeth)

Lesham—previous
Levia—join
Lewanna—moon
Lilith, Lily, Lilie, Lilah—lily
Lirit, Lirita—poetic
Livana—white
Magda, Magdalen, Magdalene,
   Magdala, Magdalena,
   Madalen, Maialen, Matxalen,
   Madel, Maidel, Madeleine,
   Madelaine, Madelene,
   Madelena, Madalyn, Malina,
   Marlene, Marlena—from the
   tower
Mahala, Mahalia—tender
Maia—bitter
Malak—messenger
Malcah, Malkah, Milcah—queen
Mangena—melody
Manuela—God is with us (form
   of Emmanuel)
Mariamne, Miriam—rebellious
Maribel, Maribelle, Maribella—
   bitter, beautiful
Marla—bitter
Marna, Marnina—joyful (form of
   Marnin)
Mary, Mara, Mae, Maria, Maren,
   Miren, Mariette, Marika,
   Mallaidh, Marie, Marion,
   Mariska, Molly, May, Marily,
   Marthe, Martha, Mirit, Miri,
   Mira, Marisha—bitter
Matea, Mattea, Matthea,
   Matthia, Mathea, Mathia—
   God's gift (form of Matthew)
Mava—pleasant
Mayah, Maia—close to God

Mazel—luck
Mehetabel, Mehitabelle,
   Mettabel, Meheytabel—
   God's favor
Meira—light
Menachemah, Menachema—
   consolation (form of
   Menachem)
Menuha—peaceful
Michelle, Micheline, Michaele,
   Michalin, Mikele, Michaela,
   Michaelina—who is like God
   (form of Michael)
Mitzi, Mieze—small, bitter
Moria, Moriah, Morit, Moriel,
   Morice, Morise—God
   teaches
Moselle—from the water
Naamah, Naomi, Neomi, Navit—
   pleasant
Naamit—bird
Naavah, Naava—beautiful
Nathania—gift from God (form
   of Nathaniel)
Naysa—miracle of God
Nechama, Nehama—comfort
Nedivah, Nediva—giving
Neorah, Nora, Norah—light
Neta, Nita—grace
Nili—success
Nina, Nana, Nan, Nanna, Nancy,
   Nanelle, Nanelia, Nanette,
   Nanetta, Nanine, Nanny,
   Nannie, Nancsi, Ninacska,
   Nusi, Nusa, Nainsi, Nin—
   grace
Niria, Nira—plow

Nirit, Nurit, Nurita, Nureet—
plant
Nisi—emblem
Nitzanah, Nizana, Nitza—
blossom
Noga—sparkle
Noy—decoration
Odeda, Odede—strong
Odelia—praise to God
Ofra, Ofrah—fawn
Ona, Onit—graceful
Ora, Orah, Oralee, Orali, Orlee—
light
Ornah, Ornette, Ornetta, Orna—
cedar tree
Orpha, Orprah, Orpah—fawn
Orzora—God's strength
Orzsebet—consecrated to God
(form of Elizabeth)
Paili, Polly, Pall, Poll—bitter
Pazit, Pazia, Pazice, Paz, Paza—
golden
Peninah, Penina—pearl
Perzsike, Perke, Perzsi—
devoted to God
Qeturah—incense
Raananah—unspoiled (form of
Raanan)
Rachel, Rachele, Rakel—ewe
Raizel—rose
Ranit, Ranita, Ranice, Ranica—
lovely tune
Raphaella, Rafela—healed by
God (form of Raphael)
Raquel, Rahil, Raonaid—
innocent
Reba, Rabah—fourth born
Rebecca, Reveka, Rebekah,
Rivka—captivating

Rena, Rina, Rinna, Rinnah—
joyous song
Rimona—pomegranate
Rishona—first
Rivka—captivating (form of
Rebecca)
Ronli, Rona, Ronia—my joy
Rosanne, Rosana—graceful rose
Ruth, Ruta—friend
Sabra—to rest
Sadie, Sara, Sarah, Sally, Sallie,
Sarita—princess
Salome, Salomeaex, Saloma,
Selima, Schlomit, Shulamit—
tranquil
Samantha—name of God
Samara, Shemariah—protected
by God
Samuela—asked of God (form of
Samuel)
Sapphira, Sapphire—blue jewel
Sara, Sarah—princess
Sarai—argumentative
Segulah—precious
Sela, Sele, Seleta—rock
Semadar—berry
Semira, Sheiramoth—from
heaven
Seraphina, Seraphine, Serafine,
Serefina—fiery one; angel
Shaina, Shaine—beautiful
Sharon—from the land of Sharon
Sheena—God's gift
Shelah—request
Shifra—beautiful
Shira, Shiri—tune
Sidonia, Sidonie—captivates
Simcha—joyous

TINA WAINSCOTT

Tina Wainscott published her first novel in 1994. She has published nine novels since then, her most recent being *What She Doesn't Know* (St. Martin's Paperbacks).

I must confess that one of my favorite hero names came from a real-life villain. I was reading a true crime book about a guy who shot at people on a bus, and his name totally fit the man who was forming in my mind. I changed the spelling of the name, and Silas Koole became one of my favorite heroes, appearing in *Unforgivable*.

I sometimes use real names in my books as a way to honor friends. Of course, I always get their permission. One friend didn't want to be included. I think she regretted it once the book came out.

Never force a name on a character. I have some neat names I'm dying to use, but I just haven't found the right character for them. Make sure the name feels right.

Simona, Simone—God is heard (form of Simon)

Sippora—bird

Susan, Sue, Susie, Susy—lily

Susanna, Susannah, Suzanna—graceful lily

Suzette, Suzetta—little lily

Talia, Talya, Tal—dew of heaven

Talori, Talora—morning's dew

Tamara, Tamar, Tamarah—palm tree

Tamma, Teme, Temima—without flaw

Tema—righteous

Temira—tall

Thadine, Thadina—given praise

Thirza—delightful

Thomsina, Thomasin, Tomasina, Tomasine—twin (form of Thomas)

Tikva—hope

Tivona—nature lover (form of Tivon)

Tova, Toba, Toibe—goodly

Tsifira—crown

Tzilla—defender

Tzippa, Tzipporah—bird

Tzivia—doe

Tziyona—of Zion

Urit, Urice—light

Uzziye—God's strength

Vania, Vanna—God's gift

Varda, Vardit, Vadit, Vared—rose

Vida, Vidette—dearly loved

Ya-akove—supplanter (form of Jacob)

Yachne—kind

Ya-el—wild goat

Yaffa, Yaffit—beautiful

Yardenah—from the river Jordan

Yarkona—green

Yedidah—friend

Yehudit, Yuta, Yuhudit—praise

Yelizavetam, Yelysaveta—consecrated to God (form of Elizabeth)

Yeva, Yetsye, Yevunye—life (form of Eve)

Yocheved—God's glory

Yona, Yonina, Yonita—dove (form of Yonah)

Yordana—descended from

Yoseba, Yosebe, Yosepha,

Yosephina—God adds (form of Joseph)

Yovela—rejoice

Zahavah, Zehave, Zehuva, Zehavit, Zehavi—golden

Zaneta, Zanna—God's gift

Zara, Zarah—day's awakening

Zehira—protected

Zemira, Zemirah—joyous melody

Zera, Zera'im—seed

Zerlinda, Zarahlinda—beautiful dawn

Zibiah, Zibia—doe

Zilla, Zillah—shadow

Zimra, Zimria, Zemira, Zemora, Zamora—song of praise

Zippora, Zipporah—beauty

Ziva—splendid

Zohar, Zoheret—sparkle

MALE

Aaron, Aron—high mountain; lofty

Abaddon—destruction

Abbot, Abbott—abbey father

Abbotson—son of Abbot

Abe—father of many (form of Abraham)

Abel, Abie—breath

Abijah, Abisha—the Lord is my father

Abir, Aitan, Avniel—strong

Abner—father of light

Abraham, Abram, Abramo, Avraham, Aram, Abarron, Avidor—father of many

Adam—of the red earth

Adamson—son of Adam

Adar, Adir—fire

Addai—man of God

Aderet—crown

Adin, Adiv—delicate

Adlai—witness

Adley—judicious

Admon—red peony

Adon—the Lord

Adriel, Adriyel—of God's flock

Ager, Asaph, Asaf—gathers

Akiba, Akub, Akiva—replaces

Akim—God will establish

Almon—forsaken

Alon—oak

Alter—old

Alva—exalted
Amal—work
Amasa—burden
Amichai—my parents are alive
Amiel, Ami-el—of the Lord's
people
Amikam, Amram—rising nation
Amin—honest
Amir—proclaimed
Amiram—of lofty people
Amita, Amiti, Ammitai—truth
Ammi—my people
Amnon, Amon—faithful
Amos—brave
Aran—nimble
Ardon—bronze
Ari, Arie, Ariel, Aryeh, Arye—
lion of God
Arion—melodious
Armon—castle
Arnon—roaring stream
Arvad—wanderer
Asa—healer
Asher—happy
Ashur—black
Atarah—crown
Avi, Avidan, Avidor, Aviel,
Avniel—father
Avichai—my father is alive
Avidan—God is just
Avigdor—father protection
Avimelech, Abimelech—father
is king
Avinoam—pleasant father
Aviram, Abiram—father of
heights
Avisha, Avishai—gift from God
Avital—father of dew

Aviv—young
Avner, Abner—father of light
Avrom—father of many (form of
Abraham)
Axel, Aksel, Absalom, Avshalom,
Avsalom—father of peace
Azarious, Azaryah, Azaria,
Azaryahu, Azriel—God
helps
Azzan—strength
Barabas—of Barabba
Barak—lightning
Baram—son of the nation
Barnabas, Barnaby, Barnabe,
Barna—son of prophecy
Bartholomew, Bart, Bartel,
Bartley—hill, furrow
Baruch—blessed
Bela—destruction
Ben—son
Ben-ami—son of my people
Ben-aryeh, Benroy—son of a lion
Benedictson—son of Benedict
Benjamin, Beniamino,
Benkamin, Binyamin—son
of the right hand
Benoni—son of my sorrows
Benson—son of Benjamin
Ben-tziyon, Benzion—son of
Zion
Berakhiak—God blesses
Betzalel—in God's shadow
Binah—understanding
Boas, Boaz—swift
Bogdan, Bohdan—gift from God
Bram—father of many (form of
Abraham)
Cain—possessed

Caleb—bold
Carmel—garden
Carmi, Carmine—vine dresser
Chagai—mediates
Chaim, Chayim—life
Chanan—cloud
Chanoch—initiating
Chavivi, Chaviv—dearly loved
Che, Chepe, Chepito—God will
   multiply
Chiram—noble
Choni—gracious
Dagan—grain
Daniel, Danel, Danil, Dan, Dani,
   Daniele, Dane, Danny, Deen,
   Danila—God is my judge
Dar—pearl
David, Davin, Davey, Davi,
   Dabi—beloved
Deron—free
Dor—home
Doren—gift
Dov—bear
Dovev—speaks in a whisper
Eben, Eban—rock
Ebenezer—rock of help
Efram, Efrem—fruitful
Efrat—honored
Ehud—meaning unknown
Elan—tree
Elazar—God helps
Eleazar, Elazaro, Eliezer—God
   has helped
Elhanan—God is gracious
Elias, Elihu, Elijah, Ellis, Eliot,
   Ely, Eli, Elisha, Eliseo—
   Jehovah is God
Elishama—God hears

Elisheva, Elisheba—God is my
   wrath
Elkanah—possessed by God
Elrad—God rules
Emmanuel—God is with us
Enoch—consecrated
Ephrem, Ephram, Ephraim,
   Efrayim—fruitful
Errapel—divine healer
Esau—hairy one
Esdras—help
Eshkol—grape cluster
Esra—helper
Ethan, Etan—strong
Eyou—symbol of piety
Ezechiel—strength of God
Ezra—helper
Foma—twin
Gabriel, Gavi, Gavriel, Gabriele,
   Gabrielo, Gabor, Gabi—God-
   given strength
Gal—wave
Gamaliel—God's reward
Gedalya, Gedaliah, Gedalyahu—
   God has made great
Gedeon, Gideon—destroyer
Geremia—God is high
Gersham, Gershom—exiled
Gideon—mighty warrior
Gil, Gilli, Gili—happiness
Giuseppe—God adds (form of
   Joseph)
Goliath—revealing
Guri, Gurion—my lion cub
Guy—valley
Habib—beloved
Hadar—glory
Hanan—grace

Hananel—God is gracious
Hans, Hansell—gracious God
    (form of John)
Harel, Harrell—mountain of God
Harrod—heroic
Hayyim, Hyman—life
Herschel, Hershel—deer
Hezekiah—God is my strength
Hieremias—God will uplift
Hillel—praised
Hiram, Hyram—exalted
Hod—vigorous
Honi—gracious
Hosea—salvation
Hyam—life
Iakovos—supplanter (form of
    Jacob)
Iaokim, Iov—God will establish
Ichabod—glory has departed
Illias, Ilias—Jehovah is God
Imanol—God is with us
Ioseph, Iosep—God adds (form
    of Joseph)
Ira—descendant
Isaac, Izaak, Isaakios, Ixaka—one
    who laughs
Isaias, Isaiah, Isiah—God's
    helper
Iseabail—devoted to God
Israel, Izrael—ruling with the
    Lord
Itai—friendly
Ittamar—island of palms
Itzak, Itzaak—laughing
Ivan, Ioan, Ian, Iban, Ionnes—
    gracious God (form of John)
Jabez—sorrow
Jacob, Jack, Jock, Jake, Jacobe,

James, Jim, Jamie, Jimmy,
    Jem, Jakome, Jaques, Jacot,
    Jaap, Jov—supplanter
Jael—mountain goat
Japhet—handsome
Jared, Jori—descending
Jasper—jewel
Jedidiah, Jed, Jedi—beloved by
    God
Jephtah—firstborn
Jeremias, Jeremiah, Jeremy,
    Jeremi, Jeremie—exalted of
    the Lord
Jesse, Jessie—wealthy
Joachim—God will establish
Job—persecuted
Jocheved—God's glory
Joel—strong-willed
John, Juan, Jens, Jonam,
    Jonathan, Jonatan, Jon, Jan,
    Jenda, Joen, Jani, Janie,
    Johan, Jussi, Jukka, Juka,
    Jean, Jeannot, Jancsi, Jonas,
    Jankia, Janko, Janos, Jantje,
    Jannes—gracious God
Jokin—God will establish
Jordan—descended
Joseph, Joosef, Jooseppi,
    Josephus, Joop, Jopie,
    Joseba—God adds
Joshua, Josue, Josias—God is
    salvation
Josiah—God heals
Josu—God saves
Judd, Judy, Jude, Judah, Judas,
    Jud—praised
Jurrien, Jurre, Jore, Jorie, Jory—
    God will uplift

Kabos—swindler
Kaleb—devoted
Kaniel—reed
Karmel—vineyard
Kiva—protected
Laban, Lavan—white
Label—lion
Lamech—powerful
Lapidos, Lapidoth—torch
Lazarus, Lazzaro, Lazar—God will help
Leb—heart
Lemuel—consecrated to God
Leshem—precious stone
Levi, Lev, Levey, Lewi—united
Lot—veiled
Machum, Menachem—comfort
Mahir—industrious
Mai-ron, Miron, Myron—holy place
Malachy, Mal, Malachi—messenger of God
Manasses, Menassah—forgetful
Manuel, Mannie, Manny—God is with us (form of Emmanuel)
Marnin—joyful
Mathew, Matthias, Mattias, Mate, Matyas, Matai, Mathews, Mads, Matthieu, Mathe, Matz—God's gift
Mayar, Mayer, Mayir, Meyer, Meir—enlightens
Meilseoir, Melchior—king
Menachem, Mendel—consolation
Michael, Mikael, Mikkel, Mitchell, Mikel, Mikko, Michel, Michon, Michele,
Michau, Makis, Misi, Mikhail, Mikhalis, Mikhos, Maichail, Mihaly, Miska, Mika, Micah—who is like God
Mordechai, Mordecai—warrior
Moses, Mosheh—taken from the water
Naaman—pleasant
Nadav—gives
Nadiv—noble
Naftali, Naftalie—wreath
Nahum, Nachman—compassionate
Nathan, Nathaniel, Nathanael, Natanael, Nethanel—gift from God
Nehemiah, Nechemya—comforted by God
Nimrod—great hunter
Nissim—wonders
Noadiah—God's assembler
Noe, Noah, Noach—comfort
Nuri—my fire
Obadiah, Ovadiah, Ovadyam, Obediah—serves God
Oded—encourages
Ofer—fawn
Ophir—meaning unknown
Oren, Orin, Oris—tree
Ori, Orneet, Ornet—my light
Osip—God adds (form of Joseph)
Oved, Ovid—worker
Ozi, Ozzie, Ozzi—strong
Palti, Palt-el—God liberates
Pascal, Paschal—born on Passover
Paz—golden

Pessach, Pesach—spread
Phineas—oracle
Pinochos—dark-skinned
Raanan—unspoiled
Ranit, Ronit, Rani, Roni, Ron—
lovely tune
Ranon, Ranen—joyful
Raphael, R'phael, Rafal—healed
by God
Ravid—wanderer
Rechavia—broad
Reuben, Ruben, Rueban, Rouvin,
Re'uven—behold a son
Saadya—God's helper
Sakeri—remembered by God
Samson, Sampson, Shimshon—
bright sun
Samuel, Schmuel—asked of God
Sanson—sun's man
Sasson, Simcha—joy
Saul, Sha-ul—longed for
Schmaiah—God hears
Seanan, Senen, Sinon, Shane—
gift from God
Seosamh, Seosaph—God adds
(form of Joseph)
Seraphim, Serafin, Serafim—
fiery one; angel (form of
Seraphina)
Seth—anointed
Shet, Set—compensation
Shulamith—peaceful
Simeon, Simon, Symeon,
Siomon, Simen, Simao,
Symon—God is heard
Simpson, Simson, Shim'on—son
of Simon
Sinai—from the clay desert

Sivan—ninth month
Solomon, Salamon, Shelomo,
Shalom—peaceful
Taaveti, Taavi—beloved
Talman—to oppress
Taneli—God is my judge (form
of Daniel)
Tapani, Teppo—victorious
Teman—right hand
Thaddeus—wise
Thomas, Tomas, Tuomas,
Thoma, Tamas, Tomek—
twin
Timur—iron
Tivon—nature lover
Tobias, Tobin, Toby, Tovi,
Tuvya, Tobiah, Turyahu—
God is good
Tsidhqiyah—God's justice
Tzadok—just
Tzefanyah, Tzefanyahu—
treasure by God
Tzion—sunny mountain
Tzuriel—God is my rock
Tzvi—deer
Udeh—praise
Uriah, Uri, Uriel—God is my light
Uzziel, Uzziah—God is mighty
Veniamin, Venamin, Venjamin—
son of the right hand (form
of Benjamin)
Ximen, Ximon, Ximun—God is
heard (form of Simon)
Yaakov—supplanter (form of
Jacob)
Yadon—judge
Yael—wild goat
Yagil—He will rejoice

Yair—enlighten

Yakov, Yago—supplanter (form of Jacob)

Yan, Yannis, Yehoash, Yehonadov—gift from God

Yaphet—handsome

Yardane—descendant

Yaron—singer

Yavin—understanding

Yechurun—meaning unknown

Yedidyah, Yedidiah, Yerucham—beloved by God

Yeeshai—rich gift

Yehoshua—God's help

Yehuda, Yehudi—praised

Yerachmiel—loves God

Yerik, Yarema, Yaremka—appointed by God

Yeshaya—God lends

Yiftach—opens

Yigil, Yigol—shall be redeemed

Yisrael—God's prince

Yissachar—reward

Yitzchak—humorous

Yo-el, Yoel—God prevails

Yonah—dove

Yusaf—God adds (form of Joseph)

Zabulon—exalted

Zacharias, Zachariah, Zachary, Zachery, Zachaios—remembered by God

Zadok—just

Zamir—songbird

Zared, Zarad—ambush

Zayit—olive

Zebadiah, Zebediah, Zane, Zani—gift from God

Zebulon—from the dwelling place

Zedekiah—God's justice

Zephaniah, Zephan—treasured by God

Z'ev, Ze'ev—wolf

Zevulun, Zebulun, Zebulon—habitation

Zimra—song of praise

Ziv—bright

Zohar—sparkle

Zuriel—stone

HUNGARIAN

In Hungary, the surname is placed before the given name. When traveling abroad, Hungarians will often reverse the order so people accustomed to seeing the given name first will not be confused. Surnames are taken from descriptive, place, occupational, and patronymic names, and they are passed down from father to children.

An interesting fact is that a married woman, instead of using a title indicating her marital status (like Mrs.), will add -né to her husband's given name. For example, if Nagy Ilona (Nagy is the surname) marries Varga Péter (Varga is the surname), she becomes Varga Péterné. If she wishes, she may keep her name and become Varga Péterné Nagy Ilona or Vargàné Nagy Ilona.

Before World War II, suffixes often gave a clue about the social standing of the bearer. During the communist period after WWII, many people with aristocratic suffixes changed their names to avoid persecution.

Aristocratic suffix:	Corresponding suffix for the lower classes:
-cz	-c
-th	-t
-eö	-ö
-ss	-zs
-ew	-ö
-ff	-f
-gh	-g
-oo	-o
-y	-i

The suffixes -i and -y are resident names showing that the original bearer was from a particular city, village, town, etc.

A few surnames:

Balogh	Deme
Bodizsár	Domokos
Deák	Dömötör
Dékány	Fábián

Horváth
Kálmán
Kelemen
Kiss
Kovács

Molnár
Nagy
Szabö
Töth
Varga

FEMALE

Agotha, Agoti, Agi, Aggie—good (form of Agatha)
Alberta—noble, intelligent (form of Albert)
Alexandra, Alexa—defender of mankind (form of Alexander)
Aliz, Alisz—sweet, noble (form of Alice)
Anasztaizia—one who will be reborn (form of Anastasia)
Anci—graceful
Angyalka—messenger
Aurelia, Aranka—gold (form of Aurelio)
Bella, Bela, Belle—beautiful
Bertuska, Berta—brave
Borbala, Borsala, Bora, Borka, Brosca, Broska, Boriska—stranger (form of Barbara)
Cili—blind (form of Cecil)
Czigany—gypsy
Darda—dart
Dorika, Dorottya—God's gift (form of Dorothy)
Duci—wealthy gift
Erika—eternal ruler (form of Eric)
Ernesztina, Erna—serious (form of Ernest)

Erssike, Erzsi, Erzsok, Erzebet—consecrated to God (form of Elizabeth)
Eszti—star
Etilka, Etel—noble (form of Ethel)
Evike, Evacska—life (form of Eve)
Ferike, Fereng, Franciska—free (form of Francis)
Firenze, Florka—flower
Frici—peaceful ruler (form of Frederick)
Gisella, Gizi—pledge
Gitta—pearl (form of Margaret)
Hajna—grace
Ibolya—violet
Ica, Ilona, Ilka—light
Ildiko—fierce warrior
Irenke—peaceful
Janka—gracious God (form of John)
Jolan—flower blossom
Jucika, Juci—praised
Juliska, Julcsa—youthful (form of Julius)
Karolina, Karola—manly (form of Charles)
Katinka, Katakin, Kat, Katalin, Katarina—pure (form of Katherine)

Krisztina, Kriszta—believes in Christ (form of Christian)
Lenci—light
Linka—mannish
Liza—consecrated to God (form of Elizabeth)
Lujza—myth name
Malika, Malcsi—industrious
Marcsa, Mara, Marika, Martuska, Marianna—bitter, grace
Nancsi, Nusa, Ninacska, Nusi—graceful
Orzsebet—consecrated to God (form of Elizabeth)
Paliki—little
Panna—graced by God
Piroska, Pirioska—ancient (form of Priscilla)
Rez—copper-haired
Rozalia, Roza—rose (form of Rosa)
Sarika, Sasa—princess (form of Sarah)
Teca, Treszka—reaper (form of Theresa)
Tunde—meaning unknown
Tzigane—gypsy
Vicuska, Viva—life
Viktoria—victorious (form of Victor)
Virag—flower
Zigana—gypsy
Zsa Zsa, Zsuzsanna, Zsuzsi, Zsuska—lily (form of Susan)
Zsofia, Zsofika—wise (form of Sophia)

MALE

Adelbert, Albert—noble, intelligent
Adony—meaning unknown
Adorjan—dark (form of Adrian)
Agoston—staff of God (form of Gustav)
Ambrus—immortal (form of Ambrose)
Andor—manly (form of Andrew)
Arpad—wanderer
Asztrik—made from ashenwood
Atalik—like his father
Attila—myth name
Bajnok—victor
Bars—pepper
Bartalan—hill, furrow (form of Bartholomew)
Becse—kite
Bela—noble, intelligent (form of Albert)
Bence—victorious
Benci—blessed
Beriszl—honored
Bod—branch
Bodi, Boldizsar—God bless the king
Bodor—curly
Botond—warrior with a mace
Csaba—myth name
Cseke—carrier
Csenger—meaning unknown
Deli—warrior
Denes—wine
Domokos—God's own

Egyed—shield-bearer
Elek—defender of mankind
(form of Alexander)
Endre—manly (form of Andrew)
Ervin—mariner
Farkas—wolf
Ferenc, Ferko—free (form of
Francis)
Fodor—curly hair
Folkus—famous
Fredek—peaceful ruler (form of
Frederick)
Frigyes—peace
Fulop—lover of horses (form of
Philip)
Gabor—God-given strength
(form of Gabriel)
Gara—goshawk
Gazsi—protects the treasure
Gedeon—destroyer
Gergo—watchful
Gerzson—banished one
Gyurka—farmer
Gyuszi, Gyala—youthful
Hont—friend of dogs
Huba—meaning unknown
Imre—innocent
Istvan—crowned in victory
(form of Stephen)
Izsak—one who laughs (form of
Isaac)
Jenci—well-born
Jozsef, Joska, Jozsi—God adds
(form of Joseph)
Kada—meaning unknown
Kadosa—meaning unknown
Kalman—manly, strong
Kapolcs—meaning unknown

Kardos—swordsman
Karsa—falcon
Kartal—eagle
Kelemen, Kellman—gentle
Keve—pebble, small stone
Kolos—scholar
Kristof—Christ-bearer (form of
Christopher)
Laborc—panther
Ladomer—trapper
Lantos—musician, lute
Laszlo—famous ruler
Lorant—victory
Lorenca—laurel (form of
Lawrence)
Lukacs—light (form of Luke)
Medard—strong
Menyhert—royal
Miksa—godlike
Moricz—Moorish
Mozes—taken from the water
(form of Moses)
Neci—ardent
Nyek—borderlands
Odon—protector
Orban—born in the city
Ormos—cliff
Oszkar—divine spear (form of
Oscar)
Pellegrin—pilgrim
Peterke—rock (form of Peter)
Pista, Pisti—victorious
Piusz—pious
Poldi—patriotic
Pongor—mighty
Radomer—peaceful
Rendor—peacekeeper

Rez—copper-headed

Rikard—strong ruler (form of Richard)

Robi—famous

Samuka—God hears

Sandor—defender of mankind (form of Alexander)

Sebes—quick, fast

Sebestyen, Sebo—revered (form of Sebastian)

Solt—honored name

Solyom—falcon

Soma—horn

Szemere—destroyer

Szever—serious

Tabor—drum

Taksony—content

Tardos—bald

Tarjan—honored name

Tass—myth name

Teteny—chieftain

Timur—iron

Titusz—honored

Tivadar—gift from God

Uros—little lord

Varad—of the fort

Vayk—prosperous, rich

Vencel—victorious

Vidor, Viktor, Vincze— victorious (form of Victor)

Vilmos—resolute protector (form of William)

Vitez—courageous soldier

Zador—violent

Zalan—fighter

Zarand—precious, golden

Zerind—Serb

Zobor—group, gathering

Zombor—buffalo

Zsolt—honored name

INDIAN

India is primarily Hindu in religion, with Islam the next largest religion in the country. Although many languages are spoken in India, the most common language in India is Hindi, which is why there is a separate listing of Hindi names in this section.

However, due to the variety of languages (over two hundred spoken) and cultures of India, It would be impossible to list all the various naming taboos, customs, and history in this work.

In some areas of India (especially northern India), names generally consist of a first, middle, and surname. In these areas, surnames are passed down from father to children. A female child is usually given her father's first name as a middle name. Upon marriage, her middle name will change to her husband's first name, and she will take her husband's surname. In the past, the husband could also change his wife's first name, but this custom is falling out of practice. It is also becoming more common for a married woman to hyphenate her last name, especially if she is known by her maiden name in her profession.

In other areas of India (especially in the south), there are no surnames. Patronymic, occupational, caste or place names may be substituted for identification in these areas, or the first initial of the father's name may be used before a name: P. Vijay. People often address their elders or superiors with titles like Sahib, Aiyya, Amma, or even Sir. However, it is becoming more common to create a surname from the father's name when traveling or doing business with Europeans or Americans.

One prevalent custom is that of giving a child two or three names. At one time, one of the names was kept secret (to prevent bad luck), and when a child entered puberty, a new name was often chosen.

Children are never named after a parent. Though at one time children were given offensive names, especially if a sibling has already died, to make the demons think this child was beneath their notice and not worth taking, this is rarely practice today.

The gamut of naming practices and rules is far too extensive to cover here. I would encourage any writer working on this culture to research the nomenclature of the language, caste, and area of the story's setting.

A few surnames:

Balin	Naidu
Chettiar	Pathan
Chetty	Pillai
Coundar	Rao
Dalal	Reddy
Dandin	Redivary
Kapoor	Sahir
Kedar	Shah
Kesin	Singh
Khan	Takeri
Kistna	Thevar
Konar	Vasin
Mudali	Yamuna
Mudaliar	

FEMALE

Abhirati—mother of five hundred children; a mother goddess; myth name

Adya—born on Sunday

Ahalya—night

Akshamala—meaning unknown

Amaravati—full of ambrosia

Amba, Ambi, Ambika—mother

Ambrosia—food of the gods

Amrita—immortality

Anahita—goddess of the waters; myth name

Anasuya—charitable

Anga—from Anga

Angirasa—of the Luminous Race; myth name

Annapurna—goddess of bread; myth name

Anumati—moon; myth name

Apala—woman cursed with a skin disorder; myth name

Apsaras—from the water's stream

Arundhati—morning star

Arya—noble goddess; myth name

Behula—perfect wife; myth name

Bha—star

Bhadraa—cow

Bhagiratha—goddess

Bhairavi—meaning unknown

Bhikkhuni—nun

Bhimadevi—frightening goddess; myth name

Bhu, Bhudevi—earth; myth name
Chamunda—aspect of Durga; myth name
Chanda, Chandi—fierce
Channa—chickpea
Charumati—daughter of Buddha
Chhaya—shade
Daeva, Div—evil spirit; myth name
Dakini—demon; myth name
Dakshina—competent
Damayanti—name of a princess
Danu—meaning unknown
Deva—superior
Devaki—black
Devamatar—mother of the gods; myth name
Devayani—daughter of Shukra; myth name
Dharani—earth; myth name
Diti—daughter of Daksha; myth name
Gandhari—name of a princess
Garudi—bird of prey
Gatha, Gita—song
Gayatri—singer
Haimati—snow queen; myth name
Hariti—goddess of smallpox; myth name
Indrani—goddess of the sky; myth name
Indumati—daughter of Vidarbha; myth name
Ishani—lady
Jaganmata—mother of the world; myth name

Janna—paradise
Jayanti—victory
Jivanta—gives life
Jyotis—light of the sun
Kadru—daughter of Daksha; myth name
Kailasa—silver mountain
Kalindi—daughter of the sun god; myth name
Karma—destiny
Karuna—compassion
Kawindra—meaning unknown
Kerani—sacred bells
Khasa—daughter of Daksha; myth name
Kirati—from the mountain
Krodha—anger
Kumari—princess
Kumudavati—owns lotuses
Kunti—lover of the sun god; myth name
Lakya—born on Thursday
Leya—lion
Madri—wife of Pandu; myth name
Mahadevi—great goddess; myth name
Mahamari—killer
Maheshvari—great lady
Mahila—woman
Marisha—dew; myth name
Mehadi—flower
Mira—name of a princess; myth name
Nidra—goddess of sleep; myth name
Nipa—stream
Nirveli—from the water

HOMER HICKAM

Homer Hickam is author of the No. 1 best-selling memoir *Rocket Boys* and three follow-up novel-memoirs, *The Coalwood Way*, *Sky of Stone*, and *We Are Not Afraid*. He is also author of the novel *The Keeper's Son*, the first in his new series.

The sound or look of a name can make a big difference in the perception of a character, so I usually give each name careful thought and try them on for a while, just to make certain they fit. I've gone back more than once and modified a name when the personality of the character changed during the writing. Sometimes, I go against type, simply for effect.

For instance, in my novel *The Ambassador's Son*, there is a be-witching, hot-blooded young woman discovered by my hero, Josh Thurlow, in the jungles of the Solomon Islands. Her name? Penelope! Readers will immediately wonder why and how a half-naked, volup-tuous, and savage woman could have such a prim name—thus, through this simple device, adding to the page-turning qualities of the novel.

Josh Thurlow, the hero of my series of World War II adventure-romantic novels, got his name because I wanted one that exuded strength. Just for the fun of it, I sometimes give characters the names of my friends. In *The Keeper's Son*, the beach patrol rider has nearly the same name as my good friend and fellow dinosaur fossil-hunter Frank Stewart. When Frank found the bones of a T. rex, I named the character Rex Stewart.

In my series of memoirs that began with *Rocket Boys*, I used many real names, but the occasional composite character required some thought. I usually combined actual West Virginia names because they had an authentic sound to them, but I was also careful to make certain the name reflected certain subjective qualities. One of my favorite char-acters in that series is a womanizer and a drunk, yet he is also a wise and thoroughly decent man. After trying a number of combinations, the name Jake Mosby just seemed to fit. It must have worked. Jake gets lots of fan mail, especially from women!

Odra—from Odra
Pandara—wife
Pishachi—shrew
Pithasthana—wife of Shiva; myth name
Pramlocha—nymph; myth name
Rana—royal
Rashmika—sweet
Rati—wife of Pradyumna; myth name
Ravati—princess; myth name
Riddhi—wealthy
Rudrani—meaning unknown
Ruma—queen of the apes; myth name
Sakari—sweet
Sakra—from India
Sakujna—bird
Samvarta—mare; myth name
Sandhya—twilight
Sanjna—conscientious
Sanya—born on Sunday
Sarama—quick
Sati, Satyavati—true
Saura—of the Saura
Savarna—same color
Savitari—daughter of Ashvapati; myth name
Sevti—white rose
Shaibya—faithful wife; myth name
Shakini—demon; myth name
Shakra—owl
Shanta—meaning unknown
Shapa—cursed
Sharada—lute
Sharama—dog of dawn; myth name

Shasti—goddess of childbirth; myth name
Shitala—goddess of smallpox; myth name
Shraddha—faithful
Shri—wealthy
Sita—furrow
Sur—sharp-nosed
Tapati—daughter of the sun god; myth name
Tara—goddess of the sea; myth name
Taraka—demon; myth name
Trisna, Trishna—desired
Tulsi—basil
Upala—opal
Ushas—dawn; myth name
Vach, Vac—well-spoken
Varaza—boar
Varunani—goddess of wine; myth name
Vema—goddess of sex; myth name
Vina—stringed instrument
Vinata—daughter of Daksha; myth name
Vineeta—simple
Vivika—wisdom
Yamuna—from the Yamuna river
Yasiman, Yasmine, Yasmina—jasmine
Zudora—labors

HINDI
Aditi—free
Ahisma—not violent
Ajaya—invincible

Alka—long hair
Ambar—sky
Ambika—goddess of the moon;
    myth name
Amritha—precious
Anala—fiery
Ananda—bliss (form of Anand)
Ananta—name of a serpent;
    myth name
Anila—meaning unknown
Arpana—dedicated
Aruna—radiant
Avasa—independent
Avatara—descending (form of
    Avatar)
Baka—crane
Bakula—meaning unknown
Bela—jasmine
Bharati—India
Bina—musical instrument;
    intelligence
Chaitra—meaning unknown
Chandi—angry
Chandra—moon
Changla—active
Chitra—bright
Corona—kind
Daru—pine
Deepa—meaning unknown
Devi—noble; myth name
Divya—divine
Drisana—sun's daughter; myth
    name
Durga—impenetrable
Ellama—meaning unknown
Ganesa—from Ganas
Garuda—sacred bird who
    carried Vishnu; myth name

Gauri—yellow
Girisa—meaning unknown
Hanita—divine grace
Hara—aspect of Shiva; myth
    name
Hema—golden
Indi—Indian
Indra—supreme god; myth
    name
Jarita—bird; myth name
Jaya, Jayne—victory
Kala—black
Kalinda—sun
Kamala—lotus (form of Kamal)
Kantha—wife
Kanya—virgin
Karka—crab
Kasi—from Kasi
Kaveri—from the sacred river
    Kaveri
Kesava—of the beautiful hair
Kiran—ray
Kumuda—flower
Lakini—meaning unknown
Lakshmi—wife of Vishnu; myth
    name
Lalasa—love
Lalita—named for the Lalita-
    Vistara
Lanka—from Lanka
Latika—meaning unknown
Madhur—gentle
Mahesa—wife of Shiva; myth
    name
Makara—meaning unknown
Malini—meaning unknown
Manda—pivotal
Mandara—from Mandara

Matrika—divine mother; myth name
Mythili—meaning unknown
Nandini—cow; myth name
Narmada—gives us pleasure
Natesa—dancer
Neerja—lily
Nishkala—meaning unknown
Padma—lotus flower
Pandita—studious
Pavithra—meaning unknown
Pinga—tawny
Prabha—light
Radha—cowgirl; myth name
Rajni—night
Ramya—beautiful
Rani, Ranee, Rania, Ran—queen
Ratna—jewel
Rekha—fine
Rohana—sandalwood
Rohini—woman
Sandhya—twilight
Sarisha—sophisticated
Seema—limit
Shanata—tranquil
Shashi—moonlight
Sita—goddess of the land; myth name
Sitara—morning star
Soma—moon
Subha—beautiful
Supriya—beloved
Sur—knife
Tira—arrow
Tirtha—ford
Trisha—thirst
Uma—bright
Usha—princess and daughter of Bana; myth name
Vairocana—king of the demons; myth name
Varouna—infinite
Vayu—vital force; myth name
Vedas—eternal laws; myth name
Vijaya—victory (form of Vijay)

MALE

Abhaya—has no fear
Abhimanyu—killed by Lakshmana; myth name
Abjaja—born of a lotus
Acharya—spiritual teacher
Achir—new
Adharma—lawless
Adi—aspect of Vasishtha; myth name
Aditya, Arun—sun
Agastya—name of a wise man
Agneya—son of Agni
Agnimukha—face of fire
Ahriman—evil spirit; myth name
Airavata—child of water
Aja—goat
Akash—sky
Akshobhya—one of the Dhyani-Buddhas; myth name
Ameretat—immortal
Amitabha—one of the Dhyani-Buddhas; myth name
Amma—supreme god; myth name

Amol, Amolik, Amulya—
  priceless
Ananda—half-brother of
  Buddha
Ananga—without body
Anish—born without a master
Arpan—offering
Aruna—god of the dawn; myth
  name
Asad—lion
Ashoka—name of an emperor
Asipatra—meaning unknown
Asura—demon; myth name
Atal—unshaking
Atraiu—great warrior
Atul—incomparable
Ayodhya—from Ayodhya
Badal—cloud
Balarama, Balahadra—brother
  of Krishna; myth name
Balbir—strong
Bali, Balin—mighty warrior
Bhaga—god of luck; myth name
Bhagwandas—serves God
Bhavaja—god of love; myth
  name
Bhavata—dearly loved
Bhikkhu—monk
Bhima, Bhishma—terrible
Bodhi—awakens
Brahman, Brahma—absolute
Brahmaputra—son of Brahma
Chakra—symbol of the sun;
  myth name
Chandaka—charioteer of
  Buddha; myth name
Chandra—moon
Chinja—son

Daksha—brilliant
Das, Dasa—slave
Dasras—handsome
Dasya—he serves
Deven—for God
Dhenuka—demon; myth name
Dhumavarna—color of smoke
Duhkha—sorrowful
Durvasas—son of Atri; myth
  name
Dushkriti—sum of all sins
Dyaus—sky
Ekadanta—has one tooth
Frashegird—wonderful
Gada—mace
Gadhi—father of Vishvamitra;
  myth name
Gajra—garland of flowers
Garuda—sacred bird who
  carried Vishnu; myth name
Girisha—storm god; myth name
Guga—serpent god; myth name
Gulab—rose
Haidar—lion
Halim—kind
Hari—tawny
Haripriya—loved by Vishnu
Harischandra—name of a king
Hasin—laughs
Hastimukha—face of an
  elephant
Hemakuta—from Hemakuta
Indra—supreme god; myth
  name
Isha, Ishana, Ishvara—lord
Jafar—little stream
Jahnu—name of a sage
Jambha—jaws

Jambhala—god of wealth; myth name
Jatinra—legend name
Javras—quick
Jivin—gives life
Josha—satisfied
Jyotish—moon
Kabandha—ugly giant; myth name
Kakar—grass
Kala, Kali—black
Kalari—aspect of Shiva; myth name
Kalki, Kalkin—white horse
Kami—loving
Kanaka—gold
Kanishka—name of a king
Kantu—myth name
Karu—legend name
Kashi, Kasi—meaning unknown
Kavi—poet
Kedar—meaning unknown
Keshi—long-haired
Kotari—unclothed
Kritanta—god of death; myth name
Kumar—prince
Kumara—youthful
Lais—lion
Lakshmana—lucky omen
Lusila—leader
Madhava—god of spring; myth name
Mahakala—aspect of Shiva; myth name
Malajit—victorious
Manoj—meaning unknown
Mehtar—prince

Mesha—ram
Mithra, Mitra—god of the sun; myth name
Mukul—blossoming
Muni—silent
Nadisu—meaning unknown
Nandin—myth name
Nara—man
Nehru—canal
Nila—blue
Omparkash—light of God
Palash—flowering tree
Panchika—husband of Abhirati; myth name
Pandu—pale
Pani—pagan
Pavaka—purifies
Pavit—pious
Pitamaha—grandfather
Pitar, Pitri—father
Poshita—dearly loved
Priyamkara—favorite son of Abhirati; myth name
Pumeet—innocent
Rajak—meaning unknown
Raji—name of king
Rajnish—king of the gods; myth name
Rakshasa—demon; myth name
Raktavira—demon; myth name
Raktim—bright red
Ranjan—delights his parents
Ravana—unjust king
Rishi—name of a priest
Rohin—meaning unknown
Rudra—howls
Sachi—descended from the sun god; myth name

Sahan—falcon
Sahen—above
Sahir—friend
Sajag—watchful
Samantaka—destroys peace
Sanjiv—long life
Saubhari—name of a hermit
Shaitan, Shetan—demon; myth name
Shaka, Saka—from the Shaka
Shaktar—name of a hermit
Shakti—powerful
Shalya—throne
Shamba—son of Krishna; myth name
Shami—husband
Shankara—grand
Shashida—ocean
Shesha—king of serpents; myth name
Shiva—destroyer; myth name
Shudra—born to the lowest caste
Skanda—god of war; myth name
Sunreet—pure
Taj—crown
Takshaka—carpenter
Tandu—god of dancing; myth name
Tathagata—walks the straightway
Tayib—good
Tripada—god of fever; myth name
Uja—grow
Utathya—name of a wise man
Valmiki—name of a poet
Varuna—infinite

Vasin—ruler
Vasistha, Vasu—wealthy
Vibishana—frightening
Visha—poison
Vivek—wise
Vrishni—manly
Vritra—demon; myth name
Vyasa—name of a poet

HINDI

Adri—rock
Agni—fire
Anand—bliss
Arun—sun
Ashwin—meaning unknown
Atman—self
Avatar—descending
Bharani—meaning unknown
Bharat—name of a saint
Bhaskar—sun
Brahma—born to the highest caste
Chander—moon
Darshan—meaning unknown
Ganesh—lord of the dwarves; myth name
Girish—lord of the mountains
Hansh—meaning unknown
Hanuman—monkey
Hari—golden
Hastin—elephant
Hiranyagarbha—golden egg; myth name
Inay—meaning unknown
Inder, Indra—supreme god; myth name
Iswara—personal god; myth name

Jalil—meaning unknown
Kabir—meaning unknown
Kala—god of time; myth name
Kalkin—white horse
Kamal—lotus
Kapil—from Kapilavastu
Karthik—meaning unknown
Kesin—long-haired beggar
Kintan, Kiritan—crowned
Kistna—meaning unknown
Lal—beloved
Loknoth—meaning unknown
Mahadeva—great god
Manu—ruler of the earth; myth name
Markandeya—name of a sage; myth name
Marut—storm god; myth name
Matsya—fish
Mohan—delightful
Murali—meaning unknown
Nandin—named for Shiva's bull, Nandi; myth name
Narain—meaning unknown
Naraka—hell
Narayan—moving water
Natesha—lord of dance; myth name
Onkar—meaning unknown
Purdy—recluse
Ravi—sun; myth name
Salmalin—claw
Sanat—ancient
Sarad—born during the fall
Srinath—meaning unknown
Surya—god of the sun; myth name
Timin—meaning unknown
Vadin—speaker
Valin—meaning unknown
Varun—infinite
Vasuki—serpent; myth name
Vijay—victory
Vishnu—protector of the worlds; myth name
Yama—god of death; myth name

INDIAN

IRISH

Ireland has some of the oldest surnames. Almost all are patronymic. Surnames became popular in the tenth and eleventh centuries and by the twelfth century were widespread. Names that derive from place or occupation are much newer than the older, patronymic ones.

Common prefixes:

M', Mc, Mac—son of
O—grandson or descendant of
ni—daughter of
ban—wife of
giolla—follower of
moal—servant of

In the original Gaelic, the apostrophe isn't used after *O-* or *M-*. Women were never referred to as *Mac* or *Mc*, but always by *-ni* if they were unmarried, *-ban* if they were married. Ciara ni Suileabhan might become Ciara ban Gorman.

The *fitz* suffix is not traditionally Irish but was brought in by Anglo-Norman invaders. *K* was also imported by the invaders. The letters J, K, Q, V, W, X, Y, and Z didn't exist in the Gaelic alphabet, so names containing these letters are likely to be anglicizations or simplifications. The name Kennedy, for example, may have originated from the name O'Cinneide.

A few surnames:

Adair	Fitzgerald
Boyle	Flynn
Brennan	Gallagher
Byrne	Hannigan
Cavanagh	Kelly
Connolly	Kennedy
Connor	Lafferty
Coughlin	Lynch
Delaney	Macartan
Doyle	MacAuley
Dunne	MacAuliffe

MacBride
MacCormack
MacElroy
MacMurra, MacMaureadhaigh
MacNamara
MacQuaid
Maguire
Malloy
McCann
McCarthy
McLoughlin
Moore
Murphy
Murray
O'Brien
O'Callaghan
O'Connell

O'Connor
O'Doherty
O'Donnell
O'Neill
O'Reilly
O'Shea
O'Sullivan
O'Toole
Quinn
Reardon
Ryan
Shaughnessy
Smith
Sullivan
Sweeney
Teague
Walsh

FEMALE

Abiageal—gives joy (form of Abigail)

Adara, Athdara—from the ford by the oak tree (form of Adair)

Africa, Afric, Aifric—pleasant

Agata, Agate—good (form of Agatha)

Aghadreena—from the field of the sloe bushes

Aghamora—from the great field (form of Aghamore)

Aghaveagh, Aghavilla—from the field of the old tree

Aghna—pure (form of Agnes)

Ahana—from the little ford (form of Ahane)

Aibrean, Aibreann—April

Aidan, Adan, Adeen, Aideen—fiery one

Aigneis—pure (form of Agnes)

Ailbe—white

Aileen, Ailey, Aili, Ailia—light (form of Eileen)

Ailis, Ailise, Ailisa—sweet, noble (form of Alice)

Aine—bright, radiant

Aingeal—angel

Aislinn, Aislin, Aisling, Ashling—vision

Alanna, Alaine, Alayne, Allene, Allyn, Alina, Alana—beautiful

Alastrina, Alastriona—avenger (form of Alastair)

Alison, Allsun, Allison, Alyson—honest

Alma—loving

Alvy—olive

Annabla—lovely grace (form of Annabelle)

Aodhnait—meaning unknown

Aoibheann—fair

Aoife—life (form of Eve)

Ardala—high honor (form of Ardal)

Arleen, Arlene, Airleas, Arlena, Arleta, Arlette, Arline, Arlyne—oath (form of Arlen)

Assane, Assana—waterfall (form of Assan)

Asthore—loved one

Attracta, Athracht—saint name

Augusteen—great (form of August)

Aurnia—golden lady

Avonmora—from the great river (form of Avonmore)

Bab, Babe—meaning unknown

Baibre—strange

Banba—myth name

Barran—little top

Bebhinn, Bevin—harmonious

Bellinagara—meaning unknown (form of Bellinagar)

Benvy—meaning unknown

Berneen—strong as a bear (form of Bernard)

Blaine—thin

Blanaid, Blathnaid—flower

Blinne—meaning unknown

Bluinse—white

Brenda, Breandan—little raven

Brenna, Brann—raven

Brianna, Briana, Breanne, Brianne, Brina, Bryana, Bryanna, Bryna—strong (form of Brian)

Brighid, Bidelia, Biddy, Bidina, Breeda, Bride, Brid—strong (form of Bridget)

Brodie—ditch

Brona, Bronagh—sorrow

Buan—goodness

Cadhla—beautiful

Caffara, Caffaria—helmet (form of Caffar)

Cahira—warrior (form of Cahir)

Cailin—small girl

Cait, Caitie, Caitlin, Caitlan, Caitrin, Catlee, Cattee, Cat—pure (form of Katherine)

Caley—slender

Caoilainn—pure white, slender

Caoimhe, Kevay—beauty, grace, gentleness

Cara, Caraid—friend

Caragh—love

Carleen—manly (form of Charles)

Casey, Cathasach—brave

Cassidy, Casidhe—clever

Cavana—from Cavan

Christian, Cristin, Christa, Christona—believes in Christ

Ciannait, Keenat, Kinnat—archaic

Ciar, Ciara, Ceire, Keara—saint name

Cliona, Cleona—shapely
Clodagh—from Clodagh
Colleen—girl
Colmcilla—dove of the church
Comyna—shrewd
Concepta—reference to the Immaculate Conception
Conchobarre, Conchobarra, Conchobara—strong-willed (form of Connor)
Congalie, Connal—constant
Cumania—saint name
Daireann—fruitful
Damhnait, Devent, Downeti, Dymphna, Devnet, Downett—bard
Dana—from Denmark
Dara—of the oak
Darby—free of envy
Darerca—saint name
Davan—adored
Dearbhail, Dearbhal, Derval—true desire
Dechtire—mother of Cuchulainn; myth name
Decla—saint name (form of Declan)
Deirbhile—daughter of the poet
Dervla, Dearbhail, Dervilia—daughter of Ireland
Dervorgilla, Derforgal, Derforgala—servant of Dervor
Dierdre, Dedre—sorrowful; myth name
Doireann, Doreen—sullen
Dominica—of the Lord; born on Sunday (form of Dominic)

Donelle—ruler of the world (form of Donald)
Donla—lady in brown
Doon—from Doon
Duana, Dubhain—dark maid
Duvessa, Dubheasa—dark beauty
Dympna—saint name
Eachna—horse, steed
Ealga—noble
Eavan—fair
Edana, Ena, Ethna, Eithna, Etney—fiery one (form of Aidan)
Eileen, Eibhlhin, Eily—light
Eilinora—light (form of Eleanor)
Eilis, Ailis—consecrated to God (form of Elizabeth)
Eistir—star (form of Esther)
Eithne, Ethna, Etney—fiery, ardent
Elan—light (form of Helen)
Emer—myth name
Ena, Enat, Eny—ardent
Enda—like a bird
Ennis, Inis—from Ennis
Erin, Erina—from Ireland
Eveleen—light; gives life (form of Evelyn)
Etain—sparkling
Ethna, Eithne—graceful
Fainche—free
Fallon—leader
Faoiltiarna—wolf lady
Feenat, Fianait—deer
Fenella, Fionnghuala, Finella—white shoulders (form of Finola)

Fidelma—saint name
Fineena—beautiful child (form of Fineen)
Fiona, Finna, Fionn—fair one
Fionnuala, Finola, Nuala, Fynballa—fair shoulders
Flanna—red-haired (form of Flann)
Gearoidin—meaning unknown
Glenna, Glynna—from the glen
Gobinet, Gobnait, Gobnat, Gubnat—brings joy (form of Abigail)
Gormghlaith, Gormly, Gormley—sad
Grainne—grace
Grania, Granna—myth name
Hiolair—happy (form of Hilary)
Hisolda, Izett—fair lady (form of Isolda)
Hodierna—meaning unknown
Honor, Honoria, Honora—honor
Ibernia—from Ireland
Ide, Ida, Ita—thirsty
Ierne—from Ireland
Illona—light
Iona—blessed
Isibeal—consecrated to God (form of Elizabeth)
Isleen, Islene—vision
Ismey, Ismenia—meaning unknown
Jana—gracious God (form of John)
Kathleen—pure (form of Katherine)
Kayley—slender
Keara, Kiara—saint name

Keavy—mild, lovely grace
Keely—beautiful
Keera, Keira, Kiera—dark, black
Kerry—dark one; county name
Kinnat, Keenat—archaic
Kyna—intelligent
Labhaoise—warrior-maid
Laetitia—happy (form of Letitia)
Leila, Lil—saint name
Liadan—lady in gray
Luighseach—torch bringer
Mab, Mabbina, Meadhbh—happiness
Macha—plain
Mada—from Mathilda
Madailein—from the tower (form of Madeleine)
Maebh, Maeve, Mave—joy
Maible—lovable
Maighdlin—magnificent
Maille, Mailsi—pearl
Mairead, Margaret—pearl; saint name
Maitilde, Maitilda, Maude, Maud, Maiti—strong battle-maid (form of Matilda)
Majella—saint name
Malvina—sweet
Maoli, Maola—handmaiden
Maureen, Maurine, Moire, Maire, Mare, Maura, Mearr, Moira, Moya, Maurya, Muire, Mairona, Mairia—bitter (form of Mary)
Meadhbh, Meghan, Megan—pearl
Meara—happy
Melva—ruler

Merna, Myrna, Morna—beloved
Mide, Meeda—thirsty
Moina, Moyna—noble
Mona—noblewoman
Monca—wise
Moncha—alone
Mor, More, Moreen—great
Muadhnait—little, noble one
Mugain—myth name
Muireann, Morrin—long-haired
Muirgheal, Murel, Muriel—
    knows the sea
Muirne—high spirited
Nainsi—grace (form of Anne)
Neala, Nelda—champion (form
    of Neal)
Neasa, Nessa—mother of
    Conchobhar; myth name
Niamh—daughter of the sea god;
    myth name
Noirin—meaning unknown
Nolliag—Christmas (form of
    Noel)
Nora, Norah, Noreen—honor
Nuala—lovely shoulders
Obharnait, Orna, Ornat—color
    of olive
Ohnicio, Onora—honor
Oilbhe, Olive—olive
Oona, Oonagh, Ona—one
Orghlaith, Orlaith, Orlaithe,
    Orla—golden
Orna—pale
Padraigin—noble (form of
    Patrick)
Paili—meaning unknown
Phiala—saint name
Rahda—vision

Ranait, Renny, Ranalt,
    Rathnait—wealthy,
    charming
Regan—little king
Richael, Raicheal—saint name
Riley—valiant
Rioghnach, Riona—royal
Rois, Roisin, Rosheen—rose
    (form of Rosa)
Ronan—small seal
Rory—red ruler
Rosaleen, Rosaline—beautiful
    rose
Sadbh, Sive—good
Sadhbh, Sadhbba—wise
Samhaoir—myth name
Saoirse—freedom
Saraid—excellent
Scota—named for Scotland;
    myth name
Searlait—manly (form of
    Charles)
Seosaimhthin, Seosaimhin—
    fertile
Shawn, Shauna, Seana—
    gracious God (form of John)
Sheila, Sheelah—blind (form of
    Cecil)
Sibeal—prophetess (form of
    Sybil)
Sile—youthful
Sinead, Sineidin, Sine, Siobhan—
    gracious God (form of John)
Slaine, Slany, Siany—good
    health
Sorcha—intelligent
Sosanna—lily (form of Susan)
Sybil, Sibeal—prophetess

Talulla—prosperous
Tara—rocky hill
Teamhair—where the kings met;
    myth name
Tierney—from the lord
Treasa, Treise, Toireasa—
    strong

Tullia—peaceful
Ulicia—resolute protector
Una, Uny, Unity—together
Vevila—harmony
Vevina—sweet lady
Zaira—princess (form of Sarah)
Zinna—meaning unknown

MALE

Abban—abbot
Abracham, Bram—father of
    many (form of Abraham)
Adamnan, Awnan—little Adam
Adare—from the ford by the oak
    tree (form of Adair)
Addergoole—from between two
    fords
Aderrig, Aghaderg—from the
    red ford
Adhamh—of the red earth (form
    of Adam)
Aengus, Angus, Aonghus,
    Oengus, Ungus, Enos,
    Hungas—exceptionally
    strong
Aghamore—from the great field
Aghy—friend of horses
Aguistin—great (form of August)
Ahane—from the little ford
Ahern, Ahearn—lord of the
    horses
Aichlin—meaning unknown
Aidrian—dark (form of Adrian)
Ailfrid—wise
Ailin—handsome
Aindreas—manly (form of
    Andrew)

Aineislis—glorious stand
Ainmire—great lord
Airleas, Arlen, Arlyn—pledge
Alabhaois—famous soldier
Alan, Allan, Allen, Alleyne—
    handsome
Alban—white
Alphonsus—noble and ready for
    battle (form of Alphonse)
Alroy—red-haired
Alsandair—defender of mankind
    (form of Alexander)
Amalgith—meaning unknown
Amblaoibh—relic
Ambros—divine
Anguish—myth name
Anlon, Anluan—champion
Anmcha, Amnchadh—brave
Annaduff—from the black marsh
Anntoin, Ann—priceless (form
    of Anthony)
Aodhfin, Aodhfionn—white fire
Aralt—leader
Ardagh—from the high field
Ardal, Artegal, Arthgallo—high
    honor
Arlen—oath
Ardkill—from the high church

Artur, Art—noble bear (form of Arthur)

Assan—waterfall

Auley, Auliffe, Amhlaoibh—ancestor (form of Olaf)

Avonmore—from the great river

Baethan, Beolagh—foolish

Bailintin—valiant

Baird—bard

Ballinamore—from the great river

Ballinderry—from the town of oak wood

Banan—white

Banbhan—piglet

Barram, Bairrfhoinn—handsome

Beagan—little one

Bearnard—strong as a bear (form of Bernard)

Beartlaidh—from Bart's meadow

Becan—little one

Bellinagar—meaning unknown

Benen—kind

Birr—from Birr

Blaine, Blian—thin

Blair, Blar—from the plain lands

Blathma—flower, sun

Boynton—from the white river

Brady, Bradaigh—spirited

Bran—myth name

Brandan—saint name

Branduff, Brandubh—black raven

Breandan—prince

Breasal—pain

Breen, Braoin—sadness

Brennan—little drop

Brody—from the muddy place

Brone—sorrowful

Buagh, Buach—victorious

Buckley—boy

Cacanisius—son of Nis

Cadhla—handsome

Caffar—helmet

Cahir, Cathaoir—warrior

Cairbre—myth name

Caith—from the battlefield

Caley, Caly, Caolaidhe—slender

Calhoun, Coillcumhann—from the narrow forest

Callaghan, Ceallachan—strife

Callough, Calvagh, Calbhach—bald

Canice—handsome

Caolan—slender

Caomh—lovable

Carlin—little champion

Carney, Cearnach—victorious

Carrick, Carraig—from the rocky headland

Carroll, Cearbhall—manly (form of Charles)

Carthage, Carthach—loving

Cashel, Caiseal—from Cashel

Cathal—strong in battle

Cathmor, Cathmore—great warrior

Cavan—from Cavan

Celsus—saint name

Cian, Cein, Cain, Cianan—archaic

Ciaran—black, dark

Ciarrai—county

Cillian—battle

ELAINE BARBIERI

Elaine Barbieri has written thirty-eight novels and has been published by Leisure Books, Berkley/Jove, Harlequin, Harper, Avon, and Zebra Books. Her titles have hit major best-seller lists and are published worldwide.

No one appreciates more than I do the importance of selecting the right names for characters when writing a book. I choose names for my main characters that are related to their personalities or are indicative of the type of person I intend for them to become. I have occasionally started out writing from an outline, only to discover when writing the book that the hero's or heroine's name strikes an off-key note in my mind each time I write it. In one instance, I changed the heroine's name four times before finding the one that I felt "fit."

Since it is especially important to me that my heroes be basically strong characters despite the human flaws in their personalities, I search for strong names that haven't been overworked. The hero of my book *Wings of a Dove* was named Delaney Marsh. Delaney was to my mind a particularly strong name because it was the maiden name of the hero's mother and because it "fit." In the time since, I've used names like Cassidy, Slater, Reed, Quinn, and Tanner—names more commonly known as family names—for the first names of my heroes.

In choosing the heroine's name, I'm more comfortable with a different technique. In the first book of my Dangerous Virtues series, my heroine is a captivating saloon woman who cheats at cards. I called her Honesty. Her sister in the second book is fascinated by a "half-breed." I called that heroine Purity. In the third book, the hero's sometimes less than honorable intentions are thwarted by the heroine's total innocence. No other name was more suitable for her than Chastity.

I used the name Cal (Caldwell) for the hero of *Texas Star* and Taylor for the hero of *Texas Triumph*. However, in the second book of the series, *Texas Glory*, the illegitimate daughter of Buck Star was the heroine. I deliberately named her Honor.

"A rose by any other name?" No, not when writing.

Cinneide—helmeted
Clancy—red warrior
Cleary—scholar
Cluny—from the meadow
Coghlan, Cochlain, Coughlan—
    hooded
Coinneach, Canice—handsome
Coireall—lordly
Colla, Conary, Conaire—ancient
    Irish name
Collin, Coilin—virile
Colm, Colman, Coleman,
    Columbo—dove
Colmcille—dove of the church
Coman—bent
Comhghan, Cowen, Cowan,
    Cowyn—twin
Comyn—shrewd
Conchobhar, Conor, Connor,
    Conny, Connie, Cornelius—
    strong-willed
Conlan—hero, wise
Connlaio, Conley, Conleth—
    ardent, wise
Connolly, Connacht—brave,
    wise
Conroy, Conaire—wise
Conway—hound of the plain
Cooney, Cuanaic—handsome
Corcoran—reddish skin
Corey, Cori, Cory—ravine
Cormac, Cormick, Corbmac,
    Cormic—charioteer
Crevan—fox
Crogher, Crohoore—loves
    hounds
Cronan—dark brown
Crowley, Cruadhlaoich—
    hunchbacked

Cuinn—wise
Cumhea, Cooey, Covey—hound
    of the plains
CuUladh, Cooley, Coolie, Cullo—
    hound of Ulster
Cuyler—chapel
Daghda—myth name
Dahy—quick and agile
Daibheid—dearly loved
Daimhin—little deer
Daire, Dary, Darragh, Darry—
    wealthy
Daithi—beloved (form of David)
Daley—counselor
Dallan—blind
Damhlaic—meaning unknown
Damon, Daman—tame
Davin—little deer
Declan, Deaglan—saint name
Delaney—from the river Slaney
Dempsey—proud
Dermot, Dermod, Darby—free
Desmond—from south Munster
Devine, Daimhin—poet
Diarmid—absence of envy
Dillon—faithful
Donal—ruler of the world (form
    of Donald)
Donnan, Donn—brown
Doran, Deoradhain—exile
Dougal, Dubhghall, Doyle,
    Dowle—dark stranger
Douglas—dark water
Dow, Dubg—black-haired
Driscol, Driscoll—interpreter
Dubhan, Dowan, Duggan,
    Dubhagain—black
Dubhlainn—black sword

Eachan—horseman
Eamon—guardian
Earnan—knowing
Egan, Egon, Eagon—fiery
Eimhin, Eimar, Evin—swift
Eirnin—strong, like iron
Elhe—legend name
Elroy—red-haired youth
Enan, Eanan—meaning unknown
Enda—saint name
Eoghan, Eoin—gracious God
(form of John)
Eoin Baiste—named for John the
Baptist
Erc, Earc—red
Ernan—serious (form of Ernest)
Eth—fire
Evoy—blond
Fachnan—saint name
Fagan, Hagan—little Hugh
Fahey, Fahy—from the green
field
Fallon, Fallamhain—leader
Faolan, Felan—little wolf
Fardoragh—dark
Farry—manly
Fay, Feich—raven
Ferdia—man of God
Fergal—valor
Fergus—of manly strength
Fiachra, Feary, Fiach—myth
name
Fineen—beautiful child
Finghin, Fineen, Finnin, Fionan,
Finian, Fionn, Fionnbarr,
Finbar—handsome
Flann, Flainn, Floinn, Flannan,
Flanagan, Flannagain, Flynn,
Floinn—red-haired

Fogarty, Fogerty, Fogartaigh—
exiled
Foley—plunders
Forba—owns the fields
Gaffney—calf
Gale, Gael, Gaile—stranger
Gall—stranger
Gara, Gadhra—mastiff
Garbhan, Garvan—rough
Garvey, Gairbith—rough peace
Gearoid—spear ruler (form of
Gerald)
Geraghty—from the court
Geralt—farmer
Gilchrist, Giolla Chriost, Gil,
Gilley, Gilvarry—serves
Christ
Gilibeirt—pledge (form of
Gilbert)
Giollabrighde, Gilbride—serves
Saint Bridget
Giollabuidhe—blond
Giolladhe, Gildea—golden
Glaisne, Glasny—meaning
unknown
Glaleanna—dwells in the glen
Gofraidh, Godfrey, Gorry,
Gorrie—peace from God
Gogarty—banished
Gorman, Gormain—eyes of blue
Gothfriadh—God's peace (form
of Godfrey)
Grady—noble
Greagoir, Grioghar—watchful
(form of Gregory)
Gruagh—giant
Haley—wise, smart
Hanraoi—rules the home (form
of Henry)

Hegarty—unjust
Heremon—myth name
Hewney—meaning unknown
Hickey—healer
Hiero—saint name
Higgins—intelligent
Hoireabard—soldier
Hrothrekr—famous ruler
Hurley—sea tide
Iarfhlaith—meaning unknown
Inerney—steward of church
   lands
Innis, Inis, Inys, Innes, Iniss—
   from the river island
Iollan—one who worships other
   gods
Irial—meaning unknown
Jarlath—tributary lord
Justin—just
Kealan, Kelan—slender
Keallach, Killian—battle
Keefe—handsome
Keegan, Keagan—fiery
Keely, Kealy—handsome
Keenan, Keanan—ancient
Keith—from the battlefield
Kellach, Killian, Ceallach—strife
Kelleher—loving husband
Kennedy—helmeted
Kenny, Kavan, Kaven—
   handsome
Kerry, Keary—dark one; county
   name
Kerwin, Kerwy—little black one
Kevan, Kevin—well born
Kian, Kean, Kienan, Kenan—
   archaic
Kieran, Kyran, Kieron—black

Killdaire, Kildare, Kildaire—
   from county Kildare
Kinsella, Kinsale—meaning
   unknown
Lalor, Leathlobhair—half-leper
Laoghaire—shepherd
Laughlin, Lany, Leachlainn,
   Loughlin—servant
Leary—cattle keeper
Lee, Laoidhigh—poetic
Liam—resolute protector (form
   of William)
Lochlain, Lakeland, Lochlann—
   home of the Norse
Loman—bare
Lorcan—little wild one
Lugaidh—famous warrior
Lugh—myth name
Lunn, Lun—strong
Madden—small dog
Maeleachlainn, Malachy, Milos,
   Miles, Myles—servant
Maelisa—serves Christ
Mago, Mane—great
Maher—generous
Mahon—bear
Malone, Maloney—serves Saint
   John
Mannix, Mainchin—monk
Mannuss—great
Maolruadhan, Melrone—serves
   Saint Ruadhan
Maughold—saint name
Meara, Meadhra—happy
Melchior—meaning unknown
Melvin, Melvyn, Malvin, Mal—
   chief
Miach—myth name

Mogue—saint name
Molan—servant of the storm
Molloy, Malloy—noble chief
Monohan—monk
Mooney, Maonaigh—wealthy
Moran, Morain—great
Moriarty, Muircheartaigh—
    expert seaman
Morolt—legend name
Morrissey—choice of the sea
Muireadhach, Murry, Murray—
    lord of the sea
Mulcahy—battle chief
Mulconry—hound of prosperity
Mundy—from Reamon
Murchadh, Murrough, Morgan—
    protector of the sea
Murphey, Murchadh, Murphy—
    sea warrior
Murtagh—protects the sea
Naal—saint name
Nally—poor
Naomhan, Nevan, Nevyn—holy
Neason, Nessan—saint name
Niall—champion (form of Neal)
Nolan—noble
Nulty, Nulte—from Ulster
Odanodan—of the red earth
Odhran, Oran, Odran—pale
    green
Oisin—myth name
Ossian—fawn
Owney, Oney—meaning
    unknown
Padriac, Padraig, Padraic—
    noble (form of Patrick)
Parlan, Patholon—legend name
Peadar, Peadair—rock (form of
    Peter)

Phelan—little wolf
Quaid—powerful warrior (form
    of Walter)
Queran—dark
Quigley—distaff; unruly hair
Quinlan—well-shaped
Quinn, Quin—wise
Raghnall—mighty power
Regan, Riagan—little king
Redmond—protector,
    counselor
Renny, Raighne—mighty
Riddock, Reidhachadh,
    Riddoc—from the smooth
    field
Riobard—bright, famous (form
    of Robert)
Riordan, Riodain—royal bard
Roark, Ruarc, Ruark, Rorke,
    Ruaidhri—famous ruler
Rogan, Ruadhagan, Rowe,
    Rowen, Rowyn, Rowin,
    Rowan, Ruadhan—red-
    haired
Roibhilin, Ravelin, Ravelyn,
    Revelin—meaning unknown
Roibin, Roibeard—robin
Ronan—small seal
Rooney, Ruanaidh—hero
Rory, Ruaidhri—red ruler
Ruadhan—saint name
Ryan, Rian—little king
Scanlon, Scannalan, Scanlan—
    scandal
Scully, Scolaighe—town crier
Seafra, Sheary, Seafraid—peace
    from God
Searbhreathach—judicious

Shamus, Seamus, Shemus—
supplanter (form of James)
Shanahan, Seanachan—wise
Shanley, Seanlaoch—old hero
Shannon, Seanan—little old wise
one
Shaughnessy, Seachnsaigh—
meaning unknown
Shea, Seaghda—majestic
Sheary, Sheron—God's peace
(form of Geoffrey)
Sheehan, Siodhachan—little
peaceful one
Sheridan, Seireadan—untamed
Sorley—Viking
Strahan, Sruthan—poet
Struthers, Sruthair—from the
stream
Sullivan, Suileabhan—black-
eyed
Sweeney, Suidhne—little hero
Tadhg, Tadleigh—bard
Teague, Teachue—poet

Terrence—tender
Terriss, Teris—son of Terrence
Tiarchnach, Tierney, Tier,
Tigherarnach, Tiernan—
regal
Tibbot—people's prince (form
of Theobald)
Torin, Toryn—chief
Tormey, Tormaigh—thunder
spirit
Torrance, Torrence, Torrans,
Tory—from the knolls
Treacy, Treasigh, Treasach—
fighter
Trevor, Treabhar—wise
Tully, Taicligh—peaceful
Uaid—powerful warrior (form of
Walter)
Uaine—meaning unknown
Ualtar—strong fighter
Ultan—Ulsterman
Uther—myth name
Ward—guard
Whelen—joyful

ITALIAN

Italian surnames came into use at the end of the tenth century. They became hereditary much later. Patronymic and descriptive names are most common, but surnames were also taken from place and occupation. Nicknames provided the most common pool from which surnames were drawn.

Di and *de* mean "son of." All surnames end in a vowel.

Some Italian families named their children after family members in a predictable pattern. The first son was named after the paternal grandfather, and the second son was named after the maternal grandfather. The first daughter was named after the paternal grandmother, and the second was named after the maternal grandmother.

A few surnames:

Abruzzi	Giordano
Auciello	Giuliani
Baldovino	Greco
Bertoletti	Lapaglia
Bianchi	Lombardi
Bruno	Mantegna
Calabria	Marino
Calendri	Medici
Casale	Minimi
Coppola	Moretti
Costa	Nicoletti
De Luca	Ricci
DeMitri	Rizzo
Donatelli	Romano
Esposito	Roselli
Fabrizio	Rossi
Faggini	Russo
Ferrari	Scala
Gallo	Tomei

FEMALE

Adriana, Adreana—dark (form of Adrian)

Agata—good (form of Agatha)

Agnella, Agnese—pure (form of Agnes)

Aida—help

Albinia—white (form of Alban)

Aldabella—beautiful

Alessandra—defender of mankind (form of Alexander)

Aletta—winged (form of Aleta)

Alisa—wise, truthful

Allegra—cheerful

Alonza—noble and ready for battle (form of Alphonse)

Amalea, Amalia—hardworking (form of Amelia)

Amadora—gift of love

Amata—beloved (form of Amato)

Anata, Annata, Anita—grace (form of Anne)

Andreana—manly (form of Andrew)

Angelia, Angela—angel

Aniela—heavenly messenger, angel

Annuziata—name for the Annunciation

Antonietta, Antonia—priceless (form of Anthony)

Aria—melody

Balbina—strong, stammers

Bambi—child

Battista, Bautista, Baptiste—named for John the Baptist

Beatricia, Beatrice—brings joy

Belinda—beautiful

Benedetta—blessed (form of Benedict)

Benigna—friendly

Bianca, Bellance, Blanca—white (form of Blanche)

Brunetta, Bruna—dark-haired (form of Brun)

Cadenza—rhythmic (form of Cadence)

Cameo, Cammeo—sculptured jewel

Caprice—fanciful

Cara, Carina—beloved

Carlotta—manly (form of Charles)

Carmela, Carmelina, Carmelita—garden (form of Carmel)

Carolina—manly (form of Charles)

Catarina, Catarine, Caterina—pure (form of Katherine)

Cerelia—of the spring

Chiara—bright

Cira—sun

Clarice, Clarissa, Clariss—clear, bright (form of Clare)

Concetta—from the Immaculate Conception

Constanza, Constansie, Constanzie, Stansie, Constantia, Constantina—constant (form of Constantine)

Clorinda—renowned

Claudina—lame (form of Claude)
Columbine—dove
Consolata—consolation
Delanna—soft as wool
Dona, Donna—lady
Donata—gift (form of Donato)
Edita, Editta—wealthy gift (form of Edith)
Elda—warrior
Elena, Elene, Elenora, Eleanora, Elenore—light (form of Eleanor)
Elisabetta, Elizabetta—consecrated to God (form of Elizabeth)
Emilia—hardworking (form of Emily)
Enrica, Enrichetta—rules the home (form of Henry)
Esta—from the east
Evalina—light; gives life (form of Evelyn)
Fabiana, Fabia—bean farmer (form of Fabian)
Fausta, Fortuna—lucky (form of Faust)
Felice—happy (form of Felix)
Filomena—lover of man
Fiorella—little flower (form of Fiorello)
Fiorenza—flower
Flavia, Fulvia—yellow (form of Flavian)
Francesca—free (form of Francis)
Gabriella—God-given strength (form of Gabriel)
Gaetane, Gaetana—from Gaete

Geltruda—meaning unknown
Gemma—jewel
Genevra—white wave (form of Genevieve)
Ghita—pearl (form of Margaret)
Gianna, Gianina—gracious God (form of John)
Giovanna—gracious God (form of John)
Giuditta—praised (form of Jude)
Giulia—youthful (form of Julius)
Grazia—grace (form of Grace)
Gulielma, Guillelmina—resolute protector (form of William)
Immacolata—reference to the Immaculate Conception
Iniga—fiery
Isabella—consecrated to God (form of Elizabeth)
Jolanda—violet
Leola—lion
Leonora—light (form of Eleanor)
Letizia—happy (form of Letitia)
Lia—languid
Liliana—lily
Loretta—laurel (form of Lawrence)
Lucetta, Lucianna, Lucia—light (form of Luke)
Lucrezia—profit
Luisa—famous in war (form of Louis)
Lunetta—little moon
Madonna—my lady; Virgin Mary
Margherita—pearl (form of Margaret)
Maria, Marea, Mara, Marietta, Maurizia—bitter (form of Mary)

Massima—great one
Maura—dark-skinned (form of Maurice)
Mercede—mercy
Mona—lady
Natala—born on Christmas (form of Natalie)
Nicia—victory of the people (form of Nicholas)
Octavia—born eighth
Olympia—from Olympus
Oria, Oriana—golden
Ornella—flowering ash tree
Ortense, Ortensia—gardener (form of Hortense)
Ottavia—born eighth
Paola—small (form of Paul)
Patrizia—noble (form of Patrick)
Perla—small pearl
Pia—pious
Pietra—rock (form of Peter)
Pippa—lover of horses (form of Philip)
Quorra—heart
Rachele—ewe (form of Rachel)
Regina—queen
Renata—reborn (form of Renato)
Ricadonna, Ricarda—ruling lady
Roma, Romia—from Rome (form of Romano)
Rosalba—white rose
Rosalie, Rosalia, Rozalia, Rosa—rose
Rosetta—little rose
Rufina—red-haired (form of Rufus)
Sabrina—from the border

Sancia—holy
Sebastiana, Sebastiene—revered (form of Sebastian)
Serafina—fiery one; angel (form of Seraphina)
Serena—serene
Siena, Sienna—reddish brown
Silvana—from the forest (form of Sylvester)
Simona—God is heard (form of Simon)
Speranza—hope
Susana—lily (form of Susan)
Teodora—God's gift (form of Theodore)
Teresa—reaper (form of Theresa)
Terza—born third
Tiberia—from the Tiber
Traviata—astray
Trilby, Trillare—sings with trills
Trista—full of sorrows
Valentina—valiant, strong (form of Valentine)
Vanni—grace
Vedette, Vedetta—from the guard tower
Violet, Violetta—flower
Virginia—pure
Vittoria—victorious (form of Victor)
Viviana—lively
Volante—flying
Ysabel, Ysabelle—consecrated to God (form of Elizabeth)
Zita—saint name

MALE

Aberto—noble, intelligent (form of Albert)

Abramo—father of many (form of Abraham)

Adriano—dark (form of Adrian)

Agosto—great (form of August)

Aldo—wealthy

Alessandro—defender of mankind (form of Alexander)

Alfredo—elf counselor (form of Alfred)

Allighiero—noble spear

Amadeo—loves God (form of Amadeus)

Ambrosi—immortal (form of Ambrose)

Anastagio—divine

Andrea—manly (form of Andrew)

Angelo—angel

Antonio—priceless (form of Anthony)

Armando, Armanno—soldier (form of Herman)

Arnaldo—eagle (form of Arnold)

Arrigo, Aroghetto, Alrigo—rules the estate

Arturo—noble bear (form of Arthur)

Baldassare, Baldassario—one of the three wise men (form of Bathalzar)

Beniamino—son of the right hand (form of Benjamin)

Bernardo—strong as a bear (form of Bernard)

Bertrando, Brando—bright raven (form of Bertrand)

Biaiardo—reddish-brown hair

Bruno—dark-haired (form of Brun)

Calvino—bald (form of Calvin)

Carlino, Carlo—manly (form of Charles)

Caseareo, Ceasario, Cesare—long-haired (form of Caesar)

Cecilio—blind (form of Cecil)

Ciro—sun (form of Cyrus)

Claudio—lame (form of Claude)

Constantin—constant (form of Constantine)

Corrado, Corradeo—bold

Cristoforo—Christ-bearer (form of Christopher)

Daniele—God is my judge (form of Daniel)

Dante—lasting

Davide—beloved (form of David)

Dino—religious official

Donatello, Donato—gift

Edmondo—rich protector (form of Edmund)

Eduardo, Edoardo—rich guardian (form of Edward)

Egidio, Egiodeo—shield-bearer

Elmo—worthy to be loved

Emmanuele—God is with us (form of Emmanuel)

Enea—born ninth

Enrico, Enzo—rules the home (form of Henry)

Ermanno—soldier (form of Herman)

Ernesto—serious (form of Ernest)

Este—from the east

Ettore—loyal

Eugenio—well-born (form of Eugene)

Fabio, Gabiano—bean farmer (form of Fabian)

Fabrizio—craftsman

Fabroni—blacksmith

Faust, Fausto, Felicio—lucky

Federico—peaceful ruler (form of Frederick)

Ferdinando—adventurer (form of Ferdinand)

Fidelio—faithful (form of Fidel)

Filippo, Filippio—lover of horses (form of Philip)

Fiorello—little flower

Flavio—yellow (form of Flavian)

Francesco—free (form of Francis)

Gabriele—God-given strength (form of Gabriel)

Gaetano—from Gaete

Georgio, Giorgio—farmer (form of George)

Gerardo—spear ruler (form of Gerald)

Geronimo, Geremia—sacred (form of Jerome)

Giacomo—supplanter (form of Jacob)

Gian, Gianni, Giovanni— gracious God (form of John)

Giancarlo—God's gracious gift, manly

Gilberto—pledge (form of Gilbert)

Gino—famous in war (form of Louis)

Giraldo—spear ruler (form of Gerald)

Giuliano, Giulio—youthful (form of Julius)

Giuseppe—God adds (form of Joseph)

Gregorio—watchful (form of Gregory)

Gualtiero, Galtero, Galterior— powerful warrior (form of Walter)

Guglielmo—resolute protector (form of William)

Guido—guide

Ignazio, Ignacio—fiery (form of Ignatius)

Ilario, Ilari—cheerful

Innocenzio—innocent

Kajetan—from Gaete

Leonardo, Leone—brave lion (form of Leonard)

Lorenz, Lorenzo—laurel (form of Lawrence)

Lothario—famous warrior

Luciano, Lucan, Lucio, Lucca— light (form of Luke)

Luigi—famous in war (form of Louis)

Marcello, Marco—warlike (form of Marcus)

Mario—bitter (form of Mary)

Massimo—great one

Matteo—God's gift (form of Matthew)

Maurizio—dark-skinned (form of Maurice)

Michelangelo—who is like God, angel

Michele, Michel—who is like God (form of Michael)

Nico—victory of the people (form of Nicholas)

Nino—gracious God (form of John)

Nuncio—messenger

Orazio—family name (form of Horatio)

Orfeo—Roman myth name

Orlando—famous throughout the land

Otello, Othello—rich

Ottavio—born eighth

Pancrizio—supreme ruler

Paolo—small (form of Paul)

Pasquale, Pascal, Pascual—born on Passover

Patrizio—noble (form of Patrick)

Piero, Pietro—rock (form of Peter)

Pino—lover of horses (form of Philip)

Pio—pious

Pippino, Peppino—God adds (form of Joseph)

Primo—firstborn

Rafaele, Raphael, Rafaello—healed by God

Raimondo—mighty protector (form of Raymond)

Renzo—laurel (form of Lawrence)

Ricardo, Riccardo, Ricciardo—strong ruler (form of Richard)

Rinaldo—wise power

Roberto—bright, famous (form of Robert)

Roderigo, Rodrigo—famous ruler (form of Roderick)

Rodolfo—famous wolf (form of Rudolph)

Romano—from Rome

Romeo—pilgrim to Rome

Ruggero—famous spearman (form of Roger)

Salvatore, Salvatorio—savior

Santo—sacred

Sebastiano—revered (form of Sebastian)

Sergio—servant

Silvio—silver

Stafano, Stefano—crowned in victory (form of Stephen)

Tiberio—from the Tiber

Tito—giant

Tommaso—twin (form of Thomas)

Ugo—intelligent

Umberto—famous warrior

Valentino, Valerio—valiant, strong (form of Valentine)

Vencentio, Vincenzio, Vittorio, Vito—victorious (form of Victor)

JAPANESE

In Japan, as in many Asian countries, the surname is given first, followed by the given name. Until 1868, commoners were not allowed a surname. At that time, they created a surname or chose one already in existence. Most Japanese surnames consist of two Kanji characters, and they are frequently descriptive of geographic characteristics. For instance, *moto* means base or origin, and *yama* means mountain. Yamamoto means "base of the mountain."

A woman was obligated to take her husband's surname at marriage until 1947, when it became legal for a married couple to choose either the husband's or the wife's surname. However, the vast majority of women still choose to take their husband's surname when they get married.

A few surnames:

Akimoto	Nakagawa
Endo	Narita
Eto	Nobunaga
Fujimoto	Obinata
Fukushima	Oichi
Genji	Saito
Hagiwara	Shiga
Hideki	Shinko
Horigome	Suzuki
Ichigawa	Tadeshi
Ino	Takayama
Iwasaki	Tojo
Kataoka	Umari
Kurofuji	Watanabe
Matsuo	Yamaha
Matsushita	Yamamoto
Murata	Yasuhiro

FEMALE

Ai—love
Aiko—beloved
Akako—red
Akina—spring blossom
Ami—friend
Aneko—older sister
Anzu—apricot
Ayame—iris
Azarni—thistle
Chika—near
Chizu—longevity
Cho—butterfly
Dai—great
Emiko—blessed child
Etsu—delight
Fujita—field
Gen—spring
Gin—silver
Hide—fruitful
Hiroko—generous
Hisa—long lived
Hoshi—star
Hoshiko—child of Hoshi
Iku—nourishing
Ima—now, the present
Inari—shrimp
Ishi—rock
Izanami—gracious
Kaede—maple leaf
Kagami—engine
Kaida—small dragon
Kaiya, Kaiyo—forgiveness
Kameko—tortoise child
Kaori—strong
Kei—revered
Keiko—adored

Kichi—blessed
Kiku—chrysanthemum
Kimi—without equal
Kita—north
Kiyoko—transparent
Kohana—small flower
Koko—stork
Kyoko—reflection
Leiko—arrogant
Machi—ten thousand
Machiko—fortunate
Mai—brightness
Maiko—child of Mai
Makiko—child of Maki
Mamiko—child of Mami
Mariko—circle
Masa—good
Masako—child of Masa
Mayako—child of Maya
Mayoko—child of Mayo
Mayuko—child of Mayu
Michi—righteous
Michiko—wisdom
Midori—green
Mihoko—child of Miho
Mika—new moon
Miki—flower stem
Mina—south
Minako—child of Mina
Mine—guardian
Misako—child of Misa
Mitsu—light
Mitsuko—child of Mitsu
Miyoko—beautiful child
Momoko—child of Momo
Mura—villager

Jennifer Crusie sold her first novel to Silhouette and her subsequent novels to Harlequin, Bantam, and St. Martin's Press. Her first five hardcover novels from St. Martin's were all voted into Romance Writers of America's Top Ten Favorite Books of the Year.

My character names usually have some kind of association that gives me a baseline character insight, not a pattern to follow, more of a vibe. Sophie in *Welcome to Temptation* was named after Georgette Heyer's *The Grand Sophy* (although I changed the spelling) because I loved the way she went around fixing people, and that's what my Sophie does, too, although not with the ruthless enthusiasm of Heyer's heroine. My Sophie is stuck with fixing people; Heyer's Sophy loves doing it. Plus it comes from Sophia, which means "wise," and they were both smart women. Zelda in *You Again* is named after Zelda Fitzgerald. The reason given in the story is that her mother was a Fitzgerald scholar, but the real reason is all the romance and tragedy and passion that I associate with the real Zelda. My Zelda isn't patterned on her, but there's an emotionally lost quality to her that became evident once I named her. She also took on a toughness with that name that didn't seem right at first, so I tried changing her name to Emma, which was too bland for this character, and Esme, which was too soft, and I finally gave up and left her tough and that turned out to be just what I needed. Sometimes if a book isn't going well, I change somebody's name and that often brings the story into focus. Names are so important.

Mutsuko—child of Mutsu
Nahoko—child of Naho
Nami—wave
Namiko—child of Nami
Nanako—child of Nana
Naoko—child of Nao
Nara—oak tree
Nariko—thunder
Natsu—summer born

Natsuko—child of Natsu
Nayoko—child of Nayo
Nori—belief
Noriko—believer's child
Nozomi—hope
Nyoko—treasure
Oki—ocean
Rai—trust
Rei—thankfulness

Reiko—child of Rei

Ren—water lily

Rieko—child of Rie

Rikako—child of Rika

Rinako—child of Rina

Rini—small rabbit

Risako—child of Risa

Ritsuko—child of Ritsu

Rumiko—child of Rumi

Ruri—emerald

Ryoko—child of Ryu

Sachi—joy

Sachiko—child of Sachi

Saeko—child of Sae

Saki—cape, headland

Sakiko—child of Saki

Sakuko—child of Saku

Sakura—cherry blossom

Sakurako—child of Sakura

Sanako—child of Sana

Satoko—child of Sato

Sayoko—child of Sayo

Shika—deer

Shina—good

Shoko—child of Sho

Sorano—from heaven

Suki—beloved

Suma—question

Sumi—refined

Tadako—child of Tada

Taka—honorable

Takako—child of Taka

Takara—gift, treasure

Takiko—child of Taki

Tama—gem

Tamika—people

Tamiko—child of Tami

Tanaka—villager

Tani—of the valley

Tomiko—child of Tomi

Tora—tiger

Toyo—bountiful

Umeko—plum blossom

Usagi—moon

Yachi—eight thousand

Yasu—peaceful

Yayoi—March

Yoko—affirmative

Yori—honorable, trusted

Yoshi—good

Yoshiko—good child

Yukako—child of Yuka

Yuki—snow

Yukiko—child of Yuki

Yumako—child of Yuma

Yumi—beauty

Yumiko—child of Yumi

Yuri—native

Yuriko—child of Yuri

Yutsuko—child of Yutsu

MALE

Akahata—supreme

Akio—intelligent boy

Akira—intelligent

Akiyama—autumn, mountain

Amida—name for Buddha

Botan—peony

Dai—great

Fudo—god of fire

Fujita—field

Goro—fifth son

Haru—spring born
Haruki—shines bright
Haruko—firstborn
Hiroshi—generous
Hoshi—star
Ichiro—first son
Jiro—second son
Kaemon—joyful
Kana—strong
Kanaye—zealot
Kano—god of water
Keiji—wary leader
Kin—golden
Kisho—self-assured
Kiyoshi—quiet
Kuri—chestnut
Makoto—honest
Mamoru—earth
Masa—straightforward
Masakazu—son of Masa
Matsu—pine
Miki—native
Natsu—summer born
Rafu—net
Raidon—god of thunder
Ronin—samurai with no
    allegiance
Ryo—excellent
Ryoichi—first son of Ryo
Ryozo—third son of Ryo
Ryu—dragon

Ryuichi—first son of Ryu
Seiichi—first son of Sei
Sen—wood fairy
Senichi—first son of Sen
Shigekazu—first son of Shige
Shima—island person
Shinichi—first son of Shin
Shino—bamboo stalk
Sho—thriving; brilliant
Shoichi—first son of Sho
Shuichi—first son of Shun
Takai—meaning unknown
Taku—meaning unknown
Tama—gem
Taro—firstborn
Toshi—mirror image
Tomi—red
Toyo—bountiful
Uyeda—of the rice fields
Washi—eagle
Yasuo—at peace
Yo—cultivating
Yogi—participates in yoga
Yoshi—quiet
Yoshifumi—meaning unknown
Yoshimitsu—meaning unknown
Yoshiyuki—meaning unknown
Yukio—God rewards
Yuri—native
Yutaka—meaning unknown

KOREAN

In Korean names, the family name comes first, followed by the given names (or name). Most Koreans have given names consisting of two characters, but some only have one. Korean's usually address their seniors or superiors by title and last name, but it is common to address one's junior or subordinate by given name.

The three most common family names in Korea are Kim, Lee, Park, together making up 45 percent of the population in the 1985 census. Groups with the same family name are divided by ancestry into branches (the Kim family name has about 280 branches). Traditionally, unrelated people with the same family name did not intermarry. Some people still abide by this tradition, but it is perfectly legal today for two people with the same family name and branch to marry, as long as they are not closely related.

The following surnames make up about half of the Korean population. There is more than one commonly used transliteration method for the Korean language, so names can often be written in several ways.

An (Ahn)
Bak (Park, Pak)
Choe (Choi)
Gang (Kang)
Han
Jang (Chang)
Jeong (Chung, Chong)
Jo (Cho)
Kim (sometimes transliterated as Gim)
Lee (Rhee, Yi, Ri, I)
Yu (Ryu, Yoo)
Yun (Yoon)

Some other surnames are:

Bae	Kwon
Baek	Seo
Hong	Sin
Hwang	Song

FEMALE

Bo-Bae—treasure
Cho—beautiful
Dae—great
Ha-Neul—heaven, sky
Hea—grace
Hyun—wise
Jin—gem
Joo-Eun—pearl of silver
Jung—affection

Kyon—shining
Kyung-Soon—honored and
    gentle
Min—clever
Moon—letters
Shin—belief
Soo—live
Sun—goodness
Yon—lotus blossom

MALE

Bae—inspiration
Chin—precious
Gi—courageous
Ha-Neul—heaven, sky
Ho—goodness
Jin—gem
Jin-Ho—jeweled lake

Joo-Chan—glory to God
Jung—righteous
Kwan—mighty
Seung—winner
Shin—faith, trust
Sun—goodness
Yong—courageous one

LATIN

The Romans were one of the first cultures to develop complex surnames. Unfortunately, after the decline of the empire (approximately A.D. 400), the nomenclature disappeared, not to be duplicated until hundreds of years later.

In the beginning, Romans had only a given name. Later, they added the father's or husband's name. The suffix -*ius* was added to indicate family. By 100 B.C. the long name was the norm.

Standard format for a name would be praenomen (given), nomen (clan or race), cognomen (surname). Most Romans were called by their cognomen.

Girls received given names on the eighth day after birth and boys on the ninth. The eldest son was usually given the name of the grandfather. Girls often took the feminine form of their father's name.

Women had two names, usually taken from the names of male relatives, and always in the genitive case. Military men were often given agnomina (second surname) that were taken from the names of victorious battles.

Surnames were common by 100 B.C. By the time of the empires decline in the fourth century A.D., one name had become the norm.

A few surnames:

Antius	Nipius
Augustus	Oppius
Bruttius	Petronius
Camilius	Primus
Claudius	Publicius
Desticius	Quintilius
Fabius	Rufus
Fortunatus	Sabinus
Fulvius	Secundus
Grattius	Sempronius
Helvetius	Statius
Hilarus	Tertius
Julius	Titius
Lucius	Ulpius
Maximus	Valerius

FEMALE

Academia—named for Cicero's
  villa
Acarnania—from Arcanania
Accalia—possibly from Acca
  Larentia, the she-wolf who
  nursed the twins Remus and
  Romulus; myth name
Acidalia—named for Venus;
  myth name
Adamina—of the red earth (form
  of Adam)
Adora, Adoria, Adoree—glory
Adorabelle, Adorabella—adored
  beauty
Adrasteia—unyielding
Adria, Adrian—dark
Adrie—from the Adriatic
Aea—from Aea
Aegaea—from the Aegean sea
Aegates—from the Aegates
Aegina, Aeginae—mother of
  Aeacus; myth name
Aeolia—daughter of Amythaon;
  myth name
Agrafina, Agrafine—born
  feetfirst
Agrippina, Agrippinae—born
  feet first (form of Agrippa)
Albina, Alba, Alva, Albinia,
  Alvinia—white (form of
  Alban)
Albula—from the Tiber
Albunea—meaning unknown
Alcimede—mother of Jason;
  myth name
Alcippee—mighty mare

Alcmena, Alcumena,
  Alcamene—mother of
  Hercules; myth name
Aleria, Alera—eagle
Aleta, Aletta, Alida, Alaida,
  Aluld—winged
Alexandre, Alexine, Alexina,
  Alexis, Alexandrine,
  Alexandria, Alexandrina,
  Alexandriana, Alexandrea—
  defender of mankind (form
  of Alexander)
Alma—loving
Almeta—driven
Alta—lofy
Alvita—lively
Amabel, Amabelle, Amabella,
  Amabilis—beautiful, loving
Amadis, Amadea, Amadee—
  loves God (form of
  Amadeus)
Amanda, Amadine, Amadina—
  worthy of love
Amare, Amara—beloved
Amarna—meaning unknown
Amata—beloved (form of
  Amato)
Amelia, Amalie, Amilia, Amalea,
  Amelita, Amelinda—
  hardworking
Aminta, Amyntas, Amynta—
  protector
Amity—friendly
Amorette, Amoretta—little love
Amorita—dearly loved
Amphitrite—sea goddess; aunt
  of Achilles; myth name

Amymone—daughter of Danaus; myth name

Anabel, Annabelle, Anabella—lovely grace

Anahid—meaning unknown

Anaxarete—cruel woman punished by the gods; myth name

Ancyra, Ankara—from Ankara

Andes—from the Andes

Andreana, Andria, Andriana—manly (form of Andrew)

Andromache, Andromacha—wife of Hector; myth name

Andromeda—daughter of Cassiopeia; myth name

Anemone—myth name

Angerona—goddess of anguish; myth name

Angela, Angel, Angelica, Anjelika, Angelina, Angelita, Angeline—angel

Anna Perenna, Anna—possibly the daughter of Dido; myth name

Annunciata—announces

Anona, Annona—myth name

Ansa, Anse—constant

Antandra—one of the Amazons; myth name

Antigone—daughter of Oedipus; sister of Priam; myth name

Antonia, Antonina, Antoinette, Antoinetta—priceless (form of Anthony)

Apollonis—one of the Muses worshipped at Delphi; myth name

April, Aprille, Averil, Averyl—opening, blossoming

Apulia—from the river Apulia

Aquilina, Aquiline, Akilina—eaglelike

Aquitania—from Aquitaine

Arabia—from Arabia

Araceli, Aracelia—treasure

Arachne—turned into a spider by Minerva; myth name

Arcadia—adventurous

Arcanania—from Arcanania

Ardea—from Ardea

Ardelis, Ardelle, Ardella, Ardis, Ardine, Ardene, Ardinia, Ardra, Ardeen, Ardina—ardent

Arethusa—nymph; myth name

Argenta, Argentina, Argentia—silver

Argolis—from Argos

Argous—myth name

Ariadna, Ariadne—daughter of Minos; myth name

Ariana, Ariadne—pleases

Aricia—from Aricia

Aristodeme—daughter of Priam; myth name

Armenia—from Armenia

Armida—little armed one

Armilla—bracelet

Arne—mother of Aeolus III Boeotus; myth name

Arrosa, Arrose—rose (form of Rosa)

Arva, Arvia—from the seashore

Ascra—from Ascra

Asia—mother of Atlas; myth name

Assa—mother of Sithon; myth name

Asta—holy

Astarte—Phoenician goddess of love; myth name

Asteria—star

Astraea—justice; surname for Artemis; myth name

Astynome—daughter of Chryses; myth name

Atalanta—huntress; myth name

Atella—from Atella

Atropos—one of the Moirae; myth name

Atthis, Attica—from Attica

Attracta—drawn to

Augusta, Augustine, Augustina, Austine, Austina—great (form of August)

Aulaire—well-spoken

Aulis—Praxidicae; myth name

Aura—gentle breeze

Aurelia, Aurelie, Aurea, Aurum, Aureline—gold (form of Aurelio)

Aurore, Aurora—dawn

Automatia—surname for Fortuna; myth name

Autonoe—mother of Actaeon; myth name

Avena, Avina—from the oat field

Averna—queen of the underworld; myth name

Avis—bird

Aviva, Avivah, Auvita—youthful

Azalea—dry earth

Balbina, Balbine—strong, stammers

Balere, Balara, Balera—strong

Beata, Beate—blessed

Beatrice, Beatrix, Bea, Beatriz—brings joy

Bella, Belle—beautiful

Bellona—goddess of war; myth name

Benedicta, Benita, Benetta, Benedikta, Bente—blessed (form of Benedict)

Benigna—friendly

Beroe—traveled with Aeneas; myth name

Bibiana, Bibine, Bibiane—animated

Bithynia—mother of Amycus; myth name

Bittore—victor

Blanche, Blanka, Biana, Bianca—white

Blandina, Blanda, Blandine—mild

Blasia—stutters (form of Blaise)

Bolbe—nymph; myth name

Bona Dea—related to Faunus; myth name

Bonnie, Bonny—sweet and good

Borbala, Borsala, Bora—stranger (form of Barbara)

Bremusa—one of the Amazons; myth name

Britannia—from Britain

Bryce—wife of Chthonius; myth name

Bubona—goddess of cattle; myth name

Cacia, Caca—daughter of Vulcan; myth name

Cadence—rhythmic
Caenis—daughter of Atrax; myth name
Caieta—nursed Aeneas; myth name
Cairistiona, Christine, Christina, Cristin, Christian, Cristiona—believes in Christ
Caledonia—from Scotland
Calendae—first
Cales—from Cales
Calida, Callida—fiery
Calliope—Muse of epic poetry; myth name
Callista—chalice
Callisto—nymph; mother of Arcas; myth name
Callula—beautiful
Calva—name referring to Venus; myth name
Calybe—nymph; myth name
Calyce, Calcia—mother of Cycnus; myth name
Calydona—from Calydon
Calypso—nymph; daughter of Atlas; myth name
Camella—goblet
Camilla, Camille—temple servant (form of Camillus)
Candice, Candace—sparkling
Candida, Candide—dazzling white
Canens—wife of Picus; myth name
Cantabria—from Cantabria
Cantilena—song
Cantrix—singer
Capita, Capta—name referring to Minerva; myth name

Cappadocia—from Cappadocia
Cara—doe
Cardea—protectress of hinges; myth name
Caries, Caria—rotten
Carina, Carin, Caryn, Caryna—keel
Carisa, Carissa—artistic
Carissima—dearest
Caritas, Charity, Charissa, Carissa, Carita—giving
Carmen, Carmin, Carmia, Carea—song
Carmenta, Carmentis—healer; myth name
Carna—protectress of vital organs; myth name
Carya—daughter of Dion; myth name
Casperia—second wife of Rhoetus; myth name
Cassandra—prophetess no one believed; myth name
Cate—wise
Catena—retrained
Cecilia, Cecile, Cecily, Cili—blind (form of Cecil)
Cegluse—mother of Asopus; myth name
Celaeno—one of the Harpies; one of the Pleiades; myth name
Celeste, Celesta, Celestine, Celestina, Celia, Celine—heavenly
Celine, Celina—hammer
Cerelia—of the spring
Ceres—goddess of the harvest; myth name

Chalciope—daughter of
Eurypylus; myth name
Charybdis—daughter of
Poseidon; myth name
Christabel, Christabella—
beautiful Christian
Chryse—daughter of Pallas;
myth name
Chryseis—daughter of Chryses;
prisoner of Agamemnon;
myth name
Chrysogeneia—daughter of
Halmus; myth name
Chrysonoe—daughter of
Cleitus; myth name
Cilla—daughter of Laomedon;
myth name
Cinxia—name referring to Juno;
myth name
Clara, Clare, Clareta, Clarice—
clear, bright
Clarabelle, Claribel, Claribelle,
Claribella, Clarinda,
Clarinde—shining
Clarissa, Clarisse—clear, bright
(form of Clare)
Clarita, Clarine, Clareta—clarity
Claudia, Clady—lame (form of
Claude)
Clementina, Clementine—
merciful (form of Clement)
Clonia—one of the Amazons;
myth name
Clorinda—renowned
Clotho—one of the Fates; myth
name
Clymene—one of the Amazons;
myth name

Columba—dove
Conception—understanding
Concordia, Concordea—
harmony
Constance, Constanze,
Constancia, Constantina,
Connie, Constantia—
constant (form of
Constantine)
Consuela—consolation
Cornelia—horn (form of
Cornelius)
Courtney—from the court
Crescentia—growing
Crispina—curly-haired (form of
Crispin)
Cyprien, Cypriene—from
Cyprus
Cyrilla, Cyrillia—lordly (form of
Cyril)
Dacia—meaning unknown
Damiana, Damone, Damia—
untamed
Davida—beloved (form of
David)
Dea Roma—goddess of Rome;
myth name
Decima—born tenth
Deidameia—daughter of
Bellerophon; myth name
Delicia, Deliciae, Delicea—
delight
Delora, Deloras, Deloros—from
the seashore
Demonassa—wife of
Hippolochus; myth name
Derimacheia—one of the
Amazons; myth name

Derinow—one of the Amazons; myth name
Desirata—desired
Deverra—goddess of birthing; myth name
Devota—devoted
Dextra—skillful
Diana, Diane—divine; moon goddess; myth name
Dido—queen of Carthage who killed herself; myth name
Diella, Dielle—worships God
Digna, Digne—worthy
Dionysia—named for Dionysus, god of wine
Dioxippe—one of the Amazons; myth name
Dirce—wife of Lycus; myth name
Discordia—goddess of war; myth name
Docilla, Docila—calm
Domela, Domele—mistress of the home
Domiduca—Juno's surname; myth name
Dominica, Dominique, Domitiane, Domitiana—of the Lord; born on Sunday (form of Dominic)
Domino, Damina—lady
Donata, Donica—gift (form of Donato)
Donelle—small mistress of the home
Donna, Dona—lady
Doris—myth name
Dorote, Dorothee, Dorothea, Dorottya, Dorotea—God's gift

Drusilla, Drucilla—strong
Dryope—nymph; myth name
Dulcinia, Dulcine, Dulcia, Duclea, Dulcia, Dulcy—sweet
Dyna—sister of Roma; myth name
Echidna—monster; myth name
Edulica—protectress of children; myth name
Egeria, Aegeria—water nymph; one of the Camenae; myth name
Egesta, Segesta—daughter of Phoenodamas; myth name
Eirene—goddess of peace; myth name
Elata—glorified
Electa, Elekta—selected
Eloine, Eloina—worthy
Elvera, Elvira—white
Emera, Emira—worthy of merit
Empanda, Panda, Padana—myth name
Entoria—lover of Saturn; myth name
Enyo, Enya—goddess of war; one of the Graeae; myth name
Eos—goddess of dawn; myth name
Ephyra—daughter of Oceanus; myth name
Epione—wife of Asclepius; myth name
Epona—protectress of horses; myth name
Equestris—Venus's surname

Eriboea—wife of Aloeus; myth name

Ermina—noble

Espe—hope

Estelle, Estella, Essie—star (form of Esther)

Euadne—daughter of Poseidon; myth name

Euandra—one of the Amazons; myth name

Euryale—mother of Orion; myth name

Euryanassa—mother of Pelops; myth name

Eurybia—one of the Amazons; myth name

Eurydice—wife of Orpheus; myth name

Euryganeia—wife of Oedipus; myth name

Eurymede—mother of Bellerophon; myth name

Eurynome—goddess of all things; myth name

Eustacia—tranquil

Fabiana, Fabia—bean farmer (form of Fabian)

Fabiola—bean

Faith—faithful

Fama—rumor; myth name

Fani, Fania—free

Fauna, Faula—lover of Hercules; myth name

Faustina, Faustine, Fausta, Fauste, Faust, Fortunata, Fortune, Fortuna—lucky

Felicia, Felice, Felise, Felita, Felicity, Feleta, Felisa,

Felicitas—happy (form of Felix)

Fidelity, Fidelia, Fides—faithful (form of Fidel)

Filomena, Filomina—lover of man

Flaminia, Flamina—Roman priestess

Flavia, Fulvia—yellow (form of Flavian)

Flora, Floris, Florice, Floria, Flor, Fiorenza, Forenza—flower

Florence, Florentina, Florentine, Florella, Floria, Florida, Florenza, Florentyna—blooming (form of Florian)

Fluonia—Juno's surname; myth name

Fornax—goddess of bread; myth name

Fortuna—goddess of luck; myth name

Fronde, Fronda—leafy branch

Fronia—wise

Furina, Furrina—one of the Furies; myth name

Gala—from Gaul

Galatea—myth name

Garabi, Garbi—clear

Genetrix—Venus's surname; myth name

Gill, Gillian, Gillien, Guilia, Guilie—youthful (form of Julius)

Ginger—from the ginger flower

Gladys—lame (form of Claude)

Glaucee—wife of Upis; myth name

Gloria, Gloriosa—glory

Graca, Gracinha, Grace, Grazia, Grata, Gratia, Gratina, Graciana, Graciene—grace

Gregoria—watchful (form of Gregory)

Gryne—one of the Amazons; myth name

Gustel, Gustelle, Gustella—noble

Gymnasia—one of the Horae; myth name

Hadria, Hadrea—dark

Hajnal—dawn

Harmony, Harmonia—concord

Harpinna—mare of Oenomaus; myth name

Hecuba—wife of Priam; mother of Paris and Hector; myth name

Helen—light

Henicea—daughter of Priam; myth name

Hermippe—daughter of Boeotus; myth name

Hero—daughter of Priam; myth name

Herophile—priestess of Apollo; myth name

Hersilia—married a follower of Romulus; myth name

Hesperia, Hespera, Hesperie—daughter of Cebren; one of the Hesperides; myth name

Hibernia—from Ireland

Hibiscus, Hibiskus—flower name

Hilaeira—shining

Hilary, Hilaria, Hillary—happy

Hippodameia—daughter of Briseus; myth name

Hippolyte—queen of the Amazons; myth name

Hippothoe—one of the Amazons; myth name

Honorine, Honorina, Honorata, Honoria, Honor, Honora—honor

Horacia, Horatia—timekeeper (form of Horace)

Hortense, Hortencia, Hortenciana—gardener

Humility—humble

Hyale—nymph; myth name

Hyria—daughter of Amphinomus; myth name

Iaera—nymph; myth name

Ibolya—violet

Ida—nymph; myth name

Ierne, Ierna—from Ireland

Ignacia, Igantia—fiery (form of Ignatius)

Ilia—mother of Remus and Romulus; myth name

Iliona—daughter of Priam; myth name

Immaculata—reference to the Immaculate Conception

Imogene, Imogenia, Imogen—image

Imperia—commanding

Ina—meaning unknown

Inferna—Proserpina's surname; myth name

Iniga—fiery

Intercidona—goddess of birthing; myth name

Karen Rose Smith has written fifty books since 1991. She has published with Silhouette Romance and Special Edition. Her romances have made both the *USA Today* list and Waldenbooks bestseller list for series romance.

There is power in a name. Therefore, I don't name my characters casually, not even the secondary ones. With my fiftieth romance being released in 2005, the process has become more challenging. I don't like to reuse names of heroes and heroines. Besides the books of names I've collected, I pay attention to credits scrolling at the end of movies, editorial pages in magazines, and class lists that run in the newspaper. Over the past few years when I take a research trip, I particularly note names native to that area, both first and last. As I tour a town, I watch for billboards, scan lists of doctors on clinic signs, and check out regional phone books. Through this process I develop a list.

A selection of names helps but still doesn't name my characters. My hero's and heroine's names are too important to simply throw a dart at a list! I think of the traits my character displays and the essence of the emotions he or she will deal with in the course of the book. I factor in the background as well as family ties. Then I intuitively choose a name I feel embodies it all.

Naming characters is definitely akin to naming a baby. Most parents try to give children names they will grow into, that the world will respect, that will help their child make his or her mark. Since my books are character-driven, I want my characters to be memorable. Choosing the perfect name is part of my writing process. I choose carefully, then watch my characters evolve.

Invidia—envious
Inyx—spell
Iphimedeia—daughter of
    Triopas; myth name
Iphinome—one of the Amazons;
    myth name

Irma, Irmine, Irmina—noble
Iulia, Iulius—youthful (form of
    Julius)
Jacoba—supplanter (form of
    Jacob)
Jana—moon; myth name

Jette, Jetta—jet-black
Jewel—jewel
Jinny—virgin
Jinx, Jynx—spell
Jocelyn, Jocelin, Joscelin, Joyce, Joy—happy
Juga, Jugalis—goddess of marriage; myth name
Julia, Juliet, Judith, Juliette, Julietta, Julie, Jill, Juliana, Julianna, Julianne, June, Julene, Junia, Julinka, Juliska, Juli, Julesa—youthful (form of Julius)
Juno—wife of Jupiter; myth name
Justa, Justina, Justine—fair (form of Justin)
Juturna—nymph; myth name
Juventas—youth; myth name
Juverna—from Ireland
Kalare, Kalara—shines
Katalin, Katalyn, Katlyn—pure (form of Katherine)
Kira, Kirie, Kyra—light
Kirsten, Kirsty, Kirstie—believes in Christ (form of Christian)
Klara, Klarissa, Klarisza, Klari, Klarika—clear, bright (form of Clare)
Klaudia—lame (form of Claude)
Konstanze, Konstanza—constant (form of Constantine)
Kornelia, Kornelie—horn
Lachesis—one of the Fates; myth name

Lacinia—Juno's surname; myth name
Lamia—evil spirit who abducts and devours children; myth name
Lampeto—one of the Amazons; myth name
Laodamia—daughter of Bellerophon; wife of Protesilaus; myth name
Lara—famous
Laraine, Lorraine, Larina, Larine—seagull
Larentia, Laurentia—wolf who nursed Remus and Romulus; myth name
Larissa—lover of Poseidon; myth name
Larunda—nymph; myth name
Latona, Latonia—named for Latium
Laura, Laurette, Laurel, Laurella, Laurentia, Laurene, Laureen, Laurin, Lauren, Lauryn, Laurena, Laurina, Laurica, Loris, Lorena, Lorinda, Lorita, Lorena, Lorna, Lora, Laurie, Lavra, Laurissa—laurel (form of Lawrence)
Laveda, Lavare, Lavetta, Lavette—purified
Lavinia, Lavina—wife of Aeneas; myth name
Lelia, Lela, Lelah—from Laelius
Leda—mother of Helen; myth name
Ledaea—granddaughter of Leda; myth name

Leiriope, Leirioessa, Liriope—
mother of Narcissus; myth
name
Leis—mother of Althepus; myth
name
Lena, Lina—light
Lenita, Leneta, Lenis, Lenet,
Lynet, Lynette—mild
Leonce, Leonita, Leontin,
Leontina, Leontine,
Leontyne, Leandra, Leodora,
Leoine, Leoline, Leonlina,
Lyonene, Leona, Leone,
Leoarrie, Leonelle—brave
lion (form of Leonard)
Lerola—blackbird
Leta, Lita, Letitia, Lettie, Letty,
Larissa—happy
Leuconoe—daughter of
Poseidon; myth name
Levana—uplifting
Leverna, Lativerna—goddess of
thieves; myth name
Libentina, Lubentia—Venus's
surname; myth name
Libertas, Libera—liberty
Libitina—protectress of the
dead; myth name
Lida—sparkle
Lila, Lilian, Liliane, Liliana, Lily,
Lilika, Lillian—lily
Lilybelle, Lilybet—graceful lily
Lima, Limentina—goddess of
the threshold; myth name
Linda—pretty
Livia, Livie—olive
Lorelle, Lorella, Lorilla—little
laurel

Lucania—mother of Roma; myth
name
Lucerne, Lucerna, Luceria—
circle of light
Lucia, Lucy, Luciana, Lucille,
Lucilla, Lucinda, Lukene,
Lucie, Lucine, Lucina—light
(form of Luke)
Lucrece, Lucretia—profit
Luella, Louella—make amends
Luna—moon
Luperca—nursed Romulus and
Remus; myth name
Lysimache—daughter of Priam;
myth name
Lysippe—one of the Amazons;
myth name
Mabel, Mabelle, Manda—lovable
Madonna—my lady; Virgin Mary
Maera—daughter of Atlas; myth
name
Maia, Maya, May—daughter of
Atlas; myth name
Majesta—majestic
Malache—Lemnian woman;
myth name
Malvina, Malvinia—sweet friend
Mana—protectress of stillborn
babies; myth name
Mania—mother of souls; myth
name
Manto—prophetess; myth name
Marica—nymph; myth name
Marina, Marea, Marnia, Meris,
Merise, Merissa, Marine—of
the sea
Marpe—one of the Amazons;
myth name

Marpesia—one of the Amazons; myth name

Marpessa—daughter of Alcippe and Evenus; myth name

Martina, Martine, Martella, Marcia, Marsha, Marcie, Marcy, Marcella, Marciane, Marcelline, Marcellina, Marsil, Marsile, Marsilla, Marsila—warlike (form of Marcus)

Matuta—goddess of the morning; myth name

Maura, Maure, Maureen, Maurine, Maurita—dark-skinned (form of Maurice)

Mavra—Moorish

Maxina, Maxime, Massima, Maxine—best

Medea—wife of Jason who murders her children; myth name

Medesicaste—daughter of Priam; myth name

Meditrina—goddess of healing; myth name

Melanippe—nymph; myth name

Melia—nymph; myth name

Melissa—honeybee; nymph; myth name

Mellona—honey

Mercedes—mercy

Merle, Meryl, Merula, Merlina, Myrlene, Merrill, Merolla—blackbird

Messina, Messena, Messinia—middle child

Meta—goal

Minerva—goddess of wisdom; myth name

Miranda, Mirande—deserves admiration

Modesta, Modesty, Modeste—modest

Moirae, Moira—fate

Molpe—one of the Sirens; myth name

Monica, Monika—counselor

Morag—blind

Muta—goddess of silence; myth name

Myra, Mira, Merta, Merte, Myrilla, Mirilla, Mirillia—marvelous

Myrina—one of the Amazons; myth name

Myrtoessa—nymph; myth name

Naenia—lamenting; myth name

Naida, Naia, Naiadia—named for the nymphs

Napea, Napia—nymph; myth name

Narda, Nardia—fragrant

Nascio—goddess of childbirth; myth name

Natalie, Nathalie, Natalia—born on Christmas

Nautia—from the sea

Nebula, Nebulia—misty

Neci—ardent

Nelia, Nelly, Nellie, Nella—horn

Neptunine—Thetis's surname; myth name

Nerine, Nerina, Neris—named for the Nereides, sea nymphs; myth name

Nerio—wife of Mars; myth name
Nevada—snowy
Nila, Nilia, Nilea—from the Nile
Nixi—goddess who helped with childbirth; myth name
Nola—olive
Noleta, Nolita—unwilling
Nona—born ninth
Nonna—sage
Nora, Norah, Norina, Norine—honor
Norma—typical
Nortia—lucky
Novia, Novea, Nova—young
Nox—goddess of night; myth name
Numeria—goddess who assisted with childbirth; myth name
Nunciata, Nunzia—announces
Nydia—refuge
Nyx—goddess of night; myth name
Octavia, Octavie—born eighth
Ocyale—one of the Amazons; myth name
Oenone—daughter of Cebren; lover of Paris; myth name
Olethea, Olithia, Olethia, Olethe—honest
Olinda—fragrant
Olive, Olivia, Olivie—olive
Oma—named for Bona Dea
Ona—only child
Ops—goddess of plenty; myth name
Ora—pray
Oralie, Oriel, Oralia, Oriana, Oria, Orial, Orlena, Orlene—golden

Orbona—protectress of sick children; myth name
Orella, Oracular—divine message
Oribel, Oribelle, Oribella—beautiful, golden child
Oris—mother of Euphemus; myth name
Ornora, Ornoria—honor
Orphe—lover of Dionysus; myth name
Ortensia, Ortensie, Ortensiana—gardener (form of Hortense)
Otrera—mother of the Amazons; myth name
Ovia—egg
Pales—goddess of shepherds and flocks; myth name
Pallantia—daughter of Hercules; myth name
Pallas—wise; another name for Athene; myth name
Palma, Palmira, Palmyra—palm tree
Pamela, Pammeli, Pamelina, Pameline, Pamella—made from honey
Pantxike, Pacquita—free
Panya—crowned in victory
Paola, Paula, Paulina, Pauline, Paulette, Pauletta, Paulita, Pauleta, Pauli, Pavlina, Pavla—small (form of Paul)
Paphos—mother of Cinyras; myth name
Parcae, Parcia, Parca—named for the Furies; myth name

Pasithea—mother of Pandion;
myth name

Patience, Patientia, Patiencia—
patient

Patricia, Patrice—noble (form of
Patrick)

Pax—peace; myth name

Pearl, Pearla, Pearline, Pearlina,
Pearle—precious

Peirene—lover of Poseidon;
myth name

Pellkita, Pellikita—happy

Pellonia—invoked to ward off
enemies; myth name

Penthesilea—queen of the
Amazons; myth name

Perdita—lost

Perdix—sister of Daedalus;
myth name

Peregrine, Peregrina—wanderer

Pero—mother of Asopus; myth
name

Perpetua—continual

Persis—from Persia

Pertunda—Juno's surname;
myth name

Petra, Petronia, Petronella,
Petronilla—rock (form of
Peter)

Phaedra—daughter of Minos;
myth name

Phoebe—one of the Titans; myth
name

Phoenice—mother of Torone;
myth name

Phrygia—head goddess of
Cybele; myth name

Phylo—handmaiden of Helen;
myth name

Pia—pious

Pilumnus—goddess of birthing;
myth name

Placida, Placidia—tranquil

Polemusa—one of the Amazons;
myth name

Polyxena—daughter of Priam;
myth name

Pomona, Pomonia—fertile

Pompeia—from Pompeii

Poppy—flower

Portia—offering

Potina—blesses the food of
children; myth name

Praenestins—Fortuna's
surname; myth name

Prima, Primalia—firstborn

Primavera—born at the
beginning of spring

Primrose—first rose

Priscilla, Prisca, Piroska, Piri—
ancient

Procris—lover of Hercules;
myth name

Proserpina—goddess of the
underworld; myth name

Prosperia, Prospera—
prosperous (form of
Prospero)

Prudence, Predentia—prudent

Prunella, Prunellia—plum

Quies—tranquillity; myth name

Quintina—born fifth

Raidne—one of the Sirens; myth
name

Regina, Regine, Reginy—queen

Renee, Renelle, Renella, Renata, Renate—reborn
Renita, Reneta—dignified
Reselda, Reseda—healer
Reva, Rive, Riva—regain strength
Rexana, Rexanne, Rexanna—royal grace
Rhea—wife of Cronus; mother of the gods; myth name
Rhea Silva—one of the vestal virgins; myth name
Rhode—daughter of Poseidon; myth name
Risa—laughter
Roma—Rome; myth name
Romana, Romania, Romola—from Rome (form of Romano)
Rosa, Rose, Ruzena, Rosie, Ruusu, Rosaline, Rosaleen, Rosalyn, Rosalina—rose
Rosabel, Rosabelle, Rosabella—beautiful rose
Rosalba—white rose
Rubette, Rubetta—little, precious jewel
Ruby—red jewel
Rufina, Rufine—red-haired (form of Rufus)
Rumina—protectress of sleeping babes; myth name
Runcina—protectress of crops; myth name
Sabina, Sabine, Savina—of the Sabine people
Sabria, Sabrina—from Cyprus

Salacia—wife of Neptune; myth name
Salina, Salena, Saline, Saleen—from a salty place
Salvia, Salva, Salvina, Salvinia, Sage—wise
Samia—wife of Ancaeus; myth name
Sancta, Sancia—sacred
Saturnia—Juno's surname; myth name
Scholastica—scholar
Scota—from Ireland
Season—fertile
Sebastiane, Sebastiana—revered (form of Sebastian)
Secuba—born second
Semele—mother of Dionysus; myth name
Sena, Sina—blessed
Septima—born seventh (form of Septimus)
Serena, Serina, Serene—serene
Side—wife of Orion; myth name
Sidero—evil nymph; myth name
Sidra, Sidera, Sideria, Siderea—luminous
Signa, Signe, Signia—sign
Silke, Silka, Silkie—blind
Silvia, Sylvia, Silva, Sylva, Sylvana, Sylvanna, Sylvania—from the forest (form of Sylvester)
Sinope—daughter of Ares; myth name
Solita—accustomed
Speranza—hope
Spes—hope

Stella, Stelle, Star, Stanislava—
    star
Stimula—another name for
    Semele; myth name
Suada—persuasion
Syllis—nymph; myth name
Symaethis—mother of Acis;
    myth name
Tacita—silent
Tanaquil—worshipped in the
    home; myth name
Tansy—tenacious
Tarpeia—killed for an act of
    treason against her father;
    myth name
Telephassa—wife of Agenor;
    myth name
Teles—one of the Sirens; myth
    name
Tellus, Terra—earth; myth name
Templa—sanctuary
Tertia—born third (form of
    Tertius)
Tethys—daughter of Gaea; wife
    of Oceanus; myth name
Thalassa—sea goddess; myth
    name
Thelxiepeia, Thelxepeia—one of
    the Sirens; myth name
Tiberia—from the Tiber
Tigris, Tigrisia, Tigrisa—from
    the Tigris
Timandra—sister of Helen; myth
    name
Tiryns—aunt of Hercules; myth
    name
Tita—honored
Toinette, Tonia—priceless
    (form of Anthony)

Topaz—jewel
Tosca, Toscana—meaning
    unknown
Trinity—unity
Triste, Trista—full of sorrows
Trivia—another name for Diana;
    myth name
Trixy, Trix, Trixie—happy
Tryphena, Tryphana,
    Tryphaena—delicate
Tuccia—one of the vestal
    virgins; myth name
Tullia, Tulia—meaning unknown
Tulliola—little Tullia
Tutilina—goddess of harvest;
    myth name
Una—one
Undine, Undina, Undinia—of the
    waves
Urbana, Urbania—born of the
    city
Ursule, Urzula, Ursola, Urselina,
    Urseline, Ursula—little bear
Vacuna—victory; myth name
Val, Valentina, Valeria, Valery,
    Valorous, Valari, Valarie,
    Valencia, Valentia, Valeda,
    Valora—valiant, strong
    (form of Valentine)
Valonia, Vallonia—from the vale
Vega—star
Venessa, Vanessa—named for
    Venus; myth name
Venilia—of the sea and winds;
    myth name
Venus, Venita—goddess of love
    and beauty; myth name
Vera, Veradis, Veradisia—true

Verbane, Verbena, Verbenae, Verbenia—sacred limb
Verda—unspoiled
Verna, Vernita—born in the spring
Veronica, Veronika—honest image
Vespera, Vespira, Vesperia—evening star
Vesta—goddess of the hearth; myth name
Victoria, Vincentia, Viktoria, Vittoria, Victrix, Victrixa—victorious (form of Victor)
Vigilia—alert
Viola—flower
Virdis, Virdia, Virdisia, Virdisa—young and budding
Virgilia—staff bearer (form of Virgil)
Virginia—pure
Virilis—Fortuna's surname; myth name
Virtus—virtue
Vita, Veta, Vitia—life
Vivian, Viviana, Vivienne, Vavay—lively
Volupia—sensual pleasure; myth name
Xanthe—one of the Amazons; myth name
Yuliya, Yulenka, Yulenke, Yulene, Yulia—youthful (form of Julius)
Zeuxippe—daughter of Lamedon; myth name
Zezili, Zezilia—gray eyes

MALE

Abantiades—descendant of Abas
Abas, Abasantis—meaning unknown
Absyrtus—murdered by his sister Medea; myth name
Academicus—name of a philosopher
Acarnanus—from Acarnania
Acastus—one of the Argonauts; son of Pelias; myth name
Accius—Roman poet
Ace—unity
Acestes—myth name
Achaemenius, Achaemenes—Persian
Achaeus, Achaean, Achivus—Greek
Achates—friend of Aeneas; myth name
Acheron, Acheros—river of woe; myth name
Achilles—lipless; hero of the Greeks; myth name
Achillides—descendant of Achilles
Acis—son of Faunus; lover of Galatea; myth name
Acrisioniades—descendant of Acrisius
Acrisius—father of Danae; grandfather of Perseus; myth name

Actaeon, Actaeonis—hunter torn apart by his own dogs; myth name

Actaeus—from Athens

Actor, Actoris—son of Azeus; myth name

Adrian, Adrien, Adok, Adriano, Adrik, Andrion—dark

Aeetes—Medea's father; myth name

Aegaeus, Aegeus—from the Aegean sea

Aegides—meaning unknown

Aegisthus—cousin of Agamemnon; myth name

Aegyptus—brother of Danaus; father of the Danaides; myth name

Aeneades—descended from Aeneas

Aeneas—praiseworthy

Aeolius, Aeolus—god of the winds; myth name

Aeschylus—Athenian poet

Aesclapius, Asclepius, Aesculapius—god of medicine; myth name

Aeson—father of Jason; myth name

Aethiops—Ethiopian

Agenor—son of Poseidon; myth name

Agrippa—born feet first

Ajax—one of the Greeks at Troy; myth name

Alair—happy

Alban, Avaro, Albin, Albion, Aubin, Aubyn, Albano, Alvar, Alver, Albinus, Alva, Albus—white

Albion—from Britain

Alcaeus—Greek poet

Alcibiades—name of an Athenian polititian

Alcides—descended from Alcaeus

Alcinous—father of Nausicaa; helped Odysseus return home; myth name

Aleron, Alerio—eagle

Aloysius, Alois—famous in war

Alroy—regal

Amadeus, Amadis, Amadeo, Amadio, Amado—loves God

Americus, Amerigo—meaning unknown

Amiphitryon—meaning unknown

Amphiaraus—one of the Seven against Thebes; myth name

Amphitryo, Amphitryon—husband of Alcmene; myth name

Amory, Amery—meaning unknown

Amulius—myth name

Amyas, Amias—loves God

Anacreon—name of an ancient poet

Anaxagoras—name of a Greek philosopher

Anaximander—name of a Greek philosopher

Anchises—father of Aeneas; myth name

Ancile—king of Rome; myth
name
Andoni, Antton, Antonin, Antal,
Antoine, Antoin, Antanas,
Ante, Antanelis, Antanukas,
Antony—priceless (form of
Anthony)
Andronicus—name of a Roman
poet
Anguis—dragon
Anius—myth name
Antenor—elder of Troy; myth
name
Anteros—brother of Eros; myth
name
Antilochus—son of Nestor; myth
name
Antiphates—king of the
Laestrygones; myth name
Antisthenes—name of a
philosopher
Apelles—name of an artist
Apollo—manly beauty; myth
name
Apollodorus—name of a Greek
writer
Aquilino—eagle
Arar, Araris—from the Arar
Aratus—name of a Greek author
Arber, Arbor—sells herbs
Arcas—son of Callisto and Zeus;
myth name
Archer—bowman
Archimedes—name of a
scientist
Arcitenens—archer
Arctophylax—myth name
Arctos—myth name

Arcturus—myth name
Arden, Ardin—fervent
Ardmore—ardent
Ares—god of war; myth name
Argus—monster; myth name
Aries—ram
Ariobarzanes—name of a king
Arion—name of a Greek poet
Aristoteles—intelligent (form of
Aristotle)
Arruns, Aruns—killed Turnus;
myth name
Arval, Arvalis—from the
cultivated land
Ascanius—son of Aeneas; myth
name
Astyanax—son of Hector; killed
at Troy; myth name
Atabulus—southeastern wind
Athamas—brother of Sisyphus;
father of Phrixus and Helle;
myth name
Atlas—one of the Titans; myth
name
Atreus—father of Agamemnon;
myth name
Atrides—descended from
Atreus
Attalus—name of a king
Attis—name of a priest
Aufidus—from the river Apulia
Augeas—king of Elis; myth name
Augustus, Augusty, Augustine,
August, Augustin, Austin,
Agoston—great
Aurelian, Aurelien, Aurelio—
gold
Auriga, Aurigo—wagoner

Avernus—portal to Hades; myth
name
Axenus—from the Black Sea
Bacchus, Bromius—god of wine;
myth name
Balbo, Balbas—speaker
Balendin, Balen—brave
Balint, Baline—strong and
healthy
Bellerophon—son of Glaucus;
slew Chimera; myth name
Belus—king of Tyre; myth name
Benedict, Benedicte, Bennett,
Benin, Bent, Benoit,
Benedikte, Benedetto,
Benedek, Benke, Bence,
Benci, Benen, Beinean,
Binean, Bendik, Bengt—
blessed
Binger, Bittor—conqueror
Blaise, Blase, Ballas, Balaza,
Braz—stutters
Blandon, Bland—mild
Bonaventure—lucky
Boniface, Bonifacy, Bonifacio—
good
Boreas—north wind; myth name
Brencis—crowned with laurel
Brutus—stupid
Bucer—horned
Cacus—son of Vulcan; myth
name
Cadmus—from the east; son of
Agenor; myth name
Caduceus—myth name
Caesar, Cesar, Cesario, Cezar—
long-haired
Cajetan—rejoiced

Calais—son of Boreas; myth
name
Calchas—seer; myth name
Caligula—name given to Gaius
Ceasar when he was a child
Calix, Callixtus—chalice
Calleo—knowing
Callimachus—name of a poet
Callosus—callous
Calvin, Calvinus—bald
Camillus, Camilo—temple
servant
Canis—son of Vulcan; myth
name
Cantor—singer
Capys—myth name
Carcer—prisoner
Carmine—crimson
Carneades—name of a
philosopher
Carsten, Christiann, Cristiano,
Christian, Carston—
believes in Christ
Cassius, Cass, Cash—vain
Castor—twin of Pollux and
brother of Helen of Troy;
myth name
Cato, Catus, Caton—shrewd
Catullus—name of a poet
Cavillor—critical
Cecil, Cecilio, Caecelius—blind
Cecrops—founder of Athens;
myth name
Celeres—paladin
Celestin, Celistine, Celestun—
heavenly
Centaurus—half man, half
horse; myth name

Cephalus—husband who killed Procris; myth name

Cepheus—father of Andromeda; myth name

Cereberus—guard of Hades; myth name

Chauncey, Chaucor, Chaucer, Chauncory—chancellor

Chester—camp

Chryses—priest of Apollo; myth name

Ciceron, Cicero—chickpea

Clarence, Clare, Clarensis—clear, bright

Claud, Claude, Cladian, Claus, Claudio, Claudion, Clodius, Claudius—lame

Clement, Clemence, Clem, Clemente—merciful

Cocles—hero who saved Rome; myth name

Collatinus—myth name

Colon—dove

Constantine, Constant, Constantios, Constantino—constant

Corbin, Cowin—raven

Cornelius, Cornelio—horn

Crispin—curly-haired

Curt—short

Damon—loyal friend

Danaus—king of Argos; father of the Danaides; myth name

Daphnis—shepherd blinded for his infidelity; myth name

Dardanus—founder of Troy; father of Erichthonius; myth name

Deiphobus—son of Priam; myth name

Delmar, Delmer—of the sea

Demodocus—blind bard; myth name

Deucalion—son of Prometheus; myth name

Dexter—right

Dezso—desired

Dis—Hades; myth name

Dolon—Trojan spy; myth name

Domiducus—Jupiter's surname; myth name

Dominic, Dominick, Domeka, Domiku, Dominico, Domokas, Domo, Dome, Dom, Dedo—of the Lord; born on Sunday

Donato, Donatello—gift

Dorjan—dark

Duke—leader

Durant, Duran, Durand—enduring

Eligius—worthy

Elvio—blond

Emil, Emilian, Emile—excellent

Erichthonius—founder of Troy; myth name

Errol—wandering

Euphorbus—Trojan soldier; myth name

Eurus—god of the east wind; myth name

Eurypylus—soldier against Greece in the Trojan War; myth name

Eurystheus—cousin of Hercules; myth name

Evander—fought with Aeneas; myth name

Fabian, Fabiano, Fabiyan—bean farmer

Fabrice, Fabrizio—craftsman

Fabron—mechanic

Faunus—god of forests; myth name

Fausto, Faust—lucky

Favonius—west wind; myth name

Felician, Felix, Feliks, Felice, Felicio—happy

Ferenc, Feri, Ferke, Ferko—free (form of Francis)

Fidelio, Fidelis, Fidel, Fedele—faithful

Flavian, Flavio, Flawiusz—yellow

Florian, Florentin, Floren, Florentyn—blooming

Forrest—dwells in the forest

Foster—keeper of the forest

Ganymede—cup-bearer to the gods; myth name

Garai—conqueror

Genius—guardian spirit; myth name

Germain—has same parents

Giles—kind

Gilroy—serves the king

Giuliano—youthful (form of Julius)

Glaucus—son of Minos; myth name

Graham, Graeme, Gram—grain

Grant—great

Gratian—grateful

Gustave, Gusztav—staff of God (form of Gustav)

Guy, Guido, Gwidon—life

Gyala—young

Halirrhothius—son of Poseidon; myth name

Harpocrates—Horus, Egyptian god of the sun; myth name

Hector—brother of Paris; myth name

Helenus—son of Priam; myth name

Hercules—Hera's glory; myth name

Herminius—hero who saved Rome; myth name

Hieronymous—sacred

Hilary, Hillary, Hillery, Hilarion—happy

Hippocampus—Neptune's horse; myth name

Honorato—honor

Horace, Horatio, Horaz, Horacio—timekeeper

Horatius—hero who saved Rome; myth name

Idaeus—meaning unknown

Idomeneus—king of Crete; myth name

Ignatius, Inaki, Inigo, Ignac—fiery

Ilari, Ilarion, Ilarius—cheerful

Illan, Illian, Illius—youth

Ilus—founder of Troy; myth name

Inachus—river god; father of Io; myth name

Ince, Innocenty, Innocent—innocent

Inek—small

Inuus—god of fertility; myth name

Iphicles—twin of Hercules; myth name

Iphis—lover who hanged himself over unrequited love; myth name

Iphitus—brother of Iole; myth name

Iulus—son of Aeneas; myth name

Janus—god of beginnings; myth name

Jerolin, Jerome—sacred

Jove—another name for Jupiter; myth name

Julius, Julen, Jules, Juliusz, Julian, Jullian, Jullien, Junus, Junius, Julio—youthful

Jupiter—supreme god; myth name

Justin, Justus, Joost, Justyn—just

Kasen—helmeted

Kauldi, Klaudi, Klaudius, Klaude—lame (form of Claude)

Kelman, Klemens, Klemenis, Kliment—merciful

Kerstan—believes in Christ (form of Christian)

Kester—from the Roman camp

Killian, Kilian—blind

Kinden, Kindin—born fifth

Konstantin, Kostas, Konstantinus—constant (form of Constantine)

Korneli, Kees, Krelis, Kornel—horn

Lacy—from Latius's estate

Laocoon—son of Priam; myth name

Laomedon—father of Priam; myth name

Lapis—myth name

Lares—god of the household; myth name

Lars—Roman hero; myth name

Lartius—hero who saved Rome; myth name

Latinus—king of Latium; myth name

Laudalino, Lino—praise

Laurence, Lawrence, Laurel, Lorin, Loren, Lauren, Lorne, Lauran, Lorentz, Lawron, Laurent, Laurentios, Lenci, Lorant, Loreca, Lorenc, Lorine, Lorenzo, Loretto, Labrencis—laurel

Leo, Leon, Leone, Leonidas, Leonide, Leonid, Lyonya, Lyonechka, Lew, Lon, Leontis, Leander, Leandros—brave lion (form of Leonard)

Leroy—regal

Lester, Leicester—from the legion's camp

Liber—another name for Dionysus; myth name

Lichas, Lycus, Licus—friend of Hercules; myth name

Lionel—little lion

JULIE ORTOLON

Julie Ortolon has published romance novels with Dell and St. Martin's Press and has upcoming books with Signet. Of her five published books, three are part of the Pearl Island trilogy. She is also working on her second romantic trilogy.

For the first names of my main characters, I try to stay simple since anything too unusual tends to trip the reader's eye. Then comes the angst-ridden process of pairing that name with the perfect last name, which can take days away from the writing process. The two names need to have the right rhythm and balance. If you have a short, common first name, you can go with a longer, more unusual last name, and vice versa. Plus, when possible, the name should add a layer to your characterization and even the story.

In *Drive Me Wild*, I named the news anchor hero Brent Michael Zartlich and had him go by Brent Michaels in his professional life. Dropping his last name when he left his small East Texas hometown to go into broadcasting seems obvious on the surface. What sort of name is Zartlich for a news anchor? But a whole lot of emotional baggage was attached to that last name, and that was the core of his story.

Lombard, Longobard—long beard
Lorimer, Lorrimer—saddle maker
Lucious, Lucian, Lucien, Luke, Lucas, Lucaas, Luken, Lukas, Loukas, Luciano, Lucio—light
Lysander—liberator
Magnus, Max, Maximilian, Maximillian, Maximos, Maghnus, Manus, Maxime, Maximus—great
Mallory—ill-fated

Manvel, Manvil—from a great estate
Marcel, Marcellus, Marcian, Marco, Marcus, Mario, Marius, Mark, Marc, Marus, Marcellin, Markos, Markus, Marci, Marcely—warlike
Maren, Marinos—of the sea
Mars—god of war; myth name
Martial, Martin, Martinus, Marcel, Martinien, Marceau, Martel, Marton, Martino, Mairtin, Marek, Marion, Marian—warlike (form of Marcus)

Maurice, Morie, Morris, Maury, Mauritins—dark-skinned

Mayer, Mayor—great

Mazentius—meaning unknown

Memnon—killed by Achilles in the Trojan War; myth name

Mercer—merchant

Mercury—messenger of the gods; myth name

Metabus—father of Camilla; myth name

Miles, Myles—soldier

Miller—miller

Minos—king of Crete; son of Zeus; myth name

Misenos, Misenus—drowned for hubris; myth name

Modeste, Modestus—modest

Moneta—admonishes

Montague—from the peaked mountain

Morrell, Morel—swarthy

Mortimer—dwells by the still water

Mulciber—meaning unknown

Munroe, Munro, Monroe—from the red marsh

Nelek—horn

Nemesio, Nemesus—named for Nemesis, goddess of vengeance

Neon—strong

Neptune—god of water; myth name

Nereus—god of the sea; father of the Nereids; myth name

Neville—from the new town

Nigel—dark

Nikki, Niki—of the lord

Noble, Nobilus—noble

Notus—south wind; myth name

Numa—king of Rome; myth name

Nuncio, Nunzio—messenger

Octavian, Octavius, Octavio, Ottavio—born eighth

Oistin—revered

Oliver, Ollie, Olvan, Olliver, Olivier, Oliverio, Oliverios—affectionate

Orban—born in the city

Orcus—underworld; myth name

Orson—bear

Ovid—Roman poet

Paganus—villager

Paine, Payne—rustic

Pales—god of cattle; myth name

Palinurus—pilot of Aeneas's boat; myth name

Palmer—pilgrim

Pandarus—Trojan soldier killed for breaking a truce; myth name

Paris—son of Priam; abductor of Helen of Troy; myth name

Parnassus—from Parnassus

Pastor—shepherd

Patricio, Patrizio—noble

Patroclus—friend of Achilles; myth name

Paul, Paulin, Pauli, Paavo, Paola, Pauls, Paulus, Pavlis—small

Pax—peace

Peli—happy

Penates—god of the household; myth name

Pephredo—dread; myth name

Percival, Parzifal—destroyer

Perdix—apprentice Daedalus murdered; myth name

Periphetes—son of Hephaestus; myth name

Phoebus—shining

Picus—father of Faunus; myth name

Pierpont, Pierrepont—lives by the stone bridge

Pius, Pio, Pious—pious

Placyd, Placid, Placidio—tranquil

Pluto—god of the underworld; myth name

Plutus—wealthy; myth name

Pluvius—meaning unknown

Pollux—Roman name for Polydeuces, the twin of Castor and brother of Helen of Troy; myth name

Polydamas—Trojan soldier; myth name

Polydorus—son of Priam; myth name

Polyeidus—seer; myth name

Polymestor—son-in-law of Priam; myth name

Pompilius—meaning unknown

Pontifex—priest

Porter—gatekeeper

Portumnus—god of the sea; myth name

Prentice—scholar

Priam—king of Troy; myth name

Prince—prince

Prior, Pryor—head of a monastery

Proctor, Procurator—manager

Prosper, Prospero—prosperous

Publius—hero who saved Rome; myth name

Pygmalion—king of Cyprus; myth name

Quartus—born fourth

Quintus, Quentin, Quincy, Quinton—born fifth

Quirinus—lesser war-god; myth name

Ray—radiant

Remus—founder of Rome; myth name

Renato—reborn

Renzo—laurel (form of Lawrence)

Rex—king

Rhadamanthus—judge in the underworld; myth name

Rhesus—king of Thrace; myth name

Rodhlann, Roland, Rowland—famous

Romain, Romney, Romano—from Rome

Romeo—pilgrim to Rome

Romulus—founder of Rome; myth name

Royal, Royce—regal

Rufus, Russell, Rufin, Rufeo, Rufio—red-haired

Rule—ruler

Sabino, Sabin, Sabinus—of the Sabine people

Salmoneus—king of Elis who, during Trojan War, pretended to be Zeus; myth name

Salvador, Salvator—savior (form of Salvatore)

Sargent—military attendant

Sarpedon—Trojan soldier killed by Patroclus during the Trojan War; myth name

Saturn—god of the harvest; myth name

Savill—from the willow farm

Sebastian, Sebastianus—revered

Segundo—born second

Septimus—born seventh

Sereno, Serenus—serene

Sergius, Sergios, Serguei, Sergio, Serge—attendant

Severin, Seweryn—severe

Sibley—prophetic

Sichaeus—husband of Dido; myth name

Silas, Silos, Sylvester, Silvester, Silvanus, Sylvanus, Sill, Sil, Silio, Silvain, Silvius, Sylvan, Silvanos—from the forest

Sinclair—hardworking

Sinon—convinced the Trojans to pull the horse inside the city walls; myth name

Siseal—blind

Sisyphus—son of Aeolus; myth name

Sixtus, Sextus—born sixth

Sol—sun

Somnus—sleep; myth name

Spurius—hero who saved Rome; myth name

Stacy, Stacey—dependable

Tarchon—myth name

Tavey—born eighth

Terence, Terrence, Terry—smooth

Terminus—myth name

Tertius—born third

Tithonus—lover of Aurora; myth name

Titus, Tito—saved

Tony—above praise

Tracy, Thrasius—bold

Trent, Torrentem—swift

Tristan—noisy

Tristram—full of sorrows

Triton—sea god; son of Poseidon; myth name

Troilus—son of Priam; myth name

Tros—founder of Troy; myth name

Tulio—lively

Tullius—name of a king

Tully, Tullus—meaning unknown

Turner—works on the lathe

Turnus—killed by Aeneas; myth name

Txanton—meaning unknown

Txomin—like God

Tyre—from Tyre

Uiseann—conqueror

Ulysses—Roman name for Odysseus, the Greek hero whose return from the Trojan War took ten years; myth name

Urban, Urbain—born of the city

Valens, Valentine, Valentino, Valerian, Valerius, Val,

Valerio, Valentin, Valerii, Valera, Valerik—valiant, strong

Varian—fickle

Venedictos—blessed

Vergil, Virgil, Virgilio—staff bearer

Verne, Vernus—youthful

Vernon—springlike

Vertumnus—god of seasons; myth name

Viator—traveler

Victor, Victorin, Victorien, Viktor, Vidor, Vincent, Vincien, Vincens, Vincenzio, Vincenzo, Vittorio, Vito—victorious

Vital, Vitus, Veit, Vitale, Vito, Vivien—lively

Vulcan—god of fire; myth name

Walerian—brave, strong

Waring—true

Wincent, Wicek, Wicus, Wicenty—victorious (form of Vincent)

Wit—life

Xanthus—immortal horse belonging to Achilles; myth name

Zethus—brother of Amphion; myth name

Zeuxippus—son of Apollo; myth name

Zorian—happy

MAORI

The Maoris are the indigenous people of New Zealand. They are of Polynesian ancestry, and were probably established in the North and South Islands of New Zealand by the fourteenth century. All Maori names and words end with a vowel, and consonants are always separated by vowels.

Traditionally, Maori were given one name at birth. The meaning of the name was very important. Names often referred to a significant event or circumstance at the time of birth, and an individual's name could change in commemoration of a special event in his or her life. Some Maori given names still follow this tradition.

Modern Maori names usually follow the Western pattern of first name, middle name, surname (although some people don't have a middle name). Surnames were introduced by missionaries, who arrived in New Zealand in the early nineteenth century. Many Maori adopted as a surname the Christian name of the missionary who baptized them. Descendants of Western missionaries, sailors, whalers, and colonists may also have Western surnames. Other surnames incorporate elements of ancestral names, such as the name of the head of the family. Sometimes these names were complex, and if various family members took different parts of the name, different surnames could result within the same family. Surnames are passed from father to children. Women usually take their husband's surname at marriage, but it is becoming more common for a woman to keep her original surname.

A few surnames:

Aotea	Moeke
Hakaraia	Oneroa
Heretini	Paranihi
Hoepo	Raharuhi
Hohapata	Rerekura
Hokotoki	Rihare
Kaiteke	Tiweka
Kerapa	Waaka
Kereru	Wiritana

FEMALE

Aka—affection
Akenehi—pure
Akona—to enthuse
Amiria—hardworking (form of Amelia)
Ani—grace (form of Anne)
Aputa—open space
Aroha—love, affection
Awhina—to help, assist
Hera—princess (form of Sarah)
Hinamoki—place name
Hine—girl, young lady
Huhana—lily (form of Susan)
Irihapeti, Erihapeti—consecrated to God (form of Elizabeth)
Kuia, Kui—elderly woman
Kura—treasure
Maata—mistress (form of Martha)
Makareta—pearl (form of Margaret)
Marama—light of the world
Marika—quiet, careful
Mate—signifying death

Mere—bitter (form of Mary)
Moana—sea
Mokai—pet
Ngaio—native mangrove tree of New Zealand
Ngaire, Nyree—flaxen
Omaka—where the river flows
Pania—sea-maiden; myth name
Pare—bitter (form of Polly)
Pounamu—treasured gift
Puti—flower
Rangi—sky father; myth name
Rawinia—myth name (form of Lavinia)
Reka—sweet
Rere—waterfall
Reremoana—to fly or skip across the ocean
Tahupotiki—beloved child
Tangiwai—crying water, tears
Te Tapiri—place name
Tiaki—supplanter (form of Jacqueline)
Wikitoria—victorious (form of Victoria)

MALE

Akahata—supreme
Amahau—gatherer
Amiri—east wind
Anaru—manly (form of Andrew)
Anewa—to fall
Arama—of the red earth (form of Adam)

Enoka—consecrated (form of Enoch)
Eruera—rich guardian (form of Edward)
Hare—manly (form of Charles)
Haruru—rumble, thunder
Hemi—supplanter (form of James)

Hohepa—God adds (form of Joseph)

Hone—gracious God (form of John)

Huatare—famous Maori chieftain

Huirau—gathering of the hundreds

Kura—knowledge; treasure; darling

Maaka—warlike (form of Marcus)

Matiu—God's gift (form of Matthew)

Pita, Petera—rock (form of Peter)

Pouwhare—pillar of support

Rangi—sky father; myth name

Rangiamo—day of gathering

Rawiri—beloved (form of David)

Rongo—god of rain and fertility; myth name

Ruka—light (form of Luke)

Tama—boy, son

Tamati—twin (form of Thomas)

Taua—army, expedition of warriors

Tane—god of man and forests; myth name

Tewi—beloved (form of David)

Tiare—manly (form of Charles)

Timoti—God-fearing (form of Timothy)

Tipeni, Tipene—crowned in victory (form of Stephen)

Toko—support

Wiremu—resolute protector (form of William)

NATIVE AMERICAN

This section lists given names by tribe, when the tribe of origin is known. But each gender list begins with names whose tribes of origin are difficult (or impossible) to determine. Since many tribes were migratory, they passed on and borrowed names from other tribes, making it difficult to know in which tribe a name originated.

Names were bestowed upon a person at the various epochs of life after careful consideration and, in some cases, with extreme ceremony. When Native Americans learned to speak English, they automatically translated their names; because certain phrases and distinctions didn't translate verbatim, many Native Americans were left with names that sound odd to most European descendants. Indeed, in a similar fashion, many Blancs became White and Schmidts became Smiths after migrating to America.

Writers should not generalize; names and habits changed profoundly from one group to the next, even within a single nation.

During the nineteenth century, many nations and tribes were forced by law to take on Christian names and surnames. Often they chose the names of soldiers or towns. One tribe of the Apaches was so adamant in their refusal that they were issued numbers by the government to serve as names.

Today, problems still exist with hereditary surnames among certain tribes and nations. Depending on the nation/tribe and individual, a last name may be either a translated version of a native name (such as White-Cloud), a Christian name (Smith), or a native name in its original form (Eponi).

FEMALE

Adoette—large tree
Aiyana—eternal blossom
Alameda—grove of cottonwood
Alaqua—sweet gum tree
Aleshanee—plays at all times
Algoma—valley of flowers
Amitola—rainbow

Anevay—superior
Angeni—spirit
Aponi—butterfly
Aquene—peace
Awendela—morning
Awentia—fawn
Ayita—worker

Bena—pheasant
Benquasha—daughter of Ben
Bhimalis—bluebird
Bly—tall
Chenoa—dove
Chilaili—snowbird
Chimalis—bluebird
Chitsa—fair
Cholena—bird
Cocheta—stranger
Dena—valley
Dyani—deer
Enola—solitary
Etenia—rich
Eyota—great
Flo—arrow
Gaho—mother
Halona—of happy fortune
Imala—disciplines
Istas—snow
Ituha—sturdy oak
Izusa—white stone
Kaniya, Niya—meaning unknown
Kineks—rosebud
Kiona—brown hills
Lakota—friend
Leotie—flower of the prairie
Lomasi—pretty flower
Lulu—rabbit
Luyu—wild dove
Magena—moon
Mahal, Mahala—woman
Mai—coyote
Maralah—born during an earthquake
Mausi—plucks flowers
Meda—prophetess

Memdi—henna
Miakoda—power of the moon
Mika—intelligent raccoon
Minal—fruit
Minda—knowledge
Mitena—future moon
Mitexi—holy moon
Nara—from Nara
Nashota—twin
Nata—speaker
Natane—female child
Neka—wild goose
Nina—strong
Nita—grower of beans
Nitika—angel
Nituna—daughter
Nuna—land
Ogin—wild rose
Olathe—beautiful
Onawa—wide awake
Onida—the one searched for
Petunia—flower name
Rozene—rose (form of Rosa)
Sakari—sweet
Satinka—magical dancer
Shada—pelican
Shako—mint
Sisika—bird
Tacincala—deer
Taima—thunder
Tainn—new moon
Tala—wolf
Tallulah—running water
Tama—thunder
Tayen—new moon
Tehya—precious
Utina—meaning unknown
Waneta—charger

Wenona, Wenonah—firstborn
daughter
Winema—chief
Wyanet—beautiful
Yepa—snow woman
Zaltana—high mountain

ALGONQUIN
Alawa—pea
Alsoomse—independent
Anna—mother
Chepi—fairy
Hausis, Hausisse—old woman
Hurit—beautiful
Kanti—sings
Keegsquaw—virgin
Kimi—secret
Makkitotosimew—she has large
breasts
Nadie—wise
Nijlon—mistress
Nittawosew—she is not sterile
Numees—sister
Nuttah—my heart
Oota Dabun—day star
Pauwau—witch
Pules—pigeon
Sokanon—rain
Sokw—sour
Sooleawa—silver
Tahki—cold
Wikimak—wife

BLACKFOOT
Koko—night
Peta—golden eagle
Sinopa—fox

CHEROKEE
Adsila—blossom
Amadahy—forest water
Awenasa—my home
Awinita—fawn
Ayita—first to dance
Galilahi—attractive
Salali—squirrel
Tayanita—young beaver

CHEYENNE
Abedabun—sight of day
Abequa, Abeque—stays at home
Ayashe, Ayasha—little one
Keezheekoni—burning fire
Kiwidinok—of the wind
Meoquanee—wears red
Migisi—eagle
Namid—star dancer
Nokomis—grandmother
Odahingum—rippling water
Ominotago—beautiful voice
Sheshebens—small duck
Tis-see-woo-na-tis—she who
bathes with her knees

CHOCTAW
Atepa—wigwam
Fala—crow
Isi—deer
Nita—bear
Poloma—bow
Talulah—leaping water

DAKOTA
Wicapi Wakan—holy star
Zitkala—bird

HOPI

Angwusnasomtaqa—crow mother spirit
Ankti—repeat dance
Catori—spirit
Cha'kwaina—one who cries
Cha'risa—elk
Chochmingwu—corn mother
Chosovi—bluebird
Chosposi—bluebird eye
Chu'mana—snake maiden
Hakidonmuya—time of waiting moon
Hehewuti—warrior mother spirit
Honovi—strong deer
Humita—shelled corn
Kachina—spirit; sacred dancer
Kakawangwa—bitter
Kasa—dressed in furs
Kaya—elder sister
Kokyangwuti—spider woman at middle-age
Kuwanlelenta—to make beautiful surroundings
Kuwanyamtiwa—beautiful badger going over the hill
Kuwanyauma—butterfly showing beautiful wings
Lenmana—flute girl
Lomahongva—beautiful clouds arising
Mahu—myth name
Mansi—plucked flower
Muna—overflowing spring
Nova—chases butterfly
Nukpana—evil
Pakwa—frog
Pamuya—water moon
Pavati—clear water
Polikwaptiwa—butterfly sitting on a flower
Powaqa—witch
Shuman—rattlesnake handler
Sihu—flower
Soyala—time of the winter solstice
Sunki—to catch up with
Tablita—tiara
Takala—corn tassel
Tansy—name of a flower
Tiponi—child of importance
Tiva—dance
Totsi—moccasins
Tuwa—earth
Una—remember
Waki—shelter
Wuti—woman
Yamka—blossom
Yoki—rain
Zihna—spins

IROQUOIS

Onatah—of the earth
Orenda—magic power

MIWOK

Amayeta—meaning unknown
Awanata—turtle
Helki—touch
Huata—carrying seeds in a basket
Huyana—falling rain
Kaliska—coyote chasing deer
Kolenya—coughing fish

ALEXANDER MCCALL SMITH

Alexander McCall Smith has written over fifty books, including the detective novel *The No. 1 Ladies' Detective Agency*, which received two Booker Judge's Special Recommendations. *The No. 1 Ladies' Detective Agency* is now a series that sells around the world.

In my forthcoming trilogy of Portuguese Irregular Verbs books, which will soon be published by Anchor Books, I have three main protagonists, Professor Dr. Moritz-Maria Von Igelfeld, Professor Dr. Detlev Amadeus Unterholzer and Professor Dr. Florianus Prinzel. I chose Von Igelfeld's name because it is wonderfully absurd. *Igel* in German means "hedgehog," and the whole name therefore means "hedgehog field." In spite of this absurdity, my main character is proud of his name and of his doctorate, as all German professors are.

Liluye—singing chicken hawk that soars

Litonya—darting hummingbird

Malila—fast salmon swimming up a rippling stream

Mituna—wraps salmon in willow leaves

Omusa—misses with arrows

Oya—jacksnipe

Pakuna—deer jumping downhill

Papina—vine growing around an oak tree

Pati—break by twisting

Posala—farewell to spring flowers

Sanuye—red cloud at sundown

Sitala—of good memory

Suletu—flies

Taipa—spread wings

Tolinka—coyote's flapping ear

Wauna—singing snow goose

NAVAJO

Altsoba—all war

Anaba—returns from war

Asdza—woman

At'eed—girl

Dezba—goes to war

Dibe—sheep

Doba—no war

Doli—bluebird

Haloke—salmon

Kai—willow tree

Manaba—return to war

Mosi—cat

Nascha—owl

Ooljee—moon

Sahkyo—mink

Shadi—older sister

Shideezhi—younger sister
Shima—mother
Shimasani—grandmother
Sitsi—daughter
Yazhi—little one

OMAHA
Abetzi—yellow leaf
Abey—leaf
Abeytu—green leaf
Donoma—sight of the sun
Migina—returning moon
Mimiteh—new moon
Nidawi—fairy
Tadewi—wind
Tadita—one who runs
Taigi, Taini—returning moon
Urika—useful to all

OSAGE
Misae—white sun
Niabi—fawn

SHOSHONE
Kimama—butterfly

SIOUX
Anpaytoo—radiant

Chapa—beaver
Chumani—dewdrops
Ehawee—laughing maiden
Hantaywee—faithful
Kimimela—butterfly
Macawi—generous
Magaskawee—graceful
Maka—earth
Makawee—mothering
Mapiya—sky
Nahimana—mystic
Ptaysanwee—white buffalo
Takchawee—doe
Talutah—bloodred
Wachiwi—dancer
Wakanda—possesses magical
    power
Weeko—pretty
Wihakayda—little one
Winona, Wenona, Wenonah—
    giving
Witashnah—virginal

ZUNI
Liseli—meaning unknown
Malia—bitter
Mankalita—meaning unknown
Meli—bitter

MALE

Ahmik—beaver
Akando—ambush
Akule—looks up
Anoki—actor
Apenimon—worthy of trust
Awan—somebody
Bemossed—walker

Bimisi—slippery
Bodaway—fire-maker
Chesmu—gritty
Dakota—friend
Delsin—he is so
Demothi—talks while walking
Dichali—speaks a lot

Dohosan—bluff
Dyami—eagle
Elan—friendly
Elsu—flying falcon
Elu—full of grace
Enyeto—walks as a boar
Etu—sun
Ezhno—solitary
Gosheven—leaper
Guyapi—frank
Hahnee—beggar
Hakan—fire
Helaku—full of sun
Hinun—myth name
Honovi—strong
Igasho—wanders
Inteus—has no shame
Istu—sugar
Iye—smoke
Jacy—moon
Jolon—valley of the dead oaks
Kaga—chronicler
Kajika—walks without sound
Knoton—wind
Lakota—friend
Langundo—peaceful
Lenno—man
Lonato—flint
Manipi—amazing
Maska—strong
Masou—myth name
Milap—charitable
Mingan—gray wolf
Mojag—never silent
Motega—new arrow
Muraco—white moon
Nahele—forest
Namid—dancer

Nawat—left-handed
Nayati—he who wrestles
Neka—wild goose
Nigan—ahead
Nikiti—round, smooth
Nitis—friend
Nodin—wind
Ohanko—reckless
Ouray—arrow
Paco—eagle
Pallaton—warrior
Pat—fish
Patamon—tempest
Patwin—man
Payat, Pay, Payatt—he is coming
Pilan—godly essence
Pinon—myth name
Sahale—falcon
Sakima—king
Siwili—tail of the fox
Songan—strong
Tate—he who talks too much
Tyee—chieftain
Wakiza—desperate warrior
Wapi—lucky
Wemilat—of wealthy parents
Wilny—meaning unknown
Wynono—firstborn
Yancy—Englishman
Yoskolo—meaning unknown
Yuma—chief's son

ALGONQUIN
Abooksigun—wildcat
Abukcheech—mouse
Achak—spirit
Ahanu—he laughs
Anakausuen—worker

Aranck—stars
Askook—snake
Askuwheteau—he keeps watch
Chansomps—locust
Chogan—blackbird
Eluwilussit—holy one
Enkoodabooaoo,
    Enkoodabaoo—one who
    lives alone
Etchemin—canoe man
Etlelooaat—shouts
Hassun—stone
Huritt—handsome
Keme—secret
Kesegowaase—swift
Kestejoo—slave
Kitchi—brave
Machk—bear
Makkapitew—he has large teeth
Matchitehew—he has an evil
    heart
Matchitisiw—he has bad
    character
Matunaaga—fights
Matwau—enemy
Megedagik—kills many
Melkedoodum—conceited
Mukki—child
Nixkamich—grandfather
Nootau—fire
Nosh, Noshi—father
Pajackok—thunder
Pannoowau—he lies
Powwaw—priest
Rowtag—fire
Segenam—lazy
Sucki—black
Sunukkuhkau—he crushes

Taregan—crane
Tihkoosue—short
Togquos—twin
Wematin—brother

CHEROKEE
Adahy—lives in the woods
Dustu—meaning unknown
Tooantuh—spring frog

CHEYENNE
Ahtunowhiho—one who lives
    below
Avonaco—lean bear
Hahkethomemah, Harkahome—
    little robe
Heammawihio—wise one above
Heskovizenako—porcupine
    bear
Hevataneo—hairy rope
Hevovitastamiutsto—whirlwind
Hiamovi—high chief
Hohnihohkaiyohos,
    Neeheeoeewootis—high-
    backed wolf
Honiahaka—little wolf
Hotuaekhaashtait—tall bull
Kohkahycumest—white crow or
    white antelope
Kuckunniwi—little wolf
Mantotohpa—four bears
Meturato, Mokatavatah,
    Moketavato, Moketaveto,
    Moketoveto, Mokovaoto,
    Motavato—black kettle
Minninnewah—whirlwind
Nahcomence—old bark
Nahiossi—has three fingers

Ocumwhowurst,
Ocunnowhurst—yellow wolf
Ohcumgache, Okhmhaka—little
wolf
Otoahhastis—tall bull
Otoahnacto—bull bear
Tahkeome—little robe
Tahmelapachme—dull knife
Vaiveahtoish, Vaive Atoish—
alights on the cloud
Viho—chief
Vipponah—slim face
Vohkinne—Roman nose
Voistitoevitz, Voisttioevetz—
white cow
Vokivocummast—white
antelope
Wahanassatta—he who walks
with his toes turned
outward
Waquini—hook nose
Wohehiv—dull knife
Wokaihwokomas—white
antelope

DAKOTA
Ciqala—little one
Hinto—blue
Maza Blaska—flat iron
Tasunke—horse
Tatanka-ptecila—short bull
Tokala—fox
Wambli-waste—good eagle
Wicasa—sage

HOPI
Ahiliya—meaning unknown
Ahote—restless one

Alo—spiritual guide
Alosaka—myth name
Aponivi—where the wind blows
down the gap
Ayawamat—one who follows
orders
Cha'akmongwi—crier chief
Cha'tima—caller
Chavatangakwunua—short
rainbow
Cheveyo—spirit warrior
Chochmo—mud mound
Chochokpi—throne for the
clouds
Chochuschuvio—white-tailed
deer
Choovio—antelope
Choviohoya—young deer
Chowilawu—joined together by
water
Chu'a—snake
Chuchip—deer spirit
Chunta—cheating
Hania—spirit warrior
Hawiovi—going down the ladder
Honani—badger
Honaw—bear
Hototo—warrior spirit who
sings; he who whistles
Istaqa—coyote man
Kachada—white man
Kele—sparrow
Kolichiyaw—skunk
Kotori—screech owl spirit
Kwahu—eagle
Kwatoko—bird with big beak
Lansa—lance
Lapu—cedar bark

Len—flute
Machakw—horny toad
Makya—eagle hunter
Masichuvio—gray deer
Mochni—talking bird
Moki—deer
Mongwau—owl
Nukpana—evil
Omawnakw—cloud feather
Pachu'a—feathered water snake
Pahana—lost white brother
Pivane—weasel
Qaletaqu—guardian of the people
Qochata—white man
Sikyahonaw—yellow bear
Sikyatavo—yellow rabbit
Sowi'ngwa—black-tailed deer
Tangakwunu—rainbow
Tocho—mountain lion
Tohopka—wild beast
Wikvaya—one who brings

MIWOK

Elki—meaning unknown
Helki—touch
Hesutu—yellow jacket's nest rising out of the ground
Honon—bear
Howi—turtledove
Kono—meaning unknown
Kosumi—fishes for salmon with spear
Lanu—meaning unknown
Leyati—shaped like an abalone shell
Lise—salmon's head rising above water

Liwanu—growl of a bear
Lokni—rain falls through the roof
Misu—rippling brook
Molimo—bear walking into shade
Momuso—meaning unknown
Mona—gathers jimson weed seed
Muata—yellow jackets inside a nest
Oya—jacksnipe
Sewati—curved bear claw
Telutci, Tuketu—bear making dust
Tupi—to pull up
Uzumati—bear
Wuyi—soaring turkey vulture

NAVAJO

Ahiga—he fights
Ashkii—boy
Ata'halne'—he interrupts
Bidziil—he is strong
Bilagaana—white person
Gaagii—raven
Gad—juniper tree
Hastiin—man
Hok'ee—abandoned
Naalnish—he works
Naalyehe Ya Sidahi—trader
Nastas—curve like foxtail grass
Niichaad—swollen
Niyol—wind
Sani—old one
Shilah—brother
Shiye—son
Shizhe'e—father

Sicheii—grandfather
Sike—he sits at home
Sik'is—friend
T'iis—cottonwood
Tse—rock
Tsiishch'ili—curly-haired
Yanisin—ashamed
Yas—snow
Yiska—the night has passed

PAWNEE
Kuruk—bear
Shiriki—coyote

SIOUX
Akecheta—fighter
Chankoowashtay—good road
Chayton—falcon
Enapay—brave
Hotah—white
Howahkan—of the mysterious voice
Kangee—raven
Kohana—swift
Lootah—red
Mahkah—earth
Mahpee—sky

Matoskah—white bear
Napayshni—strong, courageous
Odakota—friend
Ogaleesha—wears a red shirt
Ohanzee—shadow
Ohitekah—brave
Otaktay—kills many
Paytah—fire
Skah—white
Takoda—friend to everyone
Teetonka—talks too much
Wahchinksapa—wise
Wahchintonka—has much practice
Wahkan—sacred
Wamblee—eagle
Wambleeska—white eagle
Wanageeska—white spirit
Wanahton—charger
Wanikiya—savior
Weayaya—setting sun
Yahto—blue

WINNEBAGO
Chas-chunk-a—wave
He-lush-ka—fighter
Nawkaw—wood

NORWEGIAN

Before surnames became common in Norway, people were identified by their given name plus their father's name, the name of their residence, or a distinctive trait. Traditional surnames started in urban areas around the sixteenth century and spread to the rural areas in the late nineteenth century. Surnames were used first by the nobility and military officers and then spread down the social ladder. The first surnames were patronymic and included the suffixes *-sen* or *-son* (son) or *-datter* or *-dotter* (daughter). Rural people were identified by their given name along with their father's, followed by the name of their residence, (frequently called a farm name) which was subject to change whenever they moved. But in 1923 a law was passed requiring everyone to have a fixed surname.

A few surnames based either on a patronymic or a place name:

Adrisson	Kittelsen
Ambjornsen	Mortenson
Amundsen	Nansen
Anderson	Nilsen
Arnfindatter	Olavson
Austreim	Olsen
Bjornson	Olessdatter
Eiriksdatter	Opstvedt
Elvestad	Pedersdatter
Gasdeilde	Rasmusdatter
Halvorsen	Sjursen
Hamsun	Skredsvig
Hansen	Solheim
Heyerdahl	Stenerud
Holfeldt	Torkjelson
Ibsen	Trondhjem
Jacobsen	Undset
Johansseson	

FEMALE

Aase—tree-covered mountain
Alfdis—spirit
Amma—grandmother
Andras—breath
Anselma—divine helmet (form of Anselm)
Arna—eagle (form of Arnold)
Arnbjorg—eagle protection
Arndis—eagle spirit
Arnora—light eagle
Arnthrud—meaning unknown
Asdis—divine spirit
Ase, Asta—tree
Ashild, Ashilde, Ashilda—god-fighting
Aslaug—devoted to God
Astrid, Astra, Astred, Astryd, Astryr, Astrud—divine strength
Aud, Auda—wealthy
Audhild, Audhilde, Audhilda—rich, warrior-woman
Audney—newfound wealth
Audun, Auduna—deserted
Bera—spirited
Bergdis—spirit protection
Bergthora—Thor's spirit (form of Bergthor)
Bjork—meaning unknown
Bo—householder
Bodil, Bodile, Bodilla—fighting woman
Borgny—help
Botilda—commanding
Brenda—sword
Brita, Britta, Brit—from Britain

Brynhild, Brynhilde, Brunhilda, Brunhild, Brunnehilde—armored battle-maid
Brynja—dark
Dagmar—maiden of the day
Dagna—splendid day
Dagny—joy of the Danes
Dahlia, Dalr—from the valley
Dale—lives in the valley
Disa, Diss—spirited
Dyrfinna—deer, Finn
Edda, Eda—poetic
Eldrid—fiery spirit
Elle—old age
Ellisif—consecrated to God (form of Elizabeth)
Embla—from an elm
Erica, Erika, Ricci, Rika—eternal ruler (form of Eric)
Fjarskafinn—meaning unknown
Flos—chieftain
Frida, Frieda—beautiful
Frikka, Frika—peaceful ruler
Frodis—meaning unknown
Gala, Gale—lovely voice
Gerd, Gerda, Gerdie, Garthf—protected
Gjaflaug—meaning unknown
Gro, Groa—gardener
Gudrun, Guro, Gudrid—divine knowledge
Gunhilde, Gunnhild, Gunhilda, Gunnhildr—battle-maid
Gunnvor—meaning unknown
Guri—lovely
Gyda, Gytha, Guthr—warlike

Hakan—noble
Haldana—half-Dane
Haldis, Halldis—firm helper
Haldora, Halldora—half-spirited
Halfrid, Hallfrid, Halfrida—
peaceful heroine
Halla, Hallgerd, Hallgerda—
half-protected
Halveig, Hallveig—meaning
unknown
Haralda—army ruler (form of
Harold)
Hekja—saga name
Helga, Helge—holy
Helle—meaning unknown
Hildegunn, Hildigunn—warrior-
woman
Hulda—hidden
Hvergelmir—home of Nidhug;
myth name
Idona, Idun, Iduna, Idunn—
active in love
Ingeborg, Injerd, Ingibjorg—
Ing's protection
Ingemar—of the sea
Inger—daughter of a hero
Ingrid, Ingrit, Ingrida—beauty of
Froy
Ingunn—loved by Froy
Jorunn—chief's love
Katla—meaning unknown
Kelda—fountain
Kelsey, Kelci, Kelda—from the
ship's island
Kirsten—believes in Christ
(form of Christian)
Linnea—lime tree
Liv—life

Magna—strong
Magnild, Magnilde, Magnilda—
strong fighter
Marianne—bitter grace
Mildri—mild and lovely
Norberta, Njorthrbiartr—bright
hero (form of Norbert)
Oda, Odd—point
Oddfrid—beautiful point
Oddny—new point
Oddveig, Oddnaug—pointed
woman
Ola—ancestor (form of Olaf)
Olaug—of the ancestors
Olga—holy
Ragnfrid, Ragni, Randi—lovely,
goddess
Ragnild, Ragnilde, Ragna,
Ragnhild—one who is wise
in battle
Rana, Rania—nobility
Ranveig, Rannveig, Ronnaug—
housewoman
Reidun—lovely in the nest
Rona, Runa—mighty strength
Ronalda—mighty, powerful
(form of Ronald)
Sigourney—conqueror
Sigrid, Sigrath—victorious
counselor
Sissell—without sight
Siv—kinswoman
Solveig—housewoman
Svanhild, Svanhile, Svenhilda,
Svenhilde—swan, warrior
Thorberta, Thorbiartr,
Torberta—brilliance of Thor
Thorbjorg—protected by Thor

Thordis, Thordissa, Thoridyss, Thordia—spirit of Thor
Thorgerd—Thor's protection
Thorgunna, Torgunna, Thorgunn—Thor's fighter
Thorhild, Thorhilda—Thor's maiden
Tora, Tordis, Thora, Thorir—Thor, goddess
Toril—Thor-inspired fighting woman

Torne, Torny, Torney—Thor, new
Torunn—Thor's love
Tove—good
Trine—innocent
Trude, Truda—strong
Uald—ruler
Unn, Unne—love
Valda—spirited in war
Valgerd—ruling protection
Yule—born during Yule

MALE

Aage, Age, Ake—ancestors
Aesire, Aegir—of the gods
Afi—grandfather
Alf—dead and living in the underworld
Alfgeir—elfin spear
Alfrothul—of the sun
Alvis, Alviss—wise
Amhlaoibh, Auliffe—relic from the ancestor
Amund, Amundi—bridal gift
Ander—manly (form of Andrew)
Annar—father of the world
Aren—eagle (from of Arnold)
Aricin, Arkin, Arkyn—eternal king's son
Arild—battle commander
Arngeir—eagle spear
Arngrim—saga name
Arnlaug—eagle; devoted
Arnljot—frightens eagles
Arons—from the river's mouth
Arvid, Arve—eagle tree
Asbiorn, Asbjorn—divine bear

Asgaut—divine Goth
Asgeir, Ansgar, Asgerd—spear of the gods
Ask—from the ash tree
Audolf—wolf's friend
Audun—friend of wealth
Bard—good fighter
Bekan—meaning unknown
Bergthor—Thor's spirit
Birger—rescuer
Bjarne, Bjorn, Bjarni—bear
Bjornolf—bear-wolf
Blund—saga name
Bo—householder
Bodil—leader
Bodolf—wolf leader
Bond—peasant farmer
Booth, Bothi, Bothe—herald
Borg—from the castle
Brand, Brander, Brandr—sword
Brede—broad
Brian, Bryan—strong
Bruin—legend name
Buri—meaning unknown

Burnaby, Bionbyr—warrior's estate
Burr—young
Busby, Busbyr—dwells at the village
Cadby—from the warrior's settlement
Canute, Cnute, Cnut—knot
Carr—from the marsh
Cawley, Cauley—relic
Colby—from the dark village
Cort, Cortie—short
Crosby—dwells by the town cross
Dag—day
Dana, Dain, Dane, Denby, Danb, Den, Denny, Derby, Danby—from Denmark
Darby—from the deer estate
Davin, Davyn—intelligent
Delling, Dellingr—shining
Desiderio—desired (form of Desirata)
Digby, Dikibyr—from the dike settlement
Donner—meaning unknown
Dreng—warrior
Duartr—rich guardian (form of Edward)
Dustin—warrior
Dyre, Dyri—dear
Egil, Eigil—inspires fright
Einar, Enar—fighter
Elphin—meaning unknown
Elvis—sage
Eric, Erik, Erick, Eirik, Eryk, Eikki—eternal ruler
Erland—leader

Erling—chief's son
Esbjorn—bear of the gods
Eske—spear of the gods
Eskil—vessel of the gods
Eystein, Eistein—lucky
Faste—firm
Fell, Fjall—from the rough hill
Finn—finder
Freystein—rock-hard
Frode—wise
Gamble—old
Garth, Garrett, Garet—defender
Garton—farmer
Gaute—great
Geir, Geiri—spear
Geirleif—spear descendant
Geirolf—wolf spear
Geirstein—rock-hard spear
Gilby—pledge
Gjest—stranger
Gudbrand, Gudbrande—weapon of the gods
Gunnar—bold warrior
Gunnbjorn—fighting bear
Gunnolf—fighting wolf
Gus, Gustav—staff of God
Hakon, Haaken—of the chosen race
Hallam—from the hillside
Hallbjorn—rock bear
Halvdan, Halden—half-Dane
Halvor, Halvard—rock defender
Hamar, Hammer—hammer
Hans—legend name
Harald, Harold, Haral, Herrick, Harry, Hal, Herryk—army ruler
Hauk—hawk

Havelock, Hafleikr—sea war
Helgi—holy (form of Helga)
Hesketh—horseracing
Hilario—happy (form of Hilary)
Holger—spear, weapon
Howe—burial hill
Hrani—meaning unknown
Hringham—meaning unknown
Hrolf—wolf (form of Rolf)
Hrolleif—old wolf
Hugin—thoughtful
Inger, Ingharr—son's army
Inghram, Ingram—Ing's raven
Ingmar, Ingemar, Ingemur—famous son
Ingolf—Ing's wolf
Ivar, Ivor—archer
Johannes, Johanne—legend name
Kali—meaning unknown
Kare, Kari—tremendous
Karli—manly (form of Charles)
Karr, Kerr, Kiarr—from the marsh
Kell, Keldan—from the spring
Kelsey, Kiollsig, Kelsig—from the ship's island
Kirby, Krikjabyr—from the church village
Kirk—dwells at the church
Kleng—has claws
Knud—kind
Knut, Knutr—knot
Kol—dark
Kolbyr—from the dark settlement
Koll, Kolli—dark
Kollvein—dark, young
Kolskegg—meaning unknown
Kort—short
Krossbyr—dwells at the shrine of the cross
Kuanbyr—from the woman's estate
Lamont, Lamond, Lagmann—lawyer
Lang—tall
Latham—division
Leidolf—wolf descendant
Leif, Lief—descendant
Lunt—from the grove
Magnor, Magnild, Magne, Magnus—strong fighter
Mikkel—who is like God (form of Michael)
Narfi—meaning unknown
Norbert, Norberto, Njorthrbiartr—bright hero
Odd—point
Oddleif—point descendant
Oddvar—pointable
Odell—wealthy
Olave, Oilibhear, Olaf, Olin, Olyn, Olen, Ola, Ole, Olav, Olof—ancestor
Oleif—relic descendant
Oliver, Olvaerr, Olvir—affectionate
Os—divine
Oscar, Oskar—divine spear
Osgood—divine god
Ottar—fighter
Ove—ancestor
Oysten, Ostein, Osten—happy
Quemby, Quimby—from the woman's estate

Lynn Emery sold her first novel, *Night Magic*, to Kensington Publishing. It went on to be recognized for Excellence in Romance Fiction for 1995 by *Romantic Times* magazine. Her third novel, *After All*, became a movie produced by BET. She has also published her multicultural romances with Harper Torch and Jove Books.

Raenette "Rae" Dalcour, blues singer and guitarist, is the heroine in my novel *Sweet Mystery*. In the backstory she explains that her mother was a Ray Charles fan. Since his backup female group was known as the Raelettes, Rae's mother added *ette* to her name to honor both. I love the blues more than any other music genre, but I can't play the guitar or sing. I got to live my dream through that character.

My favorite character name is Hercule Poirot, the Belgian detective from Agatha Christie's wonderful mystery novels. The name suits him perfectly. The very sound of it implies someone of fastidious habits, which of course he is. *Mon Dieu!*

THE LISTS

NORWEGIAN

Ragnor, Ragnar, Raynor, Rainer—wise warrior

Reidar, Reider—fighter of the nest

Reynard—legend name

Ric—honorable ruler

Roald—mighty, powerful (form of Ronald)

Roar—fighter of praise

Rolf—wolf

Roscoe, Raskogr—from the deer forest

Rothwell, Rauthuell—dwells near the red spring

Royd, Riodhr—from the forest clearing

Rune—secret

Rutland, Rotland—from the root land

Saxby—from the farm of the short sword

Sigurd, Sigvard, Sigurdhr, Siv, Sijur, Syver, Sigvat—victorious defender

Skerry, Skereye—rocky island

Skipp—ship's captain

Skule, Skuli—hide

Stein—stone

Steinar—rock-hard fighter

Steinbjorn—rock bear

Steinolf—rock wolf

Steinthor—Thor's rock

Stian—swift

Storr—great

Sutherland, Suthrland—from the south

Svan, Svann—swan

Svend, Svein, Svewn, Sveyn—young

Tait, Tayte—happy

Terje, Torgeir, Torger, Tarjei—spear of Thor

Thorald, Thorualdr, Torald, Torvald—Thor ruler

Thorbert, Thorbiartr—the glorious Thor

Thorbjor, Throburn—bear of Thor

Thorleif—Thor's descendant

Thorolf—Thor's wolf

Thororm—saga name

Thorstein—Thor's rock

Thurlow—from Thor's hill

Torgny—Thor's loud weapon

Torquil—Thor's cauldron

Trigg, Trygg, Tryggr—true

Trond, Tron—growing

Trygve—brave victory

Turpin, Thorfinn—Finnish man of Thor

Tuxford—from the spearman's ford

Uigbiorn, Ugbjorn—war bear

Ulf—wolf

Ulmer, Ulfmaerr—famous wolf

Ura—from the corner property

Vegard—protection

Vegeir—great sacrificer

Vidar—tree-fighter

Vigrid—battleground

Wray—from the corner property

Wyborn, Wybjorn—war bear

PERSIAN

Persia is a geographic region roughly corresponding to Iran, but the Persian ethnicity, language, and culture extends into some regions of India, Tajikistan, Afghanistan, and Uzbekistan. Iran was called Persia until 1935. The primary religion in Iran is Islam, but Iran is 50 to 70 percent Persian in ethnicity. The language of Iran is Persian, also called Farsi.

Names in Iran usually consist of a first name and surname. Surnames were not used until 1926, when new laws forced everyone to register a surname and all married women to take the name of their husband's family. Nicknames were not tolerated. Surnames are passed down from father to children. Many citizens added a place name to their surname with a hyphen. The place name is usually followed by the suffix -i.

A few surnames:

Agassi	Maybodi
Alavi	Mehran
Amini	Moazami
Ansari	Naderi
Baraheri	Neekzad
Borzorg	Nemazi
Borzorg-Alavi	Pahlavi
Bozorgi	Pakravan
Caspari	Reyahni
Dulabi	Sattar
Firouzi	Shamsi
Ghaffari	Sharifi
Habibi	Sherafat
Hedayat	Talavi
Hosseini	Tehrani
Kazemi	Vali

FEMALE

Amira—king (form of Amir)
Arezou—wishful
Azadeh—without possessions
Azar, Azara—scarlet
Azura, Azur—blue
Cyra—moon
Daria, Darya—preserver
Darice—queen
Esther—star
Farah—happy
Farideh—delightful
Gatha—song
Gelsey—flower
Golnar—fire
Hester, Hetty, Hestia—star
Jaleh—rain
Jasmine, Jessamine—jasmine
Kira—sun
Kismet—fate
Laleh—flower
Lila, Lilac—lilac
Marjan—coral
Minau—heaven
Mitra—angel's name
Nahid—myth name

Narda—anointed
Nasrin—wild rose
Pari—myth name
Parisa—angelic
Parvaneh—butterfly
Roshan—glorious light
Roxana, Roxanne—bright; dawn
Sadira—dreamy
Shabnan—raindrop
Shahdi—happy
Shahin—eagle
Shahnaz—ruler's pride
Shirin—charming
Sholeh—fire
Simin—silver
Soraya—name of a princess
Soroushi—happiness (form of
    Soroush)
Taraneh—song
Vashti—beautiful
Yasmin, Yasmina, Yasmine,
    Yasmeen, Yasmena—
    jasmine
Zenda—womanly
Zuleika—wise beauty

MALE

Ahura Mazda—lord
Amir—king
Asha—protector of fire; myth
    name
Assim—great one
Bahar, Baharak—spring
Bahram—name of a Persian king
Balthasar—war adviser

Behrooz—lucky
Caspar, Casper—treasurer
Cyrus—sun
Dareh—rich
Darioush—name of a king
Darius—preserver
Fariel—meaning unknown
Feroz—lucky

Gaspar, Gazsi—treasurer (form of Casper)

Ghebers, Guebers—followers of ancient Persian religion

Jamsheed—Persian

Jasper—treasurer (form of Casper)

Kansbar—treasure master

Kaveh—name of a hero

Khorshed—sun

Ksathra—ruler

Kurush—myth name

Majeed—superior

Majnoon—a historical name

Mehrdad—gift from the sun

Melchior—king

Nasim—breeze

Rashne—judge

Roshan—light bearer

Saeed, Said, Soroush—happy

Sarosh—prayer

Shabouh—meaning unknown

Shah—king

Shatrevar—power; myth name

Sohrab—name of a hero

Soroush—happiness

Tab, Tabb, Tabor—drum

Tallis—wise one

Val—high hill

Xerxes—prince

Zoroaster—star

POLISH

Polish surnames are patronymic, occupational, or descriptive. Place names are also used. By 1500, most of the nobility had surnames ending with -*ski* or -*ska* that were distributed by the king as a way of honoring them. Surnames derived from saints' names were used by the urban classes.

Common suffixes:

-yk, -ak, -ek, -czyk, -czak, -czek—little
-slaw (males), -slawa (female)—glory
-dski, -cki, -ski (male), -ska (female)—these suffixes linked aristocrats' names with the estates they owned.

When used with a Christian name by the lower classes, these suffixes meant "son of" or "daughter of":

-owski—place name
-lis—male
-lisowa—married woman
-lisowna—unmarried female

A few surnames:

Adamczyk	Klimek
Banaszak	Kowalksi
Brzezinski	Krupinski
Bykowski	Kryszka
Cegielski	Kurowski
Chodakowsk	Levitsky
Chudzik	Ludwiczak
Dabrowski	Makowski
Dekownik	Michalski
Denys	Nowakowski
Dlugosz	Ostrowski
Dolinski	Pulawski
Frankowski	Robak
Jankowski	Staszak
Karpinski	Wojno
Klimas	Zwolinski

FEMALE

Adelajda—noble (form of Adelaide)

Albinka—blonde

Aldona—old

Alina—beautiful

Alka—intelligent

Anastazja—one who will be reborn (form of Anastasia)

Ania, Anka—grace (form of Anne)

Aniela—heavenly messenger, angel

Antonina—priceless (form of Anthony)

Balbina—strong, stammers

Basha, Basia—stranger

Beate, Beata—blessed

Bodgana, Bohgana, Bogna—gift from God (form of Bohdan)

Celinka, Celek—myth name

Danuta—little deer

Dorota—God's gift (form of Dorothy)

Edyta—wealthy gift (form of Edith)

Elwira—white (form of Elvira)

Elzbieta—consecrated to God (form of Elizabeth)

Euzebia—pious

Ewa—life (form of Eve)

Felka, Fela, Felcia—lucky

Franciszka—free (form of Francis)

Gizela—pledge

Grazyna—grace (form of Grace)

Gutka—good

Halina—light (form of Helen)

Henka, Heniuta—rules the home (form of Henry)

Hortensja—gardener (form of Hortense)

Iwona—bow of yew (form of Yvonne)

Jadwiga—refuge in war

Janecska, Jana, Jasia, Joanka—gracious God (form of John)

Jolanta—violet

Kamilka, Kamilla—ceremonial attendant

Karol—manly (form of Charles)

Kassia, Kasienka, Kaska—pure (form of Katherine)

Katarzyna, Katrine, Katya, Katine—pure (form of Katherine)

Klaudia—lame (form of Claude)

Krystynka, Krysta, Krystka, Krystyn—believes in Christ (form of Christian)

Kunigunde, Kunegundy—name of a queen

Lechsinska—wood nymph

Lidia—from Lydia

Lila—of the people

Lilka, Ludka, Lodoiska, Luisa—famous battle-maid

Lucja, Lucyna—light (form of Luke)

Malgorzata, Margisia—pearl (form of Margaret)

Marta, Marsia, Marysia, Macia—bitter (form of Mary)

Marzina—warlike

Matylda—strong battle-maid (form of Matilda)

Mela, Melka—dark

Minka—strong

Morela—apricot

Nadzia, Nata, Natia—hope

Nelka—stone

Olesia—defender of mankind (form of Alexandra)

Otylia—lucky heroine

Paulina—small (form of Paul)

Petronela, Petra—rock (form of Peter)

Rahel—ewe (form of Rachel)

Rasia—regal

Rasine—rose

Rayna—queen

Roch—glory

Rozyczka, Roz, Roza, Rozalia—rose (form of Rosa)

Sylwia—from the forest (form of Sylvester)

Takli—divine fame (form of Tekla)

Teodory, Teodozji—God's gift (form of Theodore)

Tesia—loved by God

Tola—priceless

Valeska—glorious ruler

Vanda—wanderer (form of Wanda)

Weronika—honest image (form of Veronica)

Wiktoria, Wiktorja, Wikta—victorious (form of Victoria)

Wirke, Wira—white

Yachne—kind

Zanna—God's gracious gift

Zefiryna—zephyr

Zofia, Zosia—wise (form of Sophia)

Zuzanny, Zuzanna—lily (form of Susan)

Zytka, Zyta—strong

MALE

Adok—dark

Adolf—noble wolf (form of Adolph)

Albin—white (form of Alban)

Aleksander, Aleksy—defender of mankind (form of Alexander)

Andrzej—manly (form of Andrew)

Apoloniusz—manly beauty; myth name (form of Apollo)

Armand, Armandek—soldier (form of Herman)

Aron—high mountain; lofty (form of Aaron)

Artur—noble bear (form of Arthur)

Augustyn—great (form of August)

Aurek, Aureli—blond

Bazyli—kingly

Bendyk, Bendek—blessed (form of Benedict)

Bialy, Bialas—white-haired

Bogumil—God's peace

Boguslaw—God's glory
Borys—stranger
Boryslaw—stranger, glory
Casimir, Kazmer—destroys peace
Cyprian—from Cyprus
Cyrek, Cyryl—lordly (form of Cyril)
Czeslaw—fortress glory
Dionizy—god of wine (form of Dionysus)
Dobieslaw—glory of Dionysus
Dobry—goodly
Dodek—hero
Donat—gift (form of Donato)
Dorek—gift from God
Dymitr—meaning unknown
Elek—blond
Emilian—active
Erek, Eryk—lovable
Feliks—happy (form of Felix)
Flawiusz—yellow (form of Flavian)
Florian—blooming (form of Florian)
Franciszek—free (form of Francis)
Fryderyk—peaceful ruler (form of Frederick)
Gerik—wealthy spearman
Gerwazy—warrior
Grzegorz—watchful (form of Gregory)
Henryk—rules the home (form of Henry)
Hieronim—sacred (form of Jerome)
Holleb—dove

Jacek—lily
Jack, Janek, Jan—God's gracious gift
Jarek, Januarius—born in January
Jedrik, Jedrek, Jedrus—strong
Jerzy—farmer (form of George)
Josep, Jozef—God adds (form of Joseph)
Kazimierz—destroys peace (form of Casimir)
Konstanty—constant (form of Constantine)
Krzysztof—Christ-bearer (form of Christopher)
Laiurenty—laurel (form of Lawrence)
Lech—founder of Poland; myth name
Liuz—light
Lubomir—loves peace
Lucjan—light (form of Luke)
Ludoslaw, Luboslaw—loves glory
Ludwik—famous in war (form of Louis)
Lukasz—light (form of Luke)
Maksym, Maksymilian—great (form of Maximillian)
Mandek, Mandex—warrior
Marek, Marcin, Marcinek—warlike
Maury, Maurycy—dark-skinned (form of Maurice)
Mikolaj, Mikolai—victory of the people (form of Nicholas)
Miron—peace
Nelek—horn

Nikodem—conqueror of the people
Oles—defender of mankind (form of Alexander)
Onufry—meaning unknown
Patryk—noble (form of Patrick)
Pawelek, Pawel, Pawl—small (form of Paul)
Piotr, Pietrek—rock (form of Peter)
Radoslaw—loves peace
Rafal—healed by God (form of Raphael)
Rajmund—mighty protector (form of Raymond)
Rufin—red-haired (form of Rufus)
Ryszard—strong ruler (form of Richard)
Sergiusz—servant (form of Sergio)
Seweryn—severe (form of Severin)
Stefan, Szczepan—crowned in victory (form of Stephen)
Szymon—God is heard (form of Simon)
Tanek—immortal
Telek—cuts iron
Teodor—God's gift (form of Theodore)
Tomasz—twin (form of Thomas)
Tomislaw—glory of the twin
Tolek, Teos—gift of God
Tytus—Old Roman name
Waldemar—strong ruler
Walenty—strong, healthy
Walerian, Waleron—brave, strong
Wienczyslaw—victory
Wiktor—victorious (form of Victor)
Wincenty, Wicus—victorious (form of Vincent)
Wit—life
Zarek—God protect the king
Ziven—lively
Zygmunt—conquering protection

POLYNESIAN

Polynesia is a large group of islands in the South Pacific, including Hawaii, Tahiti, Samoa, and Tonga. Polynesians speak a number of closely related languages. Naming practices vary not only island by island, but within groups on the islands as well. Be sure to research carefully before you name your Polynesian characters.

Polynesian given names almost always carry a meaning. They may contain components of ancestor names or refer to significant events at the time of the person's birth or in the family history. Some names are phrases and can be very long compared to traditional European names. Before foreigners came to the islands, a Polynesian went by one given name, but it was not unusual for a person to change his name or be given a new name in honor of a special event in that person's life.

When missionaries and foreign governments came to the Polynesian islands, they often began a campaign against native languages and customs. Surnames were introduced and Christian first names were assigned in addition to or instead of Polynesian names. For some time, parents would give their children a Polynesian name only as a middle name, if at all. Recently, there has been a resurgence in pride in the native cultures, and children are more likely to be given a Polynesian first name. In Hawaii, natives were required by law to adopt European naming conventions starting in 1860. Only in 1967 did it become legal to carry a Hawaiian, rather than Christian, first name.

A person's lineage was (and is) very important in Polynesia. Surnames are a foreign introduction, but in Hawaii, a person's name would occasionally be followed by a patronymic: the word *a* (of) and the father's given name. A matronymic (*a* plus the mother's first name) would be used if her bloodline was more prominent. Modern Polynesian surnames may contain elements of ancestors' given names. Many Polynesian surnames are foreign in origin because of the influence of missionaries and colonial governments as well as intermarriage with outsiders. In Hawaii, for instance, there are many American, Chinese, Japanese, Korean, and Philippine surnames.

A few surnames:

Aheona
Ahina
Hanohano
Hapai
Inouye
Iokepa
Kaapuiki
Kaaua
Kahananoku

Kaneapua
Kaulupali
Kealoha
Naikelekele
Nailima
Nalatu
Tatupu
Tonono
Topeni

FEMALE

Ema—beloved
Heirani—sky crown
Hika—daughter
Hine—maiden
Hirawa—silver
Hoku—star
Inas—wife of the moon
Kaimi—seeker
Kaula—prophet
Kiri—tree bark
Kohia—passionflower
Kura—red
Lana—float
Lani, Loni—sky
Leilani—heavenly flower
Mahina—moon
Mahuru—spring goddess
Maru—kind
Matahina—goddess eyes

Maylea—wildflower
Mere—bitterly wanted child
Moeata—sleeping cloud
Moerani—sleeping sky
Mohea—beautiful princess
Nahini—total woman
Nani—beautiful
Poehina—moon pearl
Puaiti—little flower
Rangi—heaven
Ranitea—clear sky
Rata—chieftain
Rewa—slender
Tama—son
Taranga—legendary figure
Tehani—floral caress
Tera—sun
Teora, Ora—life
Turua—beautiful
Ulani—cheerful

MALE

Alika—defender
Amana—ruler
Anui—large canoe
Arana—handsome
Arava—lusty child
Ariki—chief
Atiu—eldest
Hori—farmer
Ihorangi—rain
Irawaru—legendary figure
Kauri—tree
Keoni—righteous
Kereteki—myth name
Konane—bright moon
Kupe—explorer
Lani—sky
Manu—man of birds
Marama—man of the moon

Matareka—smiling one
Maui—legendary hero
Ora—life
Oroiti—slow
Ra'anui—sacred
Rahiti—rising sun
Rangi—heaven
Rata—chieftain
Rongo—god of rain
Tama—son
Tane—god name
Tangaroa—from the sea
Tawhiri—storm
Teva—name of a clan
Tiki—spirit
Turi—chieftain name
Ulani—cheerful
Whetu—star

PORTUGUESE

A Portuguese name consists of a first name and two last names: the mother's surname and the father's surname, in that order. A woman may add her husband's surname when she gets married, but this is becoming less common. When she marries Duarte Costa Silva, Olivia Dias Salazar may keep her name as is, add her husband's surname (Olivia Dias Salazar Silva), or drop her mother's surname and append her husband's (Olivia Salazar Silva). The two surnames a child receives are his grandfathers' surnames—in other words, the father's surname from each of his parents: Gloria Salazar Silva.

Just as English-speaking people use suffixes like Jr. and III to differentiate between family members with the same name, the Portuguese use Filho (son), Neto (grandson), and occasionally Sobrinho (nephew). These suffixes were treated as part of the name, but their use is falling out of practice.

A few surnames:

Andrade	Magellan
Azocar	Oliveira
Barreto	Paneira
Barros	Rios
Caldeira	Salazar
Costa	Serrão
Da Silva	Silva
Dias	Souza
Dourado	Travada
Figuiera	Vento
Lapuente	

FEMALE

Adelina—noble (form of Adelaide)

Amalia, Amelia—hardworking

Andrea, Andreia—manly (form of Andrew)

Assuncao—assumption

Benigna—friendly (form of Benigno)

Branca—white, fair

Bruna—dark-haired (form of Brun)

Calisto—beautiful

Carmo—garden

Catarina—pure (form of Katherine)

Cecilia—blind (form of Cecil)

Celia—heaven (form of Celio)

Cintia—woman of Kynthos; the moon; myth name

Clara, Clarissa—clear, bright (form of Clare)

Cristina—believes in Christ (form of Christian)

Daniela—God is my judge (form of Daniel)

Diamantina—diamond

Dores—sorrow (form of Dolores)

Doroteia—God's gift (form of Dorothy)

Edite—wealthy gift (form of Edith)

Efigenia, Eugenia—well-born (form of Eugene)

Elena—light (form of Eleanor)

Elzira—gift to God

Emilia, Emiliana—rival (form of Emil)

Estela, Ester—star (form of Esther)

Eufemia—well-spoken

Eulalia—well-spoken

Fabiana—bean farmer (form of Fabian)

Fatima—name of pilgrimage site

Felicidade—happy (form of Felix)

Fia—weaver

Filipa—lover of horses (form of Philip)

Filomena—lover of man

Flavia—yellow (form of Flavian)

Fortunata—fortunate

Gertrudes—strong with a spear (form of Gertrude)

Glaucia—bluish gray (form of Glaucio)

Gloria—glory

Graca—grace (form of Grace)

Guiomar—famous in battle

Herminia—from the Roman god Hermes

Imaculada—clean, immaculate

Ines, Inez—pure (form of Agnes)

Irma—whole, strong

Isabel, Isabela—consecrated to God (form of Elizabeth)

Isadora, Isidora—gift of Isis

Isaura—from Isauria

Jacinta—hyacinth (form of Hyacinth)

Jesusa—God saves (form of Jesus)

Joana—gracious God (form of John)

Josefa—God adds (form of Joseph)

Jovita—from the Roman god Jove

Julia, Juliana, Liana—youthful (form of Julius)

Laura, Lorena—laurel (form of Lawrence)

Leocadia—bright, clear; saint's name

Leonor—light (form of Eleanor)

Leticia—happy (form of Letitia)

Lidia—from Lydia

Ligia—beautiful voice

Lilian—lily

Livia—envious

Lourdes, Lurdes—place name, pilgrimage site

EVAN MARSHALL

Evan Marshall is the president of the Evan Marshall Agency, a literary agency that specializes in representing novelists. He is the international best-selling author of the Marshall Plan series of novel writing guides. He also writes the popular Jane Stuart and Winky mysteries.

The first question I ask myself when naming a character is whether a name I have in mind fits the character's personality as I've defined it so far. This is a "gut" thing; we all have preconceived ideas of how people with certain names look and act. I never select a name first and then define the character, because when I do this I find that the character's personality ends up suiting the name.

When weighing names, I keep these questions in mind:

- Does the character's background suggest any names or types of names?
- Would the character's parents have been likely to choose a certain name or kind of name?
- What names were in fashion when the character was born?
- Would a nickname or less formal version of a name be appropriate for this person?

Additionally, I apply these rules:

- I try (at least with my major characters) to have all first and last names start with a different letter. I keep a simple alphabetical list.
- I vary the sound and length of characters' first and last names.
- I avoid using all Anglo names.
- I avoid using names that end alike or similarly.
- I try to avoid using names that end in s, which make for awkward possessives.
- I avoid overly long names, especially for my major characters. The star of my mystery series is simply Jane.

Lucia, Luciana, Lucinda—light (form of Luke)
Luisa, Luiza—famous in war (form of Louis)
Madeira—wine
Mafalda—strong battle-maid (form of Matilda)
Manuela—God is with us (form of Emmanuel)
Marcia, Mariana, Marina— warlike (form of Marcus)
Margarida—pearl (form of Margaret)
Maria, Marisa—bitter (form of Mary)
Matilde—strong battle-maid (form of Matilda)
Monica—counselor
Natalia, Nathalia—born on Christmas (form of Natalie)
Neves—snowy
Ofelia—helper
Olivia—olive
Palmira—from the city of palms
Primitiva—firstborn
Rafaela—healed by God (form of Raphael)
Raquel—ewe (form of Rachel)
Rebeca—captivating (form of Rebecca)

Renata—reborn (form of Renato)
Rosa, Rosalina—rose
Rute—friend (form of Ruth)
Sabina—of the Sabine people
Sanrevelle—meaning unknown
Severina—severe (form of Severin)
Silvia—from the forest (form of Sylvester)
Sol—sun
Sonia—wise (form of Sonya)
Susana, Suzana—lily (form of Susan)
Telma—will
Teodora—God's gift (form of Theodore)
Teresa, Teresinha, Tereza, Terezinha—reaper (form of Theresa)
Ursula—little bear
Valeria—strength (form of Valerius)
Veronica—honest image
Vidonia—vine branch
Virginia—pure
Vitoria—victorious (form of Victor)
Zara—flower blossom

MALE

Abel—breath
Adalberto—noble, intelligent (form of Albert)
Adao—of the red earth (form of Adam)

Afonso—noble and ready for battle (form of Alphonse)
Agostinho—great (form of August)
Alvaro—guardian

Amancio—loving

Amaro—dark, Moorish

Ambrosio—immortal (form of Ambrose)

Amilcar—friend of the Phoenician god Melqart (form of Hamilcar)

Anacleto, Cleto—invoked; papal name

Anselmo—divine helmet (form of Anselm)

Atilio—ancient Etruscan name

Benigno—friendly

Bento—blessed (form of Benedict)

Bernardino, Bernardo—strong as a bear (form of Bernard)

Bras—lisping

Bruno—dark-haired (form of Brun)

Carlito, Carlo, Carlos—manly (form of Charles)

Casimiro—destroys peace (form of Casimir)

Celio—heaven

Celso—tall

Cesar, Cezar—long-haired (form of Caesar)

Cristiano—believes in Christ (form of Christian)

Cristovao—Christ-bearer (form of Christopher)

Daniel, Danilo—God is my judge

Demetrio—saint's name

Diago, Diogo—teacher (form of Diego)

Duarte, Eduardo—rich guardian (form of Edward)

Eleuterio—free

Elias—Jehovah is God

Elpidio—hope

Eneas—praise

Enrique—rules the home (form of Henry)

Estevao—crowned in victory (form of Stephen)

Eusebio—historian; historical name

Evaristo—pleasing

Fabiano, Fabio—bean farmer (form of Fabian)

Fabricio—craftsman

Felipe—lover of horses (form of Philip)

Fernando, Fernao—adventurer (form of Ferdinand)

Fortunato—fortunate

Gil, Gilberto—pledge (form of Gilbert)

Glaucio—bluish gray

Goncalo, Gonsalvo—warrior

Guiomar—famous in battle

Heitor—possess, hold

Herberto, Heriberto—shining warrior (form of Herbert)

Inacio—fire

Jacinto—hyacinth (form of Hyacinth)

Jaime—supplanter (form of James)

Javier—owner of a new home (form of Xavier)

Joao—gracious God (form of John)

Joaquim—God will establish; saint name (form of Joachim)

Jorge—farmer (form of George)

Leandro, Leonardo—brave lion (form of Leonard)

Lourenco—laurel (form of Lawrence)

Lucian, Luciano, Lucio—light (form of Luke)

Luis, Luiz—famous in war (form of Louis)

Manoel, Manuel—God is with us (form of Emmanuel)

Marcelino, Marcelo, Marco, Marcos, Martinho—warlike (form of Marcus)

Mateus, Matheus—God's gift (form of Matthew)

Maximiano, Maximiliano, Maximino—great (form of Maximillian)

Miguel—who is like God (form of Michael)

Narcisco—sleep

Nicolau—victory of the people (form of Nicholas)

Nuno—ninth

Olavo—ancestor (form of Olaf)

Osvaldo—God's rule

Otavio—born eighth

Paulino, Paulo—small (form of Paul)

Placido—tranquil

Rafael—healed by God (form of Raphael)

Raimundo, Raymundo—mighty protector (form of Raymond)

Remigio—oarsman

Rodrigo—famous ruler (form of Roderick)

Rubens—son

Salomao—peaceful (form of Solomon)

Sergio—servant

Simao—God is heard (form of Simon)

Tadeu—heart

Teodoro, Teodosio—God's gift (form of Theodore)

Teofilo—friend of God

Thiago, Tiago—teacher (form of Diego)

Tomas—twin (form of Thomas)

Tristao—noisy (form of Tristan)

Valerio—strength (form of Valerius)

Vasco—crow

Victor, Victorino, Vitor—victorious

Xavier—owner of a new home

Zeferino—breeze

RUSSIAN

Modern-day Russians have a given name, a patronymic, and a surname. The patronymic is the father's first name modified with a suffix appropriate to the gender of the child: -evich or -ovich for a boy and -evna or -ovna for a girl. If the father's first name is Ivan, for instance, the son's patronymic would be Ivanovich and the daughter's would be Ivanovna. The polite form of address is by first name and patronymic, rather than by a title (like Mr. or Mrs.) and the surname. Aleksandra Denisovna Petrova would be addressed as Aleksandra Denisovna.

As a general rule, male first names, patronymics, and surnames end in a consonant (Some male names end in -i or -y when transliterated into English—these names end in a letter that is a consonant in Cyrillic alphabet.) Female names end in -a, and it is not uncommon for nicknames or diminutives to end in -a, even for males: Aleksandr becomes Sasha and Mikhail becomes Misha. If a family's surname is Petrov, the females in the family will add an -a at the end to form Petrova.

Because Russian is written in the Cyrillic alphabet, English transliterations of Russian names can vary widely. The Russian equivalent of Peter, pronounced PYO-ter, might be spelled as Pyotr, Petr, or Piotr.

Russians began to use surnames in the fifteenth century. The naming system was originally used only by princes; then it was adopted by the rest of the nobility. Commoners used their given name combined with a nickname.

Certain suffixes were controlled by the czar or czarina. Under Empress Catherine, for example, the right to use -ovich was extended to include the first five grades of civil servants. The sixth to the eighth grades could use -ov (-ova) or -ev (-eva). Later, the rest of the populace was allowed to use -ev (-eva) and -ov (-ova).

Common suffixes:

-sky, -ski, -ska—nature of or like
-ov, -ova, -ovna, -ev, -eva, -evna—of
-oy—used for nicknames
-ik—occupational names

Married couples decide which surname to use. If the wife's surname is chosen, the couple will later decide which name their children will use.

A few surnames:

Babin(a)
Alliluyev(a)
Antipov(a)
Bakhtin(a)
Baklanov(a)
Balakirev(a)
Borodin(a)
Chapaev(a)
Chukovsky (Chukovskaya)
Dubov(a)
Dyakonov(a)
Gagarin(a)
Golitsin(a)
Golubov(a)
Ivanov(a)
Kalugin(a)
Kaminsky (Kaminskaya)
Kazakov(a)

Krestyanov(a)
Lebedev(a)
Mayakovsky
   (Mayakovskaya)
Mayorsky (Mayorskaya)
Nevsky (Nevskaya)
Orlov(a)
Petrov(a)
Rybin(a)
Sergeyev(a)
Shirokii (Shirokaya)
Smirnov(a)
Tumanov(a)
Varvarinski (Varvarinskaya)
Volkov(a)
Yermakov(a)
Zhilkin(a)

FEMALE

Agafia—good (form of Agatha)
Agrafina—born feet first (form of Agrippa)
Agnessa—pure (form of Agnes)
Akilina—eagle
Aksana—glory to God
Alena—light (form of Helen)
Alexandra, Aleksandra— defender of mankind (form of Alexander)
Alina—beautiful
Alla, Allochka—meaning unknown

Amaliji—hardworking (form of Amelia)
Ana—one who will be reborn (form of Anastasia)
Anastasia, Stasya, Nastya—one who will be reborn
Anstice—resurrected
Antonina—priceless (form of Anthony)
Anya, Anitchka, Anna, Anechka, Asenka—grace (form of Anne)
Arkadina—meaning unknown

Avdotya—meaning unknown

Avel—breath

Bohdana—gift from God (form of Bohdan)

Charlotta—manly (form of Charles)

Cyzarine—royalty

Dasha, Doroteya—God's gift (form of Dorothy)

Devora—bee (form of Deborah)

Dimitra—from Demeter, spring

Dominika—of the Lord; born on Sunday (form of Dominic)

Dunyasha—meaning unknown

Duscha—ghost; divine spirit

Ekaterina—pure (form of Katherine)

Elga—holy

Evalina, Eva—life (form of Eve)

Evgenia—well-born (form of Eugene)

Fayina—free

Feodora—God's gift (form of Theodore)

Galenka, Galina, Galine, Galya—God has redeemed

Helenka—light (form of Helen)

Helga—holy

Helina—sunlight

Ilia—God is Lord

Irena, Irina—peace (form of Irene)

Irisa—rainbow

Ivana, Ivane, Ivanna—gracious God (form of John)

Jelena—bright light

Kira, Kirochka—light (form of Helen)

Kisa—kitten

Kiska, Katya, Katarina, Katyenka, Katyuska, Katherina—pure (form of Katherine)

Ksana, Ksanochka—praise be to God

Lada—Slavic goddess of beauty; myth name

Lara, Larisa, Larissa, Lanassa—happy

Lenusya—flower

Lidija, Lidia, Lidiya, Lidochka, Lida—from Lydia

Lubmilla—loving

Lyudmila, Lyuba, Lyubochka, Luda, Ludmila—love of the people

Margarete, Margosha—pearl (form of Margaret)

Marianne, Marianna—bitter grace

Marinochka, Marina, Marinka—of the sea

Masha, Mara, Marisha, Manya, Mura, Maruska, Marusya—bitter (form of Mary)

Mavra—dark

Milena, Mila—favored

Nadia, Nadezhda, Nadyenka, Nadenka—hope

Narkissa—daffodil

Natasha, Natascha, Nitca, Natasia, Natalia, Natyashenka—born on Christmas (form of Natalie)

Nesha, Nessa, Nesya—pure (form of Agnes)

Nikita—victory of the people (form of Nicholas)

Nikolaevna, Nika—belongs to
God
Ninockha, Nina—grace
Oksanochka, Oksana—praise be
to God
Olena—light (form of Helen)
Olga, Olya, Olenka, Olechka—
holy
Orlenda—eagle
Parasha, Parashie, Pasha—born
on Good Friday
Pauline, Paulina—small (form of
Paul)
Rahil—ewe (form of Rachel)
Raisa—adaptable
Ranevskaya, Ranya—meaning
unknown
Sabina—of the Sabine people
Sacha, Sasha, Sashenka—
defender of mankind (form
of Alexander)
Sinovia, Sinya—stranger
Sonia, Sonya, Sonechka—wise
Stephania, Stefanya, Stesha,
Panya—crowned in victory
(form of Stephen)
Svetlana, Sveta—luminescent
Talia, Talya—born on Christmas
(form of Natalie)
Tanya, Tania, Tanechka,
Tatyana, Tatiana,
Tanichka—myth name
Tasya—resurrected

Theodosia, Theda, Thedya—
God's gift (form of
Theodore)
Ursola, Ursula—little bear
Valentina—valiant, strong (form
of Valentine)
Valeska—glorious ruler
Vania, Vanya—God's gift
Vanka—grace
Varvara, Varya, Varinka,
Varushka—stranger
Vassillissa, Vasilissa, Vasya—
regal (form of Basil)
Velika—wonderful
Verochka, Vera—true
Vilma—resolute protector (form
of William)
Viveka—beautiful voice
Yalena, Yalenchka—light (form
of Helen)
Yelizaveta—consecrated to God
(form of Elizabeth)
Yeva—life (form of Eve)
Yuliya, Yulenka—youthful (form
of Julius)
Zaneta—God's gift
Zenevieva—white wave (form of
Genevieve)
Zenochka, Zena—from Zeus
Zenya, Zenechka—well-born
(form of Eugene)
Zinerva—wise (form of Minerva)
Zoyechka, Zoyenka, Zoya—life

MALE

Adrik—dark

Alek, Alik, Aleksandr, Aleksis, Aleksi, Alexei—defender of mankind (form of Alexander)

Aloyoshenka, Aloysha—defends mankind

Anatolii—from the east (form of Anatole)

Andrusha, Andrya, Andrei—manly (form of Andrew)

Antosha, Antinko, Anton—priceless (form of Anthony)

Arman—soldier (form of Herman)

Bogdashka, Bohdan—gift from God

Bolodenka—peaceful

Borya, Boryenka, Boris—fighter

Brencis—crowned with laurel

Brody—from Brody

Burian—lives near the weeds

Cheslav—lives in a strong camp

Danya—God's gift

Demyan—tame

Deniska—myth name

Dima—strong fighter

Dimitri—from Demeter, spring

Edik, Eduard—rich guardian (form of Edward)

Egor—farmer (form of George)

Evgenii—well-born (form of Eugene)

Fabiyan, Fabi—bean farmer (form of Fabian)

Fadeyka, Fadey, Faddei—brave

Fedor, Fedya, Fyodor, Fedyenka—God's gift (form of Theodore)

Feliks—happy (form of Felix)

Fiers—meaning unknown

Filip—lover of horses (form of Philip)

Foma—twin (form of Thomas)

Fredek—peaceful ruler (form of Frederick)

Gavril, Ganya, Gav, Gavrel, Gavrilovich—worships God

Gayeff—meaning unknown

Grisha, Grigori, Grigorii, Girsha—watchful (form of Gregory)

Hedon—destroyer

Helge—holy (form of Helga)

Igoryok, Igor—farmer (form of George)

Ilya—meaning unknown

Ioakim, Iov—God will establish (form of Joachim)

Ivan—gracious God (form of John)

Jasha—supplanter

Jermija—exalted of the Lord (form of Jeremiah)

Jov—persecuted (form of Job)

Jurg, Jeirgif—farmer (form of George)

Karolek, Karol—manly (form of Charles)

Kiryl, Kiril—noble

Kolenka, Kolya—of the conquering people

Kostenka, Kostya, Konstantin—
constant (form of
Constantine)
Laurentij—laurel (form of
Lawrence)
Leonide, Lenya, Lyonechka,
Levushka, Levka, Lyonya,
Lev, Levka—brave lion
(form of Leonard)
Lesta—meaning unknown
Lopahin—meaning unknown
Lukasha, Lukyan, Luka—light
(form of Luke)
Maks, Maksim, Maksimillian—
great (form of Maximillian)
Matvey, Motka, Matyash—God's
gift (form of Matthew)
Mishenka, Mishe, Misha,
Mikhail—who is like God
(form of Michael)
Moriz—Moorish
Naum—comforter
Nicolai, Nikita—victory of the
people (form of Nicholas)
Oleg, Olezka—holy
Osip—God adds (form of Joseph)
Pashenka, Pavlushka, Pavla,
Pavlya, Pavel, Pavlov—small
(form of Paul)
Petenka, Pyotr, Petya—rock
(form of Peter)
Romochka, Roman—Roman
Rurik—famous ruler
Sacha, Sasha, Shura, Shurochka,
Sanya, Shurik, Shashenka—
defender of mankind (form
of Alexander)
Semyon—God is heard (form of
Simon)
Seriozha, Seriozhenka, Serge,

Serguei—servant (form of
Sergio)
Stanislov, Slavik—glory
Stefan, Stepka, Stephan—
crowned in victory (form of
Stephen)
Tolenka, Tolya—from the east
Tosya, Tusya—beyond
expectation
Trofimoff—meaning unknown
Uri, Uriah, Urie, Uriel—God is
my light
Vadim—powerful ruler
Valerik, Valerii—strength (form
of Valerius)
Vanechka, Vanyusha—God's gift
Vassily, Vassi, Vasya, Vas,
Visilii—regal (form of Basil)
Vitenka, Viktor—victorious
(form of Victor)
Vladislav, Vladik, Vyacheslav—
glorious ruler
Vladmir, Vladmiri—has peace
Vladsislas—meaning unknown
Volodya, Valdik, Vladya—
peaceful
Yakov—supplanter (form of
Jacob)
Yaremka, Yerik—appointed by
God
Yasha—defends mankind (form
of Alexander)
Yermolay—meaning unknown
Yuri, Yurii, Yurik, Yura,
Yurochka—farmer (form of
George)
Zhenechka, Zhenya—noble
Zhorah, Zorya—farmer
Ziven, Zivon—lively

SCANDINAVIAN (OLD NORSE)

Strictly speaking, Scandinavia consists of Norway, Sweden, and Denmark, which have closely related Germanic languages descended from Old Norse. Many consider Iceland and Finland to be part of Scandinavia, and these countries do share Scandinavia's Nordic cultural heritage. It should be noted, however, that the Finnish language is not a member of the Indo-European language group, as are Norwegian, Swedish, Danish, and Icelandic. Names originating in the Finnish language will therefore be markedly different from other Scandinavian names.

The myth names in the following lists are names of Norse gods, the places where they lived, their servants, and various other creatures that inhabited the world of the gods. Saga names are human names taken from epic stories written in the twelfth and thirteenth centuries chronicling historical and legendary events.

For specific information about the development and use of surnames in the various Scandinavian countries, see the sections on Danish, Norwegian, Swedish, and Finnish names.

FEMALE

Aegileif—daughter of Hrolf Helgason; saga name

Angerbotha, Angerboda, Angrboda—giant; myth name

Annaliese—grace of God

Anrid—wife of Ketil Fjorleifarson; saga name

Asvor, Asvora—wife of Asrod; saga name

Audhumbla, Audumla—giant cow that nursed Ymir; myth name

Bestla—mother of Odin; myth name

Bifrost—bridge from earth to Asgard; myth name

Birgit, Birgitta, Birgitta—strong (form of Bridget)

Borghild, Borghlide, Borghilda— wife of Sigmund; myth name

Brisingamen—Freya's necklace; myth name

Bryngerd—mother of Tongue-Stein; saga name

Dalla—mother of Kormak; saga name

Dana—myth name

Victoria Alexander is the *Romantic Times* Book Club Historical Story-teller of the Year (2004). Her novels have made it to the *New York Times* and *USA Today* best-seller lists and have been Doubleday book club selections.

A few books ago I created a country that I called the Kingdom of Greater Avalonia. The name was taken more or less from the Isle of Avalon and the country itself based loosely on the country of Ruthania where my father-in-law was born. (The country no longer exists.) I needed a ruling family, so I borrowed the family name of some of my favorite people — my mother-in-law's family. Thus the ruling family of the Kingdom of Greater Avalonia became the House of Pruzinsky.

Darda—dart

Donalda—ruler of the world (form of Donald)

Draupnir—Odin's magic ring; myth name

Edda—myth name

Eir—goddess of healing; myth name

Elin—daughter of the Russian king Boleslaw; saga name

Elli—giant; myth name

Erika—eternal ruler (form of Eric)

Erna—wife of Jarl; myth name

Fjorgyn—mother of Thor; myth name

Freya, Freydis—noblewoman; goddess of love and fertility; myth name

Frigga, Frig—myth name

Frigga—goddess of matrimonial love; myth name

Fulla—one of Frigga's ladies-in-waiting; myth name

Geirbjorg—sister of Bersi the Godless; saga name

Geirrid—sister of Geirrod; saga name

Gimle—new heaven; myth name

Ginnungagap—abyss that births all living things; myth name

Gjalp—giant; myth name

Gna—one of Frigga's ladies-in-waiting; myth name

Greip—giant; myth name

Grid—wife of Odin; myth name

Grima—saga name (form of Grim)

Grimhild, Grimhilda, Grimhilde—mother of Gudrun; myth name

Gullveig—witch; myth name

Gunnlod—mother of Bragi;
    myth name

Gutrune—myth name

Hedda—vigorous battle-maid

Heidrun—goat who supplies
    mead for the gods; myth
    name

Hel, Hela—goddess of the
    underworld; myth name

Herdis—Bolli's daughter;
    saga name

Hilde, Hild, Hilda, Hildur—
    Valkyrie; myth name

Hiordis—second wife of
    Sigmund; myth name

Hjordis—sword goddess;
    myth name

Hlif—mother of Atli; saga name

Hrefna—daughter of Asgeir;
    saga name

Hrodny—mother of Hoskuld;
    saga name

Hyndla—giant; myth name

Hyrna—saga name

Hyrrokkin—ogre; myth name

Inga, Inge, Ingunna, Ingaborg—
    daughter of a hero

Ingigerd—sister of Dagstygg;
    saga name

Iwona—archer

Jarngerd—saga name

Jarnsaxa—giant; myth name

Jofrid—saga name

Jord—daughter of Night;
    myth name

Joreid—saga name

Karita—benevolent

Katrine, Katrina, Karen—pure
    (form of Katherine)

Kirsten—believes in Christ
    (form of Christian)

Kjolvor—saga name

Klara—clear, bright (form of
    Clare)

Kolfinna—saga name

Kriemhild, Kriemhilda,
    Kriemhilde—wife of
    Siegfried; myth name

Lene, Line—light

Linne—cascade

Lin—one of Frigga's ladies-in-
    waiting; myth name

Ljotunn—saga name

Lofn—goddess of lust; myth
    name

Lofnheid, Lyngheid—sister of
    Otter; myth name

Lopthaena—saga name

Maeva—saga name

Maria—bitter; name not
    originally Norse, but it
    appears in several sagas,
    and is the name of King
    Harald Sigurdsson's
    daughter (form of Mary)

Marny—of the sea

Melkorka—deaf and mute
    concubine; saga name

Menglad—won by Svipdag;
    myth name

Mia—bitter

Mista—Valkyrie; myth name

Nada—hope

Nanna—wife of Balder; myth
    name

Nerthus—mother of earth; myth
   name
Nissa, Nisse, Nysse, Nyssa—
   friendly elf
Norna, Norn—goddess of fate;
   myth name
Noss—daughter of Frey;
   myth name
Ola—ancestor (form of Olaf)
Osk—mother of Hild; saga name
Otkatla—saga name
Quenby—womanly
Rakel—ewe (form of Rachel)
Ran—sea goddess; myth name
Ray, Rae—doe
Rinda, Rind—giant; myth name
Saehild—saga name
Saeunn—mother of Bergthora;
   saga name
Saga—drank with Odin in her
   hall; myth name
Sangrida—Valkyrie; myth name
Sif—Thor's second wife;
   myth name
Sign, Sigun, Signy—daughter of
   Volsung; myth name
Sigyn—wife of Loki; myth name
Sinmora—wife of Surt;
   myth name
Skade—goddess of skiers;
   myth name
Skalm—saga name
Skuld—Norn of the future;
   myth name
Snor, Snora—wife of Karl;
   myth name
Snotra—self-discipline; myth
   name

Steinunn—saga name
Steinvorr—saga name
Swanhild, Swanhilda,
   Swanhilde—daughter of
   Sigurd; myth name
Syn—invoked during trials;
   myth name
Thaukt—giant; myth name
Thir—wife of Thrall; myth name
Thjodhild, Thjodhilda—saga
   name
Thokk—female disguise Thor
   used to keep Balder from
   returning to life; myth name
Thorarin—saga name
Thorfinna—wife of Thorstein
   Kuggason; saga name
Thorhalla—daughter of Asgrim;
   saga name
Thorkatla—wife of Mord; saga
   name
Thorunn, Thorunna, Torunn—
   mother of Bishop Bjorn;
   saga name
Thrud—promised to Alvis;
   myth name
Thurid—wife of Thorstein the
   Red; saga name
Ulrike—ruler of all
Urd—Norn of the past; myth
   name
Vaetild, Vaetilda—mother of the
   Skraeling children; saga
   name
Valdis—daughter of Thorbrand;
   saga name
Valkyrie—Freya's priestesses;
   myth name

Vanja—gracious God (form of John)
Var—punishes adulterers; myth name
Velaug—wife of Bjorn Buna; saga name
Vendela—meaning unknown
Verdandi—Norn of the present; myth name
Vigdis—wife of Killer-Hrapp; saga name
Villborg—saga name
Viveca, Viveka—life
Volva—prophetess; myth name
Vor—omniscient goddess; myth name
Woglinda—myth name
Yggsdrasil—tree that binds heaven, hell, and earth; myth name
Yngvild—mother of Bishop Brand; saga name
Ywla—wolf

MALE

Aevar—son of Ketil; saga name
Alberich—dwarf; myth name
Alfarinn, Alfarin—son of Hlif; saga name
Alfrigg—dwarf; myth name
Amund—divine protection
Anders—manly (form of Andrew)
Andvaranaut—Brunhild's ring; myth name
Andvari—treasure guardian; myth name
An—son of Grim Hairy-Cheek; saga name
Apsel—father of peace
Arles—pledge
Armod—blood brother of Geirleif; saga name
Arni—in Njal's saga, killer of Althing; saga name
Arvakl—horse; myth name
Asgard—city of the gods; myth name
Asgrim—in Njal's saga, chieftain of Tongue; saga name
Ashby—from the ash tree farm
Ashiepattle—legend name
Asi—saga name
Askel, Askell—son of Dufniall; saga name
Aslak—supporter of Thorgest; saga name
Asolf—kinsman of Jorund; saga name
Asrod—husband of Asvor; saga name
Asvald—son of Ulf; saga name
Atli—king of the Huns; myth name
Aud—son of night; myth name
Avaldamon—name of a king; saga name
Avang—Irishman; saga name
Balder, Baldur, Baldr—son of Odin; myth name
Balki—son of Blaeng; saga name

Balmung—Siegfried's sword; myth name

Bardi—son of Gudmund; saga name

Baug—son of Raud; saga name

Beinir—name of a smith; saga name

Bergelmir—giant; myth name

Bergen, Bergin—mountain dweller

Bergren, Berggren—from the mountain brook

Bersi—son of Balki; saga name

Bifrost—bridge from earth to Asgard; myth name

Bjolf—blood brother of Lodmund; saga name

Bodmod—son of Oleif; saga name

Bodvar—son of Thorleif; saga name

Bolli—son of Thorleik; saga name

Bolthor—giant; myth name

Bolverk—disguise of Odin; myth name

Bor—father of Odin; myth name

Borg—from the castle

Bori—father of Bor; myth name

Bork—killed by Gunnar; saga name

Bragi—god of poetry; myth name

Branstock—tree in Volsung's palace; myth name

Bresi—saga name

Brisingamen—Freya's necklace; myth name

Brokk—dwarf; myth name

Brondolf—son of Naddodd; saga name

Bruni—son of Earl Harek; saga name

Brynjolf—killed Atli; saga name

Carrson—son of Carr

Crow-Hreidar—son of Ofeig Dangle-Beard; saga name

Daegal—dawn

Dain—dwarf; myth name

Dana, Dane, Dain—from Denmark

Davin, Daven, Dagfinnr—intelligent

Denby—from the Danish settlement

Draupnir—Odin's magic ring; myth name

Durin—dwarf; myth name

Dyre—dear one

Ederyn—myth name

Eggther—guardian for the giants; myth name

Eilif—wounded in an attack on Hlidarend; saga name

Eitri—dwarf; myth name

Eldgrim—killed by Hrut Herjolfsson; saga name

Erp—son of Meldun; saga name

Etzel—Attila the Hun; myth name

Eyfrod—farmed at Tongue; saga name

Eyjolf—killed by Kari; saga name

Eyvind—son of Lodin; saga name

Fafnir, Fafner—dragon; myth name

Fasolt—killed by Fafnir; myth name

Fenrir, Fenris—monster wolf; myth name

Finnbogi—merchant; saga name

Floki—heroic Viking; saga name

Flosi—chieftain; saga name

Forseti—son of Balder; myth name

Frans—free (form of Francis)

Freki—Odin's wolf; myth name

Frey, Freyr—god of weather; myth name

Freyvid—saga name

Fridleif—father of Ari; saga name

Galm—father of Thorvald; saga name

Gamel—elder

Ganger—founder of Normandy; saga name

Garder—son of Svafar; saga name

Gardi—ghost; saga name

Garm—guards the gate of Hel; myth name

Geirmund—son of Gunnbjorn; saga name

Geirrod—brother of Geirrid; myth name

Gest—son of Oddleif; saga name

Gils—father of Hedin; saga name

Gimle—new heaven; myth name

Gizur—leader of the attack on Hlidarend; saga name

Gjallar—horn sounded for Ragnorok; myth name

Gleipnir—magic net woven to hold Fenrir; myth name

Glistenheath—place where Sigurd killed Fafnir; myth name

Glum—outlaw; saga name

Gnup—took refuge in Iceland after several killings he performed; saga name

Gram—Sigurd's sword; myth name

Grani—son of Gunnar; saga name

Grenjad—son of Hermund; saga name

Greyfell—Sigurd's horse; myth name

Grimkel—son of Ulf; saga name

Grim—son of Njal; saga name

Gris—man freed by Skallagrim; saga name

Gudlaug—son of Asbjorn; saga name

Gudmund—chieftain; saga name

Gullinbursti—boar ridden by Freyr; myth name

Gulltopp—horse of Heimdall; myth name

Gungir—Odin's spear; myth name

Gunlaug, Gunnlaug—son of Illugi; saga name

Gunther—brother of Kriemhild; myth name

Guttorm—brother of Gudrun; myth name

Gymir—father of Gerd; myth name

Gynt—legend name

Gyrd—saga name

Hafgrim—settler of Greenland; saga name

Hafnar—father of Thorgeir Cheek-Wound; saga name

Hafthor—saga name

Hagen—killed Siegfried; myth name

Haki—name of a slave; saga name

Halldor—son of Gunnbjorn; saga name

Hallfred—son of Ottar; saga name

Hallkel—brother of Ketilbjorn; saga name

Hall—son of Helgi the Godless; saga name

Hallstein—Thorolf; saga name

Hallvard—fought in the Battle of Hafursfjord; saga name

Hamund—son-in-law of Helgi the Lean; saga name

Harald—army ruler (form of Harold)

Hardar—saga name

Hardbein—son of Helga; saga name

Hastein—son of Atli; saga name

Hedin—son of Thorstein Troll; saga name

Heimdal—guardian of Bifrost; myth name

Herjolf—father of Vapni; saga name

Hermod—messenger of the gods; myth name

Hermund—brother of Gunnlaug; saga name

Hersir—chieftain; saga name

Hoder, Hodur, Hodr—blind son of Odin; myth name

Hoenir, Honir—brother of Odin; myth name

Hofud—myth name

Hogna, Hogni—saga name

Holmstein—supported Flosi; saga name

Hord—father of Asbjorn; saga name

Hoskuld—son of Thorstein; saga name

Hrafn—saga name

Hrapp—father of Hrodgeir; saga name

Hreidmar—dwarf king; myth name

Hrifla—saga name

Hrimfaxi—horse of night whose bridle drips the morning dew; myth name

Hroald—brother of Eyvind Weapon; saga name

Hrodgeir—son of Hrapp; saga name

Hromund—son of Thori; saga name

Hrosskel—son of Thorstein; saga name

Hrut—son of Herjolf; saga name

Hugi—giant; myth name

Hunbogi—son of Alf; saga name

Hvergelmir—home of Nidhug; myth name

Igor—hero

Illugi—son of Aslak; saga name

Im—giant; myth name

Ingimund—saga name

Ingjald—son of Helga; saga name

Ingmar—famous son

Ing—myth name

Ing—myth name

Ingvar—Ing's army

Isleif—brother of Isrod; saga name

Isolf—son of Hrani; saga name

Isrod—brother of Isleif; saga name

Ivor, Ivar, Iver—archer

Jakob—supplanter (form of Jacob)

Jens—gracious God (form of John)

Jolgeir—brother of Radorm; saga name

Jormungand—serpent who encircles the earth; myth name

Jorund—son of Hrafn the Foolish; saga name

Jostein—saga name

Kalf—son of Asgeir; saga name

Kalman—man from Ireland; saga name

Karl—manly (form of Charles)

Ketil—son of Thori; saga name

Kjarr, Kjartan—son of Olaf the Peacock; saga name

Klepp—saga name

Knut—knot

Kodran—father of Thjodgerd; saga name

Kolbein—son of Sigmund of Vestfold; saga name

Kolgrim—son of Hrolf; saga name

Konal—saga name

Konstantin—constant (form of Constantine)

Kotkel—sorcerer; saga name

Kristoffer—Christ-bearer (form of Christopher)

Kveld—saga name

Kvist—saga name

Kylan—son of Kara; saga name

Lambi—son of Thorbjorn the Feeble; saga name

Lamont—lawyer

Lars—laurel (form of Lawrence)

Larson—son of Lars

Latham—division

Lidskjalf—throne of Odin; myth name

Lodmund—blood brother of Bjolf; saga name

Lodur—giver of senses; myth name

Loki—god of destruction; myth name

Ludvig—famous in war (form of Louis)

Lyting—brother of Thorstein Torfi; saga name

Magni—one of the seven gods of the Aesir; myth name

Mani—father of Ketil; saga name

Mar—son of Naddodd; saga name

Mjolnir, Miolnir—Thor's hammer; myth name

Modan—saga name

Modi—son of Thor; myth name

Modolf—saga name

Mord—saga name

Mottul—saga name

Munin—memory; myth name

Myrkjartan—saga name

Nagelfar—ship that will carry the dead to Ragnarok; myth name

Niels, Nils—champion (form of Neal)

Nighug, Nighogg—dragon; myth name

Niklaus—victory of the people (form of Nicholas)

Nithhogg—myth name

Njal, Njall—son of Thorgeir; saga name

Njord—father of Freya; myth name

Odin, Othin—god of the sky; myth name

Olaf—ancestor

Onund—son of Viking; saga name

Orebjorn—saga name

Orlyg—son of Valthjof; saga name

Orm—son of Ulf; saga name

Orn—father of Idunn; saga name

Ornolf—son of Armod; saga name

Ospak—brother of Gudrun; saga name

Osvif—father of Gudrun; saga name

Otkel—saga name

Ovaegir—father of the Skraeling children; saga name

Ove—popular name

Ozur—son of Thorleif; saga name

Paavo—small (form of Paul)

Pedar, Per—rock (form of Peter)

Quinby—from the woman's estate

Radorm—brother of Jolgeir; saga name

Ragi—saga name

Ragnarok—final battle of the gods; myth name

Ragnar—wise warrior (form of Ragnor)

Raud—father of Ulf; saga name

Ref—saga name

Regin—blacksmith; myth name

Reist—son of Bjarn-Isle; saga name

Rikard—strong ruler (form of Richard)

Rognvald—earl of Orkney; saga name

Royd—from the forest clearing

Rungnir—giant killed by Thor; myth name

Runolf—son of Ulf; saga name

Rurik—famous ruler

Saehrimnir—magic boar; myth name

Siggeir—king of the Goths; myth name

Sigmund—son of Volsung; saga name

Sindri—dwarf; myth name

Sinfiotli—son of Siggeir; myth name

Skagi—son of Skopta; saga name

Skalla—saga name

Skamkel—saga name

Skapti—saga name

Skarp, Skarphedin—saga name

Skefil—saga name

Skeggi—son of Bodolf; saga name

Skidbladnir—magical ship of Freyr; myth name

Skinfaxi—stallion of the daylight; myth name

Skirnir—servant of Freyr;
   myth name
Skjold—meaning unknown
Skorri—saga name
Skrymir—king of the giants;
   myth name
Skum—saga name
Sleipnir—Odin's horse;
   myth name
Snaebjorn—son of Eyvindar;
   saga name
Snorre—meaning unknown
Snorri—son of Thorfinn;
   saga name
Solmund—saga name
Solve—meaning unknown
Solvi—farmer; saga name
Soren—god of thunder; myth
   name (form of Thor)
Starkadhr—fierce warrior;
   myth name
Starkad—saga name
Stigandi—son of Kotkel;
   saga name
Strifebjorn—father of Ornolf;
   saga name
Sturla—saga name
Styr—supporter of Erik; saga
   name
Sumarlidi—son of Killer-Hrap;
   saga name
Surtr—giant; myth name
Svaldifari—stallion; myth name
Svart, Svartkel—father of
   Thorkel; saga name
Sverting—son of Runolf Ulfsson;
   saga name
Tait—happy

Tanni—saga name
Tarnkappe—cloak that renders
   its wearer invisible; myth
   name
Thangbrand—missionary;
   saga name
Thialfi, Thjalfi—servant of Thor;
   myth name
Thor, Tor—god of thunder;
   myth name
Thorarin—son of Thorkol;
   saga name
Thord—son of Viking;
   saga name
Thorfinn—killed Einar;
   saga name
Thorgils—father of Ingjald; saga
   name
Thorgrim—brother of Onund
   Bild; saga name
Thorhadd—son of Stein; saga
   name
Thorhall, Thorhalli—saga name
Thorir—son of Asa; saga name
Thorkel—sorcerer; saga name
Thorlak—bishop of Skalholt;
   saga name
Thorleik—son of Bolli; saga name
Thormod—son of Odd;
   saga name
Thorvald—son of Asvald; saga
   name
Thorvid—son of Ulfar; saga name
Thrain—saga name
Thrand—brother of Eyvind the
   Easterner; saga name
Thrasi—son of Thorolf; saga
   name

Throst—son of Hermund; saga name

Thrym—giant; myth name

Thurston—Thor's stone

Tind—saga name

Tjasse—giant; myth name

Torfi—saga name

Torrad—son of Osvif; saga name

Turfeinar—son of Rognvald; saga name

Tyr, Tiu—god of war; myth name

Tyrkir—German; saga name

Ulfar—saga name

Ull—god of skiers; myth name

Uni—Dane; myth name

Utgard-Loki—king of the giants; myth name

Valbrand—saga name

Valgard—saga name

Vali—son of Odin; myth name

Valthjof—son of Orlyg; saga name

Vandrad—son of Osvif; saga name

Vanir—god of rain; myth name

Ve—giver of feeling; myth name

Velief—saga name

Vestar—son of Thorolf; saga name

Vestein—son of Vegeir; saga name

Vibald—saga name

Vifil—father of Thornbjorn; saga name

Vigfus—saga name

Vigsterk—saga name

Viking—father of Thord; saga name

Vili—giver of reason; myth name

Volsung—ruler of the Huns; saga name

Waldemar—strong ruler

Welby—from the farm by the spring

Whitby—from the white farm

Ymir—giant; myth name

Yngvar—saga name

Yrar—saga name

SCOTTISH

As recently as the nineteenth century, Scottish children were named after their relatives according to birth order. Sons would be named after the paternal grandfather, then the maternal grandfather, then the father. Daughters were named after first the maternal grandmother, then the paternal grandmother, then the mother. Subsequent children were named after aunts and uncles.

Many Scottish surnames originated as patronymics and begin with a prefix like Mack-, Mac-, Ap-, and P-, (which mean "son of"). Some of the other Scottish surnames are based on place names, occupation, or a nickname.

In the Highlands of Scotland, clans formed from large family groups with a common male ancestor. Each clan had its own clan name and tartan. However, it was possible for many surnames to fall under the same clan name. While "native men" (men born to the clan and related by blood) shared the clan name, "broken men" (men from other clans who are under the clan's protection) would retain their original surname or clan name. Although clans were distinctly a Highland feature, it has become common to refer to large families of the lowlands as clans.

The surnames of Highland women were often different from the clan name because, until the late nineteenth century, it was not common practice for a woman to take her husband's surname at marriage. (Even in modern-day Scotland, a married woman's legal identity is her original surname; if a woman takes her husband's surname, it is recognized as an alias.) The female lines and unrelated families that fell under the umbrella of a clan name are called septs. Septs were also given the privilege of wearing the clan tartan.

Like Irish names, Scottish surnames are among the oldest in Europe. Highlander surnames developed separately from those in the Lowlands. The Lowlander surnames were more like the English and borrowed many English descriptive and place names.

In retaliation for acts by the clan against the crown, the name MacGregor was abolished from 1617 until 1661; to bear that name during the ban invited execution.

A few surnames:

Affleck	MacDonnough
Anderson	MacDougal
Argyle	MacDuff
Bane	MacEwen
Barr	MacFadden
Berryman	MacFarlane
Brodie	MacFie
Campbell	MacGillivray
Chalmers	MacGinnis
Crawford	MacGowan
Crichton	MacGregor
Douglas	MacIntyre
Duncan	MacIver
Ferguson	MacKay
Gibson	MacKenzie
Gilchrist	MacKinley
Gordon	MacKinnon
Grant	MacLachlan
Henderson	MacLaine
Kilgour	MacLean
Kinnear	MacLeod
Lawson	MacMillan
Lithgow	MacNab
Lochhead	MacNaughton
MacAdam	MacNeill
MacAlister	MacNicol
MacAlpine	MacPherson
MacArtney	MacQuarrie
MacAulay	MacQueen
MacAuslan	MacRae
MacAvoy	Marshall
MacBain	Moffat
MacBeth	Reagh
MacCallum	Russell
MacClennan	Scott
MacCloud	Shaw
MacCulloch	Stewart
MacDonald	Weir

FEMALE

Aila—from the strong place

Aileana—from the green meadow

Aileen—light (form of Eileen)

Ailsa—rocky inlet

Ainsley—meadow

Akira—anchor

Alpina—blonde

Anice—grace (form of Anne)

Annabel, Annabella—lovely grace (form of Annabelle)

Athdara, Adaira, Adairia—from the oak-tree ford (form of Athdar)

Beathas—wise

Blair—from the plain lands

Bonnie, Bonny—sweet and good

Bradana—salmon

Cadha—from the steep place

Cailleach, Caillic—hag

Cairistiona—believes in Christ (form of Christian)

Caroline—manly (form of Charles)

Christel, Christal, Christie, Christy—believes in Christ (form of Christian)

Coira, Cora—seething pool

Colina—victory of the people (form of Nicholas)

Cullodena, Cullidina—from the marsh (form of Culloden)

Cumina—from Comines

Daracha—from the oak (form of Darach)

Donalda—ruler of the world (form of Donald)

Eara, Earie—from the east

Edina, Edine, Edeen—from Edinburgh

Edme—rich protector (form of Edmund)

Eiric, Eirica—eternal ruler (form of Eric)

Erskina—from the top of the cliff

Evanna, Evina—right-handed

Fearchara, Fearcharia—dear one

Fenella—white shoulders (form of Finola)

Fia—dark of peace

Fiona—fair one

Firtha—arm of the sea (form of Firth)

Forba, Forbia—headstrong

Fyfa—from Fifeshire

Gara, Garia, Gaira—short

Gavina, Gavenia—white hawk (form of Gavin)

Gilbarta—pledge

Gordania, Gordana—hero (form of Gordan)

Grear, Greer, Grier—vigilant

Grizel, Grizela—gray battle-maid (form of Griselda)

Gunna—white (form of Gunn)

Inghean, Inghinn—daughter

Iona—place name, island in Hebrides

Isobel, Iseabal—consecrated to God (form of Elizabeth)

Jean—gracious God (form of John)

Kirstie—believes in Christ (form of Christian)

Kyla—from the straits
Lainie, Leana—serves John
Lair, Laire, Lara—mare
Larena, Laren, Laria—serves
    Lawrence
Lassie—little girl
Leslie, Lesley, Lioslaith—from
    the gray fortress
Lindsay, Lindsey, Lyndsey,
    Lynsey—from the island of
    the linden tree
Machara—plain
Mairead—pearl (form of
    Margaret)
Mairi, Moire—bitter (form of
    Mary)
Maisie, Mai, May, Maggie—pearl
    (form of Margaret)
Malise—God's servant
Malmuira, Malmuirie—dark-
    skinned
Marcail—pearl (form of
    Margaret)
Moibeal—lovable (form of Mabel)
Moireach—lady
Morag—great one
Muira, Muire—from the moor
    (form of Muir)
Nairne, Nairna—from the alder-
    tree river
Nathaira, Nathara—snake (form
    of Nathair)

Nessa, Nessia—from the
    headland (form of Ness)
Nighean, Nighinn—young woman
Odara, Odaria—meaning
    unknown
Raoghnailt—ewe
Robena, Robina—robin
Rona—island name
Rose—rose (form of Rosa)
Rossa—meadow
Seonaid, Sheena, Shona—
    gracious God
Sileas—youthful
Sima—listener
Siubhan—gracious God (form of
    John)
Siusan—lily (form of Susan)
Skena—from Skene
Struana—stream (form of Struan)
Tam—twin
Tara—hill where the kings met;
    myth name
Tavia, Teva—twin (form of
    Thomas)
Tira, Tyra—land
Torra—from the castle
Vika—from the creek
Wynda—from the narrow
    passage
Zena—defender of mankind
    (form of Alexander)

MALE

Abernethy—name of a river
Abhainn, Aibne—river
Acair, Akir, Acaiseid—anchor
Achaius—friend of a horse

Adair—from the ford by the oak
    trees
Adhamh—of the red earth (form
    of Adam)

Ailbert—noble (form of Albert)
Ailean—handsome
Ailein—from the green meadow
Aillig, Ail—from the stony place
Aindreas—manly (form of Andrew)
Ainsley—meadow
Alan, Allan, Allen, Alleyne—handsome
Alastair, Alasdair—avenger
Albanact—myth name
Alpin—blond
Amhuinn—lives at the alder-tree river
Angus, Aengus, Aonghus—exceptionally strong
Aoidh—spirited
Argyle, Arregaithel—from the land of the Gauls
Armstrong, Armstrang—strong arm
Artair—noble bear (form of Arthur)
Athdar, Adair—from the oak-tree ford
Athol—new Ireland
Bac, Bhaic—bank
Baird—from Baird
Balfour—from the pastureland
Balgair, Balgaire—fox
Balloch—from the pasture
Balmoral—from the majestic village
Barclay—from Berkeley
Bean, Baen—fair-skinned
Bearnard—strong as a bear (form of Bernard)
Beathan—son of the right hand

Beth—lively
Bhaltair—strong fighter
Biast, Beiste—beast
Birk—from a birch tree
Blair—from the plain lands
Both, Bothan, Bothain—from the stone house
Bowie—blond
Boyd—blond
Braden, Bhradain—salmon
Braigh, Bhraghad—from the upper part
Breac, Bhreac, Brice, Bryce, Bhric—speckled
Broc—badger
Brochan, Brochain—broken
Brodie—from Brodie
Bruce—woods
Buchanan—from the cannon's seat
Busby—meaning unknown
Cailean, Caillen—child
Caladh—harbor
Callum—bald dove
Cam, Chaim, Crom, Cruim—crooked
Camden, Camdin, Camdan, Camdyn—from the winding valley
Cameron, Camshron—crooked nose
Campbell, Cam, Camp, Cambeul—crooked mouth
Carlton, Caraidland—from the land between the streams
Carmichael—friend of Saint Michael
Carr, Cathair—from the marsh

Cat, Chair—catlike

Cawley, Cauley, Camhlaidh—relic

Ceard, Ceardach—smith

Chalmer, Chalmers—rules the home

Chattan—clan of the cats

Chisholm—from Chisolm

Christie, Christy—believes in Christ (form of Christian)

Clach—stone

Cleit—rocky eminence

Clennan—Finnian's servant

Clunes—resting place

Clyde—name of a river

Colin—victory of the people (form of Nicholas)

Colquhoun—from Colquhoun

Corey, Cory, Coire—seething pool

Craig—dwells at the crag

Crannog—lake dweller

Creighton—from the town by the creek

Cromwell—from the crooked stream

Culloden—from the marsh

Cumin, Comyn, Cumming—from Comines

Cunningham—from Cunningham

Dallas, Daileasss—dwells by the waterfall

Dalziel, Dalyell—from the little field

Damh, Daimh—ox

Darach—from the oak

Davis, Dave, Davidson, MacDaibhidh—David's son

Dearg—red

Doire, Dhoire—from the grove

Don, Donald, Donel, Donell, Domhnull—ruler of the world

Doughall, Dougal—dark stranger

Douglas, Dubhglas—dark water

Dour—from the water

Drummand, Drummond—at the ridge

Duff, Dubh—dark-faced

Duncan, Donnchadh, Donnachadh—dark warrior

Dunmore, Dunmor—from the fortress on the hill

Eachan—dark horse

Eanruig—rules the home (form of Henry)

Ear, Earie—from the east

Earvin—place name

Eideard—rich guardian (form of Edward)

Eigg—meaning unknown

Eilig—from the deer pass

Ellar—steward, servant

Elliot—old Welshman

Errol—wandering

Erskine—from the top of the cliff

Euan, Ewan—of the yew

Evan—right-handed

Fang, Faing—from the sheep pen

Farlan, Farlane—son of the furrows

Farquhar—dear one

Farquharson—son of the dear one

Feandan—from the narrow glen

Fearchar—dear one
Fergus—of manly strength
Fergusson, Ferguson—son of
Fergus
Fie—dark of peace
Fife, Fyfe—man of Fife
Fingal—fair stranger
Finlay—fair soldier
Firth—arm of the sea
Fletcher—feathers arrows
Forbes—headstrong
Fraser—strawberry flowers
Fyfe, Fibh—from Fifeshire
Gare, Gair—short
Gavin, Gawain, Gawen, Gawyn,
Gaven—white hawk
Gilleabart—pledge (form of
Gilbert)
Gilleasbuig—bold
Gillecriosd—Christ-bearer
Gillivray—servant of judgment
Gilmer—servant of the Virgin
Mary
Goraidh—God's peace
Gordan, Gordain, Gordy—hero
Gow, Gobha, Gowan—smith
Graham—from the gray home
Grant—great
Gregor, Griorgair—watchful
(form of Gregory)
Gunn—white
Guthrie—free wind
Hamilton—from Hameldone
Hamish—supplanter (form of
James)
Harailt—leader
Hay, Haye—from the stockade
Henson, Henderson,
MacKendrick—son of Henry

Home, Hume—from the cave
Houston—from Hugh's town
Iagan—fiery one
Ian, Iain—gracious God (form of
John)
Innes—from Innes
Irvin, Irving—from the city
Iver—archer (form of Ivar)
Jock—gracious God (form of
John)
Johnson—son of John
Johnston—from John's farm
Kay, Kai—fiery
Keir—dark
Keith—from the battlefield
Kelso—place name
Kelvin—from the narrow river
Ken, Kenneth, Kenny—
handsome
Kennedy—helmeted
Kenzie—fair
Kermichil—from Michael's
fortress
Kerr—man of strength
Kinnon—fair born
Kinny, Kin—from the top of the
cliff
Kirk, Kerk—dwells at the church
Kyle—from the straights
Lachlan, Laochailan—warring
Laine, Lean, Leane—serves John
Laird—lord
Lamont—lawyer
Laren—serves Lawrence
Leith, Leathan—wide river
Len, Lennie, Lenox—from a
Scottish surname and
district

Leod—ugly

Lesley, Leslie—from the gray
fortress

Lindsay—from the island of the
linden tree

Livingstone—from Livingston

Logan—Finnian's servant

Lundie, Lundy—from the island
grove

Luthais—famous in war

Malcolm, Mealcoluim—servant
of Saint Columba

Maolmuire—dark-skinned

Math, Mathe—bear

Matheson—bear's son

Maxwell—from Maxwell

Menzies—from Mesniers,
Normandy

Minas—great one

Moffatt—long plain

Moncreiffe—from the hill of the
sacred bough

Montgomery—from
Montgomerie

Moray—land by the sea

Morrison—son of the servant of
Mary

Muir—from the moor

Muirfinn—dwells near the
beautiful sea

Munro, Munroe—man from Ro

Murdoc, Murdock, Murdoch—
protector of the sea

Murray, Morogh—man of the
sea

Nab—abbot

Nairn, Nairne—from the alder-
tree river

Nathair, Nathrach,
Nathraichean—snake

Naughton, Nachton, Nechtan—
pure

Nealcail—victorious people

Ness—from the headland

Niall—champion (form of Neal)

Norval—from the north valley

Odar—meaning unknown

Ogilvie, Ogilbinn—from the high
peak

Oidhche—night

Oliphant—great strength

Padruig—noble (form of
Patrick)

Parlan—farmer

Payton, Paden, Paton, Peyton—
royal

Pherson—Parson

Quarrie, Quarry—proud

Rab, Rabbie, Raibeart—bright,
famous (form of Robert)

Rae, Ray—grace

Ramsey—from Ram's island

Robertson—son of Robert

Rob Roy—red Rob

Ronald—mighty, powerful

Ross, Ros—from the peninsula

Roy—red

Sandy—defender of mankind
(form of Alexander)

Scot, Scott—wanderer

Scrymgeour—fighter

Shaw, Shawe—terse

Sheiling—from the summer
pasture

Sim—heard

Sinclair—from Saint-Clair-sur-
Elle

Skene—from Skene
Strahan—small valley
Struan—stream
Sutherland—from Sutherland
Tarsuinn—meaning unknown
Tavis, Tavey, Tevis, Tamnais, Tavish—twin (form of Thomas)
Tearlach—manly (form of Charles)

Thurso—place name
Todd—fox
Tormod—meaning unknown
Uilleam—resolute protector (form of William)
Urquhart—from the fount on the knoll
Wallace—from Wales

SLAVIC

Slavs form Europe's largest ethnic and linguistic group. The Slavic peoples who inhabit much of Eastern Europe can be subdivided into three main groups: East Slavs, West Slavs, and South Slavs. East Slavs include Russians, Ukrainians, and Belarusians. West Slavs include Poles, Czechs, and Slovaks. Bulgarians, Macedonians, Serbs, Bosniaks, Croats, and Slovenians are all South Slavs. There has been much debate on the origins of Slavs, but historians generally agree that Slavs migrated into their western-most territories in the fifth and sixth centuries A.D.

Ancient Slavs did not use surnames. See the sections in this book on Czech and Russian names for surnames and more given names that developed from Slavic languages.

FEMALE

Bronya—protector
Chesna—peaceful
Danica, Danika—morning star
Dobrilla—kind
Fania, Fanya, Fanny—free (form of Francis)
Fedosia, Feodora—God's gift (form of Theodore)
Gavrila, Gavrilla—God give me strength
Hedy—strife (form of Hedwig)
Ilka—flattering
Jarka—spring
Jarmila—spring's grace
Katarina—pure (form of Katherine)
Kasmira, Kazatimiru—commanding peace
Lala—tulip
Lilia—mauve

Ludmilla, Ljudumilu—loved by the people
Marika, Marya—bitter (form of Mary)
Milka—industrious
Mira, Myra—famous
Nada, Nadia, Nadege, Nadezhda, Nadya, Nadyenka, Nadyuiska, Nadine—hope
Neda—born on Sunday
Rada—happy
Radinka—active
Radmilla, Radilu—works for the people
Sonja—wise (form of Sonya)
Valeska, Valdislava—glorious ruler
Varvara, Varina—stranger
Valika, Velika—great
Zora, Zorah, Zorana—dawn

MALE

Anatol—from the east (form of Anatole)

Andrej—manly (form of Andrew)

Bogdan—gift from God (form of Bohdan)

Boguslaw, Bohuslav—God's glory

Boleslaus—sorrowful

Bolodenka, Dimka—universal

Boris, Borysko—fighter

Bronislaw—weapon of glory

Casimir—destroys peace

Cestmir—fortress

Dragan—beloved, dear

Jaroslav—spring's glory

Karel, Karol—manly (form of Charles)

Kazatimiru, Kasimer—destroys peace (form of Casimir)

Kersten—believes in Christ (form of Christian)

ELIZABETH GEORGE

Elizabeth George is *The New York Times* and international best-selling author of thirteen novels of psychological suspense set in England. She is the recipient of literary awards from France, Germany, and the United States.

Charles Dickens taught me the importance of the names of characters. Uriah Heep. Ebenezer Scrooge. Miss Havisham. . . . Dickens always positioned the reader with reference to the characters by naming them in such a way that aspects of personality were suggested merely from the choice of name. He was the master of this, of course. No one else has ever come close.

Today, however, writers have to be a bit more subtle because realism is the name of the game. So in the past I've gone for names like Clive Pritchard, Robin Payne, Colin Shepherd, Polly Yarkin, and Robin Sage to make a more delicate point about my people.

But British names also are suggestive of class, level of education, economic status, and social origin, so I also have to be careful there.

In a pinch, I turn to the British tabloids for help. In the tabloids I can find every kind of name: from the Duke of Widgy-wak to the dustman on the street. It's an invaluable tool for an American whose novels are all set in England.

Laci, Laszlo, Lacko, Lazlo—famous ruler

Ladislas, Ladislav—glorious

Lew—lion

Milos—pleasant

Miroslav—peaceful glory

Nicholai, Nikolai—victory of the people (form of Nicholas)

Pavel—small (form of Paul)

Pjotr, Pyotr—rock (form of Peter)

Rostislav—glory

Rurik—famous ruler

Sandor—defender of mankind (form of Alexander)

Slava, Slavochka—glory

Stanislaus, Stanislas, Stannes, Slavik, Stanislav, Stas—military glory

Stasio—stand of glory

Tibor—holy place

Upravda—upright

Vaclar, Vasek, Valdik, Vladya—wreath of glory

Vassily—regal (form of Basil)

Vladimer, Vimka, Vladimir, Volodya, Vova, Vladimiru—universal ruler

Vladislava, Vyacheslav, Vladislav—glorious ruler

Wenceslaus, Wenceslava—great glory

Zakarij—meaning unknown

Zbigniew—release anger

Ziven, Ziv, Zivon—lively

Zoran—sunrise, dawn

SPANISH

Surnames began in the mid-ninth century and became hereditary in the thirteenth century. Before they were used, the father's name was listed in the genitive form (indicates who the person's parents are/ were) after the given name.

Most given names came from the Visigoths and the Moors. The majority of surnames derived from descriptive or occupational names, but some were patronymic and place names.

As was customary in most of Europe, the nobility took the names of the estates they owned. Occasionally, the father's name was used in conjunction with the estate name.

The standard format of a Spanish full name has been given name first, then the father's family name, *y* (and), and the mother's family name. However, in more recent years, the y is often omitted and the mother's family name tends to come before the father's name.

A few articles and suffixes:

-ez, -es—son of
y—and
viuda—widow of
de—of
la, le—the
de la, de le, de los, del—of the

Married women may add their husband's name to their own with the article *de*. Example: Agueda Padilla y de la Fuente de Chavez. Translated: Agueda (given name) Padilla (father's surname) y (and) de la Fuente (mother's maiden name) de (of) Chavez (husband's name). If *viuda* came before *de Chavez*, it would indicate that this woman was a widow. Names are always traced through the father.

A few surnames:

Alvarez	Cruz
Aznar	Delgado
Benitez	Diaz
Carrera	Diego
Chavez	Fernandez

Flores
Garcia
Gomez
Gonzalez
Guzman
Hernandez
Herrera
Lopez
Luna
Martinez
Mendoza
Menendez
Ortega
Ortiz

Perez
Ramirez
Riviera
Rodriguez
Romero
Ruiz
Salazar
Sanchez
Santiago
Torres
Valdez
Vargas
Vasquez
Vega

FEMALE

Abrienda—open
Adelina, Adelita—noble (form of
   Adelaide)
Adoncia—sweet
Adoracion—adoration
Adriana—dark (form of Adrian)
Agnese—pure (form of Agnes)
Agueda, Agata, Agacia—good
   (form of Agatha)
Agurtzane—meaning unknown
Aida, Aidia—help
Ainhoa, Ainhoe—meaning
   unknown
Aintzane—glory
Aitziber—meaning unknown
Alameda—promenade
Alatea—truth
Alazne—miracle
Albertine, Albertina—noble,
   intelligent (form of Albert)
Aldonza, Aldonsa—nice

Alegria, Allegra—cheerful
Alejandra, Alejandrina—
   defender of mankind (form
   of Alexander)
Aleta—winged
Aletea, Aletia—honest
Alfonsa—noble and ready for
   battle (form of Alphonse)
Alfreda—elf counselor (form of
   Alfred)
Alicia—sweet, noble (form of
   Alice)
Alita—noble
Alma—spirit
Almira—from Almeira
Almunda, Almundena,
   Almundina—reference to
   the Virgin Mary
Alona—light
Alonsa—noble and ready for
   battle (form of Alphonse)

Alva—white
Amaia—end
Amalia—hardworking (form of Amelia)
Amalur, Amalure—homeland
Amanda—worthy of love
Amaranta—flower (form of Amarantha)
Amata—beloved (form of Amato)
Amor, Amora—love
Andeana—leaving
Andere, Andera, Andrea—manly (form of Andrew)
Angela, Angelina, Angelia—angel
Anitia, Anita, Anica—grace (form of Anne)
Antonina, Antonia—priceless (form of Anthony)
Anunciacion—of the Annunciation
Aquilina—eagle (form of Aquilino)
Aracelia, Araceli—altar of heaven
Arama—reference to the Virgin Mary
Arcadia—adventurous
Arcelia—treasure
Armada—armed one
Arrate—meaning unknown
Artemisia—perfection
Ascencion—reference to the Ascension
Asuncion—born during the Feast of Assumption
Atalaya, Athalia—guard tower
Aureliana, Aurelia—gold (form of Aurelio)

Aurkene, Aurkena—present
Beatriz, Beatrisa—brings joy
Belicia—dedicated to God
Belinda—attractive
Belita—beautiful
Bella—beautiful
Benigna—friendly
Benita—blessed
Bibiana—animated
Bienvenida—welcome (form of Bienvendido)
Blanca—white (form of Blanche)
Blasa—stutters (form of Blaise)
Bonita—pretty
Brigidia, Brigida—strong (form of Bridget)
Buena—good
Calandria—lark
Calida—fiery
Calvina—bald (form of Calvin)
Camila—temple servant (form of Camillus)
Candida—dazzling white
Carilla, Carla, Carlita, Carletta, Carlotta, Carlota—manly (form of Charles)
Carmelita, Carmela—garden
Carmencita, Carmen, Carmina—song
Carmita—rosy
Carona—crowned
Casild, Casilda—meaning unknown
Casta, Catalina—pure
Catalonia—region of Spain; place name
Cenobia—born of Zeus (form of Zenobia)

Cesara—long-haired (form of Caesar)

Charo—nickname for Rosario

Chiquita—little one

Cipriana—from Cyprus (form of Cipriano)

Clareta—brilliant

Clarinda—beautiful

Clarissa—clear, bright (form of Clare)

Claudia—lame (form of Claude)

Clementina—merciful (form of Clement)

Clodovea—famous warrior (form of Clodoveo)

Concepcion, Concetta, Conchetta, Conshita—reference to the Immaculate Conception

Constanza—constant (form of Constantine)

Consuelo, Consuela, Consolacion, Consolata, Chela—consolation

Corazon—heart

Cristina—believes in Christ (form of Christian)

Dalila—gentle

Damita—little noble

Danita—God is my judge (form of Daniel)

Daria—rich

Deiene, Deikun, Deina—religious holiday

Delcine, Dulcine, Dulcina, Dulce, Dulcinea, Dulcinia—sweet

Delicia—delight

Delma, Delmar, Delmara—of the sea

Desideria—desired (form of Desirata)

Devera—task

Dia—day

Diega—supplanter (form of Diego)

Digna—worthy

Dionis, Dionisa—god of wine (form of Dionysus)

Dolores, Doloritas, Dolorita—sorrow

Dominga—of the Lord; born on Sunday (form of Dominic)

Dorbeta—reference to the Virgin Mary

Dorota, Doroteia, Dorotea—God's gift (form of Dorothy)

Drina—defender of mankind (form of Alexander)

Duena—chaperon

Dulcinea—sweet

Elbertina—noble, glorious (form of Elbert)

Eldora—golden

Elena—light (form of Eleanor)

Elisa—consecrated to God (form of Elizabeth)

Elsa—truth

Elvira—white

Ema—grandmother

Emilia, Emilie—flattering (form of Emilio)

Encarnacion—reference to the Incarnation

Engracia—graceful

Enrica, Enriqueta, Enriqua—rules the home (form of Henry)

Erendira, Erendiria—name of a princess

Ernesta—serious (form of Ernest)

Eskarne, Eskarna—merciful

Esma, Esme, Esmerelda—emerald

Esperanza—hope

Estebana, Estefana, Esteva—crowned in victory (form of Stephen)

Estella, Estrella, Ester—star (form of Esther)

Eva, Evita—life (form of Eve)

Exaltacion—reference to the cross

Faqueza—weakness

Fe—trust

Felipa, Filipa—lover of horses (form of Philip)

Fermina—strong (form of Fermin)

Fidelia—faithful (form of Fidel)

Florentina, Florida, Florinia, Flor, Florencia—blooming (form of Florian)

Fonda—profound

Fortuna, Fausta, Faustina, Felisa—lucky

Francisca—free (form of Francis)

Freira—sister

Frescura—freshness

Fuensanta—holy fountain

Gala—from Gaul

Galena, Galenia—small intelligent one

Garaitz—victory

Garbine, Garbina, Garabine, Garabina—purification

Gaspara—treasurer (form of Casper)

Gechina—graceful

Generosa—generous (form of Generoso)

Gertrudes, Gertrudis—strong with a spear (form of Gertrude)

Gezane, Gezana—reference to the Incarnation

Ginebra, Ginessa—white

Gitana—gypsy

Godalupe, Guadalupe—reference to the Virgin Mary

Gorane—holy cross

Gotzone—angel

Gracia, Graciana—grace (form of Grace)

Gregoria—watchful (form of Gregory)

Guillelmina—resolute protector (form of William)

Gustava—staff of God (form of Gustav)

Havana—from the capital of Cuba

Henriqua—rules the home (form of Henry)

Hermelinda—shield of power

Herminia—myth name

Hermosa—beautiful

Honor, Honoria, Honoratas—honor

Idoia, Idurre, Iratze, Izazkun—reference to the Virgin Mary

Ignacia—fiery (form of Ignatius)

Igone—reference to Christ's Ascension

Ikerne—visitation

Iluminada—illuminated

Imelda—floret

Immaculada—reference to the Immaculate Conception

Inez, Ines—pure (form of Agnes)

Inocencia, Inocenta—innocent

Irene—peace

Irmina—meaning unknown

Irune—reference to the Holy Trinity

Isabella, Isabel—consecrated to God (form of Elizabeth)

Isidora—gifted with many ideas

Isleta—small island

Itsaso—sea

Itxaro—hope

Izar, Izarre, Izarra—star

Jacinta, Jakinda—hyacinth (form of Hyacinth)

Jade—jewel

Jaimica—supplanter

Jaione—reference to the Nativity

Jasone—assumption

Javiera—owner of a new home (form of Xavier)

Jesusa, Josune—God saves (form of Jesus)

Jimena—heard

Joaquina—God will establish (form of Joachim)

Josefa, Josefina—God adds (form of Joseph)

Juana, Juanita—gracious God (form of John)

Kemena, Kemina—strong (form of Kemen)

Kesare, Kesara—youthful

Landa, Legarre, Leira, Lera, Lorda, Lourdes, Louredes, Lucita—reference to the Virgin Mary

La Reina—queen

Laura, Larunda, Laurencia—laurel (form of Lawrence)

Latoya—victorious

Leonora, Leonor—light (form of Eleanor)

Leya—loyalty

Liana—to bind; youth

Linda, Lindy, Lynda, Lyndey—pretty

Lititia, Laetizia—happy (form of Letitia)

Lola, Lolita, Loleta, Lolitta—manly (form of Charles)

Lona—solitary

Lore, Lora—flower

Loretta—laurel (form of Lawrence)

Lucetta, Lucia, Lucita, Lucrecia, Luz—light (form of Luke)

Luisa—famous in war (form of Louis)

Lujuana—Lu

Lupe—wolf

Lur—earth

Madra, Madre—mother

Maite, Maitea—love

Malaya—free

Manda—battle-maid

Manuela—God is with us (form of Emmanuel)

Marcela—warlike (form of Marcus)

Margarita—pearl (form of Margaret)

Mariquita, Marquilla, Marisa, Marisol, Madalena, Maria, Marietta, Marita—bitter (form of Mary)

Maribel—bitter, beautiful

Mariposa—butterfly

Marta—mistress (form of Martha)

Melisenda, Melosa, Melosia—honeybee

Mendi, Molara—reference to the Virgin Mary

Mercedes—mercy

Milagros, Milagrosa, Milagritos, Mirari, Mireya—miracle

Miranda—deserves admiration

Modesta, Modeste—modest

Monica—counselor

Mora—little blueberry

Naiara—reference to the Virgin Mary

Nalda—strong (form of Naldo)

Narcisa—daffodil

Natalia—born on Christmas (form of Natalie)

Natividad—reference to the Nativity

Nazaret—of Nazareth

Nekane, Nekana—sorrows

Nelia—yellow

Nerea—mine

Neta, Nita—serious (form of Neto)

Neva, Nieve, Nevada—snowy

Nicanora—victorious army

Nina—girl

Ofelia—helper

Oihane—from the forest

Olalla—soft spoken

Olinda—protector of property

Oliveria—affectionate (form of Oliver)

Olivia—olive

Ora—gold

Orlanda—famous throughout the land (form of Orlando)

Orquidea, Orquidia—orchid

Osane, Osana—health

Pabla—small (form of Paul)

Paciencia—patient

Palba—blond (form of Palban)

Palmira—from the city of palms

Paloma—dove

Paquita—free

Pastora—shepherdess

Patia—leaf

Patricia—noble (form of Patrick)

Paulina, Paulita—small (form of Paul)

Paz—peace

Pedra—rock (form of Peter)

Pepa, Pepita—God adds (form of Joseph)

Perfecta—perfect

Perla—small pearl

Pia—pious

Pilar—pillar

Placida—tranquil

Primavera—born at the beginning of spring

Prudencia—prudent

Puebla—from the city (form of Pueblo)

Pureza, Pura, Purisima—pure
Querida—beloved
Quinta—born fifth
Raeka—unique
Ramira—judicious
Ramona, Raimunda—mighty
    protector (form of
    Raymond)
Raquel—ewe (form of Rachel)
Reina, Regina—queen
Remedios—remedy
Ria—from the river's mouth
Rica, Ricarda—strong ruler
    (form of Richard)
Rio—river
Rita—pearl (form of Margaret)
Roana—reddish-brown skin
    (form of Roano)
Rocio—dewdrops
Roderiga—famous ruler (form of
    Roderick)
Roldana—famous
Romana—from Rome (form of
    Romano)
Rosa, Rosalind, Rosalinda,
    Rosalinde, Roslyn,
    Rosario—rose
Rosamaria, Rosemarie—bitter
    rose
Rufa, Rufina—red-haired (form
    of Rufus)
Sabina—of the Sabine people
Salbatora, Salvatora,
    Salvadora—savior (form of
    Salvatore)
Sancia, Sancha—holy
Sandia—watermelon
Sarita, Sara—princess (form of
    Sarah)

Saturnina—gift of Saturn
Savanna, Savannah, Sabana—
    from the open plain
Segunda—born second (form of
    Segundo)
Seina—innocent (form of Sein)
Senalda—sign
Senona—lively (form of Senon)
Serafina—fiery one; angel (form
    of Seraphina)
Serena—serene
Sevilla—from Seville
Shoshana, Susana—lily (form of
    Susan)
Simona—God is heard (form of
    Simon)
Socorro—helps
Sofia—wise (form of Sophia)
Solana—sunshine
Soledad, Soledada—solitary
Suelita—little lily
Tabora—drum
Terceira—born third (form of
    Terceiro)
Tia—aunt; princess
Tierra—earth
Trella—star
Trinidad—of Trinidad, the
    island
Ursula, Ursulina—little bear
Usoa—dove
Valentina—valiant, strong (form
    of Valentine)
Ventura—good fortune
Verdad—honest
Veta—intelligent (form of Veto)
Vicenta—victorious (form of
    Vincent)

Vina—from the vineyard
Virginia—pure
Vittoria—victorious (form of Victor)
Xalbadora, Xalvadora—savior (form of Salvatore)
Xaviera, Xevera, Xeveria—owner of a new home (form of Xavier)
Xuxa, Xylia—queen

Yanamaria, Yanamarie—bitter grace (form of Annamarie)
Ynes—pure (form of Agnes)
Yoana—God's gift
Yolanda—violet
Yomaris—I am the sun
Ysabel—consecrated to God (form of Isabel)
Zamora—from Zamora
Zita—little hope
Zurine, Zurina—white

MALE

Abejundio—of the bees
Adriano—dark (form of Adrian)
Agustin—great (form of August)
Alano—handsome (form of Alan)
Alarico—noble ruler (form of Alaric)
Alberto—noble, intelligent (form of Albert)
Alejandro—defender of mankind (form of Alexander)
Alfonso, Alonso, Alonzo—noble and ready for battle (form of Alphonse)
Aluino—noble friend
Amadeo, Amado—loves God (form of Amadeus)
Amador—lover
Amato—beloved
Ambrosio—immortal (form of Ambrose)
Amistad—friendship
Anastasio—one who will be reborn (form of Anastasia)

Andres—manly (form of Andrew)
Angel, Angelo—angel
Anibal—graced by God
Anselmo—divine helmet (form of Anselm)
Antonio, Anton—priceless (form of Anthony)
Aquilino—eagle
Archibaldo—bold (form of Archibald)
Arlo—barberry
Armando—soldier (form of Herman)
Arturo—noble bear (form of Arthur)
Aurelio—gold
Bartolo, Bartoli, Bartolome—hill, furrow (form of Bartholomew)
Basilio—regal (form of Basil)
Beltran—bright raven
Benedicto—blessed (form of Benedict)

Bernardo—strong as a bear (form of Bernard)

Bernbe—son of prophecy (form of Barnaby)

Berto—intelligent

Bienvenido—welcome

Blanco—blond

Blas—stutters (form of Blaise)

Bonifaco, Bonifacio—good (form of Boniface)

Calvino—bald (form of Calvin)

Camilo—temple servant (form of Camillus)

Carlomagno—Charles the Great

Carlos—manly (form of Charles)

Casimiro—destroys peace (form of Casimir)

Castel—of the castle

Caton—wise

Cesar, Cesaro—long-haired (form of Caesar)

Chale—manly

Chico, Currito, Curro—free

Ciceron—chickpea

Cipriano—from Cyprus

Cirilo—noble

Ciro—sun

Claudio—lame (form of Claude)

Clodoveo—famous warrior

Colon—dove

Conrado—able counsel (form of Conrad)

Constantino—constant (form of Constantine)

Cornelio—horn (form of Cornelius)

Cristo, Cristiano—believes in Christ (form of Christian)

Cristobal—Christ-bearer (form of Christopher)

Cuarto, Cuartio—born fourth

Curcio—polite

Damian—tame

Darien, Dario—rich

Delmar—of the sea

Desiderio—desired (form of Desirata)

Devante—fight for good

Diego—supplanter

Domingo—of the Lord; born on Sunday (form of Dominic)

Edmundo—rich protector (form of Edmund)

Eduardo—rich guardian (form of Edward)

Efrain—fruitful

Eloy—famous fighter

Elvio—blond

Emilio—flattering

Eneas—praised

Enrique—rules the home (form of Henry)

Erasmo—friendly

Ernesto—serious (form of Ernest)

Esteban, Estefan—crowned in victory (form of Stephen)

Eugenio—well-born (form of Eugene)

Fabio—bean farmer (form of Fabian)

Farruco, Frasco, Frascuelo—free

Fausto, Felix—lucky (form of Faust)

Federico—peaceful ruler (form of Frederick)

Felipe—lover of horses (form of Philip)

Fermin—strong

Fernando—adventurer (form of Ferdinand)

Fidel, Fidele—faithful

Flaminio—meaning unknown

Flavio—yellow (form of Flavian)

Florentino, Florinio—blooming (form of Florian)

Fraco—weak

Francisco, Cisco—free (form of Francis)

Franco—free (form of Francis)

Fresco—fresh

Gabino, Gabriel, Gabrio—God-given strength

Galeno—small intelligent one

Garcia—brave in battle

Gaspar, Gaspard—treasurer (form of Casper)

Generoso—generous

Gerardo—spear ruler (form of Gerald)

Geronimo—sacred (form of Jerome)

Gervasio, Gervaso, German—warrior

Gil—squire

Gilberto—pledge (form of Gilbert)

Godofredo, Godfredo—God's peace (form of Godfrey)

Gomez—man

Gregorio—watchful (form of Gregory)

Gualterio, Galtero—powerful warrior (form of Walter)

Guillermo—resolute protector (form of William)

Guido—guide

Gustavo—staff of God (form of Gustav)

Hector—steadfast

Heriberto—shining warrior (form of Herbert)

Hernando—adventuresome

Hilario—happy (form of Hilary)

Honorato—honor

Horacio—timekeeper (form of Horace)

Humberto, Hugo—intelligent

Iago—supplanter (form of James)

Ignacio, Ignazio, Incendio—fiery (form of Ignatius)

Inocencio, Inocente—innocent

Isidoro, Isidro—gifted with many ideas

Ivan—gracious God (form of John)

Jacinto—hyacinth (form of Hyacinth)

Jago, Jaime—supplanter (form of James)

Javier, Javiero—owner of a new home (form of Xavier)

Jeremias—exalted of the Lord (form of Jeremiah)

Jeronimo—sacred (form of Jerome)

Jesus—God saves

Joaquin—God will establish (form of Joachim)

Jonas—dove

Jorge—farmer (form of George)

Jose—God adds (form of Joseph)

Josue—God is salvation (form of Joshua)

Juan, Juanito—gracious God (form of John)

Julian, Julio—youthful (form of Julius)

Kemen—strong

Lazaro—God will help

Leandro, Leonardo, Leon, Leonides—brave lion (form of Leonard)

Lorenzo—laurel (form of Lawrence)

Lucio, Lucero—light (form of Luke)

Luis—famous in war (form of Louis)

Macario—happy

Manuel—God is with us (form of Emmanuel)

Marco, Marcos, Mario, Martin, Martino, Martinez—warlike (form of Marcus)

Mateo, Matro—God's gift (form of Matthew)

Mauricio, Mauro—dark-skinned (form of Maurice)

Miguel—who is like God (form of Michael)

Moises—taken from the water (form of Moses)

Naldo—strong

Natal, Natalio—born on Christmas (form of Natalie)

Natanael, Nataniel—gift from God (form of Nathaniel)

Nemesio—named for Nemesis, goddess of vengeance

Neron—strong

Nestor—wisdom

Neto, Nesto—serious

Nevada—snowy

Nicanor—victorious army

Noe—peace

Norberto—bright hero (form of Norbert)

Oleos—holy oil

Oliverio, Oliverios—affectionate (form of Oliver)

Orlando—famous throughout the land

Oro—gold

Pablo—small (form of Paul)

Pacifico—peaceful

Paco, Pacorro, Pacho—free

Palban, Palben—blond

Patricio—noble (form of Patrick)

Paz—peace

Pedro—rock (form of Peter)

Pepe, Pepillo—God adds (form of Joseph)

Pirro—red-haired

Placido—tranquil

Platon—broad-shouldered

Ponce—born fifth

Porfirio, Porfiro—purple stone

Primeiro—firstborn

Prospero—prosperous

Pueblo—from the city

Quinton—born fifth

Quirce—martyr's name

Quirino—martyr's name

Rafael—healed by God (form of Raphael)

Ramiro, Ramirez—judicious

Ramon, Raimundo—mighty protector (form of Raymond)

Raul, Raulo—wise

Renaldo—wise ruler

Rey—king

Rico, Ricardo—strong ruler (form of Richard)

Roano—reddish-brown skin

Roberto—bright, famous (form of Robert)

Rodas—rose garden

Roderigo, Rodrigo—famous ruler (form of Roderick)

Rodolfo—famous wolf (form of Rudolph)

Rogelio—famous soldier

Roldan—famous

Roman, Romeo, Roman—from Rome (form of Romano)

Ruben—son

Rufo, Rufio—red-haired (form of Rufus)

Sabino—of the Sabine people

Salbatore, Salvatore, Salvadore, Salvador—savior

Salomon—peaceful (form of Solomon)

Sancho, Santos—saint

Santiago—named for Saint James

Santos—of the saints

Saturnin—gift of Saturn

Saul—longed for

Sebastiano—revered (form of Sebastian)

Segundo—born second

Sein—innocent

Senon—lively

Serafin—fiery one; angel (form of Seraphina)

Stefano—crowned in victory (form of Stephen)

Tabor—drum

Tadeo—praise

Tajo—day

Teodoro—God's gift (form of Theodore)

Terciero—born third

Tito—giant

Tobias—God is good

Toli—plowman

Tomas—twin (form of Thomas)

Tulio—lively

Turi—bear

Urbano—born of the city

Veto—intelligent

Victor, Victoro, Vittorio—victorious (form of Victor)

Vincente—victorious (form of Vincent)

Virgilio—staff bearer (form of Virgil)

Vito, Vidal—vital

Xalbador, Xalvador, Xabat—savior (form of Salvatore)

Xavier, Xever—owner of a new home

Ximen, Ximenes, Ximens—God is heard (form of Simon)

Yago—supplanter (form of Jacob)

Zacarias—remembered by God

Zavier—owner of a new home (form of Xavier)

SWEDISH

Swedish surnames appeared in the seventeenth century and were first used by the military for administrative purposes. By the eighteenth century, others began using hereditary surnames, but these names weren't standardized until the nineteenth century.

Before the nineteenth century, most Swedes used their given name with the father's name, to which they attached the suffix -*son* (for a male child) or -*dotter* for a female child). In 1901, laws were enacted to regulate surnames. Under these laws, only the king could change names. In 1946, the National Bureau of Statistics was granted the right to make name changes.

The suffix -*son* was used mostly by the lower classes. The upper classes preferred:

-berg	-strom
-gren	-in
-lund	-man
-quist	

A few surnames:

Almgren	Linberg
Andersson	Lindstrom
Bergman	Ljungren
Bergstrom	Lundquist
Blomquist	Nilsson
Buss	Nordman
Davidsson	Nygard
Dolk	Nyman
Eriksson	Olsson
Hanson	Ostergard
Harald	Pettersson
Hellman	Rank
Hellqvist	Sandberg
Holm	Silversten
Johansson	Soderlund
Kristofferson	Svensson
Larsson	

FEMALE

Adrian—dark

Agda, Agata, Agaton, Agneta—
pure (form of Agnes)

Aina—joy

Alexandra—defender of
mankind (form of
Alexander)

Algot—pearl

Alicia—sweet, noble (form of
Alice)

Alma—loving

Amalia—hardworking (form of
Amelia)

Anna, Annika, Annike—grace
(form of Anne)

Anna Cristina—graceful
Christian

Annalina—graceful light

Anneli, Annalie, Annali—
graceful meadow

Antonetta—priceless (form of
Anthony)

Astrid—divine strength

Atalie, Atali—pure

Barbro—stranger (form of
Barbara)

Beata—blessed

Berit, Berta—intelligent

Blenda—heroine

Botilda—commanding

Brigetta, Birgitta, Birget, Britta,
Britt, Brite—strong (form of
Bridget)

Carina, Carine, Caren—pure
(form of Karen)

Cecilia—blind (form of Cecil)

Cristina, Christina—believes in
Christ (form of Christian)

Dagmar—maiden of the day

Devnet—Danish home

Ebba, Ebbe—strength

Edit—wealthy gift (form of
Edith)

Eleonora, Elin—light (form of
Eleanor)

Elisabet—consecrated to God
(form of Elizabeth)

Elsa—truth

Emilia—hardworking (form of
Emily)

Emma—universal

Erika—eternal ruler (form of
Eric)

Eva, Evelina—life (form of Eve)

Filippa—lover of horses (form of
Philip)

Frederika—peaceful ruler (form
of Frederick)

Freya—myth name

Frida, Frideborg, Fritjof—
peaceful

Gabriella—God-given strength
(form of Gabriel)

Gala—lovely voice

Gerda—protected

Germund—defender of man

Gertrud—strong with a spear
(form of Gertrude)

Gote, Gota, Gotilda—strong

Greta—pearl (form of Margaret)

Guda—supreme

Gudny—unspoiled

Gudrun, Gudruna—divine
knowledge
Gunilla, Gunnel—battle-maid
Gustava—staff of God (form of
Gustav)
Hakan, Hakana—noble
Hanna—gracious God (form of
John)
Hedwig—strife
Helena—light (form of Helen)
Helga—holy
Henrika—rules the home (form
of Henry)
Hildegard, Hilda—stronghold
Hulda—hidden
Inga, Ingrid, Inge, Inger—Ing's
daughter
Ingaborg, Ingeborg, Ingegard—
Ing's helper
Ingalill—Ing's lily
Jaythen—meaning unknown
(form of Jay)
Johanna—gracious God (form of
John)
Judit—praised (form of Jude)
Julia—youthful (form of Julius)
Karin, Karen—pure
Karla, Karolina—manly (form of
Charles)
Katarina, Katrina, Katrine,
Kaysa—pure (form of
Katherine)
Kate—legend name
Kerstin, Kristina—believes in
Christ (form of Christian)
Kolina—maiden
Klara—clear, bright (form of
Clare)

Lage—from the sea
Laura—laurel (form of
Lawrence)
Lena, Lina—light
Lotta—masculine
Lovisa—renowned battle-maid
Lydia—from Lydia
Mai—sea jewel
Maj, Maja—pearl
Malena, Malene, Malin—from
the tower (form of
Madeleine)
Margareta, Margit—pearl (form
of Margaret)
Maria, Marita—bitter (form of
Mary)
Marta—mistress (form of
Martha)
Martina—warlike (form of
Marcus)
Matilda—strong battle-maid
Mikaela—who is like God (form
of Michael)
Monika—counselor (form of
Monica)
Nanna—graceful
Olga—holy
Olivia—olive
Paulina, Paula—small (form of
Paul)
Petra, Petronella—rock (form of
Peter)
Pia—pious
Quinby, Quenby—from the
woman's estate
Ragnara, Ragnhild—wise
warrior (form of Ragnor)
Rakel—ewe (form of Rachel)

Rigmor, Rigmora—name of a
 queen
Rosel, Roselle, Rosa—rose
Rut—beautiful
Sibylla—prophetess (form of
 Sybil)
Signe, Signild, Signilda, Sigrid—
 victorious
Soasan—legend name
Sofia—wise (form of Sophia)
Solveig—housewoman
Sonya, Sonja—wise
Stella—star
Stina—pure
Svante—myth name
Svea—myth name
Tekla—divine fame

Teresia—reaper (form of
 Theresa)
Tilda—mighty in war
Tora—victor
Trilby—meaning unknown
Trind, Trina, Trine—innocent
Ulla, Ulrika—has willpower
Vedia, Vedis—myth name
Vega—star
Viktoria—victorious (form of
 Victor)
Vilhelmina, Vilma—resolute
 protector (form of William)
Viola—flower
Virginia—pure
Viveka—little woman

MALE

Adolphus, Adolph, Dolph—
 noble wolf
Ake—ancient
Alberik—blond ruler
Albert—noble, intelligent
Alexander—defender of
 mankind
Alf, Alfred—wise
Alfonso, Alfons—noble and
 ready for battle (form of
 Alphonse)
Alrik—all-ruler
Alvar—dwarf shrub
Ambrosius—immortal (form of
 Ambrose)
Anderson—son of Ander
Andreas, Anders—manly (form
 of Andrew)

Ansgar—divine spear
Antonius, Anton—priceless
 (form of Anthony)
Arn, Arne, Arnold—eagle
Aron—high mountain; lofty
 (form of Aaron)
Artur—noble bear (form of
 Arthur)
Arvid—of the people
Axel—father of peace
Balder—god of light; myth name
Baltasar—protected by God
Bartholomeus—hill, furrow
 (form of Bartholomew)
Basilius—regal (form of Basil)
Beck—brook
Bengt, Benedikt—blessed (form
 of Benedict)

Beowulf—myth name
Berg—mountain
Bergren, Bergron—from the mountain brook
Bertil—intelligent
Birger—rescuer
Bjorn—bear
Blasius—stutters (form of Blaise)
Bodil, Bo—commanding
Borg, Borje—from the castle
Brand—sword
Burr—young
Caesar—long-haired
Cowbelliantus—legend name
David—beloved
Davin—intelligent
Denholm—home of the Danes
Eddy—unresting
Edvard—rich guardian (form of Edward)
Emil—lively
Enar—warrior
Erik—eternal ruler (form of Eric)
Erling, Erland—stranger
Ernst—serious (form of Ernest)
Esbjorn—bear of the gods
Eskil—vessel of the gods
Eugen—well-born (form of Eugene)
Evert—bear
Fabian—bean farmer
Felix—happy
Filip—lover of horses (form of Philip)
Fisk—fish
Frans, Franz—free (form of Francis)

Fredrik, Fredek, Frederek—peaceful ruler (form of Frederick)
Gabriel—God-given strength
Garth—defender
Georg, Goran, Gorin—farmer (form of George)
Gerhard—spear ruler (form of Gerald)
Greger—watchful (form of Gregory)
Gunner, Gunnar—bold warrior
Hadrian—dark
Halvard—rock enclosure
Hans, Hansel—gracious God (form of John)
Harald—army ruler (form of Harold)
Helmer, Helmar—fighting fury
Hemming, Harry, Henrik, Henning, Hendrik—rules the home (form of Henry)
Herbert—shining warrior
Hermann—soldier (form of Herman)
Hilmar, Hjalmar—name of a noble
Hugo—intelligent (form of Hugh)
Humfrid—peaceful Hun (form of Humphrey)
Ingmar, Ingemar—famous
Ingvar—famous fighter
Isak—one who laughs (form of Isaac)
Ivar—archer
Jakob—supplanter (form of Jacob)

Jan, Jonam, Jens, Johan—gracious God (form of John)

Jesper—jasper stone

Jonas—dove

Jorgen—farmer (form of George)

Justus—just (form of Justin)

Kalle, Kjell, Karl—manly (form of Charles)

Klas—victory of the people (form of Nicholas)

Knut—knot

Kolbjorn—black bear

Konrad—able counsel (form of Conrad)

Konstantin—constant (form of Constantine)

Krister, Kristar, Krist, Kristian—believes in Christ (form of Christian)

Kristofer—Christ-bearer (form of Christopher)

Lang—tall

Lars, Larry, Larz, Lorenz, Lorens—laurel (form of Lawrence)

Leif—descendant

Lennart—brave lion (form of Leonard)

Lucio, Lukas—light (form of Luke)

Ludvik—famous in war (form of Louis)

Lunt—from the grove

Magnild, Magnus—strong fighter

Malkolm—servant of Saint Columba (form of Malcolm)

Manfred—peaceful

Markus, Mark—warlike (form of Marcus)

Matteus, Mattias, Mats—God's gift (form of Matthew)

Melker—king

Mikael—who is like God (form of Michael)

Nansen—Nancy's son

Natanael—gift from God (form of Nathaniel)

Nels, Nils—chief

Niklas, Nikolaus—victory of the people (form of Nicholas)

Noak—rest

Olof, Olaf—ancestor

Oskar—divine spear (form of Oscar)

Otto—rich

Ove—egg

Patrik—noble (form of Patrick)

Pavel—small (form of Paul)

Per, Peder, Petter—rock (form of Peter)

Perchnosius—legend name

Poul, Pol—small (form of Paul)

Ragnar, Ragnor—wise warrior

Ragnvard—powerful fighter

Rikard—strong ruler (form of Richard)

Roald—mighty, powerful (form of Ronald)

Roland—famous

Rolf—wolf

Rune—secret

Rurik—famous ruler

Rutger—famous spearman (form of Roger)

Samson, Simson—son of
Samuel; heard
Samuel—asked of God
Saul—longed for
Saxe—legend name
Set—compensation
Sigurd, Sigvard—victorious
defender
Skamelson—legend name
Soren—reddish-brown hair
Staffan, Stefan—crowned in
victory (form of Stephen)
Sten—stone
Stig—from the mount
Sven, Svend, Svens—young
Svenbjorn—young bear
Tage—day
Tait—happy
Tobias—God is good
Tor, Thor, Tore—god of
thunder; myth name

Torbjorn, Torborg—thunder
bear
Torgny—Thor's loud weapon
Torkel—Thor's kettle
Torsten—Thor's stone
Ture—meaning unknown
Twigmuntus—legend name
Ulf—wolf
Valborg—powerful mountain
Valdemar—famous ruler
Valentin—valiant, strong (form
of Valentine)
Valfrid—powerful peace
Valter—powerful warrior (form
of Walter)
Vatt—legend name
Verner—protecting friend
Vilhelm—resolute protector
(form of William)
Yngve—master

TEUTONIC

Teutonic—also called Germanic—tribes and cultures spread across Europe in the first millennium A.D. Teutonic languages, culture, and names can be found to some degree in several modern countries: Austria, Belgium, Denmark, England, France, Germany, Iceland, Ireland, the Netherlands, Norway, Scotland, Sweden, and Switzerland. The Germanic languages spoken by Teutonic tribes were distinct from the Celtic languages that also influenced several of these regions.

Surnames were not used among the loosely affiliated Teutonic tribes. See the sections on Danish, Dutch, English, French, German, Irish, Scottish, and Swedish names to learn more about the surname practices that evolved in those areas.

FEMALE

Ada—happy
Adabel, Adbelle—lovely, happy
Adela, Adel, Adeline, Adelina, Adaline, Adalina, Adelicia, Adalia, Adalie, Adal—noble (form of Adel)
Adima—famous
Adolpha, Adolphina, Adolphine—noble wolf (form of Adolph)
Ailsa, Alyssa, Alisa—good humor
Aimiliana, Amialiona, Aimilionia—hardworking (form of Amelia)
Alarica, Alaricia, Alarice—noble ruler (form of Alaric)
Alberta, Alberte, Albertine, Albertina—noble, intelligent (form of Albert)
Alda, Aldea—wealthy (form of Aldo)

Alfonsa, Alphonsa, Alphonza, Alphosine, Alonza, Alphosina—noble and ready for battle (form of Alphonse)
Alfreda, Alfrieda—elf counselor (form of Alfred)
Algiane, Algiana—spear
Alice, Alix, Allis, Alys, Alyce, Alicia, Alisa, Alissa, Alithia, Allys, Alicea—sweet, noble humor
Aline, Alina—noble
Alison, Allison—divine fame
Aloysia—famous in war (form of Aloysius)
Alvernia, Alverna, Alvina, Alvinia, Alvira, Alvera—dearly loved
Amelia, Amalie, Amalia, Amelie, Amalija—hardworking

Andromache—wife of Hector; myth name

Anselma—divine helmet (form of Anselm)

Ara, Aria—beautiful eagle

Arabella—eagle, heroine

Ardith—wealthy gift

Arilda, Arilde—hearth maiden

Arlette—eagle

Armilda, Armilde—armored battle-maiden

Armina—warrior maid

Arnalda, Aroldine, Arnoldina—eagle (form of Arnold)

Astrid, Astred—divine strength

Asvoria—divine wisdom

Auberta—intelligent

Audris, Audrisa—rich

Audrey—noble strength

Axelle—father of peace (form of Axel)

Azalea—noble

Bathilda, Bathilde, Bathild—heroine

Bera—bear

Bernadine, Berdine, Bernardina, Bertine—intelligent maiden

Bernadette—strong as a bear (form of Bernard)

Beronika—honest

Bertha, Berta—bright (form of Bert)

Bertild, Bertilde, Bertilda—bright battle-maid

Bertilla, Bertille—outstanding warrior-maiden

Blenda, Blanda—glory

Brend, Brenda—sword

Bruna, Brunella—dark-haired (form of Brun)

Brunhild, Brunhilda, Brunhilde—armored battle-maid

Burga, Burgha—from the town

Carly, Carlen—womanly

Clotild, Clotilde, Clotilda—renowned for war

Dagmar—maiden of the day

Dagna—splendid day

Dale—lives in the valley

Didrika—ruler of the people (form of Dietrich)

Dova—dove

Druella—elfin

Eberta, Elberta—intelligent

Edburga, Edra, Edrea—wealthy defender

Edeline, Edelina—noble

Edith, Editta, Edyte, Edyta—wealthy gift

Edolie, Edolia—good humor

Edwige—refuge from war

Elda, Elde—warrior

Eldora—gift of wisdom

Elfreda, Elfrida—threatens the elves

Elga—holy

Elke—industrious

Elmina, Elmine—intimidating fame

Eloise—famous in war

Elsa—noble

Elvira—white

Emily, Emlyn, Emeline, Emiline, Emelina, Emelin, Emilie—hardworking

Emma, Ema—universal

Engelberta—bright angel

Enrica, Enrika, Enriqueta—rules the home (form of Henry)

Erica, Erika—eternal ruler (form of Eric)

Ermelinda, Ermelinde, Erma—serpent

Ernestina, Ernestine, Ernesta, Erna—serious (form of Ernest)

Erwina—honorable

Ethel—noble

Ethelda, Ethelde—wise adviser

Ethelinda, Ethelind, Ethelinde—noble serpent

Etta—ruler of the home

Fanny, Fannie, Frances, Francine, Fanchon, Franziska, Franze, Frantiska, Francoise, Francique, Francesca, Francisca, Fotina, Franci, Fereng, Ferike, Ferika—free (form of Francis)

Felda—from the field

Fernande, Fernanda—adventurer (form of Ferdinand)

Fleda, Flede, Fleta, Flita—swift

Freda, Frida—tranquil

Frederica, Fredrika, Farica, Fryda, Fritzi, Fritzie, Farica, Farika, Friederike, Friederika, Friedegard, Friedegarde—peaceful ruler (form of Frederick)

Frideborg, Fritjog—tranquil aide

Frodine, Frodina—sage friend

Galiena—lofty maiden

Garda, Garde, Gerda, Gerde—guarded

Gari—spear-maid

Gay—lively

Geralda, Geraldine, Geraldina, Girelda—spear ruler (form of Gerald)

Gerlinda, Gerlinde—weak spear

Germaine, Germane—armed

Gertraud, Gertrud, Gertruda—strong with a spear (form of Gertrude)

Gilberta, Gilberte—pledge (form of Gilbert)

Gilda—sacrifice

Gisele, Gisel, Gizela, Gizi, Gizike, Gizus—pledge

Griselda, Griselde, Griseldis, Grissel, Grizel—gray battle-maid

Gusta, Gustaafa, Guusa, Gustha, Gustava—staff of God (form of Gustav)

Haldis, Haldisa—spirit of stone

Halfrida—peaceful heroine

Harelda, Harelde, Harolda, Harole, Hally, Hallie—army ruler (form of Harold)

Harriet, Harriette, Harrietta—army ruler (form of Harold); rules the home (form of Henry)

Hazel—commander

Hedwig, Hedy, Hadwig, Hedda—strife

Henriette, Henrietta, Hatty, Hattie, Henrika, Henie, Hennie, Hen, Henny, Henka,

Henia, Henuita, Henuite—
rules the home (form of
Henry)
Hertha, Herthe, Heartha—
mother earth
Hilda, Hilde, Hild—battle-maid
Hildegard, Hildegarde—
stronghold
Holda—concealed
Holli, Hollye—holly
Huberta, Huberte—intelligent
(form of Hubert)
Huette—intelligent (form of
Hugh)
Ida, Ide—active
Idaline, Idalina—working noble
Idelia—noble
Idelle, Idette, Idetta—merry
Idona, Ilke, Ilka, Idone—
hardworking
Ilda—heroine
Ildiko—fierce warrior
Ilsa, Ilse—noble maid
Inge, Inger, Ingeborg, Inga, Inkeri,
Ingria—daughter of a hero
Ingrid, Ing—myth name
Irma—whole, strong
Isa—devoted to God
Jadryga, Jada, Jadriga—refuge
in war
Jarvia—sharp weapon
Jetje—ruler of the home
Kelly—born on the farm during
the spring
Kerttu, Kerta—strong with a
spear (form of Gertrude)
Koldobike, Koldobika—
renowned holiness

Kundegunde, Kundegunda—
name of a princess
Laobhaoise, Loes, Lois—holy
Lelia—loyal
Leoda—of the people
Leola—dear
Lorelle, Lorrella, Lorilla—little
laurel
Lou, Louisa, Louise, Lulita, Lulu—
famous in war (form of Louis)
Magan—powerful
Marcella—warlike (form of
Marcus)
Marelda, Marelde—elfin Mary
Matilda, Mathilda, Matilde,
Mathilde, Mathild—strong
battle-maid
Maude, Maud—strong in war
Melcia—ambitious
Milia, Malia—hardworking
Milicent, Millicent, Milicente,
Melicent, Mellicent—strong
Mimi, Minka—resolute
Minna, Minnie, Minny—love
Mona—loner
Nette, Nettie—clean
Nordica—from the north
Oda, Odile, Odelia, Odila—
wealthy
Oktobriana, Octobriana—myth
name
Olga—holy
Ordelia—elfin spear
Orinda—fire serpent
Orlanthe, Orlantha—famous
throughout the land (form of
Orlando)
Ortrud, Ortrude, Ortruda—
serpentine

SHERRILYN KENYON

Sherrilyn Kenyon is *The New York Times* best-selling author of several series, including the Dark-Hunters, Brotherhood of the Sword, the Mac-Allisters, Sex Camp Diaries, and BAD Boys. Her novel *Fantasy Lover* was voted one of the top ten romances of 2002 by Romance Writers of America.

I've always been entranced by Greek mythology, so when I started my ancient Greek based vampire series, I turned to my primary sources. In Hades, there are four main rivers. In order to get from the world of Man to the Underworld (something that is prophetic to say the least in the series since my characters are caught between the world of the living and the world of the dead), there are two main rivers to cross: Styx, which everyone knows, and Acheron. Styx is the river of Hatred, and Acheron is the river of Woe, two names that really capture the nature of the characters' two lives. I knew Styx was traditionally a female goddess name, but I wanted these two names to represent the twins who are primary characters in the Dark-Hunter world. So I decided to add an extra *x* to Styxx's name and make jokes in the series about the fact that he has a female name. Acheron's name is old and holds that ancient cadence that is part of him, but since Acheron is a character who has changed and evolved through the ages (he likes to blend with the popular culture of the current time period he's living in), his name has evolved from being pronounced *Ack-uh-rahn* to *Ash-uh-rahn* to now *Ash* for short. His last name Par-thenopaeus is also very important to the series, but the exact nature of that will come out in future books.

Ottilie, Ottilia—lucky battle-maiden
Pastora, Pastore—shepherdess
Proinnseas—free
Queena, Queeny, Queenie—queen
Ragnild, Reinheld, Renilde, Renilda, Renilde, Ragnilde,

Renild, Reinhelda—one who is wise in battle
Raina, Raine—strong
Ramona—mighty protector (form of Raymond)
Ricarda—strong ruler (form of Richard)
Rikka—tranquil leader

Rilla—stream

Roberta, Robina, Robine—bright, famous (form of Robert)

Roderica—famous ruler (form of Roderick)

Rolanda, Rolande, Rollande, Rollanda—famous (form of Roland)

Romilda, Romilde, Romelde, Romelda—glorious battle-maid

Ronalda, Ronalde—mighty, powerful (form of Ronald)

Rosamund, Rosemond, Rosamunde—noted protector

Rudelle—famous

Saxona—of Saxony

Selma—helmet

Serilda, Serilde—armored battle-maid

Sigismonda, Sigismunda—victorious defender

Sunhild, Sunhilde, Sunhilda, Sonnehilda, Sonnehilde—sun battle-maid

Swanhilda, Swanhilde—swan battle-maid

Theda—of the people

Thora, Tora—god of thunder; myth name (form of Thor)

Tilda, Tilde, Tille—mighty in war

Uald, Ualda—brave

Uda—prosperous

Ulrike, Ulrica, Ulrika—ruler of all

Ulva—she wolf

Ute—fortunate

Valda—spirited in war

Vala—chosen one

Vanda—wanderer (form of Wanda)

Vedia, Vidis, Vedis—holy spirit of the forest

Veleda, Velda—inspired intelligence

Verena, Verina—protector

Vigdis—myth name

Vilhelmina, Vilma—resolute protector (form of William)

Walburgha, Walburga—strong defender

Waltraud—strength

Wandis, Wanda, Wenda, Wende, Wendelin, Wendeline, Wendelina—wanderer

Wilhelmina, Wileen, Willa, Willette, Wilmet, Wilhemine, Wilhemina, Wilna—resolute protector (form of William)

Wilva—determined

Winifred, Wynifred, Winifrid, Winfreda, Wynfreda—peaceful friend

Zelda, Zelde—gray battle-maid (form of Griselda)

Zerelda, Zerelde, Zereld—armored battle-maid

Zerlina—serene beauty

Zissi, Ziske, Ziska—free

MALE

Abelard, Allard, Alard—resolute

Adal, Adel—noble

Adalard, Adelard, Adler, Adlar—brave, noble

Adalbert, Adelbert, Ambert—noble, intelligent (form of Albert)

Addo—happy

Adelric, Adalric, Aric, Arik—noble ruler

Adolf, Adolph, Adolphus—noble wolf

Agilard—glowing

Ahren—eagle

Aimery—industrious

Aimon—home

Alajos—famous holiness

Alard, Alaric, Alirick, Alric, Alrik—noble ruler

Alber—brilliant

Alberic—skillful ruler

Albern—noble warrior

Albert—noble, intelligent

Alcuin—noble friend

Aldo, Audwin, Audwyn—wealthy

Aldous—wise

Aldrich, Aldridge—wise ruler

Alfred—elf counselor

Alger—noble spearman

Alison, Allison—divine fame

Alonso, Alonzo, Alphonse, Alphonso, Alfonso—noble and ready for battle

Aloysius, Alaois, Aloys—famous in war

Altman—old wise man

Alvin, Alvyn, Alvan, Alwan, Alwin, Alwyn—noble friend

Ambert—shining bright light

Amerigo, Amery, Amory—hardworking

Ancel, Ancil—like God

Annraio, Arrigo, Arrighetto, Alrigo—rules an estate

Anselm, Ansel, Ancil, Anzelm, Anzel, Amselmo—divine helmet

Ansgar—divine spear

Archibald—bold

Ardmore—ardent

Armon, Armin, Armonno, Armino, Armando—warrior

Arnall—kind eagle

Arnold, Arnaldo, Aroldo—eagle

Arvin—friend of the people

Aubrey, Aubrian—rules the elves

Aylmer, Aylmar—infamous

Aylsworth—of great worth

Aylward—noble protector

Aylwin, Aylwyn—great friend

Baldric—bold ruler

Baldwin, Baldwyn—bold friend

Ballard—bold, strong

Barnard, Barnardo, Bernard, Bernardo, Burnard—strong as a bear

Barrett—bear

Barron, Barin, Barrin, Baron, Baran—noble fighter

Bayard—reddish-brown hair

Belden, Beldan, Beldane—lives in the beautiful glen
Berger—of the mountains
Bert, Bertold—bright
Bertin, Berton, Bertwin, Bertwyn—shining friend
Bertram, Bertrand, Bartram, Bertok—bright raven
Bevis—archer
Bodo—leader
Booth—from the market stall
Boyce—dwells in the woods
Brainard—bold raven
Brandon—from the beacon hill
Brant, Brantley—firebrand
Bruno—dark-haired (form of Brun)
Burchard—strong as a castle
Burke—stronghold
Burleigh, Burley—from the meadow by the hill
Byron—from the cottage; bear
Canute—hill
Cavell—bold
Chalmer, Chalmar, Chalmers—rules the home
Charles—manly
Clay, Clayborn, Claybourne—mortal
Clayton—from the town on the clay bed
Clinton—from the headland estate
Clovis—famous warrior
Colbert—seaman
Cole, Coleman—dark
Conrad, Cort—able counsel
Crosby—dwells by the town cross

Culbert, Colbert—cool and intelligent
Curt—wise counselor
Dale, Dail—lives in the dale
Dannel—God is my judge (form of Daniel)
Darrick, Derek, Dedrick, Dedrik, Dedric, Dick—rules the people
Delwyn, Delwin—valley friend
Derwin, Derwyn—friend of wild animals
Dirk—dagger
Dixon, Dickson—strong leader
Dolph—wolf
Dustin—warrior
Dwight—blond
Earnest—serious (form of Ernest)
Eberhard—strong as a boar
Edrigu—famous leader
Edsel—noble one
Egan, Egon—formidable
Egbert—shining sword
Ehren—honorable
Einri—intelligent
Elbert—noble, glorious
Elden, Eldon—elder
Eldred, Eldridge—wise adviser
Elgar—shining spear
Ellard—brave
Ellery, Ellary—lives by the alder tree
Elmar, Elemer, Elmer—awe-inspiring
Elvin—wise
Emeric, Emrik, Emric—leader
Emilian, Emil, Emile—excellent

Emory, Emery—joint ruler
Engelbert—bright angel
Enrico, Enzo, Enrique—rules the
home (form of Henry)
Erramun, Erroman, Ermanno—
mighty defender
Erhard—honor
Ethelred—nobel counsel
Everard—brave as a boar
Evgenii—well-born (form of
Eugene)
Ewald—powerful
Farand—pleasant
Faxon—thick-haired
Ferdinand—adventurer
Filbert—brilliant
Fitz—son of
Fitz Gerald, Fitzgerald—son of
Gerald
Fitz Patrick, Fitzpatrick—son of
Patrick
Fletcher—feathers arrows
Folke—people's guard
Francis, Franchot, Frank,
Franklin, Frantisek, Franta,
Francois, Franz, Franziskus,
Franciscus, Frantisek—free
Frederic, Frederick, Fred, Fredi,
Fritz, Frits, Friedel,
Friedrich, Fredek, Frigyes,
Frici, Fryderyk, Fredrick,
Fredrik—peaceful ruler
Friedhelm—true peace
Fydor, Fedya, Fadyenka—divine
gift
Gandolf—wolf's progress
Gardell, Garner—defender
Gardener, Gardiner—farmer

Garrick, Garek—rules by the
spear
Garvin—spear friend
Gautier, Gauthier—powerful
warrior (form of Walter)
Gavin—white hawk
Geoffrey—God's peace
Gerald, Gerry, Gerold, Geraud,
Giraud, Gerard, Girard,
Garret, Garret, Gearoid,
Garcia—spear ruler
Gervais—serves the spear
Gifford—gift of bravery
Gilamu, Gillen, Guillame, Gellert,
Guilerme—resolute fighter
Gilbert, Gilberto, Gilburt,
Gilen—pledge
Gilfred, Gilfrid—oath of peace
Gilmer—famous hostage
Goddard, Gotthard—divinely
stern
Goodwin, Godwyn, Godwin—
God's friend
Gorman—eyes of blue
Gottfrid, Godfrey, Godfried,
Gottfried, Goffredo,
Godofredo, Giotto—God's
peace
Govert—divine peace
Graham—from the gray home
Griswald, Griswold—from the
gray forest
Gualtiero, Galtero—powerful
warrior (form of Walter)
Guglilmo, Gwilym—resolute
protector (form of William)
Gunner, Gunnar—bold warrior
Gunther—battle army

Gustave, Gustavus, Gustaof, Gusztav—staff of God (form of Gustav)

Guy, Gert, Gerwazy, Gervasy, Gervazy, German, Gervasio—warrior

Hadwin, Hadwyn—friend in war

Hagan, Hagen—strong defender

Haines, Hanes, Hane, Haine—dwells in the hedged enclosure

Halbert—shining jewel

Halden, Haldan—half-Dane

Hale—robust

Hallam—from the hillside

Hamlin—rules the home

Hardie, Hardy—strong

Harlan, Harland—from the land of strength

Harman—of the army

Harold, Hal, Harry—army ruler

Harris—son of Harry

Harte, Hart—stag

Hartman—strong

Hartwell—lives near the stag's spring

Hartwig, Hass—strong adviser

Harvey, Herman, Hermann, Harm, Harme, Herve—soldier

Haydon, Hayden—from the hedged-in valley

Helmer—fighting fury

Hendrik, Henrik, Henerik, Harry, Henning, Henri, Heinroch, Heike, Harro, Hinrich, Henrich, Hannraoi, Hank, Henryk, Heromin, Henry—rules the home

Herbert, Heribert, Heriberto—shining warrior

Herwyn, Herwin—loves war

Hew, Hewitt—heart and mind

Hildebrand, Hildebrandt—war sword

Hilliard—defender in war

Holden—gracious

Holman—from the river island

Holmes—son of Holman

Howard—chief guardian

Hrorek—famous ruler

Hubert, Hobart, Hugo, Hugh, Hugues, Huberto, Humberto, Huw—intelligent, brilliant mind

Humbert—shining support

Humfried, Hunfredo, Hunfried—peaceful Hun (form of Humphrey)

Humphrey, Humfrey—peaceful Hun

Ibon, Ivar, Ivor, Ive, Iver, Iomhar, Ives, Ifor—archer

Imre—hardworking

Inglebert—bright angel

Ingram—Ing's raven

Jarratt, Jarvis, Jervis—sharp as a spear

Jerrold, Jarold—strong with a spear

Jeff, Jeffrey—God's peace (form of Geoffrey)

Kelby, Kilby—from the farm by the water

Kerbasy, Kerbasi—warrior

Kirby, Kerby—from the church village

Kirk—dwells at the church
Konrad—able counsel (form of Conrad)
Lali, Lajos, Lajcsi, Laji—famous holiness
Lamar, Lambert, Lamerto—famous around the land
Latham—dwells by the barn
Lear—of the sea
Learoyd, Leroy—from the cleared meadow
Ledyard—nation's defender
Leonard, Len, Leonardo, Leonaldo, Lennart, Leonhard—brave lion
Leopold, Leo, Leupold, Luitpold, Leorad—bold for his people
Liam—resolute protector (form of William)
Lindsay, Lindsey—from the island of the linden tree
Lombard—long beard
Lopolda, Lopold, Lopoldi, Lipot—patriotic
Loring—from Lorraine
Lothar, Lothair—famous warrior (form of Lothario)
Louis, Lewis, Luther—famous in war
Lydon—from the linden-tree hill
Madison—son of Maud
Mandel—almond
Manfred, Manfrid—peaceful
Marvin, Marwin, Marwyn, Mervin, Merwin, Merwyn—mariner
Marshall—steward
Mason—stone worker
Maynard, Meinrad—brave

Medwin, Medwyn—strong friend
Merrell, Merrill—famous
Merrick, Merek—strong ruler
Naldo—strong
Nevin, Nevyn—nephew
Norbert, Noberto—bright hero
Norman, Norris, Novin, Norvyn—from the north
Norward—guardian of the north road
Notker, Notcher—compelling spear
Obert—wealthy
Odo, Odilo, Otto, Ota, Otik, Oto, Otokars, Otomars, Ode, Orton—rich
Olaf—ancestor
Orlando, Orland—famous throughout the land
Ormond, Orman—mariner
Osborn, Osbourne—divine bear
Osgood—divine god
Osmund, Osmond—divine protection
Osric, Osrik—divine ruler
Oswald, Oswaldo, Osvald—divine power
Othmar—happy fame
Otway, Ottoway—lucky in war
Outram—wealthy raven
Patxi, Proinnsias, Paquito, Panchito—free
Paxton, Paxon—trader
Philibert—sharp-willed
Pippen—father
Podi—bold for the people
Pollard—short-haired
Raghnall, Ragnol, Randal,

Randahl, Renaud, Rinaldo,
Ranaldo, Randolf, Randolph,
Rendell—mighty power
Ram—raven
Rambert—mighty; intelligent
Ramsey, Ramsay—from Ram's
island
Raoul, Ralph, Raul—wolf (form
of Rolf)
Rawdon—from the hill
Raymond, Raymund, Raimund,
Reamonn, Raimondo,
Raimundo, Rajmund, Ramon,
Redmond, Redmund,
Richmond, Ramone,
Reinhold—mighty protector
Reginald, Reynold—strong ruler
Renard, Rennard, Raynard—fox
Renfred, Renfrid—peacemaker
Renwick, Renwyk—where the
ravens nest
Richard—strong ruler
Ritter—knight
Robert, Roberto, Robin, Rob,
Rab, Robby, Raibert,
Robinet, Roibeard, Riobart,
Rupert—bright, famous
Roderick, Roderic, Rodrick,
Rurik, Ruaidhri, Ruairidh,
Roderigo, Rogelio—famous
ruler
Roger, Rudger, Rutger, Rotger,
Rudiger, Rogerio, Ruggero,
Ruggiero, Rodrigue—
famous spearman
Roland, Rowland, Rolando,
Rolden, Rodney—famous
Rolf, Rolfe, Rolph, Rolphe—wolf

Rollo, Rollin, Rollins—famous
(form of Roland)
Rory—red ruler
Roscoe—from the deer forest
Roswell, Roswald, Ross—mighty
horse
Rudolph, Rudolf—famous wolf
Saxon—swordsman
Searle, Serle—armed
Selby—from the manor farm
Seldon, Selden—from the manor
house
Sewell, Seymour—mighty at sea
Siegbert—famous victory
Siefried, Sigfrid, Sigfried,
Seifred—victorious peace
(form of Siegfried)
Sigmund, Sigmond, Sigismund,
Seigmund, Sigismondo—
victorious defender
Sprague—alert
Steen, Sten—stone
Stig—from the mount
Swain—young
Tage, Tag, Tajo—day
Tancred—adviser
Tedman, Tedmund, Theomund—
national protector
Terrill, Tirell, Terrell—thunder
ruler
Terriss, Terris—son of Terry
Thayer—nation's army
Theobald—people's prince
Theodoric, Theodric, Theodrik,
Thierry, Terry, Till,
Tillmann, Tilman, Thilo,
Til—people's rule
Thorley—from Thor's meadow

Thorpe—from the village
Thurborn—dwells by the stream
Tibald, Tybalt—people's prince
Torbert, Thorbert—glorious as Thor
Tormod—from the north
Torquil, Torkel—Thor's cauldron
Torsten, Thorsten, Thurston— Thor's stone
Traugott—God's truth
Tyson—son of a German
Ugo—spirit
Uilliam, Uileog, Ulik—resolute protector (form of William)
Uistean, Ustean, Uisdean, Uberto, Ubert—intelligent
Uland—from the noble land
Ulbrecht—splendor
Ulfred—wolf of peace
Ulrik, Ulric—ruler of all
Uther—myth name
Uwe, Udo—universal ruler
Valdis—spirited in war
Valter, Vater—powerful warrior (form of Walter)
Varick, Varik—defending ruler
Verner—protecting friend
Vilhelm, Viljo, Vilo, Vilhelms, Vilis—resolute protector (form of William)
Vilmos, Vili—resolute protector (form of William)
Volker—people's guard
Volney—of the people
Waldram—mighty raven
Wallace, Wallis—from Wales
Walter, Walt, Walther, Wlader, Wat, Watt, Wouter,

Waldemar, Waldemarr, Walden, Waldo—powerful warrior
Ward—guard
Waring—heedful
Warner, Werner, Wuhur, Werhar—protecting army
Warren—protecting friend
Warrick, Warwyk, Warwick— protecting ruler
Washington—active
Weldon—from the spring by the hill
Wendel, Wendell—wanderer
Wies—famous fighter
Wilfrid, Wilfred—resolute peace
Willard—resolute, brave
William, Will, Wilhelm, Wilhelmus, Willem, Wim— resolute protector
Wilmer, Wilmar—resolute; famous
Wilmot—resolute spirit
Wilson—Will's son
Windsor, Winsor—from the bend of the river
Winefeld, Winfield—friend of the soil
Winfred, Wynfred, Winfryd— friend of peace
Winthrop—from the friendly village
Wolfe, Wolf—wolf
Wolfgang—advancing wolf
Wolfgar—wolf spear
Wolfram—wolf-raven
Zsigmond, Zsiga, Zygmunt— victorious defender

THAI

Thai names consist of a given name and a surname, but are listed surname first. In addition to that, a Thai person usually has a short nickname, which is the name most commonly used. In fact, the surname is rarely used by anyone except in official records. Common nicknames are Noom ("young man") and Lah ("young lady"). Women take their husband's surnames when they marry.

Very long Thai surnames often belong to families that immigrated to Thailand from China and then applied for Thai surnames. Under the law, they were not allowed to choose names already in existence. In their attempts to create totally unique names, they inevitably had to create very long names.

A few surnames:

Adoonyadayt
Adulyadej
Aromdee
Bunyasarn
Chaiprasit
Gosayotin
Jetjirawat
Kadesadayurat
Kaothai
Kongsangchai
Kosayodhin
Kunakorn
Leekpai
Lertkunakorn
Meesang

Narkhirunkanok
Ornlamai
Paowsong
Parnthong
Rattamondhree
Rojumanong
Sakda
Sangsorn
Thumying
Udomprecha
Vipavakit
Wattanapanit
Wongmontha
Yongjaiyut

FEMALE

Daw—stars
Kama—love
Kanya—young woman
Mali—flower
Pakpao—kite

Phailin—sapphire
Prasert—meaning unknown
Ratana—crystal
Sirikit—queen
Solada—listener

Suchin—beautiful thoughts
Sumalee—lovely blossom
Sunee—good

Tasanee—beautiful view
Vanida—girl

MALE

Aran—forest
Aroon—daybreak
Chet—brother
Kama—love
Kiet—honor
Mongkut—crown

Niran—eternal
Pravat—history
Rama—king
Sakda—power
Sunan—good word
Virote—power

UKRAINIAN

Some Ukrainian surnames are patronymic. Others refer to place or occupation or are descriptive. A sequence of three names is the standard: given name, father's name (in the genitive case), and surname.

Ukrainian names are written in a Cyrillic alphabet. When they are transliterated into English, the new spelling can vary widely. For instance, the suffix pronounced SKEE, common to many Russian and Ukrainian names, can be written as -ski, -skii, -skji, -sky, -skyi, -ckyj, -ckii, etc.

Common surname suffixes:

-enko, -vych, -ovych, -uk, -iuk, -yshyn—son of
-oviat, -iat—ancient forms of "son of"
-ivna—daughter of
-kha—widow
-ska, -cka—female
-skyi, -ckyj, -ec, -iak, -ianyn—from

A few surnames:

Andrukhovych	Kupchenko
Andrushko	Makarovskyi
Bilynskyj	Michalovic
Bobrovnyk	Pashkowskyj
Boiko	Paslawskyj
Braniski	Petriv
Danylovych	Petrowycz
Demidas	Podrova
Denisovich	Rudnyk
Dimitrenko	Savchenko
Dyachenko	Skriabin
Glinski	Teslenko
Khristin	Tesler
Kimko	Volynskji
Klimus	Witkowski
Kliubova	Yaroshcenko

FEMALE

Aleksandra—defender of mankind (form of Alexander)
Alias—noble
Aneta, Anita, Anichka—grace (form of Anne)
Bohuslava—God's glory (form of Bohuslav)
Hannah—gracious God (form of John)
Ionna—God's gift
Ivanna—gracious God (form of John)
Katerina, Katrya—pure (form of Katherine)
Klarysa—clear, bright (form of Clare)
Lavra—laurel (form of Lawrence)
Leysa, Lyaksandra—defender of mankind (form of Alexander)
Luba—love
Lukina—bright
Lyudmyla—love of the people
Mariya, Marynia, Maryska—bitter (form of Mary)
Mikayla—who is like God (form of Michael)
Nastasiya, Nastunye—rebirth
Natalka—born on Christmas (form of Natalie)
Nyura—graceful
Oksana, Oxana—hospitality
Olena—light (form of Helen)
Orynko—peace
Pavla—small (form of Paul)
Sofiya, Sofiyko—wise (form of Sophia)
Yaryna—peaceful
Yelysaveta—consecrated to God (form of Elizabeth)
Yevtsye, Yeva—life (form of Eve)

MALE

Aleksander—defender of mankind (form of Alexander)
Andriy—manly (form of Andrew)
Bohdan, Bohdanko, Bogdan, Bodashka—gift from God
Bohuslav—God's glory
Borysko—warrior
Burian—lives near the weeds
Danya—God's gift
Danylets, Danylko—God is my judge (form of Daniel)
Dymtrus—supplanter (form of James)
Fadey, Faddei, Fadeyka, Fadeyushka—brave
Hadeon—destroyer
Heorhiy—farmer
Ivan—gracious God (form of John)
Krystiyan—believes in Christ (form of Christian)
Lyaksandro—defender of mankind (form of Alexander)
Marko—warlike (form of Marcus)
Matviyko—God's gift

DAVID MORRELL

David Morrell is the award-winning author of *First Blood*, the novel in which Rambo was created. He is the author of nineteen novels, including six *New York Times* best sellers.

A rose by any other name would smell as sweet. Nonetheless many authors have an almost mystical attachment to the names they give characters. I once had a heated discussion with a fellow author who insisted that "Decker" was better than "Becker." The artist hero of my novel *Burnt Sienna* was originally called Kincaid, but my editor got nervous because there was a real-life artist with that name (although spelled differently), so in anguish I changed Kincaid to Malone. For about a week, I felt intense loss. Now I have trouble recalling the original name. In the end, I decided that names are merely abstractions, and when we consider them as such, we can avoid a lot of problems. For example, at the start of a project I make a list of characters' names to ensure that each begins with a different letter of the alphabet, thus preventing a repetition of Anna, Albert, and Anastasia. The list also helps me avoid a lot of names with similar endings—Harry, Bobby, and Tommy. Note that those names also have the same syllables, as do Corrigan, Matheson, and Faraday, names that would be rhythmically wearying if all three were in the same story. With audio books now widely available, I also try to avoid names with *s* in them. "Susan said" challenges even the best actor. For me, the goal is to choose names that don't inadvertently draw attention to themselves and distract the reader from the story.

Mykhailo, Mykhaylo, Mychajlo, Mykhaltso—who is like God (form of Michael)

Oleksander—defender of mankind (form of Alexander)

Osip—God adds (form of Joseph)

Pavlo—small (form of Paul)

Petro, Petruso—rock (form of Peter)

Taras—meaning unknown

Vanko—gracious God

Vasylko—noble

Volodymyr, Wolodymyr—to rule with greatness

Yevheniy, Yevhen—noble

Yure, Yuri, Yuriy—farmer (form of George)

VIETNAMESE

Vietnamese list the family name first and then their middle and given names.

Few given names are exclusively masculine or feminine. Children are not usually named after parents.

The words *Van* and *Thi* occur often in the middle name position in Vietnamese names. In fact, they are articles indicating gender: *Van* for male and *Thi* for female. A boy may have *Huu, Duc, Dinh, Xuan, Ngoc, Quang,* or *Cong* in place of *Van*. Birth order for sons can also be indicated in the middle name position: *Manh* for the firstborn, then *Trong* and *Qui* for second and third. All subsequent sons use *Gia. Ba* and *Thuc* are used to indicated older and younger brothers, respectively. A typical name might be *Nguyen Thi Mai*, in which *Nguyen* is the surname and *Mai* is the given name.

Many surnames in Vietnam are Chinese in origin. The surname *Nguyen* is shared by almost half the population.

A few surnames:

Banh	Mai
Cao	Ngo
Che	Nguy
Chu	Nguyen
Dam	Pham
Dang	Phan
Dao	Phung
Dinh	Ta
Do	Tang
Doan	Thach
Du	Thieu
Duong	Ton
Hoang	Tran
Hua	Trinh
Huynh	Trouong
Lam	Tu
Le	Vanh
Luong	Vo
Ly	Vu

FEMALE

Ai—beloved, gentle
Anh—intelligent
An—peace
Be—baby or doll
Bian—hidden, secret
Bich—jade
Binh—peaceful
Cai—meaning unknown
Cam—orange fruit; sun
Chau—pearls
Chi—tree branch, twig
Cuc—chrysanthemum
Dao—peach blossoms; Tet
   flower
Dep—beautiful
Diep—leaves
Diu—gentle
Doan Vien—happy reunion
Dong—winter
Giang—river
Hai—fairy shoe
Han—faithful, moral
Hang—angel in the full moon
Hanh Phuc—blessing from
   above
Ha—river
Hien—gentle, nice
Hoa—flower
Hong—rose pink
Hue—lily
Khanh—precious stone
Khiem—virtue
Kieu—graceful
Kim Cuc—golden lion
Kim Ly—chrysanthemum yellow
Kim—golden one

Lam—jungle
Lang—sweet potato
Lanh—gentle spirit
Lan—orchid
Le—pear; tears
Lien—lotus
Lieu—willow
Mai—cherry blossom
Mychau—great
My-Duyen—pretty
Ngoc—precious stone
Nguyet—moon
Nhung—velvet
Nhu—wish
Nu—girl
Phuong—destiny; phoenix
Quyen—bird
Quy—precious
Sang—upper class
Suong—fog
Tam—heart
Tham—discreet
Thanh—bright, sunny
Thao—sweet, kind
Thi—poem; common middle
   name
Thuy—friendly; pussy willow
Tien—fairy
Trinh—virginal girl
Truc—wish
Tuyen—angel
Tuyet—snow white
Uoc—wishes
Van—cloud
Xuan—spring
Yen—a swallow; peace

MALE

Anh Dung—heroism
Bao—protection
Bay—reddish brown
Binh—peaceful
Cadeo—folk song
Cam—orange fruit; sun
Chien—battle
Chinh—correct
Cuong—prosperous
Danh—fame
Duc—desire
Due—virtuous
Dung—heroic
Duong—virility
Giang—river
Hai—river
Hao—good
Hien—nice, kind, gentle
Hieu—dutiful
Hoc—to study
Hung—prosperity
Huy—light, bright
Huynh—elder brother
Kim—golden one
Lam—all-knowing
Lanh—street smart
Minh—bright
Ngai—herb
Nhat—long life
Nhung—velvet
Phuoc—good fortune
Phuong—destiny; phoenix
Quang—good reputation

Quan—soldier
Quy—precious
Ritchell—gross
Sang—bright
Sinh—birth
Son—mountain
Tai—talented
Thai—many
Thang—victory
Thanh—accomplished
Thinh—prosperous
Tho—long lived
Thuan—tamed
Thu—autumn
Tinh—aware
Toan—complete
Tong—fragrant
Trai—oyster
Tran—family name
Trang—honored
Trieu—tide
Trong Tri—not of small mind
Trong—respected
Truc—bamboo
Trung—loyalty
Tuan—brilliant
Tung—a type of coniferous tree
Tu—star, brilliant, quick-minded
Van—traditional middle name
Vien—completion
Vuong—prosperous
Xuan—spring

WELSH

Traditionally, Welsh children were named after certain family members in order of birth. Though variations existed, the general pattern was as follows: The first son would be named after the paternal grandfather, the second son after the maternal grandfather. The first daughter would be named after the maternal grandmother, and the second daughter after the paternal grandmother. The third son and daughter would be named after the parent of the appropriate sex, and the following children were named after aunts and uncles in birth order.

Despite evidence in medieval records that some Welsh border dwellers used their father's name as a surname as far back as the twelfth century, Wales was one of the last countries in Europe to adopt the use of hereditary surnames. In the sixteenth century, Welshmen who dealt regularly with the English began to use surnames, as did some of the nobility. However, it was not until the nineteenth century that surnames became common throughout the country.

Even today, in remote Welsh districts, some individuals cling to the old custom of adding *ap-* or *ab-* to their father's name rather than using a true hereditary surname.

Most surnames are patronymic in origin, but some are related to place, description, or occupation.

Patronymic names are prefixed by *B-, P-, ap-,* or *ab-,* or suffixed with *-s.*

Originally, a Welshman used his given name followed by a list of all his male ancestors' names, which he linked with *ap-* or *ab-.*

A few surnames:

Adda	Carne
Benyon	Cogan
Bevan (ap Evan)	Crowther
Bowen (ab Owen)	Don
Brace	Ellis
Brice (ab-Rhys)	Evans
Broderick (ap-Roderick)	Glace
Cardiff	Goff

Griffith
Jenkins
Maddox
Nash
Parry (ap Harry)
Powell (ap-Howell)
Price (ap-Rhys)
Pritchard (ap Richard)

Prosser
Pugh (ap-Hugh)
Stackpoole
Teague
Trevor
Tudor
Vaughan

In the list below, traditional names are names that have a long historical record of use in Wales. Legend names are those that are found in Welsh legends such as *The Mabinogion* (the Welsh tales of King Arthur), and myth names are those that are found in Welsh mythology.

FEMALE

Aberfa—from the mouth of the river
Abertha—sacrifice
Adain, Adenydd—winged
Adara—catches birds
Addfwyn—meek
Addiena, Addien—beautiful
Aderyn—bird
Adyna—wretched
Aelwyd—from the hearth
Almedha—shapely
Amser—time
Anghard, Angharad—loved greatly
Angwen—handsome
Argel—refuge
Arglwyddes—lady
Argoel—omen
Argraff—impression
Arial—vigorous
Ariana, Arian, Arien, Ariene—silver (form of Arian)

Arianrhod—daughter of Don; myth name
Arlais—from the temple
Armes—prophetess
Artaith—torment
Arthes—she-bear
Arwydd—sign
Asgre—heart
Atgas—hateful
Awel—breeze
Awsta—majestic
Aylwen—fair
Banon—queen
Bari—spear thrower
Berth—beautiful
Berthog—wealthy
Berwyn—bright friend
Bethan—consecrated to God (form of Elizabeth)
Betrys—she who brings joy
Blodwen, Blodwyn—white flower

Jodi Picoult is the best-selling author of eleven novels, her most recent being *My Sister's Keeper* (Atria). In 2003, she was awarded the New England Bookseller Award for Fiction.

The best thing about having children is that you can recycle your baby name books when it comes to naming characters. So what if no one else realizes that Brendan means "raven; sword"? You do, and that's what counts. Some names, of course, are a matter of common sense; when I wrote *Plain Truth*, which is about the Amish, I wasn't about to name someone Julio or Pierre. But often, the first place I start when I want to name a character, I ask myself if something about his name might provide a clue to the journey he will be undertaking. For example, when I created Ross Wakeman in *Second Glance*, it was with the knowledge that he was going to have to literally have a rebirth of consciousness. When I named Nina Frost in *Perfect Match*, it was with the understanding that her character arc would involve a "thawing." The little girl at the heart of *Keeping Faith* is named by the title of the book, which not only explores the nature of spiritual belief but a custody battle revolving around young Faith White. And Delia Hopkins, in *Vanishing Acts*, is rechristened by her father after he kidnaps her during a custody visit . . . and named after King Lear's most loyal daughter. So what's the one name you'll probably never find in a main character in one of my books? Tim. I'm married to one, and I'd find it too disconcerting to have a fictional heroine calling my husband's name!

THE LISTS

WELSH

Braith—freckled
Bregus—frail
Briallan—primrose
Bronwen, Bronwyn, Brangwen, Brangwy, Branwenn—dark and pure
Bryn, Brynna—hill
Buddug—victorious (form of Victor)

Cadi, Catrin—pure (form of Katherine)
Cadwyn—chain
Caethes—slave
Cafell—oracle
Caniad—song
Carryl—love
Carys—beloved
Cath—cat

Ceinwen—blessed
Ceridwen—fair poet
Cordelia, Creiddylad—jewel of the sea
Corsen—reed
Cragen—shell
Crisiant—crystal
Cymreiges—Welsh woman
Dai—beloved
Dee, Du, Dierdre, Delia—dark
Delwyn, Delyth—neat and fair
Dera, Daere—fiend
Derryth, Derwen—from the oak tree
Dicra—slow
Difyr—amusing
Dilys—steadfast
Drysi—thorn
Ebrill—born in April
Efa—life (form of Eve)
Eheubryd—daughter of Kyvwlch; legend name
Eiddwen—beloved fair one
Eira, Eirwen—snow
Eirian—silver
Elen—light (form of Helen)
Eleri—river name
Ellylw—daughter of Neol Hang Cock; legend name
Eluned—waterfall
Eneuawg—daughter of Bedwyr; legend name
Enit, Enid—spirit
Enrhydreg—daughter of Tuduathar; legend name
Erdudvyl—daughter of Tryffin; legend name
Eres—wonderful

Esyllt—fair lady (form of Isolda)
Eurneid—daughter of Clydno; legend name
Eurolwyn—daughter of Gwydolwyn; legend name
Eurwen, Eyslk—fair
Ffanci—fancy
Ffraid—strong (form of Bridget)
Garan—stork
Gaynor—soft and fair
Gladys, Gwladys, Gleda—lame (form of Claude)
Glan—from the shore
Glenda, Glenys, Glyn, Glynnis—from the glen
Goewin—daughter of Pebin; legend name
Goleuddydd—bright day
Gorasgwrn—daughter of Nerth; legend name
Gorawen—joy
Gryffyn—myth beast
Gwaeddan—daughter of Kynvelyn; legend name
Gwanwyn—spring
Gwen, Gwyn, Guinevere, Gwenhwyvar, Gwyneth, Gwynedd, Gwynne—white
Gwenabwy—daughter of Caw; legend name
Gwendoline, Gwendolen, Gwyndolen—of the white brow
Gwener—goddess of love (form of Venus)
Gwenledyr—daughter of Gwawrddur Hunchback; legend name

Gwenn Alarch—daughter of Kynwal; legend name
Hafwan—summer beauty
Heledd—traditional name
Indeg—daughter of Garwy; legend name
Iola—valued by the lord
Isolde, Isolda—fair lady
Kelemon—daughter of Kei; legend name
Kenwyn—saint name
Keyna—jewel
Kieve—myth name
Kigva—wife of Partholon's son; legend name
Lilybet—God's promise
Lowri—laurel (form of Lawrence)
Lyn, Lynn—attractive
Mabli—lovable (form of Mabel)
Mair—bitter (form of Mary)
Mali—bitter (form of Mary)
Marged, Margred, Mererid, Megan, Meghan—pearl (form of Margaret)
Meinwen—slender, fair
Melva—sweet place
Mercia—from Mercia
Meredith, Maredud, Meredydd—protector of the sea
Modlen—from the tower (form of Madeleine)
Morgan, Morgana, Morgant—lives by the sea
Morvudd—daughter of Uryen; legend name
Morwenna—maiden
Myfanawy—my fine one

Nerys—lady
Nesta—chaste
Neued—daughter of Kyvwlch; legend name
Olwen, Olwyn, Olwina, Olwyna—white footprint
Owena—young warrior (form of Owen)
Penarddun—daughter of Beli; legend name
Rathtyen—daughter of Clememyl; legend name
Rhan—fate
Rhawn—coarse, long hair
Rhedyn—fern
Rhiain—maiden
Rhiannon—pure maiden
Rhianwen, Rhianwyn—comely maiden
Rhonwen—white-haired (form of Rowena)
Rhosyn—rose
Saeth—arrow
Saffir—sapphire
Sarff—snake
Seren—star
Seirian, Seiriol—sparkling
Sian, Sioned—gracious God (form of John)
Talaith—diadem
Talar—from the headland in the field
Tangwen—daughter of Gweir; legend name
Tarian—shield
Tarren—from the knoll
Tegan—doelike
Tegwen—blessed

Teleri—daughter of Peul; legend name
Telyn—harp
Terrwyn—brave
Tirion—gentle
Toreth—abundant
Torlan—from the river bank
Torri—break

Vala—chosen one
Valimai—mayflower
Vanora, Una—white wave
Winnifred, Wynnifred—white wave
Wynne, Wyn—fair
Ysbail—spoiled

MALE

Aberthol—sacrifice
Adda—of the red earth (form of Adam)
Addolgar—devout
Adwr—coward
Aedd—king of Ireland; legend name
Aethlem—meaning unknown
Ahasferus—meaning unknown
Alawn—harmony
Albanwr—from Scotland
Aled—offspring
Alun—legend name
Alwyn, Alwin—from Alwyn
Amathaon—son of Don; legend name
Amerawdwr—emperor
Amhar—son of Arthur; legend name
Amlawdd—father of Goleuddydd; legend name
Amren—son of Bedwyr; legend name
Amynedd, Amyneddgar—patient
Anarawd—father of Iddig; legend name

Andreas—manly (form of Andrew)
Aneirin, Aneurin—myth name
Anfri—disgrace
Angawdd—son of Caw; legend name
Anghrist—Antichrist
Angor—anchor
Angwyn—handsome
Anwar—wild
Anwas—father of Twrch; legend name
Anwell, Anwyl, Anwyll, Anwill, Anwil—beloved
Anwir—liar
Anynnawg—son of Menw; legend name
Anyon—anvil
Ardwyad—protector
Arglwydd—lord
Arian—silver
Arthur, Arthwr—noble bear
Arvel, Arval, Arvil—cried over
Atawn—harmony
Avaon—son of Talyessin; legend name
Awstin—august

Baddon—from Baddon

Baeddan, Badan, Badden—boar

Barris, Barrys—son of Harry

Beda—name of a priest (form of Bede)

Bedwyr—son of Pedrawd; legend name

Bedyw—son of Seithved; legend name

Beli, Beli Mawr—brother-in-law of the Virgin Mary; legend name

Bendigeidfran—blessed raven

Berth—son of Cadwy; legend name

Berwyn—son of Kerenhyr; legend name

Beven, Bevyn, Bevin—young soldier

Blathaon—son of Mwrheth; legend name

Bleidd, Bledig—wolf

Bowen—son of Owen

Brac—free

Brad—treason

Bradwen—son of Moren; legend name

Bradwr—traitor

Braen—corrupt

Bran—raven

Brannock, Brannoc—meaning unknown

Brathach—son of Gwawrddur; legend name

Brian—son of Turenn; legend name

Brychan—freckled

Brynmor—hill

Brynn—from the hill

Brys—son of Brysethach; legend name

Bwlch—son of Cleddyv Kyvwlch; legend name

Cadarn—strong

Caddock, Caddoc, Cadawg—battle-sharp

Cadell, Cadel—battle

Cadellin—father of Gweir; legend name

Cadman, Cadmon—warrior

Cadwallen—battle dissolver

Cadwgawn—son of Iddon; legend name

Cadwr—son of Gwryon; legend name

Cadwy—son of Gereint; legend name

Cadyryeith—well-spoken

Caer Llion—from Caerleon

Caerwyn—holy fortress

Cai—rejoicer

Cain—clear water

Calcas—on of Caw; legend name

Caledvwlch—Excalibur; legend name

Cant—white

Caradawg, Caradog—father of Eudav; legend name

Caradoc—beloved

Cardew—from the black fortress

Carey, Caerau, Cary—from the fortress

Carnedyr—son of Govynyon; legend name

Carwyn—blessed love

Cas—son of Seidi; legend name

Casnar—nobleman; legend name

Casswallawn, Caswallon—son of Beli; legend name

Caw—legend name

Cawrdav—son of Caradawg; legend name

Ceithin—uncle of Lugh; legend name

Cledwyn—blessed

Clud—lame (form of Claude)

Clust—son of Clustveinydd; legend name

Clyde, Clywd—loud-voiced

Cnychwr—son of Nes; legend name

Coch—son of Caw; legend name

Coed—dwells in the woods

Conway—holy water

Conyn—son of Caw; legend name

Corryn—spider

Cors—myth name

Craddock, Caradoc, Cradoc—beloved

Cranog—heron

Crist—believes in Christ (form of Christian)

Cubert—son of Daere; legend name

Culhwch—son of Kilydd; legend name

Culvanawd—son of Gwryon; legend name

Custenhin—father of Erbin; legend name

Cymry—from Wales

Cynbel, Cynbal—warrior chief

Cynfor—great chieftain

Cystennin—constant (form of Constantine)

Dadweir—legend name

Dafydd, Dewi—beloved (form of David)

Dalldav—son of Cunyn Cov; legend name

Daned—son of Oth; legend name

Deverell, Deverril—from the riverbank

Dewi, Dewey—belonging to the lord

Digon—son of Alar; legend name

Dillus—son of Eurei; legend name

Dirmyg—son of Caw; legend name

Drem—sign

Dremidydd—father of Drem; legend name

Drew, Dryw—wise

Druce, Drywsone, Druson—son of Drew

Drudwas—son of Tryffin; legend name

Drudwyn—meaning unknown

Drwst—legend name

Drych—son of Kibddar; legend name

Drystan—noisy (form of Tristan)

Duach—son of Gwawrddur; legend name

Dwnn—meaning unknown

Dyffryn—meaning unknown

Dylan, Dilan, Dillie, Dillon—born near the sea

Dyngannon—legend name

Dyvynarth—son of Gwrgwst; legend name
Dyvynwal—legend name
Dyvyr—son of Alun; legend name
Dywel—son of Erbin; legend name
Earwine, Erwyn, Earwyn, Erwin—white river
Edern—son of Nudd; legend name
Edlym—legend name
Edmyg—honor
Ehangwen—legend name
Eiddoel—son of Ner; legend name
Eiddon—legend name
Eiddyl—legend name
Eiladar—son of Penn Llarcan; legend name
Einion, Einian—anvil
Eiryn—son of Peibyn; legend name
Eivyonydd—legend name
Elidyr—legend name
Elphin—son of Gwyddno; legend name
Emlyn—waterfall
Emrys—immortal (form of Ambrose)
Ennissyen—legend name
Erbin—son of Custenhin; legend name
Ercwlff—Hera's glory; myth name (form of Hercules)
Ergyryad—son of Caw; legend name
Erim—legend name
Ermid—son of Erbin; legend name

Erwm—legend name
Eryi—from Snowdon
Eudav—son of Caradawg; legend name
Eurosswydd—legend name
Eus—son of Erim; legend name
Evan—young fighter
Evrawg—from York
Evrei—legend name
Ewyas—legend name
Fercos—son of Poch; legend name
Fflam—son of Nwyvre; legend name
Fflergant—king of Brittany; legend name
Fflewdwr—son of Naw; legend name
Ffodor—son of Ervyll; legend name
Ffowc—of the people
Fotor—legend name
Fychan—small
Fyrsil, Fferyll—staff bearer (form of Virgil)
Gallgoid—legend name
Gamon—legend name
Gandwy—legend name
Garanhon—son of Glythvyr; legend name
Garanwyn—white shank
Garnock, Garnoc, Gwernach—dwells by the alder-tree river
Garselid—legend name
Garwyli—son of Gwyddawg Gwyr; legend name
Garym—legend name
Gavin, Gwalchmai—white hawk

Gawl—myth name

Geraint—father of Cadwy; legend name

Gilbert—son of Cadgyffro; legend name

Gilvaethwy—son of Don; legend name

Gleis—son of Merin; legend name

Glew—son of Ysgawd; legend name

Glewlwyd—legend name

Glinyeu—son of Taran; legend name

Gloyw—legend name

Glyn, Glenn, Glynn—dwells in the glen

Glythvyr—legend name

Gobrwy—son of Echel Pierced Thighs; legend name

Gogyvwlch—legend name

Goreu—son of Custenhin; legend name

Gormant—son of Rica; legend name

Goronwy—legend name

Gorsedd—from the mound

Govan—son of Caw; legend name

Govannon—son of Don; legend name

Govynyon—legend name

Gower, Gwyr, Gowyr—pure

Granwen—son of Llyr; legend name

Greid—son of Eri; legend name

Greidyawl—legend name

Griffin, Griffen, Gryphon, Gryphin—strong in faith

Griffith, Griffeth, Gruffudd, Grufydd—red-haired

Gruddyeu—son of Muryel; legend name

Gruffin, Gruffen, Gruffyn—fierce lord

Grugyn—legend name

Gryn—legend name

Gusg—son of Achen; legend name

Gwalchmei—son of Gwyar; legend name

Gwales—legend name

Gwalhaved—son of Gwyar; legend name

Gwallawg—son of Llenawg; legend name

Gwallter—powerful warrior (form of Walter)

Gwarthegydd—son of Caw; legend name

Gwastad—legend name

Gwawl—son of Clud; legend name

Gwawrddur—legend name

Gweir—son of Cadellin Silver; legend name

Gwenwynwyn—son of Naw; legend name

Gwern—old

Gwerthmwl—legend name

Gwevyl—son of Gwastad; legend name

Gwiawn—legend name

Gwiffred—legend name

Gwilenhin—king of France; legend name

Gwilym—resolute protector (form of William)

Gwitart—son of Aedd; legend name

Gwlgawd—legend name
Gwlwlwyd—legend name
Gwlyddn—legend name
Gwrddnei—legend name
Gwrddywal—son of Evrei;
    legend name
Gwres—son of Rheged; legend
    name
Gwrgwst—legend name
Gwrhyr—legend name
Gwri—legend name
Gwrtheyrn—meaning unknown
Gwryon—legend name
Gwyddawg—son of Menestyr;
    legend name
Gwydre—son of Arthur;
    legend name
Gwydyon—son of Don;
    legend name
Gwyn, Gwynn—handsome; son
    of Nudd
Gwyngad—son of Caw; legend
    name
Gwynnan—legend name
Gwyr—from Gower
Gwys—legend name
Gwystyl—son of Nwython;
    legend name
Gwythyr—son of Greidyawl;
    legend name
Heilyn—son of Gwynn; legend
    name
Hen Beddestyr—son of Erim;
    legend name
Hen Was—old servant
Hen Wyneb—old face
Hetwn—legend name
Heveydd—legend name

Howel, Howell—eminent
Hu, Huw—intelligent (form of
    Hugh)
Huabwy—son of Gwyron;
    legend name
Huarwar—son of Avlawn;
    legend name
Hueil—son of Caw; legend name
Hydd—deer
Iaen—legend name
Iago—supplanter (form of
    James)
Iau—supreme ruler of the gods;
    myth name (form of Zeus)
Iddawg—son of Mynyo; legend
    name
Iddig—son of Anarawd;
    legend name
Ioan, Iwan—gracious God (form
    of John)
Iona—king of France; legend
    name
Iorwerth—son of Maredudd;
    legend name
Iustig—son of Caw; legend name
Kay—fiery
Kei—son of Kynyr; legend name
Keith—dwells in the woods
Kelli—from the wood
Kelyddon—legend name
Kelyn—son of Caw; legend name
Kenehyr—legend name
Kenn, Ken—clear water
Kent—white
Kenyon—from Ennion's mound
Kethtrwm—legend name
Keudawg—legend name
Kevyn—from the ridge

Kian—father of Lugh; legend
name
Kibddar—legend name
Kilwich—myth name
Kilydd—son of Kelyddon;
legend name
Kim—ruler
Kimball, Kimble—warrior chief
Kyledyr—son of Nwython;
legend name
Kynan—chief
Kynddilig—legend name
Kynedyr—son of Hetwn; legend
name
Kynlas—son of Kynan;
legend name
Kynon—son of Clydno;
legend name
Kynwal—son of Caw;
legend name
Kynwas—legend name
Kynwrig—legend name
Kynwyl—name of a saint
Kynyr—legend name
Kyvwlch—legend name
Llacheu—Arthur's son;
legend name
Llaesgymyn—legend name
Llara—meek
Llassar—son of Llassar Llaes;
legend name
Llawr—son of Erw; legend name
Llawvrodedd—legend name
Llenlleawg—legend name
Llue—legend name
Llevelys—son of Beli; legend
name
Llewelyn, Llewellyn, Llyweilun—
lion

Lloyd, Llwyd—gray
Lludd, Llundein—from London
Llwch—legend name
Llwyarch—legend name
Llwybyr—son of Caw; legend
name
Llwyd—son of Kil Coed;
legend name
Llwydawg—legend name
Llwydeu—son of Nwython;
legend name
Llwyr—son of Llwyryon; legend
name
Llwyrddyddwg—legend name
Llyn—from the lake
Llyr—from the sea
Lug, Luc—light (form of Luke)
Mabon—son of Modron;
legend name
Mabsant—son of Caw; legend
name
Madawg—son of Teithyon;
legend name
Maddock, Madawc, Madoc,
Maddoc, Madog, Maddog—
beneficent
Mael—son of Roycol; legend
name
Maelgwyn—prince of the
hounds
Maelwys—son of Baeddan;
legend name
Mallolwch—king of Ireland;
legend name
Manawydan—son of Llyr; legend
name
March—son of Meirchyawn;
legend name

Maredudd—legend name

Math, Mathonwy—myth name

Mawrth—god of war; myth name (form of Mars)

Maxen—legend name

Medyr—son of Medyredydd; legend name

Meilyg—son of Caw; legend name

Menw—son of Teirwaedd; legend name

Mercher—messenger of the gods; myth name (form of Mercury)

Meredith, Meridith, Meredydd—protector of the sea

Merin—legend name

Meurig—dark-skinned (form of Maurice)

Mihangel—who is like God (form of Michael)

Mil—son of Dugum; legend name

Moesen—taken from the water (form of Moses)

Mordwywr—sailor

Moren—son of Iaen; legend name

Morgan, Morcan, Morcar—lives by the sea

Morgannwg—from Glamorgan

Morgant—legend name

Morthwyl—hammer

Morvran—son of Tegid; legend name

Myrddin—falcon (form of Merlin)

Naw—son of Seithved; legend name

Neb—son of Caw; legend name

Neifion—god of water; myth name (form of Neptune)

Ner—legend name

Nerth—son of Cadarn; legend name

Nerthach—son of Gwawrddur; legend name

Neued—father of Tringad; legend name

Newlin, Newyddllyn, Newlyn—from the new spring

Nissyen—son of Eurosswydd; legend name

Nodawl—legend name

Nudd—legend name

Nynnyaw—son of Beli; legend name

Odgar—son of Aedd; legend name

Odyar—myth name

Ofydd—Roman poet (form of Ovid)

Ol—son of Olwydd; legend name

Olwydd—tracker

Ondyaw—son of a French Duke; legend name

Osla—legend name

Oswallt—divine power (form of Oswald)

Oth—legend name

Owein, Owyn, Owen, Owin, Owain—young warrior

Padrig—noble (form of Patrick)

Panawr—legend name

Parry, Perry—son of Harry

Pebin—legend name

Pedr—rock (form of Peter)

Pedrawd—legend name
Peibyn—legend name
Peissawg—king of Brittany; legend name
Pembroke—lives in the headland
Pendaran—meaning unknown
Penkawr—myth name
Penllyn—from the lake's headland
Penn—from the peak
Penryn—legend name
Penvro—from Pembroke
Peredur—son of Evrawg; legend name
Powell—son of Howell
Powys—legend name
Price, Prys, Preece—son of Rhys
Pryderi—son of Pwyll; myth name
Prydwen—handsome
Puw—son of Hugh (form of Pugh)
Pwyll—son of Howell
Pyrs—rock (form of Peter)
Ren, Ryn—ruler
Renfrew, Rhinffrew—from the still river
Rheged—father of Gwres; legend name
Rheidwn—legend name
Rheu—legend name
Rhioganedd—prince of Ireland; legend name
Rhisiart—strong ruler (form of Richard)
Rhobert—bright, famous (form of Robert)

Rhun—son of Beli; legend name
Rhuvawn—son of Deorthach; legend name
Rhyawdd—son of Morgant; legend name
Rhychdir—from the plow land
Rhyd—from the ford
Rhynnon—legend name
Rhys, Rice, Reece, Rees—ardent
Romney, Rumenea—dwells near the curving river
Sach—legend name
Sadwrn—god of the harvest; myth name (form of Saturn)
Sanddev—legend name
Sawyl—legend name
Sayer, Saer, Sayre, Sayers, Sayres—carpenter
Seissyllwch—legend name
Seith, Saith—seven
Seithved—legend name
Sel—son of Selgi; legend name
Selyf—peaceful (form of Solomon)
Selyv—son of Kynan; legend name
Siencyn—God is gracious (form of Jenkin)
Sinnoch—son of Seithved; legend name
Sion—gracious God (form of John)
Sior—farmer (form of George)
Steffan—crowned in victory (form of Stephen)
Sugyn—son of Sugynedydd; legend name
Sulyen—son of Iaen; legend name

Syvwlch—son of Cleddyv Kyvwlch; legend name
Tad, Tadd—father
Taffy—beloved
Taliesin, Talyessin—handsome
Tallwch—legend name
Taran—legend name
Tarawg—legend name
Taredd—legend name
Tarrant, Tarran, Taryn, Taren—thunder
Tathal—legend name
Tawy—legend name
Tegvan—legend name
Tegyr—legend name
Teir—legend name
Teirnon—legend name
Teirwaedd—legend name
Teithi—son of Gwynnan; legend name
Teregud—son of Iaen; legend name
Timotheus—God-fearing (form of Timothy)
Trachmyr—legend name
Trahern, Trahayarn—strong as iron
Tremayne, Tremen—lives in the house by the rock
Trent, Trynt—dwells near the rapid stream
Trevelyan, Trevelian—from Elian's home

Tringad—son of Neued; legend name
Tristan, Trystan—noisy
Tristram—full of sorrows
Tryffin—legend name
Tudor, Tewdwr—God's gift
Twm—twin (form of Thomas)
Twrch—legend name
Twrgadarn—tower of strength
Tywysog—prince
Uchdryd—son of Erim; legend name
Unig—legend name
Uryen—legend name
Vaddon—from Bath
Vaughn, Vychan—small
Wadu—son of Seithved; legend name
Waljan—chosen
Werbenec—meaning unknown
Wmffre—peaceful Hun (form of Humphrey)
Wren—ruler
Wrnach—legend name
Wynn, Wyn, Winn—handsome
Ynyr—legend name
Ysberin—son of Fflergant; legend name
Ysberyr—legend name
Ysgawyn—son of Panon; legend name
Ysgithyrwyn—legend name
Ysgonan—legend name
Yspadaden—myth name

TOP TEN U.S. NAMES BY YEAR

This list is taken from the Social Security Administration's Web site www.ssa.gov/OACT/babynames/index.html. You can view this site for more naming information.

1880

1 John	1 Mary
2 William	2 Anna
3 Charles	3 Elizabeth
4 George	4 Margaret
5 James	5 Minnie
6 Joseph	6 Emma
7 Frank	7 Martha
8 Henry	8 Alice
9 Thomas	9 Marie
10 Harry	10 Annie, Sarah (tie)

1881

1 John	1 Mary
2 William	2 Anna
3 Charles	3 Elizabeth
4 James	4 Margaret
5 George	5 Emma
6 Joseph	6 Minnie
7 Frank	7 Sarah
8 Henry	8 Alice
9 Edward,	9 Bertha
10 Harry, Thomas (tie)	10 Grace

1882

1 John	1 Mary
2 William	2 Anna
3 Charles	3 Elizabeth
4 James	4 Emma, Margaret (tie)
5 George	
6 Frank	6 Minnie
7 Joseph	7 Bertha
8 Henry	8 Mabel
9 Thomas	9 Florence,
10 Harry	Ida (tie)

1883

1 John	1 Mary
2 William	2 Anna
3 Charles	3 Margaret
4 George	4 Emma
5 James	5 Elizabeth
6 Joseph	6 Florence
7 Frank	7 Bertha
8 Harry, Henry (tie)	8 Alice
	9 Sarah
10 Thomas	10 Clara, Rose (tie)

1884

1 John	1 Mary
2 William	2 Anna
3 George	3 Elizabeth
4 Charles	4 Emma
5 James	5 Margaret
6 Frank	6 Minnie
7 Joseph	7 Alice,
8 Harry	Florence
	(tie)
9 Henry	9 Clara
10 Thomas	10 Bertha,
	Rose (tie)

1885

1 John	1 Mary
2 William	2 Anna
3 Charles	3 Elizabeth
4 Joseph	4 Margaret
5 George,	5 Emma
James (tie)	6 Ida
7 Frank	7 Rose
8 Robert	8 Minnie
9 Henry	9 Bertha
10 Edward	10 Annie

1886

1 John	1 Mary
2 William	2 Anna
3 George	3 Elizabeth
4 James	4 Emma
5 Charles	5 Clara
6 Joseph	6 Margaret
7 Frank	7 Minnie
8 Henry	8 Bertha
9 Thomas	9 Rose
10 Edward,	10 Ida, Sarah
Walter	(tie)
(tie)	

1887

1 John	1 Mary
2 William	2 Anna
3 George	3 Emma
4 Charles	4 Margaret
5 James	5 Bertha
6 Frank,	6 Elizabeth,
Joseph	Minnie
(tie)	(tie)
8 Harry	8 Florence
9 Robert	9 Mabel
10 Thomas	10 Bessie,
	Helen,
	Jennie (tie)

1888

1 John	1 Mary
2 William	2 Anna
3 George	3 Margaret
4 Joseph	4 Elizabeth
5 James	5 Bertha
6 Charles	6 Emma
7 Frank	7 Ethel
8 Harry	8 Rose
9 Robert	9 Bessie
10 Thomas	10 Ida, Minnie
	(tie)

1889

1 John	1 Mary
2 William	2 Anna
3 George	3 Elizabeth
4 James	4 Margaret
5 Charles	5 Minnie
6 Joseph	6 Helen,
7 Frank	Rose (tie)
8 Harry	8 Bertha
9 Edward	9 Alice,
10 Robert	Emma (tie)

1890

1 John	1 Mary
2 William	2 Anna
3 James	3 Elizabeth
4 George	4 Emma
5 Charles	5 Margaret
6 Joseph	6 Rose
7 Frank	7 Ethel
8 Harry	8 Florence
9 Henry	9 Ida
10 Edward	10 Bertha,
	Helen (tie)

1891

1 John	1 Mary
2 William	2 Anna
3 James	3 Margaret
4 George	4 Florence
5 Joseph	5 Elizabeth
6 Charles	6 Clara
7 Frank	7 Rose
8 Henry	8 Helen
9 Harry	9 Emma,
10 Robert	Ethel (tie)

1892

1 John	1 Mary
2 William	2 Anna
3 James	3 Margaret
4 George,	4 Florence
Joseph	5 Elizabeth
(tie)	
6 Charles	6 Rose
7 Frank	7 Ruth
8 Harry	8 Ethel
9 Thomas	9 Helen,
10 Robert	Minnie (tie)

1893

1 John	1 Mary
2 William	2 Anna
3 George	3 Margaret
4 Joseph	4 Elizabeth
5 Charles	5 Helen
6 James	6 Ruth
7 Frank	7 Florence
8 Edward	8 Bertha
9 Thomas	9 Ethel
10 Walter	10 Rose

1894

1 John	1 Mary
2 William	2 Anna
3 George	3 Margaret
4 James	4 Helen
5 Joseph	5 Elizabeth
6 Charles	6 Ruth
7 Frank	7 Florence
8 Harry	8 Ethel
9 Thomas	9 Marie
10 Robert	10 Rose

1895

1 John	1 Mary
2 William	2 Anna
3 James,	3 Elizabeth
Joseph	4 Helen
(tie)	
5 George	5 Ruth
6 Charles	6 Margaret
7 Frank	7 Florence
8 Henry,	8 Marie,
Walter (tie)	Rose (tie)
10 Harry	10 Ethel

1896

1 William	1 Mary
2 John	2 Anna
3 James	3 Helen
4 George	4 Margaret
5 Joseph	5 Ruth
6 Frank	6 Marie
7 Charles	7 Elizabeth
8 Harry	8 Rose
9 Robert	9 Ethel
10 Edward	10 Florence

1897

1 John	1 Mary
2 William	2 Anna
3 James	3 Helen
4 George	4 Ruth
5 Joseph	5 Margaret
6 Charles	6 Florence
7 Frank	7 Rose
8 Robert	8 Marie
9 Harry	9 Elizabeth
10 Edward	10 Lillian

1898

1 John	1 Mary
2 William	2 Anna
3 George	3 Helen
4 James	4 Margaret
5 Joseph	5 Ruth
6 Charles	6 Elizabeth
7 Frank	7 Florence
8 Edward	8 Rose
9 Robert	9 Lillian
10 Henry	10 Ethel,
	Marie (tie)

1899

1 John	1 Mary
2 William	2 Anna
3 George	3 Margaret
4 James	4 Helen
5 Joseph	5 Marie
6 Charles	6 Elizabeth
7 Frank	7 Florence
8 Robert	8 Ruth
9 Henry	9 Ethel
10 Edward	10 Alice

1900

1 John	1 Mary
2 William	2 Helen
3 James	3 Anna
4 George	4 Margaret
5 Charles	5 Ruth
6 Joseph	6 Elizabeth
7 Frank	7 Marie
8 Henry	8 Rose
9 Robert	9 Florence
10 Harry	10 Bertha

1901

1 John	1 Mary
2 William	2 Helen
3 James	3 Anna
4 Joseph	4 Margaret
5 George	5 Elizabeth
6 Charles	6 Ruth
7 Frank	7 Marie
8 Henry	8 Gladys
9 Robert	9 Florence
10 Edward	10 Rose

1902

1 John	1 Mary
2 William	2 Helen
3 James	3 Anna
4 George	4 Margaret
5 Joseph	5 Ruth
6 Charles	6 Elizabeth
7 Robert	7 Marie
8 Frank	8 Lillian
9 Edward	9 Florence
10 Walter	10 Alice, Rose (tie)

1903

1 John	1 Mary
2 William	2 Margaret
3 James	3 Helen
4 George	4 Anna
5 Joseph	5 Ruth
6 Charles	6 Marie
7 Robert	7 Elizabeth
8 Frank	8 Florence
9 Walter	9 Dorothy
10 Henry	10 Lillian

1904

1 John	1 Mary
2 William	2 Helen
3 George, James (tie)	3 Margaret
	4 Ruth
5 Joseph	5 Anna
6 Charles	6 Dorothy, Elizabeth (tie)
7 Robert	
8 Frank	8 Marie
9 Edward	9 Alice, Florence (tie)
10 Walter	

1905

1 John	1 Mary
2 William	2 Helen
3 James	3 Margaret
4 George	4 Anna
5 Charles	5 Ruth
6 Joseph	6 Dorothy
7 Frank, Robert (tie)	7 Elizabeth
	8 Mildred
9 Edward	9 Lillian
10 Thomas	10 Marie

1906

1 John	1 Mary
2 William	2 Helen
3 James	3 Margaret
4 Joseph	4 Ruth
5 George	5 Anna
6 Charles	6 Elizabeth
7 Robert	7 Dorothy

8 Frank
9 Henry
10 Edward

8 Marie
9 Alice
10 Florence

7 Charles
8 Frank
9 Edward
10 Henry,
  Walter (tie)

7 Elizabeth
8 Mildred
9 Marie
10 Alice

1907

1 John
2 William
3 James
4 George
5 Charles
6 Joseph
7 Robert
8 Frank
9 Thomas,
  Walter (tie)

1 Mary
2 Helen
3 Margaret
4 Anna
5 Ruth
6 Dorothy
7 Elizabeth
8 Mildred
9 Alice
10 Ethel

1910

1 John
2 William
3 James
4 Robert
5 Joseph
6 Charles,
  George
  (tie)
8 Edward
9 Frank
10 Henry

1 Mary
2 Helen
3 Margaret
4 Dorothy,
  Ruth (tie)
6 Anna
7 Mildred

8 Elizabeth
9 Alice
10 Ethel

1908

1 John
2 William
3 James
4 George
5 Joseph
6 Charles
7 Robert
8 Frank
9 Edward
10 Henry

1 Mary
2 Helen
3 Margaret
4 Anna
5 Ruth
6 Dorothy
7 Elizabeth
8 Mildred
9 Frances
10 Florence

1911

1 John
2 William
3 James
4 Joseph

5 Charles,
  Robert
  (tie)
7 George
8 Frank
9 Edward
10 Walter

1 Mary
2 Helen
3 Dorothy,
  Margaret
  (tie)
5 Ruth
6 Anna

7 Mildred
8 Elizabeth
9 Marie
10 Gladys

1909

1 John
2 William
3 James
4 George
5 Joseph
6 Robert

1 Mary
2 Helen
3 Margaret
4 Dorothy,
  Ruth (tie)
6 Anna

1912

1 John
2 William

1 Mary
2 Helen

3 James   3 Dorothy
4 Robert   4 Ruth
5 George   5 Margaret
6 Joseph   6 Anna
7 Charles   7 Mildred
8 Frank   8 Frances
9 Edward   9 Elizabeth
10 Thomas,   10 Marie
   Walter (tie)

1913

1 John   1 Mary
2 William   2 Helen
3 James   3 Dorothy
4 Robert   4 Margaret
5 Joseph   5 Ruth
6 Charles   6 Mildred
7 George   7 Elizabeth
8 Frank   8 Anna
9 Edward   9 Marie
10 Thomas   10 Florence

1914

1 John   1 Mary
2 William   2 Helen
3 James   3 Dorothy
4 Robert   4 Margaret
5 Joseph   5 Ruth
6 George   6 Mildred
7 Charles   7 Anna
8 Frank   8 Elizabeth
9 Edward   9 Evelyn
10 Walter   10 Marie

1915

1 John   1 Mary

2 William   2 Helen
3 James   3 Dorothy
4 Robert   4 Margaret
5 Joseph   5 Ruth
6 Charles   6 Anna
7 George   7 Mildred
8 Edward   8 Evelyn
9 Frank   9 Virginia
10 Thomas   10 Elizabeth

1916

1 John   1 Mary
2 William   2 Helen
3 James   3 Margaret
4 Robert   4 Dorothy
5 Charles   5 Ruth
6 George   6 Mildred
7 Joseph   7 Anna
8 Edward   8 Frances
9 Frank   9 Elizabeth
10 Walter   10 Marie

1917

1 John   1 Mary
2 William   2 Helen
3 James   3 Dorothy
4 Robert   4 Margaret
5 Joseph   5 Ruth
6 George   6 Anna
7 Charles   7 Frances
8 Edward   8 Elizabeth
9 Frank   9 Mildred
10 Thomas,   10 Marie
   Walter (tie)

1918

1 John	1 Mary
2 William	2 Helen
3 Robert	3 Dorothy
4 James	4 Margaret
5 Joseph	5 Ruth
6 Charles	6 Frances
7 George	7 Virginia
8 Edward	8 Anna
9 Frank	9 Mildred
10 Thomas	10 Elizabeth

1919

1 John	1 Mary
2 William	2 Helen
3 James	3 Dorothy
4 Robert	4 Margaret
5 Charles	5 Ruth
6 Joseph	6 Virginia
7 George	7 Elizabeth
8 Edward	8 Mildred
9 Frank	9 Frances
10 Thomas	10 Anna

1920

1 John	1 Mary
2 William	2 Dorothy
3 James	3 Helen
4 Robert	4 Margaret
5 Joseph	5 Ruth
6 Charles	6 Virginia
7 George	7 Elizabeth
8 Edward	8 Anna
9 Thomas	9 Mildred
10 Frank	10 Betty

1921

1 John	1 Mary
2 Robert	2 Dorothy
3 James	3 Helen
4 William	4 Margaret
5 George	5 Ruth
6 Charles	6 Mildred
7 Joseph	7 Betty
8 Edward	8 Virginia
9 Frank	9 Elizabeth
10 Thomas	10 Anna

1922

1 John	1 Mary
2 Robert	2 Dorothy
3 James	3 Helen
4 William	4 Margaret
5 Joseph	5 Ruth
6 Charles	6 Betty
7 George	7 Frances
8 Edward	8 Elizabeth
9 Richard	9 Virginia
10 Frank	10 Anna

1923

1 John	1 Mary
2 Robert	2 Dorothy
3 William	3 Helen
4 James	4 Margaret
5 Charles	5 Betty
6 George	6 Ruth
7 Joseph	7 Mildred
8 Edward	8 Virginia
9 Frank	9 Frances
10 Richard	10 Elizabeth

1924

1 John	1 Mary
2 Robert	2 Dorothy
3 James	3 Helen
4 William	4 Betty
5 Charles	5 Margaret
6 Joseph	6 Ruth
7 George	7 Virginia
8 Edward	8 Frances
9 Richard	9 Doris
10 Donald	10 Mildred

1925

1 John	1 Mary
2 Robert	2 Dorothy
3 James	3 Betty
4 William	4 Helen
5 Charles	5 Margaret
6 Joseph	6 Ruth
7 George	7 Doris
8 Richard	8 Virginia
9 Edward	9 Elizabeth
10 Donald	10 Evelyn, Mildred (tie)

1926

1 Robert	1 Mary
2 John	2 Dorothy
3 William	3 Helen
4 James	4 Betty
5 Charles	5 Margaret
6 George	6 Ruth
7 Richard	7 Virginia
8 Joseph	8 Doris
9 Edward	9 Jean
10 Donald	10 Maria

1927

1 Robert	1 Mary
2 James	2 Betty
3 John	3 Dorothy
4 William	4 Helen
5 Charles	5 Margaret
6 Richard	6 Ruth
7 George	7 Virginia
8 Joseph	8 Doris
9 Donald	9 Maria
10 Edward	10 Shirley

1928

1 Robert	1 Mary
2 John	2 Betty
3 James	3 Dorothy
4 William	4 Helen
5 Charles	5 Margaret
6 Richard	6 Ruth
7 Donald	7 Barbara
8 George	8 Doris
9 Joseph	9 Maria
10 Edward	10 Patricia

1929

1 Robert	1 Mary
2 John	2 Betty
3 James	3 Dorothy
4 William	4 Helen
5 Charles	5 Margaret
6 Donald	6 Ruth

7 Richard
8 George
9 Joseph
10 Edward

7 Doris
8 Maria
9 Barbara
10 Shirley

4 William
5 Charles
6 Richard
7 Donald
8 George
9 Joseph
10 Thomas

4 Dorothy
5 Joan
6 Patricia
7 Shirley
8 Margaret
9 Doris
10 Helen

1930

1 Robert
2 James
3 John
4 William
5 Richard
6 Charles
7 Donald
8 George
9 Joseph
10 Edward

1 Mary
2 Betty
3 Dorothy
4 Helen
5 Barbara
6 Margaret
7 Maria
8 Patricia
9 Doris
10 Joan, Ruth
(tie)

1933

1 Robert
2 James
3 John
4 William
5 Richard
6 Donald
7 Charles
8 Joseph
9 George
10 Thomas

1 Mary
2 Betty
3 Barbara
4 Dorothy
5 Joan
6 Patricia
7 Maria
8 Helen
9 Margaret
10 Doris

1931

1 Robert
2 James
3 John
4 William
5 Richard
6 Charles
7 Donald
8 George
9 Joseph
10 Thomas

1 Mary
2 Betty
3 Dorothy
4 Barbara
5 Joan
6 Helen
7 Maria
8 Patricia
9 Margaret
10 Shirley

1934

1 Robert
2 James
3 John
4 William
5 Richard
6 Charles
7 Donald
8 George
9 Thomas
10 Joseph

1 Mary
2 Betty
3 Shirley
4 Barbara
5 Joan
6 Patricia
7 Dorothy
8 Maria
9 Margaret
10 Helen

1932

1 Robert
2 John
3 James

1 Mary
2 Betty
3 Barbara

1935

1 James

1 Mary

2 Robert
3 John
4 William
5 Richard
6 Charles
7 Donald
8 Thomas
9 Ronald
10 David

2 Shirley
3 Barbara
4 Betty
5 Patricia
6 Joan
7 Dorothy
8 Margaret
9 Maria
10 Helen

2 James
3 John
4 William
5 Richard
6 Charles
7 Donald
8 David
9 George
10 Ronald,
Thomas
(tie)

2 Barbara
3 Patricia
4 Betty
5 Shirley
6 Nancy
7 Carol,
Maria (tie)
9 Margaret
10 Joan

1936

1 Robert
2 James
3 John
4 William
5 Donald
6 Richard
7 Charles
8 Ronald
9 George
10 Joseph

1 Mary
2 Shirley
3 Barbara
4 Betty
5 Patricia
6 Maria
7 Dorothy,
Nancy (tie)
9 Joan
10 Margaret

1939

1 Robert
2 James
3 John
4 William
5 Richard
6 Charles
7 David
8 Thomas
9 Donald
10 Ronald

1 Mary
2 Barbara
3 Patricia
4 Betty
5 Shirley
6 Maria
7 Margaret
8 Carol
9 Nancy
10 Judith

1937

1 Robert
2 James
3 John
4 William
5 Richard
6 Donald
7 Charles
8 David
9 George
10 Thomas

1 Mary
2 Barbara
3 Patricia
4 Shirley
5 Betty
6 Maria,
Nancy (tie)
8 Dorothy
9 Carol
10 Margaret

1940

1 James
2 Robert
3 John
4 William
5 Richard
6 Charles
7 David
8 Thomas
9 Donald
10 Ronald

1 Mary
2 Barbara
3 Patricia
4 Carol
5 Judith
6 Betty
7 Nancy
8 Maria
9 Margaret
10 Linda

1938

1 Robert

1 Mary

1941

1 Robert	1 Mary
2 John	2 Barbara
3 James	3 Patricia
4 William	4 Carol
5 Richard	5 Linda
6 Charles	6 Judith
7 David	7 Sandra
8 Thomas	8 Maria
9 Ronald	9 Betty
10 Donald	10 Nancy

1942

1 James	1 Mary
2 Robert	2 Barbara
3 John	3 Patricia
4 William	4 Carol
5 Richard	5 Linda
6 Charles	6 Nancy
7 David	7 Betty
8 Thomas	8 Sandra
9 Ronald	9 Maria
10 Joseph	10 Judith

1943

1 James	1 Mary
2 Robert	2 Barbara
3 John	3 Patricia
4 William	4 Linda
5 Richard	5 Carol
6 David	6 Sandra
7 Charles	7 Nancy,
8 Thomas	Sharon
	(tie)
9 Ronald	9 Judith
10 Michael	10 Betty

1944

1 Robert	1 Mary
2 James	2 Barbara
3 John	3 Patricia
4 William	4 Linda
5 Richard	5 Carol
6 David	6 Nancy
7 Charles	7 Sandra
8 Thomas	8 Sharon
9 Michael	9 Judith
10 Ronald	10 Maria

1945

1 James	1 Mary
2 Robert	2 Linda
3 John	3 Barbara
4 William	4 Patricia
5 Richard	5 Carol
6 David	6 Maria
7 Thomas	7 Sandra
8 Charles	8 Nancy
9 Michael	9 Sharon
10 Ronald	10 Susan

1946

1 James	1 Mary
2 Robert	2 Linda
3 John	3 Patricia
4 William	4 Barbara
5 Richard	5 Carol
6 David	6 Susan
7 Michael	7 Nancy
8 Charles	8 Sandra
9 Thomas	9 Maria
10 Ronald	10 Sharon

1947

1 James	1 Linda
2 John	2 Mary
3 Robert	3 Patricia
4 William	4 Barbara
5 Richard	5 Sandra
6 David	6 Susan
7 Michael	7 Maria
8 Thomas	8 Carol
9 Charles	9 Nancy
10 Larry	10 Sharon

1948

1 Robert	1 Linda
2 James	2 Mary
3 John	3 Patricia
4 William	4 Barbara
5 David	5 Susan
6 Richard	6 Maria
7 Michael	7 Carol
8 Thomas	8 Nancy,
9 Charles	Sandra
	(tie)
10 Ronald	10 Sharon

1949

1 James	1 Linda
2 Robert	2 Mary
3 John	3 Patricia
4 David,	4 Barbara
William	5 Susan
(tie)	
6 Michael	6 Sandra
7 Richard	7 Maria
8 Thomas	8 Nancy

9 Charles	9 Carol
10 Larry	10 Sharon

1950

1 John	1 Linda
2 James	2 Mary
3 Robert	3 Patricia
4 William	4 Barbara
5 Michael	5 Susan
6 David	6 Maria
7 Richard	7 Sandra
8 Thomas	8 Nancy
9 Charles	9 Deborah
10 Gary	10 Kathleen

1951

1 Robert	1 Linda
2 James	2 Mary
3 John	3 Patricia
4 Michael	4 Barbara
5 David	5 Deborah
6 William	6 Susan
7 Richard	7 Nancy
8 Thomas	8 Maria
9 Charles	9 Kathleen
10 Gary	10 Karen,
	Sandra
	(tie)

1952

1 James	1 Linda
2 Robert	2 Mary
3 John	3 Patricia
4 Michael	4 Deborah

5 David   5 Barbara
6 William   6 Susan
7 Richard   7 Maria
8 Thomas   8 Nancy
9 Charles   9 Debra
10 Gary   10 Kathleen

1953

1 Michael	1 Mary
2 Robert	2 Linda
3 James	3 Deborah
4 John	4 Patricia
5 David	5 Susan
6 William	6 Barbara
7 Richard	7 Debra
8 Thomas	8 Maria
9 Gary	9 Nancy
10 Charles	10 Karen

1954

1 Robert	1 Mary
2 Michael	2 Deborah
3 John	3 Linda
4 James	4 Debra
5 David	5 Patricia,
6 William	Susan (tie)
7 Richard	7 Barbara
8 Thomas	8 Maria
9 Mark	9 Karen
10 Gary	10 Nancy

1955

| 1 Michael | 1 Mary |
| 2 James | 2 Deborah |

3 David,	3 Debra,
Robert	Linda (tie)
(tie)	
5 John	5 Patricia
6 William	6 Susan
7 Richard	7 Maria
8 Mark	8 Barbara
9 Thomas	9 Karen
10 Charles,	10 Nancy
Steven	
(tie)	

1956

1 Michael	1 Mary
2 Robert	2 Susan
3 David	3 Debra
4 James	4 Linda
5 John	5 Deborah
6 William	6 Patricia
7 Richard	7 Karen
8 Mark	8 Maria
9 Thomas	9 Barbara
10 Steven	10 Donna

1957

1 Michael	1 Mary
2 James	2 Susan
3 Robert	3 Linda
4 David	4 Karen
5 John	5 Patricia
6 William	6 Deborah,
7 Richard	Debra (tie)
8 Mark	8 Cynthia
9 Thomas	9 Maria
10 Steven	10 Nancy

1958

1 Michael	1 Mary
2 David	2 Linda
3 Robert	3 Susan
4 John	4 Patricia
5 James	5 Karen
6 William	6 Maria
7 Mark	7 Debra
8 Richard	8 Cynthia
9 Thomas	9 Deborah
10 Charles	10 Barbara

1959

1 Michael	1 Mary
2 David	2 Susan
3 James	3 Linda
4 John	4 Donna,
5 Robert	Patricia
	(tie)
6 Mark	6 Maria
7 William	7 Karen
8 Richard	8 Debra
9 Thomas	9 Cynthia
10 Steven	10 Deborah

1960

1 David	1 Mary
2 Michael	2 Susan
3 John	3 Maria
4 James	4 Karen
5 Robert	5 Lisa
6 Mark	6 Linda
7 William	7 Donna
8 Richard	8 Patricia
9 Thomas	9 Debra
10 Steven	10 Deborah

1961

1 David	1 Mary
2 Michael	2 Lisa
3 John	3 Susan
4 James	4 Maria
5 Robert	5 Karen
6 Mark	6 Linda
7 William	7 Patricia
8 Richard	8 Donna
9 Thomas	9 Sandra
10 Kenneth,	10 Brenda
Steven	
(tie)	

1962

1 Michael	1 Lisa
2 John	2 Mary
3 David	3 Maria
4 Robert	4 Karen
5 James	5 Susan
6 Mark	6 Linda
7 William	7 Patricia
8 Richard	8 Donna
9 Thomas	9 Cynthia
10 Jeffrey	10 Debra

1963

1 David	1 Lisa
2 John,	2 Mary
Michael	3 Maria
(tie)	

4 James
5 Robert
6 Mark
7 Richard,
  William
  (tie)
9 Thomas
10 Kevin

4 Susan
5 Karen
6 Patricia
7 Linda
8 Donna

9 Sandra
10 Deborah

1964

1 Michael	1 Lisa
2 John	2 Mary
3 David	3 Maria
4 Robert	4 Susan
5 James	5 Karen
6 Mark	6 Patricia
7 William	7 Donna
8 Richard	8 Linda
9 Thomas	9 Kimberly
10 Joseph	10 Elizabeth

1965

1 Michael	1 Lisa
2 James	2 Maria
3 John	3 Karen
4 David	4 Mary
5 Robert	5 Kimberly
6 William	6 Susan
7 Richard	7 Patricia
8 Mark	8 Cynthia
9 Thomas	9 Linda
10 Jeffrey	10 Donna

1966

1 Michael	1 Lisa

2 David	2 Maria
3 John	3 Mary
4 James	4 Kimberly
5 Robert	5 Michelle
6 William	6 Patricia
7 Richard	7 Susan
8 Mark	8 Karen
9 Thomas	9 Sandra
10 Jeffrey	10 Deborah,
Elizabeth
(tie)

1967

1 Michael	1 Lisa
2 David	2 Maria
3 James	3 Kimberly
4 John	4 Michelle
5 Robert	5 Mary
6 William	6 Karen
7 Mark	7 Susan
8 Richard	8 Angela
9 Jeffrey	9 Melissa
10 Christopher	10 Jennifer

1968

1 Michael	1 Lisa
2 David	2 Michelle
3 James	3 Kimberly
4 John	4 Maria
5 Robert	5 Jennifer
6 William	6 Melissa
7 Mark	7 Tammy
8 Christopher	8 Angela
9 Richard	9 Mary
10 Brian	10 Susan

1969

1 Michael	1 Lisa
2 David	2 Jennifer
3 John	3 Michelle
4 Robert	4 Kimberly
5 James	5 Maria
6 William	6 Melissa
7 Richard	7 Amy
8 Christopher	8 Mary
9 Mark	9 Elizabeth
10 Brian	10 Karen

1970

1 Michael	1 Jennifer
2 David	2 Lisa
3 John	3 Kimberly
4 James	4 Michelle
5 Robert	5 Angela
6 Christopher	6 Maria
7 William	7 Amy
8 Mark	8 Melissa
9 Richard	9 Mary
10 Brian	10 Tracy

1971

1 Michael	1 Jennifer
2 John	2 Michelle
3 David	3 Lisa
4 James	4 Kimberly
5 Robert	5 Angela
6 Christopher	6 Amy
7 William	7 Maria
8 Jason	8 Melissa
9 Brian	9 Mary
10 Scott	10 Christine

1972

1 Michael	1 Jennifer
2 Christopher	2 Michelle
3 David	3 Lisa
4 John	4 Angela
5 James	5 Kimberly
6 Robert	6 Amy
7 Jason	7 Maria
8 Brian	8 Melissa
9 William	9 Heather
10 Matthew	10 Nicole

1973

1 Michael	1 Jennifer
2 Christopher	2 Michelle
3 James	3 Amy
4 Jason	4 Lisa
5 Robert	5 Kimberly
6 David	6 Maria
7 John	7 Angela
8 Brian	8 Melissa
9 William	9 Heather
10 Daniel	10 Stephanie

1974

1 Michael	1 Jennifer
2 Jason	2 Amy
3 Christopher	3 Michelle
4 David	4 Angela
5 James	5 Kimberly
6 John	6 Heather
7 Robert	7 Lisa
8 Brian	8 Melissa
9 William	9 Maria
10 Daniel	10 Stephanie

1975

1 Michael	1 Jennifer
2 Christopher	2 Amy
3 Jason	3 Michelle
4 David	4 Heather
5 James, Robert (tie)	5 Angela
	6 Melissa
7 John	7 Kimberly
8 Brian	8 Lisa
9 Matthew	9 Maria
10 Daniel, William (tie)	10 Stephanie

1976

1 Michael	1 Jennifer
2 Jason	2 Amy
3 Christopher	3 Melissa
4 David	4 Heather
5 John	5 Michelle
6 James	6 Angela
7 Robert	7 Jessica
8 Brian	8 Lisa
9 Matthew	9 Maria
10 Joseph	10 Kimberly

1977

1 Michael	1 Jennifer
2 Jason	2 Amy
3 Christopher	3 Melissa
4 David, James (tie)	4 Heather
	5 Jessica
6 John	6 Michelle
7 Robert	7 Angela
8 Brian	8 Kelly
9 Matthew	9 Sarah
10 Joseph	10 Amanda

1978

1 Michael	1 Jennifer
2 Jason	2 Jessica
3 Christopher	3 Melissa
4 David	4 Heather
5 James	5 Amy
6 John	6 Sarah
7 Robert	7 Angela
8 Matthew	8 Amanda
9 Brian	9 Michelle
10 Joseph	10 Elizabeth

1979

1 Michael	1 Jennifer
2 Jason	2 Melissa
3 Christopher	3 Amanda
4 David	4 Jessica
5 James	5 Sarah
6 Matthew	6 Amy
7 Robert	7 Heather
8 John	8 Angela, Kimberly (tie)
9 Joshua	
10 Daniel	10 Michelle

1980

1 Michael	1 Jennifer
2 Jason	2 Jessica
3 Christopher	3 Amanda
4 David	4 Melissa

5 James	5 Sarah
6 Matthew	6 Nicole
7 John	7 Heather
8 Joshua	8 Amy
9 Robert	9 Michelle
10 Daniel	10 Elizabeth

1981

1 Michael	1 Jennifer
2 Christopher	2 Jessica
3 Jason	3 Amanda
4 Matthew	4 Melissa
5 David	5 Sarah
6 Joshua	6 Nicole
7 James	7 Elizabeth
8 John	8 Michelle
9 Robert	9 Amy
10 Daniel	10 Stephanie

1982

1 Michael	1 Jennifer
2 Christopher	2 Jessica
3 Matthew	3 Amanda
4 Jason	4 Sarah
5 James	5 Melissa
6 David	6 Michelle
7 John	7 Nicole
8 Joshua	8 Elizabeth
9 Justin	9 Crystal
10 Robert	10 Amy

1983

| 1 Michael | 1 Jennifer |
| 2 Christopher | 2 Jessica |

3 Matthew	3 Ashley
4 David	4 Amanda
5 Daniel	5 Sarah
6 Jason	6 Melissa
7 James	7 Nicole
8 Robert	8 Elizabeth
9 Joshua	9 Stephanie
10 Joseph	10 Heather

1984

1 Michael	1 Jennifer
2 Christopher	2 Jessica
3 Matthew	3 Ashley
4 Joshua	4 Amanda
5 David	5 Sarah
6 Daniel	6 Stephanie
7 James	7 Nicole
8 Robert	8 Elizabeth
9 John	9 Heather
10 Ryan	10 Melissa

1985

1 Michael	1 Jessica
2 Christopher	2 Ashley
3 Matthew	3 Jennifer
4 Joshua	4 Amanda
5 David	5 Nicole
6 Daniel	6 Sarah
7 James	7 Stephanie
8 Joseph	8 Heather
9 Robert	9 Melissa
10 John	10 Elizabeth

1986

| 1 Michael | 1 Jessica |

2 Christopher	2 Ashley
3 Matthew	3 Amanda
4 Joshua	4 Jennifer
5 David	5 Sarah
6 Daniel	6 Stephanie
7 Andrew	7 Brittany
8 James	8 Heather
9 Robert	9 Elizabeth, Megan (tie)
10 John	

1987

1 Michael	1 Jessica
2 Christopher	2 Ashley
3 Matthew	3 Amanda
4 Joshua	4 Jennifer
5 Andrew	5 Sarah
6 Daniel	6 Stephanie
7 David	7 Nicole
8 Justin	8 Brittany
9 James	9 Elizabeth
10 Robert	10 Heather

1988

1 Michael	1 Ashley
2 Christopher	2 Jessica
3 Matthew	3 Amanda
4 Joshua	4 Jennifer
5 David	5 Brittany
6 Daniel	6 Sarah
7 Andrew	7 Stephanie
8 Justin	8 Samantha
9 Robert	9 Heather
10 Joseph	10 Elizabeth

1989

1 Michael	1 Jessica

2 Christopher	2 Ashley
3 Joshua	3 Amanda, Brittany (tie)
4 Matthew	
5 David	5 Sarah
6 Daniel	6 Jennifer
7 Andrew	7 Stephanie
8 Joseph	8 Samantha
9 Justin	9 Elizabeth
10 John	10 Lauren

1990

1 Michael	1 Jessica
2 Christopher	2 Ashley
3 Joshua	3 Brittany
4 Matthew	4 Amanda
5 David	5 Stephanie
6 Daniel	5 Jennifer
7 Andrew	7 Samantha
8 Joseph	8 Sarah
9 Justin	9 Megan
10 James	10 Lauren

1991

1 Michael	1 Ashley
2 Christopher	2 Jessica
3 Matthew	3 Amanda
4 Joshua	4 Brittany
5 Daniel	5 Stephanie
6 Andrew	6 Samantha
7 Robert	7 Sarah
8 David, Nicholas (tie)	8 Elizabeth
	9 Jennifer
10 James, William (tie)	10 Megan

1992

1 Michael	1 Jessica
2 Christopher	2 Ashley
3 Joshua	3 Sarah
4 Matthew	4 Brittany
5 Brandon	5 Amanda
6 Andrew	6 Samantha
7 Daniel	7 Emily
8 Joseph	8 Elizabeth
9 Tyler	9 Jennifer
10 David	10 Stephanie

1993

1 Michael	1 Jessica
2 Christopher	2 Ashley
3 Joshua	3 Sarah
4 Matthew	4 Taylor
5 Daniel	5 Emily
6 Tyler	6 Samantha
7 Andrew	7 Brittany
8 David,	8 Amanda
Ryan (tie)	9 Rachel
10 Jacob	10 Lauren

1994

1 Michael	1 Jessica
2 Matthew	2 Ashley
3 Christopher	3 Emily
4 Joshua	4 Samantha
5 Zachary	5 Sarah
6 Nicholas	6 Brittany
7 Daniel	7 Amanda
8 Jacob	8 Taylor
9 Tyler	9 Elizabeth
10 Brandon	10 Nicole

1995

1 Michael	1 Emily
2 Jacob	2 Ashley
3 Matthew	3 Jessica
4 Joshua	4 Sarah
5 Christopher	5 Samantha
6 Daniel	6 Taylor
7 Nicholas	7 Amanda
8 Tyler	8 Brittany
9 Brandon	9 Elizabeth
10 Austin	10 Rachel

1996

1 Michael	1 Emily
2 Matthew	2 Jessica
3 Jacob	3 Ashley
4 Joshua	4 Sarah
5 Christopher	5 Samantha
6 Daniel	6 Taylor
7 Nicholas	7 Hannah
8 Andrew,	8 Rachel
Tyler (tie)	9 Alexis
10 Joseph	10 Megan

1997

1 Michael	1 Emily
2 Jacob	2 Sarah
3 Matthew	3 Taylor
4 Christopher	4 Jessica
5 Nicholas	5 Ashley
6 Austin	6 Samantha
7 Joshua	7 Madison
8 Andrew	8 Hannah
9 Joseph	9 Kayla
10 Brandon	10 Alexis

1998

1 Michael	1 Emily
2 Jacob	2 Hannah
3 Matthew	3 Samantha
4 Joshua	4 Ashley
5 Christopher	5 Sarah
6 Nicholas	6 Alexis
7 Brandon	7 Taylor
8 Tyler	8 Jessica
9 Andrew	9 Madison
10 Austin	10 Elizabeth

1999

1 Jacob	1 Emily
2 Michael	2 Hannah
3 Matthew	3 Alexis
4 Joshua	4 Samantha
5 Christopher	5 Sarah
6 Nicholas	6 Ashley
7 Andrew	7 Madison
8 Joseph	8 Taylor
9 Daniel	9 Jessica
10 Tyler	10 Elizabeth

2000

1 Jacob	1 Emily
2 Michael	2 Hannah
3 Matthew	3 Madison
4 Joshua	4 Ashley
5 Christopher	5 Sarah
6 Nicholas	6 Alexis
7 Andrew	7 Samantha
8 Joseph	8 Jessica
9 Daniel	9 Taylor
10 Tyler	10 Elizabeth

2001

1 Jacob	1 Emily
2 Michael	2 Madison
3 Matthew	3 Hannah
4 Joshua	4 Ashley
5 Christopher	5 Alexis
6 Nicholas	6 Samantha
7 Andrew	7 Sarah
8 Joseph	8 Abigail
9 Daniel	9 Elizabeth
10 William	10 Jessica

2002

1 Jacob	1 Emily
2 Michael	2 Madison
3 Joshua	3 Hannah
4 Matthew	4 Emma
5 Ethan	5 Alexis
6 Joseph	6 Ashley
7 Andrew	7 Abigail
8 Christopher	8 Sarah
9 Daniel	9 Samantha
10 Nicholas	10 Olivia

2003

1 Jacob	1 Emily
2 Michael	2 Emma
3 Joshua	3 Madison
4 Matthew	4 Hannah
5 Andrew	5 Olivia
6 Joseph	6 Abigail
7 Ethan	7 Alexis
8 Daniel	8 Ashley
9 Christopher	9 Elizabeth
10 Anthony	10 Samantha

3 THE INDEXES

...bound raging

...eal, Grete, Gretel, Gredel, Gr,
...er · Cassidy, Casidhe clever · Valentino,
...a sweet · Pakuna deer jumping downhill · Quem...
...reza, Terezinha summer harvest · Helenka light · Kons
...yuiska, Nadine hope · Marco, Marcos, Mario, Martin, Marti...
...oibeard, Riobart, Rupert bright fame · Tasanee beautiful view · C
...asper treasure · Xavier new house · Odelia, Odella, Odelina, Odelin...
..., Asia, Ashia, Asha lively · Krikor *Armenian form of Gregory* watchful · Antton
...asty name, bright moon · Alzbeta *Czechoslovakian form of Elizabeth* consecrat
...eous · Faith, Faithe, Fayth faithful · Burton, Burhtun lives in the fortified to...
...ngelique, Angela, Angilia, Ange, Angeline, Angelina, Angelika angel · Yoland...
...dant · Glen, Glenn, Glenna, Glennis, Glynnis, Glynis from the glen · Bren...
..., Diarmad free man · Lorelei, Lurline, Lurlina, Lurleen, Lurlene temptress · Konrad, K
...oralina, Coralin from the coral of the sea · Kora, Katakin, Katoka, Katica, Katus, Kot
...s leaving · Debora, Deborah, Debra, Devora, Devoria bee · Mayah, Maia, Michell...
...raim, Efrayim fruitful · Viktoria *Hungarian form of Victoria* victorious · Tardos bald · Sakar
...re, Maire, Mare, Maura, Mearr, Moira, Moya, Maurya, Muire, Mairona, Mairia b...
...Violet, Violetta flower · Rafaele, Raphael, Rafaello God has healed · Kaiya,
...Essie star · Pamela, Pammeli, Pamelina, Pameline, Pamella made of honey · '
...d · Meoquanee wears red · Kaliska coyote chasing deer · Pannoowau he li...
...na, Yasmine, Yasmeen, Yasmena sweet flower · Saeed, Said, Soroush h...
...Nahini total woman · Raanui sacred · Fatima abstain, name of pilgrimag
...a, Natyashenka born at Christmas · Nicolai, Nikita *Russian form of Nichola*
...npion · Evanna, Evina right-handed · Tira, Tyra land · Alan, Allan, Al'
...e hope · Wenceslaus, Wenceslava great glory · Boris, Borysko
...lation · Tia aunt, princess · Horacio *Spanish form of Horace* t'
...Rolf wolf · Fanny, Fannie, Frances, Francine, Fanc'
...ewitt heart and mind · Wolfgang wolf's way · '
...le with greatness · Lieu willow · Tuyet snow wl
...the sea · Tad, Tadd father · Catherine, Cathryn, (
...peaceful gift · Shelby from the ledge farm · Cary, C
...Damiane, Damia, Damiana untamed · Orson, Ourso
...s · Duhkha sorrowful · Sofiya, Sofiyko wisdom · Jia love...
...eli, Helja, Helli, Eila, Elina, Leena *Finnish form of Helen* (light) · V
...ey, Bromleah, Bromleigh, Bromly from the broom-covered me...

...ebora, D... ...a, Devor... ...Devi... ...vah, Am... ...Mi... ...ne, M... ...ale,
...n fruitful... ...ctori... ...*rian form for victori*... ...ictoricus... ...erdo... ...ald · Sakari swe... ...e stru...
...Mare, Ma... ...Me... ...M... ...a, M... ...rya, Muir... ...airo... ...Mairia bitter · Bra... ...laigh s
...loletta fl... ...· Ra... ...aele, Ra... ...llo God has... ...Kaya, Ka... ...yo fork... ...es · Akat...
...er · Pam... ...Pam... ...eli, P... ...i, Pa... ...line, Par... ...made of honey · Teren... ...ce, Te... ...st
...oquane... ...Kali... ...oyote chasing... ...awau he lies... ...· Kel...
...Yasmine... ...smen... ...Yasmer... ...wee... ...ed, Sa... ...oozyczka...
...hini total woman · Raanui sacred · Fatima abstain, name of pilgrimage site · Monica advisor · Fer
...talia, Natyashenka born at Christmas · Nicolai, Nikita *Russian form of Nicholas* victory of the people · Ya
...champion · Evanna, Evina right-handed · Tira, Tyra land · Alan, Allan, Allen, Alleyne handsome · Too
..., Nadine hope · Wenceslaus, Wenceslava great glory · Boris, Borysko fighter · Brigidia, Brigida *Spanis*
...a consolation · Tia aunt, princess · Horacio *Spanish form of Horace* timekeeper · Salbatore, Salvatore, Salv
...ncient · Rolf wolf · Fanny, Fannie, Frances, Francine, Fanchon, Franziska, Franze, Frantiska, Francoi
...· Hew, Hewitt heart and mind · Wolfgang wolf's way · Solada listener · Niran eternal · Hannah grace ·
...yr to rule with greatness · Lieu willow · Tuyet snow white · Tuan brilliant · Sang bright · Cordelia, Creide
...near the sea · Tad, Tadd father · Catherine, Cathryn, Catheryn, Cate innocent · Lora, Loretta small sag
...off peaceful gift · Shelby from the ledge farm · Cary, Carey from the river · Myrna, Merna, Mirna, Moina
..., Damiane, Damia, Damiana untamed · Orson, Ourson little bear · Azizah, Aziza cherished · Sabira, Sal
...s · Duhkha sorrowful · Sofiya, Sofiyko wisdom · Jia lovely and good · Li strength · Wen ornamental · Pan
...eli, Helja, Helli, Eila, Elina, Leena *Finnish form of Helen* (light) · Veli, Veikko, Veijo brother · Ada, Aida, Adda, Ad
..., Bromleah, Bromleigh, Bromly from the broom-covered meadow · Harlan, Harland from the hare's land
...ves · Ida, Idaia, Idna, Idalie active · Anton *German form of Anthony* beyond praise · Clovis, Chlodwig famous w
...oisa, Eloisee famous in war · Julie, Julia, Juliette, Juliet, Julietta, Julita youthful · Simone heard · Lance, i
...ly dwells at the ash-tree meadow · Farook, Farouk One who knows the truth · Gadara, Gadarine from th
...beak · Morgan, Morgance, Morgane, Morgana dweller of the sea · Mulan magnolia blossom · Josef God v
...ght · Ella, Elle beautiful fairy · Ralph, Ralf, Raff, Rolf, Rolfe red wolf · Susanna, Sanna lily · Karel, Karl, Kaarl
...tis strong and masculine · Deirdre, Deidra, Deardriu raging · Bernard, Bernon, Bernot, Barnard, Benat, Bai
...ardyn brave as a bear · Greta, Gretal, Grete, Gretel, Gredel, Gryta, Ghita, Gretchen pearl · Isaac, Izaak, Isa
...· Narayan moving water · Cassidy, Casidhe clever · Valentino, Valerio brave, strong · Hiroshi generous ·

REVERSE LOOKUP

Beautiful

Adabel, 360; Adah, 184; Adara, 156; Adbelle, 360; Addien, 382; Addiena, 382; Aglaia, 156; Alain, 134; Alaine, 215; Alana, 134, 215; Alane, 54; Alanna, 54, 134, 215; Alayne, 134, 215; Aldabella, 229; Alene, 54; Alina, 54, 134, 215, 297, 311; Aline, 54; Allene, 134, 215; Allyn, 134, 215; Amabel, 243; Amabella, 123, 243; Amabelle, 123, 243; Amabilis, 243; Apollo, 171, 261; Apoloniusz, 171, 298; Areta, 157; Arete, 157; Aretha, 157; Bela, 199; Belinda, 229; Belita, 342; Bella, 199, 245, 342; Belle, 199, 245; Berth, 382; Bonita, 342; Buthaynah, 31; Cadhla, 216; Calida, 158; Calisto, 304; Calla, 158; Calli, 158; Callie, 158; Callista, 158; Callula, 246; Caoimhe, 55, 216; Charis, 159; Cho, 241; Cinnia, 55; Cinnie, 55; Clarinda, 343; Dep, 379; Doreen, 160; Dubheasa, 217; Duvessa, 217; Fayre, 88; Frida, 286; Frieda, 286; Guri, 286; Hafwan, 385; Hasna, 32; Hermosa, 344; Hurit, 276; Husain, 35; Hussain, 35; Hussein, 35; Isabis, 17; Jaffa, 187; Jafit, 187; Jafita, 187; Jamila, 32, 79; Jamilah, 32; Jia, 64; Jolie, 126; Jun-Chhoun, 52; Keeley,

135; Keelia, 55; Keelin, 55; Keely, 55, 135, 218; Kennis, 135; Kennocha, 55; Kevay, 216; Krasava, 68; Lind, 147; Linda, 147, 253, 345; Lindie, 147; Lindy, 345; Lynda, 345; Lyndey, 345; Maribel, 188, 346; Maribella, 188; Maribelle, 188; Maysun, 32; Mee, 64; Mildri, 287; Mirabella, 127; Mirabelle, 127; My-Duyen, 379; Naava, 188; Naavah, 188; Nabelung, 18; Nani, 302; Narkeasha, 18; Niamh, 136; Olathe, 275; Omorose, 80; Oribel, 255; Oribella, 255; Oribelle, 255; Ragnfrid, 287; Ragni, 287; Ramya, 209; Randi, 287; Rut, 356; Shaina, 189; Shaine, 189; Shakila, 18; Shifra, 189; Siran, 40; Siroun, 40; Subha, 209; Turua, 302; Vashti, 294; Wasima, 33; Weeko, 279; Wyanet, 276; Yaffa, 191; Yaffit, 191; Yue, 65; Yue, 66; Yumi, 238; Zayna, 33; Zerlina, 365; Zi, 65; Zippora, 191; Zipporah, 191; Zuleika, 294; Zuri, 129; Zuria, 129; Zurie, 129

Beloved

Ai, 379; Aiko, 236; Amara, 243; Amare, 243; Amata, 229, 243, 342; Amato, 348; Anwell, 57, 386; Anwil, 386; Anwill, 386; Anwyl, 57, 386; Anwyll, 386; Armas,

120; Cara, 229; Caradoc, 57, 387, 388; Carina, 229; Carys, 383; Cheryl, 124; Craddock, 388; Cradoc, 388; Dabi, 193; Dafydd, 388; Dai, 384; Daibhidh, 139; Daithi, 223; Davet, 130; Davey, 193; Davi, 185, 193; David, 193, 357; Davida, 185, 247; Davide, 232; Davin, 193; Davina, 185; Davinah, 185; Davinia, 185; Davitah, 185; Davite, 185; Dawud, 34; Dewi, 388; Dodie, 186; Dragan, 338; Eiddwen, 384; Ema, 302; Femi, 17; Habib, 35, 193; Habiba, 31; Habibah, 78; Holda, 147; Holde, 147; Holle, 147; Hulda, 147; Hulde, 147; Jed, 194; Jedi, 194; Jedidiah, 194; Lal, 213; Leof, 26; Loefel, 97; Louvel, 131; Lovell, 97, 131; Lowe, 131; Lowell, 97, 131; Luvena, 90; Luvina, 90; Luvyna, 90; Lyfing, 97; Merna, 56, 219; Milan, 69; Milos, 69; Mirna, 56; Moina, 56; Morna, 56, 219; Moyna, 56; Myrna, 56, 136, 219; Olufemi, 80; Querida, 347; Rawiri, 273; Suki, 238; Supriya, 209; Taaveti, 196; Taavetti, 121; Taavi, 121, 196; Taffy, 395; Tahupotiki, 272; Tewi, 273; Thais, 168; Thandiwe, 18; Yedidiah, 197; Yedidyah, 197; Yerucham, 197

Brave

Adalard, 149, 366; Adalhard, 149; Adelard, 366; Adlar, 366; Adler, 366; Aethelhard, 91; Akins, 81; Alhhard, 91; Allard, 91; Amos, 192; Amnchadh, 220; Anmcha, 220; Balen, 262; Balendin, 262; Bealantin, 137; Berta, 199; Bertuska, 199; Caci, 135; Caflice, 24; Casey, 57, 135, 138, 216; Cathasach, 135, 138, 216; Connacht, 223; Connolly, 223; Donnally, 58; Donnelly, 58; Ealhhard, 95; Eallard, 95; Edel, 150; Eferhard, 95; Ellard, 95, 367; Enapay, 284; Ever, 95; Everard, 95, 368; Everhart, 77; Faddei, 314, 376; Fadey, 314, 376; Fadeyka, 314, 376; Fadeyushka, 376; Farrel, 59; Farrell, 59; Ferda, 69; Garcia, 350; Hardwin, 96; Hardwyn, 96; Heardwine, 96; Helmut, 151; Helmutt, 151; Jabari, 82; Kenway, 26, 97; Kim, 26; Kimball, 26; Kitchi, 281; Lander, 177; Leander, 177, 265; Leandra, 253; Leandro, 177, 309, 351; Leandros, 265; Len, 370; Lennart, 358, 370; Lenya, 315; Leo, 265; Leoarrie, 253; Leocadie, 131; Leodegrance, 131; Leodora, 253; Leoine, 253; Leoline, 253; Leon, 131, 265, 351; Leona, 126, 253;

Tivadar, 181, 202; Todor, 181; Tolek, 300; Tuder, 181; Tudor, 181, 395; Vanechka, 315; Vania, 190, 313; Vanna, 190; Vanya, 313; Vanyusha, 315; Yan, 197; Yannis, 197; Yehoash, 197; Yehonadov, 197; Yoana, 348; Zane, 197; Zaneta, 191, 313; Zani, 197; Zanna, 191; Zebadiah, 197; Zebediah, 197

Gentle
Ai, 379; Adiva, 31; Anana, 17; Caoimhe, 55, 216; Caoimhghin, 57; Dalila, 78, 343; Damara, 160; Damaris, 160; Diu, 379; Halim, 35; Halima, 17, 32, 78; Hien, 379, 380; Kelemen, 201; Kellman, 201; Kevay, 216; Kyung-Soon, 241; Lateef, 82; Lateefah, 18; Latif, 35; Latifa, 32; Latifah, 32; Madhur, 208; Malinda, 164; Melinda, 164; Metea, 165; Shu, 65; Sopheap, 52; Stilleman, 100; Stillman, 28, 100; Stillmann, 100; Tirion, 386

Grace
Ana, 184; Anabal, 134; Anabel, 244; Anabella, 244; Anais, 184; Analise, 184; Anata, 229; Ance, 184; Anci, 199; Ane, 184; Anechka, 311; Aneta, 184, 376; Anetta, 184; Ani, 272; Ania, 297; Anica, 184, 342; Anice, 330; Anichka, 184, 376; Anicka, 68; Anika, 76, 185; Aniki, 185; Aniko, 185; Anita,

184, 229, 342, 376; Anitchka, 311; Anitia, 342; Anitra, 184; Anja, 119; Anka, 184, 297; Anke, 76; Anki, 76; Anku, 184; Ann, 184; Anna, 68, 119, 184, 229, 311, 354; Annabel, 134, 330; Annabella, 134, 330; Annabelle, 134, 244; Annabla, 216; Annaliese, 184, 316; Annalisa, 184; Annata, 229; Anne, 119, 184; Anneli, 119; Anneliese, 184; Annette, 184; Anni, 119; Annie, 184; Annika, 354; Annike, 354; Annikka, 185; Annikke, 185; Annikki, 119, 185; Annora, 184; Annorah, 184; Annukka, 119; Anny, 184; Annze, 184; Anora, 184; Antje, 184; Anu, 119; Anya, 311; Anyuta, 184; Asenka, 184, 311; Asenke, 184; Asya, 184; Ayn, 184; Caoimhe, 55, 216; Chana, 185; Chanah, 185; Charis, 159; Cherise, 159; Eithne, 217; Elu, 280; Engracia, 343; Ethna, 217; Gechina, 50, 344; Ghada, 31; Gloriana, 88; Gloriane, 88; Glorianna, 88; Graca, 250, 305; Grace, 88, 250; Gracia, 88, 250, 344; Graciana, 250, 344; Gracie, 88; Graciene, 250; Gracinha, 250; Grainne, 135, 218; Grata, 250; Gratia, 250; Gratina, 250; Grazia, 230, 250; Grazina, 186; Grazinia, 186; Grazyna, 186, 297; Hajna, 199; Hanan, 193; Hea, 241;

Hubbard, 151; Hulbard, 151; Hulbart, 151; Hulbert, 151; Huldiberaht, 151; Ionanna, 187; Keavy, 218; Kevay, 216; Kieu, 379; Linette, 56; Linnette, 56; Lynet, 56; Lynette, 56; Magaskawee, 279; Mara, 200; Marcsa, 200; Marianna, 200; Marika, 200; Martuska, 200; Nainsi, 188, 219; Nan, 188; Nana, 188; Nancsi, 188, 200; Nancy, 188; Nanelia, 188; Nanelle, 188; Nanetta, 188; Nanette, 188; Nanine, 188; Nanna, 188, 355; Nannie, 188; Nanny, 188; Nanon, 127; Neta, 188; Nin, 188; Nina, 188, 313; Ninacska, 188, 200; Ninette, 127; Ninockha, 313; Ninon, 127; Nita, 188; Nusa, 188, 200; Nusi, 188, 200; Nyura, 376; Ona, 189; Onit, 189; Rae, 335; Rahimat, 37; Rahimateh, 32; Ray, 335; Rexana, 257; Rexanna, 257; Rexanne, 257; Ting, 65; Vanka, 313; Vanni, 231; Zarifa, 33; Zi, 65

Happiness
Ada, 86, 145, 360; Adabel, 360; Adbelle, 360; Adda, 86; Addo, 366; Adia, 86; Agalia, 156; Aida, 86; Alair, 260; Asher, 192; Bliss, 21, 24, 87, 92; Bliths, 87; Dakarai, 19, 81; Farah, 294; Feleta, 249; Felice, 230, 249, 264; Felicia, 125, 249; Felician, 264; Felicidade, 305; Felicienne, 125; Felicio, 264;

Felicitas, 249; Felicity, 125, 249; Feliks, 264, 299, 314; Felisa, 249; Felise, 249; Felita, 249; Felix, 264, 357; Filicia, 125; Glad, 88; Gleda, 88; Gil, 193; Gili, 193; Gilli, 193; Hana, 31; Hilaire, 126; Hilaria, 250; Hilario, 290, 350; Hilarion, 264; Hilary, 250, 264; Hillary, 250, 264; Hillery, 264; Hiolair, 218; Jocelin, 252; Jocelyn, 88, 252; Jocelyne, 88; Joscelin, 252; Josceline, 88; Joscelyne, 88; Joy, 252; Joyce, 252; Laetitia, 218; Laetizia, 345; Lanassa, 312; Lara, 312; Larisa, 312; Larissa, 164, 253, 312; Larisse, 164; Leitis, 136; Leta, 253; Leticia, 305; Letitia, 253; Letizia, 230; Lettie, 253; Letty, 253; Lita, 253; Lititia, 345; Mab, 218; Mabbina, 218; Macario, 351; Meadhbh, 218; Meadhra, 225; Meara, 218, 225; Merry, 90; Nara, 136; Oseye, 80; Ostein, 290; Osten, 290; Oysten, 290; Peli, 267; Pellikita, 256; Pellkita, 256; Rada, 337; Radek, 70; Rafa, 32; Saeed, 295; Said, 295; Saidah, 18; Shahdi, 294; Soroush, 295; Soroushi, 294; Tait, 23, 90, 100, 292, 326, 359; Taite, 23; Tarub, 33; Tate, 23, 90, 100; Tatum, 90; Tayt, 100; Tayte, 23, 90, 100, 292; Trix, 258; Trixie, 258; Trixy, 258; Xin, 65; Yi, 65; Zelig, 154; Zorian, 270; Zorion, 51

THE INDEXES

REVERSE LOOKUP

INDEX

Aeacus, 169; Aeaea, 156; Aeccestane, 92; Aedd, 386; Aedon, 156; Aedre, 21; Aeetes, 169, 260; Aefentid, 21; Aefre, 21; Aegaea, 243; Aegaeus, 260; Aegates, 243; Aegea, 156; Aegelmaere, 92; Aegelweard, 92; Aegeria, 248; Aegeus, 169, 260; Aegides, 260; Aegileif, 316; Aegina, 156, 243; Aeginae, 243; Aegir, 288; Aegis, 169; Aegisthus, 169, 260; Aegyptus, 169, 260; Aeldra, 86, 91; Aelfdane, 91; Aelfdene, 91; Aelfraed, 86, 91; Aelfric, 92; Aelfwine, 86; Aelle, 23; Aello, 156; Aelwyd, 382; Aeneades, 260; Aeneas, 169, 260; Aenedleah, 91; Aenescumb, 91; Aengus, 56, 220, 332; Aeolia, 243; Aeolius, 260; Aeolus, 169, 260; Aerlene, 22; Aerwyna, 87; Aescby, 102; Aeschylus, 260; Aesclapius, 260; Aescleah, 92; Aesclin, 92; Aesctun, 92; Aesculapius, 169, 260; Aescwine, 92; Aescwyn, 92; Aesire, 288; Aesoburne, 102; Aeson, 169, 260; Aethelbald, 23; Aethelbeorht, 95; Aethelbeorn, 91; Aethelberht, 91; Aethelbert, 23, 91; Aethelflaed, 21; Aethelfrith, 23; Aethelhard, 91; Aethelhere, 23; Aethelisdun, 91; Aethelmaer, 91; Aethelmaere, 92; Aethelred, 23; Aethelreda, 88; Aethelstan, 24; Aethelstun, 91; Aethelthryth, 21; Aethelweard, 92; Aethelwine, 86; Aethelwulf, 23; Aethelwyne, 86; Aetheston, 91; Aethiops, 260; Aethlem, 386; Aethra, 156; Aethretun, 102; Aetna, 156; Aevar, 320; Affrica, 134; Afi, 288; Afonso, 307; Afra, 184; Afraima, 31; Afric, 54, 215; Africa, 54, 134, 215; Afrodille, 123; Agacia, 341; Agafia, 156, 311; Agalaia, 156; Agalia, 156; Agamedes, 169; Agamemnon, 169; Agape, 156; Agastya, 209; Agata, 156, 215, 229, 341, 354; Agate, 156, 215; Agatha, 145, 156; Agathe, 123, 145; Agathi, 156; Agaton, 354; Agaue, 156; Agave, 156; Agda, 354; Age, 288; Agenor, 170, 260; Ager, 51, 191; Agestes, 169; Aggie, 199; Aghaderg, 220; Aghadreena, 215; Aghamora, 215; Aghamore, 220; Aghaveagh, 215; Aghavilla, 215; Aghna, 215; Aghy, 220; Agi, 199; Agiefan, 23; Agilard, 366; Agilberht, 23; Aglaeca, 23; Aglaia, 156; Aglaral, 44; Aglarale, 44; Aglauros, 156; Aglaval, 44; Agna, 156; Agnek, 156; Agnella, 156, 229; Agnes, 156; Agnese, 156, 229, 341; Agnessa, 311; Agneta, 72, 156, 354; Agneya, 209; Agni, 212; Agnimukha, 209; Agostinho, 307; Agosto, 232; Agoston, 200, 261; Agotha, 156, 199; Agoti, 199; Agrafina, 243, 311; Agrafine, 243; Agramant, 129; Agravain, 44; Agrican, 129; Agrippa, 260; Agrippina, 243; Agrippinae, 243; Agueda, 156, 341; Aguistin, 220; Agurtzane, 50, 341; Agustin, 348; Agyfen, 23; Agymah, 80; Ahalya, 204; Ahana, 215; Ahane, 220; Ahanu, 280; Ahasferus, 386; Ahava, 184; Ahave, 184; Ahearn, 56, 220; Aheawan, 23; Ahebban, 23; Aherin, 137; Ahern, 56, 137, 220;

Aherne, 137; Ahiga, 283; Ahiliya, 282; Ahisma, 207; Ahmed, 34; Ahmik, 279; Ahote, 282; Ahreddan, 23; Ahren, 149, 366; Ahriman, 129, 209; Ahtunowhiho, 281; Ahuda, 184; Ahura Mazda, 294; Ahuva, 184; Ai, 236, 379; Aibne, 331; Aibrean, 215; Aibreann, 215; Aichlin, 220; Aickin, 91; Aida, 86, 123, 229, 341; Aidan, 23, 134, 137, 215; Aideen, 215; Aiden, 137; Aidia, 341; Aidoios, 156; Aidrian, 220; Aife, 54; Aifric, 54, 215; Aiglentina, 123; Aiglentine, 123; Aigneis, 54, 134, 156, 215; Aiken, 23, 91; Aikin, 91; Aiko, 236; Ail, 332; Aila, 119, 330; Ailat, 184; Ailbe, 56, 149, 215; Ailbert, 332; Ailean, 137, 332; Aileana, 330; Aileen, 215, 330; Ailein, 332; Ailen, 137; Ailey, 215; Ailfrid, 220; Aili, 119, 145, 215; Ailia, 215; Ailidh, 54; Ailill, 56; Ailin, 137, 220; Ailis, 54, 134, 145, 215, 217; Ailisa, 215; Ailise, 215; Aillig, 332; Ailsa, 72, 184, 330, 360; Ailse, 145; Ailsie, 184; Aimee, 123; Aimery, 366; Aimil, 134; Aimiliana, 360; Aimilionia, 360; Aimon, 366; Ain, 78, 91; Aina, 54, 354; Aindreas, 137, 170, 220, 332; Aindriu, 170; Aine, 54, 134, 215; Aineislis, 220; Aingeal, 54, 215; Aingealag, 134; Aingeru, 51; Ainhoa, 50, 341; Ainhoe, 341; Ainmire, 220; Aino, 119; Ainsley, 91, 330, 332; Ainslie, 91; Ainsworth, 101; Aintzane, 50, 341; Airavata, 209; Airdsgainne, 137; Airell, 56; Airla, 156; Airleas, 134, 137, 216, 220; Airlia, 156; Aisha, 31; A'ishah, 31; Aisley, 21, 86, 92; Aislin, 215; Aisling, 215; Aislinn, 215; Aisly, 21; Aissa, 17; Aiston, 92; Aitan, 18, 191; Aithne, 54; Aitziber, 50, 341; Aiya, 185; Aiyana, 274; Aja, 209; Ajani, 18; Ajax, 170, 260; Ajaya, 207; Aka, 272; Akahata, 238, 272; Akakia, 156; Akako, 236; Akando, 279; Akantha, 156; Akash, 209; Akbar, 34; Ake, 288, 356; Akecheta, 284; Akenehi, 272; Akhenaten, 80; Aki, 120; Akiba, 184, 191; Akibe, 184; Akiiki, 80; Akil, 34, 51, 80, 170; Akila, 31, 78; Akilah, 31; Akilina, 244, 311; Akim, 191; Akina, 236; Akins, 81; Akio, 238; Akir, 331; Akira, 238, 330; Akiva, 184, 191; Akiyama, 238; Akker, 101; Akona, 272; Akram, 34; Aksana, 311; Aksel, 150, 192; Akshamala, 204; Akshobhya, 209; Akub, 191; Akule, 279; Alabhaois, 220; Alacoque, 123; Aladdin, 34; Alai, 137; Alaida, 243; Alain, 44, 129, 134; Alaine, 215; Alair, 260; Alajos, 366; Alake, 18; Al'alim, 34; Alameda, 274, 341; Alan, 56, 220, 332; Alana, 134, 215; Alane, 54; Alanna, 54, 134, 215; Alano, 348; Alanson, 56; Alaois, 366; Alaqua, 274; Alard, 366; Alaric, 149, 366; Alarica, 145, 360; Alarice, 145, 360; Alaricia, 360; Alarick, 149; Alarico, 348; Alarik, 149; Alasdair, 170, 332; Alastair, 170, 332; Alaster, 137; Alastor, 170; Alastrina, 54, 215; Alastrine, 54; Alastriona, 54, 215; Alatea, 156, 341; Alawa, 276; Alawn, 386; Alayne, 134, 215;

Alazne, 50, 341; Alba, 243; Alban, 220, 260; Albanact, 332; Albano, 260; Albanwr, 386; Albaric, 129; Alber, 366; Alberic, 366; Alberich, 320; Alberik, 356; Albern, 91, 366; Albert, 91, 149, 200, 356, 366; Alberta, 86, 145, 199, 360; Alberte, 360; Alberteen, 86; Albertina, 86, 123, 145, 341, 360; Albertine, 86, 123, 145, 341, 360; Alberto, 348; Albertyna, 86; Albertyne, 86, 145; Albin, 260, 298; Albina, 243; Albinia, 229, 243; Albinka, 297; Albinus, 23, 260; Albion, 44, 260; Albiona, 42; Albracca, 123; Albrecht, 149; Albula, 243; Albunea, 243; Alburn, 91; Alburt, 91; Albus, 260; Alcaeus, 260; Alcamene, 243; Alcestis, 156; Alchfrith, 23; Alcibiades, 260; Alcides, 260; Alcimede, 243; Alcina, 123, 156; Alcinoos, 170; Alcinous, 170, 260; Alcippe, 156; Alcippee, 243; Alcmaeon, 170; Alcmena, 243; Alcmene, 156; Alcott, 101; Alcuin, 366; Alcumena, 243; Alcyone, 156, 162; Alcyoneus, 170; Ald, 149; Alda, 145, 360; Aldabella, 229; Aldan, 91; Aldara, 156; Aldea, 360; Alden, 23, 91; Alder, 101; Aldercy, 86; Aldfrith, 23; Aldhelm, 23; Aldin, 23; Aldis, 86, 101; Aldo, 91, 149, 232, 366; Aldona, 145, 297; Aldonsa, 341; Aldonza, 341; Aldora, 86, 156; Aldous, 101, 366; Aldred, 23, 91; Aldric, 91; Aldrich, 91, 129, 366; Aldrick, 129; Aldrid, 91; Aldridge, 366; Aldrik, 91, 150; Aldtun, 91; Aldus, 101; Aldwin, 91; Aldwine, 91; Aldwyn, 23, 91; Aldys, 86; Alec, 170; Alecta, 156; Aled, 386; Aleda, 86, 145; Aleeza, 184; Aleezah, 184; Alegria, 341; Alejandra, 341; Alejandrina, 341; Alejandro, 348; Alek, 314; Aleka, 156; Aleksander, 298, 376; Aleksandr, 170, 314; Aleksandra, 311, 376; Aleksandur, 170; Aleksanteri, 120; Aleksi, 120, 314; Aleksia, 72; Aleksis, 314; Aleksy, 170, 298; Alemannus, 149; Alena, 156, 311; Alene, 54; Aler, 101; Alera, 243; Aleria, 243; Alerio, 260; Aleris, 156; Alerissa, 156; Aleron, 129, 260; Alesandere, 156; Alesandese, 50; Aleser, 34; Aleshanee, 274; Alesia, 156; Alessandra, 229; Alessandro, 170, 232; Aleta, 86, 243, 341; Aletea, 341; Alethea, 156; Aletheia, 156; Alethia, 156; Aletia, 341; Aletta, 229, 243; Alex, 170; Alexa, 156, 199; Alexander, 170, 356; Alexandina, 156; Alexandra, 156, 199, 311, 354; Alexandras, 170; Alexandre, 44, 129, 243; Alexandrea, 243; Alexandria, 243; Alexandriana, 243; Alexandrina, 243; Alexandrine, 123, 243; Alexandros, 170; Alexandrukas, 170; Alexei, 170, 314; Alexia, 156; Alexina, 156, 243; Alexine, 156, 243; Alexio, 170; Alexis, 123, 156, 170, 243; Aleyn, 44; Alf, 288, 356; Alfarin, 320; Alfarinn, 320; Alfdis, 286; Alfgeir, 288; Alfons, 356; Alfonsa, 341, 360; Alfonsine, 145; Alfonso, 149, 348, 356, 366; Alford, 91; Alfred, 23, 91, 356, 366;

Alfreda, 86, 341, 360; Alfredo, 91, 232; Alfrida, 86; Alfrieda, 360; Alfrigg, 320; Alfrothul, 288; Algar, 23; Alger, 23, 149, 366; Algernon, 129; Algiana, 360; Algiane, 360; Algoma, 274; Algot, 354; Algrenon, 129; Alhhard, 91; Alhmarric, 149; Alhraed, 86; Alhric, 92; Alhrick, 92; Alhrik, 92; Alhsom, 149; Alhwin, 149; Ali, 31, 34; Alias, 376; Alice, 54, 145, 360; Alicea, 360; Aliceson, 91; Alicia, 145, 156, 341, 354, 360; Alicides, 170; Alida, 145, 243; Alik, 314; Alika, 303; Alim, 34; Alima, 31; Alina, 54, 134, 156, 215, 297, 311, 360; Aline, 54, 360; Alirick, 366; Alis, 44; Alisa, 229, 360; Alison, 91, 145, 216, 360, 366; Alissa, 360; Alisz, 145, 199; Alita, 86, 123, 341; Alithia, 360; Alitza, 184; Alix, 170, 360; Alixandre, 44; Aliya, 31; Aliz, 145, 199; Aliza, 184; Alizah, 184; Alka, 208, 297; All, 91; Alla, 311; Allan, 56, 220, 332; Allard, 91, 366; Allegra, 123, 229, 341; Allen, 56, 220, 332; Allene, 134, 215; Allete, 123; Alleyne, 220, 332; Allighiero, 232; Allis, 360; Allison, 216, 360, 366; Allister, 137; Allochka, 311; Allona, 184; Allonia, 184; Allred, 91; Allsun, 216; Allura, 86; Allyn, 56, 134, 215; Allys, 360; Alma, 54, 216, 243, 341, 354; Almedha, 382; Almer, 92; Almeta, 72, 243; Almira, 31, 341; Almo, 91; Almon, 191; Almund, 23; Almunda, 341; Almundena, 341; Almundina, 341; Alo, 282; Alodia, 21; Alodie, 21; Aloeus, 170; Aloin, 129; Alois, 149, 260; Aloisia, 146; Alon, 191; Alona, 50, 184, 341; Alonia, 184; Alonsa, 146, 341; Alonso, 348, 366; Alonza, 229, 360; Alonzo, 348, 366; Alosaka, 282; Aloyoshenka, 314; Aloys, 366; Aloysha, 314; Aloysia, 146, 360; Aloysius, 260, 366; Alpha, 157; Alphenor, 170; Alpheus, 170; Alphonsa, 360; Alphonse, 366; Alphonsine, 145; Alphonso, 149, 366; Alphonsus, 220; Alphonza, 360; Alphosina, 360; Alphosine, 360; Alpin, 332; Alpina, 330; Alric, 366; Alrigo, 232, 366; Alrik, 149, 356, 366; Alroy, 137, 220, 260; Alsandair, 220; Alson, 91; Alsoomse, 276; Alston, 91; Alta, 243; Altair, 31, 34; Altaira, 31; Alter, 191; Altha, 86; Althaea, 157; Althaia, 156; Althea, 157; Altheda, 86, 157; Althia, 86; Altman, 149, 366; Altmann, 149; Alton, 91; Altsoba, 278; Aluin, 129; Aluino, 348; Alula, 31; Auld, 243; Aluma, 184; Alumit, 184; Alun, 386; Alura, 86; Alurea, 86; Alva, 76, 146, 192, 243, 260, 342; Alvan, 366; Alvar, 146, 260, 356; Alvara, 146; Alvarie, 146; Alvaro, 307; Alver, 260; Alvera, 360; Alverna, 360; Alvernia, 360; Alvie, 146; Alvin, 149, 366; Alvina, 86, 360; Alvinia, 243, 360; Alvira, 360; Alvis, 288; Alviss, 288; Alvita, 243; Alvord, 91; Alvy, 149, 216; Alvyn, 366; Alwalda, 23; Alwan, 366; Alwin, 23, 149, 366, 386; Alwyn, 366, 386; Alyce, 360; Alycesone, 91; Alyda, 145; Alyosha, 170; Alyoshenka, 170; Alys, 54, 145, 360; Alysia,

244; Argentina, 244; Argi, 50; Argia, 157; Argie, 157; Arglwydd, 386; Arglwyddes, 382; Argo, 171; Argoel, 382; Argolis, 244; Argos, 171; Argous, 244; Argraff, 382; Argus, 73, 171, 261; Argyle, 57, 332; Ari, 192; Aria, 86, 229, 361; Ariadna, 244; Ariadne, 157, 244; Arial, 382; Arian, 24, 382, 386; Ariana, 157, 244, 382; Ariane, 157; Arianrhod, 382; Arianrod, 21; Aric, 92, 149, 366; Aricia, 244; Aricin, 288; Arick, 149; Aridatha, 185; Arie, 192; Ariel, 185, 192; Ariela, 185; Arielle, 185; Ariellel, 185; Arien, 382; Ariene, 382; Arienh, 54, 134; Aries, 261; Arietta, 86; Ariette, 86; Arif, 34; Arik, 92, 149, 366; Ariki, 303; Arild, 288; Arilda, 361; Arilde, 361; Ariobarzanes, 261; Arion, 171, 192, 261; Aristaeus, 171; Aristid, 171; Aristodeme, 244; Aristoteles, 261; Aristotle, 171; Arje, 76; Arkadina, 311; Arkin, 288; Arkwright, 101; Arkyn, 288; Arlais, 382; Arlan, 57; Arlana, 54; Arland, 57; Arledge, 102; Arleen, 54, 216; Arleigh, 102; Arlen, 57, 137, 220; Arlena, 216; Arlene, 54, 216; Arles, 320; Arleta, 54, 216; Arlette, 54, 216, 361; Arley, 102; Arlice, 24; Arlie, 102; Arlin, 57; Arlina, 54; Arline, 54, 216; Arlo, 92, 348; Arlyn, 57, 220; Arlyne, 216; Arlys, 24; Arlyss, 24; Armada, 342; Arman, 314; Armand, 129, 150, 298; Armandek, 298; Armando, 232, 348, 366; Armanno, 232; Armas, 120; Armelle, 54; Armen, 40; Armenia, 244; Armenouhie, 40; Armes, 382; Armida, 244; Armilda, 361; Armilde, 361; Armilla, 244; Armin, 366; Armina, 146, 361; Armino, 366; Armod, 320; Armon, 192, 366; Armonno, 366; Armstrang, 102, 332; Armstrong, 102, 332; Arn, 356; Arna, 286; Arnald, 150; Arnalda, 146, 361; Arnaldo, 232, 366; Arnall, 150, 366; Arnatt, 92; Arnaud, 129, 150; Arnbjorg, 286; Arnd, 150; Arndell, 92; Arndis, 286; Arndt, 150; Arne, 76, 150, 244, 356; Arnell, 150; Arnet, 92, 150; Arnett, 92, 150; Arney, 150; Arngeir, 288; Arngrim, 288; Arnhold, 150; Arni, 150, 320; Arnlaug, 288; Arnljot, 288; Arno, 129, 150; Arnold, 150, 356, 366; Arnoldina, 361; Arnoll, 150; Arnon, 192; Arnora, 286; Arnot, 150; Arnott, 92, 150; Arnou, 129; Arnoux, 129; Arnt, 150; Arnthrud, 286; Arnwolf, 150; Aroghetto, 232; Aroha, 272; Aroldine, 361; Aroldo, 366; Aron, 191, 298, 356; Arons, 288; Aroon, 374; Arpad, 200; Arpan, 210; Arpana, 208; Arpiar, 40; Arrate, 50, 342; Arregaithel, 137, 332; Arridano, 129; Arrighetto, 366; Arrigo, 232, 366; Arrosa, 50, 244; Arrose, 244; Arruns, 261; Arsene, 171; Arsenio, 171; Arshavir, 40; Art, 57, 137, 221; Artair, 23, 332; Artaith, 382; Artaxiad, 40; Artegal, 220; Artemas, 171; Artemesio, 171; Artemia, 157; Artemis, 157; Artemisia, 157, 342;

Artemus, 171; Arth, 23; Arthes, 382; Arthgallo, 44, 92, 220; Arthur, 23, 44, 57, 386; Arthwr, 386; Artur, 57, 137, 221, 298, 356; Arturo, 57, 232, 348; Artus, 129; Arub, 31; Aruba, 31; Arun, 52, 209, 212; Aruna, 208, 210; Arundel, 92; Arundhati, 204; Aruns, 261; Arva, 157, 244; Arvad, 192; Arvada, 72; Arvakl, 320; Arval, 261, 386; Arvalis, 261; Arve, 288; Arvel, 386; Arvia, 244; Arvid, 288, 356; Arvil, 386; Arvin, 150, 366; Arwood, 107; Arwydd, 382; Arwyroe, 24; Arya, 204; Arye, 192; Aryeh, 192; Arziki, 17; Asa, 192; Asabi, 17; Asad, 34, 210; Asaf, 191; Asaph, 191; Asbiorn, 288; Asbjorn, 288; Ascalaphus, 171; Ascanius, 261; Ascencion, 342; Asclepius, 260; Ascot, 102; Ascott, 102; Ascra, 244; Asdis, 286; Asdza, 278; Ase, 286; Aselma, 134; Asenka, 184, 311; Asenke, 184; Asentzio, 51; Asfour, 34; Asfoureh, 31; Asgard, 320; Asgaut, 288; Asgeir, 288; Asgerd, 288; Asgre, 382; Asgrim, 320; Asha, 31, 294; Ashburn, 102; Ashby, 102, 320; Asher, 192; Ashford, 102; Ashia, 31; Ashiepattle, 320; Ashild, 286; Ashilda, 286; Ashilde, 286; Ashira, 185; Ashkii, 283; Ashley, 21, 86, 92; Ashlin, 92; Ashling, 134, 215; Ashly, 92; Ashoka, 210; Ashraf, 34; Ashtaroth, 129; Ashton, 92; Ashur, 192; Ashwin, 92, 212; Ashwyn, 92; Asi, 320; Asia, 31, 157, 244; Asim, 34, 81; Asima, 31; Asipatra, 210; Asis, 17; Ask, 288; Askel, 320; Askell, 320; Asklepios, 169; Askook, 281; Askuwheteau, 281; Aslak, 320; Aslaug, 286; Asolf, 320; Asopus, 171; Aspasia, 157; Asrod, 320; Assa, 245; Assan, 221; Assana, 216; Assane, 216; Assim, 294; Assuncao, 304; Asta, 157, 245, 286; Astarte, 78, 245; Astennu, 84; Asteria, 245; Asthore, 216; Astolat, 42; Astolpho, 129; Astra, 157, 286; Astraea, 157, 245; Astrea, 157; Astred, 286, 361; Astrid, 72, 286, 354, 361; Astrud, 286; Astryd, 286; Astryr, 286; Astyanax, 171, 261; Astynome, 245; Astyrian, 24; Asuncion, 342; Asura, 210; Asvald, 320; Asvor, 316; Asvora, 316; Asvoria, 361; Aswad, 34, 81; Asya, 184; Asztrik, 200; Ata, 81; Atabulus, 261; Ata'halne', 283; Atal, 210; Atalanta, 158, 245; Atalante, 158; Atalaya, 342; Atali, 354; Atalia, 185; Atalie, 185, 354; Atalik, 200; Atara, 185; Atarah, 185, 192; Atawn, 386; Ate, 158; At'eed, 278; Atelic, 24; Atella, 245; Atemu, 81; Aten, 81; Atepa, 276; Atera, 185; Ateret, 185; Atgas, 382; Athaleyah, 185; Athalia, 185, 342; Athalie, 185; Athamas, 171, 261; Athan, 170; Athanasia, 158; Athanasios, 171; Athanasius, 170; Athangelos, 40; Athdar, 137, 332; Athdara, 137, 215, 330; Athelstan, 24; Athelston, 91; Athelward, 92; Athemar, 91; Athena, 158; Athene, 158; Atherton, 102; Athilda, 86; Athmarr, 91; Athmore, 102; Athol, 332; Athracht, 216; Atia, 31; Atifa, 31; Atilda, 86;

356; Balthasar, 171, 294; Baltsaros, 171; Bambi, 229; Ban, 44; Bana, 24; Banain, 137; Banaing, 102; Banan, 24, 221; Banba, 216; Banbhan, 221; Banbrigge, 102; Bancroft, 92; Bankole, 81; Bannan, 150; Banning, 24, 102, 137; Bannruod, 150; Banon, 382; Bao, 380; Baptista, 158; Baptiste, 171, 229; Bar, 24; Bara, 68; Barabal, 134; Barabas, 192; Barabell, 134; Barak, 192; Baraka, 31; Barakah, 31, 34; Baram, 192; Baran, 137, 366; Barbara, 158; Barbora, 68; Barbro, 354; Barclay, 24, 92, 332; Bard, 137, 288; Bardalph, 92; Bardan, 92; Bardaric, 92; Bardarik, 92; Bardawulf, 92; Barden, 92, 103; Bardene, 103; Bardi, 321; Bardo, 73; Bardolf, 92; Bardolph, 92; Bardrick, 92; Bardulf, 92; Barend, 76; Barhloew, 102; Bari, 34, 54, 382; Barin, 366; Barkarna, 50; Barkarne, 50; Barke, 19; Barlow, 102; Barna, 192; Barnabas, 192; Barnabe, 192; Barnaby, 192; Barnard, 150, 366; Barnardo, 366; Barnett, 92; Barney, 150; Barnum, 102; Baron, 92, 366; Barr, 92; Barra, 57, 137; Barram, 221; Barran, 216; Barre, 92; Barret, 150; Barrett, 150, 366; Barrie, 130; Barrin, 366; Barris, 387; Barron, 92, 366; Barry, 57, 130, 137; Barrys, 387; Bars, 200; Bart, 102, 192; Bartalan, 200; Bartel, 192; Barth, 92; Bartholomeus, 76, 356; Bartholomew, 192; Barthram, 92; Bartleah, 102; Bartleigh, 102; Bartlett, 130; Bartley, 102, 192; Bartoli, 348; Bartolo, 348; Bartolome, 348; Barton, 102; Bartram, 92, 367; Baruch, 171, 192; Baruti, 81; Barwolf, 92; Basha, 297; Basham, 158; Bashira, 31; Bashiyra, 31; Bashshar, 34; Basia, 297; Basil, 57, 171; Basile, 171; Basilia, 158; Basilio, 171, 348; Basilius, 76, 356; Basim, 34; Basima, 31; Basimah, 31; Bast, 78; Baste, 171; Bastet, 78, 83; Bastiaan, 171; Bastien, 171; Batair, 137; Bathild, 146, 361; Bathilda, 146, 361; Bathilde, 146, 361; Bathsheba, 185; Battista, 229; Battseeyon, 185; Battzion, 185; Batul, 31; Batula, 31; Batya, 185; Baucis, 158, 171; Baug, 321; Bautista, 229; Bav, 54; Bawdewyn, 24; Bawdewyne, 24; Bax, 102; Baxter, 102; Bay, 92, 380; Bayard, 130, 366; Bayen, 24; Bayhard, 92; Bayley, 130; Bazyli, 171, 298; Be, 379; Bea, 245; Beacan, 57; Beacher, 92; Beadu, 87; Beadurinc, 24; Beadurof, 24; Beadutun, 102; Beagan, 137, 221; Beagen, 137; Beal, 44; Bealantin, 137; Bealohydig, 24; Beaman, 102; Beamer, 102; Bean, 332; Bearach, 57, 137; Bearchan, 57; Bearn, 24; Bearnard, 137, 221, 332; Bearrocsir, 21; Beartlaidh, 221; Beata, 245, 297, 354; Beate, 245, 297; Beatha, 54; Beathag, 185; Beathan, 138, 332; Beathas, 330; Beatie, 138; Beaton, 102; Beatrice, 229, 245; Beatricia, 229; Beatrisa, 342; Beatrix, 245; Beatriz, 245, 342; Beattie, 138; Beatty, 138; Beaufort, 130; Beaumains, 44;

Beauvais, 130; Beb, 81; Bebeodan, 24; Bebhinn, 134, 138, 216; Bebti, 81; Becan, 57, 138, 221; Beceere, 92; Beck, 92, 356; Becky, 185; Becse, 200; Beda, 87, 387; Bede, 24, 92; Bedegrayne, 42; Bedivere, 44; Bedrich, 69; Bedrosian, 40; Bedver, 44; Bedwyr, 44, 57, 387; Bedyw, 387; Beecher, 92; Behdeti, 81; Behrooz, 294; Behula, 204; Beinean, 262; Beinir, 321; Beircheart, 24; Beiste, 332; Beitris, 134; Bek, 92; Bekan, 288; Bel, 68; Bela, 68, 192, 199, 200, 208; Belakane, 43; Belda, 124; Beldan, 102, 367; Beldane, 102, 367; Belden, 102, 367; Beldene, 102; Beldon, 102; Beli, 387; Beli Mawr, 387; Belia, 68; Belicia, 342; Belinda, 229, 342; Belisarda, 124; Belita, 342; Bell, 68, 130; Bella, 185, 199, 245, 342; Bellamy, 130; Bellance, 229; Bellangere, 45; Belle, 199, 245; Bellerophon, 171, 262; Bellinagar, 221; Bellinagara, 216; Bellinus, 24; Bellona, 245; Beltane, 130; Beltran, 348; Belus, 262; Bemeere, 102; Bemossed, 279; Ben, 192; Bena, 275; Ben-ami, 192; Ben-aryeh, 192; Benat, 51, 150; Bence, 200, 262; Benci, 200, 262; Bendek, 298; Bendigeidfran, 57, 387; Bendik, 262; Bendyk, 298; Benecroft, 92; Benedek, 262; Benedetta, 229; Benedetto, 262; Benedict, 262; Benedicta, 245; Benedicte, 262; Benedicto, 348; Benedictson, 192; Benedikt, 356; Benedikta, 245; Benedikte, 262; Benen, 221, 262; Benetta, 245; Bengt, 262, 356; Beniamino, 192, 232; Benigied Vran, 45; Benigna, 229, 245, 304, 342; Benigno, 308; Benin, 262; Benita, 245, 342; Benjamin, 192; Benkamin, 192; Benke, 262; Bennett, 262; Bennu, 78; Benoic, 24; Benoit, 262; Benoni, 192; Benoyce, 45; Benquasha, 275; Benroy, 192; Benson, 192; Bent, 73, 262; Benta, 185; Bente, 245; Bentleah, 102; Bentleigh, 102; Bentley, 102; Bento, 308; Benton, 102; Bentziyon, 192; Benvy, 216; Benwick, 24; Benzion, 192; Beolagh, 221; Beomann, 102; Beore, 92; Beorht, 92; Beorhthilde, 87; Beorhthram, 92; Beorhthramm, 92; Beorhttun, 102; Beorn, 24; Beornet, 92; Beornham, 102; Beornia, 21; Beornwulf, 24; Beorthtraed, 87; Beowulf, 24, 357; Ber, 150; Bera, 286, 361; Berakhiak, 192; Berangari, 87; Berangaria, 124; Berchtwald, 150; Bercilak, 45; Bercleah, 92; Berde, 73; Berdina, 146, 158; Berdine, 146, 158, 361; Berdy, 150; Berend, 150; Berengaria, 87; Berenice, 158; Beresford, 102; Beretun, 102; Berford, 102; Berg, 76, 150, 357; Bergdis, 286; Bergelmir, 321; Bergen, 321; Berger, 367; Berggren, 321; Bergin, 321; Bergitte, 72; Bergren, 321, 357; Bergron, 357; Bergthor, 288; Bergthora, 286; Berinhard, 150; Beriszl, 200; Berit, 54, 146, 354; Berkeley, 24, 92; Berkley, 92; Bern, 150; Bernadette, 124, 146, 361;

Carson, 103; Carsten, 262; Carston, 262; Carswell, 93; Carter, 103; Cartere, 103; Carthach, 221; Carthage, 221; Cartimandua, 22; Carvel, 93; Carvell, 93; Carver, 103; Carwyn, 387; Cary, 55, 57, 387; Carya, 246; Caryn, 135, 246; Caryna, 246; Carys, 383; Cas, 387; Caseareo, 172, 232; Casey, 57, 135, 138, 216; Cash, 262; Cashel, 221; Casidhe, 135, 138, 216; Casild, 342; Casilda, 342; Casimir, 299, 338; Casimiro, 308, 349; Casnar, 388; Caspar, 294; Casper, 294; Casperia, 246; Cass, 262; Cassandra, 158, 246; Cassia, 185; Cassibellaunus, 93; Cassidy, 135, 138, 216; Cassie, 158; Cassiopeia, 158; Cassius, 262; Cassivellaunus, 57; Cassondra, 158; Casswallawn, 388; Casta, 158, 342; Castalia, 158; Castel, 349; Caster, 103; Castor, 172, 262; Caswallan, 57; Caswallon, 388; Cat, 216, 333; Catalin, 50, 158; Catalina, 342; Catalonia, 342; Catalyn, 158; Catarina, 158, 229, 305; Catarine, 229; Cataya, 17; Cate, 22, 246; Cateline, 124; Catena, 246; Caterina, 229; Cath, 45, 383; Cathair, 57, 332; Cathal, 57, 138, 221; Cathaoir, 57, 221; Cathaoirmore, 138; Catharina, 158; Cathasach, 135, 138, 216; Cathbad, 57; Catherin, 158; Catherine, 22, 158; Catheryn, 22, 158; Catheryna, 158; Cathleen, 158; Cathlin, 158; Cathlyn, 158; Cathmor, 138, 221; Cathmore, 138, 221; Cathryn, 22, 158; Catia, 158; Catlee, 216; Cato, 262; Caton, 262, 349; Catori, 277; Catrin, 383; Catriona, 135; Cattee, 216; Catterick, 45; Catterik, 45; Catullus, 262; Catus, 262; Cauley, 289, 333; Cavalon, 45; Cavan, 138, 221; Cavana, 216; Cavell, 367; Cavillor, 262; Caw, 45, 388; Cawley, 289, 333; Cawrdav, 388; Cayden, 138; Cayle, 93; Cayleigh, 135; Ceallach, 135, 138, 225; Ceallachan, 221; Ceanach, 138; Ceannfhionn, 138; Ceapmann, 103; Ceara, 135; Cearbhall, 130, 221; Cearbhallan, 138; Ceard, 333; Ceardach, 333; Cearnach, 221; Cearo, 22; Ceasario, 232; Ceaster, 93; Ceastun, 93; Ceawlin, 24; Cebriones, 172; Cecil, 262; Cecile, 246; Cecilia, 246, 305, 354; Cecilio, 232, 262; Cecilius, 76; Cecily, 246; Cecrops, 172, 262; Cedd, 24; Cedric, 57, 93; Cegluse, 246; Ceileachan, 138; Cein, 138, 221; Ceinwen, 384; Ceire, 216; Ceit, 135; Ceithin, 388; Celaeno, 158, 246; Celandina, 158; Celandine, 158; Celdtun, 105; Celek, 297; Celena, 159; Celeres, 262; Celesta, 246; Celeste, 246; Celestin, 262; Celestina, 246; Celestine, 246; Celestun, 262; Celeus, 172; Celia, 246, 305; Celidon, 45; Celidone, 45; Celina, 159, 246; Celine, 246; Celinka, 297; Celio, 308; Celistine, 262; Celosia, 159; Celso, 308; Celsus, 221; Celyddon, 57; Cemal, 34; Cendrillon, 124;

Cenehard, 93; Ceneward, 93; Cenewig, 93; Cenewyg, 93; Cenobia, 159, 342; Cenon, 172; Centaurus, 262; Cenwalh, 25; Ceolbeorht, 94; Ceolfrith, 25; Ceolwulf, 25; Cephalus, 172, 263; Cepheus, 172, 263; Cerberus, 172; Cercyon, 172; Cerdic, 25; Cerdwin, 55; Cereberus, 263; Cerelia, 229, 246; Ceres, 159, 246; Ceridwen, 384; Cerin, 138; Cesar, 262, 308, 349; Cesara, 343; Cesare, 172, 232; Cesario, 262; Cesaro, 349; Cestmir, 69, 338; Cestus, 159; Cetewind, 103; Ceto, 159; Cetus, 172; Ceyx, 172; Cezar, 262, 308; Cha'akmongwi, 282; Chaba, 185; Chabah, 185; Chad, 25, 58, 93; Chadburn, 93; Chadburne, 93; Chadbyrne, 93; Chadwick, 103; Chadwik, 103; Chadwyk, 103; Chafulumisa, 81; Chagai, 193; Chaim, 193, 332; Chair, 333; Chaitra, 208; Chaka, 185; Chakra, 210; Cha'kwaina, 277; Chalciope, 247; Chale, 349; Chalmar, 367; Chalmer, 333, 367; Chalmers, 333, 367; Chamunda, 205; Chan, 66; Chana, 185; Chanah, 185; Chanan, 193; Chance, 93; Chancellor, 93; Chancey, 93; Chanda, 205; Chandaka, 210; Chander, 212; Chandi, 205, 208; Chandler, 130; Chandra, 208, 210; Changla, 208; Chankoowashtay, 284; Chankrisna, 52; Chanler, 130; Channa, 205; Channary, 52; Channing, 130; Chanoch, 193; Chansomps, 281; Chantel, 124; Chantrea, 52; Chao, 64; Chapa, 279; Chapalu, 45; Chapin, 130; Chapman, 25, 103; Chappel, 130; Chappell, 130; Charis, 159; Cha'risa, 277; Charissa, 159, 246; Charity, 246; Charleen, 124; Charlene, 124; Charles, 93, 130, 367; Charleton, 93; Charline, 124; Charlot, 130; Charlotta, 312; Charlotte, 124; Charlton, 93; Charmaine, 87, 124; Charo, 343; Charon, 172; Charraigaich, 138; Charumati, 205; Charybdis, 159, 247; Chas-chunk-a, 284; Chasidah, 185; Chasya, 185; Chasye, 185; Chata, 19; Chatha, 81; Chatham, 103; Cha'tima, 282; Chattan, 333; Chatuluka, 81; Chatwin, 93; Chatwyn, 93; Chau, 379; Chaucer, 263; Chaucor, 263; Chaunce, 93; Chaunceler, 93; Chauncey, 93, 263; Chauncory, 263; Chava, 185; Chavatangakwunua, 282; Chaviv, 193; Chaviva, 185; Chavive, 185; Chavivi, 193; Chay, 52; Chaya, 185; Chayim, 193; Chayka, 185; Chayton, 284; Che, 45, 193; Cheche, 17; Chedva, 185; Chela, 343; Chelinda, 43; Chelinde, 43; Chelsea, 22, 87; Chen, 64, 66; Chenda, 52; Cheney, 130; Cheng, 66; Chenoa, 275; Chenzira, 81; Cheops, 81; Chepe, 193; Chephzibah, 185; Chepi, 276; Chepito, 193; Cher, 124; Cheree, 124; Cheri, 124; Cherie, 124; Cherise, 124, 159; Cherry, 124; Cheryl, 124; Cheslav, 314; Chesmu, 279; Chesna, 337; Chester, 93, 263; Cheston, 93; Chet, 374; Chetwey, 103; Chetwin, 103; Cheveyo, 282;

Conary, 223; Concepcion, 343; Concepta, 217; Conception, 247; Concetta, 229, 343; Conchetta, 343; Conchobar, 58; Conchobara, 217; Conchobarra, 217; Conchobarre, 217; Conchobhar, 223; Concordea, 247; Concordia, 247; Condan, 58; Condon, 58; Condwiramurs, 43; Cong, 64, 66; Congalie, 217; Conlan, 139, 223; Conlaoch, 58; Conleth, 223; Conley, 223; Conlin, 139; Conn, 58, 139; Connacht, 223; Connal, 217; Connell, 57; Connie, 223, 247; Connla, 58; Connlaio, 223; Connlan, 139; Connolly, 223; Connor, 223; Conny, 223; Conor, 223; Conrad, 150, 367; Conradin, 150; Conradina, 146; Conradine, 146; Conrado, 150, 349; Conroy, 58, 139, 223; Conshita, 343; Consolacion, 343; Consolata, 230, 343; Constance, 247; Constancia, 247; Constansie, 229; Constant, 263; Constantia, 229, 247; Constantin, 232; Constantina, 229, 247; Constantine, 263; Constantino, 263, 349; Constantios, 263; Constanza, 229, 343; Constanze, 247; Constanzie, 229; Consuela, 247, 343; Consuelo, 343; Conway, 58, 139, 223, 388; Conyn, 388; Cooey, 223; Cooley, 223; Coolie, 223; Cooney, 223; Cooper, 105; Coopersmith, 105; Cora, 159, 330; Coral, 159; Coralie, 124, 159; Coralin, 159; Coralina, 159; Coraline, 159; Corann, 58; Corazon, 343; Corbenic, 45; Corbin, 263; Corbmac, 223; Corcoran, 139, 223; Corcurachan, 139; Cord, 150; Cordelia, 55, 87, 384; Corella, 159; Coretta, 124, 159; Corette, 124, 159; Corey, 25, 55, 139, 223, 333; Cori, 139, 223; Coridan, 172; Corin, 159; Corineus, 172; Corinna, 159; Corinne, 159; Corliss, 87; Cormac, 58, 139, 223; Cormack, 139; Cormic, 223; Cormick, 139, 223; Cornelia, 247; Cornelio, 263, 349; Cornelius, 223, 263; Corona, 208; Coronis, 159; Corradeo, 232; Corrado, 150, 232; Corryn, 388; Cors, 388; Corsen, 384; Cort, 130, 150, 289, 367; Cortie, 289; Corwan, 94; Corwin, 94; Corwine, 94; Corwyn, 94; Cory, 139, 223, 333; Corybantes, 172; Corydon, 172; Cos, 172; Cosette, 124; Cosima, 172; Cosimia, 159; Cosma, 159; Cosmas, 172; Cosmo, 172; Cotovatre, 43; Cottus, 172; Coughlan, 223; Court, 130; Courtland, 25, 105, 130; Courtnay, 25, 130; Courtney, 25, 130, 247; Covell, 105; Coventina, 22, 55; Covey, 223; Covyll, 105; Cowan, 139, 223; Cowbelliantus, 357; Cowen, 223; Cowin, 263; Cowyn, 223; Coyle, 139; Cradawg, 58; Craddock, 388; Cradoc, 388; Cragen, 384; Craig, 139, 333; Crandall, 105; Crandell, 105; Cranleah, 105; Cranley, 105; Cranly, 105; Crannog, 333; Cranog, 388; Cranston, 105; Cranstun, 105; Crawford, 105; Creag, 139; Creiddylad, 384; Creiddyladl, 43;

Creighton, 105, 333; Creissant, 124; Creketun, 105; Creon, 172; Crescent, 124; Crescentia, 247; Cressida, 159; Cretiein, 130; Cretien, 172; Creusa, 159; Crevan, 223; Crichton, 105; Criostoir, 139; Crisdean, 139; Crisiant, 384; Crispin, 263; Crispina, 247; Crist, 388; Cristiano, 262, 308, 349; Cristin, 216, 246; Cristina, 305, 343, 354; Cristiona, 246; Cristo, 349; Cristobal, 349; Cristoforo, 172, 232; Cristophe, 172; Cristovao, 308; Crocale, 159; Croften, 105; Crofton, 105; Crogher, 223; Crohoore, 223; Crom, 332; Crombwiella, 105; Crompton, 105; Cromwell, 105, 333; Cronan, 139, 223; Cronus, 172; Crosby, 289, 367; Crosleah, 105; Crosleigh, 105; Crosley, 105; Crosly, 105; Crow-Hreidar, 321; Crowley, 223; Cruadhlaoich, 223; Crudel, 45; Cruim, 332; Crystal, 159; Csaba, 200; Cseke, 200; Csenger, 200; Csilla, 185; Cuanaic, 223; Cuartio, 349; Cuarto, 349; Cubert, 388; Cuc, 379; Cuchulainn, 58; Cuilean, 139; Cuimean, 138; Cuini, 135; Cuinn, 58, 139, 223; Culain, 58; Culann, 58; Culbart, 94; Culbert, 94, 367; Culhwch, 46, 58, 388; Cullan, 139; Cullen, 58; Culley, 139; Cullidina, 330; Cullin, 139; Cullo, 223; Culloden, 333; Cullodena, 330; Cully, 139; Culvanawd, 388; Culver, 94; Culyer, 55; Cumania, 217; Cumhea, 223; Cumin, 333; Cumina, 330; Cumming, 333; Cundrie, 43; Cundry, 43; Cunningham, 333; Cuong, 380; Cupere, 105; Curadhan, 139; Curcio, 130, 349; Curney, 139; Curr, 139; Curran, 139; Currito, 349; Curro, 349; Curt, 130, 263, 367; Curtice, 130; Curtis, 130; Custenhin, 388; Custennin, 46, 58; Cuthbeorht, 94; Cuthbert, 25, 94; Cutler, 94; CuUladh, 223; Cuyler, 223; Cwen, 22, 87; Cwene, 22; Cwentun, 105; Cy, 172; Cybele, 159; Cycnus, 172; Cym, 87; Cyma, 159; Cymbeline, 46; Cymbelline, 94; Cymberly, 87; Cymreiges, 384; Cymry, 388; Cynara, 159; Cynbal, 388; Cynbel, 388; Cynburleigh, 87; Cyne, 87; Cyneburhleah, 87; Cynegils, 25; Cyneheard, 25; Cyneleah, 94; Cyneley, 94; Cynere, 159; Cyneric, 25, 94; Cynerik, 94; Cynewulf, 25; Cynfarch, 46; Cynfor, 388; Cynhard, 93; Cyning, 94; Cynn, 25; Cynric, 25, 94; Cynrik, 94; Cynthia, 159; Cynward, 93; Cynyr, 58; Cyprian, 172, 299; Cypriana, 159; Cyprien, 247; Cypriene, 247; Cypris, 159; Cyr, 172; Cyra, 159, 294; Cyrano, 172; Cyrek, 172, 299; Cyrena, 159; Cyrene, 159; Cyril, 172; Cyrilla, 159, 247; Cyrillia, 247; Cyrus, 172, 294; Cyryl, 172, 299; Cyst, 22, 25; Cystennin, 388; Cythera, 159; Cytherea, 160; Cytheria, 160; Cyzarine, 312; Czeslaw, 299; Czigany, 199

D'Arcy, 124, 130; D'Ary, 139; Da Xia, 64; Daba,

193; Derora, 186; Derorice, 186; Derorit, 186; Derrick, 150; Derry, 139, 150; Derryth, 384; Derval, 217; Dervilia, 217; Dervla, 135, 217; Dervorgilla, 217; Derwan, 94; Derward, 94; Derwen, 384; Derwin, 94, 367; Derwyn, 94, 367; Desdemona, 160; Desideria, 124, 343; Desiderio, 289, 349; Desirat, 124; Desirata, 248; Desire, 124, 130; Desiree, 124; Desma, 160; Desmoa, 160; Desmon, 139; Desmona, 160; Desmond, 25, 58, 139, 223; Deucalion, 173, 263; Deunoro, 51; Deutsch, 150; Deva, 55, 205; Devaki, 205; Devamatar, 205; Devan, 139; Devante, 349; Devayani, 205; Deven, 210; Devent, 217; Devera, 343; Deverell, 58, 388; Deverra, 248; Deverril, 388; Devi, 208; Devin, 58, 139; Devine, 223; Devlin, 139; Devlyn, 139; Devnet, 217, 354; Devon, 25; Devona, 22, 55, 87; Devonna, 87; Devora, 185, 312; Devoria, 185; Devota, 248; Devyn, 25, 58, 139; Devyna, 87; Dewain, 58; Dewei, 66; Dewey, 388; Dewi, 388; Dexter, 130, 263; Dextra, 248; Dezba, 278; Dezso, 263; Dharani, 205; Dhenuka, 210; Dhimitrios, 173; Dhoire, 333; Dhumavarna, 210; Dia, 160, 343; Diago, 308; Diallo, 19; Diamanta, 125; Diamantina, 305; Diamond, 105; Diamont, 105; Diana, 125, 248; Diane, 125, 248; Diantha, 160; Dianthe, 160; Diarmad, 139; Diarmaid, 139; Diarmid, 139, 223; Diata, 17; Dibe, 278; Dice, 160; Dichali, 279; Dick, 150, 367; Dickran, 40; Dickson, 105, 367; Dicra, 384; Didier, 130; Dido, 160, 248; Didrika, 146, 361; Diederich, 150; Diederik, 73; Diega, 343; Diego, 349; Diella, 248; Dielle, 248; Diep, 379; Diera, 22; Dierck, 150; Dierdre, 217, 384; Dieter, 150; Dietrich, 150; Dietz, 150; Difyr, 384; Digby, 289; Digna, 248, 343; Digne, 248; Digon, 388; Dike, 160; Dikesone, 105; Dikibyr, 289; Dikran, 40; Dikranouhi, 40; Dilan, 388; Dillie, 388; Dillion, 58; Dillon, 139, 223, 388; Dillus, 388; Dilys, 384; Dima, 314; Dimitra, 312; Dimitri, 314; Dimka, 338; Dina, 87, 186; Dinadan, 46; Dinah, 186; Dinas, 46; Dino, 94, 160, 232; Dinsmore, 58; Diogo, 308; Diolmhain, 139; Diomasach, 139; Diomedes, 173; Dion, 173; Diona, 160; Dione, 160; Dionis, 343; Dionisa, 343; Dionizy, 299; Dionysia, 160, 248; Dionysie, 160; Dionysios, 173; Dionysius, 173; Dionysus, 173; Diorbhall, 135; Dioxippe, 248; Dirce, 160, 248; Dirck, 76; Dirk, 76, 150, 367; Dirmyg, 388; Dirran, 31; Dis, 263; Disa, 286; Discordia, 248; Diss, 286; Diti, 205; Diu, 379; Div, 205; Diva, 55; Divone, 55; Divsha, 186; Divshah, 186; Divya, 208; Dixie, 125; Dixon, 105, 367; Diya al din, 34; Djoser, 81; Doan Vien, 379; Doane, 58, 105; Doba, 278; Dobhailen, 139; Dobieslaw, 299; Dobrilla, 337; Dobry, 299; Docila, 248; Docilla, 248; Dodek, 299; Dodie, 186; Dodinel,

46; Dohosan, 280; Dohtor, 22; Doire, 333; Doire-Ann, 135; Doireann, 135, 217; Doli, 278; Dolius, 173; Doll, 160; Dollie, 160; Dolly, 160; Dolon, 263; Dolores, 343; Dolorita, 343; Doloritas, 343; Dolph, 356, 367; Dom, 263; Dome, 263; Domeka, 263; Domela, 248; Domele, 248; Domhnall, 58; Domhnull, 139, 333; Domhnulla, 135; Domiduca, 248; Domiducus, 263; Domiku, 263; Dominga, 343; Domingart, 46; Domingo, 349; Dominic, 263; Dominica, 217, 248; Dominick, 263; Dominico, 263; Dominika, 312; Dominique, 125, 248; Domino, 248; Domitiana, 248; Domitiane, 248; Domo, 263; Domokas, 263; Domokos, 200; Don, 22, 58, 333; Dona, 230, 248; Donaghy, 58; Donahue, 139; Donal, 58, 223; Donald, 58, 139, 333; Donalda, 135, 317, 330; Donall, 58; Donat, 58, 299; Donata, 230, 248; Donatello, 232, 263; Donatien, 130; Donato, 232, 263; Donel, 333; Donell, 333; Donella, 55; Donelle, 217, 248; Dong, 379; Donia, 55, 135; Donica, 248; Donkor, 81; Donla, 135, 217; Donn, 223; Donna, 230, 248; Donnachadh, 333; Donnally, 58; Donnan, 223; Donnchadh, 58, 139, 333; Donnelly, 58; Donner, 289; Donogh, 58; Donoma, 279; Donovan, 58; Dooley, 139; Doon, 217; Dor, 193; Dora, 160; Doralia, 160; Doralice, 160; Doralie, 160; Doralis, 160; Doran, 58, 173, 223; Dorbeta, 343; Dorcas, 160; Dordei, 160; Dordie, 160; Dore, 125; Dorea, 160; Doreen, 55, 125, 135, 160, 217; Doreena, 55; Dorek, 299; Dorelia, 160; Doren, 193; Dorene, 125, 135; Dores, 305; Doretta, 160; Dorette, 160; Doria, 160; Dorian, 160, 173; Doriana, 160; Dorice, 160; Dorien, 160; Dorika, 199; Dorinda, 160; Dorine, 125; Doris, 160, 248; Dorita, 160; Dorjan, 263; Dorkas, 160; Dorlisa, 160; Dorota, 297, 343; Dorote, 248; Dorotea, 119, 248, 343; Doroteia, 305, 343; Doroteya, 312; Dorothea, 72, 76, 160, 248; Dorothee, 248; Dorothy, 160; Dorottya, 199, 248; Dorran, 58; Dorte, 160; Dory, 125; Dougal, 25, 58, 223, 333; Doughal, 58; Doughall, 333; Doughlas, 58; Douglas, 25, 58, 223, 333; Doune, 105; Dour, 333; Dov, 193; Dova, 361; Dovev, 193; Dow, 223; Dowan, 223; Dowle, 223; Downeti, 217; Downett, 217; Doy, 58; Doyle, 58, 223; Draca, 94; Dragan, 338; Drake, 94; Draupnir, 317, 321; Drefan, 25; Drem, 58, 388; Dremidydd, 388; Dreng, 25, 289; Dreogan, 25; Drew, 25, 58, 160, 388; Dridan, 105; Driden, 105; Drina, 343; Drisana, 208; Driscol, 58, 223; Driscoll, 58, 223; Driskell, 58; Dristan, 46; Drostan, 58; Druas, 46; Druce, 25, 58, 388; Drucilla, 248; Drud, 150; Drudwas, 388; Drudwyn, 46, 58, 388; Druella, 361; Drugi, 150; Drummand, 333; Drummond, 58, 333; Drusilla, 248; Druson, 388; Drust, 46; Drwst, 388; Drych,

Eidothea, 160; Eigg, 333; Eigil, 289; Eija, 119; Eikki, 120, 289; Eila, 119; Eiladar, 389; Eileen, 135, 217; Eileithyia, 160; Eilidh, 135; Eilif, 321; Eilig, 333; Eilinora, 217; Eilionoir, 135; Eilis, 135, 217; Eily, 217; Eimar, 224; Eimhin, 224; Einar, 289; Einhard, 150; Einhardt, 150; Einian, 389; Einion, 59, 389; Einri, 367; Eir, 317; Eira, 384; Eirene, 160, 248; Eirian, 384; Eiric, 330; Eirica, 330; Eirik, 289; Eirnin, 224; Eirwen, 384; Eiryn, 389; Eisa, 34; Eistein, 289; Eistir, 217; Eithna, 217; Eithne, 135, 217; Eitri, 321; Eivyonydd, 389; Ejnar, 73; Ekadanta, 210; Ekaterina, 160, 312; Ekerd, 151; Ekhard, 151; Ektor, 46; Elaine, 43, 160; Elan, 193, 217, 280; Elata, 248; Elayne, 43; Elazar, 51, 193; Elazaro, 193; Elbert, 367; Elberta, 88, 361; Elberte, 88; Elbertina, 88, 343; Elbertine, 88; Elbertyna, 88; Elda, 22, 230, 361; Eldan, 106; Elde, 361; Elden, 106, 367; Elder, 106; Eldgrim, 321; Eldon, 106, 367; Eldora, 343, 361; Eldoris, 160; Eldred, 25, 367; Eldreda, 88; Eldrid, 25, 286; Eldrida, 22, 88; Eldride, 22; Eldridge, 367; Eldur, 106; Eldwin, 25; Eldwyn, 25; Eleanor, 125, 160; Eleanora, 160, 230; Eleanore, 160; Eleazar, 193; Electa, 248; Electra, 160; Elefteria, 160; Eleftherios, 173; Elek, 173, 201, 299; Elekta, 248; Elemer, 367; Elen, 384; Elena, 160, 230, 305, 343; Elene, 22, 230; Eleni, 160; Elenitsa, 160; Elenora, 230; Elenore, 230; Eleonora, 354; Eleora, 186; Elepheteria, 160; Elephteria, 160; Eleri, 384; Eleta, 125; Elethea, 88; Elethia, 88; Eleuterio, 308; Eleutherios, 173; Elfie, 88; Elfreda, 88, 361; Elfrida, 88, 361; Elfrieda, 88; Elga, 22, 312, 361; Elgar, 367; Elhanan, 193; Elhe, 224; Eli, 173, 193; Elia, 186; Eliana, 186; Eliane, 186; Elias, 193, 308; Eliaures, 46; Elica, 146; Elida, 88; Elidor, 59; Elidure, 46, 95; Elidyr, 389; Elienor, 125; Eliezer, 193; Eligius, 263; Elihu, 193; Eliisa, 120; Elijah, 193; Elin, 317, 354; Elina, 119; Elinore, 125; Eliora, 186; Eliot, 130, 193; Eliott, 130; Elisa, 125, 343; Elisabet, 120, 161, 186, 354; Elisabeth, 125, 161, 186; Elisabetta, 230; Elisavet, 186; Elisaveta, 186; Elise, 125; Eliseo, 193; Elisha, 193; Elishama, 193; Elisheba, 193; Elisheva, 186, 193; Elisia, 161; Eliska, 68; Elissa, 161; Elita, 88, 125; Elivina, 88; Eliza, 125, 186; Elizabeth, 43, 186; Elizabetta, 230; Elizaveta, 186; Elka, 186; Elkanah, 193; Elke, 186, 361; Elki, 283; Ella, 88; Ellama, 208; Ellar, 139, 333; Ellard, 95, 367; Ellary, 367; Ellder, 106; Elle, 88, 286; Ellema, 17; Ellen, 25, 160; Ellenweorc, 22; Ellery, 151, 367; Ellette, 22; Elli, 186, 317; Ellice, 161, 186; Ellinor, 125; Elliot, 130, 333; Ellis, 193; Ellisif, 286; Ellison, 106; Ellwood, 106; Ellylw, 384; Elma, 161; Elmar, 367; Elmas, 40; Elmer, 25, 95, 367; Elmina, 361; Elmine, 361; Elmira, 88; Elmo, 232;

Elmoor, 95; Elmore, 95; Elmyra, 88; Elne, 25; Elnora, 160; Eloina, 248; Eloine, 248; Eloisa, 125; Eloise, 125, 361; Eloisee, 125; Elon, 17; Elora, 160, 186; Eloy, 151, 349; Elpenor, 173; Elphin, 289, 389; Elpida, 161; Elpide, 161; Elpidio, 308; Elrad, 193; Elroy, 224; Els, 186; Elsa, 43, 120, 146, 343, 354, 361; Elsdon, 106; Else, 72, 146; Elsha, 54, 146; Elsie, 146, 186; Elsje, 146; Elspeth, 186; Elsu, 280; Elsworth, 106; Elswyth, 22; Elthia, 88; Elton, 106; Elu, 280; Eluned, 384; Eluwilussit, 281; Elva, 22, 88; Elvena, 88; Elvera, 248; Elvey, 95; Elvia, 22, 88; Elvie, 88; Elvin, 88, 367; Elvina, 22, 88; Elvine, 88; Elvio, 263, 349; Elvira, 248, 343, 361; Elvis, 289; Elvy, 95; Elvyne, 88; Elwald, 95; Elwell, 95; Elwen, 95; Elwin, 95; Elwine, 22; Elwira, 297; Elwold, 95; Elwood, 106; Elwyn, 95; Elwyna, 22; Ely, 151, 193; Elyse, 146; Elyta, 88; Elzbieta, 297; Elzira, 186, 305; Ema, 302, 343, 361; Embla, 286; Emelin, 361; Emelina, 361; Emeline, 361; Emer, 217; Emera, 248; Emeraude, 125; Emeric, 95, 367; Emerick, 95; Emery, 95, 151, 368; Emiko, 236; Emil, 263, 357, 367; Emile, 263, 367; Emilia, 119, 230, 305, 343, 354; Emilian, 263, 299, 367; Emiliana, 305; Emilie, 146, 343, 361; Emiline, 361; Emilio, 349; Emily, 361; Emir, 34; Emira, 248; Emlyn, 361, 389; Emma, 119, 146, 354, 361; Emmanuel, 193; Emmanuele, 232; Emmanuella, 186; Emmanuelle, 186; Emmeline, 125; Emmi, 119; Emogen, 55; Emogene, 55; Emory, 151, 368; Empanda, 248; Emric, 367; Emrik, 367; Emrys, 59, 389; Emunah, 186; Emyr, 46; Ena, 55, 135, 217; Enan, 224; Enapay, 284; Enar, 289, 357; Enat, 217; Encarnacion, 343; Enceladus, 173; Enda, 135, 217, 224; Endocia, 161; Endora, 160, 186; Endre, 174, 201; Endymion, 174; Enea, 174, 232; Eneas, 174, 308, 349; Enerstina, 88; Enerstyne, 88; Eneuawg, 384; Engel, 22, 151; Engelbert, 368; Engelberta, 362; Engelbertha, 146; Engelbertina, 146; Engelbertine, 146; Engl, 55; Englbehrt, 151; Englebert, 151; Engleberta, 146; Engracia, 343; Engres, 46; Enid, 43, 55, 88, 384; Enide, 43; Enit, 88, 384; Enite, 43; Enkoodabaoo, 281; Enkoodabooaoo, 281; Ennea, 161; Ennis, 59, 217; Ennissyen, 389; Enno, 150; Eno, 150; Enoch, 193; Enok, 73; Enoka, 272; Enola, 275; Enora, 161; Enos, 220; Enrhydreg, 384; Enrica, 230, 343, 362; Enrichetta, 230; Enrico, 232, 368; Enrika, 362; Enriqua, 343; Enrique, 308, 349, 368; Enriqueta, 343, 362; Entoria, 248; Eny, 217; Enya, 248; Enyd, 88; Enyeto, 280; Enygeus, 43; Enyo, 161, 248; Enys, 55; Enzo, 232, 368; Eoforwic, 106; Eoghan, 139, 174, 224; Eoghann, 59, 139; Eoin, 59, 224; Eoin Baiste, 224; Eorl, 25, 94; Eorland, 106; Eorlland, 106; Eorlson, 106; Eos, 161, 248;

376; Fadey, 314, 376; Fadeyka, 314, 376; Fadeyushka, 376; Fadil, 34, 81; Fadila, 31; Fadilah, 31; Fadyenka, 368; Fae, 125; Faegan, 95; Faer, 95; Faerrleah, 106; Faerwald, 95; Fafner, 321; Fafnir, 321; Fagan, 95, 224; Fagen, 140; Fagin, 140; Fahd, 34; Fahey, 224; Fahy, 224; Fai, 66; Fain, 95; Fainche, 217; Faing, 333; Fairfax, 25, 106; Fairlie, 106; Faisal, 34; Faith, 88, 249; Faithe, 88; Faiza, 31; Faizah, 17; Faki, 81; Fala, 276; Falala, 17; Falerina, 125; Fallamhain, 224; Fallon, 217, 224; Fama, 249; Fanchon, 125, 362; Fanchone, 125; Fane, 95; Fanetta, 125; Fanette, 125; Fang, 333; Fani, 249; Fania, 249, 337; Fannie, 362; Fanny, 337, 362; Fantina, 125; Fantine, 125; Fanya, 337; Faodhagan, 140; Faoiltiarna, 217; Faolan, 140, 224; Faqueza, 344; Farah, 294; Faraji, 19; Faran, 25; Farand, 368; Fardoragh, 224; Farica, 362; Farid, 35; Faridah, 31; Farideh, 294; Fariel, 294; Farika, 362; Faris, 35; Farkas, 201; Farlan, 333; Farlane, 333; Farleigh, 106; Farley, 106; Farly, 106; Farmon, 25; Farnall, 106; Farnell, 106; Farnham, 106; Farnley, 106; Farold, 95; Farook, 35; Farouk, 35; Farquhar, 140, 333; Farquharson, 333; Farr, 95; Farran, 35; Farrel, 59; Farrell, 59, 140; Farris, 174; Farriss, 140; Farrs, 106; Farruco, 349; Farry, 224; Fars, 106; Farson, 106; Faruq, 35; Fasolt, 321; Faste, 289; Fate, 161; Fatima, 31, 305; Fatin, 31, 35; Fatina, 31; Fatinah, 31; Faula, 249; Faun, 125; Fauna, 125, 249; Faunia, 125; Faunus, 264; Faust, 233, 249, 264; Fausta, 230, 249, 344; Fauste, 249; Faustina, 249, 344; Faustine, 249; Fausto, 233, 264, 349; Favonius, 264; Favor, 125; Fawnia, 125; Faxhir, 35; Faxon, 368; Fay, 125, 224; Faye, 125; Fayette, 125; Fayina, 312; Fayme, 125; Fayne, 95; Fayola, 17; Fayre, 88; Faysal, 34; Fayth, 88; Fe, 344; Fealthy, 125; Feandan, 333; Fearbhirigh, 140; Fearchar, 334; Fearchara, 330; Fearcharia, 330; Fearcher, 140; Fearghall, 140; Fearghus, 59, 140; Fearnhamm, 106; Fearnhealh, 106; Fearnleah, 106; Feary, 224; Fedele, 264; Fedelm, 55; Federico, 233, 349; Federikke, 72; Fedor, 174, 314; Fedora, 161; Fedosia, 337; Fedya, 314, 368; Fedyenka, 314; Feenat, 217; Feich, 224; Feirefiz, 46; Fela, 297; Felabeorht, 88, 95; Felamaere, 95; Felan, 224; Felberta, 88; Felcia, 297; Felda, 146, 362; Felding, 106; Feldon, 106; Feldtun, 106; Feldun, 106; Feleta, 249; Felice, 230, 249, 264; Felicia, 125, 249; Felician, 264; Felicidade, 305; Felicienne, 125; Felicio, 233, 264; Felicitas, 249; Felicity, 125, 249; Feliks, 264, 299, 314; Felipa, 344; Felipe, 308, 350; Felisa, 249, 344; Felisberta, 146; Felise, 249; Felita, 249; Felix, 25, 264, 349, 357; Felka, 297; Fell, 289; Felton, 106; Femi, 17, 78; Fenella, 55, 217, 330; Feng, 64; Fenice, 43;

Fenrir, 322; Fenris, 322; Fenton, 106; Fenuku, 81; Fenyang, 81; Feodor, 174; Feodora, 312, 337; Feodras, 174; Feran, 25; Ferchar, 59; Fercos, 389; Ferda, 69; Ferdia, 224; Ferdiad, 59; Ferdinand, 368; Ferdinando, 233; Ferenc, 201, 264; Fereng, 199, 362; Fergal, 224; Ferghus, 59, 140; Fergus, 59, 140, 224, 334; Ferguson, 334; Fergusson, 334; Feri, 264; Ferika, 362; Ferike, 199, 362; Ferke, 264; Ferko, 201, 264; Fermin, 350; Fermina, 344; Fern, 88, 161; Fernald, 106; Fernanda, 362; Fernande, 362; Fernando, 308, 350; Fernao, 308, 362; Feroz, 35, 294; Ferragus, 130; Ferran, 35; Ferrau, 130; Ferrex, 95; Ferris, 59, 140; Ffanci, 384; Fferyll, 389; Fflam, 389; Fflergant, 389; Fflewdwr, 389; Ffodor, 389; Ffowc, 389; Ffraid, 384; Fia, 305, 330; Fiach, 224; Fiachra, 224; Fiacra, 59; Fiacre, 59; Fiallan, 59; Fiamain, 59; Fianait, 217; Fianna, 55; Fibh, 334; Fidel, 264, 350; Fidele, 350; Fidelia, 249, 344; Fidelio, 233, 264; Fidelis, 264; Fidelity, 249; Fidelma, 218; Fides, 249; Fie, 334; Fielding, 106; Fiers, 314; Fife, 334; Fifi, 125; Fifine, 125; Fifna, 186; Fifne, 186; Filbert, 95, 368; Filberta, 88; Filburt, 95; Filia, 161; Filicia, 125; Filip, 314, 357; Filipa, 305, 344; Filipina, 161; Filippa, 354; Filippio, 233; Filippo, 174, 233; Filips, 174; Filmarr, 95; Filmer, 95; Filmore, 95; Filomena, 161, 230, 249, 305; Filomenia, 161; Filomina, 249; Fina, 186; Finan, 25; Finbar, 59, 140, 224; Findabair, 55; Findlay, 140; Fineas, 81; Fineen, 224; Fineena, 218; Finella, 217; Fingal, 59, 140, 334; Finghin, 224; Fingula, 55; Finian, 59, 224; Finlay, 140, 334; Finn, 59, 95, 140, 289; Finna, 218; Finnbar, 59; Finnbogi, 322; Finnin, 224; Finnobarr, 59; Finola, 218; Fiona, 55, 135, 218, 330; Fionan, 224; Fionn, 59, 140, 218, 224; Fionnbarr, 224; Fionnghuala, 135, 217; Fionnlagh, 140; Fionnlaoch, 140; Fionnuala, 218; Fiorella, 230; Fiorello, 233; Fiorenza, 230, 249; Firdos, 35; Firenze, 199; Firman, 25, 95; Firth, 334; Firtha, 330; Fisk, 357; Fiske, 95; Fisseha, 17; Fitch, 95; Fitche, 95; Fitsadam, 106; Fitz, 106, 130, 368; Fitz Adam, 106; Fitz Gerald, 106, 368; Fitz Gibbon, 106; Fitz Gilbert, 106; Fitz Hugh, 106; Fitz James, 106; Fitz Patrick, 106, 368; Fitz Simon, 106; Fitz Walter, 106; Fitz Water, 106; Fitzgerald, 106, 368; Fitzgibbon, 106; Fitzgilbert, 106; Fitzhugh, 106; Fitzjames, 106; Fitzpatrick, 106, 368; Fitzsimmons, 106; Fitzsimon, 106; Fitzsimons, 106; Fitzwalter, 106; Fitzwater, 106; Fjall, 289; Fjarskafinn, 286; Fjorgyn, 317; Flainn, 224; Flamina, 249; Flaminia, 249; Flaminio, 350; Flanagan, 224; Flann, 140, 224; Flanna, 135, 218; Flannagain, 224; Flannan, 140, 224; Flavia, 230, 249, 305; Flavian, 264; Flavio, 233, 264, 350; Flawiusz,

Garafeld, 107; Garai, 81, 264; Garaitz, 50, 344; Garan, 384; Garanhon, 389; Garanwyn, 389; Garatun, 95; Garberend, 26; Garbhach, 140; Garbhan, 140, 224; Garbi, 249; Garbina, 344; Garbine, 344; Garcia, 350, 368; Garda, 362; Garde, 362; Gardell, 368; Gardener, 368; Garder, 322; Gardi, 322; Gardiner, 107, 368; Gardner, 107; Gare, 334; Garek, 368; Garet, 95, 289; Gareth, 26, 46; Garfield, 107; Gari, 362; Garia, 330; Gariland, 107; Garland, 107, 125, 131; Garm, 95, 322; Garman, 95; Garmangabis, 22; Garmann, 95; Garmon, 95; Garmond, 95; Garmund, 95; Garner, 368; Garnet, 95; Garnett, 95; Garnoc, 389; Garnock, 389; Garr, 26, 95; Garrard, 95; Garret, 368; Garrett, 26, 95, 289; Garrick, 95, 368; Garrman, 95; Garroway, 95; Garrson, 107; Garselid, 389; Garson, 107; Garsone, 107; Garth, 289, 357; Garthf, 286; Garton, 95, 289; Garuda, 208, 210; Garudi, 205; Garvan, 224; Garvey, 140, 224; Garvin, 95, 368; Garvyn, 95; Garwig, 95; Garwin, 95; Garwine, 95; Garwood, 107; Garwyli, 389; Garwyn, 95; Gary, 95; Garym, 389; Gascon, 131; Gaspar, 131, 295, 350; Gaspara, 344; Gaspard, 131, 350; Gaston, 131; Gatha, 205, 294; Gaukroger, 95; Gauri, 208; Gaute, 289; Gauthier, 131, 368; Gautier, 131, 368; Gauvain, 46; Gav, 314; Gaven, 334; Gavenia, 330; Gavi, 193; Gavin, 334, 368, 389; Gavina, 330; Gavivi, 17; Gavra, 186; Gavrel, 314; Gavriel, 193; Gavril, 314; Gavrila, 186, 337; Gavrilla, 186, 337; Gavrilovich, 314; Gawain, 46, 95, 334; Gawen, 95, 334; Gawl, 390; Gawyn, 95, 334; Gay, 88, 125, 362; Gayane, 40; Gayatri, 205; Gayeff, 314; Gayle, 88, 95, 186; Gayleen, 186; Gaylen, 140; Gaylene, 186; Gayner, 140; Gaynor, 140, 384; Gazali, 19; Gazit, 186; Gazsi, 201, 295; Gear, 140; Gearald, 140; Gearoid, 224, 368; Gearoidin, 218; Geary, 95; Geb, 81; Gechina, 50, 344; Gedaliah, 193; Gedalya, 193; Gedalyahu, 193; Gedeon, 193, 201; Geela, 186; Gehard, 95; Geir, 289; Geirbjorg, 317; Geiri, 289; Geirleif, 289; Geirmund, 322; Geirolf, 289; Geirrid, 317; Geirrod, 322; Geirstein, 289; Gelasia, 161; Gelasius, 174; Gelban, 59; Gellert, 368; Gelsey, 294; Gelsomina, 72; Geltruda, 230; Gemina, 161; Gemma, 125, 230; Gen, 236; Generosa, 344; Generoso, 350; Genetrix, 249; Geneva, 125; Genevieve, 55, 125, 147; Genevra, 230; Genevre, 125; Genius, 264; Genji, 64; Genoveva, 147; Genowefa, 147; Gentza, 51; Genymede, 174; Geoff, 26; Geoffrey, 26, 95, 131, 368; Geol, 96; Geordie, 174; Georg, 151, 174, 357; George, 174; Georges, 131, 174; Georget, 174; Georgette, 125, 161; Georgia, 161; Georgiana, 161; Georgine, 161; Georgio, 233; Georgitte, 125; Geraghty, 224; Geraint, 26, 390; Gerald, 368; Geralda, 362;

Geraldina, 147, 362; Geraldine, 147, 362; Geralt, 224; Geranium, 162; Gerard, 151, 368; Gerardo, 95, 233, 350; Geraud, 368; Gerd, 95, 286; Gerda, 147, 286, 354, 362; Gerde, 147, 362; Gerdie, 147, 286; Geremia, 193, 233; Gergely, 175; Gergo, 201; Gergor, 175; Gerhard, 151, 357; Gerhardina, 147; Gerhardine, 147; Gerik, 299; Gerlach, 151; Gerlinda, 362; Gerlinde, 362; Germain, 125, 131, 264; Germaine, 55, 125, 362; German, 350, 369; Germana, 125; Germane, 362; Germano, 131; Germund, 354; Gerold, 368; Geronimo, 233, 350; Gerrit, 95; Gerry, 95, 368; Gersham, 193; Gershom, 193; Gert, 369; Gertraud, 362; Gertrud, 147, 354, 362; Gertruda, 147, 362; Gertrude, 147; Gertrudes, 305, 344; Gertrudis, 344; Gertrut, 147; Gervais, 368; Gervase, 96; Gervasio, 350, 369; Gervaso, 350; Gervasy, 369; Gervazy, 369; Gervin, 140; Gerwalt, 147; Gerwalta, 147; Gerwazy, 299, 369; Geryon, 174; Gerzson, 201; Gesnes, 46; Gest, 322; Geva, 186; Gezana, 344; Gezane, 344; Ghada, 31; Ghassan, 35; Ghebers, 295; Gheorghe, 174; Gherardo, 95; Ghislain, 151; Ghislaine, 147; Ghita, 162, 230; Ghleanna, 135; Ghoukas, 40; Gi, 241; Giacomo, 233; Gian, 233; Giancarlo, 233; Giancinta, 162; Giancinte, 162; Giang, 379, 380; Gianina, 230; Gianna, 230; Gianni, 233; Gibbesone, 107; Gibson, 107; Gideon, 193; Gifford, 96, 131, 368; Giflet, 46; Gifre, 26; Gifuhard, 96; Gijs, 88, 96; Gil, 131, 193, 224, 308, 350; Gila, 186; Gilah, 186; Gilal, 186; Gilala, 186; Gilamu, 368; Gilana, 186; Gilat, 186; Gilbarta, 330; Gilbert, 96, 368, 390; Gilberta, 147, 362; Gilberte, 362; Gilberto, 233, 308, 350, 368; Gilbride, 224; Gilburt, 96, 368; Gilby, 289; Gilchrist, 224; Gilda, 55, 88, 362; Gildan, 88; Gildas, 26, 46, 55, 59, 96; Gildea, 224; Gilen, 368; Giles, 175, 264; Gilford, 107; Gilfred, 368; Gilfrid, 368; Gili, 186, 193; Gilia, 186; Gilibeirt, 224; Gilit, 186; Gill, 131, 249; Gilleabart, 334; Gilleasbuig, 140, 151, 334; Gillecriosd, 334; Gille-Eathain, 140; Gillen, 368; Gilles, 175; Gilley, 314; Gilli, 193; Gillian, 249; Gillien, 249; Gillivray, 334; Gilmar, 96; Gilmer, 96, 334, 368; Gilmore, 59, 140; Gilpin, 96; Gilroy, 59, 140, 264; Gils, 322; Gilvaethwy, 390; Gilvarry, 224; Gimbya, 17; Gimle, 317, 322; Gimm, 26; Gin, 236; Gina, 162; Ginebra, 55, 344; Ginerva, 55; Ginessa, 55, 344; Ginger, 249; Ginnungagap, 317; Gino, 233; Ginton, 35; Giolla Chriost, 224; Giollabrighde, 224; Giollabuidhe, 224; Giolladhe, 224; Giollamhuire, 140; Giollanaebhin, 140; Giollaruaidh, 140; Gionnan, 140; Giorgio, 233; Giorsal, 135; Giotto, 368; Giovanna, 230; Giovanni, 233; Giraldo, 233; Girard, 46, 59, 368; Giraud, 368; Girelda, 362; Girflet, 46; Girisa, 208;

175; Guillame, 368; Guillelmina, 230, 344; Guillermo, 350; Guin, 140; Guinevere, 43, 55, 384; Guiomar, 305, 308; Guivret, 46; Gulab, 210; Gulielma, 230; Gullinbursti, 322; Gulltopp, 322; Gullveig, 318; Gungir, 322; Gunhilda, 286; Gunhilde, 286; Gunilla, 147, 355; Gunlaug, 322; Gunn, 334; Gunna, 330; Gunnar, 289, 357, 368; Gunnbjorn, 289; Gunnel, 147, 355; Gunner, 357, 368; Gunnhild, 286; Gunnhildr, 286; Gunnlaug, 322; Gunnlod, 318; Gunnolf, 289; Gunnvor, 286; Gunther, 322, 368; Gurgalan, 46; Guri, 193, 286; Gurice, 186; Gurion, 193; Gurit, 186; Guro, 286; Gurutz, 51; Gus, 289; Gusg, 390; Gust, 76; Gusta, 76, 362; Gustaafa, 362; Gustaof, 369; Gustav, 289; Gustava, 344, 355, 362; Gustave, 264, 369; Gustavo, 350; Gustavus, 369; Gustel, 147, 250; Gustella, 250; Gustelle, 250; Gustha, 362; Gusztav, 264, 369; Guthr, 286; Guthrie, 140, 334; Gutka, 297; Gutrune, 318; Guttorm, 322; Guusa, 362; Guy, 59, 131, 193, 264, 369; Guyapi, 280; Gvenour, 43; Gwaeddan, 384; Gwalchmai, 59, 389; Gwalchmei, 390; Gwales, 390; Gwalhaved, 390; Gwallawg, 390; Gwallter, 390; Gwanwyn, 384; Gwarthegydd, 390; Gwastad, 390; Gwawl, 59, 390; Gwawrddur, 390; Gwefl, 59; Gweir, 390; Gwen, 384; Gwenabwy, 384; Gwenddydd, 43; Gwendlolen, 43; Gwendolen, 55, 384; Gwendolin, 55; Gwendoline, 384; Gwendoloena, 43; Gwener, 384; Gweneth, 55; Gwenhwyfach, 43; Gwenhwyvar, 384; Gwenith, 55; Gwenledyr, 384; Gwenn, 55; Gwenn Alarch, 385; Gwenneth, 55; Gwenwynwyn, 390; Gwenyver, 55; Gwern, 59, 390; Gwernach, 59, 389; Gwerthmwl, 390; Gwevyl, 390; Gwiawn, 390; Gwidon, 264; Gwiffred, 390; Gwilenhin, 390; Gwilym, 368, 390; Gwitart, 390; Gwladys, 384; Gwlgawd, 391; Gwlwlwyd, 391; Gwlyddn, 391; Gwrddnei, 391; Gwrddywal, 391; Gwres, 391; Gwrgwst, 391; Gwrhyr, 391; Gwri, 59, 391; Gwrtheyrn, 391; Gwryon, 391; Gwyddawg, 391; Gwydre, 391; Gwydyon, 391; Gwyn, 384, 391; Gwyndolen, 384; Gwyndolin, 55; Gwynedd, 384; Gwyneth, 384; Gwyngad, 391; Gwynham, 59; Gwynith, 55; Gwynn, 55, 391; Gwynnan, 391; Gwynne, 384; Gwyr, 46, 390, 391; Gwys, 391; Gwystyl, 391; Gwythyr, 391; Gyala, 201, 264; Gyasi, 81; Gyda, 286; Gyes, 175; Gylda, 88; Gyldan, 88; Gymir, 322; Gymnasia, 250; Gynt, 322; Gyoergy, 174; Gyongy, 125; Gyorgy, 174; Gypsy, 88; Gyrd, 322; Gytha, 72, 88, 286; Gyuri, 174; Gyurka, 174, 201; Gyuszi, 201; Gzifa, 17

Ha, 379; Haagley, 107; Haaken, 289; Haalstead, 107; Haarac, 98; Haben, 19; Habib, 35, 193; Habiba, 31; Habibah, 78; Habika, 17; Hacket, 151; Hackett, 151; Hada, 17; Hadar, 186, 193;

Hadara, 186; Hadassah, 186; Haddad, 35; Hadden, 107; Haddon, 107; Haden, 107; Hadeon, 376; Hadil, 31; Hadiya, 31; Hadley, 107; Hadon, 107; Hadrea, 250; Hadria, 250; Hadrian, 107, 357; Hadu, 147; Haduwig, 147; Hadwig, 362; Hadwin, 96, 369; Hadwyn, 96, 369; Hadya, 31; Haefen, 96; Haele, 96; Haemon, 175; Haesel, 88; Haestingas, 96; Haethowine, 96; Hafgan, 59; Hafgrim, 322; Hafiz, 35; Hafleikr, 290; Hafnar, 322; Hafsah, 78; Hafthor, 323; Hafwan, 385; Hagaleah, 108; Hagalean, 107; Hagan, 140, 224, 369; Hagar, 186; Hagaward, 108; Hagen, 77, 323, 369; Hagly, 107; Hagop, 40; Hahkethomemah, 281; Hahnee, 280; Hai, 379, 380; Haidar, 210; Haidee, 162; Haifa, 31; Haig, 40, 107; Haimati, 205; Haine, 369; Haines, 369; Haji, 81; Hajiri, 19; Hajna, 199; Hajnal, 250; Hakan, 280, 287, 355; Hakana, 355; Hakeem, 35; Haki, 323; Hakidonmuya, 277; Hakim, 35; Hakizimana, 82; Hakon, 289; Hal, 289, 369; Hala, 31; Halag, 147; Halah, 31; Halbart, 96; Halbert, 96, 369; Halburt, 96; Halcyone, 162; Haldan, 369; Haldana, 287; Halden, 289, 369; Haldis, 287, 362; Haldisa, 362; Haldora, 287; Hale, 96, 369; Halebeorht, 96; Halette, 125; Haley, 135, 224; Halford, 107; Halfrid, 147, 287; Halfrida, 147, 287, 362; Halfrith, 88; Halfryta, 88; Hali, 175, 186; Halia, 162; Halifrid, 147; Halig, 26, 88; Haligwiella, 107; Halim, 35, 210; Halima, 17, 78; Halimeda, 162; Halina, 162, 297; Halirrhothius, 175, 264; Halithersis, 175; Hall, 107, 323; Halla, 287; Hallam, 107, 289, 369; Hallbjorn, 289; Halldis, 287; Halldor, 323; Halldora, 287; Halley, 107; Hallfred, 323; Hallfrid, 287; Hallfrita, 88; Hallgerd, 287; Hallgerda, 287; Hallie, 362; Halliwell, 107; Hallkel, 323; Hallstein, 323; Hallvard, 323; Hallveig, 287; Hallwell, 107; Hally, 362; Haloke, 278; Halona, 275; Halsey, 107; Halsig, 107; Halton, 107; Halvard, 289, 357; Halvdan, 289; Halveig, 287; Halvor, 289; Halwende, 26; Halwn, 59; Ham, 26; Hamadi, 82; Hamal, 35; Hamar, 289; Hamden, 37; Hamdun, 37; Hamelatun, 107; Hamia, 22; Hamid, 37; Hamilton, 107, 131, 334; Hamish, 334; Hamlet, 151; Hamlett, 151; Hamlin, 151, 369; Hammad, 37; Hammer, 289; Hamoelet, 151; Hamund, 323; Ha-Neul, 241; Han, 151, 379; Hana, 31; Hanan, 186, 193; Hananel, 194; Hanbal, 82; Hand, 107; Handord, 107; Hane, 369; Hanes, 369; Hang, 379; Hanh Phuc, 379; Hania, 282; Hanif, 82; Hanita, 208; Hank, 369; Hanley, 107; Hanly, 107; Hann, 151; Hanna, 35, 119, 186, 355; Hannah, 186, 376; Hanne, 72, 186; Hannela, 186; Hannele, 119, 186; Hannelora, 147; Hannelore, 147; Hanno, 151; Hannraoi, 369; Hanraoi, 224; Hanrietta, 125; Hanriette, 125; Hans, 73, 151,

55, 147, 385; Isolde, 43, 55, 385; Isole, 147; Isolf, 324; Isoud, 43; Isoude, 43; Isra, 32; Israel, 194; Israt, 32; Isrod, 324; Issa, 82; Issay, 19; Istaqa, 282; Istas, 275; Istu, 280; Istvan, 176, 201; Iswara, 212; Ita, 135, 218; Itai, 194; Ither, 47; Itsaso, 345; Ittamar, 194; Ituha, 275; Itxaro, 345; Itzaak, 194; Itzak, 194; Iulia, 251; Iulius, 251; Iulus, 265; Iustig, 391; Iuwine, 26; Iva, 126, 187; Ivan, 176, 194, 314, 350, 376; Ivana, 68, 187, 312; Ivane, 187, 312; Ivanko, 176; Ivanna, 163, 187, 312, 376; Ivar, 290, 324, 357, 369; Ive, 369; Iven, 131; Iver, 324, 334, 369; Ives, 97, 369; Ivey, 88; Ivor, 290, 324, 369; Ivy, 88, 163; Iwan, 391; Iwdael, 97; Iwona, 297, 318; Ixaka, 51, 194; Ixidor, 176; Ixion, 176; Iye, 280; Izaak, 77, 194; Izabella, 187; Izanami, 236; Izar, 345; Izarra, 345; Izarre, 345; Izazkun, 344; Izett, 218; Izmirlian, 40; Izrael, 194; Izsak, 201; Izso, 187; Izusa, 275

Jaakkima, 120; Jaakkina, 119; Jaana, 119; Jaantje, 187; Jaap, 194; Jabari, 82; Jabbar, 35; Jabez, 194; Jabilo, 19; Jabir, 35; Jabulani, 19; Jacek, 299; Jacinta, 163, 305, 345; Jacintha, 163; Jacinthe, 163; Jacinto, 176, 308, 350; Jack, 97, 194, 299; Jackson, 108; Jacob, 194; Jacoba, 187, 251; Jacobe, 194; Jacot, 194; Jacquelin, 131; Jacqueline, 126; Jacquenetta, 126; Jacquenette, 126; Jacques, 131; Jacy, 280; Jada, 187, 363; Jade, 345; Jadriga, 363; Jadryga, 363; Jadwiga, 297; Jael, 187, 194; Jaen, 187; Ja'far, 35; Jafar, 210; Jafari, 82; Jaffa, 187; Jafit, 187; Jafita, 187; Jafuru, 19; Jaganmata, 205; Jager, 108; Jagger, 108; Jago, 350; Jahi, 82; Jahnu, 210; Jahzara, 17; Jaime, 308, 350; Jaimica, 345; Jaine, 187; Jaione, 50, 345; Jake, 194; Jakinda, 50, 345; Jakob, 73, 77, 151, 324, 357; Jakoba, 147, 187; Jakobah, 187; Jakobe, 147; Jakobie, 147; Jakome, 51, 194; Jakub, 69; Jala, 32; Jaleel, 35; Jaleh, 294; Jalil, 213; Jalmari, 121; Jamal, 35; Jambha, 210; Jambhala, 211; James, 97, 194; Jamie, 194; Jamil, 35; Jamila, 32, 79; Jamilah, 32; Jamo, 121; Jamsheed, 295; Jan, 77, 187, 194, 299, 358; Jana, 68, 187, 218, 251, 297; Jancsi, 194; Jane, 187; Janecska, 297; Janek, 299; Janet, 187; Janetta, 187; Janette, 187; Jani, 121, 194; Janice, 187; Janie, 187, 194; Janina, 187; Janine, 187; Janis, 187; Janita, 187; Janka, 187, 199; Jankia, 194; Janko, 194; Janna, 205; Janne, 121, 187; Jannes, 194; Janos, 194; Jans, 187; Jansje, 187; Jantje, 194; Januarius, 299; Janus, 265; Japhet, 151, 194; Jaquelina, 187; Jaqueline, 187; Jaquenette, 187; Jaques, 194; Jaquetta, 187; Jarda, 69; Jardena, 187; Jardina, 187; Jared, 194; Jarek, 299; Jari, 121; Jarina, 163; Jarine, 163; Jarita, 208; Jarka, 337; Jarkko, 121; Jarlath, 225; Jarman, 151; Jarmann, 151; Jarmila, 337; Jarmo,

121; Jarngerd, 318; Jarnsaxa, 318; Jarold, 369; Jaroslav, 69, 338; Jarratt, 369; Jarvia, 363; Jarvis, 151, 369; Jasha, 314; Jasia, 297; Jasmine, 294; Jason, 176; Jasone, 345; Jasper, 97, 131, 194, 295; Jasun, 176; Jatinra, 211; Javier, 131, 308, 350; Javiera, 345; Javiero, 350; Javras, 211; Jawhar, 35; Jay, 131, 151, 176; Jaya, 208; Jayanti, 205; Jaye, 131, 151; Jayne, 187, 208; Jaythen, 355; Jayvyn, 19; Jean, 131, 194, 330; Jean Baptiste, 131; Jeanetta, 126; Jeanette, 126; Jeanne, 126; Jeannot, 194; Jed, 194; Jedi, 194; Jedidiah, 35, 194; Jedrek, 299; Jedrik, 299; Jedrus, 299; Jeff, 369; Jefferson, 108; Jeffrey, 26, 131, 369; Jehan, 32; Jehane, 126; Jeirgif, 314; Jelani, 19; Jelena, 312; Jem, 194; Jemima, 187; Jemina, 187; Jen, 73; Jenci, 201; Jencir, 176; Jenda, 187, 194; Jendayi, 17, 79; Jennifer, 55; Jenny, 55; Jennyfer, 55; Jennyver, 55; Jeno, 163, 176; Jens, 73, 194, 324, 358; Jensina, 187; Jensine, 72, 187; Jeoffroi, 131; Jephtah, 194; Jeremi, 194; Jeremiah, 194; Jeremias, 77, 194, 350; Jeremie, 194; Jeremy, 194; Jermija, 314; Jeroen, 176; Jerolin, 265; Jerome, 176, 265; Jeronimo, 350; Jerrold, 369; Jerusha, 187; Jervis, 369; Jerzy, 299; Jerzyr, 176; Jesper, 131, 358; Jessamina, 126; Jessamine, 126, 294; Jesse, 194; Jessica, 187; Jessie, 187, 194; Jesus, 350; Jesusa, 305, 345; Jetje, 363; Jetta, 252; Jette, 252; Jewel, 126, 252; Jia, 64; Jibade, 82; Jibril, 35; Jie, 64, 66; Jill, 88, 252; Jilt, 77; Jim, 194; Jimena, 345; Jimmy, 194; Jin, 64, 66, 241; Jin-Ho, 241; Jinny, 252; Jinx, 252; Jira, 17; Jirair, 40; Jiri, 69, 176; Jirina, 68; Jirka, 69; Jirkar, 176; Jiro, 239; Jivanta, 205; Jivin, 211; Joachim, 194; Joakima, 187; Joan, 187; Joana, 305; Joanka, 297; Joanna, 126, 187; Joao, 308; Joaquim, 308; Joaquin, 350; Joaquina, 187, 345; Joaquine, 187; Job, 194; Jobina, 187; Jobyna, 187; Jocasta, 163; Jocelin, 187, 252; Joceline, 187; Jocelyn, 88, 187, 252; Jocelyne, 88; Jochebed, 187; Jocheved, 194; Jock, 194, 334; Jodie, 187; Joel, 194; Joella, 187; Joelle, 187; Joelliana, 187; Joelliane, 187; Joen, 73, 194; Jofrid, 318; Johan, 121, 151, 194, 358; Johann, 151; Johanna, 119, 147, 187, 355; Johanne, 290; Johannes, 121, 151, 290; Johari, 17; Johfrit, 47; John, 194; Johnson, 334; Johnston, 334; Joka, 187; Jokin, 194; Jokina, 187; Jokine, 187; Jola, 187; Jolan, 147, 199; Jolanda, 230; Jolanka, 147; Jolanta, 297; Jolgeir, 324; Joli, 147; Jolie, 126; Jolon, 280; Jon, 194; Jonam, 194, 358; Jonas, 194, 350, 358; Jonatan, 194; Jonathan, 194; Jonati, 187; Jone, 187; Joo-Chan, 241; Joo-Eun, 241; Joop, 194; Joosef, 121, 194; Joosep, 121; Jooseppi, 121, 194; Joost, 77, 265; Jopie, 194; Jora, 187; Jord, 318; Jordan, 187, 194; Jordane, 187; Jore, 194; Joreid, 318;

205; Kay, 47, 163, 334, 391; Kaya, 277; Kayley, 218; Kayne, 60, 140; Kaysa, 355; Kazatimiru, 337, 338; Kazemde, 82; Kazi, 19; Kazia, 187; Kazimierz, 299; Kazimir, 69; Kazmer, 299; Ke, 45; Keagan, 225; Keaghan, 60; Kealan, 225; Keallach, 225; Kealy, 225; Kean, 225; Keanan, 97, 225; Keane, 60, 97; Keara, 216, 218; Kearn, 141; Kearney, 60; Keary, 60, 225; Keavy, 218; Kebira, 32; Kedalion, 176; Kedar, 35, 211; Keefe, 140, 225; Keegan, 60, 140, 225; Keegsquaw, 276; Keeley, 135; Keelia, 55; Keelin, 55; Keely, 55, 135, 218, 225; Keenan, 97, 225; Keenat, 216, 218; Keene, 60, 97; Keera, 135, 218; Kees, 77, 265; Keeya, 18; Keezheekoni, 276; Kefira, 187; Kegan, 60, 140; Kei, 47, 236, 391; Keifer, 140; Keiji, 239; Keiko, 236; Keir, 60, 334; Keira, 135, 218; Keisha, 18; Keith, 60, 225, 334, 391; Kek, 82; Keket, 79; Kelan, 225; Kelby, 369; Kelci, 287; Kelda, 287; Keldan, 290; Kele, 282; Kelemen, 201; Kelemon, 385; Keleos, 163; Kelilah, 187; Kell, 290; Kellach, 225; Kellan, 135; Kelleher, 225; Keller, 141; Kelley, 141; Kelli, 391; Kellie, 136; Kellman, 201; Kelly, 136, 141, 363; Kelman, 265; Kelsey, 287, 290; Kelsig, 290; Kelso, 334; Kelula, 187; Kelvin, 60, 141, 334; Kelvyn, 60; Kelwin, 60; Kelwyn, 60; Kelyddon, 391; Kelyn, 391; Kemal, 35; Kembell, 60; Kemble, 60; Keme, 281; Kemen, 51, 351; Kemena, 345; Kemina, 345; Kemp, 97; Kempe, 97; Ken, 97, 334, 391; Kenan, 225; Kendal, 60; Kendall, 60, 97; Kendhal, 60; Kendra, 22, 55; Kendrick, 26, 60, 108, 141; Kendrik, 108; Kendryck, 26; Kendryk, 108; Kenehyr, 391; Kenelm, 97; Kengsley, 108; Kenley, 108; Kenly, 108; Kenn, 60, 391; Kennard, 97; Kennedy, 141, 225, 334; Kenneth, 60, 97, 334; Kennis, 135; Kennocha, 55; Kenny, 225, 334; Kenric, 26; Kenrick, 97; Kenrik, 97; Kenryk, 97; Kent, 26, 60, 97, 391; Kentigern, 60; Kenton, 97; Kenward, 97; Kenway, 26, 97; Kenwyn, 385; Kenyi, 19; Kenyon, 141, 391; Kenzie, 334; Keon, 19; Keoni, 303; Kepa, 50, 163; Kepe, 163; Keran, 187; Kerani, 205; Kerbasi, 51, 369; Kerbasy, 369; Kerby, 369; Keren, 187; Keres, 163; Kereteki, 303; Keriam, 135; Keril, 176; Kerk, 334; Kerman, 131; Kermeilde, 88; Kermichael, 141; Kermichil, 141, 334; Kermilda, 88; Kermilla, 88; Kermillie, 88; Kermit, 60, 141; Kermode, 60; Kern, 141; Kerne, 141; Kerr, 141, 290, 334; Kerrie, 88; Kerry, 60, 88, 135, 141, 218, 225; Kerstan, 265; Kersten, 338; Kerstin, 355; Kerta, 363; Kerttu, 120, 363; Kerwen, 141; Kerwin, 60, 141, 225; Kerwy, 225; Kerwyn, 60, 141; Keryn, 187; Kesara, 345; Kesare, 345; Kesava, 208; Kesegowaase, 281; Keshi, 211; Keshia, 18; Kesi, 79; Kesia, 18; Kesin, 213; Kestejoo, 281; Kester, 108, 176, 265; Kestorr, 176; Kethryn, 163;

Kethtrwm, 391; Ketil, 324; Ketura, 187; Ketzia, 187; Keudawg, 391; Kevan, 60, 225; Kevay, 216; Keve, 201; Keverne, 136; Kevin, 60, 141, 225; Kevork, 40; Kevyn, 60, 141, 391; Key, 141; Keyna, 385; Kezia, 187; Khachig, 40; Khafra, 82; Khaldun, 35, 82; Khalfani, 82; Khalid, 35, 82; Khalidah, 32; Khalif, 35; Khalil, 35; Khanh, 379; Kharouf, 35; Khasa, 205; Khayri, 35; Khayyat, 35; Khentimentiu, 82; Khepri, 79, 82; Khiem, 379; Khnemu, 82; Khnum, 82; Khons, 82; Khorshed, 295; Khoury, 35; Khristos, 176; Khrustina, 163; Khrystiyanr, 176; Khufu, 82; Kian, 225, 392; Kianga, 18; Kiara, 218; Kiarr, 290; Kiba, 187; Kibddar, 392; Kichi, 236; Kiden, 18; Kienan, 225; Kiera, 218; Kieran, 60, 141, 225; Kieron, 225; Kiet, 374; Kieu, 379; Kieve, 385; Kigva, 385; Kiku, 236; Kilby, 369; Kildaire, 225; Kildare, 225; Kilian, 60, 265; Killdaire, 225; Killian, 60, 225, 265; Kilwich, 392; Kilydd, 392; Kim, 26, 88, 97, 379, 380, 392; Kim Cuc, 379; Kim Ly, 379; Kimama, 279; Kiman, 52; Kimball, 26, 60, 392; Kimberly, 88; Kimble, 392; Kimbra, 88; Kimbro, 88; Kimbrought, 88; Kimi, 236, 276; Kimimela, 279; Kimoni, 19; Kin, 239, 334; Kinden, 265; Kindin, 265; Kineks, 275; Kineta, 163; Kinetikos, 163; King, 97; Kingdon, 108; Kingston, 109; Kingswell, 109; Kinnard, 141; Kinnat, 216, 218; Kinnell, 141; Kinneret, 187; Kinnette, 187; Kinnon, 334; Kinny, 334; Kinsale, 225; Kinsella, 225; Kinsey, 97; Kintan, 213; Kiollsig, 290; Kiona, 275; Kip, 109; Kipp, 109; Kippar, 109; Kippie, 109; Kipr, 176; Kira, 252, 294, 312; Kiran, 208; Kirati, 205; Kirby, 290, 369; Kiri, 52, 53, 302; Kirie, 252; Kiril, 176, 314; Kiritan, 213; Kirk, 97, 290, 334, 370; Kirkley, 109; Kirkly, 109; Kirkwood, 109; Kirochka, 312; Kirsi, 120; Kirsten, 72, 163, 252, 287, 318; Kirsti, 120; Kirstie, 163, 252, 330; Kirsty, 163, 252; Kirwin, 60; Kirwyn, 60; Kiryl, 314; Kirylr, 176; Kisa, 312; Kisho, 239; Kiska, 312; Kismet, 294; Kissa, 18, 79; Kistna, 213; Kit, 163; Kita, 236; Kitchi, 281; Kitr, 176; Kitty, 163; Kiva, 187, 195; Kivi, 187; Kiwidinok, 276; Kiyoko, 236; Kiyoshi, 239; Kjarr, 324; Kjartan, 324; Kjell, 358; Kjolvor, 318; Klaas, 77, 176; Klára, 68; Klara, 252, 318, 355; Klari, 252; Klarika, 252; Klarissa, 252; Klarisza, 252; Klarysa, 376; Klas, 358; Klaude, 265; Klaudi, 265; Klaudia, 252, 297; Klaudius, 265; Klaus, 73, 153, 176; Klazina, 163; Kleef, 109; Klemenis, 265; Klemens, 265; Kleng, 290; Kleopatra, 163; Klepp, 324; Kliment, 265; Kneph, 82; Knight, 97; Knocks, 109; Knoton, 280; Knox, 109; Knud, 73, 290; Knut, 290, 324, 358; Knutr, 290; Kodran, 324; Koen, 153; Koenraad, 77, 153; Kohana, 236, 284; Kohia, 302; Kohkahycumest, 281; Kojo, 19; Koko, 236,

252; Latonia, 252; Latoya, 345; Laudalino, 265; Laudegrance, 47; Laudine, 43; Laughlin, 225; Launcelot, 47, 131; Launder, 109; Launfal, 47; Laura, 252, 305, 345, 355; Lauran, 265; Laureen, 252; Laurel, 126, 252, 265; Laurella, 252; Lauren, 126, 252, 265; Laurena, 252; Laurence, 265; Laurencia, 345; Laurene, 126, 252; Laurent, 265; Laurentia, 252; Laurentij, 315; Laurentios, 265; Laurette, 126, 252; Lauri, 121; Laurica, 252; Laurie, 252; Laurin, 252; Laurina, 252; Laurissa, 252; Lauritz, 73, 77; Lauryn, 252; Lausanne, 43; Lavan, 195; Lavare, 252; Laveda, 252; Lavena, 55; Laverna, 126; Lavernia, 126; Lavetta, 252; Lavette, 252; Lavina, 252; Lavinia, 252; Lavra, 252, 376; Law, 109; Lawe, 109; Lawford, 109; Lawler, 141; Lawley, 109; Lawly, 109; Lawrence, 265; Lawron, 265; Lawson, 109; Lawton, 109; Lay, 109; Layla, 32, 79; Laylie, 187; Layna, 164; Layton, 109; Lazar, 195; Lazaro, 351; Lazarus, 195; Lazlo, 339; Lazzaro, 195; Le, 64, 66, 379; Lea, 90, 164, 187; Leachlainn, 225; Leah, 90, 136, 187; Leal, 97, 131; Leala, 126; Lealia, 126; Leamhnach, 141; Lean, 334; Leana, 331; Leander, 177, 265; Leandra, 253; Leandro, 177, 309, 351; Leandros, 265; Leane, 334; Leanian, 26; Leannan, 141; Lear, 97, 370; Learoyd, 370; Leary, 225; Leathan, 334; Leathlobhair, 225; Leax, 26; Leb, 195; Lech, 299; Lechsinska, 297; Leda, 164, 252; Ledaea, 252; Ledah, 187; Ledyard, 370; Lee, 60, 90, 97, 225; Leena, 119; Leeto, 19; Legarre, 345; Legget, 131; Lehana, 18; Lei, 64; Leia, 90; Leicester, 109, 265; Leidolf, 290; Leif, 290, 358; Leigh, 60, 90, 97; Leighton, 109; Leiko, 236; Leila, 32, 218; Leilani, 302; Leira, 345; Leirioessa, 253; Leiriope, 253; Leis, 253; Leith, 60, 334; Leitha, 164; Leitis, 136; Leksi, 177; Lela, 252; Lelah, 252; Leland, 109; Lele, 97; Lelia, 164, 252, 363; Leman, 97; Lemuel, 195; Lemuela, 187; Len, 283, 334, 370; Lena, 164, 253, 355; Lenci, 164, 200, 265; Lene, 76, 318; Lenet, 253; Leneta, 253; Lenge, 26; Lenis, 253; Lenita, 253; Lenka, 68; Lenmana, 277; Lennart, 358, 370; Lennie, 334; Lenno, 280; Lennon, 141; Lennox, 141; Lenore, 164; Lenox, 334; Lenusya, 312; Lenya, 315; Leo, 97, 265, 370; Leoarrie, 253; Leocadia, 305; Leocadie, 131; Leod, 335; Leoda, 147, 363; Leodegan, 47; Leodegrance, 131; Leodegraunce, 47; Leodora, 253; Leof, 26; Leoine, 253; Leola, 230, 363; Leoline, 253; Leoma, 90; Leon, 131, 265, 351; Leona, 126, 253; Leonaldo, 370; Leonard, 370; Leonarda, 126, 164; Leonardo, 233, 309, 351, 370; Leonce, 131, 253; Leone, 126, 131, 233, 253, 265; Leonelle, 126, 253; Leonhard, 370; Leonid, 265; Leonidas, 265; Leonide, 265, 315; Leonides, 351; Leonie, 126; Leonita, 253; Leonlina, 253; Leonor, 305,

345; Leonora, 164, 230, 345; Leonore, 164; Leontin, 253; Leontina, 253; Leontine, 253; Leontis, 265; Leontyne, 253; Leopold, 153, 370; Leopolda, 147; Leopoldina, 147; Leopoldine, 147; Leopoldo, 153; Leora, 164; Leorad, 370; Leota, 147; Leotie, 275; Leppa, 120; Lera, 345; Lerola, 253; Leroy, 131, 265, 370; Lesham, 188; Leshem, 195; Lesley, 55, 60, 136, 141, 331, 335; Leslie, 55, 60, 136, 141, 331, 335; Lesta, 315; Lester, 265; Leta, 253; Letha, 164; Lethe, 164, 177; Lethia, 164; Leticia, 305; Letitia, 253; Letizia, 230; Letje, 126; Lettie, 253; Letty, 253; Letya, 126; Leucippe, 164; Leuconoe, 253; Leucothea, 164; Leucothia, 164; Leupold, 370; Leute, 147; Lev, 195, 315; Levana, 253; Levene, 90; Leveret, 131; Leverett, 131; Leverna, 253; Leverton, 109; Levey, 195; Levi, 195; Levia, 188; Levina, 90; Levka, 315; Levushka, 315; Levyna, 90; Lew, 97, 265, 339; Lewanna, 188; Lewi, 195; Lewis, 370; Lewy, 153; Lexina, 164; Lexine, 164; Ley, 90; Leya, 205, 345; Leyati, 283; Leyman, 97; Leysa, 376; Li, 64, 66; Lia, 164, 230; Liadan, 218; Liam, 141, 225, 370; Lian, 64; Liana, 126, 305, 345; Liane, 126; Liang, 66; Libentina, 253; Liber, 265; Libera, 253; Libertas, 253; Liberty, 90; Libitina, 253; Libusa, 68; Libuse, 68; Lichas, 177, 265; Licus, 265; Lida, 68, 253, 312; Lidia, 297, 305, 312; Lidija, 312; Lidio, 177; Lidiya, 312; Lidmann, 26; Lidochka, 312; Lidoine, 43; Lidskjalf, 324; Liealia, 126; Lief, 290; Lien, 64, 76, 379; Liesbet, 187; Liesbeth, 187; Lieu, 379; Lifton, 109; Ligia, 164, 305; Liisa, 120; Lil, 218; Lila, 164, 253, 294, 297; Lilac, 294; Lilah, 188; Lilch, 164; Lili, 136, 164; Lilia, 164, 337; Lilian, 253, 305; Liliana, 230, 253; Liliane, 253; Lilie, 188; Lilika, 253; Lilis, 164; Lilith, 188; Lilka, 297; Lilla, 164; Lillian, 253; Lillis, 164; Liluye, 278; Lily, 164, 188, 253; Lilybelle, 253; Lilybet, 253, 385; Lima, 253; Limber, 18; Limentina, 253; Lin, 26, 90, 318; Lina, 32, 76, 164, 253, 355; Lincoln, 60, 109; Lind, 97, 147; Linda, 147, 253, 345; Lindael, 97; Lindberg, 153; Linddun, 97; Lindeberg, 153; Lindell, 97; Lindie, 147; Lindisfarne, 109; Lindleigh, 109; Lindley, 109; Lindly, 109; Lindsay, 90, 331, 335, 370; Lindsey, 90, 331, 370; Lindy, 345; Line, 109, 318; Linette, 22, 56, 126; Linford, 97; Ling, 64; Link, 109; Linka, 200; Linleah, 109; Linley, 109; Linly, 109; Linn, 22, 26; Linne, 90, 318; Linnea, 287; Linnette, 56; Lino, 265; Linton, 109; Lintun, 109; Linus, 177; Lionel, 47, 265; Lioslaith, 331; Liosliath, 141; Lipot, 370; Lipp, 177; Lippi, 177; Lippio, 177; Lippo, 121; Lir, 60, 97; Liriene, 126; Lirienne, 126; Liriope, 253; Lirit, 188; Lirita, 188; Lisa, 148; Lisabet, 187; Lisabette, 187; Lisavet, 187; Lisbet, 72; Lise, 72, 148, 187, 283; Liseli,

392; Mabuz, 47; Mac, 60; Mac Adhaimh, 141; Mac Ailean, 141; Mac Alasdair, 141; Mac Artuir, 141; Mac Asgaill, 141; Mac a'bhaird, 141; Mac a'bhiadhtaiche, 141; Mac an Aba, 141; Mac an Bhaillidh, 141; Mac an Bharain, 141; Mac an Bhreatannaich, 141; Mac an Tsagairt, 141; Mac an t-Saoir, 141; Mac Bheathain, 141; Mac Bhriain, 141; Mac Daraich, 141; Mac Ghille Aindries, 141; Mac Ghille Mhicheil, 142; Mac Ghille-Bhuidhe, 141; Mac Ghille-Dhuibh, 141; Mac Ghille-Dhuinn, 142; Mac Ghille-Easpuig, 142; Mac Ghille-Laider, 142; MacAdam, 141; MacAdhaimh, 141; MacAilean, 141; MacAladair, 141; MacAllen, 141; MacAllister, 141; MacArthur, 141; MacArtuir, 141; Macaire, 177; Macaria, 164; Macario, 351; Macawi, 279; Maccus, 26, 60; MacDaibhidh, 333; Macha, 218; Machakw, 283; Machaon, 177; Machara, 331; Machi, 236; Machiko, 236; Machk, 281; Machum, 195; Macia, 297; MacKendrick, 334; Mack, 60; Macklin, 60; Macklyn, 60; MacLean, 141; MacNab, 141; MacNair, 142; Mada, 218; Madailein, 218; Madalen, 188; Madalena, 346; Madalyn, 188; Madawc, 392; Madawg, 392; Maddalen, 148; Maddalena, 148; Maddalene, 148; Maddalyn, 148; Madden, 225; Maddoc, 392; Maddock, 60, 392; Maddog, 392; Maddox, 60; Madeira, 307; Madel, 188; Madelaine, 188; Madeleine, 188; Madelena, 188; Madelene, 188; Madelhari, 148, 153; Madge, 164; Madhava, 211; Madhur, 208; Madison, 109, 370; Madoc, 47, 392; Madog, 392; Madonna, 230, 253; Mador, 47; Madora, 164; Madra, 90, 345; Madre, 90, 345; Madri, 205; Mads, 195; Madu, 82; Mady, 90, 148; Mae, 22, 188; Maebh, 218; Maed, 110; Maegth, 90; Mael, 392; Maeleachlainn, 225; Maelgwyn, 392; Maelisa, 225; Maelwine, 97; Maelwys, 392; Maera, 253; Maeret, 97; Maerewine, 98; Maertisa, 90; Maethelwine, 97; Maetthere, 97; Maeva, 318; Maeve, 56, 218; Maeveen, 56; Mafalda, 307; Mafuane, 79; Magaere, 164; Magan, 26, 363; Maganhildi, 148; Magar, 41; Magaskawee, 279; Magd, 148; Magda, 148, 188; Magdala, 188; Magdalen, 188; Magdalena, 188; Magdalene, 188; Magena, 275; Maggie, 331; Maghnus, 266; Magna, 287; Magne, 290; Magnhilda, 148; Magni, 324; Magnild, 148, 287, 290, 358; Magnilda, 148, 287; Magnilde, 148, 287; Magnolia, 126; Magnor, 290; Magnus, 73, 266, 290, 358; Mago, 225; Mahadeva, 213; Mahadevi, 205; Mahakala, 211; Mahal, 275; Mahala, 32, 188, 275; Mahalia, 188; Mahamari, 205; Mahault, 76; Mahdi, 18; Maheloas, 47; Maher, 225; Mahesa, 208; Maheshvari, 205; Mahieu, 132; Mahila, 205; Mahina, 302; Mahir, 35, 195; Mahkah, 284; Mahmoud, 37; Mahmud,

37; Mahon, 225; Mahpee, 284; Mahu, 277; Mahuru, 302; Mai, 236, 275, 331, 355, 379; Maia, 164, 188, 253; Maialen, 188; Maibe, 79; Maible, 218; Maichail, 195; Maida, 22, 90; Maidel, 90, 188; Maidie, 90; Maighdlin, 218; Maija, 120; Maikki, 120; Maiko, 236; Mailhairer, 131; Maille, 218; Mailsi, 218; Mainchin, 225; Mair, 385; Maire, 136, 218; Mairead, 218, 331; Mairearad, 136; Mairghread, 136; Mairi, 136, 331; Mairia, 218; Mairin, 136; Mai-ron, 195; Mairona, 218; Mairtin, 266; Maisie, 331; Maitane, 90; Maite, 90, 345; Maitea, 345; Maitena, 90; Maiti, 218; Maitilda, 218; Maitilde, 218; Maitland, 109; Maizah, 18; Maj, 355; Maja, 355; Majeed, 295; Majella, 218; Majesta, 253; Majida, 32; Majnoon, 295; Maka, 279; Makalani, 82; Makalo, 19; Makara, 53, 208; Makareta, 272; Makarim, 32; Makarioa, 177; Makawee, 279; Makeen, 35; Makiko, 236; Makin, 35; Makis, 195; Makkapitew, 281; Makkitotosimew, 276; Makoto, 239; Maks, 315; Maksim, 315; Maksimillian, 315; Maksym, 299; Maksymilian, 299; Makya, 283; Mal, 195, 225; Malache, 253; Malachi, 195; Malachy, 195, 225; Malagigi, 131; Malaika, 18; Malajit, 211; Malak, 32, 188; Malaya, 345; Malcah, 188; Malcolm, 60, 142, 335; Malcsi, 200; Malduc, 47; Maledysaunte, 43; Malena, 355; Malene, 148, 355; Malgorzata, 297; Mali, 373, 385; Malia, 279, 363; Malik, 35; Malika, 32, 200; Malila, 278; Malin, 97, 355; Malina, 188; Malinda, 164; Malini, 208; Malise, 136, 331; Malkah, 188; Malkolm, 358; Mallaidh, 188; Malleville, 132; Mallolwch, 392; Mallory, 131, 148, 153, 266; Malloy, 226; Malmuira, 331; Malmuirie, 331; Malone, 225; Maloney, 142, 225; Malva, 164; Malvin, 60, 97, 142, 225; Malvina, 56, 136, 164, 218, 253; Malvine, 164; Malvinia, 253; Malvyn, 60, 97; Malyn, 97; Mamiko, 236; Mamoru, 239; Mana, 253; Manaba, 278; Manal, 32; Manar, 32; Manara, 32; Manasses, 195; Manawydan, 392; Manchu, 66; Manda, 208, 253, 345; Mandara, 208; Mandek, 299; Mandel, 131, 153, 370; Mandex, 299; Mandisa, 18, 79; Mane, 225; Manette, 126; Manfred, 97, 153, 358, 370; Manfrid, 97, 370; Manfried, 153; Manfrit, 153; Mangena, 188; Mani, 324; Mania, 253; Manipi, 280; Mankalita, 279; Manley, 109; Manly, 109; Mann, 26, 97; Manneville, 131; Mannie, 195; Manning, 97; Mannis, 142; Mannix, 225; Mannleah, 109; Mannuss, 225; Manny, 195; Manoel, 309; Manoj, 211; Mansa, 19; Mansfield, 109; Mansi, 277; Mansoor, 37; Mantel, 131; Manto, 253; Manton, 26, 109; Mantotohpa, 281; Manu, 82, 213, 303; Manuel, 195, 309, 351; Manuela, 188, 307, 345; Manus, 142, 266; Manvel, 266; Manvil, 266; Manville, 131; Manya,

Maxina, 254; Maxine, 254; Maxwell, 27, 97, 335; May, 22, 188, 253, 331; Maya, 253; Mayah, 188; Mayako, 236; Mayar, 195; Mayda, 22, 90; Mayde, 90; Mayer, 195, 267; Mayfield, 110; Mayhew, 132; Mayir, 195; Maylea, 302; Maynard, 153, 370; Mayo, 142; Mayoko, 236; Mayor, 267; Maysun, 32; Mayuko, 236; Maza Blaska, 282; Mazel, 188; Mazentius, 267; Mbizi, 82; Mead, 110; Meadghbh, 56; Meadhbh, 218; Meadhra, 225; Mealcoluim, 335; Meara, 218, 225; Mearr, 218; Meda, 275; Medard, 201; Medb, 56; Medea, 164, 254; Medesicaste, 254; Meditrina, 254; Medora, 164; Medoro, 132; Medr, 60; Medredydd, 60; Medrod, 47; Medus, 177; Medusa, 164; Medwin, 97, 370; Medwine, 97; Medwyn, 97, 370; Medyr, 393; Mee, 64; Meeda, 219; Megan, 22, 218, 385; Megara, 164; Megedagik, 281; Meghan, 22, 218, 385; Mehadi, 205; Mehemet, 37; Mehetabel, 188; Meheytabel, 188; Mehitabelle, 188; Mehrdad, 295; Mehtar, 211; Meht-urt, 79; Meilseoir, 195; Meilyg, 393; Meinhard, 153; Meinke, 153; Meino, 153; Meinrad, 153, 370; Meinwen, 385; Meinyard, 153; Meir, 195; Meira, 188; Mela, 298; Melampus, 177; Melania, 164; Melanie, 164; Melanippe, 254; Melanippus, 177; Melantha, 164; Melanthe, 164; Melanthius, 177; Melantho, 164; Melborn, 110; Melbourne, 110; Melburn, 110; Melbyrne, 110; Melchior, 47, 195, 225, 295; Melcia, 363; Meldon, 110; Meldrick, 110; Meldrik, 110; Meldryk, 110; Meleagant, 47; Meleager, 177; Melecertes, 177; Melechan, 47; Meleda, 165; Melek, 32; Melena, 164; Meleta, 165; Meletios, 177; Meli, 279; Melia, 254; Meliadus, 47; Melicent, 363; Melina, 164; Melinda, 164; Meliodas, 47; Melisande, 127; Melisenda, 346; Melissa, 43, 164, 254; Melisse, 164; Melita, 165; Melka, 298; Melkedoodum, 281; Melker, 358; Melkorka, 318; Melleta, 165; Mellicent, 363; Mellisa, 164; Mellona, 254; Melodie, 127; Melosa, 346; Melosia, 346; Melpomene, 165; Melrone, 225; Melusina, 127; Melva, 56, 218, 385; Melville, 60, 132; Melvin, 60, 97, 225; Melvina, 56; Melvyn, 60, 97, 225; Melwas, 47; Melyon, 47; Memdi, 275; Memnon, 267; Memphis, 79, 82; Menachem, 195; Menachema, 188; Menachemah, 188; Menassah, 195; Mendel, 195; Mendi, 346; Menelaus, 177; Menes, 82; Meng, 53; Menglad, 318; Menkaura, 82; Menoeceus, 177; Mensah, 82; Mentor, 177; Menuha, 188; Menw, 60, 393; Menyhert, 201; Menzies, 335; Meoquanee, 276; Mercede, 231; Mercedes, 254, 346; Mercer, 110, 132, 267; Mercher, 393; Merci, 127; Mercia, 22, 90, 385; Mercury, 267; Mercy, 90, 127; Mere, 272, 302; Meredith, 56, 385, 393; Meredydd,

385, 393; Merek, 370; Mererid, 385; Merestun, 110; Merewode, 110; Merewood, 110; Meridith, 393; Meriel, 32; Merin, 393; Meris, 253; Merise, 253; Merissa, 253; Merle, 132, 254; Merlin, 47, 60, 132; Merlina, 254; Merlion, 132; Merlow, 109; Merlyn, 60; Merna, 56, 219; Merolla, 254; Merope, 165; Merrell, 370; Merrick, 370; Merrill, 254, 370; Merritt, 97; Merry, 90; Mersc, 110; Mert, 79; Merta, 165, 254; Merte, 254; Mertice, 90; Mertise, 90; Merton, 27, 110; Mert-sekert, 79; Mertysa, 90; Merula, 254; Mervin, 98, 370; Mervyn, 98; Merwin, 370; Merwyn, 98, 370; Meryl, 32, 254; Mesha, 211; Mesi, 79; Meskhenet, 79; Mesrop, 41; Messena, 254; Messina, 254; Messinia, 254; Meta, 72, 254; Metabus, 267; Metanira, 165; Metea, 165; Methena, 127; Methina, 127; Metis, 165; Mettabel, 188; Mettalise, 72; Mette, 177; Meturato, 281; Meurig, 393; Meyer, 195; Mezentius, 177; Mia, 120, 318; Miach, 225; Miakoda, 275; Micah, 195; Michael, 195; Michaela, 69, 188; Michaele, 188; Michaelina, 188; Michal, 69; Michalin, 188; Michau, 195; Micheil, 142; Michel, 132, 195, 234; Michelangelo, 234; Michele, 132, 195, 234; Micheline, 188; Michelle, 188; Michi, 236; Michiko, 236; Michon, 195; Midas, 177; Mide, 219; Midori, 236; Mielikki, 120; Mieze, 188; Migina, 279; Migisi, 276; Mignon, 127; Mignonette, 127; Miguel, 309, 351; Mihaly, 195; Mihangel, 393; Mihoko, 236; Miia, 120; Miika, 121; Miikka, 121; Miina, 119; Mika, 121, 195, 236, 275; Mikael, 121, 195, 358; Mikaela, 355; Mikayla, 376; Mikel, 51, 195; Mikele, 188; Mikhail, 195, 315; Mikhalis, 195; Mikhos, 195; Miki, 236, 239; Mikkel, 73, 195, 290; Mikko, 121, 195; Miklos, 69; Mikolai, 299; Mikolaj, 299; Mikolas, 51, 177; Mikolaus, 51; Miksa, 201; Mil, 393; Mila, 69, 312; Milada, 69; Milagritos, 346; Milagros, 346; Milagrosa, 346; Milan, 69; Milap, 280; Milburn, 110; Milbyrne, 110; Milcah, 188; Mildraed, 90; Mildread, 136; Mildred, 22, 90; Mildri, 287; Mildrid, 90; Mildryd, 90; Milena, 69, 312; Miles, 177, 225, 267; Milford, 110; Milia, 363; Milicent, 363; Milicente, 363; Milja, 119; Milka, 69, 337; Milla, 119; Millard, 132; Miller, 110, 267; Millicent, 127, 148, 363; Millicente, 127; Millman, 110; Milman, 110; Milo, 177; Milos, 69, 225, 339; Miloslav, 70; Milton, 110; Milward, 110; Mimi, 127, 363; Mimis, 177; Mimiteh, 279; Mimmi, 119; Min, 82, 241; Mina, 76, 148, 236; Minako, 236; Minal, 275; Minas, 335; Minau, 294; Minda, 275; Mindy, 148; Mine, 236; Minerva, 165, 254; Minetta, 127; Minette, 127; Ming, 64, 66; Mingan, 280; Mingmei, 64; Minh, 380; Minka, 298, 363; Minkah, 82; Minna,

THE INDEXES

INDEX

Olabisi, 80; Olaf, 73, 290, 325, 358, 370; Olalla, 346; Olathe, 275; Olaug, 287; Olav, 290; Olave, 290; Olavi, 121; Olavo, 309; Oldrich, 70; Ole, 73, 290; Olechka, 313; Oleda, 90; Oleg, 315; Oleif, 290; Oleisia, 166; Oleksander, 377; Olen, 290; Olena, 166, 313, 376; Olenka, 313; Oleos, 351; Oles, 178, 300; Olesia, 298; Oleta, 90; Olethe, 255; Olethea, 255; Olethia, 255; Olezka, 315; Olga, 287, 313, 355, 363; Olii, 121; Olin, 290; Olina, 166; Olinda, 148, 255, 346; Oliphant, 335; Olita, 90; Olithia, 255; Olive, 219, 255; Oliver, 132, 267, 290; Oliveria, 346; Oliverio, 267, 351; Oliverios, 267, 351; Olivia, 255, 307, 346, 355; Olivie, 255; Olivier, 132, 267; Ollaneg, 110; Ollie, 267; Olliver, 267; Olney, 110; Olof, 290, 358; Olufemi, 80; Olvaerr, 290; Olvan, 267; Olvir, 290; Olwen, 56, 385; Olwina, 385; Olwydd, 393; Olwyn, 44, 56, 385; Olwyna, 385; Olya, 313; Olympe, 127, 166; Olympia, 127, 166, 231; Olyn, 290; Oma, 32, 255; Omaka, 272; Omar, 37; Omari, 83; Omawnakw, 283; Omer, 37; Ominotago, 276; Ommar, 37; Omorose, 80; Omparkash, 211; Omphale, 166; Omusa, 278; On, 66; Ona, 189, 219, 255; Onaedo, 18; Onatah, 277; Onawa, 275; Ondra, 70; Ondras, 70; Ondrej, 70; Ondrus, 70; Ondyaw, 393; Onella, 166; Oney, 226; Onfroi, 132; Oni, 80; Onida, 275; Onit, 189; Onkar, 213; Onora, 136, 219; Onslow, 110; Onslowe, 110; Ontibile, 18; Onufry, 300; Onund, 325; Onuris, 83; Ooljee, 278; Oona, 219; Oonagh, 219; Oota Dabun, 276; Ophelia, 127, 166; Ophelie, 127, 166; Ophion, 178; Ophir, 195; Ophira, 166; Oppida, 56; Ops, 255; Ora, 23, 90, 189, 255, 302, 303, 346; Orabel, 90; Orabelle, 90; Oracular, 255; Orah, 189; Orahamm, 110; Oralee, 189; Orali, 189; Oralia, 255; Oralie, 90, 255; Oram, 110; Oran, 61, 142, 226; Orane, 127; Oratun, 111; Orazio, 234; Orban, 201, 267; Orbart, 153; Orbert, 153; Orbona, 255; Orcus, 267; Ord, 27; Ordalf, 148; Ordelia, 363; Ordella, 148; Ordland, 110; Ordman, 110; Ordmund, 111; Ordsone, 111; Ordwald, 98; Ordway, 27; Ordwin, 90, 98; Ordwina, 90; Ordwine, 98; Ordwyn, 90; Ordwyna, 90; Orea, 166; Orebjorn, 325; Oreias, 178; Orelia, 90; Orella, 255; Oren, 142, 195; Orenda, 277; Oreste, 178; Orestes, 178; Orfeo, 234; Orford, 110; Orghlaith, 219; Orguelleuse, 44; Orham, 110; Ori, 195; Oria, 166, 231, 255; Orial, 255; Oriana, 56, 231, 255; Oribel, 255; Oribella, 255; Oribelle, 255; Orick, 98; Oriel, 127, 255; Orik, 98; Orin, 61, 142, 195; Orinda, 363; Oringo, 19; Orion, 178; Oris, 195, 255; Orithyia, 166; Orla, 219; Orlaith, 219; Orlaithe, 219; Orlan, 110; Orland, 110, 370; Orlanda, 346; Orlando, 234, 351, 370; Orlantha, 363; Orlanthe, 363; Orlee, 189; Orlege, 27;

Orlena, 255; Orlenda, 313; Orlene, 127, 255; Orliena, 127; Orlina, 127; Orlyg, 325; Orm, 325; Orman, 110, 370; Ormazd, 127; Ormeman, 110; Ormemund, 111; Ormod, 27; Ormond, 111, 370; Ormos, 201; Ormund, 111; Orn, 325; Orna, 136, 189, 219; Ornah, 189; Ornat, 219; Orneet, 195; Ornella, 231; Ornet, 195; Ornetta, 189; Ornette, 189; Ornolf, 325; Ornora, 255; Ornoria, 255; Oro, 351; Oroiti, 303; Orpah, 189; Orpha, 189; Orphe, 255; Orpheus, 178; Orprah, 189; Orquidea, 346; Orquidia, 346; Orran, 142; Orren, 142; Orrick, 98; Orrik, 98; Orrin, 142; Orsen, 111; Orson, 111, 132, 267; Ortense, 231; Ortensia, 231, 255; Ortensiana, 255; Ortensie, 255; Orthros, 178; Orton, 111, 370; Ortrud, 363; Ortruda, 363; Ortrude, 363; Ortun, 111; Ortygia, 166; Ortzi, 51; Orva, 23, 90, 127; Orval, 98; Orvil, 98; Orville, 98, 132; Orvin, 27, 98; Orvyn, 27, 98; Orwald, 98; Orynko, 376; Orzora, 189; Orzsebet, 189, 200; Os, 98, 290; Osahar, 83; Osama, 37; Osana, 346; Osane, 50, 346; Osaze, 83; Osbart, 98; Osbeorht, 98; Osbeorn, 98; Osberga, 23; Osbert, 98; Osborn, 98, 370; Osbourne, 98, 370; Osburga, 23; Osburn, 98; Osburt, 98; Oscar, 61, 290; Osckar, 61; Oseye, 80; Osgood, 290, 370; Osip, 195, 315, 377; Osiris, 83; Osk, 319; Oskar, 61, 290, 358; Oskari, 121; Osker, 61; Osla, 48, 393; Osman, 37; Osmar, 98; Osmarr, 98; Osmond, 98, 370; Osmont, 98; Osmund, 98, 370; Ospak, 325; Osraed, 98; Osred, 98; Osric, 27, 98, 370; Osrick, 98; Osrid, 98; Osrik, 98, 370; Osryd, 98; Ossian, 61, 226; Ostein, 290; Osten, 290; Osvald, 370; Osvaldo, 309; Osvif, 325; Oswald, 27, 98, 153, 370; Oswaldo, 370; Oswallt, 393; Osweald, 98; Oswell, 98; Oswine, 27; Oswiu, 27; Oswy, 27; Oszkar, 201; Ota, 370; Otakar, 70; Otaktay, 284; Otavio, 309; Otello, 234; Oth, 393; Otha, 23; Othello, 234; Othilia, 23; Othin, 325; Othman, 153; Othmann, 153; Othmar, 370; Otho, 153; Othomann, 153; Otieno, 19; Otik, 70, 370; Otilie, 148; Otis, 178; Otka, 69, 148; Otkatla, 319; Otkel, 325; Oto, 70, 370; Otoahhastis, 282; Otoahnacto, 282; Otokars, 370; Otomars, 370; Otos, 178; Otrera, 255; Ottah, 83; Ottar, 290; Ottavia, 231; Ottavio, 234, 267; Otthild, 148; Otthilda, 148; Otthilde, 148; Ottila, 148; Ottilia, 148, 364; Ottilie, 23, 364; Otto, 153, 358, 370; Ottokar, 153; Ottoway, 370; Otus, 178; Otway, 370; Otylia, 148, 298; Oubastet, 83; Ouray, 280; Ourson, 132; Outram, 370; Ovadiah, 195; Ovadyam, 195; Ovaegir, 325; Ove, 56, 290, 325, 358; Oved, 195; Ovia, 255; Ovid, 195, 267; Owain, 48, 393; Owein, 393; Owen, 61, 178, 393; Owena, 385; Owin, 61, 393; Owney, 226; Owyn, 61, 393; Oxa, 27; Oxana, 376; Oxford, 111; Oxley,

Reetta, 120; Reeve, 99; Reeves, 112; Ref, 325; Regan, 56, 61, 90, 136, 219, 226; Regenfrithu, 99; Regenweald, 99; Reggie, 154; Reghan, 61; Regin, 325; Regina, 231, 256, 347; Reginald, 99, 154, 371; Reginberaht, 153; Regine, 256; Reginhard, 154; Reginy, 256; Re-Harakhty, 83; Rehema, 80; Rei, 237; Reid, 99; Reidar, 291; Reider, 291; Reidhachadh, 226; Reidun, 287; Reiko, 238; Reina, 127, 347; Reine, 127; Reiner, 153; Reinhard, 153, 154; Reinheld, 364; Reinhelda, 364; Reinhold, 371; Reist, 325; Reit, 167; Reka, 272; Rekha, 209; Remedios, 347; Remi, 132; Remigio, 309; Remington, 112; Remus, 268; Remy, 132; Ren, 99, 238, 394; Rena, 167, 189; Renaldo, 352; Renard, 371; Renata, 231, 257, 307; Renate, 257; Renato, 268; Renaud, 370; Rendell, 370; Rendor, 201; Rene, 127, 132; Renee, 127, 257; Renella, 257; Renelle, 257; Renenet, 80; Reneta, 257; Renfield, 111; Renfred, 99, 371; Renfrew, 61, 394; Renfrid, 99, 371; Renild, 364; Renilda, 364; Renilde, 364; Renita, 257; Renke, 153; Rennard, 371; Renny, 219, 226; Renshaw, 112; Renton, 112; Renweard, 27; Renwick, 371; Renwyk, 371; Renzo, 234, 268; Reod, 99; Rere, 272; Reremoana, 272; Reseda, 257; Reselda, 257; Reshef, 83; Resi, 167; Reta, 167; Reuben, 196; Reule, 133; Re'uven, 196; Reva, 257; Reve, 99; Reveka, 189; Revelin, 226; Rewa, 302; Rex, 268; Rexana, 257; Rexanna, 257; Rexanne, 257; Rexford, 112; Rexley, 112; Rexton, 112; Rey, 132, 352; Reyburn, 112; Reynard, 154, 291; Reynold, 371; Rez, 200, 202; Rezi, 167; Reznik, 70; Rhadamanthus, 180, 268; Rhan, 385; Rhawn, 385; Rhea, 167, 257; Rhea Silva, 257; Rheda, 23; Rhedyn, 385; Rheged, 27, 394; Rheidwn, 394; Rhesus, 180, 268; Rheta, 167; Rhete, 167; Rheu, 394; Rhiain, 385; Rhiannon, 56, 385; Rhianwen, 385; Rhianwyn, 385; Rhinffrew, 394; Rhioganedd, 394; Rhisiart, 394; Rhobert, 394; Rhoda, 167; Rhodantha, 167; Rhodanthe, 167; Rhode, 257; Rhodes, 112; Rhodia, 167; Rhoecus, 180; Rhongomyant, 48; Rhonwen, 385; Rhosyn, 385; Rhun, 394; Rhuvawn, 394; Rhyawdd, 394; Rhychdir, 394; Rhyd, 394; Rhydderch, 48; Rhynnon, 394; Rhys, 394; Ria, 347; Riagan, 226; Rian, 226; Riane, 136; Ric, 291; Rica, 347; Ricadene, 99; Ricadonna, 231; Ricarda, 90, 148, 231, 347, 364; Ricardo, 154, 234, 352; Riccardo, 154, 234; Ricci, 286; Ricciardo, 234; Rice, 27, 394; Rich, 99, 154; Richael, 219; Richard, 99, 154, 371; Richman, 99; Richmond, 154, 371; Rickard, 154; Ricker, 99; Rickman, 99; Rickward, 99; Ricman, 99; Rico, 154, 352; Ricweard, 99; Riddhi, 207; Riddoc, 226; Riddock, 226; Rider, 99; Ridere, 99;

Ridge, 112; Ridgeley, 99; Ridgely, 99; Ridley, 99; Ridpath, 112; Rieko, 238; Rigby, 99; Rigg, 99; Riggs, 112; Rigmor, 72, 356; Rigmora, 356; Rihana, 32; Riika, 120; Riikka, 120; Riitta, 120; Rika, 286; Rikako, 238; Rikard, 154, 202, 325, 358; Rikka, 148, 364; Rikkard, 99, 121; Riku, 121; Rikward, 99; Riley, 136, 142, 219; Rilla, 148, 365; Rille, 148; Rilletta, 90; Rillette, 90; Rillia, 148; Rillie, 148; Rima, 32; Rimona, 189; Rina, 167, 189; Rinako, 238; Rinaldo, 234, 370; Rinan, 27; Rinc, 27; Rind, 319; Rinda, 319; Ring, 99; Rini, 238; Rinna, 189; Rinnah, 189; Rio, 347; Riobard, 226; Riobart, 371; Riocard, 154; Riodain, 226; Riodhr, 291; Rioghbhardan, 142; Rioghnach, 219; Rion, 48; Riona, 219; Riordan, 142, 226; Ripley, 27, 112; Risa, 70, 257; Risako, 238; Rishi, 211; Rishona, 189; Risley, 112; Risteard, 142, 154; Risto, 121, 180; Riston, 112; Rita, 167, 347; Ritchell, 380; Rithisak, 53; Ritsa, 167; Ritsuko, 238; Ritter, 154, 371; Ritva, 120; Ritza, 167; Riva, 127, 257; Rivalen, 48; Rivalin, 61; Rive, 127, 257; Rivka, 189; Riyad, 37; Rizpah, 167; Ro, 27; Roald, 154, 291, 358; Roan, 99, 142; Roana, 347; Roano, 352; Roar, 291; Roark, 226; Rob, 371; Rob Roy, 335; Robby, 371; Robena, 331; Robert, 132, 371; Roberta, 90, 365; Robertia, 90; Roberto, 234, 352, 371; Robertson, 335; Robi, 202; Robin, 371; Robina, 331, 365; Robine, 365; Robinet, 371; Robinetta, 127; Robinette, 127; Roch, 133, 148, 154, 298; Roche, 133; Rocio, 347; Rocke, 133; Rodas, 180, 352; Roderic, 371; Roderica, 148, 365; Roderick, 154, 371; Roderiga, 347; Roderigo, 234, 352, 371; Roderika, 148; Rodes, 112; Rodhlann, 268; Rodman, 112; Rodney, 371; Rodolfo, 234, 352; Rodor, 27; Rodrick, 371; Rodrigo, 234, 309, 352; Rodrigue, 371; Rodrik, 154; Rodwell, 112; Roe, 27, 99; Roesia, 127; Rogan, 226; Rogelio, 352, 371; Roger, 371; Rogerio, 371; Rognvald, 325; Rohais, 127; Rohana, 209; Rohin, 211; Rohini, 209; Roho, 19; Roial, 127; Roibeard, 226, 371; Roibhilin, 226; Roibin, 226; Rois, 137, 219; Roisin, 137, 219; Roland, 268, 358, 371; Rolanda, 148, 365; Rolande, 148, 365; Rolando, 371; Roldan, 352; Roldana, 347; Rolden, 371; Rolf, 98, 291, 358, 371; Rolfe, 27, 98, 371; Rollanda, 365; Rollande, 365; Rollin, 371; Rollins, 371; Rollo, 371; Rolph, 371; Rolphe, 371; Roma, 231, 257; Romain, 133, 268; Romaine, 127; Roman, 315, 352; Romana, 127, 257, 347; Romania, 257; Romano, 234, 268; Romelda, 365; Romelde, 365; Romeo, 234, 268, 352; Romhild, 148; Romhilda, 148; Romhilde, 148; Romia, 231; Romilda, 148, 365; Romilde, 148, 365; Romney, 112, 268, 394; Romochka, 315; Romola, 257; Romulus, 268; Ron, 48, 196; Rona, 189, 287, 331; Ronald, 99,

THE INDEXES

INDEX

Ulf, 292, 359; Ulfar, 327; Ulfmaerr, 292; Ulfred, 100, 372; Ulger, 100; Uli, 149, 154; Ulicia, 220; Ulik, 372; Ulima, 33; Ulka, 149; Ull, 327; Ulla, 149, 356; Ullock, 100; Ullok, 100; Ulmar, 100; Ulmarr, 100; Ulmer, 292; Ulric, 372; Ulrica, 149, 365; Ulrich, 154; Ulrik, 73, 372; Ulrika, 356, 365; Ulrike, 149, 319, 365; Ultan, 227; Ulva, 365; Ulvelaik, 100; Ulysses, 181, 269; Ulz, 154; Uma, 209; Umar, 37; Umarah, 37; Umayma, 80; Umberto, 234; Umeko, 238; Umi, 84; Umm, 80; Una, 56, 134, 220, 258, 277, 386; Unai, 51; Undina, 258; Undine, 258; Undinia, 258; Ungus, 220; Uni, 327; Unig, 395; Unika, 84; Unity, 220; Unn, 288; Unne, 288; Un-nefer, 83; Unwin, 100; Unwine, 100; Unwyn, 100; Uny, 220; Uoc, 379; Uolevi, 121; Upala, 207; Upchurch, 115; Upendo, 20; Upravda, 339; Upton, 28, 115; Uptun, 115; Upwode, 115; Upwood, 115; Ur, 84; Ur-Atum, 84; Ura, 292; Urania, 168; Uranus, 181; Urbain, 269; Urban, 269; Urbana, 258; Urbania, 258; Urbano, 352; Urbi, 80; Urd, 319; Uri, 196, 315; Uriah, 196, 315; Urian, 181; Urice, 190; Urie, 315; Uriel, 196, 315; Urien, 48; Uriens, 48; Urika, 279; Urit, 190; Uros, 202; Urquhart, 336; Ursa, 168; Ursel, 168; Urselina, 258; Urseline, 258; Ursola, 258, 313; Ursula, 168, 258, 307, 313, 347; Ursule, 258; Ursulina, 347; Urtzi, 51; Uryen, 395; Urzula, 258; Usagi, 238; Usenech, 61; Usha, 209; Ushas, 207; Usi, 84; Usko, 121; Usk-water, 62; Usoa, 347; Ustean, 372; Utathya, 212; Ute, 365; Utgard-Loki, 327; Uth, 53; Uther, 48, 227, 372; Uthman, 84; Utina, 275; Uwaine, 48; Uwayne, 48; Uwe, 372; Uyeda, 239; Uzumati, 283; Uzziah, 196; Uzziel, 196; Uzziye, 190

Vac, 207; Vach, 207; Vachel, 133; Vaclar, 339; Vaclav, 70; Vacuna, 258; Vaddon, 395; Vaden, 133; Vadim, 315; Vadin, 213; Vadit, 190; Vaetild, 319; Vaetilda, 319; Vahe, 41; Vail, 100, 133; Vaino, 121; Vairocana, 209; Vaive Atoish, 282; Vaiveahtoish, 282; Val, 258, 269, 295; Vala, 365, 386; Valara, 129; Valari, 258; Valarie, 258; Valborg, 359; Valborga, 149; Valbrand, 327; Valda, 288, 365; Valdemar, 154, 359; Valdemarr, 154; Valdik, 315, 339; Valdis, 319, 372; Valdislava, 337; Vale, 100; Valeda, 258; Valencia, 258; Valens, 269; Valentia, 258; Valentin, 73, 269, 359; Valentina, 231, 258, 313, 347; Valentine, 269; Valentino, 234, 269; Valera, 269; Valeraine, 129; Valere, 129; Valeria, 129, 258, 307; Valerian, 269; Valerii, 269, 315; Valerik, 269, 315; Valerio, 234, 269, 309; Valerius, 269; Valery, 258; Valeska, 298, 313, 337; Valfrid, 359; Valgard, 327; Valgerd, 288; Vali, 327; Valiant, 100, 133; Valika, 337; Valimai, 386; Valin, 213; Valkoinen, 121; Valkyrie, 319;

Vallis, 133; Vallois, 133; Vallonia, 258; Valmiki, 212; Valonia, 258; Valora, 258; Valorous, 258; Valpuri, 120; Valter, 359, 372; Valthjof, 327; Valtteri, 121; Van, 379, 380; Vance, 100; Vanda, 149, 298, 365; Vande, 149; Vandrad, 327; Vanechka, 315; Vanessa, 258; Vania, 168, 190, 313; Vanida, 374; Vanir, 327; Vanja, 320; Vanka, 313; Vanko, 181, 377; Vanna, 52, 168, 190; Vannes, 100; Vanni, 231; Vanny, 168; Vanora, 386; Vanya, 313; Vanyusha, 315; Vappu, 120, 121; Var, 320; Vara, 168; Varad, 202; Varaza, 207; Varda, 190; Vardan, 133; Varden, 62, 133; Vardit, 190; Vardon, 62, 133; Vared, 190; Varian, 270; Varick, 372; Varik, 372; Varin, 53; Varina, 337; Varinka, 313; Varney, 62; Varouna, 209; Vartan, 41; Vartoughi, 40; Varun, 213; Varuna, 212; Varunani, 207; Varushka, 313; Varvara, 168, 313, 337; Varya, 313; Vas, 315; Vasco, 309; Vasek, 70, 339; Vasha, 18; Vashti, 294; Vasileios, 181; Vasilis, 181; Vasilissa, 313; Vasin, 212; Vasistha, 212; Vasos, 181; Vassi, 315; Vassillissa, 313; Vassily, 315, 339; Vasu, 212; Vasuki, 213; Vasya, 313, 315; Vasyl, 181; Vasylko, 181, 377; Vasyltso, 181; Vater, 372; Vatt, 359; Vaughn, 62, 395; Vavara, 168; Vavay, 259; Vavrin, 70; Vavrinec, 70; Vayk, 202; Vayle, 100, 133; Vayu, 209; Ve, 327; Veasna, 53; Veata, 52; Vedas, 209; Vedetta, 129, 231; Vedette, 129, 231; Vedia, 356, 365; Vedis, 356, 365; Vega, 33, 258, 356; Vegard, 292; Vegeir, 292; Veijo, 121; Veikko, 121; Veit, 77, 270; Velaug, 320; Velda, 365; Veleda, 365; Veli, 121; Velief, 327; Velika, 313, 337; Vellamo, 120; Velouette, 91; Velvet, 91; Vema, 207; Venamin, 196; Vencel, 202; Vencentio, 234; Venda, 18; Vendela, 320; Venedictos, 270; Venessa, 168, 258; Venetia, 56; Veniamin, 196; Venilia, 258; Venita, 258; Venjamin, 196; Ventura, 347; Venus, 258; Vera, 258, 313; Veradis, 258; Veradisia, 258; Verbane, 259; Verbena, 259; Verbenae, 259; Verbenia, 259; Verda, 259; Verdad, 347; Verdandi, 320; Verddun, 133; Verel, 133; Verena, 149, 365; Verene, 149; Verge, 28; Vergil, 270; Verina, 149, 365; Verna, 259; Vernados, 154; Vernay, 133; Verne, 270; Verner, 359, 372; Verney, 133; Vernita, 259; Vernon, 133, 270; Vernus, 270; Verochka, 313; Veronica, 168, 259, 307; Veronicha, 168; Veronika, 168, 259; Veronique, 129; Verrall, 133; Verrell, 133; Verrill, 133; Vertumnus, 270; Verushka, 69; Veryl, 133; Vespera, 259; Vesperia, 259; Vespira, 259; Vesta, 259; Vestar, 327; Vestein, 327; Veta, 259, 347; Veto, 352; Vevila, 220; Vevina, 220; Viator, 270; Vibald, 327; Vibeke, 72, 149; Vibishana, 212; Vibol, 53; Vic, 133; Vicenta, 347; Vick, 133; Vicq, 133; Victor, 270, 309, 352; Victoria, 259;

Welford, 116; Welles, 101; Wellington, 28, 116; Wells, 101; Welsa, 91; Welsh, 101; Welsie, 91; Welton, 116; Wematin, 281; Wemilat, 280; Wen, 66; Wenceslaus, 339; Wenceslava, 339; Wenda, 91, 365; Wende, 365; Wendel, 154, 372; Wendelin, 365; Wendelina, 365; Wendeline, 365; Wendell, 154, 372; Wendlesora, 116; Wenhaver, 43; Wenona, 276, 279; Wenonah, 276, 279; Wentworth, 116; Weolingtun, 116; Weorth, 117; Werbenec, 395; Werhar, 372; Werian, 28; Werner, 154, 372; Weronika, 298; Wes, 116; Wesley, 101; West, 116; Westbroc, 116; Westbrook, 116; Westby, 116; Westcot, 116; Westcott, 116; Westleah, 101; Westley, 101; Weston, 116; Westun, 116; Wetherby, 116; Wetherly, 116; Wethrby, 116; Wethrleah, 116; Weyland, 116; Weylin, 62; Weylyn, 62; Wharton, 116; Wheatley, 116; Wheeler, 116; Whelen, 227; Whetu, 303; Whistler, 116; Whitby, 116, 327; Whitcomb, 116; Whitelaw, 116; Whitfield, 116; Whitford, 116; Whitlaw, 116; Whitley, 116; Whitlock, 101; Whitman, 101; Whitmoor, 116; Whitmore, 116; Whitney, 23, 28, 101; Whittaker, 116; Whytlok, 101; Wiatt, 101, 133; Wicapi Wakan, 276; Wicasa, 282; Wiccum, 116; Wicek, 270; Wicenty, 270; Wichamm, 116; Wickam, 116; Wickley, 116; Wicleah, 116; Wicus, 270, 300; Widad, 33; Widjan, 33; Wido, 149; Wiellaburne, 116; Wiellaby, 116; Wielladun, 116; Wiellaford, 116; Wiellatun, 116; Wienczyslaw, 300; Wies, 372; Wigburg, 76; Wigmaere, 101; Wigman, 101; Wihakayda, 279; Wikimak, 276; Wikitoria, 272; Wikta, 298; Wiktor, 300; Wiktoria, 298; Wiktorja, 298; Wikvaya, 283; Wilbart, 154; Wilbert, 101, 154; Wilbur, 28, 101, 154; Wilburt, 101, 154; Wilda, 23, 149; Wilde, 149; Wildon, 116; Wileen, 365; Wilford, 116; Wilfred, 101, 154, 372; Wilfrid, 28, 101, 154, 372; Wilfryd, 101; Wilhelm, 154, 372; Wilhelmina, 149, 365; Wilhelmine, 72, 149; Wilhelmus, 372; Wilhemina, 365; Wilhemine, 365; Will, 101, 372; Willa, 23, 91, 101, 365; Willaburh, 101; Willamar, 154; Willan, 28; Willaperht, 154; Willard, 101, 372; Willem, 372; Willesone, 116; Willette, 365; Willhard, 101; William, 101, 133, 372; Williamon, 154; Williams, 116; Williamson, 116; Willifrid, 154; Willimod, 154; Willis, 116; Willmar, 154; Willmarr, 154; Willoughby, 116; Wilmar, 154, 372; Wilmer, 154, 372; Wilmet, 365; Wilmod, 154; Wilmot, 154, 372; Wilna, 365; Wilny, 280; Wilona, 23; Wilone, 23; Wilpert, 154; Wilson, 116, 372; Wilton, 116; Wilva, 365; Wim, 77, 372; Win, 101; Wincel, 101; Wincent, 270; Wincenty, 300; Winchell, 28, 101; Windgate, 117; Windham, 117; Windsor, 116, 372; Wine,

28, 101; Winefeld, 372; Winefield, 116; Winefrith, 101; Winema, 276; Winetorp, 117; Winfield, 116, 372; Winfred, 101, 372; Winfreda, 365; Winfrid, 101; Winfryd, 372; Wing, 65, 66; Wingate, 117; Winifred, 149, 365; Winifrid, 149, 365; Winifrida, 149; Winifride, 149; Winn, 101, 395; Winnie, 56; Winnifred, 386; Winola, 149; Winona, 279; Winslow, 117; Winslowe, 117; Winsor, 116, 372; Winston, 117; Winswode, 117; Winta, 18; Wintanweorth, 116; Winter, 28, 101; Winthrop, 117, 372; Winton, 117; Winward, 117; Winwodem, 117; Winwood, 117; Wira, 298; Wireceaster, 117; Wiremu, 273; Wirke, 298; Wirt, 28; Wissian, 28; Wit, 270, 300; Witashnah, 279; Withypoll, 91; Witt, 101; Witta, 101; Wittahere, 101; Wittatun, 117; Witter, 101; Witton, 117; Wlader, 372; Wmffre, 395; Wodeleah, 117; Woden, 28; Woglinda, 320; Wohehiv, 282; Wokaihwokomas, 282; Wolcott, 117; Wolf, 101, 372; Wolfcot, 117; Wolfe, 101, 372; Wolfgang, 154, 372; Wolfgar, 372; Wolfram, 372; Wolfric, 154; Wolfrick, 154; Wolfrik, 154; Wolodymyr, 377; Wolter, 77; Woodley, 117; Woodman, 101; Woodrow, 101; Woodruff, 101; Woodward, 117; Woolcott, 117; Woolsey, 101; Worcester, 117; Worden, 101; Wordsworth, 117; Worrell, 117; Worth, 117; Worthington, 29; Worton, 117; Wotan, 154; Wouter, 372; Wray, 292; Wregan, 29; Wren, 395; Wright, 29, 117; Wrnach, 395; Wryhta, 117; Wudoweard, 117; Wuhur, 372; Wulf, 29, 101; Wulfcot, 117; Wulffrith, 101; Wulfgar, 29, 101; Wulfhere, 29; Wulfsige, 101; Wulfweardsweorth, 117; Wurt, 28; Wuti, 277; Wuyi, 283; Wyanet, 276; Wyatt, 101, 133; Wybjorn, 292; Wyborn, 292; Wycliff, 117; Wyclyf, 117; Wylie, 29; Wyligby, 116; Wylingford, 116; Wylltun, 116; Wyman, 29, 101; Wymer, 101; Wyn, 386, 395; Wynchell, 28; Wynda, 331; Wyndham, 117; Wyne, 28, 101; Wynfield, 116; Wynfred, 372; Wynfreda, 365; Wynfrid, 101; Wynfrith, 101; Wynifred, 365; Wynn, 395; Wynne, 56, 62, 386; Wynnie, 56; Wynnifred, 386; Wynono, 280; Wynston, 117; Wynter, 101; Wynthrop, 117; Wynward, 117; Wynwode, 117; Wyrttun, 117; Wyth, 117; Wythe, 117

Xabat, 352; Xabier, 51; Xalbador, 352; Xalbadora, 348; Xalvador, 352; Xalvadora, 348; Xantha, 168; Xanthe, 168, 259; Xanthia, 168; Xanthus, 181, 270; Xanti, 51; Xarles, 133; Xavier, 37, 51, 309, 352; Xaviera, 348; Xavierra, 129; Xavierre, 129; Xenia, 168; Xeno, 181; Xenophon, 181; Xenos, 181; Xerxes, 181, 295; Xever, 352; Xevera, 348; Xeveria, 348; Xhosa, 18; Xi Wang, 65, 66; Xia, 65; Xiang, 65; Xiao, 65,

18; Ziska, 365; Ziske, 365; Zissi, 365; Zita, 169, 231, 348; Zitkala, 277; Ziv, 197, 339; Ziva, 191; Ziven, 300, 315, 339; Zivon, 315, 339; Ziyad, 84; Zobor, 202; Zoe, 169; Zoel, 169; Zoelie, 169; Zoelle, 169; Zofia, 169, 298; Zofie, 169; Zohar, 191, 197; Zoheret, 191; Zohra, 33; Zoia, 169; Zoltan, 38, 182; Zoltar, 182; Zombor, 202; Zondra, 168; Zophie, 69; Zora, 337; Zorah, 337; Zoran, 339; Zorana, 337; Zorian, 270; Zorion, 51; Zoroaster, 295; Zorya, 315; Zosia, 298; Zosima, 169; Zotikos, 182; Zowie, 143; Zoya, 169, 313; Zoyechka, 313; Zoyenka, 313; Zsa Zsa, 200; Zsiga, 372; Zsigmond, 372; Zsofia, 169, 200; Zsofie, 169; Zsofika, 200; Zsolt, 202; Zsuska, 200; Zsuzsanna, 200; Zsuzsi, 200; Zuberi, 84; Zudora, 207; Zuhayr, 38; Zuka, 84; Zula, 18; Zuleika, 33, 294; Zulema, 33; Zulu, 20; Zuri, 129; Zuria, 129; Zurie, 129; Zuriel, 197; Zurina, 50, 348; Zurine, 50, 348; Zuza, 69; Zuzana, 69; Zuzanna, 298; Zuzanny, 298; Zuzka, 69; Zygmunt, 300, 372; Zyphire, 169; Zyta, 169, 298; Zytka, 298

Reg shelf